RETAILING

THE IRWIN SERIES IN MARKETING

Gilbert A. Churchill, Jr., Consulting Editor
University of Wisconsin, Madison

Alreck & Settle
The Survey Research Handbook, *1/e*

Arens & Bovee
Contemporary Advertising, *5/e*

Belch & Belch
Introduction to Advertising and Promotion: An Integrated Marketing Communications Approach, *2/e*

Bernhardt & Kinnear
Cases in Marketing Management, *6/e*

Bonoma & Kosnik
Marketing Management: Text & Cases, *1/e*

Boyd & Walker
Marketing Management: A Strategic Approach, *1/e*

Boyd, Westfall & Stasch
Marketing Research: Text and Cases, *7/e*

Burstiner
Basic Retailing, *2/e*

Cadotte
The Market Place: A Strategic Marketing Simulation, *1/e*

Cateora
International Marketing, *8/e*

Churchill, Ford & Walker
Sales Force Management, *4/e*

Cole
Consumer and Commercial Credit Management, *9/e*

Cravens
Strategic Marketing, *4/e*

Cravens & Lamb
Strategic Marketing Management Cases, *4/e*

Crawford
New Products Management, *4/e*

Dillon, Madden & Firtle
Essentials of Marketing Research, *1/e*

Dillon, Madden & Firtle
Marketing Research in a Marketing Environment, *3/e*

Engel, Warshaw & Kinnear
Promotional Strategy, *8/e*

Faria, Nulsen & Roussos
Compete, *4/e*

Futrell
ABC's of Selling, *4/e*

Futrell
Fundamentals of Selling, *4/e*

Hawkins, Best & Coney
Consumer Behavior, *5/e*

Kerin, Hartley, Rudelius & Berkowitz
Marketing, *4/e*

Lambert & Stock
Strategic Logistics Management, *3/e*

Lehmann & Winer
Analysis for Marketing Planning, *3/e*

Lehmann
Market Research and Analysis, *4/e*

Lehmann & Winer
Product Management, *1/e*

Levy & Weitz
Retailing Management, *1/e*

Mason, Mayer & Wilkinson
Modern Retailing, *6/e*

Mason, Mayer & Ezell
Retailing, *5/e*

Mason & Perreault
The Marketing Game!, *2/e*

McCarthy & Perreault
Basic Marketing: A Global-Managerial Approach, *11/e*

McCarthy & Perreault
Essentials of Marketing: A Global-Managerial Approach, *6/e*

Patton
Sales Sim, *1/e*

Peter & Donnelly
A Preface to Marketing Management, *6/e*

Peter & Donnelly
Marketing Management: Knowledge and Skills, *3/e*

Peter & Olson
Consumer Behavior and Marketing Strategy, *3/e*

Peter & Olson
Understanding Consumer Behavior, *1/e*

Quelch & Farris
Cases in Advertising and Promotion Management, *4/e*

Quelch, Dolan & Kosnik
Marketing Management: Text & Cases, *1/e*

Smith & Quelch
Ethics in Marketing, *1/e*

Stanton, Buskirk & Spiro
Management of a Sales Force, *8/e*

Thompson & Stappenbeck
The Marketing Strategy Game, *1/e*

Walker, Boyd & Larréché
Marketing Strategy: Planning and Implementation, *1/e*

Weitz, Castleberry & Tanner
Selling: Building Partnerships, *1/e*

RETAILING

Fifth Edition

J. Barry Mason
Morris L. Mayer
Hazel F. Ezell

all of
Graduate School of Business
College of Commerce and Business Administration
The University of Alabama

IRWIN
Burr Ridge, Illinois
Boston, Massachusetts
Sydney, Australia

Executive editor:	Rob Zwettler
Senior developmental editor:	Nancy Barbour
Project editor:	Lynne Basler
Production manager:	Ann Cassady
Designer:	Larry J. Cope
Photo research coordinator:	Patricia A. Seefelt
Compositor:	Carlisle Communications, Ltd.
Typeface:	10/12 Times Roman
Printer:	R.R. Donnelley & Sons Company
Cover photo:	Paul Rung, Photographer

Library of Congress Cataloging-in-Publication Data

Mason, Joseph Barry.
Retailing / J. Barry Mason, Morris L. Mayer, Hazel F. Ezell.—5th ed.
p. cm.—(The Irwin series in marketing)
Includes bibliographical references and index.
ISBN 0-256-12002-1
1. Retail trade—Management. I. Mayer, Morris Lehman. II. Ezell, Hazell F. III. Title. IV. Series.
HF5429.M327 1994
658.8′7—dc20 93–21286

Printed in the United States of America
1 2 3 4 5 6 7 8 9 0 DOC 0 9 8 7 6 5 4 3

To Linda, Judy, and Chuck

Preface

For the career-oriented student, few topics are more exciting and dynamic than retailing. Studying the subject paves the way for the most diversified career opportunities available in the marketplace of the 1990s and beyond. Our fifth edition has been designed to reflect the dynamics of retailing and to make study of the field rewarding for both students and instructors.

APPROACH OF THE TEXT

This text uses a "how-to" approach but also emphasizes strategic planning and the need for a marketing focus. We address all issues likely to concern a person interested in a retail career as an owner, a manager, or an employee who is uncertain of future directions. These issues are addressed from a pragmatic point of view, but we have not sacrificed the conceptual and analytical foundation necessary for a complete introduction to the field. The approach we have taken assumes no prior knowledge of retailing. Thus, the material is presented in simple, straightforward language. With the assumption of "no prerequisites needed," we have defined all terms carefully. We also provide many real-life examples.

The stage is set in the first chapter, which introduces and captures the excitement of retailing today. The strategic framework of the book is presented in Chapter 2.

The objectives of this text are to address:

- The status of retailing today.
- What must be considered to plan for situations over which management has no control, in other words, the external environments of retailing.
- Key decisions to be made as part of a successful retail strategy.
- The ways a retailer can ensure that operations will be profitable.
- Whether retailing is a viable career (or investment) in your future.

This book presents the broad spectrum of opportunities that exist for the aspiring retailer. What types of stores are out there? Large ones like J.C. Penney and small ones like your local 7-Eleven; fancy ones like Neiman-Marcus, and no-frills operations such as Price Club and F&M deep discount drugstores all exist successfully.

Where will the action in retailing be in the mid-1990s? The small, secondary markets look good to many strategic planners. Will the outlying regional malls in metropolitan areas still be attractive investments? What about downtown (the central business district)? Will the winning format be the combination food and general merchandise operation?

Which names are part of the big retail action? Nordstrom, The Limited, The Gap, and the Neiman-Marcus Group are well known in upscale fashion apparel. As the 1980s ended, Sears' "everyday low price" strategy was too little, too late. We are encouraged about the future of Federated and Allied Stores following the massive Campeau debacle. Some interesting downtown investments include A&S Plaza in the old Gimbel's property in New York City as well as Trump Tower with Prentempts from Paris replacing the defunct Bonwit Teller; San Diego's Horton Plaza; Chicago's Michigan Boulevard; and New York's Madison Avenue. Do these developments indicate a trend in downtown renovation? What about the mega malls—the West Edmonton Mall in Alberta and the Mall of America in suburban Minneapolis–St. Paul—are they part of a trend? Hypermarkets? Open air fashion stores? Bulk food stores? Polish up the crystal ball and you will see continuing growth and success in services retailing. Yes, retailing is dynamic, diverse, and exciting; and retail organizations need people to manage all functions that exist to serve the customer.

ORGANIZATION OF THE TEXT

The book flows in a logical sequence since each topic fits into a planned framework. Part 1 of the framework, Structural Dynamics and Strategic Planning, discusses what retailing is like today (Chapter 1) by quickly initiating you into the retailing fraternity! Chapter 2 introduces students to the essence of strategic planning as a way of defining the purposes of the firm and deciding how to compete. Part 2 introduces students to the environmental factors affecting retail strategy development, including the key legal and public policy issues (Chapter 3) and the critical dimensions of the demographic, social, competitive, and technological environments (Chapter 4). The focus of Chapter 5 is management information systems.

Part 3 focuses on the issue of selecting markets in which to compete. Chapter 6 asks and answers critical questions about the consumer. Lifestyle merchandising is the topic of Chapter 7. Part 4 introduces students to the resources needed to compete, including issues in organizing and financing the new retail enterprise (Chapter 8). Chapter 9 presents the key issues in location, site, and building decisions; Chapter 10 discusses critical issues in the recruiting, selecting, and motivating of employees.

Part 5 focuses on positioning for competitive advantage and introduces students to merchandise and planning and control (Chapter 11); evaluating retail performance (Chapter 12); buying and inventory management (Chapter 13); determining retail prices (Chapter 14); physically handling and securing merchandise (Chapter 15); store design and layout and merchandise presentation (Chapter 16); keys to successful selling (Chapter 17); advertising, sales promotion, and publicity (Chapter 18); and sales-support services (Chapter 19).

Part 6 focuses on retailing issues, opportunities, and outlook. Franchising operations are discussed in Chapter 20; service retail organizations and nonstore retailing are the topics of Chapter 21. The text ends with Chapter 22, which provides an overview of trends, social dimensions, and prospects that affect retailing. Following this chapter is a comprehensive careers appendix to help students make better decisions about the many facets of a career in retailing.

SOME OTHER THINGS ABOUT THE BOOK

We have tried to make this book interesting and to reflect the excitement of retailing. Some of the premier retail firms have provided excellent photographs. The introductory retailing capsule at the beginning of each chapter and the two cases at the end of each chapter bring a high degree of realism to the material.

HOW TO STUDY RETAILING WITH THIS BOOK

Look carefully at the first page or two of each chapter. The information provided here is valuable. It indicates topics covered in the chapter and spells out the specific chapter learning objectives.

Each chapter includes study questions to make you think about what you've read and to test your memory and understanding of the chapter. Practice problems are given in some chapters so you can check your understanding of skills explained in the book. Always work the problems. Each chapter also includes two cases. These cases let you confront a real situation to make a decision or to judge someone else's actions. These cases are fun and good learning experiences.

We have also created an exciting series of computer assisted problems and exercises. These exercises will help you "crunch the numbers" and see the relationships between various sets of data in making retail decisions. Additionally, we have provided your instructor with several videos that highlight specific companies and situations discussed in the text. Study the videos with care. They will provide useful insights into how progressive companies make decisions.

Other additions to the text include a profile in excellence vignette in each chapter which highlights the personalities of senior executives who have helped shape the U.S. retailing scene. Each chapter also contains an ethics vignette to help you think through the ethical implications of decisions made by retailers on a daily basis.

In addition to the key terms highlighted in the chapter, a glossary has been added at the end of the text.

ACKNOWLEDGMENTS

Colleagues who have taught the book for the past several years have given us valuable suggestions for improvements. People from both the business world and the academic world have been helpful in assisting us throughout this experience.

Our sincere appreciation is extended to the following people who graciously assisted in the preparation of the manuscripts for one or more editions: Gemmy S. Allen, Mountain View College; Mark I. Alpert, University of Texas at Austin; Jill Ataway, University of Kentucky; Ronald Bernard, Diablo Valley College; Dave Bradley, University of Central Arizona; David Burns, Purdue University; Bob Bush, Memphis State University; Martin R. Clayman, University of Tulsa; Kathy Cochran, University of Wisconsin; Jerry A. Cooper, Southern Oregon State College; Barnett Greenburg, Florida International University; Wilma S. Greene, The University of Alabama; Blaine Greenfield, Bucks County Community College; Larry G. Gresham, Memphis State University; James Healey, Chabot College; Tony Henthorne, University of Southern Mississippi; Judith S. Leonard, Eastern Kentucky University; Richard O. Leventhal, Metropolitan State College; Michael F. O'Neill, California State University, Chico; Elisabeth K. Ryland, Farmville, Virginia; Robert H. Solomon, Stephen F. Austin State University; Robert Stephens, University of Tennessee at Martin; and Robert E. Witt, University of Texas at Austin.

The following firms have been generous with their time and materials. We extend our gratitude to: The A&P Company, Aronov Realty, Dillard's, IBM, Macy's, National Cash Register, Parisian, The Jewel Companies, J.C. Penney Company, Inc., Sears, Kmart, The Doody Co., Neiman-Marcus, Mercantile Stores, and The Fannie Farmer Company.

J. Barry Mason
Morris L. Mayer
Hazel F. Ezell

Contents in Brief

Contents

PART 5 Positioning for Competitive Advantage: The Marketing Plan

CASE NAMES AND DESCRIPTIONS

PART 1

Structural Dynamics and Strategic Planning

The size and complexity of retailing become apparent when we think about its structure. Millions of retail outlets in the United States generate billions of dollars in annual sales. All of us are familiar with such giants as Sears Roebuck, Wal-Mart, and J. C. Penney. Yet small, independent retail and franchised outlets far outnumber the larger well-known chains.

The number of retail outlets continues to increase at a much faster rate than the population. As more and more markets have become saturated with retail stores, competition has become increasingly strong. Thus in recent years, the development of strategic plans as the essence of competitive strategy has become as important as merchandising skills. Retailers are now more careful about choosing the markets in which they compete, as well as the competitive strategies and retailing-mix variables they use.

Chapter 1 reviews the essence of retailing structure to help students understand the complexity, excitement, and dynamic nature of retailing. Chapter 2 provides an overview of the ingredients of retail strategy development and is designed to help students understand how retailers develop strategies for competing in today's marketplace.

C H A P T E R

1

Retailing Today

THIS CHAPTER:

Relates retailing to the marketing discipline.

Explains and describes the current retail institutional structure.

Presents the concept of the retail life cycle and reviews several explanations of retail institutional change.

RETAILING CAPSULE

WAREHOUSE CLUBS: GROWING AND SUCCESSFUL

One of the fastest-growing sectors in retailing is warehouse club stores, such as Sam's, Price Club, Costco, PACE, and B.J.'s Wholesale Club. These members-only discount chains sell just about everything, typically in industrial-size quantities. Most items are name-brand products, not seconds.

About one-third of the stores' customers (who account for approximately 60 percent of sales) are business owners, using their warehouse memberships to buy goods in bulk for their restaurants, gas stations, or small offices. Individuals used to be able to get a membership at no cost but had to pay a surcharge on posted prices. In some places this procedure is still used; however, most warehouse clubs are switching to all paid memberships, usually $25 a year and eliminating the surcharge. Most chains won't accept just anybody as a member. Consumers must prove that they belong to a certain credit union or work for the government or an approved school, hospital, or company.

Although there is little sales assistance, no decor, no deliveries, and no frills, consumers flock to warehouse clubs to take advantage of their incredible bargains. Goods are marked up 8 to 10 percent, as opposed to the typical 20 to 30 percent markup in a regular discount store or the 35 to 50 percent markup in a department store. At Costco, for example, a $600 Ralph Lauren suit sells for $269.99, and two 32-ounce bottles of Scope mouthwash, regularly $9.78, sell for $6.99.

With 3,500 items per store, warehouse clubs don't have large selections in each merchandise category. Therefore, consumers still need to visit supermarkets, department stores, and office-supply stores for special needs.

However, the warehouse formula works, and market analysts predict that the warehouse-club boom should continue well into the 1990s.

Source: Based on Dori Jones Yang, "Bargains by the Forklift," *Business Week,* July 15, 1991, p. 152; Dori Jones Yang and Geoffrey Smith, "Corn Flakes, Aisle 1., Cadillacs, Aisle 2," *Business Week,* April 29, 1991, pp. 68–70; Peter Annin, "You Have to Join to Pay," *Newsweek,* August 5, 1991, p. 65.

We believe that introducing Chapter 1 with a discussion of warehouse clubs is most appropriate because they represent a type of retail institution that is currently experiencing success and growth. However, as the opening section of this chapter indicates, not all forms of retailing are currently classified as successful.

RETAILING: CURRENT REALITIES

In 1989 David Glass, CEO of Wal-Mart, rocked the retailing industry by predicting that 50 percent of all retailers would not be around in the year 2000. Now he fears he made a mistake: He believes he underestimated his figure.[1] In 1991 more than 15,000 retail firms filed for bankruptcy; 20 percent of the nation's department stores were owned by companies that were bankrupt.[2] What's the problem? The answer is that the United States is overstored, many retailers are overloaded with debt, consumers are not spending like they did in the 1980s, and many retailers are not adapting to meet the needs of a changing marketplace.

In 1990, the United States had 18 square feet of retail space for every man, woman, and child—twice the amount that it had in 1972.[3] Part of this buildup of retail capacity was the result of retail prosperity during the 1970s and 1980s. Mall expansion, the emergence of new types of retail institutions, and the expansion efforts of existing chains—adding stores, merchandise lines, and new store formats—are factors that have led to overstoring. The problem of overstoring becomes even more severe with decreases in consumer spending. Adjusted for inflation, retail sales per square foot have steadily declined since the mid-1980s. Retail sales growth is predicted to be only 2.5 percent or less in the 1990s, compared to the growth of 4 percent or more from the mid-1970s through the 1980s.[4]

Who will be successful retailers in the future? The consensus is that retailers destined for growth and success are those that will provide consumers with value and convenience, that will be technologically advanced and light on debt, and that will be narrowly focused on specific customers or products.

EXHIBIT 1–1

Courtesy The Price Company

Warehouse stores are the hottest segment in retailing today. At this Price Club store in Fountain Valley, California, you can get everything from groceries to copiers, but service is minimal.

Consumers at all socioeconomic levels have discovered the value and convenience of discounters, such as Wal-Mart, Kmart, and Target; warehouse clubs, such as Price Club and Costco, discussed in the Retailing Capsule (see Exhibit 1–1); and superstores that combine a supermarket and a discount store all under one roof.

At the same time, a strategy of unique products targeted to increasingly narrow audiences underscores the success of specialty retailers. Some, who focus on a customer lifestyle, not only offer merchandise that meets the needs of that market, but also then reinforce their product offerings with ambience. Examples include retailers such as Banana Republic, Ralph Lauren, and the various Limited stores (see A Profile in Excellence). Other successful specialty retailers are focusing on a product category or customer need. Retailers such as Toys 'R' Us, Home Depot, Crate & Barrel, and Circuit City are examples. Other retailers who are expected to be successful include catalog retailers and other nonstore retailers who are increasingly using sophisticated computers and ordering and delivery systems to provide unusual specialty-niche products.[5]

We hope that this brief introduction to retailing has provided you with a basic understanding of the diversity, complexity, and risk inherent in this industry. Before we discuss the structure and dynamics of retailing in this

A Profile in Excellence

LESLIE H. WEXNER

In 1963 Leslie Wexner borrowed $5,000 from his aunt and created a store that carried a narrow line of sportswear for women in the Columbus, Ohio, market. This was the beginning of the highly successful chain of stores called The Limited. By 1976, Wexner owned 100 stores.

Currently, Wexner has over 2,500 stores across the country and has diversified his portfolio of retail outlets. In addition to The Limited, his business units include Lane Bryant, Victoria's Secret, The Limited Express, Sizes Unlimited, Henri Bendel, and Abercrombie and Fitch.

Owing to the rapid growth of The Limited's portfolio, the corporation's financial resources became strained and its debt-to-equity ratio grew to 55 percent. Wexner decided to turn over the debt-load management to his chief financial officer so that he could focus on his innate talent for finding new markets and getting the right merchandise to the right stores before competition could react.

Wexner's continuing desire for growth and accomplishment is exemplified by one of his favorite quotes: "I'd like to believe that trees can grow to the sky. None have yet, but that doesn't mean it's impossible."

country in more detail, we must define some essential retail-related terms and describe the role played by retailing in getting products and services into the marketplace.

THE ROLE OF RETAILING

Retailing can be described in several ways: (1) in terms of activities, (2) as part of a process, (3) as having structure, and (4) as an intermediary in a channel of distribution.

Retailing consists of all activities involved in the sale of goods and services to the ultimate consumer. A retail sale occurs whenever an individual purchases groceries at a supermarket, a meal at McDonald's, a haircut at the barber shop, or a cassette at a video store. Not all sales are made in a store that is open for business. Direct sales are common—Tupperware and Mary Kay are examples.

Retailing is part of the process of marketing. **Marketing** is defined by the American Marketing Association as the process of planning and executing the conception, pricing, promotion, and distribution of ideas, goods, and services to create exchanges that satisfy individual and organizational objectives. Thus, by satisfying individual objectives, retailing is the final part of the marketing process.

Structure is the arrangement of parts, elements, or constituents that are considered as a whole. Thus, the **retail structure** comprises all retail outlets through which goods or services move to the ultimate consumer. The structure is complex and, as we will discuss later in the chapter, can be classified in various ways to help one understand its components.

Finally, retailing is conducted by organizations that act as intermediaries in a channel of distribution. A **channel of distribution** is an interorganizational system through which products or services are marketed. Refer to Figure 1–1 to see typical channel-of-distribution structures. The longest channel is an indirect one: products move from the producer, through the functional middleman (an agent or a broker), to a wholesaler, to the retailer who serves the consumer. An example of this channel is a widely distributed food product: the producer needs a sales force (for example, a broker) to sell to the wholesale market (a merchant wholesaler in a local market) from whom small retailers buy. The producer-to-retailer channel is appropriate for large retailers who have their own distribution centers and who perform the wholesale functions themselves. For example, J. C. Penney operates in this manner. The direct channel is represented by catalog companies, direct sellers, and electronic home shopping.

Alternative Ways to Classify the Retail Structure

The complexity, magnitude, and dynamics of retailing can best be understood by analyzing its structure and also by evaluating the explanations of structural changes. Retail markets can be structured in a variety of ways, and any number of dimensions or criteria can be used to group retailers. The criteria chosen are dependent on the purpose or use of the classification scheme. For example, government agencies or trade associations may use particular classifications to analyze the effect of retailing on the economy or to report data based on the size, growth, and future outlook of various components of the retail structure. On the other hand, market researchers may use different classification schemes to evaluate the competitive positioning of a retailer's outlets or to study changes in retail institutions. The classification schemes will be discussed under two headings: descriptive and strategic (see Figure 1–2).

Descriptive Classifications

Classification schemes that group retailers by descriptive characteristics are often used for reporting retail data. As shown in Figure 1–2, descriptive classifications include type of ownership, type of merchandise carried, kind of business, and location.

Type of Ownership. The most common classification is based on ownership. Trade associations and industry consultants typically report retail performance data (for instance, average store sales, sales per square foot, and gross profit percentage) by ownership status. Retailers use these data to evaluate company or store performance and to track shifts in retail

FIGURE 1–1

TYPICAL CHANNEL STRUCTURES

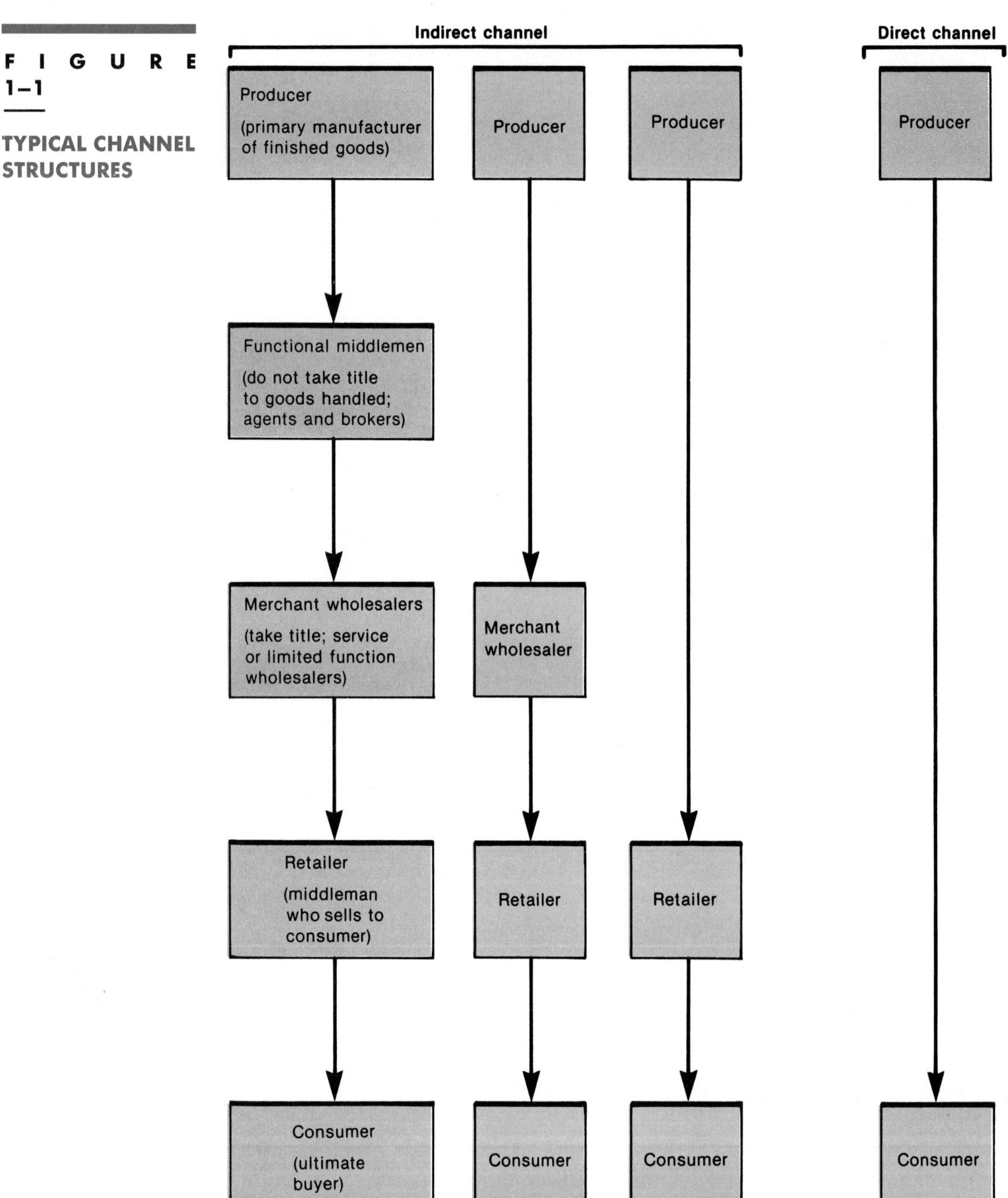

Indirect channel—Involves the use of intermediaries between producer and consumer.
Direct channel—Allows the movement of goods or services directly from producer to consumer.

Descriptive classifications
- Type of ownership
- Type of merchandise carried
- Kind of business
- Location

Strategic classifications
- Margin/Turnover
- Retail price/ Service strategy
- Strategic group analysis

FIGURE 1–2

ALTERNATIVE WAYS FOR CLASSIFYING THE RETAIL STRUCTURE

concentration. For example, the Food Marketing Institute reports retail grocery sales made through chain stores versus independents.

Independent. The independent operator with a single store dominates retailing in terms of numbers of outlets, accounting for approximately 80 percent of all retail establishments. Sales by such establishments constitute just over 52 percent of all retail sales. These independents tend to be small businesses operated by family members.

Chain. A chain (or multiunit organization) is characterized by the sale of similar merchandise in more than one outlet, a similar architectural format, centralized buying, and common ownership. Chains account for 37 percent of total retail sales. This general statistic, however, hides the importance of chains in certain kinds of business. For example, chains account for approximately 93 percent of general merchandise store sales, 60 percent of grocery store sales, but only about 27 percent of eating-establishment sales.

Manufacturer-Owned. Some manufacturers practice forward integration and operate their own retail outlets. Examples are Firestone retail stores and manufacturer-owned gasoline outlets, such as Texaco. Manufacturers own their own outlets for the following reasons: (1) they believe ownership offers the most profitable distribution alternative; (2) they desire total control over distribution; and (3) they wish to experiment with merchandising methods and product innovations.

Government-Owned. Occasionally, governments operate retail establishments. State-owned stores that sell liquor for off-premise consumption are typical examples. Military commissaries or post exchanges are also examples.

Farmer-Owned. Some farmers operate a limited number of retail outlets as seasonable roadside stands. More permanent farmer-owned retail outlets involve purchasing other producers' output for resale to consumers. Such open-air markets are experiencing a resurgence across the nation.

Public Utility-Owned. For many years, public utilities have sold stoves, refrigerators, and other types of appliances to boost the consumption of natural gas or electricity. In times of energy shortages, however, such sales decline.

Consumer-Owned. Consumer cooperatives are retail stores owned by consumers and operated by hired managers. Such cooperatives have not been important in the U.S. retail structure because the advantages of membership have been important only in isolated instances where the population has some strong reason—usually social—for wanting to associate for mutual benefit. Co-ops operate on the one person, one vote principle, no matter how much stock a member owns. Prices are competitive and, at the end of the year, members receive patronage dividends based on the dollar amount of purchases during the year. The country's largest cooperative is Consumers Cooperative of Berkeley, Inc., in California.

Type of Merchandise Carried

Retail establishments may be classified by the variety and assortment of their merchandise. **Variety** refers to the number of lines of merchandise carried; **assortment** refers to the choices offered within a line. For example, a store specializing in the sale of television sets will not have the large variety of other electrical appliances found in a discount department store. However, the assortment of TVs would be greater, with the consumer being able to choose among many different prices, cabinet styles, sizes, and other features. Figure 1–3 illustrates a classification framework based on variety and assortment. Variety can be broad or narrow; assortment can be shallow or deep. Based on these dimensions, four quadrants emerge.

Variety can also be thought of as the width of a store's merchandise offerings. Assortment, in turn, can be thought of as the depth of a store's merchandise selection, including sizes, colors, and types of material. Figure 1–4 illustrates the concepts of width (variety) and depth (assortment) for infants' wear in department, specialty, and discount stores.

Kind of Business

Retail establishments can be classified by the kind of business they engage in, or by the merchandise group they belong to. Figure 1–5 shows the retail categories, along with the percentage of retail sales accounted for by each category in 1988. Because most government statistics on retailing are reported for these categories, analysts use this classification scheme to report historical trends and sales for types of stores. However, the data mask important changes in the retail structure and may not be useful for strategic analyses.

For example, large supermarkets typically sell a broad mix of merchandise, including food, drugs, liquor, and general merchandise. Such a mix

Varying Retail Strategies – From L. L. Bean to Cub Foods

RETAILERS HAVE VARYING *DIRECT* WAYS TO REACH CUSTOMERS

(Courtesy of L. L. Bean)

L. L. Bean, the renowned sporting goods marketer, reaches the market through its catalog and retail stores.

(Courtesy of Home Shopping Network)

Home Shopping Network contacts customers directly through the electronic media.

(Courtesy Gurnee Mills)

Gurnee Mills offers name-brand marketers the opportunity to sell directly to the customers in a factory-outlet-mall setting.

Wal-Mart, the nation's *number one retailer,* employs varying strategies (strategic business units) to reach diverse markets

(Courtesy Wal-Mart Stores, Inc.)

Preparing to open a Wal-Mart Discount Center — the discount store known by consumers in the smallest and largest trading centers.

(Courtesy Sam's Club)

Sam's Club is Wal-Mart's format in the fast-growing wholesale club segment of retailing. "Members" include small retailers and individuals.

(Courtesy Hypermart USA)

Hypermart USA is Wal-Mart's entry in the European-developed megastore (in the 250,000-square foot range). A joint venture with a food chain, the format is already being strategically downsized.

UPSCALE, FASHION-ORIENTED GENERAL MERCHANDISE STORES EMPLOY VARYING STRATEGIES TO DEFINE THEIR MARKET NICHES IN DIFFERENT PARTS OF THE COUNTRY

Philadelphia-based John Wanamaker, one of the finest names in department store retailing.

(Courtesy John Wanamaker)

(Courtesy The Neiman-Marcus Group)

The mystique of Dallas-originated Neiman-Marcus, one of the world's most famous purveyors of "the best."

Parisian brings music to create style in this Alabama-headquartered, regional fashion apparel chain.

(Courtesy Parisian)

STRATEGIES OF FOOD MERCHANTS COME IN ALL SHAPES AND SIZES

West Point Market, in Akron, Ohio, is the Neiman-Marcus of food stores – fashion, elegance, and service.

(Courtesy Design Management)

(Courtesy Cub Foods)

Cub Foods, Minneapolis, bases its competitive strategy almost entirely on price in a warehouse-style setting.

FIGURE 1–3 **TYPE OF MERCHANDISE CARRIED—CLASSIFICATION BASED ON VARIETY AND ASSORTMENT**

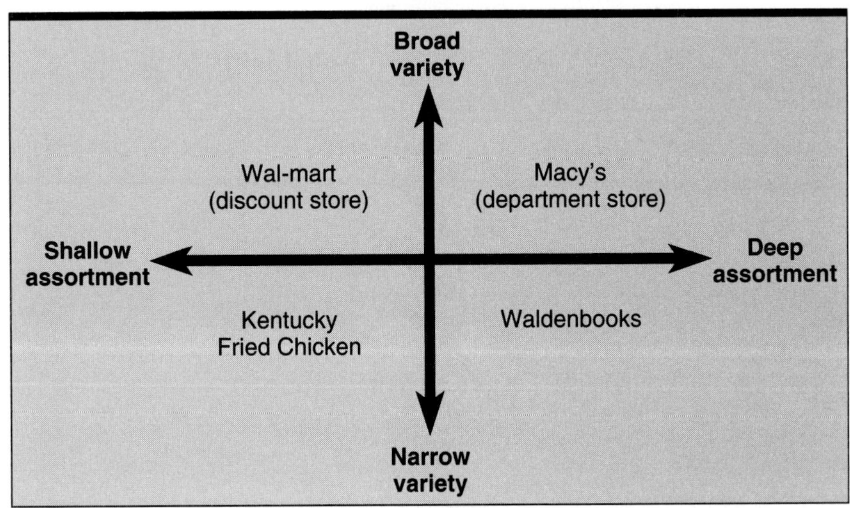

creates problems with classification and data accuracy because the supermarket will be classified as a particular kind of business depending on which type of merchandise has the highest percentage of sales. Also, each category may include retailers that follow different strategic formats, such as convenience food stores, conventional supermarkets, superstores, warehouse food stores, and other types of food stores. As a result, sales and profitability trends for strategic formats within a category cannot be analyzed.

Location

The nature and characteristics of location decisions are addressed in Chapter 9. The material in this chapter will therefore be limited to a brief discussion of the following location alternatives: the central business district, shopping centers, and stand-alone locations.

The Central Business District. During the 19th century, as cities grew in this country, the central business district (CBD) was the focal point of retailing. The major transportation arteries converged in these downtown areas, and small single-line and specialty stores were joined by the department store, which offered one-stop shopping for general merchandise. In the food sector, mom-and-pop grocery stores were the outlets of choice until the Great Depression, when the supermarket was born. Until the years immediately following World War II, all stores were essentially CBD or inner-city–neighborhood bound. The suburbanization of the

FIGURE 1–4 MERCHANDISE LINE WIDTH AND DEPTH FOR INFANTS' WEAR IN THREE TYPES OF RETAIL STORES

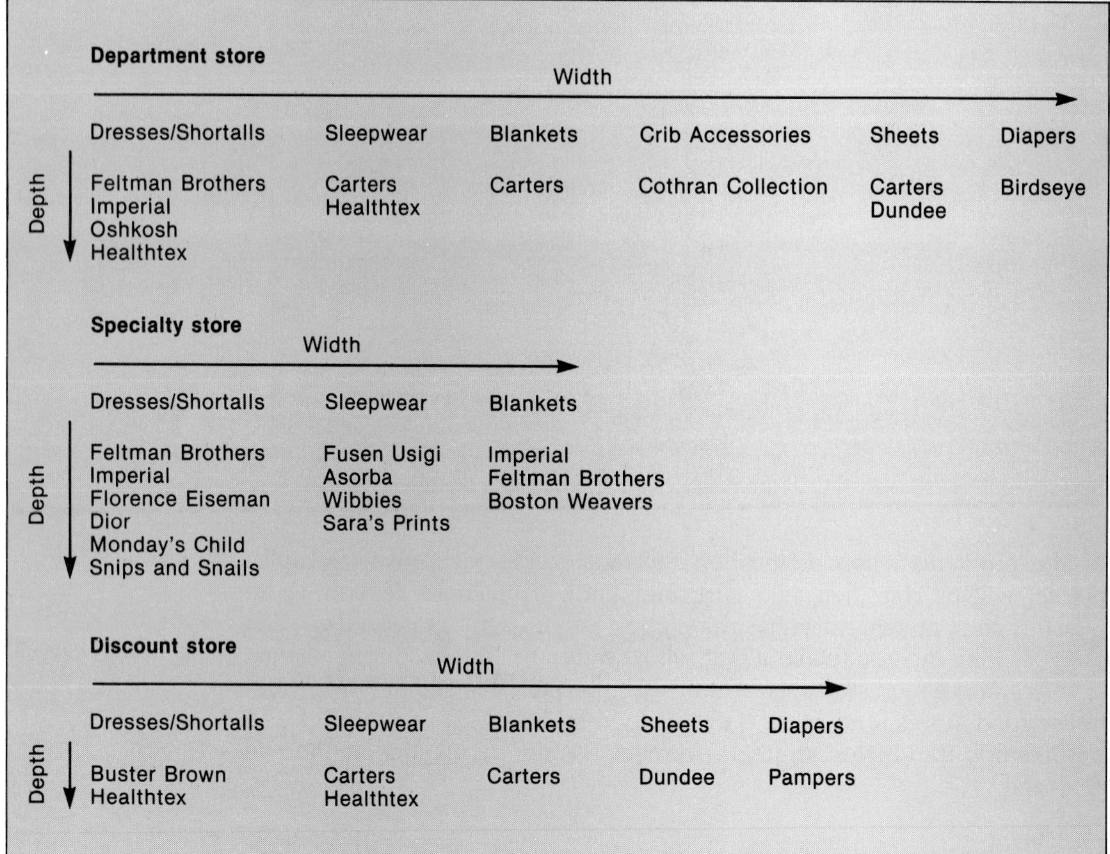

United States was a phenomenon of the 1950s and 1960s, when retailing followed the movement of the people who were leaving the cities for a new suburban lifestyle. This suburbanization led to the birth of the shopping center but to the decline of many central business districts.

Many cities have attempted, however, to revitalize their downtown areas. Downtown malls, with trees, foliage, sculpture, playgrounds, and fountains, were developed in many cities to beautify downtown areas in an attempt to attract shoppers. Many of these efforts have failed to meet expectations. But there are many examples of exciting and successful central-city developments. The CBD in New Orleans, for example, boasts three developments—Riverwalk, on the site of the disappointing 1984 Louisiana World Exposition; Canal Place, anchored by Saks; and New Orleans Centre, a 12-acre development anchored by Macy's and Lord

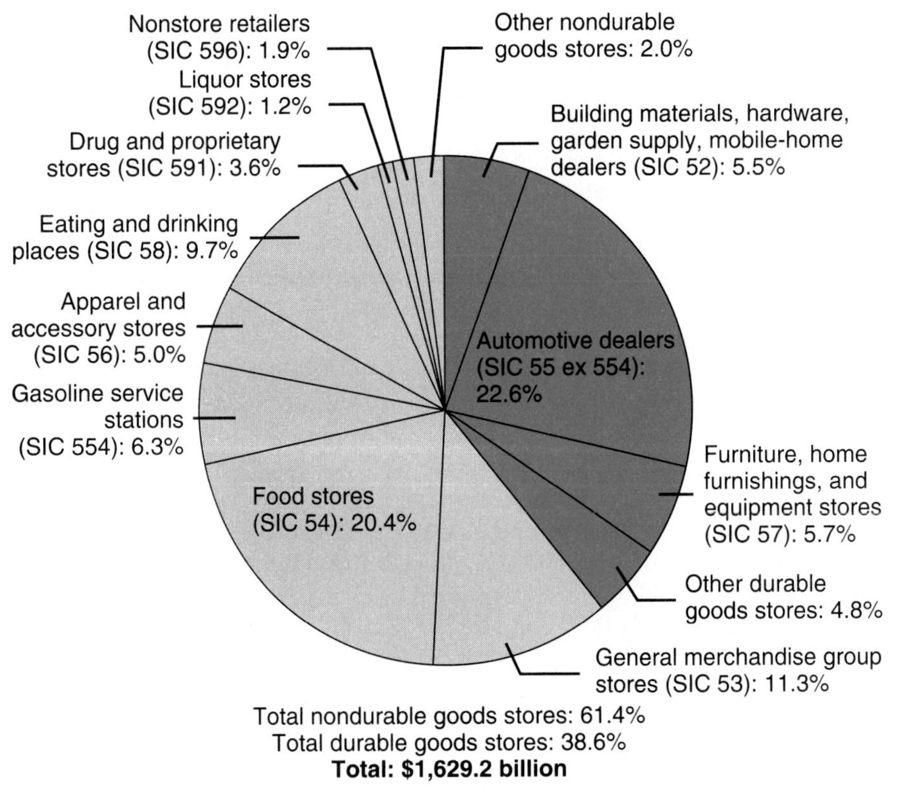

FIGURE 1–5

RETAIL TRADE: 1988 SALES BY KIND OF BUSINESS

Source: U.S. Bureau of the Census, *Statistical Abstract of the United States: 1990,* 110th ed. (Washington, D.C.: U.S. Government Printing Office, 1990), p. 772.

Taylor, that includes over 110 specialty stores. El Paseo, in the inner city of Santa Barbara, is a vintage CBD shopping center often referred to as the "jewel in the crown of Southern California." Another urban center, The Country Club Plaza in Kansas City, Missouri, may be the nation's most innovative, different, and beautiful development. The architectural motif is Spanish, dominated by red-tiled roofs, imported filigree ironwork, murals, art, and sculpture from around the world. Over 150 stores comprise this mixed-use development, as well as world-class hotel accommodations and apartment and condo dwellings.

Another example of revitalized urban development is the festival market. Probably the most famous is Faneuil Hall Marketplace in Boston, consisting of three 19th-century market buildings adjacent to Faneuil Hall. More than 155 merchants occupy space in the three buildings, not counting the pushcart operators. Baltimore's Inner Harbor has been transformed from a stagnant, commercially ignored backwater of Chesapeake Bay into a tastefully planned marketplace, Harborplace, whose retail core was modeled after the Faneuil Hall development. Another adaptive-use festival center is Union Station in St. Louis. In 1985 the ornate Union Station with its magnificent steel train shed, abandoned by Amtrack in 1978, was opened after having been restored and turned into a complex of restaurants, promenades, shops, and a hotel. It even contains a boat pond and a beer garden.

Shopping Centers. As indicated previously, shopping centers emerged during the late 1950s and 1960s to meet the needs of suburban consumers. Over time, dynamic changes have occurred with respect to shopping centers as a location alternative. For example, traditional shopping malls are currently being designed and renovated to be more consumer friendly (see Focus 1–1). Over time new forms of shopping centers have been developed. Some malls, for example, have successfully combined retailing with entertainment. One such mall, the West Edmonton Mall, located in Canada, includes over 800 shops and 11 department stores, complete with a theme park and much more. The U.S. answer to Edmonton is the Mall of America, located in Bloomington, Minnesota (see Case 2 at the end of the chapter). Another exciting development in shopping centers is the power, or destination, center. A power center is an oversized strip center ranging in size from 225,000 to 400,000 square feet, located on or near major highways or their arteries. Power centers are generally anchored by retailers such as toy, electronics, or home improvement superstores; off-price apparel outlets; or discount department stores or drugstores. Also popular among consumers today are the off-price centers and factory outlet malls (see A Question of Ethics).

Stand-Alone Locations. Stand-alone or freestanding locations offer several advantages: no common area maintenance charges, more space for parking and expansion, lack of close competition, and lower rent. Research conducted on store location preferences among retailers indicated that store size was a factor affecting location preferences. Of the retailers surveyed, those who preferred freestanding locations had the highest average gross leasable area. This is why many of the retailing formats such as warehouse clubs, hypermarkets, and category-dominant specialty stores often stand alone. In addition, retailers with the least number of stores (1 to 10) had the largest number of freestanding locations.[6]

Strategic Classifications

From strategic classification schemes, retailers gain competitive insights that assist them in assessing market opportunities and in developing strategies. As shown in Figure 1–2, strategic classifications include margin-turnover, retail price and service strategy, and strategic group analysis.

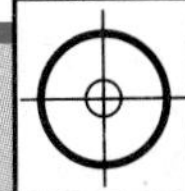

FOCUS 1–1

A CONSUMER-FRIENDLY APPROACH TO MALL DESIGN AND RENOVATION

A consumer-friendly approach is being used to design and renovate regional shopping malls. The objective is to attract consumers and to keep them coming back.

In the 1970s, malls were unique enough to draw people just because all the shops were there together. Today malls have to be larger and regionally oriented to attract shoppers. Malls are therefore being designed and renovated to reflect the location of the mall and the expectations of those who shop there. For example, the Volusia Mall in Daytona Beach, Florida, is being renovated so that the mall's new look will be reminiscent of the coastal mansions that sprang up in the state in the 1920s. Vegetation native to Florida, such as palm trees and sea grapes, and Florida limestone for columns are being used.

The customer-friendly aspects of the regional mall extend to spatial ambience as well. The "caves" of the 1960s and 1970s are being opened up by skylights to create the illusion of open-air shopping. For example, in Lewisville, Texas, an 80-foot-high oval cupola surrounded by rows of smaller pyramidal glass ceiling coffers presents an ever-changing view of the center's roof. At night the cupola and coffers are illuminated and, like giant lanterns, act as beacons, drawing shoppers to the center.

The increased use of skylights also focuses more attention on the design of center court areas. These areas must function as individual points of interest, separate from the retail tenants, to draw shoppers to them and to guide shoppers to other areas of the mall. Increasingly, center court areas are multipurpose, with courts being used for entertainment, after-hours events, and community-oriented programs. Kiosks are also becoming more commonplace in the common areas.

As many malls are increasing in size to more than 1 million square feet, developers are concerned with keeping mall corridors to a walkable length. Some developers are designing curved malls. With a curved mall, even if the corridor is long, it seems shorter. It also makes storefronts stand out for shoppers down the mall. In a straight-shot mall, shoppers can't see a storefront until they are in front of the store. Another idea is to run the mall directly through anchor stores. The concept would make the anchors' departments look like individual shops along the mall. Vertical centers are also becoming more common, although architects most often cite getting people to the upper floors as a problem.

Because mall retailers find that more open storefronts attract more customers, retailers are being encouraged to use storefronts that are higher and more visually open. Some stores have as much as two-thirds of the front open. Even the closed part of the storefront is usually made of glass to provide better merchandise visibility and a sense of openness.

Finally, some market analysts believe that major department stores will have less influence on a center in the future than they did in the past. They predict that there will be less department store space and more specialty store space.

Source: Adapted from Geoffrey Richards, "Atmosphere Key to Mall Design," *Shopping Center World,* August 1990, pp. 23–29.

A Question of Ethics

FACTORY OUTLET MALLS ANGER RETAILERS AS STORE SUPPLIERS TURN INTO COMPETITORS

Factory outlet malls are one of the fastest-growing segments of the retail industry. Between 1986 and 1990, the number of factory outlet malls nationwide more than doubled, with 275 such malls in existence in 1990. During that time period, sales grew to about $6.3 billion.

Decades ago, manufacturers opened outlet malls near their factories and used them to unload seconds, imperfect goods, and merchandise that was overproduced or sent back unsold by retailers. Now, even though most apparel manufacturers keep their outlets stocked with clothes that are at least a season behind, most of the merchandise is flawless and deep in size and selection. Furthermore, department stores may not have the edge over the outlet malls in terms of service. In a survey of 818 outlet shoppers, a majority indicated that service at outlet stores is superior to that at department stores.

Even though developers usually locate outlet malls outside big cities in towns too small to boast a big retail industry, the off-the-beaten-path locations and older merchandise aren't much comfort to retailers within an hour of the malls. The growth in outlet malls has angered retailers, who don't want their suppliers competing against them. In fact, a few groups, such as the National Sporting Goods Association and the National Shoe Association, have urged members to reduce or eliminate purchases from manufacturers operating units in outlet malls. But that strategy could backfire because of consumers' desire for certain trendy brands. Some retail consultants say that dropping a line to punish a manufacturer could be like cutting off the nose to spite the face.

How do we explain the growth and success of outlet malls? What are the manufacturers' benefits of opening outlets in such malls? Are retailers justified in their concerns? Are there any strategies that retailers could implement to compete more effectively against the outlet malls? If so, what are they?

Source: Based on Kevin Halliker, "Thriving Factory Outlets Anger Retailers as Store Suppliers Turn into Competitors," *The Wall Street Journal*, October 8, 1991, pp. B1 and B8; Gretchen Morgenson, "Cheapie Gucci," *Forbes*, May 27, 1991, pp. 43–44.

Margin-Turnover Classification

The margin-turnover framework for analyzing the retail structure, developed by Ronald Gist, may be applied to all types of outlets.[7] Based on the concepts of margin and turnover, the framework is useful for understanding basic strategy choices along financial dimensions. **Margin** is defined as the difference between cost and the retail selling price, or as the percentage markup at which merchandise is sold. **Turnover** is the number of times the average inventory is sold in a given year.

Figure 1–6 diagrams four quadrants, defined by margin and turnover, into which any retail outlet can be placed. The outlets can then be described in terms of store-level retail strategy, as shown in Table 1–1. The key strategy elements are types of merchandise sold, varieties and assort-

FIGURE 1–6 THE MARGIN-TURNOVER CLASSIFICATION

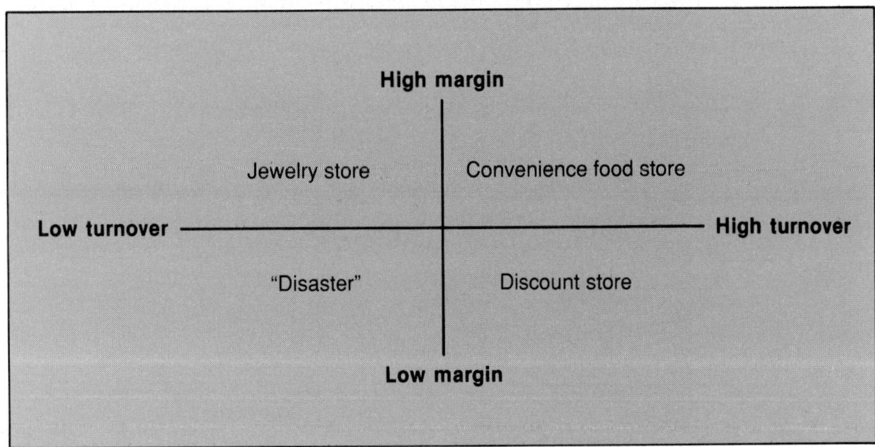

ments, services, price level, type of personal selling, type of promotion, complexity of organizational structure, and location requirements.

Retail Price and Service Strategy Classification

A second strategic classification (illustrated in Figure 1–7) utilizes two major value dimensions—price and service—to categorize firms.[8] Quadrants 1 and 4 are not viable in the long run and are in fact traps. On the other hand, quadrants 2 and 3 are promising strategic options.

In quadrant 1, even though customers would be pleased with high services and low prices, the strategy would not be profitable for the firm. Customers would not be interested in quadrant 4's poor value of low service at high prices. Retailers must monitor this strategy carefully as they reduce service in an attempt to be more price competitive.

TABLE 1–1 PROTOTYPES OF THE MARGIN-TURNOVER APPROACH TO THE CLASSIFICATION OF RETAIL INSTITUTIONS

Low-Margin—High Turnover	*High Margin—Low Turnover*
Merchandise presold or self-sold	Merchandise sold in store
Few services or "optional charge" services	Many services
Isolated locations	Cluster locations
Simple organizational characteristics	Complex organization
Variety large, assortments small	Variety smaller, assortments larger
Prices below the market	Prices above the market
Promotional emphasis on price	Promotion, institutional and merchandise-oriented

FIGURE 1–7

RETAIL PRICE/SERVICE STRATEGY CLASSIFICATION

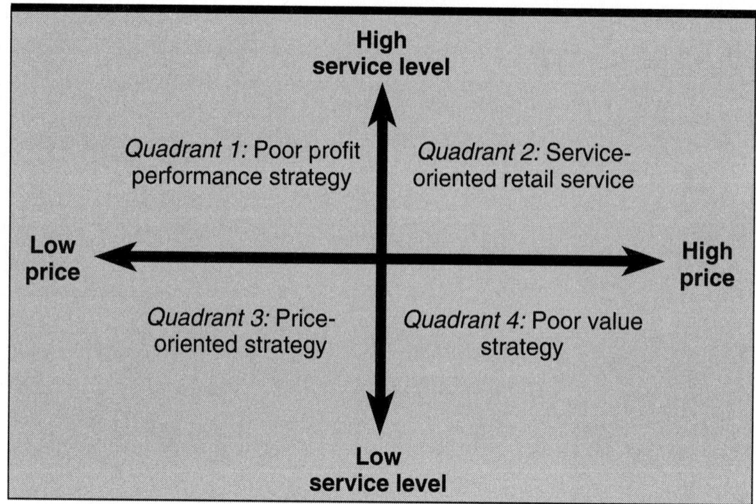

Source: George H. Lucas, Jr., and Larry G. Gresham, "How to Position for Retail Success," *Business* 38, no. 2, April–June 1988, p. 5.

Quadrant 2, classified as high price–high service, illustrates the business practices of firms such as Neiman-Marcus and Nordstrom, Bierly's Minneapolis food chain, Lands' End in catalog retailing, and Disney in entertainment retailing. Quadrant 3 illustrates a popular strategy represented by such firms as Sam's Wholesale Clubs, T.J. Maxx, and Wal-Mart.

Strategic Group Analysis

Figure 1–8 illustrates a classification format that allows a retailer to map competition in a particular line of trade—in this instance, the retail jewelry industry. The classification dimensions are price/quality on the vertical axis and product/line merchandise mix on the horizontal axis.

Assume that a small, independent jeweler with a high price/quality status carries only gold jewelry and gemstones (a highly specialized product line) and focuses strategic attention only on other small, independent guild competitors. Taking such a narrow view of competition, this jeweler is likely to take actions without considering retailers who are directly competitive though not in the identical category of small, independent guild stores. For example, Figure 1–8 indicates that small, independent stores compete with larger, national guild stores (such as Tiffany's and Cartier) as well as with prestige department stores with fine-jewelry departments (such as Neiman-Marcus and Saks Fifth Avenue).

Strategic classification formats can be applied to any line of merchandise and are flexible in terms of choice of classification dimensions. The dimensions used should be those that are important to consumers in

FIGURE 1–8

STRATEGIC GROUP ANALYSIS: RETAIL JEWELRY

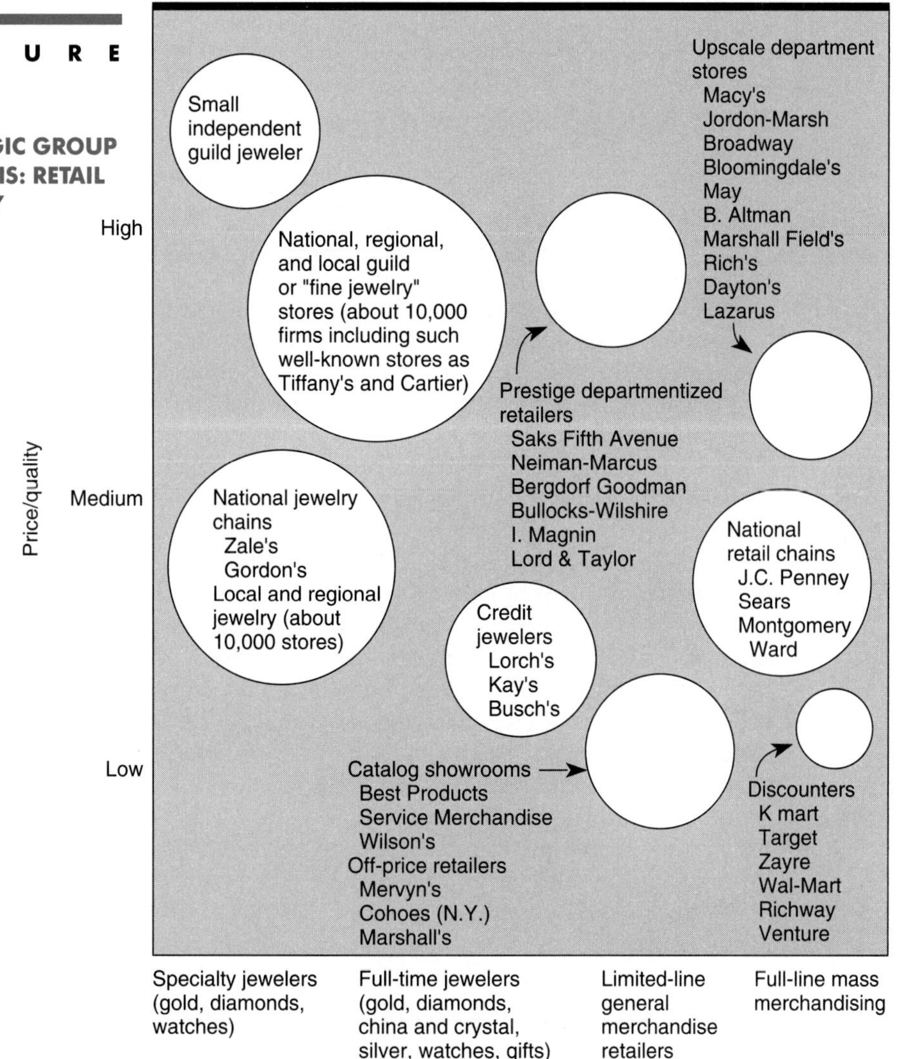

Note: The sizes of the circles are roughly proportional to the market shares of each group of competitors.

Source: Arthur A. Thompson, Jr. and A. J. Strickland III. *Strategy Formulation & Implementation: Tasks of the General Manager,* 4th ed. (Homewood, IL: BPI/Irwin, 1989), p. 96.

deciding where to shop, and the analysis should be based on shoppers' perceptions of competitors along the relevant dimensions.

DYNAMICS OF THE RETAIL STRUCTURE

The retail structure as previously classified—either descriptively or strategically—is dynamic. The institutions that comprise the structure have historically moved through a life cycle comprised of four stages: development and introduction, growth, maturity, and decline.

During the development and introduction stage, management develops concepts and strategies for the new business and attempts to stimulate consumer awareness and patronage of initial outlets. Few, if any, competitors exist, and initial outlets may be limited in number and location. Current examples of businesses at this stage are the organic food stores and retailers offering products that protect the environment. For example, Goodebodies offers a complete line of high-quality, all-natural, biodegradable, recycled body care products. During the growth stage, retailers expand into new markets and add new merchandise lines as the new store format catches on. Wholesale clubs and factory outlet centers currently are in the growth stage, as are many superspecialists and superstores. For example, office supply superstores such as WORKplace, HQ, and Staples Inc. are doubling and tripling store locations annually. In the maturity stage, the stage that characterizes today's fast-food industry, price competition is brutal in the fight for market share. Cost reduction and profitability improvement become key issues. In the decline stage, competitors drop out and the institutions may cease to exist. For example, the general store and the variety store (such as Woolworth) are virtually extinct. During the 1980s, the number of variety stores in the United States declined 38 percent—the worst decline suffered by any retail sector in that decade.[9]

In the following sections, we discuss theories and models that explain institutional development and evolution. Ideally, analysis of such change should lead to a universal model that would enable management to *predict* change. Unfortunately, the theories are descriptive at best and do not apply, without modifications, to retailing outside the United States.

Why do we devote time to the theories? Because they help retailers understand past events and their causes, thereby aiding understanding of the present and the future. For example, in the United States, the superstore format has invaded many retail sectors—food, office supplies, toys, and electronics. Observing this pattern and its causes may alert retailers in other sectors to study the phenomenon and determine its likely effect on their markets and businesses.

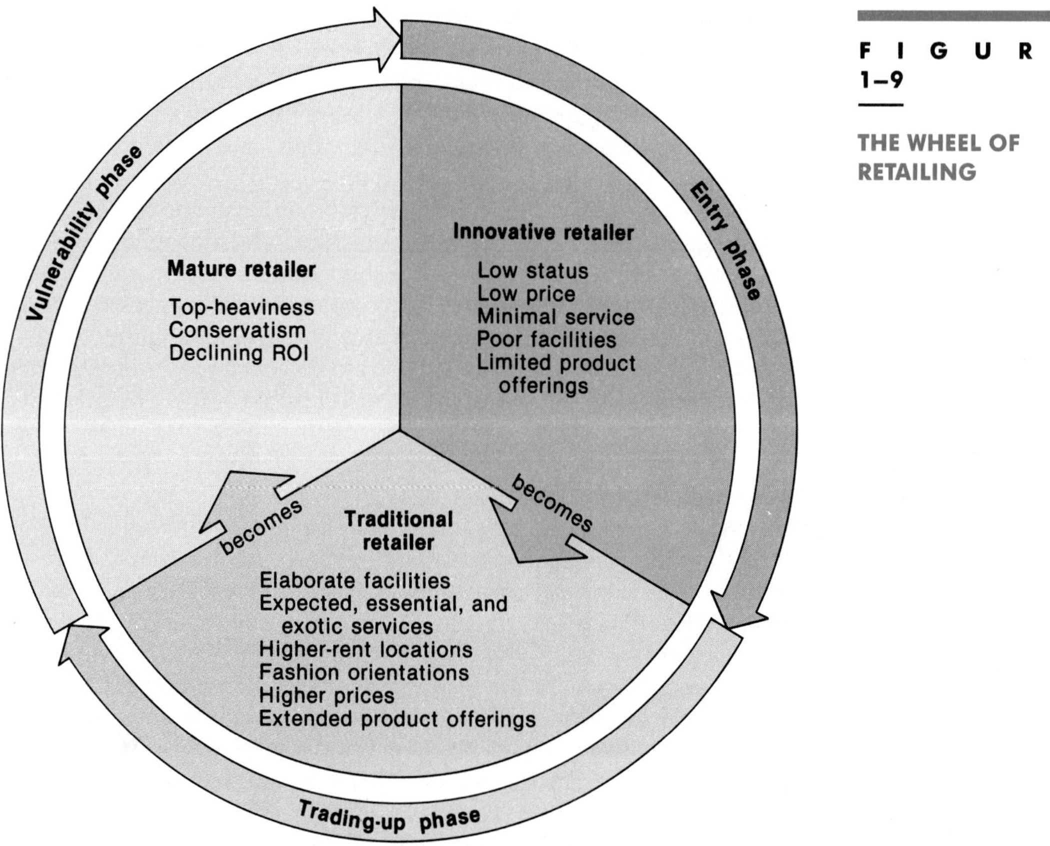

FIGURE 1–9

THE WHEEL OF RETAILING

Source: Dale M. Lewison, *Retailing* (New York: Macmillan, 1991), p. 73. Reprinted with the permission of Macmillan Publishing Company from *Retailing*, Fourth Edition by Dale M. Lewison. Copyright © 1991 by Macmillan Publishing Company. Copyright © 1989, 1986, 1982 by Merrill Publishing Company.

THEORIES OF RETAIL INSTITUTIONAL CHANGE

The Wheel of Retailing

The **wheel of retailing** hypothesis, developed by Harvard University professor Malcolm McNair, is the best-known explanation for changes in the retail structure (see Figure 1–9). McNair's theory states that new types of retail institutions enter the market as low-margin, low-price, low-status merchants (the entry phase). Gradually, during the trading-up phase, they provide new services and improve their facilities, a process that drives up expenses, margins, and consequently prices. Eventually the innovator matures as a high-cost, conservative merchant that is vulnerable to new types of institutions that enter the market as low-cost, low-price, no-frills competitors. Examples of retail institutions that entered the market as low-cost, low-price operations include warehouse or wholesale clubs, factory outlet centers, off-price retailers, discount stores, and catalog showrooms.

The wheel theory has been criticized on several points. First, not all retail operations start out as low-cost, low-price outlets. For example, department stores and automatic vending machines did not follow this model. Also, some argue that retailers tailor their outlets to match specific wheel positions and intend to remain at that point. Multibusiness retailers with operations focused on different market segments (for example, a corporation owning both gourmet and warehouse/discount food stores) would not want the various store types in their portfolios to compete openly with one another.

The Retail Accordion

An alternative explanation for changes in the retail structure is the concept of the **retail accordion.** Proponents of the theory argue that changes in the merchandising mix, not price and margins, are a better explanation for change in the retail institutional structure than the wheel of retailing. This theory is based on the premise that retail institutions evolve over time from broad-based outlets with a wide variety of merchandise to outlets offering specialized narrow lines. Eventually, outlets begin again to offer a wide variety, thus establishing a general-specific-general pattern. This evolution suggests the term *accordion,* which reflects a contraction and expansion of merchandise lines.

Modern retailing in the United States began with general stores—one-stop outlets that offered a wide variety of merchandise. General stores usually prosper where the population is too sparse to support more specialized stores. With the development of large population centers, retailers typically specialize in a merchandise line in an attempt to provide better selection and service. Thus, as cities grew in the United States, general stores gave way to small, service-oriented specialty stores such as hat stores, butcher shops, and barber shops. Then, the department store emerged as a viable store format during the post–Civil War depression. With a broader merchandise mix than specialized stores, department stores were better able to withstand the depression. Beginning in the 1950s, affluence and continued growth of cities made it easier for retailers to tailor merchandise offerings to specific market segments—hence the emergence of single-line and specialty stores, such as bookstores, clothing boutiques, and drugstores. Starting in the late 1950s, broad-based outlets again grew rapidly, even though specialized operations did not disappear. Today, the retail sector appears to be moving to such operations as large superstores, category killers (such as Toys 'R' Us), or warehouse formats. At the same

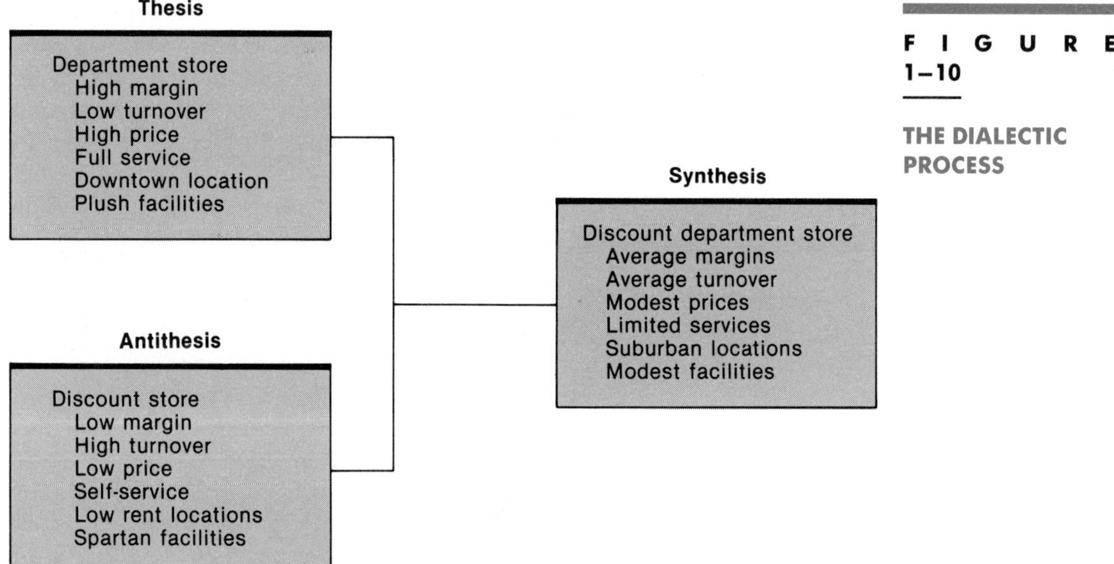

FIGURE 1–10

THE DIALECTIC PROCESS

Source: Dale M. Lewison, *Retailing* (New York: Macmillan, 1991), p. 74. Reprinted with the permission of Macmillan Publishing Company from *Retailing,* Fourth Edition by Dale M. Lewison. Copyright © 1991 by Macmillan Publishing Company. Copyright © 1989, 1986, 1982 by Merrill Publishing Company.

time, small specialty stores offering high levels of service and unique products are enjoying success.

The Dialectic Process

A third explanation for changes in the retail structure is the theory of the **dialectic process,** which is based on the premise that retailers mutually adapt in the face of competition from "opposites." When challenged by a competitor with a differential advantage, an established institutional type will adopt strategies and tactics in the direction of the advantage, thereby negating some of the innovator's attraction.

For example, as shown in Figure 1–10, the department store was originally developed as an institution offering both hard goods and soft goods, a wide array of services, and attractive surroundings (the thesis). The challenging institution (the antithesis) was the discount store, which offered merchandise similar to that of a department store but in unattractive, low-cost surroundings without customer services. The promotional or discount department store (the synthesis) then emerged as a blend of the strengths of both the department store and the discount store. Kmart provides an example of a discount department store. Other institutions that might fit the dialectic model are the self-service gasoline/convenience store and the warehouse club (retail and wholesale operations).

Adaptive Behavior and Natural Selection

Adaptive behavior states that an environmental need that exists for a certain kind of retail institution will cause the institution to evolve. When the need ceases to exist, the institution will disappear. Adaptive behavior thus explains the inception of an institution. Shopping centers, for example, emerged to meet the needs of consumers moving from downtown to suburbia. The adaptive behavior theory can be used to explain the development and growth of health spas, diet centers, and similar types of institutions that have emerged in response to American consumers' interest in health and physical fitness.

Natural selection suggests that retailing institutions that can most effectively adapt to economic, competitive, social, technological, and legal and political environmental changes are the ones most likely to prosper or survive. Department stores have lost market share because they have been slow to adapt to environmental change. They remained too long in central business locations, and when they finally did move to suburban locations, discount stores and specialty stores had already gained shoppers' acceptance. Likewise, the variety store is often cited as an institution that failed to adapt to changing environmental conditions and consequently is virtually absent from the modern retailing scene.

This section of the chapter has presented theories developed to explain retail institutional change. Each theory is different, and no one theory can explain the evolution of all retail institutions, but together they provide a more comprehensive understanding of the evolution of retail structure. However, using such theories to predict future developments in retailing is risky. Retailing is and always will be one of the most dynamic industries in a society. But the dynamic nature of retailing is one of the factors that makes careers in retailing so exciting and rewarding. This book has been written to provide you with the knowledge, information, and skills you need to pursue a successful career in this challenging yet rewarding industry.

Chapter Highlights

- Retailing is diverse, complex, and high risk. It represents the final stage of the marketing process. Retailers act as intermediaries in channels of distribution.
- The complexity, magnitude, and dynamics of retailing can best be understood by analyzing its structure and by evaluating the explanations of structural change.
- Descriptive classifications, often used for reporting retail data, include type of ownership, type of merchandise carried, kind of business, and location.
- From strategic classification schemes, retailers gain competitive insights that assist them in assessing market opportunities and in developing strategies. Examples of such classification formats include margin-turnover, retail price and service strategy, and strategic group analysis.

- Institutions comprising the retail structure have historically moved through a life cycle encompassing four stages: development and introduction, growth, maturity, and decline.
- Theories of retail institutional change help retailers understand events and their causes in retrospect, thus aiding their understanding of the present and the future. These theories include the wheel of retailing, the retail accordion, the dialectic process, and natural selection and adaptive behavior.

Study Questions

1. Define and relate the following terms: retailing, marketing, retailing structure, and channels of distribution.
2. Why is it important to classify the retail institutional structure? How might the owner of an existing store benefit from a study of the retail structure in a given market?
3. Describe the classification of retail institutions based on ownership and type of merchandise carried.
4. Discuss the margin-turnover classification model. Give an example of a type of retail outlet that may exist in each of the four quadrants of the model.
5. Discuss the differences in the operating characteristics of a low-margin/high-turnover retail firm and a high-margin/low-turnover firm.
6. Discuss the retail price and service strategy classification scheme.
7. Select a merchandise line other than jewelry (as used in the text) and illustrate the way a retail manager might utilize the concept of strategic group mapping.
8. Explain the life cycle concept as applied to retail institutions.
9. Describe the following theories of retail institutional change: the wheel of retailing, the retail accordion, and the dialectic process.
10. Discuss adaptive behavior and natural selection as theories of retail institutional change.

A P P L I C A T I O N S

CASE 1: Tuesday Morning, Inc.

Tuesday Morning, Inc., is a 150-store chain that specializes in the sale of upscale close-out merchandise such as gifts and household items. Operating hours are 9:30 A.M. to 6:00 P.M.—that is, when the stores are open at all (*they are closed more than half the year*). From "event" to "event" (as each of the four openings a year is called), nobody, not even chief executive Lloyd Ross, knows exactly what goods Tuesday Morning will offer. New customers often have trouble finding the stores at all. The one in Overland Park, Kansas, sits in a basement at a strip shopping center, its entrance facing a back alley.

Events at Tuesday Morning ironically begin on Thursday mornings. As much as an hour before opening time, Mercedes, Cadillacs, and even chauffeur-driven limos pull into the parking lot. Ninety-two percent of the store's customers are female, and their median household income is more than $55,000. Officials say that a customer once postponed her husband's open-heart surgery so that she wouldn't miss the opening of a Tuesday Morning event.

The appeal is threefold: (1) merchandise bears such names as Ralph Lauren, Wedgewood, and Laura Ashley; (2) it is offered at price reductions between 50 and 80 percent; and (3) supplies are severely limited. Generally, the better merchandise is gone after the first day of the opening. In fact, because of the limited merchandise, some customers have been observed taking merchandise from another customer's cart. Some customers go to even greater lengths than cart robbing to gain first pick of the limited stocks—some join the staff of Tuesday Morning (the chain uses all part-time help, except for store managers).

Ross founded the chain 18 years ago as an outlet for manufacturers' excess inventory. The goods are displayed on cafeteria-style tables or metal shelves. Some market analysts didn't believe that a store closed half the year would make money. However, the chain has been very successful. Since the company went public in 1984, sales and profits have grown every year, except 1988 when costs rose 24 percent (because of some one-time warehouse-construction expenses) on a 12 percent sales increase. In 1991 earnings were $5.4 million, up 15 percent from $4.7 million in 1990, on a 14 percent increase in sales of $122 million from $107 million.

Source: Adapted from Kevin Helliker, "If There's Hardly Anything Left to Buy, It's Tuesday Morning on Christmas Eve," *The Wall Street Journal*, December 23, 1991, p. B1.

Applying Retailing Principles

1. What are the ingredients that have made Tuesday Morning a successful retail operation?
2. How can Tuesday Morning offer such low prices and still operate profitably?
3. Speculate on the long-run success of such operations as Tuesday Morning.

CASE 2: Mall of America

The mammoth Mall of America opened its doors in August 1992 in Bloomington, Minnesota. Developed by Melvin Simon & Associates, it is the biggest mall in the United States. The mall cost $625 million to build and covers 4.2 million square feet. Simon has booked such stores as Bloomingdale's, Nordstrom, Sears, and 400 specialty stores. Mall of America also includes, among other attractions, 14 movie screens, six supper clubs, and a seven-acre Knott's Berry Farm with a log flume and a 70-foot-tall roller coaster.

Source: Adapted from "The Biggest Mall of All," *Money*, December 1991, p. 160.

Applying Retailing Principles

1. Consider the shopping mall as an institution in the retail structure. Utilize any of the explanations of retail evolution and provide reasons for the emergence of shopping malls that combine entertainment with shopping.
2. Do you think that shopping malls such as Mall of America that combine shopping and entertainment will be successful? Explain your answer.

Notes

1. Bill Saporito, "Is Wal-Mart Unstoppable?" *Fortune*, May 6, 1991, p. 50.
2. Bill Saporito, "Why the Price Wars Never End," *Fortune*, March 23, 1992, p. 70.
3. Laura Zinn, "Fewer Rings on the Cash Register," *Business Week*, January 14, 1991, p. 85.
4. Bill Saporito, "Retailing's Winners and Losers," *Fortune*, December 18, 1989, pp. 69–78.
5. R. Fulton Macdonald, "Shake, Rattle & Roll: The Coming Retail Revolution," *Retail Control*, April/May 1992, pp. 19–26.

6. Jane A. Black, "Centerless Anchors," *Monitor,* September 1989, p. 28.
7. Ronald R. Gist, *Retailing: Concepts and Decisions* (New York: John Wiley & Sons, 1968), pp. 37–40.
8. George H. Lucas, Jr. and Larry S. Gresham, "How to Position for Retail Success," *Business* 38, April–May–June 1988, pp. 3–13.
9. Brent Bowers, "Variety Stores Struggle to Keep the Dimes Rolling In," *The Wall Street Journal,* May 7, 1991, p. B2.

C H A P T E R

2

Strategic Retail Management

THIS CHAPTER:

Lists the steps involved In strategic retail planning.

Interprets the concept of an organization's mission statement.

Explains the difference between long- and short-term objectives.

Presents the issues involved in a situation analysis.

Discusses factors involved in selecting markets in which to compete.

Explains how retailers obtain resources needed to compete.

Reviews the components of retail positioning strategy.

Describes several strategic options available to retailers.

Focuses on the issues involved in the evaluation and control of a retail operation.

RETAILING CAPSULE

FREDERICK'S OF HOLLYWOOD: A NEW POSITIONING STRATEGY

Frederick's of Hollywood, a world-famous lingerie chain, has replaced its hard edge with an updated image. The company has developed a new positioning strategy targeted at mainstream America, and company values have shifted accordingly.

When George W. Townson assumed chairmanship of the company in 1985, sales and profits had been declining for several years. Frederick's decline was apparent on all fronts. Frederick's seemed garish and tacky compared to more elegant, romance-oriented competitors such as Victoria's Secret. Lingerie tastes had grown up, but Frederick's had not.

Although sex appeal is still the name of the game, Townson has softened and improved the image of Frederick's. The redefinition of the company's target market has led to an extensive overhaul that has affected every area of the company. Changes are most apparent in the merchandise mix and store design. Merchandise has been upgraded with better-quality fabrics, softer colors, and more modern styling. Items that might be considered of questionable taste have been dropped. To complement the new store image, Frederick's has embarked on an extensive store remodeling program. The new store has a sleek, contemporary design and a less risqué look. Even Frederick's infamous mail order catalog has a new look. It is less cluttered and less naughty looking.

Consumers have responded positively to the changes. Sales are increasing, as are net earnings. Company management expects the positive trend to continue.

Source: Based on Marianne Wilson, "The De-Sleazification of Frederick's," *Chain Store Age Executive,* September 1989, pp. 94–96; Kathleen Kerwin, "Frederick's of Hollywood Trades Its X Rating for an R," *Business Week,* December 11, 1989, p. 64.

FIGURE 2–1

STRATEGIC PLANNING

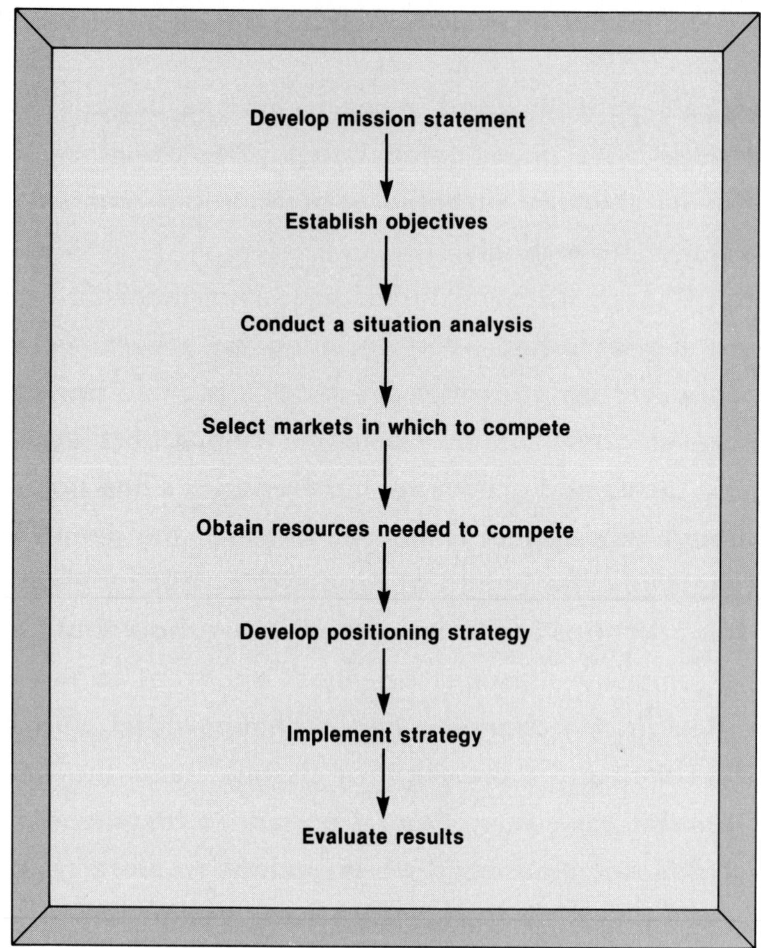

The preceding profile illustrates the concept of strategic planning in a retail organization. **Strategic planning** includes defining the overall mission or purpose of the company, deciding on objectives that management wants to achieve, and developing a plan to achieve these objectives. Frederick's of Hollywood observed marketplace alterations that required a strategic change: serving the needs of the mainstream mall shopper. Changes in all aspects of the company's operations occurred to support this new mission.

Figure 2–1 illustrates the steps involved in strategic planning. The plan begins with a statement of the mission or purpose of the organization. Management establishes its objectives. It then analyzes internal strengths and weaknesses and external threats and opportunities to help it decide the best way to carry out the organization's mission and to achieve its objectives. Management must select markets in which to compete and obtain resources. It also develops a positioning strategy that outlines how the organization will serve chosen markets. It then implements the strategy. Finally, management measures and evaluates results to ensure that the strategy is working.

DEFINING THE MISSION OR PURPOSE OF THE ORGANIZATION

Management begins the planning process by identifying the organization's mission or purpose. This definition often reflects top management's personal goals and values. Some people, by sheer force of personality, may single-handedly lead an organization to pursue a specific mission. Individuals who shaped major organizations are Ray Kroc, founder of McDonald's; Sam Walton, founder of Wal-Mart; Mary Kay Ash, creator of Mary Kay Cosmetics; and Harland Sanders, who started Kentucky Fried Chicken (see A Profile in Excellence).

The vehicle used to communicate the organization's purpose is the **mission statement.** This statement tells what the firm intends to do and how it plans to do it. A statement of mission or purpose normally includes the following elements:

1. Definitions of products and services to be offered, customers to be served, and geographic areas to be covered.
2. How the physical assets, financial assets, and human resources will be used to create customer satisfaction.
3. How the firm intends to compete in its chosen markets.

A company that has been consistent in clearly communicating its purpose is the Dayton-Hudson Corporation. Their mission statement begins with the sentence, "We are in business to please our customers," and then goes on to explain how the company does this—by emphasizing value, by having the most wanted merchandise in stock and in depth, and by giving customers a "total shopping experience that meets their expectations for service, convenience, environment, and ethical standards."[1]

Ingvar Kamprad, founder of IKEA, the world's largest home furnishing chain, developed a nine-part statement of philosophy in his "Testament of a Furniture Dealer" in 1976, when the firm opened its first stores outside Sweden. This statement begins with the firm's basic purpose: "IKEA shall offer a wide range of home furnishing items of good design and function, at prices so low that the majority of people can afford to buy them."[2]

A firm's mission statement often reflects its **corporate culture,** which establishes the values of greatest importance to the organization. When J. C. Penney was incorporated in 1913, the company formulated and

A Profile in Excellence

HARLAND SANDERS

Harland Sanders, the founder of Kentucky Fried Chicken, was forced to make his way in the world at a very young age. His father died when he was six, and he had to accept responsibility for his family. Sanders had quite a colorful life, held many odd jobs, and earned a law degree before perfecting the recipe for Kentucky Fried Chicken.

In 1929, Sanders opened a gasoline station in Corbin, Kentucky. As time passed, he began to serve his clients the Southern dishes he cooked for his family. Sanders's specialties included fried chicken, fresh vegetables, and homemade biscuits. As the popularity of his gas station–café grew, Sanders needed to find a faster way to cook the chicken that would make him famous. In 1939, he began using a pressure cooker and was able to meet the growing demand for his product without sacrificing the taste and quality of the chicken.

Sanders started selling the rights to his pressure-cooking process and the recipe for his chicken to other restaurateurs, who paid him a set fee per chicken cooked. In 1956, Sanders had to sell his café to pay his debts. He then set off on a quest to find others interested in purchasing the rights to his process. By 1960, he had found 200 people willing to cook chicken his way, and the first 200 KFC franchisees were born.

By 1963, the number of franchisees had grown to 600. One year later Sanders sold the business (with the exception of the Canadian branch) to John Young Brown. The franchise grew to 3,500 outlets by 1971. Sales currently exceed $700 million. Sanders remained involved with Kentucky Fried Chicken after the sale by serving as its spokesperson and national symbol.

adopted "The Penney Idea," a set of seven principles that guide the firm to this day. These principles, presented in A Profile in Excellence in Chapter 3, are personal standards of the founder and values the company tries to maintain.

Often, mission statements also reflect the firm's ethics. Ethical organizations pursue a sense of duty and purpose that goes beyond meeting the letter of the law. For example, some firms may elect not to sell certain products because they have been identified as harmful, even though they are legal. For a specific application of this issue, see A Question of Ethics.

Employees at all levels of an organization must understand the firm's mission statement. Sometimes even the simplest, clearest mission can be misinterpreted. Therefore, once determined, the firm's mission statement must be repeated constantly. The message must be further reinforced through signals sent by management attitudes, policies, rewards, and supporting facilities. Conflicting signals rapidly negate a carefully designed statement. Employees, for example, become frustrated when an organization says that it stresses total customer satisfaction but then imposes controls that make it difficult or impossible to deliver it.

A Question of Ethics

TO SELL OR NOT TO SELL

A survey of pharmacies located throughout the United States was conducted to determine the retailers' views concerning the sale of tobacco. The retailers were divided on the issue.

Approximately two-thirds of the retailers sell cigarettes and plan to continue doing so as long as they are manufactured. Not only do cigarettes account for nearly 6 percent of pharmacy sales, but independent retailers also believe that cigarette sales draw traffic and enable the stores to better compete with larger chains. Some of the retailers interviewed stated that people who choose to smoke have a right to do so. On the other hand, retailers who have chosen not to sell cigarettes believe that they will gain a competitive advantage from a strengthened health care image. Finally, 9 out of 10 respondents indicated that they do not sell cigarettes to minors and that they ask for proof of age.

Are the retailers who decided not to sell cigarettes following a sound strategy? Why or why not? Do you think that retailers, such as pharmacies, that are in the health care field should sell products known to be harmful? Explain your position.

Source: Adapted from Cynthia Starr, "To Sell or Not to Sell," *Drug Topics* 132, (May 2, 1988), pp. 28–34.

SETTING OBJECTIVES

After agreeing on the firm's mission, management's task is to establish objectives. **Objectives** are statements of results to be achieved. Objectives may include profit, sales volume, market share, or expansion.

Management normally sets both long-term and short-term objectives. Long-term objectives are usually set for five years or more and indicate results that the organization must achieve to remain successful over time. Short-term objectives are set in one- or two-year time frames and are designed to measure at regular intervals how well the organization is meeting its long-term objectives.

To be effective, objectives must reflect the organization's priorities. They must be precise and realistic, and they must embody quantitative and qualitative aspects. Objectives should also include a time horizon. Examples of well-stated and poorly stated objectives appear in Figure 2–2.

CONDUCTING A SITUATION ANALYSIS

Once objectives are set, management must decide on a plan for achieving them within the context of the firm's mission. This plan is based on an analysis of strengths and weaknesses of the organization and threats and opportunities in the external environments. This assessment of internal strengths and weaknesses and external threats and opportunities is referred to as a **situation analysis.**

FIGURE 2–2

EXAMPLES OF WELL-STATED AND POORLY STATED OBJECTIVES

Examples of Well-Stated Objectives	*Examples of Poorly Stated Objectives*
Our objective is to increase market share from 15 percent to 18 percent in 1993 by increasing promotional expenditures 15 percent.	Our objective in 1995 is to increase promotional expenditures.
Our objective for 1992 is to earn aftertax profits of $5 million.	Our objective is to maximize profits.
Our objective is to open three new units by 1993 in each of the following states where the chain presently has no units: Tennessee, Georgia, and Florida.	Our objective is to expand by adding units to the chain.

Internal factors evaluated in the situation analysis are variables that are largely under the control of store management. Both tangible and intangible resources should be evaluated; these include financial resources, physical assets (for example, buildings and display fixtures), merchandise lines, customer services, management skills, sales force composition, the firm's reputation with customers, and employees' attitudes toward the company. One way to develop a better understanding of critical internal strengths and weaknesses is to use a profile chart, which is a visual display of factors affecting internal organizational strengths, such as those just mentioned. Each factor is rated on a scale ranging from −2 to +2, with −2 being extremely unattractive and +2 being extremely attractive.

External factors are those that management cannot control. Chapters 3, 4, and 5 discuss these. Management studies trends in the external environments and determines whether these trends pose threats, present opportunities, or are irrelevant to the organization.

DECIDING ON MARKETS IN WHICH TO COMPETE

The ultimate value of the situation analysis is this: it helps the firm identify and capitalize on opportunities. It helps store management identify markets that offer strong opportunities for growth and profitability and avoid markets that appear undesirable.

Screening criteria are useful tools for identifying markets that are most compatible with the firm's resources and skills, as well as threats and opportunities from the external environments. Typical criteria are shown in Figure 2–3 and include such factors as the growth potential of the likely market, the investment needed to compete, and the strength of competition. The possible markets are evaluated by deciding the importance of each criterion and ranking each possible market on the criteria. Multiplying the importance of each factor by a market's score for that characteristic yields a score for each factor. The sum of factor scores for each possible market indicates to management the most attractive markets.

FIGURE 2–3

MARKET ALTERNATIVES PROFILE ANALYSIS

Critical market factors	*Importance to management*	×	*Attractiveness of the chosen market based on the factor evaluated*	=	*Total score*
Future growth potential	2		1		2
Present size	6		4		24
Investment required	5		6		30
Strength of competition	4		5		20
Ability to meet the needs of the market	1		3		3
Profit potential	3		2		6
	1 is most important		1 is most attractive to management		85

J. C. Penney serves as an excellent example of how a situation analysis can shape a firm's strategy development. Penney's management identified slower population growth, intensified competition caused by mergers, more professionally managed retail outlets, and saturated markets as factors affecting the organization's future, and it adjusted its strategy accordingly. Management chose to compete in more affluent consumer markets rather than in its traditional blue-collar market. Likewise, two of The Limited's divisions—Limited Stores and Lerner New York—are moving upscale in response to environmental dynamics and an assessment of internal operations. Case 2 at the end of the chapter gives a more in-depth look at the changes taking place in these two operations.

The markets that management decides to serve are referred to as **target markets.** As shown in Figure 2–4, retail managers may follow one of three approaches in selecting target markets: aggregation, partial segmentation, and extreme segmentation.

Aggregation

Aggregation as an approach to target market selection assumes that most consumers are alike in their needs and wants. Retailers following such an approach do not recognize varying demand curves for different groups of consumers. Such retailers focus on the common dimensions of a market. They attempt to attract the broadest possible number of buyers by relying on mass advertising and by appealing to the universal desire for low prices. Examples of retailers following such an approach are warehouse food stores and discount department stores such as Kmart and Wal-Mart.

Retailers who follow partial and extreme segmentation approaches to target market selection do not assume that consumers have the same needs and wants and thus engage in a process called market segmentation.

FIGURE 2–4 APPROACHES TO SELECTING TARGET MARKETS

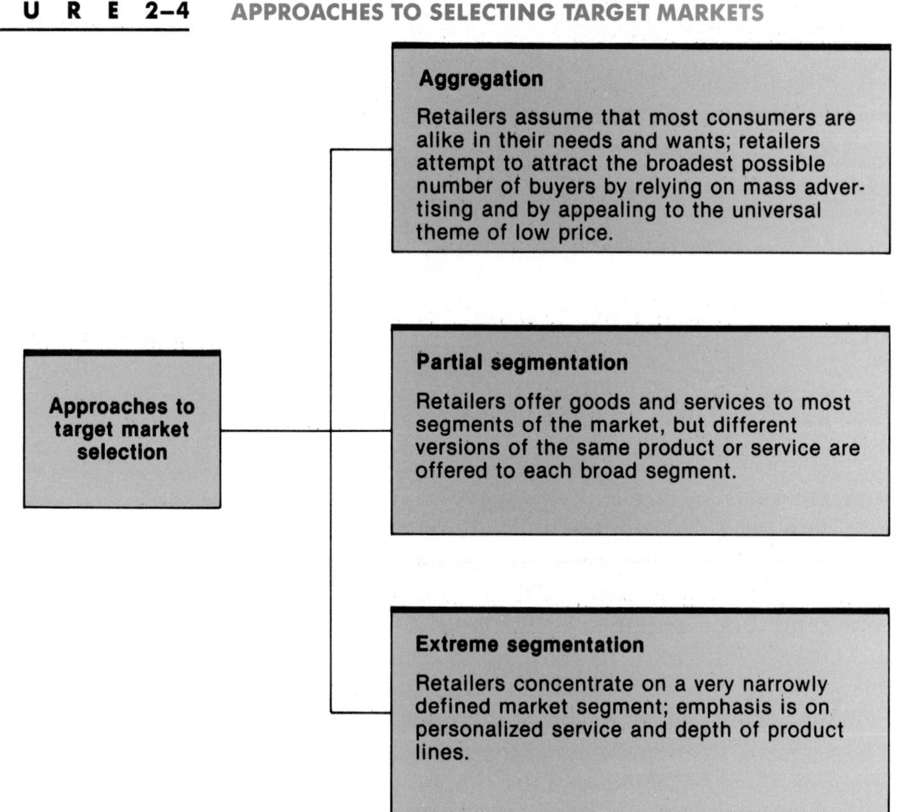

Market segmentation is the process of taking a heterogeneous market and developing homogeneous groups (segments) on the basis of some kind of similarity among consumers, such as demographic, buying behavior, or psychological traits.

Partial Segmentation

In a **partial segmentation** approach to target market selection, retailers offer goods and services to most segments of the market, but different versions of the same product or service are offered to each broad segment. A department store, for example, may have separate clothing departments for juniors; budget-conscious shoppers; and high-income, fashion-conscious consumers.

Extreme Segmentation

In an **extreme segmentation** approach, retailers concentrate on a very narrowly defined market segment. They emphasize such elements as personalized service and depth of product lines. We could give numerous examples of specialty operations that follow this approach to target market selection. Safety Zone, for example, is a chain that focuses on the security needs of consumers and sells products such as portable 12-story fire escape ladders, telephone tap detectors, portable door-knob alarms that can be used in hotel rooms, and counterfeit money testers.[3] Numerous retail firms have sprung up to meet the needs of consumers who are concerned about environmental hazards and want to help safeguard the environment. The Ecology Box, for example, offers a wide selection of environmentally sound toiletries, household cleaners, and cosmetics.[4] Other examples of specialty operations include Left Hand World, Inc., which sells merchandise exclusively for southpaws; Murder Ink, a bookstore that carries only mystery books; and Ted E. Bear and Company, which sells nothing but teddy bears.

Once retailers have chosen markets in which to compete, they must develop a plan to attract targeted consumers. The basis for this plan is a thorough understanding of those consumers—their behavior, values, motives, and expectations. Especially important is an understanding of the customer decision-making process. Because of the importance of this topic, separate chapters are devoted to a discussion of buyer behavior: Chapter 6 focuses on the consumer as a problem-solver and highlights consumer behavior, and Chapter 7 provides an in-depth look at consumer living patterns. Understanding the lifestyles of consumers helps retailers better understand their merchandise and store preferences and their shopping behavior.

OBTAINING RESOURCES NEEDED TO COMPETE

As part of the planning process, retailers must evaluate the alternatives for owning a business as well as avenues for entering a retail business. For example, a retail firm can be operated as a sole proprietorship, a partnership, or a corporation. To enter retailing, a person can start his or her own business, buy an existing business, or become part of a franchise operation. Such issues are the topics of Chapters 8 and 20. Chapter 8 focuses on such issues as the different types of ownership and factors one should consider when buying an established business. Chapter 20 is devoted to a discussion of franchising as a retail business concept.

Chapter 9 discusses store location, a crucial element of retail planning. Wal-Mart illustrates the importance of location in retail strategy. Sam Walton, founder of Wal-Mart, realized that there was a market for discounters in small towns; his rivals were concentrating on urban areas. Beyond that, he understood the importance of getting merchandise to the stores from the chain's distribution warehouses. To be successful in the small, out-of-the-way locations, he needed the same efficient merchandise deliv-

ery methods of his big-city counterparts. He achieved this goal by locating his stores in clusters.

Human resources are just as vital to the success of a retail operation as are financial resources and physical facilities. As you will see in Chapter 10, the human resources plan must be consistent with the overall strategy of the retail firm. You will also learn that human resources management involves a variety of issues such as recruiting, selecting, training, compensating, and motivating personnel and that managing these activities effectively and efficiently is essential.

DEVELOPING A POSITIONING STRATEGY

After markets are selected and resources obtained, a positioning strategy is developed. A **positioning strategy** is a plan of action that outlines how the organization will compete in chosen markets and how the firm will differentiate itself from other organizations competing for the same customers. It involves the use of retailing mix variables; the **retailing mix** consists of all variables that can be used as part of a positioning strategy for competing in chosen markets. Such variables include product, price, presentation, promotion, personal selling, and customer services. They are discussed further in Chapters 11 through 19.

An example of positioning is Rudy's Sirloin Steak Burgers, an upscale fast-service restaurant serving 100 percent sirloin on a bun. The restaurant is positioned between sit-down, full-service, liquor-serving places such as Bennigan's and TGI Friday's on the high end and fast-food operations such as McDonald's and Wendy's on the low end.[5]

To further illustrate the concept of positioning, let's look at two companies (Office Depot and Staples Inc.) that have contrasting strategies but that have both been highly successful in the office supply discount market. Both chains got started in 1986, but the paths they have followed have been quite different. Thomas Stemberg, Staples' chairman, likes high-cost urban markets such as New York and Philadelphia and prefers to invest in centralized distribution. The firm has a 136,000-square-foot distribution center in Putnam, Connecticut, and a 130,000-square-foot center in Fontana, California. These regional hubs cut the cost of handling shipments from suppliers and allow Staples to put up smaller stores because the stores do not have to stock back-up inventory. Furthermore, Mr. Stemberg advocates moderate growth rates, a decision consistent with his strategy of concentrating on costly urban areas where centralized distribution would give him a competitive advantage. In contrast, David Fuente, chairman of Office Depot, has shunned centralization, opting instead to ship goods directly from suppliers to the stores. Thus, Office Depot's outlets are much larger, with back-up inventory kept on the premises. The added expense of larger stores has been partly offset by expanding in smaller, less expensive cities, many in the Sunbelt. Fuente firmly believes that there are advantages to being first in a market, and thus advocates aggressive growth. Without ties to a regional distribution center, units can be built quickly and farther away.[6]

At times, firms may need to reposition their operations. One such firm is Banana Republic, which has shifted from the safari approach to a more upscale sportswear direction. Another example is Perry Drug Stores, based in Pontiac, Michigan. The chain, which once sold everything from pets to kitchen sinks, slashed the ancillary items in favor of core drugstore products. Perry dropped categories such as sewing notions, plants, and fishing and hunting needs. The heart of the repositioning effort was to build the pharmacy prescription business. Management believed that such a move was needed to give the drugstore a competitive edge. Perry is but one of several drugstore retailers going back to its "roots" because of dynamic market changes, including the advent of deep discount drugstores such as Drug Emporium.[7]

Strategy Implementation

A sound strategy is no guarantee of success if it cannot be successfully executed. To implement a firm's desired positioning effectively, every aspect of the store must be focused on the target market. Merchandise must be selected for it; displays must appeal to the target market; advertising must talk to it; personnel must have empathy for it; and customer service must be designed with the target customer in mind.

Our purpose in this section of the chapter is to show how the retailing mix variables can be blended to implement a store's positioning strategy. Space does not permit an extensive discussion of strategy options, but we believe that the examples we chose—market penetration, market development, and productivity improvement—will demonstrate this concept. The range of options within each strategy is shown in Figure 2–5.

Market Penetration

Retailers following a strategy of **market penetration** seek an advantage over competition by a strong market presence bordering on saturation. Such a strategy is designed to increase the number of customers, the quantity purchased by customers, and purchase frequency.

Increasing the Number of Customers. A variety of approaches may be taken to increase the number of customers. Some retailers have sought to gain customers by increasing the number of stores. McDonald's, for example, continues to add units both domestically and worldwide. Furthermore, the company is invading less conventional fast-food sites such as hospitals, airport terminals, zoos, and office buildings. Other avenues for

FIGURE 2–5 RETAIL STRATEGY OPTIONS

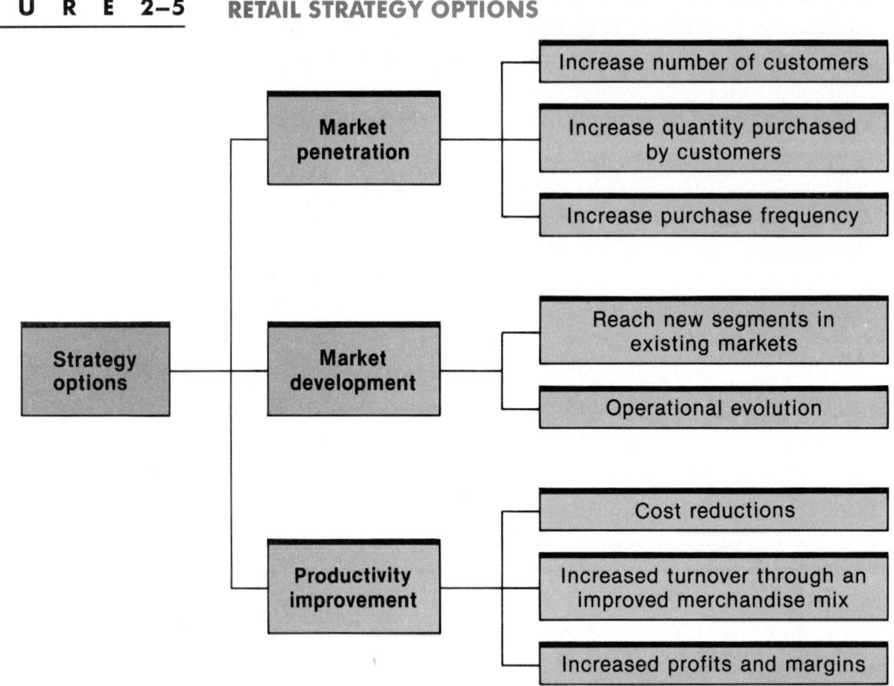

increasing the numbers of customers include adding products, services, or both; lowering prices; and advertising more intensively.

Increasing the Quantity Purchased. In following this approach, retailers attempt to get customers to spend more money while they are in the store. Kmart, for example, has improved store layout and merchandise presentation and has attempted to create an atmosphere conducive to free spending. Departments have been relocated within the store, and new display fixtures that provide shelf space and more attractive merchandise presentation have been added.

Hotels that have initiated frequent-stay plans have discovered that frequent-stay members spend more than nonmembers. Sheraton Corporation, for example, found that its frequent-stay members spend 77 percent more per stay than other guests. Frequent-stay plans, modeled after the airlines' frequent-flier programs, enable hotel guests to earn points for each dollar spent at a hotel. These points can then be cashed in for free airline tickets, hotel stays, or merchandise.

Increasing Purchasing Frequency. A firm that has been very successful in implementing a strategy designed to increase purchase frequency is

Toys 'R' Us. The firm offers a complete selection of items that sell year-round. Customers know that if they buy a toy at Christmas they will find a good selection after Christmas to accommodate returns. Toys in the low to medium price ranges, often with strong affiliations to licensed characters provide sales day in and day out. High-impulse items such as peg boards, die-cast toys, and hobby kits lead to high customer traffic. The firm capitalizes not only on birthdays and Christmas but also on other holidays and special occasions such as Valentine's Day, Easter, Halloween, and back-to-school.[8]

Market Development

A strategy of *market development* focuses either on attracting new market segments or completely changing the customer base. Market development normally involves bolder strategy shifts, more capital, and greater risk than a market penetration strategy. Examples of market development efforts include reaching new segments and operational evolution.

Reaching New Segments. Fast-food restaurants provide a good example of firms that have followed a strategy of attracting new segments in existing markets. Many fast-food chains have looked beyond the heavily saturated hamburger market and added items such as a salad bar, chicken sandwiches, breakfast items, and hot baked potatoes with different fillings. Some firms, such as Hardee's and McDonald's, have introduced a reduced-fat burger. Burger King is joining forces with Weight Watchers and is offering in some of its units nearly a dozen breakfast, lunch, and dinner items. Such menu additions help attract new segments of the market—consumers who are looking for something nonfried, less filling, lower in calories, and more nutritious than many traditional fast-food offerings.[9]

Some hotels, even a few luxury hotels, have initiated children's programs in an attempt to reach new market segments. Perhaps the most ambitious program is Hyatt Hotel's Camp Hyatt, offered at some of the organization's hotels and resorts. Camp Hyatt is a way for children to be merrily distracted by panning for gold, riding in a gondola, or taking hula lessons while their parents attend meetings, go sight-seeing, or soak in the pool. Even Club Med, once the ultimate swinging adult summer camp, introduced Baby Clubs, Mini Clubs, and children's programs at some of its locations.[10]

Operational Evolution. **Operational evolution** means changing competitive strategy over time by focusing on a new target market and developing a business concept different from the existing one. This strategy is different from that of increasing the customer base because it involves changing the customer base, rather than adding customers to it.

EXHIBIT 2–1

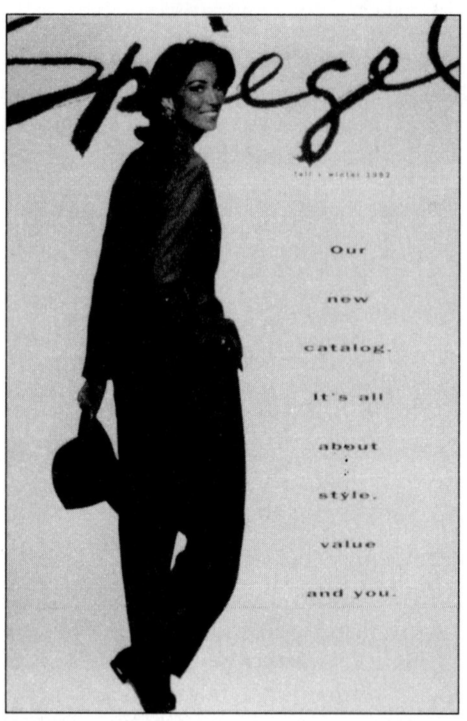

Courtesy Spiegel, Inc.

Repositioning Spiegel as a fashion-conscious sophisticated outlet for the affluent working woman

Spiegel, Inc., is a firm that has followed a strategy of operational evolution. For many years, Spiegel focused on lower-income, rural, mail-order shoppers as its target market. Management then made a major strategic decision to position the firm as a fashion catalog retailer for women's apparel and home furnishings. The new target market is fashion-conscious, sophisticated working women, as shown in Exhibit 2–1. This market consists of women 25 to 54 years of age with average household incomes of $48,000. The firm's mission for the 1990s is to be "the best specialty shopping experience in America . . . by offering real value to our customers based on a combination of product, service and price, tightly focused on their needs."

Productivity Improvement

The strategy of **productivity improvement** focuses on improved earnings through cost reductions, increased turnover through an improved merchandise mix, and increased prices and margins. Productivity improvement often occurs in firms in the mature or declining phases of their life cycles. During these stages, strategies requiring major infusions of cash are not acceptable to management. Rather, the emphasis is on squeezing as much profit as possible from the operation. The strategy is more a refinement of existing strategies than a dramatic new way of doing business.

Cost Reductions. Some retailers concentrate on cost reductions as a competitive weapon in increasing productivity. A key to such a strategy often is to increase self-service and to hold down labor costs. Reducing store hours, making better use of part-time help, and cutting back on customer services are other actions that can be taken to reduce costs. Renovation expenses are often minimized through the use of modular departments and less expensive display fixtures.

Improved Merchandise Mix. Many department stores have attempted to improve productivity by increasing their turnover through a better merchandising mix. In the past, department stores carried everything from wrist watches to kitchen sinks. Now, many department stores are reducing the number of lines carried. They are dropping such lines as appliances, toys, tools, health and beauty aids, books, and sporting goods, and are now focusing on fashion apparel, jewelry and other accessories, and cosmetics—goods that provide high margins and relatively quick turnover. Fashion is where department stores perform best, and fashion goods are the lines that department store managers are now committed to promoting.

Price and Margin Increases. Price and margin increases can be a key element in productivity-based strategies. Higher-than-normal prices may be possible on low-visibility items or infrequently purchased products. Charging for services such as delivery or installation may also be feasible. Adding high-margin items to the merchandise mix is a further dimension of such a strategy.

EVALUATING AND CONTROLLING OPERATIONS

Once a strategy is implemented, managers need feedback on its performance. Information is needed on a routine basis to help management determine whether objectives have been met. Chapters 11 and 12 discuss several types of control systems that help management assess the success of operations.

The effectiveness of the firm's long-term competitive strategy must also be evaluated periodically. Such an evaluation covers all elements of the plan, as shown in Figure 2–6. This type of evaluation guarantees that the firm's plan does not degenerate into fragmented, ad hoc efforts that are not in harmony with the overall competitive strategy of the business. Manage-

FIGURE 2–6

EVALUATING COMPETITIVE STRATEGY

Merchandising plan
1. What is the growth pattern of existing merchandise lines?
2. Is the merchandise line portfolio balanced? Should merchandise lines be added or deleted?
3. Should product line breadth or depth be modified?
4. What is the strength of the individual brands carried?
5. Are the merchandise lines properly positioned against the competition and in support of the marketing plan?
6. Does the firm have an adequate open-to-buy plan?
7. Are adequate inventory controls in place?

Pricing plan
1. What are the profit margins on the merchandise lines carried? Are they increasing or decreasing? How do they compare to those of competition?
2. Are the pricing policies, including price lines (at, equal to, or above the competition) appropriate for each target market?
3. Does pricing have a primary or secondary role in the marketing plan?
4. Is a realistic system for planned markdowns in place?

Advertising and sales promotion plan
1. Are the objectives for advertising and sales promotion clearly stated? Do they support the marketing plan?
2. Is the media mix supportive of the marketing plan?
3. Are budgets adequate to accomplish the objectives? How are budgets established?
4. Are the creative strategies compatible with the marketing plan?
5. Does the firm have weekly, monthly, and seasonal plans for such activities in place?

Distribution and sales support plan
1. Are customer service levels such as on warranties and repairs satisfactory? What weaknesses exist?
2. Are mail and telephone sales programs compatible with the overall marketing plan?
3. Are the after-sales delivery programs, if any, compatible with the marketing plan?
4. Are the credit programs offered cost effective? Should credit options be added or deleted?
5. Is the breadth and intensity of market coverage satisfactory for a firm with branches or multiple outlets?

ment can also use the process to decide what changes, if any, should be made in the future to ensure that the combination of retailing mix variables supports the firm's strategy.

CHAPTER HIGHLIGHTS

- The beginning point in developing a strategic plan is identification of the organization's purpose or mission. The mission statement tells what the firm intends to do and how it plans to do it. The mission statement often reflects the firm's values or corporate culture.
- Objectives are statements of results to be achieved. Management normally sets both long- and short-term objectives.
- The retailer's plan for achieving objectives within the context of the mission statement is based on an analysis of the strengths and

FIGURE 2–6

continued

Financial plan

1. Is a profit analysis possible, including a break-even analysis and analysis of ROI and leverage?
2. What are the profit margins by merchandise line? Are they increasing or decreasing? How do they compare to the competition? Compare with trade statistics where possible.
3. Does the firm have a sound accounting and information system?
4. What are the trends in such indicators as return on assets, earnings per share, and net profits?

Physical facilities plan

1. Is adequate emphasis placed on space productivity?
2. Is flexible fixturing used whenever possible?
3. Does signing provide adequate information to shoppers?
4. Do the atmospherics support the other elements of the marketing plan?
5. Is merchandise arranged for easy cross-selling whenever possible?

The retail information system

1. Does the merchandise information system provide the information needed for key operating decisions?
2. Is a sound, competitive shopping system in place?
3. Is someone in the firm responsible for evaluating environmental trends that can affect the continuing success of the firm?
4. Are the financial and merchandising ratios of the firm regularly compared to comparable trade statistics?

Human resources plan

1. Does the firm have the talent to execute its marketing strategies?
2. Is the firm adequately staffed?
3. Are the firm's selection and recruiting efforts and training programs adequate?
4. Are the firm's pay scales adequate? Are opportunities for promotion available? Are performance appraisals and feedback occurring?
5. If several outlets exist, are personnel decisions centralized or decentralized?
6. Are disciplinary procedures in place?
7. Do union/management relations receive adequate attention?

---

weaknesses of the organization and threats and opportunities in the external environments. Such an analysis is called a situation analysis.

- The situation analysis helps management identify markets in which to compete. The markets that management decides to serve are referred to as target markets. Retailers may follow one of three approaches in selecting target markets—aggregation, partial segmentation, or extreme segmentation. Retailers must then develop a plan for attracting targeted consumers. The basis for such planning is a thorough understanding of those consumers.
- As part of the planning process, retailers must evaluate the alternatives for owning a business as well as the avenues for entering a retail business. The planning process also involves store location decisions. A human resources plan that is consistent with the overall strategy of the firm must also be developed.
- The retailer must develop a positioning strategy, or the plan of action that outlines

how the organization will compete in chosen markets and how it will differentiate itself from other organizations competing for the same customers. The positioning strategy is developed through a combination of the retailing mix variables, which include product, price, presentation, promotion, personal selling, and customer services.

- A sound strategy is no guarantee of success if it cannot be implemented successfully. The retailing mix variables must be blended appropriately in implementing a store's positioning strategy.
- Some strategy options available to retailers include market penetration, market development, and productivity improvement. Market penetration includes strategies designed to increase the number of customers, the quantity purchased by customers, and purchase frequency. Market development strategies focus on either attracting new market segments or completely changing the customer base (operational evolution). A strategy of productivity improvement focuses on improved earnings through cost reduction, increased turnover through an improved merchandise mix, and increased prices and margins.
- Once a strategy is implemented, managers need feedback on how the organization is performing. Information is needed on a routine basis to help management determine whether objectives are being met. However, the effectiveness of the long-term competitive strategy of the firm must also be periodically evaluated.

STUDY QUESTIONS

1. Indicate the steps involved in developing a strategic plan.
2. What is meant by an organization's mission statement? What does this statement normally include?
3. What is the difference between long-term and short-term objectives?
4. What is a situation analysis? What factors are evaluated in such an analysis? What is the ultimate value and use of a situation analysis?
5. Explain the differences between the following approaches to selecting target markets: aggregation, partial segmentation, and extreme segmentation.
6. Explain the relationships between target markets, positioning strategy, and the retailing mix.
7. Discuss market penetration as a strategy option.
8. Describe the alternative means by which a strategy of market development may be pursued.
9. What specific actions might a retailer undertake following a strategy of productivity improvement?
10. How is evaluation of the short-term results of a retail operation different from evaluating the effectiveness of the firm's long-term competitive strategy?

A P P L I C A T I O N S

CASE 1: The Bigger, the Better at Think Big!

Think Big!, a New York City–based operation, specializes in selling outlandishly sized versions of everyday objects. The merchandise includes 56-inch-tall crayons, 57-inch-long toothbrushes, and 5-foot-long fountain pens. The store also carries 20-inch-tall Heinz ketchup bottles, a Chinese food take-out container with yard-long chopsticks, and giant-sized paper clips (a foot-and-one-half long). There's even a 14-inch martini glass with an equally outsized olive.

The first store, a 300-square-foot building, was opened in 1970. By 1983 Think Big! had outgrown its original location and moved to a site on West Broadway in Soho. A second store on the upper west side's trendy Columbus Avenue was opened in 1984. The owners have franchised the concept and envision a time when there will be hundreds of Think Big! stores throughout the United States and in international markets.

Source: Adapted from "The Bigger, the Better at Think Big!" *Chain Store Age,* January 1989, p. 18.

Applying Retailing Principles

1. Which approach to target market selection is Think Big! following?
2. How would you define its target market?
3. Describe Think Big!'s positioning strategy and the way in which retailing mix variables are combined in implementing this strategy.

CASE 2: Limited Stores and Lerner Moving Upscale

In 1991 Lerner and Limited Stores did roughly $2.3 billion in sales, 37 percent of the parent company's total. However, they contributed only 29 percent of The Limited Inc.'s profits. And although the corporation's sales rose 17 percent in 1991 to $6.1 billion, profit crept up only 2.1 percent to $713 million, primarily because of lackluster results at the Lerner and Limited Stores divisions. Management's solution for getting both divisions back on track is to move them upscale. Let's look more closely at each division to see what management has in mind.

Limited Stores consists of 772 stores that once catered to fashion-hungry women who were satisfied with what management calls "throwaway" clothes. As these shoppers became more value conscious, the store "got pinched." At the same time, another division, Limited Express, began to lure many of the younger Limited customers with its more cutting-edge looks. The plan is to boost Limited's quality and to distinguish it from Express. Management is trying to establish Limited Stores as a chain for more affluent, older women who are looking for clothes for work as well as play. For the first time, the stores are stocking linen. Hopefully the emphasis on the mature babyboomer will keep the chain from being further cannibalized by Express.

Lerner was a chain of moderately priced women's apparel stores bought by The Limited in 1985. The chain now has 914 outlets. Lerner's once-loyal budget customers, however, began spending more time at Wal-Mart, Kmart, and other discounters that sell the same type of clothes as Lerner did but at lower prices. Now, Lerner is trying to drive away the customer the chain tried to attract for so many years and is aiming for women with more money to spend. Management is raising prices and stocking the stores with more expensive, better-made clothing. Lower-priced lingerie, hosiery, and socks are being dropped. The chain plans to advertise aggressively to re-educate people and to keep new customers coming to the stores. Some market analysts wonder, however, whether the two divisions will focus on the same customer group as they move upscale.

Source: Based on Laura Zinn, "No Off-the-Rack Solutions Here," *Business Week*, May 25, 1991, pp. 116–18; Susan Caminiti, "In Search of the '90s Consumer," *Fortune*, September 21, 1992, p. 100; Laura Zinn, "Maybe The Limited Has Limits after All," *Business Week*, March 18, 1991, pp. 128–29.

Applying Retailing Principles

1. What environmental dynamics could explain the declining performance of the two divisions?
2. Speculate on the probable success of each division's strategy of moving upscale.

Notes

1. Jackie Bivins, "Corporate Culture," *Stores*, February 1989, pp. 9–15.
2. Mary Krienke, "IKEA's Anders Mobery," *Stores*, January 1991, p. 99.
3. Richard Behar, "Wet Seals and Whale Songs," *Time*, June 3, 1991, p. 45.
4. Laurie Freeman, "Eco-Retailers Turn Green into Gold," *Stores*, October 1991, pp. 50–51.
5. "Rudy's Courts Gourmet-Burger Lover," *Advertising Age*, December 10, 1984, p. 61-S.
6. Michael Selz, "Office Supply Firms Take Different Paths to Success," *The Wall Street Journal*, May 30, 1991, p. B2.
7. Faye Brookman, "Robinson Repositions Chain with Focus on Core Merchandise," *Stores*, April 1992, pp. 25–28.
8. Amy Dunkin, Keith H. Hammonds, and Mark Maremont, "How Toys 'R' Us Controls the Game Board," *BusinessWeek*, December 19, 1988, pp. 58–60; Joseph Pereira, "Toys 'R' Us, Big Kid on the Block, Won't Stop Growing," *The Wall Street Journal*, August 11, 1988, p. 6; Hank Gilman, "Founder Lazarus Is a Reason Toys 'R' Us Dominates Its Industry," *The Wall Street Journal*, November 21, 1985, p. 1.
9. Richard Bigson, "Burger King Lets Diners Have It Weight Watchers' Way," *The Wall Street Journal*, July 18, 1991, p. B1.
10. Nancy Gibbs, "Room Service? Get Me Milk and Cookies," *Time*, July 3, 1989, pp. 70–71.

P A R T

2

Environmental Factors Affecting Retail Strategy Development

The retail strategies discussed in Chapter 2 are not developed in a vacuum. Rather, they emerge after a careful analysis of both the firm's internal and external environments.

The environments discussed in Chapters 3, 4, and 5 are of obvious importance in shaping retailing strategies. Important considerations include consumer demographics, cultural differences between consumers, differing lifestyle patterns, and the effects of the economy on consumer behavior.

Legal and public policy issues also influence strategy development. Various federal and state laws affect all dimensions of the retailing mix, including promotion, pricing, products, and customer services decisions.

One of the most dramatic effects on retail operations in recent years has been the changing technology of retailing. The microcomputer has revolutionized the way in which retailers keep track of inventory and make decisions about what levels of merchandise to stock and when to carry them. In addition, video text, interactive home shopping networks, and in-store electronic sales aids are posing new challenges and new opportunities for today's retailers.

C H A P T E R

3

The Legal, Public Policy, and Ethical Dimensions of Retailing

THIS CHAPTER:

Reviews the regulations affecting retailers' growth strategies.

Highlights trade regulation rules affecting retail decisions.

Explains the regulations affecting retail mix decisions.

Explores ethical standards of business conduct.

Emphasizes the role of social responsibility in guiding retailer decisions.

Illustrates the increasingly global nature of retailing.

RETAILING CAPSULE

NU SKIN: PYRAMID POWER?*

Nu Skin International Inc., a direct retailer based in Provo, Utah, agreed to alter its sales practices after complaints in five states alleging that it operated as a pyramid scheme. A legal sales pyramid is a multilevel marketing system in which individuals at each successive layer of the organization participate in the commissions earned by the people below. Pyramids become illegal when their primary purpose is to generate funds by recruiting new members, not by selling products to consumers.

Nu Skin sells high-priced skin care and nutritional products to the public through a six-level organization of 100,000 independent distributors. The firm had annual sales in 1991 of over $500,000,000. It does virtually no advertising. Instead, management concentrates sales messages on distributors, noting that top producers can earn thousands of dollars a month. (A lawsuit in Connecticut claimed that, instead of earning $5,000 to $10,000 per month, as the company claims is possible for the best distributors, 98 percent of the distributors averaged only $38 per month.) The company's message—"dare to dream"—is delivered at thousands of recruiting meetings by sophisticated recruitment videos.

Management, in an agreement with the attorneys general of Ohio, Michigan, Illinois, Florida, and Pennsylvania, agreed to implement policies designed to protect its retail sales representatives and distributors from buying more products than they could sell and to eliminate incentives designed primarily to encourage sales personnel to enlist new recruits, to whom the company could sell starter kits. The agreement also included a provision for monitoring representatives to ensure that a minimum of 80 percent of their sales are to at least five customers not affiliated with Nu

Skin. Management also agreed to implement a policy that allows its retail sales representatives refunds of 90 percent for unsold products. A Nu Skin spokesman stated that the company operated legitimately in all states but that the revised policies were being implemented nationwide.

Nu Skin also encountered difficulties with the Food and Drug Administration. The FDA in 1991 warned Nu Skin about implicit claims that its hair product Nutroil could grow hair. The company agreed to change its labeling and acknowledged that some of the claims were made by overly enthusiastic retail distributors.

Source: Based on Richard L. Stern and Mary Beth Grover, "Pyramid Power?", *Forbes,* November 11, 1991, pp. 139–48; Ken Yamada, "Nu Skin to Adopt New Sales Policies in Pact with States," *The Wall Street Journal,* January 3, 1992, p. C17.

The legal wrangle between Nu Skin, the state attorneys general, and federal agencies illustrates the legal complexities that can affect retailing. Government regulations are among the most persistent issues facing retailers. Local, state, and federal laws affect virtually every aspect of retailing. The regulations are intended to keep competition at a high level, protect consumers from unfair business practices, and give consumers enough information to make wise buying decisions.

This chapter examines broad legal areas to which retailers should be alert. These areas involve regulations affecting growth; unfair competition or restraint of trade; Federal Trade Commission regulations; and laws affecting the retailing mix, including pricing, promotion, distribution, the product, credit, and methods of selling. These issues are highlighted in Figure 3–1. We also review the importance of ethical standards and social responsibility in day-to-day operations.

THE REGULATIONS AFFECTING GROWTH

The oldest regulations affecting growth are the antitrust laws. The philosophy behind the regulations is that more rigorous competition and better customer service are likely to result when all firms must compete aggressively to survive.

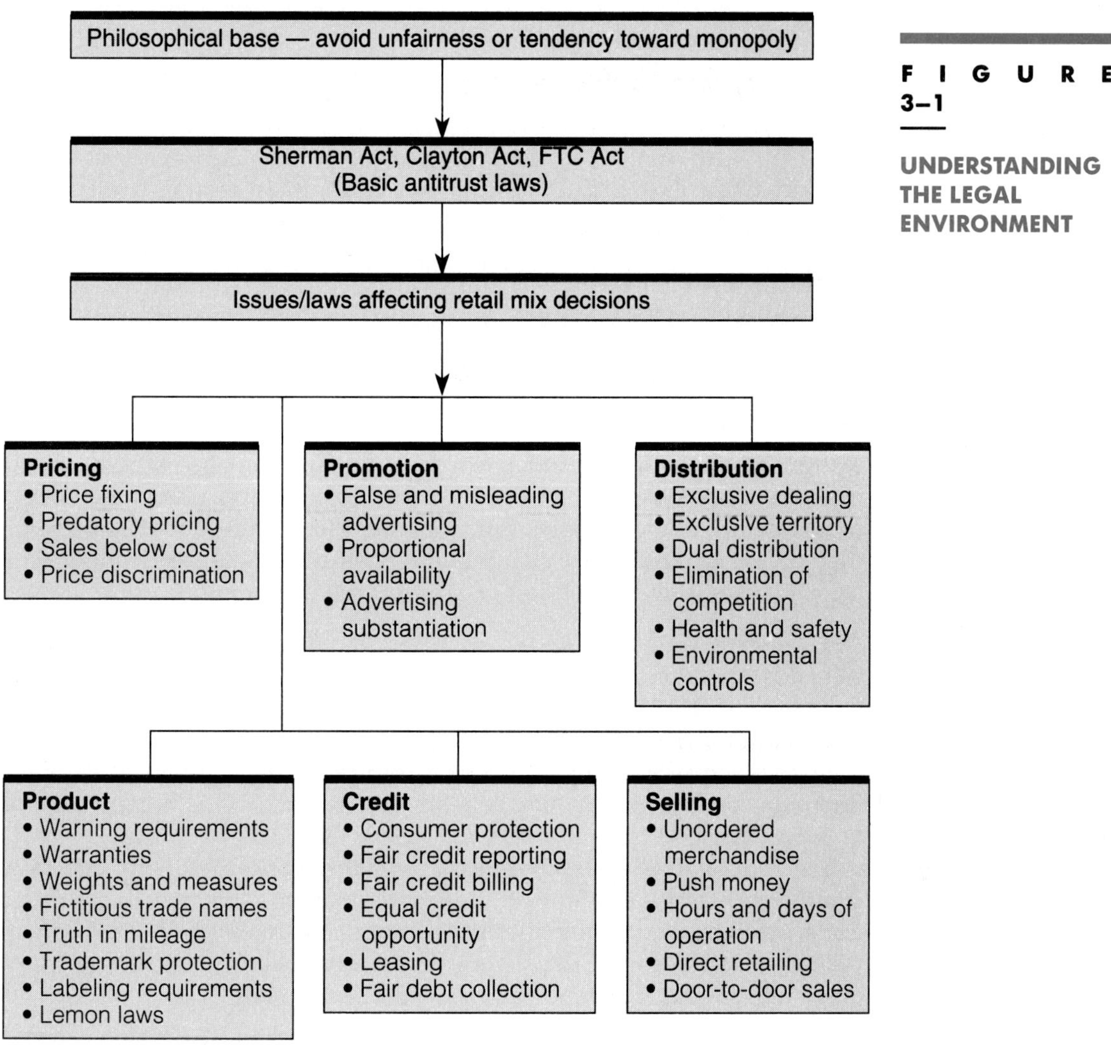

FIGURE 3–1

UNDERSTANDING THE LEGAL ENVIRONMENT

Restraint of Trade

Restraint of trade means:

1. Putting pressure on suppliers to keep them from selling products to competitors.
2. Acquiring competitors to lessen competition or to create a monopoly.
3. Fixing the price of goods sold. In other words, retailers can agree to stop price competition among themselves.
4. Underselling competitors to gain control of a market. A large chain, for example, might lower its prices to drive smaller competitors in one area out of business while maintaining higher prices in its other markets.

Key Restraint of Trade Laws

The key restraint of trade laws are the Sherman Act, the Clayton Act, and the Federal Trade Commission Act.

The Sherman Act. The Sherman Act of 1890 makes every action to restrain trade illegal. The possible forms of trade restraint are almost limitless. However, they most frequently include price fixing, dividing markets among competitors, or forcing suppliers to provide a retailer with the exclusive right to sell merchandise in a given area. In addition suppliers have required retailers to purchase a variety of products in order to get the one product they really want (tie-in sales). These activities are illegal when they tend to create a monopoly or substantially lessen competition.

The Clayton Act. The Clayton Act, passed in 1914, is more specific in its restrictions than the Sherman Act is. It declares certain practices illegal even if they do not actually restrain trade or do not constitute a monopoly or an attempt to monopolize. Furthermore, the practices are illegal even if they do not actually injure competition. Practices violate the Clayton Act if they might lessen competition or tend to create a monopoly.

The Federal Trade Commission Act. The Federal Trade Commission Act, also passed in 1914, created an independent agency, the Federal Trade Commission (FTC). The Commission's duty is to help enforce the Clayton Act and other antitrust laws. The FTC has the power to investigate and to issue cease and desist orders. Other acts or practices not in violation of the Sherman or Clayton Acts may be restrained by the FTC as unfair methods of competition.

The Federal Trade Commission is primarily concerned with interstate commerce. Its enforcement philosophy is that by removing restraints to trade, stronger price competition and better consumer service are likely to occur. FTC actions have helped encourage advertising by such professionals as attorneys, CPAs, and physicians, for example.

Mergers and Acquisitions

Mergers and acquisitions are terms often used interchangeably. These terms mean the combining of two companies into one organization by issuing stock or using some other method to pay for the assets of the merged or acquired business. Mergers and acquisitions can occur for a variety of reasons that typically include a belief that the action will improve earnings per share, provide an opportunity to achieve a stronger market position without the risk of a new start-up venture, and help offset seasonal or cyclical sales fluctuations. In addition, large size is an advantage when a firm plans to expand beyond the United States.

Leveraged buyouts have been particularly popular as a form of acquisition. Executives take on huge debt to purchase a firm and then sell off part of the assets to lower their debt. They then use its cash flow to meet the remaining debt payments. A Question of Ethics explores the effects of such actions on consumers and competitors.

Mergers between two competitors (**horizontal mergers**) are particularly risky because the courts often view such action as designed to eliminate competition. The Federal Trade Commission, for example, approved American Stores' bid to acquire Lucky Stores only after Lucky agreed to sell several of its supermarkets in California, so as to maintain an adequate level of competition. The FTC similarly gave approval to the Von Company's move to acquire Safeway stores in southern California and Nevada only after Von agreed to sell several of its California supermarkets prior to the acquisition.[1]

TRADE REGULATION RULES

Trade regulation rules are guidelines issued by the FTC that must be followed in selling certain products or services. These rules apply to specific industries and are not laws passed by Congress. For example, retailers selling items by mail must specify delivery dates. The buyer can cancel the order if the merchandise is not delivered by the stated time.

The FTC also has issued trade regulation rules that require door-to-door sellers to identify themselves as salespeople before entering a person's home, and to allow three days for the customer to decide whether to cancel an order.

Mispricing and advertising out-of-stock food items are other areas covered by trade rules. The out-of-stock rule requires retailers to stock enough of an advertised item to meet a "normal" level of demand. Mispricing is also prohibited.

Other agencies can also issue trade rules. For example, the Food and Drug Administration (FDA) has established rules concerning posting or advertising prescription drug prices.

LAWS AFFECTING THE RETAILING MIX

The retailing mix component of retailing strategy includes decisions about price, promotion, distribution, the product, length of payment, and methods of selling. Numerous laws and regulations affect the mix variables. The regulations are enforced and monitored by local, state, and federal agencies.

Price

Pricing is at the heart of a retailer's marketing plan. Pricing decisions affect profitability and market share, and can provide an advantage over the competition. Pricing decisions are monitored by a variety of agencies.

A Question of Ethics

MERGERS AND LEVERAGED BUYOUTS

A dialog among industry executives sponsored by *Progressive Grocer* on the issue of mergers and leveraged buyouts prompted widely differing perspectives, as noted in the following comments.

Hank Greenberg, president of Certified Grocers Midwest, noted that it is important to differentiate between legitimate business practices and unethical behavior. For example, he views the closing or selling of stores by highly leveraged firms as actions necessary to survive. As he put it, "that's a hard business decision. Even though people are put out of work, it isn't unethical."

But LBOs and mergers are cited by some as one cause of a decline in ethics. They have exacerbated the problem, said one executive, because of the need for quick money to pay debts because everything is judged by the next quarterly statement.

One person said that it is legitimate for a highly leveraged chain to increase its margins to help pay off its debts. But he asked whether it is ethical for competitors to raise their prices when they had been making money at their old margins. The first firm's costs went up, he said, but its competitors' didn't.

Another wholesaler executive said, "It will be shocking when higher profit margins begin to show up." In his opinion, the result of all the mergers and LBOs will be that "power elitists will be battling at both the retail and manufacturer levels, with a narrowing of competition."

Some firms maintained that neither they nor others in their markets have raised prices to pay off debts; but that assertion has been disputed. An official of one chain said that retail prices in the Los Angeles area had risen as much as 2 percent when a number of chains took on big debt burdens.

Are ethical issues inherent in mergers, acquisitions, and leveraged buyouts? If so, what are they? Are such activities likely to result in increased prices for consumers and less competition?

Source: Portions reprinted with permission from Steve Weinstein, "Changing Values in Changing Times for Business," *Progressive Grocer,* June 1989, p. 31.

Horizontal Price Fixing. **Horizontal price fixing** occurs when management agrees with competitors on the price at which identical items will be sold. The practice is illegal under the Sherman Act and the Federal Trade Commission Act.

Vertical Price Fixing. **Vertical price fixing** is an illegal practice that occurs when manufacturers set minimum prices at which their products must be sold by retailers. The practice is often referred to as **resale price maintenance,** which, as a philosophy, cannot be legislated away. Many manufacturers continue, for example, to stress "suggested retail prices" and encourage dealers to maintain these prices. They argue that retail price maintenance supports retailers who provide customers with special services or information beyond that usually expected with the product.[2]

A U.S. Supreme Court decision in the Sharp Electronics case has made it easier for manufacturers to cut off product supply to discount retailers.

The Supreme Court ruled that a manufacturer's decision to cut off a discounter at the request of a full-price competitor does not automatically violate federal antitrust laws.[3] Instead, the Court ruled that such termination agreements must be evaluated on a case-by-case basis.[4] It noted that the agreements are only automatically illegal when the manufacturer and the retailer also agree to set minimum retail prices.[5]

Predatory Pricing. **Predatory pricing** is the practice of setting prices in a deliberate effort to drive competitors from the market. Varying retail prices by community is illegal if management cannot cost justify the practice and management is trying to eliminate competition.

Sales Below Cost. Several states have laws that do not allow the sale of items at less than their cost to the retailer. These laws usually cover such product lines as milk and other dairy products, cigarettes, and gasoline. Some states allow sales below cost if they are necessary to meet the price of a competitor.

Price Discrimination. The Robinson-Patman Act, passed in 1936, amended the 1914 Clayton Act and is enforced by the FTC. As such, it is the primary law regulating price discrimination. Not all price discrimination is illegal under the Robinson-Patman Act.[6] But management should be prepared to justify price differences. The key issues are like grade and quality and the good-faith defense.

Like Grade and Quality. Price differences on goods of like grade and quality offered to various retailers are legal when differences exist in the cost of manufacturing or delivery, the price differences do not lessen competition, or both.

The Good-Faith Defense. A supplier can charge different prices to various retailers if it does so "in good faith to meet an equally low price of a competitor or the facilities furnished by a competitor." But services or facilities offered by a supplier must be available to all retailers on "proportionally equal terms."

Promotion

Local, state, and federal laws help prevent misleading or deceptive promotion. There are also laws designed to ensure that distributors do not unfairly discriminate between retailers in the type and amount of advertising support that the distributors offer.

False and Misleading Advertising. False and misleading advertising is illegal. FTC regulations affect all media advertising, promotional items sent through the mail, price lists, and similar promotional material. Retail ads cannot make false or misleading claims about prices, the value of goods, or guarantees.

The New York City Department of Consumer Affairs, for example, is in a continuing battle with electronics retailers over advertising that the Department considers to be misleading and illegal (see Case 1 at the end of this chapter).[7] Regulators and Better Business Bureaus across the country are cracking down on retailers who make misleading claims. For instance, the National Advertising Review Board, a self-regulatory panel, labeled Montgomery Ward's lowest-price ad claims as "inaccurate" and "confusing." Ward disagreed, but agreed to modify its ads.[8]

Finally, the Mail Order Consumer Protection Amendment of 1983 gave the U.S. Postal Service broadened powers to issue cease and desist orders against businesses that make fraudulent advertising claims in the print media and use the postal service in their advertising.

Proportional Availability. Section 2-E of the Robinson-Patman Act states that any service, such as advertising allowances furnished to a retailer by a supplier, must be available to all retailers on a proportionately equal basis. The law is designed to ensure that such allowances or services are not a disguised form of reduced price to a few large retailers.

Advertising Substantiation. Management must be prepared to prove the truth of their advertising claims. The FTC can require retailers to submit data to support claims about a product's safety, performance, or quality. For example, Montgomery Ward settled charges by the FTC that it made false claims in promoting its service contract agreement.[9] Similarly, Kentucky Fried Chicken and Dunkin' Donuts agreed to stop making what New York's Attorney General called misleading health claims about foods that derive half or more of their calories from fat.[10]

Distribution

Distribution regulations are designed to ensure a strong and healthy commercial environment. They help prevent retailers from unfairly eliminating competition and keep manufacturers from providing some retailers with geographic monopolies that have the effect of eliminating competition. Other regulations are designed to provide a safe and healthy environment for retail employees and shoppers.

Exclusive Dealing. **Exclusive dealing** occurs when a supplier requires a retailer not to sell a competitor's products. Under Section III of the Sherman Act, this practice is illegal when it lessens competition. Exclusive-dealing agreements, when done in good faith, can help both the retailer and the supplier: the retailer may get a more stable source of supply; the supplier gets a sure market for its merchandise.

Exclusive territories may be a problem. Exclusive territories are created by suppliers who limit the areas in which a retailer can sell a product. In return, the supplier agrees not to sell to any other retailer in the defined area. Retailers probably give more time and attention to merchandise they sell under an exclusive agreement. Many such agreements are illegal, however, in the absence of substantial and effective competition.

Congress passed a law legalizing territorial exclusive franchising in the soft drink industry. The law stipulates, however, that the product must be in substantial and effective competition with other products of the same general class before this practice will be permitted under the antitrust laws.

Gray Market Retailing. **Gray market retailers** are outlets not authorized by the manufacturer to sell the merchandise they offer for sale. They obtain the merchandise from other larger authorized retailers or wholesalers and sell it at prices 30 to 40 percent below the prices available from authorized outlets. They do not, however, provide warranty service or technical support for complex products such as cameras or electronics and undermine the efforts of legitimate retailers and manufacturers to build a strong brand name and base of consumer support by a program of advertising and promotion. Many manufacturers aggressively seek to cut off unauthorized retailers for these reasons. However, the practice is almost impossible to identify and eliminate.

Dual Distribution. **Dual distribution,** in which wholesalers operate retail outlets, is not per se illegal. However, the courts have yet to fully define legal practices in this area. Manufacturers watch this type of distribution closely to make sure that wholesalers are not selling to independent retailers at high prices and then undercutting them by reselling the same merchandise at lower prices through their own retail outlets. Independent gasoline retailers contend that company-owned gasoline stations sometimes engage in such practices, often with devastating results.

Unfair Elimination of Competitors. Retailers cannot try to unfairly eliminate competitors. Big "anchor" stores in shopping centers can no longer legally determine which other tenants may locate in the center, for example. They also cannot restrict the legal marketing practices of smaller tenants. The FTC obtained agreements with such retail firms as Federated, Gimbles, May Department Stores, and Sears to stop them from engaging in such practices.

The Free Speech Issue. Malls have become the free speech battleground of the 1990s. The U.S. Supreme Court in 1980 ruled that the First Amendment doesn't protect free speech in shopping malls because they are private property but that states have the power to offer that protection. The state Supreme Courts have tended to rule that free speech provisions do not restrain private property owners from deciding which activities will occur on their property.

Health and Safety. The Occupational Safety and Health Administration (OSHA) requires retailers to educate and inform employees who, as part of their everyday job, come in contact with hazardous chemicals. Several hundred chemicals are affected by the regulations, including some liquid hand soaps that may be considered eye irritants.[11]

OSHA is also responsible for enforcing a host of safety regulations. The U.S. Labor Department, for example, at the recommendation of OSHA, proposed penalties of more than $3 million against McCrory Stores, charging McCrory with fire safety violations in its four New York stores.[12]

In addition, the Americans with Disabilities Act of 1990 requires retailers to make their stores more accessible to disabled shoppers under regulations issued by the U.S. Justice Department. The regulations affect the number of parking spaces and the availability of handicap-accessible wheelchairs and restrooms.[13]

Environmental Control Regulations. Various environmental control regulations affect retail location decisions. The laws were passed as the result of an increasing awareness of the diminishing quality of the nation's air, water, and other natural resources.

The Clean Air Act (1970). The Environmental Protection Agency requires 10-year air quality maintenance plans for various areas of the nation. EPA strategies, which vary from area to area, include street parking restrictions, management of parking supply, and employer mass transit incentives. The result is that shopping center developers must change their notion that so many square feet of retail space translate automatically into so many parking spaces. Likewise, shopping centers are now labeled as major direct sources of pollution.

The Federal Water Pollution Control Act (1972). Of interest to retailers is the regulation of nonpoint sources of pollution. Nonpoint sources relate specifically to runoff from various types of activities. Land use controls are one control mechanism. Such controls can significantly affect the issuance of permits for construction of parking lots and various building structures.

The Coastal Zone Management Act (1972). A total of 34 states and territories are eligible to participate in this program. The act is designed to preserve, protect, develop, restore, or enhance the resources of the nation's coastal areas. The philosophy of the Corps of Engineers is a public interest determination by corps officials. These officials are required to consider whether the proposed activities are primarily dependent on wetland resources and whether feasible alternative sites are available.

The Noise Pollution Control Act (1972). This act recognized noise as a major environmental pollutant. Governments are required to set up noise limits for various kinds of equipment. These standards relate primarily to the quantity of noise emitted by products for sale and by transportation vehicles.

The National Environmental Policy Act (1970). All proposals for federal action must include an environmental impact statement. Many states now also require such statements for all significant public actions. They also require environmental impact statements for major private projects. The statements outline both the adverse and the beneficial effects of the proposed development on people, wildlife, and vegetation.

The Product

Product tampering on supermarket shelves is a growing problem, and consumers are often unable to guard themselves against the risks created by dangerous products. Both suppliers and retailers are being pressed to find better ways of informing consumers about these hazards.

Kmart, for example, paid the U.S. Justice Department $475,000 in civil penalties to settle allegations that it sold imported automotive products that didn't meet federal motor vehicle safety standards. The settlement was reported to be the largest recovery of civil penalties in the history of the National Traffic and Motor Vehicle Safety Act.

Warning Requirements. Retailers have a specific responsibility under Section 15 of the Consumer Product Safety Act to monitor the safety of the products they sell. Management is required to report any information about product hazards to the Consumer Product Safety Commission. They are also required to cooperate in product recalls. The Commission, for example, accused Sears Roebuck of violating a consent decree involving the sale of lawn darts by selling them in one or more outlets after agreeing to stop selling all lawn darts and to notify the Commission before resuming such sales.[14]

Retailers also have a duty to warn consumers whenever they have knowledge of a dangerous product and when it appears unlikely that consumers will discover the danger for themselves. Management similarly can be held criminally negligent by selling certain products such as fire-arms to minors, gasoline in unlabeled containers, or liquor to intoxicated persons.

Chemical residue on fresh fruits and vegetables has also become an issue. Supermarkets are now beginning to contract with private residue testing companies to have produce tested at receiving points and certified to reassure consumers of product safety.

Warranties. A **warranty** is a seller's guarantee regarding the quality or performance of goods. **Express warranties** are given in writing and are part of the bundle of benefits consumers receive when a product is purchased. Express warranties are covered by the Magnuson-Moss Warranty Act of 1975 and the Uniform Commercial Code.

The distinction between express warranties and sales talk that implies warranties is often vague. Management has to carefully distinguish between puffery and promise in promotional efforts. Salespeople can establish implied warranties of fitness if they make specific performance promises about the product. In addition, every sale, according to the Uniform Commercial Code, has an implied warranty of merchantability that the merchandise being offered is fit for the purpose for which it is being sold.

Express warranties may be either *full* (that is, coverage of parts and labor) or *limited* (coverage of parts only). **Extended warranties** are purchased by consumers and cover parts, and sometimes labor, for a period of time beyond the express warranty. The primary difference between express and extended warranties is that the latter are purchased separately from the product.

Service contracts and maintenance agreements are similar to extended warranties. They are also purchased separately from the product. Extended warranties typically guarantee workmanship and materials. Service contracts and maintenance agreements normally agree only to provide maintenance and repair for a specified period of time.[15]

The Magnuson-Moss Act contains three specific rules concerning written warranties:

1. Retailers are required to give warranty information to consumers before they buy a product.
2. They must state warranty terms in "simple and readily understood language."
3. They must establish a way to easily handle consumer warranty complaints.

Weights and Measures Seal. Some businesses, such as supermarkets and gasoline service stations, are inspected by a state representative from a bureau of weights and measures. The inspectors certify that the equipment is functioning accurately and then place a tag on the scales or pumps. Such equipment is also subject to periodic unannounced inspections.

Fictitious Trade Name Registration. Some states require that the fictitious name of a store must be registered with an appropriate agency within a set number of days after the business opens. This registration is necessary because the name of the firm may vary from the corporate name and often will not include the names of all owners or partners.

Truth in Mileage Act. The federal Truth in Mileage Act (1986) requires that both the buyer and seller of a vehicle must certify the vehicle's mileage before a change in title can be obtained. Exceptions include new vehicles purchased from dealers and vehicles with a model year of 1980 or earlier.

Trademark Protection. Trademarks are a form of property with a significant monetary value, as has been established by the U.S. courts over the years. McDonald's obtained a permanent injunction in U.S. District Court, for example, against Quality Inns stating that the use of the prefix "Mc" in its "McSleep Inns" infringed on the goodwill and reputation of the McDonald's Corporation.[16]

In a reverse twist, McDonald's found that Leaps and Bounds, its fledgling chain of indoor playgrounds, duplicated the name of an independent educational program in Chicago. McDonald's contends that, because it holds a federal trademark for the name, its rights supersede the state trademark. The two organizations are trying to work out a compromise.[17]

Labeling Requirements. The Nutrition Labeling and Educational Act (1990) is enforced by the U.S. Food and Drug Administration. The law affects manufacturers as well as retailers that offer private label packaging, nutritional information, and other marketing programs. The act requires manufacturers to list serving size in common household measure, number of servings per container, percentage of calories from fat, total amount of protein per serving, and a variety of additional information. Fish, fresh vegetables, and fresh fruits are also subject to nutritional descriptions by most food retailers.[18]

Some states also have specific health warning requirements. Proposition 65 in California, for example, states that the public must be warned of products that contain toxic substances in amounts that present significant health risks. Eight retail chains agreed to pay $750,000 in penalties and costs for failing to post signs about the potentially harmful effects of tobacco products.[19]

Lemon Laws. So-called state "lemon laws" are designed to protect consumers from defective automobiles. Ford and GM add charges to the base price of their vehicles in the state of New York to cover their cost of complying with the state lemon law. The New York law requires basic warranty coverage for 24 months or 18,000 miles and prevents manufacturers from charging a $100 deductible for warranty visits during that period.

Credit

Credit in its various forms is important to many consumers. Credit can also provide retailers with a competitive advantage. Numerous laws have been enacted in the past 30 years to protect consumers from abusive practices of unscrupulous retailers.

Consumer Credit Protection Act. Before 1969, the regulation of consumer credit was largely left to individual states. However, in 1969 the federal government entered the consumer credit field by passing the Consumer Credit Protection Act, commonly called the Truth in Lending Act. The law requires retailers to explain in easily understood language the dollar finance charge and annual percentage rate on merchandise they finance, the balance on which the charge is figured, the closing date of the billing cycle, and the rights and obligations of the customer.

Congress later passed a number of other laws affecting consumer credit, including the credit card provisions of the Truth in Lending Act, the Fair Credit Reporting Act, the Fair Credit Billing Act, the Equal Credit Opportunity Act, the Consumer Leasing Act, and the Fair Debt Collection Practices Act.

Fair Credit Reporting Act. The Fair Credit Reporting Act protects the consumer's right to an accurate, up-to-date, and confidential credit report. Consumers have the right to obtain information about their credit records and to ask for a reinvestigation if the completeness or accuracy of any item in the record is questionable.

Fair Credit Billing Act. The 1975 Fair Credit Billing Act sets up a billing dispute settlement procedure and imposes other requirements on retailers to ensure fair and prompt handling of credit accounts. Retailers must:

1. Include with each monthly bill a statement informing customers of their rights when they question the bill and giving the address to which all inquiries must be sent.
2. Mail billing statements to the customer at least 14 days before payments are due.
3. Settle all billing disputes within 90 days.
4. Refrain from making adverse statements to credit-reporting agencies and from turning accounts over to collection agencies when an account is in dispute.
5. Credit all payments, overpayments, and returned merchandise promptly to accounts.

The law also states that bank card issuers cannot prevent retailers from offering discounts for purchases made with cash instead of credit cards.

Equal Credit Opportunity Act. The Equal Credit Opportunity Act, passed in 1975, prohibits discrimination on the basis of sex or marital status in any aspect of a credit transaction. Later amendments expanded the act to include prohibition of discrimination based on race, color, religion, national origin, age, and receipt of income from public assistance programs.

Consumer Leasing Act. The Consumer Leasing Act, passed in 1977, applies to the leasing of personal property (such as automobiles and furniture) for more than four months and for which the total transaction cost is under $25,000. The act requires the leasing company to make an accurate and detailed disclosure of all terms and costs in leasing contracts.

Fair Debt Collection Practices Act. The Fair Debt Collection Practices Act was passed in 1978. The intent of this law, which amends the Consumer Credit Protection Act, is to "eliminate abusive debt collection practices" and to protect the consumer from harassment and unfair collection procedures. Furthermore, a Federal Trade Commission Trade Regulation Rule, issued in 1985, states that a retailer cannot require a consumer to assign a portion of his or her wages to pay debts. The retailer is also prohibited from misrepresenting the cosigner's obligation to pay a debt.

Methods of Selling

Regulations exist to protect consumers against unscrupulous retailers who engage in such practices as shipping unordered merchandise or bait and switch selling. Regulations also affect the conditions under which direct sales are possible, days and hours of operation, and door-to-door sales.

Unordered Merchandise. Retailers are not allowed to ship merchandise that the consumer has not ordered. Consumers are not required to pay for items they do not order.

Push Money (PM). "Push money" encourages the sale of specified merchandise by paying salespeople a bonus to sell it. This practice is not per se illegal. Some forms of push money are clearly illegal, however. For example, payoffs by record distributors to disc jockeys are illegal. The FTC believes that this is a deceptive practice that leads consumers to believe that the records played most often are the most popular.

Hours and Days of Operation. Many states have so-called "blue laws," which prohibit the sale of various types of merchandise on Sunday. These laws have long been controversial because they are difficult to enforce and hamper management's efforts to remain open seven days a week. The FTC also issued an unusual antitrust ruling that virtually forces automobile dealers in Detroit to remain open on Saturday, a practice the dealers had resisted for years. The FTC determined that the closings restricted competition because showroom hours are a key dimension on which new-car dealers compete.[20]

Direct Retailing. State laws prohibit interstate liquor shipments through the mail. These laws keep liquor manufacturers and retailers from capitalizing on telemarketing or mail-order sales.

Bait and Switch Advertising. Management cannot employ "bait and switch" sales tactics. In the bait and switch technique, goods are advertised at a very low price. The retailer then tries to switch customers to a higher-priced item when they come to the store.

LEGAL DIMENSIONS OF TRANSNATIONAL RETAILING

Retailers are moving to foreign countries both to locate retail outlets and to identify sources of merchandise. Large retailers often import goods directly from foreign countries. However, import restrictions make it difficult for retailers to purchase merchandise from some foreign sources. Supporters of limits on the imports of foreign merchandise, for example, were successful in getting the Federal Trade Commission to issue a country of origin labeling regulation. The regulation requires retailers to tell their customers where their garments are made. Supporters of the regulation believe that it will limit consumer purchases of imported merchandise.

The U.S. Customs Service is cracking down on apparel and textile importers for alleged import fraud. Companies such as J. C. Penney, Kmart, and Target have been caught in the customs dragnet. Customer agents have identified evidence linking some importers to such illegal trade practices as cheating on import quotas, undervaluing goods, and selling prison-made products.

The U.S. Customs Office identifies **trans shipping** as a widely practiced form of fraud in the apparel trade. Specifically, to get around U.S. quotas on the volume of goods from various countries, manufacturers will ship nearly finished apparel for final assembly to a third country that still has room in its export quota for the U.S. market.[21]

An additional problem is that foreign governments often raise barriers to keep out U.S. retailers. Among the most stringent are the restrictions in Japan. The U.S.-inspired Structural Impediments Initiative, launched in 1989, is aimed at prying open new markets for U.S. retailers in Japan. Toys 'R' Us took advantage of the U.S. initiative and opened the first American-owned discount store in Japan. Japan's large-store law traditionally had protected the country's politically powerful small merchants by allowing the Japanese Ministry of International Trade and Industry (MITI) to forestall market entry. MITI in the last few years, however, has lowered impediments to the entry of foreign retailers, which is allowing U.S. firms for the first time to crack the Japanese market.

ETHICAL STANDARDS AND BUSINESS CONDUCT

The image of retailing as a whole suffers when any firm engages in unethical or questionable business practices. On occasion, laws are passed to eliminate unethical practices. For example, the Video Privacy Protection Act of 1988 bars retailers from selling or disclosing lists of customers'

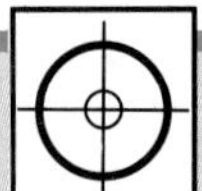

FOCUS 3–1

RALPHS SUPERMARKETS STATEMENT OF PHILOSOPHY AND COMMITMENT

1. Customers Are Number One. The success of Ralphs depends on satisfying the needs of customers. Treat them with respect and courtesy.
2. We Recognize Dedicated, Loyal Members. We are committed to Ralphs' continuing success. We work hard to achieve Company objectives and encourage and reward contribution.
3. We Are Ethical And Honest In Our Dealings With Others. We maintain the highest standards of ethics and honesty in fulfilling our job responsibilities, and in our dealings with each other, customers and suppliers.
4. We "Grow Our Own." We value our members and are alert for opportunities to help them increase their effectiveness. We take time to coach, train and develop our people as individuals and as contributing members of our organization.
5. We Listen With Respect To Each Other's Ideas To Reach Better Decisions. We seek input on concerns and needs from the people who have a stake in the decisions. We work hard to achieve agreement and mutual commitment. If a decision must be changed, it is done through appropriate channels.
6. We Look For Better Ways Of Doing Things. We're always looking to improve what we do and how we do it. New ideas and alternatives are explored and tested so that the organization remains adaptive to changing environments. In doing so, we seek to provide a working environment for all members which is not only clean, safe and attractive, but free of fear. We encourage all supervisors to maintain open channels of communication with their subordinates.
7. We Make Decisions. People are expected to make decisions appropriate to their responsibilities. We get satisfaction from successful decisions; those decisions which don't work out well are accepted as learning experiences.
8. Our Actions Reflect A Strong Sense Of Social Responsibility. We make our expertise and resources available to the communities we serve. We contribute in many ways to a wide variety of charitable and philanthropic causes. We support Affirmative Action and equal opportunity for all.
9. The Tougher The Challenge, The Better We Are. When there's a crisis, everyone willingly accepts responsibility and contributes as much as possible to solve the problem. Diverse groups submerge their own needs and join together as one when dealing with a crisis.
10. Ralphs Is In For The Long Term. We have a responsibility to ourselves, our customers and our suppliers to seek long-term growth, profits and a good return from every investment. Our planning reflects these goals.

Source: Courtesy Ralphs Supermarkets.

names and videos they have rented without those customers' permission or a court order.

Retailers establish codes of ethics and standards of behavior to make it clear to their employees that merely acting within the letter of the law is not sufficient. Such values and standards should be incorporated into the mission statement and permeate the organization, as shown in Focus 3–1,

A Profile in Excellence

JAMES CASH PENNEY

The philosophy of James Cash Penney was more than a set of guidelines designed solely to maximize profits. The son of a minister, the 27-year-old Penney opened his first store in 1902 in Kemmerer, Wyoming. He called the store the Gold Rule and catered to the needs of rural and blue-collar America by selling the basic types of merchandise demanded by all consumers. The tiny 25-by-40 foot store with its noble ideals was the cornerstone of the J. C. Penney Company and "The Penney Idea," which continues as the firm's underlying operating concept to this day.

"The Penney Idea" and the J. C. Penney Company were formalized in 1913 and were revolutionary at the time. The basic ideas still direct the organization.

1. To serve the public, as nearly as we can, to its complete satisfaction.
2. To expect for the service we render a fair remuneration and not all the profit the traffic will bear.
3. To do all in our power to pack the customer's dollar full of value, quality, and satisfaction.
4. To continue to train ourselves and our associates so that the service we give will be more and more intelligently performed.
5. To improve constantly the human factor in our business.
6. To reward the men and women in our organization through participation in what the business produces.
7. To test our every policy, method, and act in this wise: "Does it square with what is right and just?"

From these ideals, Mr. Penney dreamed of building a chain of stores premised on the Penney partnership idea. The plan allowed a store manager to purchase an equity position in a new store, provided that the manager trained a person capable of opening and managing the new link. The new manager and the manager of the existing store would jointly finance the venture. The plan allowed the J. C. Penney Company to be continually renewed from within, and to enter a period of rapid expansion.

which profiles Ralphs Supermarkets, a California-based retail organization. Statements of ethical policy are necessary but are not sufficient. Instead, retail executives must consistently communicate high standards of excellence and demonstrate them by personal example, as reflected in the pioneering efforts of James Cash Penney, highlighted in A Profile in Excellence.

Written ethics statements should be clear and comprehensive. The code of conduct should be specific to the sector of retailing for which it is written (see Case 2 at the end of the chapter, which reproduces the Neiman-Marcus ethics statement). Codes need regular updating to reflect changing environmental conditions. Sanctions should be stated; where appropriate, disciplinary actions should be taken.

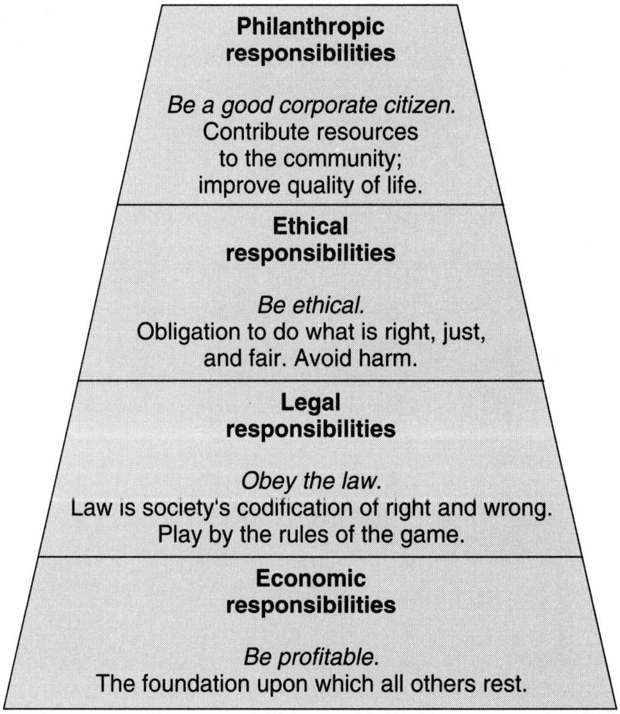

FIGURE 3–2

THE PYRAMID OF CORPORATE SOCIAL RESPONSIBILITY

Source: Archie B. Carroll, "The Pyramid of Corporate Social Responsibility: Toward Moral Management of Organizational Stockholders." Reprinted from *Business Horizons* 34, no. 4, July–August 1991, p. 42. Copyright 1991 by the Foundation for the School of Business at Indiana University. Used with permission.

SOCIAL RESPONSIBILITY

Retailers must also exhibit thoughtful and sensitive behavior in their response to society. Retailing often suffers from the societal perception that it is an institution that generates profit for the sake of profit and that believes that the social responsibility of retailers is only to stick to business.

The concept of corporate social responsibility can be viewed as a pyramid, as shown in Figure 3–2. The pyramid reflects four kinds of social responsibilities: economic, legal, ethical, and philanthropic. **Economic responsibilities** reflect the profit motive as a primary incentive for entrepreneurship. The primary economic role is to offer goods or services that consumers need and to make an acceptable profit in the process. **Legal responsibilities** require the organization to conform to all laws and regulations at the local, state, and federal levels as part of a social "contract" with society. **Ethical responsibilities** reflect those practices that are expected or prohibited by society, even though they are not reflected in law. They embody standards or norms that reflect a concern for what employees, the community, shareholders, and consumers regard as fair and just. **Philanthropic responsibilities** accomplish actions that reflect society's expectations that retailers should be good corporate citizens.

Manifestations of social responsibility are numerous. One of retailers' most tangible responses to societal needs is charitable contributions. Some retailers give preference to participating in local community projects. The supermarket industry, for example, is heavily involved in distributing food to the needy. So-called "green marketing" is also a high priority with many retailers. Firms such as The Body Shop, Ozone Brothers, and The Ecology Box offer products for the environmentally aware. Wal-Mart gives priority to purchasing biodegradable and environmentally safe products from suppliers. Many retailers, such as supermarkets, Wal-Mart, and Oil Express house recycling depots.[22]

Chapter Highlights

- The key restraint of trade laws are the Sherman Act, the Clayton Act, and the Federal Trade Commission Act.
- Price fixing is always illegal. Management cannot agree with competitors on the price at which items will be sold. Price fixing may be either horizontal or vertical.
- Management cannot set prices so as to try to deliberately drive competition out of business. Some states also prohibit the sale of items below cost.
- The Robinson-Patman Act is the primary law regulating promotional allowances offered to retailers. FTC regulations also affect all media advertising, promotional items sent through the mail, price lists, and similar promotional material. Retail ads also cannot make false or misleading claims.
- Retailers have a specific responsibility under Section 15 of the Consumer Product Safety Act to monitor the safety of the products they sell and to report any information about product hazards to the Consumer Product Safety Commission.
- The Magnuson-Moss Warranty Act is the primary warranty law affecting retailers. The law applies to written warranties for merchandise. Additionally, every sale, according to the Uniform Commercial Code, has an implied warranty of merchantability.
- The primary credit legislation affecting retailers includes the Consumer Credit Protection Act, Fair Credit Reporting Act, Fair Credit Billing Act, Equal Credit Opportunity Act, Consumer Leasing Act, and Fair Debt Collection Practices Act.
- Ethical behavior and social responsibility are becoming increasingly important issues for retailers. The image of retailing as a whole suffers when any firm engages in unethical or questionable business practices. Retailers engage in a variety of socially responsible practices to overcome the image of being interested only in making a profit.

Study Questions

1. Summarize the key restraint of trade laws and their effect on retail activities.
2. What are trade regulation rules? What are some retail activities that are covered by trade regulation rules?

3. What is meant by the term *predatory pricing?*
4. Why do some states have laws that prevent retailers from selling certain merchandise below cost?
5. What is meant by the term *good-faith defense?*
6. What is bait and switch advertising? Is this activity illegal?
7. What is meant by the following terms that relate to the distribution aspect of the marketing plan: exclusive territories and exclusive dealing?
8. What precautions must a retailer take in advertising warranties on merchandise?
9. Review the key credit legislation of which the retailer must be aware.
10. Present arguments for and against retailers' having social responsibility beyond making a profit and obeying the laws of the land.

A P P L I C A T I O N S

CASE 1: Neiman-Marcus Group: Conflict of Interest Policy

Company policy prohibits its officers, employees, and agents from occupying positions or becoming involved in situations that place them in a conflict of interest with the company and its subsidiaries, affiliates (including General Cinema Corporation), or both. Even the potential for an appearance of a conflict of interest can be detrimental to the company.

A conflict of interest arises when an officer, employee, or agent of the company or a member of his or her family, either directly or indirectly through another person, firm, or entity, has a financial or other interest that might influence his or her judgment on behalf of the company. Because there are many situations in which a conflict of interest can arise, no attempt will be made to catalog them here.

A simple rule, one which will cover the most common problems, can be stated, however:

No officer, employee or agent of the company should do any of the following:

1. Accept a gift, whether it is in the form of cash, property (an exception may be made for token gifts customarily given during holiday seasons), or services; payment of expenses; or a loan, discount, rebate, or kickback from any person, firm, or entity that fits the description below.
2. Be employed by or consult or otherwise render services to or for such a person, firm, or entity.
3. Own or have ownership interest in (other than an insubstantial holding in a publicly held company) such a person, firm, or entity.
4. Be a creditor of such a person, firm, or entity.

Persons, firms, or entities that meet any of the following criteria are to be avoided.

1. Those that supply goods or services to the company or any of its subsidiaries or affiliates (including General Cinema Corporation).
2. Those that purchase goods or services from the company or any of its subsidiaries or affiliates (including General Cinema Corporation).
3. Those that compete with the company or any of its subsidiaries or affiliates (including General Cinema Corporation).

Obviously, a person who operates or has financial interests within the same industry as one in which the company or any of its subsidiaries or affiliates (including General Cinema Corporation) is engaged has a conflict. Anyone who may benefit from his or her position at the company's or its subsidiary's or affiliate's expense has a conflict.

If a person now is or subsequently becomes involved in a conflict of interest situation, he or she should advise his or her supervisor in writing. The company will ordinarily expect the conflict of interest to be eliminated, but there are situations in which apparent conflict situations may be accepted, depending on all of the circumstances.

Neiman-Marcus Group is a division of the General Cinema Corporation. Reprinted with permission.

Applying Retailing Principles

1. Briefly summarize the key elements of the Neiman-Marcus statement of corporate ethics.
2. In your opinion, what items are missing? Briefly draft the additional points you believe should be included in the statement.
3. What are the advantages of having a published statement of corporate ethics and requiring employees to sign it?
4. Is the existence of a corporate ethics statement alone likely to deter unethical behavior? Why or why not? If not, what additional actions are needed?

CASE 2: New York Fights Scams of Midtown Electronics Stores

In a seamy section of midtown Manhattan near Times Square, Paul Viani browses through a West 42nd Street electronics store crammed with goods.

He quizzes a clerk on prices, and then inspects a Canon camera marked $499. A few minutes after the salesman offers the camera for $169, Viani finally reaches for his wallet.

But instead of money, Viani—like the hero of a late-night crime show—whips out a badge. An undercover inspector for the city's department of consumer affairs, he makes an ominous vow to the astonished clerk: "We're going to take a look at everything in the store."

In violation of the law, the store had omitted the manufacturer's suggested retail price on the camera and marked it nearly double that price instead. Viani and his partner also found in a one-hour inspection that almost every videocassette recorder selling as new had been used and rebuilt. The word "reconditioned" stamped on personal stereos had either been rubbed out or stripped from the boxes.

"And these guys," says Viani, "were amateurs."

The inspection was one of the city's latest attempts to curb the consumer chicanery and scams of midtown electronics stores. It is a battle New York City has been fighting—and for the most part losing—for decades.

Thousands of small businesses across the nation routinely break the law and view paying fines as the cost of doing business. But New York law enforcement officials say that many midtown electronics stores have carried this approach to remarkable levels. For example, before New York City revoked Camera World's license in July 1990 for alleged consumer violations, the firm had racked up hundreds of such allegations.

Salespeople almost routinely dicker over prices, but naive bargain hunters often find out too late that the price first quoted or marked is highly inflated. Viani explains the scenario: "The salesman says, 'It's a slow day. Give me $300 for the camera.' You walk away feeling, 'I really made a coup.' You turn the corner and see it for $250. I don't know how many times I've heard that story."

Other stores litter their floors with newspapers and boxes and hang large going out of business banners outside. "There have been people going out of business here as long as I can remember," says Thomas Cusick, president of the Fifth Avenue Association, a group of much posher midtown retailers.

Source: Portions reproduced with permission from Mark Robichaux, "New York Fights Scams by Midtown Electronics Stores," *The Wall Street Journal,* October 24, 1990, p. B2. Reprinted by permission of THE WALL STREET JOURNAL,

Applying Retailing Principles

1. Identify the illegal or unethical practices discussed in the case. Should consumers be expected to recognize these incidences when they occur?
2. Based on your experience and the experience of your friends, what is the frequency with which you have encountered the retailing practices described in the case? In what types of retailing do unethical practices appear to be most pervasive?

NOTES

1. "FTC Tentatively O.K.s Two Big Deals," *Supermarket News,* June 6, 1988, p. 2; "FTC Halts Red Food's Kroger Deal," *Supermarket News,* April 10, 1989, p. 1.
2. Ross A. Fabricant, "Special Retail Services and Retail Price Maintenance: The California Wine Industry," *Journal of Retailing* 66 (Spring 1990), p. 10.
3. Robert La Russa, "High Court Rules on Price Setting," *Supermarket News,* May 9, 1988, p. 2.
4. Ray O. Werner, ed., "Legal Developments in Marketing," *Journal of Marketing,* October 1990, p. 106.
5. Paul M. Barnett, "Nintendo's Latest Novelty Is a Price-Fixing Settlement," *The Wall Street Journal,* April 11, 1991, p. B1.
6. Norton E. Marks and Neely S. Inlow, "Price Discrimination and Its Impact on Small Business," *The Journal of Consumer Marketing* 5 (Winter 1988), pp. 31–38.
7. Mark A. Robichaux, "New York Fights Scams by Mid-Town Electronics Stores," *The Wall Street Journal,* October 24, 1990, p. B32.
8. Francine Schwadel, "Lowest-Price Ad Claims in Ad Stir Dispute," *The Wall Street Journal,* August 8, 1988, p. 17; "Wards Rapped for 'Lowest Price' Ads," *Advertising Age,* July 25, 1988, p. 4.
9. "Montgomery Ward Settles FTC Charges on Service Contracts," *The Wall Street Journal,* August 17, 1988, p. 4.
10. "Food Companies Change Pitch," *Marketing News,* November 25, 1991, p. 1.
11. "OSHA Standards Eliminate Some Supermarket Hazards, *Chain Store Age Executive,* January 1989, p. 15.
12. "Four McCrory Stores Are Cited by OSHA on Fire Safety Lapses," *The Wall Street Journal,* November 8, 1991, p. A4.
13. "Retailers Get ADA Deadline," *Chain Store Age Executive,* September 1991, p. 92; Kevin Pritchett, "Provisions of Disabilities Act Puzzle Many Firms," *The Wall Street Journal,* November 29, 1991, p. B1.
14. "Retailer Pays U.S. $475,000 to Settle Suit about Safety," *The Wall Street Journal,* June 5, 1991, p. A4.
15. Craig A. Kelly, Jeffrey S. Conant, and Jacqueline Brown, "Extended Warranties: Retail Management and Public Policy Implications," in Gary Frazier et al 1988, *American Marketing Association Educators Proceedings* (Chicago: American Marketing Association, 1988), pp. 261–66.
16. "Judges 'McPinion': McSleep Inns Infringed on McDonald's Trademarks," *Marketing News,* October 10, 1988, p. 5.
17. "McDonald's Takes Leap into Trouble," *Advertising Age,* September 30, 1991, p. 42.
18. Emily Denitto, "FDA's Labeling Attacks Are Creating Uncertainty," *Supermarket News,* June 17, 1991, p. 1; Russell Shaw, "Retailers Must Prepare for Labeling Law," *Supermarket News,* February 25, 1991, p. 15.
19. Elliot Zwiebach, "California Chains Penalized on Tobacco," *Supermarket News,* December 3, 1990, p. 4.
20. Michael Galen and Jeffrey Rothfeder, "The Right to Privacy: There Is More Loophole than Law," *BusinessWeek,* September 4, 1989, p. 77.
21. Amy Borrus, Pete Engardio, Laura Zinn, and Joyce Baranathan, "Customs Tears into the Chinese Rag Trade," *BusinessWeek,* December 30, 1991, p. 51; Joyce Baranathan, "It's Time to Put the Screws to China's Gulag Economy," *BusinessWeek,* December 30, 1991, p. 52.
22. Patricia Strand, "Kmart Expands Environmental Plan, Sets Rubbermaid Tie," *Advertising Age,* February 18, 1991, p. 33; Christopher Power and Mark Landler "And Now, Finger-Lickin' Good for Ya?" *Business Week,* February 18, 1991, p. 60; Alan Sloan, "The Selling of the Simple Life," *Worth,* February/March 1992, pp. 79–82.

CHAPTER

4

Demographic, Social, Competitive, and Technological Environments

THIS CHAPTER:

Reviews the new consumer demographics.

Explores the mood of today's consumer.

Illustrates how changes in competition affect retailing.

Emphasizes the globalization of retailing.

Identifies the technological forces affecting retail strategy.

RETAILING CAPSULE

THE BODY SHOP–CHANGING THE WORLD

Anita Roddick, a former "flower child," founded The Body Shop in London in 1976. The firm has been wildly successful and has grown to over 700 stores, many of them franchisees, in 39 countries, with 150 stores being added each year. Roddick believed that people wanted to buy natural cosmetics. The firm hence sells skin creams, lotions, and shampoos made from fruit and vegetable oils rather than animal fat.

The Body Shop uses its social policies as marketing aids, thereby building brand awareness without spending money on advertising and promotion. The firm does not test its products on animals. In addition, it sells such items as bracelets made out of rain forest materials to help provide Amazon residents a livelihood without destroying the forests to create crop land. Similarly, the firm sells pins with whales on them to show the company's support for cetacean life. All literature is printed on recycled paper.

Employees are carefully selected to ensure that they share Roddick's pet passions. During job interviews they are asked about everything from personal heroes to literary tastes.

The Body Shop has prompted competitors to enter the market. Les Wexner, founder of The Limited, has opened a chain of Bath and Body Works shops that look very much like Body Shops. Estée Lauder developed Origins, a product line that uses "natural" ingredients and recycled containers and has started opening stand-alone stores. Kmart now sells Naturistics natural cosmetics in its stores. Other competitors include Seattle-based Garden Botanika and a British chain called Goodebodies.

The Body Shop practices a "value" retailing strategy whereby customers are encouraged to buy only what they need. Repeat business is fostered

through the use of returnable containers, which can be refilled. Discounts are used to reinforce the practice.

Source: Based on Jacquelines Scerbinski, "Consumers and the Environment: A Focus on Five Products," *Journal of Business Strategy,* September–October 1991, pp. 44–47; "Whales, Human Rights, Rain Forests and the Smell of Profits," *Business Week,* July 15, 1991, pp. 114–15; Allan Sloan, "The Selling of the Simple Life," *Worth,* February/March 1992, pp. 75–84; Jean Sherman Chatzky, "Changing the World," *Forbes,* March 2, 1992, pp. 83–84.

As we have just illustrated, retailing is a very competitive business. Thousands of firms fail each year. But an equal number, like The Body Shop (Exhibit 4–1), succeed. The failures range from the smallest mom-and-pop operations to such giants as Gimbels, R. H. Macy, and McCrory Stores. Other well-known giants that have had troubles in recent years include A&P, Sears, and Bloomingdale's. Still others were absorbed by competitors as a result of acquisitions or mergers.

Why is competition so fierce? People can get started in retailing without much money, most competing retailers carry essentially the same items, and most competing retailers operate in the same manner. Thus, retailers can be easily wiped out if they don't read the signs of what is going on around them.

As an example, Congress, by voting to waive federal inspection requirements for all meat-top pizza sold to non-profit institutions such as schools and hospitals, opened a multi-billion dollar market for Pizza Hut and other fresh-baked pizza purveyors.[1] The International Frozen Pizza Institute lobbied unsuccessfully against the waiver, stating that the exemption would undermine public health safeguards. Fresh-baked pizza restaurateurs pointed out that pepperoni and other precooked meats on pizza are twice inspected in the cooking process.

Environmental Dynamics

Retailers cannot always anticipate the changes that occur in the environments. Weather problems such as floods or blizzards can cause retailers to lose millions of dollars in sales. Rapid increases in interest rates led to many retail failures in the early 1980s.

Totally new forms of products or channels of distribution can make some stores almost obsolete overnight. A decade or so ago, watches were sold mostly at jewelry stores. Today, they are sold in virtually every type of retail outlet. J. C. Penney similarly has emerged as a major seller of gold jewelry. Videocassette players and the low rental fees for the videocassette movies are emerging as alternatives to movie theaters as the baby boomers become homebodies.

EXHIBIT 4–1

Courtesy The Body Shop

The Body Shop is a beauty store chain founded on the principle of environmental preservation and social activism.

Increased consumer interest in fitness and health led to the rapid growth of health spas and fitness centers and low-fat and vegetarian menus in restaurants. Environmental awareness spawned natural cosmetics outlets such as The Body Shop and has led fast-food franchisers such as McDonald's to shift to environmental-friendly packaging. The increasing number of working mothers has allowed Kinder-Care Learning Centers to become the nation's largest chain of day-care centers. Similarly, the expanding number of two-income households has pressured local governments to abolish Sunday closing laws and to keep retail stores open longer hours in the evening and on the weekend to meet the needs of working adults.

What Are the New Consumer Demographics?

Understanding the dynamics of consumer demographics is critically important because they affect the projected sizes of market segments and buying behavior. All of us have probably heard discussions of the buying behavior of the baby boomers (people born between 1946 and 1964). But changes in other population segments are equally important in affecting retail strategy. The primary changes in the population include the following:

- Smaller households.
- Two-income households.
- Increase in suburban movement.
- Age mix changes.
- An older population.
- Regional growth.
- Growth in smaller communities.
- Increasing mobility.
- Growth of subcultures and minorities.
- An increasing number of male shoppers.

Smaller Households. One- and two-person households now comprise 59 percent of all households. This group includes singles, widows, empty nesters, childless and unmarried couples, and younger couples planning to have children later. These small households are prime prospects for townhouses, condominiums, kitchen mini-appliances, and packaged goods in single servings. SSWDs (single, separated, widowed, and divorced) spend more money on travel and entertainment, but they save less and tend to buy more services.

The 1990 U.S. Census revealed that about 23 million Americans live by themselves, a 91 percent jump for women since 1970 and a 156 percent increase for men over the same period. Middle-aged singles are among the fastest growing of these groups. Singles collectively represent a market of more than $60 billion. Hyatt Hotels, in recognition of this growing market, has tested a "single" share program at its Beaver Creek Ski Resort in Colorado. Hyatt arranged to provide roommates, and thus reduced room rates, to people traveling alone.[2]

Two-Income Households. Households with two or more wage earners account for more than 70 percent of all families. They have more than two-thirds of total family buying power. These households spend more for luxuries, even though in many cases the second wage earners are working to pay off family debt. Such households offer many market opportunities. They especially want products and services that offer convenience and help save time.[3]

Growth of Suburbs. The suburbs now account for more than half of all U.S. sales. During the past decade more Americans left such areas as New York and Chicago than moved into them. Younger and more affluent people move, leaving older and poorer consumers behind. These less affluent areas tend to be understored, as retailers abandon these markets for more attractive alternatives (see A Question of Ethics). Still, some evidence indicates that residential movement to central cities is again occurring as households start to restore older, elegant, larger homes in

A Question of Ethics

WHERE THE FOOD ISN'T

Supermarkets during the 1960s and 1970s fled the inner cities, leaving the poor to pay more for less. The exodus began as the major supermarket chains followed their white customers to the suburbs. It accelerated during the merger and buyout binges of the 1980s, which affected 16 of the top 20 national supermarket chains and accelerated the trend toward fewer, larger supermarkets located in affluent urban and suburban areas, away from the inner city.

Neighborhood leaders state that the industry ignores inner-city consumers who have much food-purchasing power in spite of their low incomes. They argue that the supermarket industry, led primarily by white, suburban executives, tends to think in terms of racial stereotypes that blind them to the profit potential of low-income areas.

The industry argues that economic forces led to the exodus. They point out that the supermarket business operates on low margins—less than 1 percent net profits on sales. They also state that older urban stores are too small to accommodate the product mix they need, which includes high-profit nonfood items such as beauty aids. They also argue that high land costs and lack of suitably sized locations make it difficult to enter the inner-city markets.

What obligations, if any, do supermarket executives have for serving inner-city neighborhoods? Do you believe that their decisions are driven primarily by economics or racial stereotypes?

Based on "Where the Food Isn't," *Newsweek*, February 24, 1992, pp. 36–37.

such areas. The movement has spurred the development or redevelopment of downtown shopping plazas in some cities.

Age Mix Changes. The under-40 age group now constitutes the largest segment of the population and is dominated by post–baby boomers struggling with careers, raising families, and developing investment plans. These people now account for one-third of the U.S. population and 47 percent of all household income. The baby boomers are aging, however, and, by the year 2000 the largest adult population segment will be from 35 to 54 years of age, as shown in Table 4–1. The number of people aged 18 to 34 will have decreased 11 percent by the year 2000.[4]

The Limited, in view of these population demographics, now concentrates on a youthful but slightly older target audience—the thirty-something crowd—as opposed to the primary target of teens and women in their early twenties when the firm was founded. The Limited also has a portfolio of store types appealing to other age groups and lifestyle segments.

Over the next 10 years the baby boomers will swell the ranks of middle-aged Americans by more than 1 million a year. They will bring with them changes in lifestyles, values, and outlooks. We already are seeing some such changes. At one time the idea of a 50-year-old rock star such as

TABLE 4–1 CHANGES IN AGE MIX IN THE UNITED STATES

Population by Age: 1985–2000 (in thousands)

	1985	*1990*	*1995*	*2000*	*% change*
All Ages	238,631	249,657	259,559	267,955	12.3%
Under 15	51,861	54,582	56,724	55,903	7.8
15–24	39,717	35,548	34,110	36,088	−9.1
25–34	**41,788**	**43,529**	40,520	36,415	−12.9
35–44	**32,004**	**37,847**	**41,997**	**43,743**	**36.7**
45–54	22,464	25,402	**31,397**	**37,119**	**65.2**
55–64	22,188	21,051	20,923	23,767	7.1
65+	28,609	31,697	33,888	34,921	22.1

(bold face = baby boom generation)

U.S. Households by Age of Householder

	1985		2000	
	# in millions	*% age*	*# in millions*	*% age*
Under 35	25.5	29%	22.0	22%
35–49	23.8	27	35.0	34
Over 50	37.5	43	45.5	44
TOTAL U.S.	86.8	100	102.5	100

Aggregate Household Income by Age of Householder

	1985		2000	
	$ in billions	*% age*	*$ in billions*	*% age*
Under 35	$ 614.4	26%	$ 682.5	19%
35–49	816.3	34	1,537.0	42
Over 50	952.8	40	1,448.5	40
TOTAL U.S.	2,383.5	100	3,668.0	100

Source: The Conference Board.

Mick Jagger or Tina Turner would have been absurd. Today no one thinks twice about the phenomenon.

A baby boomlet is now underway that will last for a few years as a faint echo of the postwar baby boom of 1946–64. More babies were born in 1990 than at any other time in the past 30 years—approaching the baby boom peak of 4.3 million births recorded in 1957. The trend is a reversal of the trend in the mid-1960s and 1970s. The baby boom has spawned such specialty stores as Kids 'R' Us, GapKids, and BabyGap.[5]

Although the number of births has risen, bigger families are not making a comeback. Typically, couples are having only one child. Thus, in spite of the increasing number of babies being born, the U.S. birth rate is at an all-time low. Women today will have an average of only 1.8 children, 52 percent below the peak years of the baby boom and too low to maintain the current population level. If present trends continue, deaths in the U.S. will exceed births by the year 2034.

An Older Population. More than 50 million people over the age of 55 live in the United States, and they spend around $70 billion a year on shelter, $20 billion on apparel, and many billions more on travel, entertainment, health care, and home furnishings. This group represents almost one out of three adults and accounts for half of the nation's discretionary income. The aging American consumer is less likely to be poor than the average American.[6]

Numerically and psychologically, the older consumer of tomorrow will be quite different from the stereotypes of today. Grandparents, for example, are now buying things which historically have been beyond the means of most parents: educational toys, children's designer clothing, and imported strollers, for example. F.A.O. Schwarz, the toy giant, has added a Grandma Shop (Exhibit 4–2) to its two largest stores, and the company trains its sales force to help older consumers choose special gifts for their grandchildren. Similarly, Promises Kept, a mail-order company in Minneapolis, promotes quality toys for grandchildren in a section of its catalog.[7]

Regional Growth. The Sunbelt and western states will grow faster than the rest of the U.S. during the 1990s. The West and South now have far more than half of the U.S. population. These two regions accounted for 86 percent of U.S. population growth in the past decade. California, Texas, and Florida alone accounted for 35 percent of U.S. population growth. Many Sunbelt and western states also have a higher birthrate because of their younger populations. Utah, for example, has the youngest average age in the nation.

Management should not be misled by aggregate statistics, however. Some areas of the Sunbelt are retail losers. Certain counties have been losing population since 1940 and probably will do so at least through the year 2000.

Population density continues to remain highest in the pocket of states east of the Mississippi River and north of the Mason-Dixon line. The 10 most densely populated states are New Jersey, Rhode Island, Massachusetts, Connecticut, Maryland, New York, Delaware, Pennsylvania, Ohio, and Illinois, plus the District of Columbia. These states produce a higher dollar volume of retail sales per square mile than any of the other 40 states. As such, they are very attractive markets.

EXHIBIT 4–2

Rob Maass/Sipa Press

Grandma Shop at F.A.O. Schwarz. The toy giant trains its sales force to help Grandma choose that special gift.

Growth in Smaller Communities. The largest rate of growth continues to be in the smaller market areas—cities with populations of 50,000 to 200,000. On the average, these areas over the past decade had a population growth rate nearly four times that of the United States as a whole. Their retail sales growth rate is one and a half times the national average. Such markets allowed firms such as Wal-Mart to grow quite rapidly in the 1980s. Furthermore, these markets are becoming more attractive to national retailers as their larger market areas have become saturated. Firms such as McDonald's and Sears are experimenting with down-sized outlets which will allow them to penetrate such markets.

Mobility. Today's shoppers are quite mobile. Many households have at least two automobiles. Shoppers seeking specialty merchandise and unique experiences when they shop will travel considerable distances to make purchases. Such a phenomenon has led to lower store loyalty than in the past.

As many as 20 percent of the households in a community will move in a given year. Some of the moves are within the community, but most, of course, are not. This means that consumers often look for recognized brand names and warranties on merchandise that will be honored regardless of where they live. Such mobility favors the national chains, such as Sears.

Growth of Subcultures and Minorities. Blacks, Hispanics, and Asians now constitute nearly 30 percent of the U.S. population and have a combined income of $500 billion, a market of too many people and too much money to ignore.[8]

By the year 2000, California will have no ethnic majority. The birthrate among young immigrants in California is so high that even if California had closed its borders in 1991, the state's population would still grow by four million by the end of this decade.[9]

The Asian population is among the fastest growing, and it doubled between 1980 and 1990. This minority could grow an additional 40 percent by 2000. Asians represent 30 percent of San Francisco's population, for example.[10]

Nonwhites are majorities in 15 of the 28 U.S. cities with a population of 400,000 or more. These groups include blacks, Hispanics, Asians, and native Americans. Examples of such cities include Houston, 59.2 percent; New York, 56.5 percent; Memphis, 56.2 percent; San Francisco, 53.2 percent; Dallas, 52.2 percent; and Cleveland, 52.1 percent.[11]

The changing ethnic mix within the economy complicates the marketing process for retailers. Hiring people of different ethnicities and stocking outlets with merchandise to fill special needs (such as darker-hued cosmetics) are obvious responses. Still, even the obvious things are too often neglected in making ethnic customers feel comfortable. Sensitivity training for all employees is needed to help them avoid misunderstandings because of cultural differences. Jordan Marsh, for example, has developed a community and organizational guide to Hispanic, Asian, and black markets to use as an employee recruitment source and to help guide decisions about support of charitable organizations.[12]

Advertising programs must also be tailored to the diverse market segments. For example, firms such as McDonald's and Safeway advertise in Asian-language newspapers and magazines and on Asian television and radio stations. But retailers have found that they need to come up with six different campaigns to cover the five major Asian groups: Japanese, Korean, Chinese (who may speak Mandarin or Cantonese), Vietnamese, and Filipino.[13] Similar complications exist in serving the black and Hispanic markets (see Case 1 at the end of the chapter).

Diverse Household Roles. Retail executives are belatedly recognizing that males, single and married, are making more purchasing decisions than ever before. The trend is "altering definitions of products, how they are used and designed, and how packaging connects with the new liberated male segments. . . ."[14] Men now account for 40 percent of U.S. food-shopping dollars. Social scientists point out that, over time, men are being "reconditioned" for their broadened roles. Currently, for example, approximately 50 percent of American men at some time prepare complete meals for their families.

Retailers are being forced to redirect their promotional efforts because today's food shopper is no longer primarily female. The task becomes even more daunting when one factors in the increasingly important role of the teenager in making many of the buying decisions in two-income households.

Single-Parent Households.[15] The rise of single-parent households in the last three decades has been phenomenal. Currently, more than 19 percent of white children live with one parent. Almost 55 percent of black children live with one parent. About half of all marriages now end in divorce. Indeed, the majority of children born today are likely to spend at least part of their youth in a single-parent family.

Single-parent households have complex and long-term effects on many aspects of society. Single female-headed households with children have a poverty rate of more than 45 percent, compared to a poverty rate among married couples with children of less than 8 percent. Children in such households also often receive poor education and inadequate health care. They are less likely to complete high school and have low earnings throughout their lives. Similarly, divorce and births to single mothers fray the bonds between generations. This issue is likely to become a public policy concern during the next decade.

Apart from the social implications of this trend, such households have limited resources to spend on big-ticket items. They are unlikely to own a home or to make major purchases such as appliances and automobiles.

TODAY'S CONSUMER

Understanding shifts in demographics is not sufficient to plan for the future with confidence. Management also needs to understand how their potential consumers think and act. Changing consumer attitudes can be as important as changing economic conditions in affecting shopping behavior.

The Mood of the Consumer[16]

The current consumer mood can be described as "an age of . . . creativity, self-expression, and individualism." People are seeking a higher quality of life. Consider the following evidence:

The growing consumer tendency to reject the artificial in favor of the natural, whether in ingredients, products, appearance, or behavior.

The growing number of middle-aged adults refusing promotions because they would have to relocate.

The appearance of books on the nonfiction best-seller lists such as *Total Fitness, The Save Your Life Diet,* and *Overcoming Stress.*

The march of women into the labor force, a trend only partly caused by economic factors.

One big, new value is really quite old.[17] To this generation, old-fashioned is new-fashioned.

Old-fashioned ice cream, yogurt, hand-dipped chocolate confections, frilly nightgowns, real wood furniture, clocks with hands, clothes made of wool, wine, bottled spring water, and leather boots all reflect old-fashioned values in a new-fashioned world. Many people are still terrified of technology. They are scared of synthetics. They are concerned about commercialism. One way they fight back is to look back.

So modern marketers have a big opportunity. Consumers are not saying, "Give me the old things." They are saying, "Give me the old values." If retailers can demonstrate that modern products and services are consistent with or enhance these values, then they have a way to capture a big share of the nation's heart.

The mood today is decidedly moving from "me" to "we." Such "us-ism" leads adults to be increasingly anchored to a happy home life. The trend has resulted in the appearance of a new buzz word to describe the phenomenon: *cocooning.*

Consumers today are defining value as the extent to which a product provides experiences that are good for a person. Quality is thus defined in terms of value and satisfaction. Whenever a retailer competes on quality in trying to provide value, the measurement of consumer satisfaction becomes important.[18] The consumer demand for better service is creating a marketplace where quality and service alone, however, are not sufficient. Instead, the 1990s are requiring retailers to "create value" for customers by redefining quality in customer terms, not internal corporate terms.[19]

Americans are willing to pay a premium for quality. Well-made imports have educated retail consumer tastes. Today's consumer thus defines quality in the context of reliability, durability, ease of maintenance, a trusted brand name, and, finally, a low price. The consumer mood is also manifested in Americans' concern about nutrition and a desire to know what is in their food.[20] As a corollary, consumers are concerned about our disposable society's soiling the environment.[21] Half of consumers label themselves environmentalists. Four out of five have indicated a willingness to pay a premium for products packaged with recyclable or biodegradable materials.

Consumers will be financially pressed during the 1990s and will continue to gravitate to retail sales promotions to obtain better values. Coupons and product samples are becoming more important. Sweepstakes and premiums are more important today, and brand name purchases are down.[22]

Frequent shopper plans and premiums such as the Skaggs' Frequent Shopper Awards program and the Sears Discover Card cumulative discount program are popular examples or responses to this dimension of the consumer mood.

Component buying, whereby consumers shop at various outlets for the best buy on merchandise and abandon the department stores for clothing purchases, is a further reflection of the consumer mood. Retailers offering a limited assortment of high-turnover merchandise at significantly lower prices are growing rapidly.[23] Examples include Sam's Wholesale Club in general merchandise and Jiffy Lube in auto maintenance.

In summary, retailers are facing increasingly fragmented markets because of the demise of the traditional single-income, middle-class family and its associated values. Instead, the marketplace today is characterized by a wide range of attitudes, brand preferences, shopping patterns, and lifestyles. Such diversity provides a unique opportunity for tightly focused specialty outlets such as The Body Shop, for example. In the 1990s we will also see, because of a scarcity of time, greater use of mail-order, a continued dislike for shopping, and the growth of personal shopping services. Computer technology will also allow retailers of all sizes to know more about the buying patterns of their customers than ever before.

Changes in the Competitive Environments

The Current Competitive Environment

Exhibit 4–3 depicts the essence of the competitive environment for the 1990s. Competition is as complicated as the mood of the customer. Retailing is overstored, consumer buying power has eroded, and global competition is heating up. Many retailers remain burdened with the huge debt loads that they acquired during the merger, acquisition, and leveraged buyout binges of the 1980s. Finally, new formats attuned to the preferences of today's shoppers are making inroads into the traditional department store markets. Probable winners and losers are highlighted in Table 4–2. Department stores, a traditional mainstay of retailing, have been unable to win back customers who have abandoned them for focused stores such as The Gap and specialty discounters such as Crown Books, Toys 'R' Us, Staples (a stationery discounter), and Streamers (a discount party-supply chain).[24]

Some well-known retailers, however, continue to be winners.[25] They employ a variety of successful techniques for attracting and maintaining consumers. Nordstrom, for instance, is known for its excellent customer service. Dillard's is unique for its state-of-the-art information systems. Wal-Mart has expanded by aggressive store construction and internal

EXHIBIT 4–3

Retailers Face Cutbacks, Uncertain Future

Restaurants Search for Winning Recipes

A WHOLESALE MAKEOVER OF RETAIL?

Laura Ashley to Sell 15% Stake to Jusco

No Miracle on 34th Street for Macy's

A TAKEOVER OF AVON COULD MEAN A MAKEOVER FOR AMWAY

AMWAY'S BIG, HAPPY FAMILY IS ALL SMILES—IN JAPAN

Shrinking the Five-and-Dime

Storm warnings

CAN GOULD PUT THE BLOOM BACK ON BLOOMIE'S?

Merchants Mobilize To Battle Wal-Mart In a Small Community

Globalization: Reshaping the Retail Marketplace

How Wal-Mart hits Main St.

Tough Economic Times Are Knocking Stuffing Out of Many Furniture Stores

Signs of the times: the competitive environment of the 1990s

start-ups, and Kmart has focused on upgrading store presentations and merchandise.

One point is clear: competition in retailing will continue to be intense. The keys to success in the 1990s are value, quality, and service. The successful retailer is equally concerned about customers and competitors.[26]

TABLE 4–2

A VIEW OF COMPETITION FROM 1990 TO 2000

New Format Entries
Off-price apparel stores—Ross Stores
Superstore electronics chains—Circuit City
Wholesale warehouse clubs—Costco, Sam's Warehouse
Category killer stores—Toys 'R' Us, Sportmart
All-natural stores—The Body Shop, Goodebodies
Setbacks
Catalog showrooms—remaining key players are Service Merchandise and Best Products
Mid-size regional chains—losers include Ames, Ayr-Way, Maxway, Yellowfront Stores, Gemco
Department stores—losers are Sears, J. C. Penney, Montgomery Ward
Internationalization
Benetton—Italian apparel retailer
Laura Ashley—Wales-based retailer of women's fashions and home furnishings
Mothercare—British maternity and children's apparel store
Carrefour—French retailer that sells via the hypermarket format
IKEA—Swedish furniture seller
Taken Private
R.H. Macy, Elder Beerman
Winning Strategies
Nordstrom—customer service
Dillard's—state-of-the-art information systems
Mercantile Stores—tight financial controls in secondary markets
The Limited—diversification into related retail concepts
Kmart—upgrading store presentations and merchandise, acquisitions
Wal-Mart—aggressive store construction and internal startups of new divisions

Types of Competition

Intratype Competition. The most familiar type of competition is **intratype competition.** Intratype competition is competition between two retailers of the same type, such as two drugstore chains. Most people are familiar with intratype competition because this is the model most frequently described in basic economic texts. Examples of intratype strategic groups that compete aggressively include the following:

1. Upscale fashion department stores (Neiman-Marcus, Saks, Lord & Taylor, I. Magnin).
2. Traditional department stores (Marshall Field's, Jordan Marsh, Broadway, Dillard's).
3. Promotional department stores (Sears, J. C. Penney).
4. Traditional specialty stores (Brooks Brothers, The Limited).
5. Focused specialty stores (Benetton, The Gap, Banana Republic, Ralph Lauren, Liz Claiborne).

6. Upscale discount department stores (Target, Caldor, Bradlee's, Venture).
7. Downscale discount department stores (Kmart, Wal-Mart).
8. Off-price retailers (Marshall's, T. J. Maxx, Burlington Coat Factory, Dress Barn).
9. Value-oriented fashion mini department stores (Mervyn's, Main Street).
10. Catalogue retailers (L. L. Bean, Lands' End, Sharper Image).
11. Direct sellers (Avon, Mary Kay, Lady Love).

Intratype competition is not limited to tangible-goods retailers. It can exist, for example, between hospitals, banks, financial institutions, churches, and educational institutions.

Intertype Competition. A second competitive model is **intertype competition:** competition between different types of retail outlets selling the same lines of merchandise in the same trade area. The examples shown in Figure 4–1 reflect the competition in selling the same type of merchandise between traditional department stores, such as May Company or Dillard's, and specialty merchants such as Benetton, upscale fashion retailers such as Lord & Taylor, general merchandisers such as Sears, and low-price outlets such as Wal-Mart.

Corporate Systems Competition. This occurs when a single-management ownership links resources, manufacturing capability, and distribution networks. The Limited is an example of corporate systems competition. They manufacture some of their merchandise, handle their own storage and distribution functions, and perform all management activities necessary for the sale of goods and services at the retail level.

Total systems networks can be formed either backward or forward. In **forward integration**, a manufacturer establishes its own wholesale and retail network. Examples are Goodyear, Singer, and Sherwin Williams. **Backward integration** occurs when a retailer or wholesaler performs some manufacturing functions. Sears is an example. Sears began buying into suppliers in the 1920s when it expanded from an all-catalog store to a department store retailer and wanted a dependable source of supply.

These types of competition do not exist in isolation. Retail firms in all types of channel structures face competition from retailers in any or all of the other systems. Our comments must be regarded only as broad generalizations about the nature of competition and the various types of channel systems because numerous exceptions exist.

The New Face of Competition

The changes in the competitive structure of retailing are causing management to rethink the concepts of retail competition. The following section highlights the changes occurring in industry structure and competitive strategies.

FIGURE 4–1

INTERTYPE COMPETITION: DEPARTMENT STORES VERSUS OTHER TYPES OF RETAILERS

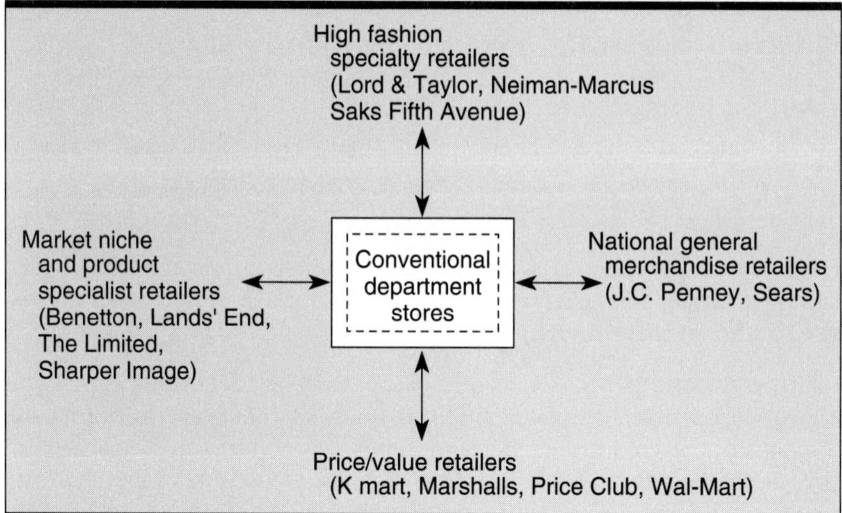

Source: *Retailing Issues Newsletter,* I, no. 1, 1987, p. 4 (Texas A&M University: Center for Retailing Studies).

Secondary Market Expansion. Secondary market expansion is an increasingly attractive move. Firms such as Wal-Mart typically face less competition, are able to pay lower wages, and encounter fewer zoning and other restrictions in smaller market areas. These are usually communities of 200,000 or fewer, and they are understored in terms of national competitors. They provide more viable markets than many of the major metropolitan markets, which are already served by almost every major retailer.

Extremes in Establishment Types. The trend today can be described as diversity in retail outlets. Broad-based merchandising firms such as Home Depot's home improvement centers and discount pricing have made major inroads into the markets of traditional hardware stores. The other high-growth market, at the opposite end of the scale, is the specialty store that carries a deep assortment of a very specialized line, often limited to a concept or "look," as opposed to commodity types. One example is Hickory Farms, shown in Exhibit 4–4. Other examples include Radio Shack, Benetton, and Laura Ashley. Their entire operations are programmed to a specific market segment, and they project a sharply defined image as a result.

EXHIBIT 4–4

Courtesy Hickory Farms of Ohio, Inc.

Hickory Farms—A fast-growth specialty retailing market

Supermarket Retailing. The supermarket concept, long familiar in the food field, has been adopted by many other types of retailers. The key elements of this type of retailing are (1) self-service and self-selection, (2) large-scale but low-cost physical facilities, (3) a strong emphasis on price, (4) simplification and centralization of customer services, and (5) a wide variety and broad assortment of merchandise. This concept has been successful in many lines of trade including sporting goods (Sportmart), home improvement (Handy Dan), furniture and housewares (IKEA), and toys (Toys 'R' Us).

Diversity in Formats. The accelerating diversity in formats can be illustrated in the context of food retailing. **Superstores** are 30,000 square feet or larger and have service departments not typically found in a conventional supermarket, including an on-premises bakery, service deli, and a wine and cheese shop. A larger percentage of sales is in general merchandise than is found in a conventional supermarket.

Hypermarkets such as Carrefour have sales as high as $40 million a year. They make heavy use of warehousing techniques, place strong emphasis on large product sizes, and experience large average purchases. They are the largest of any of the food stores. The **combination stores** are a merger of two different types of retailing operations. They offer both food and pharmacy service. They also offer many health and beauty aids as well as other nonfood items. **Warehouse markets** have a strong warehouse orientation, low prices, a limited selection of general merchandise, a low operating expense ratio compared to conventional supermarkets, and limited customer service.

Limited-assortment stores such as 7-Eleven are typically located near more conventional food stores. They have a merchandise assortment of less than 1,000 stockkeeping units, feature discount pricing, have a heavy reliance on regional and house labels, and carry only a limited assortment of perishables.

As you can see, talking about a supermarket without further description really has very little meaning in today's competitive environment.

Shortening Life Cycles. The life cycles of many types of retailing are becoming shorter, as shown in Table 4-3. Department stores, for example, moved from a period of early growth to maturity in 80 to 100 years, whereas variety stores moved from accelerated growth in the 1920s and 1930s to virtual oblivion as an institution by 1960. Other more recent retailing innovations such as video arcades and home electronics outlets covered the cycle from introduction to maturity in less than a decade.

Escalation of Price Competition. Some firms increasingly are ''buying'' a share of the market as a result of the intensified price competition emerging from the struggle for market share. However, retailers that project a strong price and value image are the ones most likely to increase their market share today. Nordstrom, a departmentalized specialty store headquartered in the Northwest, and nationally known West Point Market in Akron, Ohio, are examples.

Growing Importance of Power Marketing Programs. Many manufacturers now offer comprehensive merchandising programs to merchants; these are known as power marketing programs. The manufacturers are seeking superior results by offering a complete merchandising program to the retailer. They handle everything from price to inventory to display. The result is that they establish strong market positions in their merchandise lines. L'eggs and American Greeting Cards are examples of such programs.

Market Saturation. Many people today believe that the United States has too many stores. Sales per square foot, when adjusted for inflation, are less than they were a decade ago. Most retailers can only look forward to stiffening competition and disappointing profits in this decade. Only the smartest merchandisers will be exceptions.

TABLE 4–3 SELECTED CHANGES IN RETAIL INSTITUTIONAL STRUCTURE

Institutional Type	*Period of Fastest Growth*	*Period from Inception to Maturity (years)*	*Stage of Life Cycle*	*Representative Firms**
General store	1800–40	100	Declining/obsolete	A local institution
Single-line store	1820–40	100	Mature	Hickory Farms
Department store	1860–1940	80	Mature	Marshall Field's
Variety store	1870–1930	50	Declining/obsolete	Morgan-Lindsay
Mail-order house	1915–50	50	Mature	Spiegel
Corporate chain	1920–30	50	Mature	Sears
Discount store	1955–75	20	Mature	Kmart
Conventional supermarket	1935–65	35	Mature/declining	Winn-Dixie
Shopping center	1950–65	40	Mature	Paramus
Cooperative	1930–50	40	Mature	Ace Hardware
Gasoline station	1930–50	45	Mature	Texaco
Convenience store	1965–75	20	Mature	7-Eleven
Fast-food outlet	1960–75	15	Late growth	McDonald's
Home-improvement center	1965–80	15	Late growth	Lowes
Superspecialist	1975–85	10	Growth	Sock Shop
Warehouse retailing	1970–80	10	Maturity	Levitz
Computer store	1980–85	5	Maturity	Computerland
Electronics superstore	1980–	?	Growth	Circuit City Stores
Off-price retailer	1980–	?	Growth	Burlington Coat Factory
Warehouse club	1985	?	Growth	Sam's Wholesale Club
Electronic shopping	1990	?	Growth	Home Shopping Network

*These firms are representative of institutional types and are not necessarily in the stage of life cycle specified for the institutional group as a whole.

Some observers, however, see the problem not as one of overstoring but as a problem that has resulted from the failure of retailers to differentiate themselves in the marketplace. Some retailers are achieving success. One category of winners today are the **power retailers,** which include merchandisers such as The Limited, Inc. and The Gap. These retailers have such financial strength and marketing skills that they can bull their way into any market, however saturated, and make a profit.

Designer-Owned Retail Outlets. A trend further accelerating retail competition is the increasing tendency of designers to open their own outlets. They do so to gain greater control over the way the merchandise is presented. The growing number of designers includes Jessica McClintock, Liz Claiborne, Calvin Klein, Ralph Lauren, and other fashion names. San Francisco–based Esprit spearheaded the trend in the 1980s. Some of the European-based stores such as Benetton have further influenced it.

One of the latest entrants is Giorgio Armani's A/X Armani Exchange Outlets. Armani is seeking to capitalize on the conservative mood of the 1990s in appealing to shoppers with an interest in fashion. His outlets feature casual weekend clothes, 80 percent of which are priced under $100.[27]

Designers are attracted by the ability to control their entire presentation. They also contend that many department stores have poorly trained sales staffs, unexciting in-store merchandising, and excessive price-cutting promotions, all of which can harm their image.

Internationalization of Retailing

U.S. retailing is becoming internationalized. Retail holding companies such as Campeau Corporation of Canada acquired some of the best-known names in American retailing in the 1980s. Other retailers such as Benetton, Laura Ashley, and IKEA are rapidly becoming household names and are competing head-on with retailers in the United States. U.S. retailers are also expanding overseas.

Foreign-Based Retailers in the United States. Several factors explain the growth of foreign investment in U.S. retailing: the devaluation of the dollar, the size of the U.S. market, the stable U.S. political and legal environment, the advantages of real estate ownership associated with retailing, and a desire to learn American methods of retailing. Retailing in the United States is often a difficult challenge for foreign entrants, as seen in Focus 4–1. The United Kingdom has been the heaviest investor in U.S. markets. To a lesser extent, Dutch and German companies dominate. Some of the best-known U.S. names in retailing are owned by foreign firms, including Bloomingdale's, Brooks Brothers, and Talbot's, a womenswear and mail-order business.[28]

Foreign retailers tend to enter the U.S. market in one of three ways: by a joint venture or a franchise operation, by merger or acquisition, or by building new outlets as part of a solo venture (Table 4–4).

Many foreign retailers have expanded into U.S. markets by acquiring existing firms. For example, B.A.T. Industries of Great Britain acquired Breuners in the United States. Not all such ventures succeed. Majestic Wine Warehouses (United Kingdom) purchased the Liquor Barn, a southwestern U.S. chain, from Safeway in 1987 but failed when it made the assumption that its standard operating strategy could be used in the U.S. market.[29]

Well-known examples of franchising or licensing include The Body Shop and Gucci. Similarly, Luciano Benetton sells his clothing in the United States through licensed stores (see A Profile in Excellence).

Still other foreign retailers have built their own retailing network without involvement with U.S. firms. Examples include IKEA (Sweden), Laura Ashley, (United Kingdom), and Galleries Lafayette (France).

U.S. Retail Investment outside the United States. Most U.S. retailers have been reluctant to expand outside North America. Exceptions are specialty retailers including fast-food operators such as McDonald's and Kentucky Fried Chicken as well as convenience stores such as 7-Eleven,

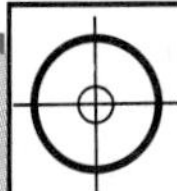

FOCUS 4–1

GALLERIES LAFAYETTE STUMBLES IN NEW YORK

Switchboard operators say "bonjour," and the sign on the fragrance counter reads "Le Bar Tous Parfums," but the new Galleries Lafayette store on Fifth Avenue and 57th Street is finding it difficult to translate French chic into American success.

When this Parisian outpost opened in 1990 on one of the most competitive retailing corners in the world, it positioned itself as a window into French culture, an enclave filled with collections of French clothes, cosmetics, and accessories offered nowhere else in America. At the same time, the showy Trump Tower location, once home to Bonwit Teller's flagship store, promised to polish the international fashion reputation of its ambitious parent, Galleries Lafayette, S.A.

It hasn't turned out that way.

Competing retailers and former suppliers say that the store has made glaring merchandising and marketing mistakes, compounded by a meager promotional budget. The clothes in some cases are too expensive, they say, and sometimes seem awkwardly styled for American women. For instance, the nipped waists of some suits are too tiny for the waistlines of many shoppers here.

Fulfilling U.S. expectations of what constitutes a French store has been a learning process, Galleries Lafayette executives say. "Part of the problem is that people want us to be more French than France—but if it is too French, we're snobbish," says Georges Meyer, chairman and chief executive officer of Galleries Lafayette, S.A. "We thought that people in New York knew France, and that we didn't need pictures of the Eiffel Tower. Probably we were wrong."

What mistakes did Galleries Lafayette make in its merchandising strategies? Suggest possible changes in competitive strategy that would help improve the firm's performance.

Portions reprinted with permission from "Galleries LaFayette Stumbles in New York," *The Wall Street Journal*, March 26, 1991, p. B1,

which are well-known in Europe and the Far East. Similarly, The Gap has outlets in the United Kingdom and is poised for further growth in Europe. Woolworth is also a player in the European market. Toys 'R' Us is making a big impact on the world market and has helped to change the way Europeans do business.[30] The firm has experienced similar success in Japan, although the cultural differences are profound.[31] Haagen-Dazs, a U.S. ice cream retailer, has also experienced strong success in both Europe and Japan.[32]

Mexico is also becoming a strong market for U.S. retailers, especially as a result of the creation of the North America Free-Trade Region, which includes the U.S., Mexico, and Canada. The agreement allows U.S. retailers to sell in Mexico with few, if any, tariffs.[33] McDonald's, Sears, Price Company, Wal-Mart, and Domino's Pizza, among others, are each planning major investments in Mexico.[34]

TABLE 4–4 EUROPEAN FIRMS ENTERING THE UNITED STATES

	Joint Venture or Franchise	Merger & Acquisition		Solo
MASS MARKET	Euromarche (Fra) & Supervalu (US) Biggs	Marks & Spencer (UK) King's	Grand Met (UK) Burger King	Marks & Spencer (UK) D'Aillard's
		Ahold (Neth) Bilo Giant First National Tops	Allied-Lyons (UK) Dunkin' Donuts Mr. Donut	Carrefour (Fra)
				Auchan (Fra)
			Docks De France (Fra) Jiffy Food	Sock Shop (UK)
		Tengelmann (Ger) A&P	Petrofina (Bel)	
		Delhaize Le Lion (Bel) Food Lion	British Petroleum (UK)	
		J. Sainsbury (UK) Shaw's		
MULTIPLE SEGMENT		Vendex (Neth) Dillard's	SuperClub (Bel) Various A/V	IKEA (Swe)
				Storehouse (UK) Conran's
		Bergner's (Swit) Carson Pirie Scott	Otto Versand (Ger) Spiegel Eddie Bauer Honeybee	Laura Ashley (UK)
		B.A.T. (UK) Ivey's Breuner's	IKEA (Swe) STOR	
SINGLE SEGMENT	The Body Shop (UK)	B.A.T. (UK) Saks Marshall Field	Dixon's (UK) Silo	Benetton (Ita)
	Printemps (Fra)		Grand Met (UK) Pearle Vision	EMI (UK) HMV Records
	Gucci (Ita)	Marks & Spencer (UK) Brooks Brothers		Galleries Lafayette (Fra)
		KBB (Bel) FAO Schwarz	Ratner's (UK) Kay Jewelers	
		Vendex (Neth) Barnes & Noble	Majestic (UK) Liquor Barn	
		W.H. Smith (UK) Wee Three Records Wall to Wall Sound	G.I.B. Group (Bel) Scotty's Central Hardware Handy Andy	

*Note: Construct indicates initial actions only. Several have been reversed or resold.
Source: Therese A. Maskulka, Gordon S. Erickson, and John K. Ryans, Jr., "EC Retail Investments in the U.S.: Motivation and Implications," a paper presented at the 1991 Triennial Academy of Marketing Science/American Collegiate Retailing Conference, p. 10. Reprinted with permission.

A Profile in Excellence

LUCIANO BENETTON

Luciano Benetton began his retail adventure in Italy in 1965 with an investment of $2,000 to sell sweaters made by his sister. His family is now among the wealthiest in the world. Benetton began its expansion into the U.S. in 1980 by opening two stores featuring the sweaters that made the Benetton name famous. Benetton now produces over 50 million garments a year in locations throughout the world and sells them in over 4,500 retail stores across the globe.

Benetton is comprised of a network of agents that handle all aspects of the retail operation (the Benetton family actually owns only five stores). These agents are responsible for selecting retailers, placing orders, and monitoring quality. Benetton hires young, motivated agents who will invest in the shops they oversee. Benetton charges its licensees no royalties but requires that each Benetton establishment carry only Benetton products. Consistency among licensees is emphasized to increase the uniformity of the Benetton experience. Licensees can select from an array of prepackaged store interiors.

Luciano Benetton has enlarged his product line to include watches, glasses, perfumes, shoes, and fabrics for home furnishings. The Benetton family has also attempted to diversify the holdings of the Benetton parent company by entering the financial services industry through acquisitions of insurance companies, Italian banks, and real estate.

The European Economic Community. Retailing is beginning to change in Europe. The European Community is a market second only to China and is larger than the combined markets of the United States and Canada.[35] Experts believe that U.S. firms positioned in Europe before 1992 will have an advantage over later entrants. Europe, however, has proved to be a difficult market for some U.S. retailers. Sears failed in Belgium and Spain, as did J. C. Penney in Belgium and Italy. Texas-headquartered Tandy spun off its money-losing foreign operations in 1987.

EMERGING TECHNOLOGIES

The remainder of this chapter is devoted to providing a perspective on the newer technological developments in retailing that affect both merchandising and consumer behavior. You may already be familiar with some of the technologies such as interactive shopping and home information services. These breakthroughs in consumer services are likely to be more widely accepted in the 1990s.

Electronic Funds Transfer

Most people have read newspaper articles that refer to a cashless and checkless society. Such a system is slowly becoming a reality.

Clearly, retailers would like to reduce their **float** (the lag between receipt of a customer's check and deposit of the funds in the retailer's account).

Automatic authorization of credit and electronic funds transfer from one account to another can eliminate float.

Some banks are now issuing a debit and credit card combination called a **combo card.** The card allows customers to use the card either as a traditional credit card or as a debit card, whereby a purchase price is deducted electronically from the customer's account.

Video Technology

Home television shopping is generating millions of dollars in annual sales, and major players such as Home Shopping Network (Exhibit 4–5) and QVC are now making a profit. Sears and IBM, among others, however, are expanding their joint-venture Prodigy service, and most of the regional Bell companies are also conducting tests. Sears now reaches over 1 million consumers through its tie-in with electronic shopping services.[36]

Videodisc Mail-Order Catalogs. Sears has led the way in experimenting with video catalogs. It has placed some of its catalogs on laser discs for in-home and at-store viewing. Sears offers an electronic order blank for its catalog, which gives consumers access to over 200,000 stockkeeping units, so that computer users can order by modem. Sears mails its electronic catalog to computer-literate people such as Prodigy customers.[37]

Interactive In-Store Video Sales Aids. Retailers often use in-store video to stimulate sales. Blockbuster Video (see the Retailing Capsule in Chapter 5) is testing interactive videos through a joint venture with IBM. Blockbuster has installed in-aisle "viewing stations" in some stores. Consumers can call up previews of nearly 100 films and critics' ratings on these titles.[38]

One of the latest dimensions of retailing to be affected by computer technology is discount grocery coupons. Shoppers in such cities as Los Angeles, Seattle, San Francisco, and New York can now get coupons from computerized machines in grocery stores.

Electronic Shelf Labels. Electronic shelf label systems allow price changes to be made electronically from a central location, rather than manually on each shelf. The hardware is being tested at major supermarkets in the United States and Canada. Loblaw Stores in Toronto is equipping some of its stores with the tags. The liquid crystal displays give a constant read-out of the cost of a product. Consumers can push a button located on each tag to find the unit cost for comparison shopping. The tags can also be programmed to provide nutritional information.

The new technology can be likened to the introduction of barcode scanning 15 years ago. Progress is still slow and expensive (as much as $100,000 per store), so many retailers are still reluctant to invest in the technology on a large scale.

EXHIBIT 4–5

Courtesy Home Shopping Network, Inc.

Home Shopping Club from the Home Shopping Network

CHAPTER HIGHLIGHTS

- The new family relationships can be described as less marriage, later marriage, and more divorce.
- The primary demographic changes of importance to retailers include smaller households, two-income households, single-parent households, growth of suburbs, changing family relationships, age mix changes, an older population, Sunbelt growth, and growth in smaller communities.
- In the mid 1980s, the under-40 age group constituted the largest segment of the population and was dominated by baby boomers. By the year 2000 the largest population segment will be people 30 to 49 years of age.
- Women are having their first child at a later age. These women are likely to continue their career after the baby is born.
- The Sunbelt is growing faster than most other areas in the United States. Population density, however, still continues to remain highest in the pocket of states east of the Mississippi river and north of the Mason-Dixon line.
- The largest population growth is in smaller market areas—cities with populations of 50,000 to 200,000 persons.
- Blacks, Asians, and Hispanics are major market segments in some parts of the United States.
- Consumers are seeking products that are low in initial cost, high in quality, resistant to

obsolescence, durable, and low in energy requirements. They also place a premium on convenience.

- The primary types of competition include intratype competition, intertype competition, and corporate systems competition.
- The competitive structure of retailing as a whole is undergoing rapid change. These changes include the following: secondary market expansion, extremes in establishment types, supermarket retailing, shortening life cycles, escalation of price competition, the growing importance of power marketing programs, and the internationalization of retailing.
- Video technology is slowly reshaping parts of the retail structure. In-home shopping, video disc catalogs, and in-store interactive video kiosks are the major advances.

STUDY QUESTIONS

1. Summarize the changes that are occurring in the demographic profiles of consumers and households in our society, and their likely effect on retail operations.
2. What geographical regions are experiencing population growth? Does this mean that opportunities for retailing will deteriorate in other parts of the United States? Explain your answer.
3. Such measures of change as the national unemployment rate and the rate of inflation may be misleading to a retailer. How can management avoid being misled by these indicators of change? What types of information would be useful at the store level?
4. Why is the U.S. market so attractive to many foreign-based retailers today?
5. What changes in the retailing mix are necessary for retailers to successfully serve black, Asian, and Hispanic markets?
6. What are the key factors underlying the mood of the consumer in the 1990s? How do these factors affect retailing strategy?
7. Retailing experts state that the U.S. retailing market is saturated and overstored. Yet retailers such as Wal-Mart, Nordstrom, and The Limited continue to experience rapid growth and expansion each year. How can you reconcile these seeming contradictions?
8. Why are fashion designers increasingly developing their own retail outlets in direct competition with their major clients, such as large department stores?
9. What impedes the rapid expansion of electronic in-home shopping? Why do companies persist in developing this option for consumers, even though they are losing money in doing so?
10. Are in-store interactive sales aids likely to be popular with consumers? Why or why not?

A P P L I C A T I O N S

CASE 1: Hispanic Supermarkets Are Blossoming

It's Sunday and time for Alicia Maruffo's weekly grocery shopping. So she and her family hop in the car and motor some 65 miles from their home in Oxnard—past at least 30 other grocers—to get to a Tianguis supermarket in Los Angeles.

As the Maruffos, originally from Mexico, stroll down aisles stocked with such items as empañadas and handmade tortillas, so does a group of mariachi singers.

"Normally, we don't drive this far for groceries," says Mrs. Maruffo, after running up a $130 bill in five hours of shopping. "But I like the people here, the products, and especially the music." Besides, adds her husband Pablo, "Everyone speaks Spanish."

Hispanic supermarkets such as Tianguis, a Southern California chain launched by Vons Cos., are hotter than jalapeño peppers. Flourishing primarily in the West and the Southwest, where the bulk of the U.S. Hispanic population is concentrated, they are changing the way many grocers in the region—and beyond—are operating in a crowded business.

"Hispanics represent a foreign consumer market within the U.S.," explains Henry Adams-Desquivel, vice-president of Market Development Inc., a San Diego–based marketing research firm. "They have special needs."

All kinds of businesses are trying to cash in on the Hispanic market, and it doesn't take a genius to figure out why. The U.S. population of Hispanics has grown 34 percent since 1980, four times the country's overall growth rate during the same period. There are now nearly as many Hispanics in the United States as there are Canadians in Canada.

Although the Hispanic market is made up largely of families with meager to modest incomes, those families' overall purchasing power is an impressive $150 billion a year. So it's perhaps no wonder that Fiesta Marts Inc., begun in the early 1970s and one of the first chains to cater to Hispanics, has become the fourth largest grocer in Houston. Its stores—some even in black and white neighborhoods—generate more than $400 million in annual sales.

To identify its customers' needs, Tianguis—the name is a Spanish adaptation of an Aztec word for "marketplace"—spent two years and $2.5 million researching the market. Store operators have made dozens of trips to Mexico and to cities in the Southwest with large Hispanic populations in their search for the right atmosphere and product mix. They consulted small Hispanic retailers and visited Mexican museums, supermarkets, cantinas, and restaurants. Some prospective products were rigorously test-marketed in Mexico.

Tianguis also worked closely with Aurrera, Mexico's largest diversified chain. Aurrera specialists trained Tianguis personnel in Los Angeles for a month, drilling them on how to cut meats, make seviche (a fish dish), and bake breads and tortillas. In exchange, Aurrera was briefed on the latest store technology.

One important lesson gleaned from all this research: most Hispanics view shopping as an eagerly awaited social event. They want to spend hours browsing and chatting; they want to eat while they shop and listen to music that reminds them of home. In short, they want a fiesta.

Tianguis obliged. The stores set up stands serving a wide variety of Mexican foods and added outdoor patios for dining. They splashed the walls with festive colors and designs and hung dozens of piñatas from the ceiling. They now feature live mariachi music four days a week and piped-in Spanish music at other times.

Attention to such details has paid off. Tianguis has become one of the most profitable chains in Southern California, according to industry analysts, raking in nearly $1.7 million in sales weekly.

Source: Alfredo Corchado, "Hispanic Supermarkets Are Blossoming," *The Wall Street Journal,* January 23, 1989. Reprinted with permission. See also Pat Lenius, "Tianguis Learning Hispanic Lessons," *Supermarket News,* October 8, 1990, p. 22; Patrick Geoghegan, "Fiesta Marks Ethnic Acumen," *Supermarket News,* November 28, 1988, p. 1; "Melting Pot," *Supermarket News,* July 30, 1990, p. 28.

Applying Retailing Principles

1. Why were supermarket operators so late in recognizing the unique advantages of serving ethnic populations?
2. What are the changes in marketing strategy necessary to serve ethnic markets?
3. Are mainstream shoppers likely to shop at ethnic outlets? Why or why not?

CASE 2: After Demographic Shift, Atlanta Mall Restyles Itself as Black Shopping Center

Minority shoppers are finally getting some attention in that icon of American shopping, the suburban mall.

On the eastern edge of Atlanta, bordered on one side by palatial homes and on the other by public housing, the South DeKalb Mall has restyled itself as an "Afrocentric retail center" and is aiming its marketing efforts squarely at blacks. If it succeeds—and early results are positive—the mall, owned by Rouse Co. of Columbia, Maryland, may serve as a model for similar centers across the country and may prompt more retailers to target minority shoppers.

"Black consumers have strong economic muscle," says Jeffrey Humphreys, a University of Georgia economist. But they "have been underserved in their local markets."

Black spending power nationally is estimated between $250 billion and $270 billion. Compared with consumers in general, blacks spend a greater portion of their incomes on apparel, footwear, and home electronics, according to *Sales & Marketing Management* magazine. A study by Stillerman Jones & Co., shopping-center consultants in Indianapolis, has found that blacks, on an average trip to a mall, spend $51.21, or 5.1 percent more than whites. And in a prime group for spending, 18 to 34 years of age, the nation's black population in the 1980s grew more than twice as rapidly as the population in general.

Malls in other areas are trying to attract other fast-growing minority groups. In the Southwest, for example, the target is Hispanics, whose population increased at a rate more than five times that of the general population in the 1980s.

A Canadian mall seeks to appeal to Asians. At the Aberdeen Centre in Richmond, British Columbia, a suburban area near Vancouver, nearly 80 percent of the merchants are Chinese-Canadians, as are 80 percent of the customers. The mall offers fashions made in Hong Kong, a shop for traditional Chinese medicines, and a theater showing Chinese movies. Kung fu demonstrations and Chinese folk dances are held in the mall on weekends. The mall developer has opened another Asian-focused mall nearby.

But malls aimed at particular groups still face obstacles. South DeKalb Mall, for example, has had to face the fact that many retailers won't locate in malls that cater to blacks, and other retailers offer blacks a limited selection. In addition, many local black professionals say that they prefer shopping elsewhere.

Several mall retailers have tried to orient their goods to blacks. Camelot Music more than doubled its selection of gospel, jazz, and rhythm-and-blues music. Foot Locker stocks styles that do well in black markets, such as suede and black athletic shoes and baseball shirts from the Negro League of the 1930s. J. C. Penney sells Gambian apparel, kufi hats, and African wooden masks. The retailer also has Malcolm X T-shirts and women's apparel in vivid colors that the store says sell well among blacks. Mall kiosks hawk black-studies books and memorabilia from black colleges.

Still, South DeKalb has had its share of problems. Although the mall has attracted national retailers such as Jeans West, several other well-known chains, citing low profits, have backed out in recent years, including Spencer Gifts, Florsheim Shoe Shop, and B. Dalton Bookseller, which took with it one of the chain's largest black-studies sections.

All this is happening despite appealing demographics nearby: in the mall's ZIP code, 42 percent of the households earn more than $50,000, according to Claritas Corp., a marketing concern in Alexandria, Virginia.

Industry executives say that the problem lies in perceptions: some retailers automatically pigeonhole blacks as lower-income people. There's a feeling that "volume won't be as great," says Jeffrey Langfelder, president of Shopping Center Group Inc., a commercial real estate broker in Atlanta. Marc Milgram, also at Shopping Center Group, adds that many retailers "unfairly equate black areas with higher crime."

Blacks themselves don't universally embrace South DeKalb. Charlie Carter, an economics professor at nearby Clark Atlanta University, says some black shoppers believe that quality suffers in black-run stores.

Source: Portions reproduced with permission from Laurie M. Grossman, "After Demographic Shift, Atlanta Mall Restyles Itself as Black Shopping Center," *The Wall Street Journal,* February 26, 1992, p. B1.

Applying Retailing Principles

1. Are ethnic malls likely to be successful? What factors will influence their success?
2. What are the difficulties in merchandising primarily to minorities? Are lifestyle and income primarily segmentation factors, or are race or ethnicity the main distinguishing variables?
3. Why do some merchants hesitate to locate in malls that primarily target blacks or other minorities?

Notes

1. Bruce Ingersoll, "Pizza Hut Gains Fast-Food Entry to Institutions," *The Wall Street Journal,* November 29, 1992, p. B1.
2. "Home Alone—with $660 Billion," *BusinessWeek,* July 29, 1991, pp. 76–77.
3. Jack Kasulis, "The Frugal Family of the 90s," *Retailing Issues Newsletter* 3, no. 5 (September 1991), pp. 1–2.
4. Gary Levin, "Boomers Leave a Challenge," *Advertising Age,* July 8, 1991, p. 1.
5. Christie Fisher, "Wooing Boomers' Babies," *Advertising Age,* July 22, 1991, p. 3.
6. Richard Leventhal, "The Aging Consumer: What's All the Fuss About Anyway?" *Journal of Consumer Marketing* 8, no. 1 (Winter 1990), p. 29.
7. "Dipping into Granny's Wallet," *Newsweek,* April 1, 1991, p. 43.
8. "Reaching Out to All Markets," *Chain Store Age Executive,* May 1991, p. 129.
9. *Time,* November 18, 1991, p. 44.
10. "Suddenly, Asian-Americans Are a Marketer's Dream," *BusinessWeek,* July 17, 1991, p. 55.
11. *U.S. News and World Report,* October 28, 1991, p. 90.
12. "Reaching Out to All Markets."
13. "Suddenly, Asian-Americans Are a Marketer's Dream."
14. Frank Tabolski, "Research a Potent Factor in Reaching the Macho Market," *Marketing News,* September 26, 1988, p. 12.
15. Based on Christopher Farsell, "Where Have All the Families Gone?" *BusinessWeek,* July 29, 1992, pp. 90 and 91.
16. Portions quoted from Larry Light, "How to Win Share and Influence Profits," *Promotion Exchange,* 1982, pp. 1–3.
17. Cyndee Miller, "P. F. Fliers Relaunch and Target Nostalgic Baby Boomers," *Marketing News,* February 17, 1992, p. 2.
18. "First Findings from Consumer Satisfaction Survey Focus on Value, Good Experiences," *Marketing News,* February 17, 1992, p. 5.
19. "Satisfaction Is. . .," *Marketing News,* February 17, 1992, p. 4.
20. "How to Deal with Tougher Customers," *Fortune,* December 3, 1990, p. 40.
21. Laurie M. Grossman, " 'Healthful' Approach Is Failing to Bring Sizzle to Kentucky Fried Chicken Sales," *The Wall Street Journal,* September 13, 1991, p. B1; Renae Rouland, "Green Laws for Green Lawns," *Discount Merchandiser,* July 1991, p. 44; Phyllis Berman, "McDonald's Caves In," *Forbes,* February 4, 1991, p. 73.
22. Barbara Marsh, "Recession Apparently Spares Housewares Industry," *The Wall Street Journal,* January 22, 1992, p. B2.
23. Albert D. Bates, "The Extended Specialty Store: A Strategic Opportunity for the 1990s," *Journal of Retailing,* 65 (Fall 1989), pp. 379–88.
24. Joseph Pereira, "Discount Department Stores Struggle against Rivals That Strike Aisle by

Aisle," *The Wall Street Journal,* June 19, 1990, p. B1.

25. Isadore Barmash, "Not All Retailers Are Living on Edge," *Birmingham Post-Herald,* February 4, 1992, p. B1.
26. Daniel C. Smith, Jonlee Andrews, and Timothy R. Blevins, "The Role of Competitive Analysis in Implementing a Market Orientation," *The Journal of Services Marketing,* 6, no. 1 (Winter 1992), pp. 23–35.
27. Jeffrey Trachtenberg, "Armani Gamble Wins Support of Big Stores," *The Wall Street Journal,* February 21, 1992, p. B1.
28. Alan Threadgold, "The Emerging Internationalization of Retailing: Present Status and Future Challenges," *Irish Marketing Review,* 5, no. 2 (1990–91), p. 17.
29. Therese A. Maskulka, Gordon Erickson, and John K. Ryans, Jr., "EC Retail Investment in the U.S.: Motivations and Implications," paper presented at the 1991 Third Triennial AMS/ACRA National Retailing Conference.
30. "Toys 'R' Us: Making Europe Its Playpen," *BusinessWeek,* January 20, 1992, p. 89.
31. Yumiko Ono, "Toys 'R' Us Learns Give and Take Game in Japan, Sets Debut for First Store," *The Wall Street Journal,* October 8, 1991, p. A18; "Selling Toys to Tokyo's Tots," *U.S. News and World Report,* December 23, 1991, p. 54.
32. Mark Maremont, "They Are All Screaming for Haagen-Dazs," *BusinessWeek,* October 14, 1991, p. 121; "Haagen-Dazs Acquiring a French Accent." *Birmingham Post-Herald,* November 14, 1990, p. 9E.
33. Stephen Baker and S. Lynne Walker, "The American Dream Is Alive and Well—in Mexico," *BusinessWeek,* September 30, 1991, p. 102.
34. "Domino's, Pizza Hut Make a Run for the Border, Continue Their War," *Marketing News,* November 11, 1991, p. 5.
35. Charles Aug, "The 1992 Integration of the European Common Market," *Chain Store Age Executive,* October 1990, p. 58.
36. "Home Shoppers Keep Tuning In—But Investors Are Turned Off," *BusinessWeek,* October 22, 1990, p. 70; see also Gary Robins, "Online Service Update," *Stores,* February 1990, p. 24.
37. "Sears Reaches One Million Patrons via Electronic Shopping," *Discount Store News,* December 17, 1990, p. 7.
38. Scott Hume, "Retailers Go Interactive," *Advertising Age,* February 24, 1992, p. 29.

C H A P T E R

5

Management Information Systems

THIS CHAPTER:

Reviews sources of data important in a retail decision support system.

Introduces the key concepts that are a part of the new technology of retailing.

Highlights the components of a merchandising information system.

Discusses the role of environmental scanning in developing and implementing retailing strategy.

Explains the evaluation and control mechanisms helpful in assessing retail performance.

The "New" Greening of America – A Sense of Social Responsibility

Promotion of a Concept Through Advertising and Packaging

(Michael J. Hruby)

Burger King switched from boxes to paper in an attempt to "make the world a nicer place to eat" by reducing trash.

(Courtesy Matrix Essentials, Inc.)

Matrix Hair Salons offer to plant a tree in honor of the person of choice – a socially conscious "gift with purchase."

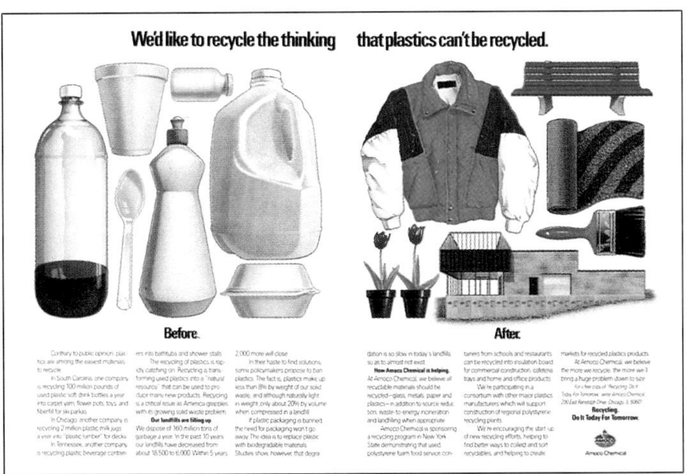

Amoco educates the public.

(Courtesy Amoco Chemical Company)

THE "GREENING" LED TO A BUMPER CROP OF ECO-SPECIALTY RETAILERS WITH AN ENVIRONMENTAL MISSION

The Body Shop is known as much for its passionate commitment to the environment as it is for the quality of the natural ingredients in its hair- and skin-care products.

(Courtesy The Body Shop)

Ozone Brothers claims to be the first store in the United States to exclusively carry environmentally safe products made from recycled fibers.

(Courtesy Ozone Brothers)

(Courtesy The Body Shop)

The Ecology Box offers products for the environmentally aware, such as safe household cleaning products, nontoxic paints and sealants, and natural foods.

(Courtesy The Ecology Box, Inc.)

RECYCLING – A SOCIAL STRATEGY

(Courtesy Oil Express)

Oil Express has developed a program that allows do-it-yourself oil changes and a convenient place to dispose of used motor oil.

(Tom Tracy)

Grocery stores face various recycling problems. This store uses a program for returning already recycled bags to the supply side of the loop.

(Tom Tracy)

Wal-Mart wants to create and control a closed-loop life cycle for its products that includes production, distribution, collection, and recycling.

RETAILING CAPSULE

BLOCKBUSTER VIDEO STAYS TUNED TO CUSTOMERS

Blockbuster Video, the world's largest distributor of movies, has experienced phenomenal growth in riding the crest of the video rental business. The firm has more than 2,000 stores, including outlets throughout the United States, Venezuela, Chile, Japan, Australia, the United Kingdom, Puerto Rico, Guam, and Canada. Since its inception in 1986, management has averaged opening a store a day and is continuing to plan for both domestic and overseas expansion.

The key to Blockbuster's success is that each store operator continually analyzes customer data on an in-store computer. Local market sensitivity, made possible by timely analysis of customer demographics and buying profiles, allows local store managers to respond to local demand and to local competition in adjusting its inventory of 10,000 video tapes.

Blockbuster places a high priority on inventory control in optimizing the flow of rental tapes across its network of stores. Information about each rental transaction is captured at the point of sale. The result is a complete record of each transaction including the tape's title, identification number, and due date. Each tape is again scanned upon its return to the store and as it is entered into inventory. The in-store database also contains information from each Blockbuster membership application. The data include the address of the membership holder, home and business phone numbers, names of other household members authorized to use the card, and employer.

Operating statistics are reported periodically to corporate headquarters, although all the information collected at the store level is also retained in the database of that store. Store-level reports enable store managers to track demand, monitor inventory performance, identify customers' preferences, and spot emerging trends.

Store-level autonomy is counterbalanced by companywide coordination and oversight. Data from geographically dispersed markets are assembled

to provide corporate management with a broad-based perspective. Management uses such information in making decisions about what to stock, how to expand market share, and when and where to advertise. The data also allow management to match multistore inventory performance with demographic information on store membership. The resulting data allow corporate personnel to determine promising locations for new stores, to project revenue by store location, and to predict video rental patterns for new stores. Corporate monitoring also allows management to identify actual and potential problem areas and to evaluate results by geographic region.

Top management views the decentralized technology strategy that undergirds Blockbuster's business strategy as the key to its rapid growth. Management has avoided the temptation to adopt a single centralized strategy in which all data come directly into corporate headquarters from each location and are processed as part of one huge database.

Source: Based on E. Portnoy, "Decentralizing Information Pays," *Enterprise*, Winter 1991–1992, pp. 44–45.

Management needs information to supplement its intuition and experience as it copes with the many issues that are part of a firm's internal and external environments. Information needs vary widely because of the diversity of management responsibilities. Management gathers and analyzes data to help understand its customers, to develop benchmark data for assessing performance, and to identify opportunities that might not otherwise be available, as noted for Blockbuster Video (see Exhibit 5–1). In that context, retailers decide what data are needed, how these data will be processed and analyzed, and how they will be used.

The process of gathering the data and transforming it into useful information occurs in a retail decision support system.

EXHIBIT 5–1

Courtesy Blockbuster Entertainment Corporation

A decentralized technology strategy undergirds Blockbuster's business strategy.

THE RETAIL DECISION SUPPORT SYSTEM

A **retail decision support system** is the structure of people, equipment, and procedures to gather, analyze, and distribute data for decision making. The data needed, as shown in Figure 5–1, include internal data, secondary data, and primary data. Data generated as a result of model building, as part of merchandise and management information systems, are similarly important.

Modeling building includes the application of statistical principles in the analysis of data important to management. The models use primary, secondary, and internal data as inputs. Examples of model building include developing sales forecasting models, site evaluation models, and performance effectiveness models. Computers are usually used to help generate these models.

Merchandise information systems are computer-based systems that primarily emphasize improved merchandise information gathering and analysis. The product of a merchandise information system is a series of computerized reports that assists retailers with seasonal planning, order management, vendor analysis, price revisions, sales promotion evaluation, and similar analyses.

FIGURE 5–1

THE INGREDIENTS OF A RETAIL DECISION SUPPORT SYSTEM

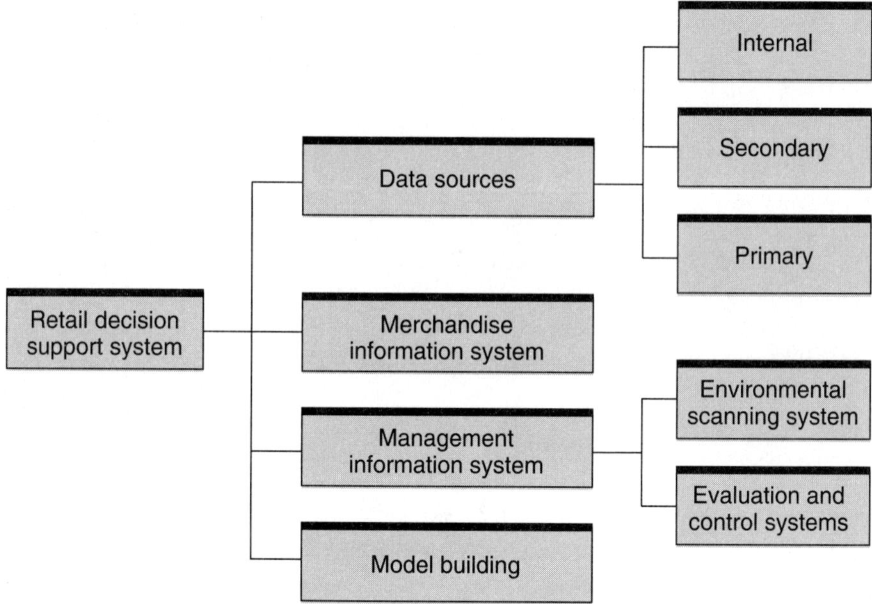

Management information systems have a broader focus than merchandising issues. They are designed to provide information on operating and macro environments and to aid in evaluation and control. Operating environments include competitors, customers, suppliers, creditors, and shareholders. The macro environments include the economic and resource environments, technological environment, social environment, and legal environment. Evaluation and control involves the application of various measures such as financial ratios in monitoring organizational performance.

Data Sources

Internal data help management determine what is going on in the firm. Examples include customer complaints, reports on out-of-stock items, information from warranty cards, and observations of customer traffic flow in a store. **Secondary data** are gathered by external groups or organizations for purposes other than the issue at hand and are made available to the firm. An example is census data. **Primary data collection** occurs when management must collect data unavailable from internal or secondary sources. Examples include analysis of the firm's image, the effectiveness of promotion, and a competitor's merchandise assortments.

Internal Data. Internal data are the least expensive type of data to collect. Some data, such as sales by merchandise line, are reported on a daily basis. Other data, though no less important to a successful operation, are collected only periodically. The personal computer and point-of-sale systems allow retailers to have ready access to a wide array of detailed internal data.

Internal data can be developed from customer records, salespeople, an analysis of customer charge accounts, and financial records.

Customer Records. Customer records can include information on product purchases and returns, warranty cards, and coupon redemptions. Customer correspondence, such as complaint letters, can also provide useful information on product quality and service problems.

Customer records are essential as part of database marketing, as shown in the Retailing Capsule. **Database marketing** is the use of customer-specific information to allow retailing programs to be narrowly targeted to specific groups of customers (see Focus 5–1). Sears, for example, has data of one sort or another on more than 68 million American households because of its store credit cards, the Discover Card, its mail-order business, and its brokerage and insurance units. Merging the files gives Sears a tremendous advantage in database marketing.[1]

Salespeople. Salespeople have the closest continuing contact with customers. They are therefore in the best position to recognize shifts and trends in consumer demand. They can also be important sources of information on missed sales opportunities because of merchandise that was out of stock or that the firm does not carry.

Many retailers require salespeople to complete "want slips" each time a customer requests merchandise the retailer does not stock. Managers have regular meetings, some daily, to generate suggestions, criticisms, and feedback from salespeople; this immediate information is not easily conveyed by a written system.

Charge Accounts. Retailers who maintain their own credit systems have a highly valuable source of information. These records can form the basis of consumer surveys to determine why some accounts are relatively inactive and others very active. Lists of customers can also be used to test special mailings or merchandise and to track consumer purchases over time. Plotting the addresses of credit card holders is also an inexpensive way of estimating a store's trading area.

Financial. Financial data such as the daily sales report can reveal a wealth of information, including sales trends over time by merchandise line, profitability by merchandise line and department, frequency of maintained markup by merchandise line, and information on merchandise turnover. Other information can be obtained on vendors, such as which vendor is offering the best financial terms, the relative popularity of selected brand names by vendor, and the frequency of unfilled or incorrect orders.

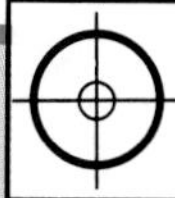

FOCUS 5–1

DATABASE RETAILING: STRENGTHENING RELATIONSHIP MARKETING

Years ago, retailers were on a first-name basis with most of their customers. They understood their tastes, needs, and preferences and strived to meet them. Retailing over the years has become more impersonal and transaction focused. The consequence is that management today often knows little about their customers and has difficulty building and maintaining customer loyalty.

The new electronic technologies are allowing retailers to once again customize merchandising strategies at the store level. The core of database retailing is the name and address of each customer, purchase frequency, and the amount, recency, and type of merchandise purchased, as we saw in the Blockbuster Retailing Capsule. Computer technology then allows retailers to develop detailed customer buying profiles and to predict selling opportunities by customer segment. Buying behavior profiles should be combined with information such as the customer's age, income, distance from the store, and other measures of purchase potential. Retailers can then use the integrated databases to develop promotion plans consistent with the customers' lifestyles and consumption patterns as reflected in prior purchases. For example, purchasers of fishing equipment are also probably candidates for camping or other outdoor equipment.

Toys 'R' Us started buyer clubs—some for kids, others for parents and grandparents—anchored in their databases. The key is the extent to which the customer can be recognized as an individual, not simply as a member of an income bracket or geographic market. Targeted groups of customers can be identified as recipients of customer newsletters, educational programs, frequent buyer award programs, and customer clubs, to strengthen customer relationships.

Source: Based on "Targeting the Right Customers," *Enterprise,* Winter 1991–1992, pp. 30–34.

Secondary Data. Information published by various sources can help management determine what is going on inside and outside the firm. Information is available from (1) syndicated services; (2) government agency reports; (3) guides, indexes, and directories; (4) trade associations; and (5) computerized searches.

Syndicated Services. Some firms specialize in collecting and selling information to clients. This information may be in the form of store audits, warehouse withdrawal services, or consumer purchase panels. Information about the movement of competitor products can be especially important in determining the threats and opportunities facing the firm.

A. C. Nielsen Company already has scanner links into nearly 5,000 stores and a pilot program in 16,000 homes where consumers can use scanner wands to record purchases when they return home. Household members each week place the wand against a telephone mouthpiece; the wand dials an 800 number and communicates the information to the

TABLE 5–1 TYPICAL SECONDARY SOURCES OF EXTERNAL INFORMATION

U.S. Censuses

1. *Census of population.* Population by state, county, metropolitan area, and census tract. Data on age, sex, race, education, occupation, and income.
2. *Census of housing.* Type, age, and size of structure; major appliances; sewage disposal; rent or mortgage; value; number and race of occupants; and condition of structure.
3. *Census of business.* Total sales, number of employees, payrolls, and number of establishments; data are available by state, county, metropolitan area, and city. Separate information is available for retail trade, wholesale trade, and selected services.
4. *Census of transportation.* All details of passenger transportation, truck usage, and bus carriers.
5. *Census of agriculture.* Data are given by county on the number of farms, their size and expenditures, crops, equipment, and number of people living on the farm.
6. *Census of government.* Number and characteristics of local governments, payrolls, and revenue.
7. *Census of retail trade.* Number of establishments, sales, characteristics of firms, and number of employees. Data are reported for states, counties, standard metropolitan statistical areas, and the central business districts of large cities. Some information is also provided for shopping centers.

Guides and Indexes

Business Periodicals Index
The Wall Street Journal Index
New York Times Index
Applied Science & Technology
Readers Guide to Periodical Literature
Public Affairs Information Service

Directories

Encyclopedia of Associations
Dollars & Cents of Shopping Centers
Directory of Advertisers
Dun & Bradstreet Million Dollar Directory
Directory of Corporate Affiliations

Nielsen computer. The information is then sold to a wide array of companies. The large databases help retailers develop successful marketing programs, but are subject to abuse, as discussed in A Question of Ethics.

Government Agency Reports. State and federal governments develop detailed information about all aspects of the economy that can be useful to management. Among the censuses conducted by the federal government are those for population, business, retailing, and government, as shown in Table 5–1. Results of these studies are available in virtually every public library. *The Statistical Abstract of the United States* also contains such information, though in encapsulated form. State agencies usually publish similar information.

Guides, Indexes, and Directories. Other valuable sources of secondary information include guides, indexes, and directories. Examples of such information are also shown in Table 5–1. Guides such as the *Business Periodicals Index* provide complete references by subject matter to articles in a wide array of journals. Specialized indexes such as *The Wall Street Journal*

A Question of Ethics

DATA MILLS DELVE DEEP TO FIND INFORMATION ABOUT U.S. CONSUMERS

Nicholas Iannelli, two days old, whines softly as a nurse's aide takes him from his hospital bassinet and positions him beneath a big metal camera. "Come on, sweetheart," she whispers, then clicks the shutter.

In a flash, Nicholas is back in the nursery, and his vital statistics embark on a lifelong journey into a vast network of direct-marketing computers.

St. Vincent's Medical Center on Staten Island sends an order card filled out by Nicholas's parents to the offices of First Foto in Red Bank, New Jersey. The Iannellis get snapshots. Their names, address, and phone number go into the files of First Foto's owner. Hasco International's hospital cameras shoot about 1.6 million newborns each year. The company passes along the data it collects to a Massachusetts outfit that does a brisk business sharing its lists with companies such as Kimberly-Clark and Sears. They will fill the Iannellis' mailbox with ads for diapers and toys.

Scavenging for the personal details of people's lives is today a high-tech, billion-dollar industry. It is the invisible engine of junk mail and junk phone calls. And it has been instrumental in the erosion of personal privacy.

The industry has its tentacles in a thousand corners where personal information resides, from car registrations to mortgage records to birth announcements. It buys data from all manner of companies. Bookstores sell lists of their customers. Magazines and newspapers sell or rent their subscription lists. The industry also plucks data directly from consumers, who don't always realize that they are feeding computers just by filling out questionnaires, entering contests, redeeming coupons, or making a simple phone call.

"You go through life dropping little bits of data about yourself everywhere," says Evan Hendricks, editor of *Privacy Times*, a Washington, D.C. monthly. "Most people don't know that there are big vacuum cleaners sucking it up.

Marketers have never been hungrier for tidbits of personal information. It is essential raw material for businesses shifting from mass-media advertising to direct marketing via mail and phone. The strategy, which costs much more per targeted consumer, makes economic sense only when they know enough about a household to consider a personal pitch worthwhile.

Are organizations acting unethically in assembling and selling data on their customers? What potentials for abuse do you see in the development and sales of such data?

Reproduced with permission from Michael W. Miller, "Data Mills Delve Deep to Find Information about U.S. Consumers," *The Wall Street Journal*, March 14, 1991, p. 1.

Index or the *New York Times Index* provide information for those specialized sources only and are available as computerized databases. Finally, the *Predicasts F and S Index of Corporations and Industries* is an index for information on specific companies and industries.

Trade Associations. Most retailers belong to trade groups, such as the National Retail Federation, that collect and publish data for association members. Such information can be useful for comparing the organization's performance to industry averages. The associations also often publish annual industry forecasts, and their predictions can guide firms as they make their own 12-month forecasts.

Computerized Searches. The amount of new information generated each year is multiplying so quickly that keeping up to date in a specialized field can be difficult. Organizations specializing in abstracting, storing, and retrieving such information by subject area are thus often the starting point in information development by management.

Strengths and Weaknesses. Secondary data can be gathered quickly and inexpensively, although using it can present problems. Some data, such as census information, can quickly become out of date.

Another problem is a lack of standardized reporting units. One organization may define the Southeast as a five-state area, and another may say that the region includes nine states. Similarly, various organizations may use different *break points* in reporting information by age or income.

A third issue is the accuracy and objectivity used in collecting the data. Management should go to the original source of data whenever possible. This limits the possibilities for errors made in publishing and republishing the information. Management also needs to know the magnitude of sampling errors and possible nonsampling errors.

Primary Data. When management cannot find what it needs to know from any existing source, it must generate first-hand information. For instance, among the research projects that Sears conducts at the corporate level are studies of credit, public relations, and home installations. Large marketing-oriented retailers conduct new-product research and test marketing with the same vigor as manufacturers do. Kmart and Wendy's, after a three-year test in a limited number of stores, decided not to go national with a plan to open Wendy's restaurants in Kmart stores. Advertising is also subject to the same intensive scrutiny.

Primary data collection can take many forms: observation, surveys, focus groups and consumer panels, and test marketing.

Observation. Observation can be an accurate method of collecting data. Competitors will not volunteer information on their prices or in-store promotional efforts. Observation is the only way to collect such data.

Comparison shopping of competitors is a time-honored example of observation. Merchants tend to look at six elements of competitor stores: (1) shifts and emphasis in merchandise classifications, (2) stock content, (3) display and presentation, (4) pricing, (5) traffic patterns, and (6) service. Most competing stores today carry basically the same merchandise, so management needs to find out what others are doing that might be different.

Au Bon Pain, a Boston-based fast-food retailer, uses observation in rewarding employees who are on their toes. They use mystery shoppers to measure whether the company's quality and service standards are being met. Anonymous company-affiliated customers buy a meal and then fill out a questionnaire about the restaurant, the food, and the service. An example of the mystery shopper questionnaire is shown in Exhibit 5–2.

Survey Research. **Survey research** often includes collection of information on consumer opinions or perceptions. It is probably management's most frequently used method of data collection. Kroger, for example, interviews up to 250,000 customers each year as part of its market monitoring efforts.

Focus Groups. A **focus group interview** is a technique used to gather information about a product or issue in an unstructured format. Respondents are typically asked broad-based questions about such topics as desired merchandise changes, changes needed in store design and layout, compliments and suggestions for improvement in existing store operations, and problems that are not being solved by the retail firm.

Panels. Retailers sometimes assemble panels of consumers to elicit information for making better merchandising decisions. A consumer advisory panel can give opinions on store services and policies, advertising copy, and merchandise assortment planning.

Test Marketing. Regional or national retail chains often test products or store concepts on a limited basis before deciding whether to introduce the changes in all outlets. Fast-food firms continually test new products for possible market entry. McDonald's, at any one time, is reportedly testing more than 100 food items ranging from tortellini to chicken fajitas.[2] Various types of joint ventures are also periodically test marketed. For example, Burger King and Amoco test marketed a gas station and fast-food operation, whereby meals could be charged to an Amoco credit card or any other major credit cards accepted by Amoco.[3] Arby's, after a successful market test, introduced turkey as a menu option at its restaurants.

Model Building

Sophisticated retailers are moving beyond ad hoc research investigations and are building models that allow them to simulate various dimensions o their businesses and answer the "what if" questions that are becoming

EXHIBIT 5–2

Frequency of the visits
Each company-owned store is visited three times over four weeks, during breakfast, lunch, and dinner shifts. There are more visits if a district manager is concerned about the service or cleanliness of a particular unit.

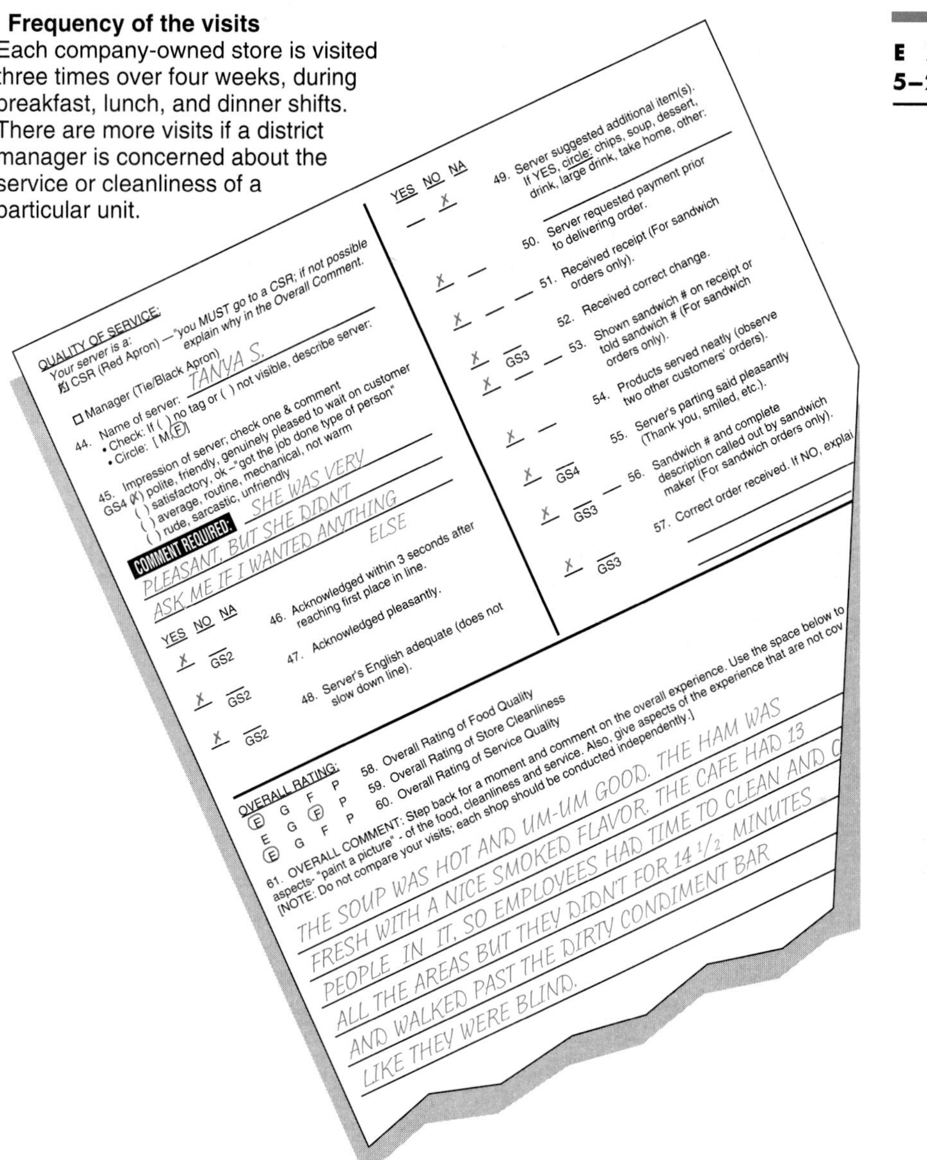

QUALITY OF SERVICE:
Your server is a:
☒ CSR (Red Apron) — "you MUST go to a CSR; if not possible explain why in the Overall Comment.
☐ Manager (Tie/Black Apron)

44. Name of server: TANYA S.
• Check: If ( ) no tag or ( ) not visible, describe server:
• Circle: [M (F)]

45. Impression of server; check one & comment
GS4 (X) polite, friendly, genuinely pleased to wait on customer
( ) satisfactory, ok – "got the job done type of person"
( ) average, routine, mechanical, not warm
( ) rude, sarcastic, unfriendly

COMMENT REQUIRED: SHE WAS VERY PLEASANT, BUT SHE DIDN'T ASK ME IF I WANTED ANYTHING ELSE

YES	NO	NA	
X	GS2		46. Acknowledged within 3 seconds after reaching first place in line.
X	GS2		47. Acknowledged pleasantly.
X	GS2		48. Server's English adequate (does not slow down line).
—	X		49. Server suggested additional item(s). If YES, circle: chips, soup, dessert, drink, large drink, take home, other:
X	—		50. Server requested payment prior to delivering order.
X	—	—	51. Received receipt (For sandwich orders only).
X	GS3	—	52. Received correct change.
X	—		53. Shown sandwich # on receipt or told sandwich # (For sandwich orders only).
X	—		54. Products served neatly (observe two other customers' orders).
X	GS4		55. Server's parting said pleasantly (Thank you, smiled, etc.).
X	GS3	—	56. Sandwich # and complete description called out by sandwich maker (For sandwich orders only).
X	GS3		57. Correct order received. If NO, explai

OVERALL RATING:
(E) G F P 58. Overall Rating of Food Quality
E G (F) P 59. Overall Rating of Store Cleanliness
(E) G F P 60. Overall Rating of Service Quality

61. OVERALL COMMENT: Step back for a moment and comment on the overall experience. Use the space below to aspects- "paint a picture" - of the food, cleanliness and service. Also, give aspects of the experience that are not cov [NOTE: Do not compare your visits; each shop should be conducted independently.]

THE SOUP WAS HOT AND UM-UM GOOD. THE HAM WAS FRESH WITH A NICE SMOKED FLAVOR. THE CAFE HAD 13 PEOPLE IN IT, SO EMPLOYEES HAD TIME TO CLEAN AND C ALL THE AREAS BUT THEY DIDN'T FOR 14 1/2 MINUTES AND WALKED PAST THE DIRTY CONDIMENT BAR LIKE THEY WERE BLIND.

The Au Bon Pain Mystery Shopper program

EXHIBIT 5–3

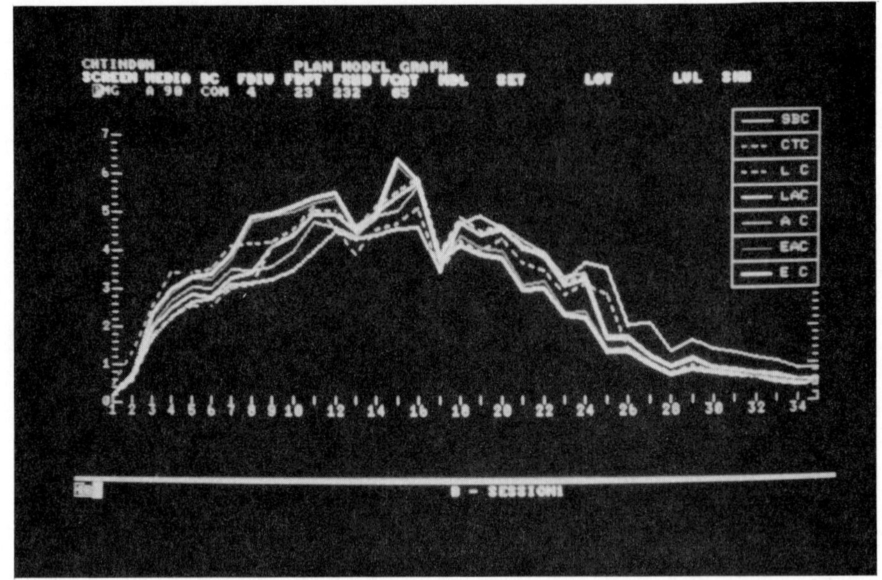

Courtesy J. C. Penney Catalog

The J. C. Penney catalog sales forecasting system forecasts the overall sales of each item for a catalog's 35-week selling period.

necessary in today's environment. Many retailers use sophisticated models to forecast sales, test the price elasticity of selected merchandise, and plan the size and timing of promotions.

J. C. Penney, the nation's largest department store chain, in 1991 received the second annual Retail Innovation Technology Award (RITA) for the forecasting system it developed in its catalog division (see Exhibit 5–3). The system has built-in models that allow management to conduct "what if" analyses to determine whether an idea makes sense before it is implemented throughout the organization. Inventory control specialists who think that a new item is similar to one from the previous year might access the model for the previous year's item and then use it to develop forecasts for the new one.

Information Systems

Recall from Figure 5–1 that additional components of the retail decision support system are the merchandise information system and the management information system. Such systems tend to be technology driven. Today, virtually all retail decisions, including on-the-floor activities, merchandise replenishment, inventory control, and other essential dimensions of implementing competitive strategy are computer driven. Personal computers have proliferated throughout retailing and have helped to streamline decision making.

A Profile in Excellence

WILLIAM DILLARD

William Dillard was born in rural Arkansas, graduated from the University of Arkansas, and earned a master's degree in retailing from Columbia University. Early in his career Dillard gained valuable retail experience working for Sears, Roebuck & Company. After World War II, Dillard realized that shoppers were no longer flocking to downtown stores. He decided instead that the future was in suburban locations and untapped smaller and rural communities. Dillard purchased a single store in rural Arkansas, and the rest is history.

Today the corporation consists of over 100 stores in 11 states. Led by a rigorous acquisition campaign, nearly one-third of these stores were purchased from failing competitors. Because of his astute purchases, Dillard has been dubbed as *the* expert of turning around department store failures.

A key to Dillard's success has been his continuing investment in management information systems to ensure that the right merchandise mix is always available. Dillard was an early pioneer in point-of-sale terminals, bar coding of all merchandise, automatic inventory replenishment from company warehouses, and electronic data interchange with vendors to expedite merchandise movement. The result is fewer and smaller markdowns than competitors, lower expense ratios than the industry norm, and a higher level of in-store purchases. Dillard's, because of its sophisticated technology, is also able to quickly spot trends and respond in time to take advantage of "hot sellers."

The emphasis on computer technology is complemented by an equal emphasis on marketing research. Management relies on both focus groups and one-on-one interviews to judge customer likes and dislikes. Dillard's is also experimenting with computer-aided design software to gauge consumer preferences for various sizes and colors of merchandise. William Dillard's pioneering ideas helped usher in a new era of sophistication in merchandise planning and control.

Source: Based on Gretchen Morgenson, "A Midas Touch," *Forbes,* February 4, 1991, p. 42.

Dillard's department stores, headquartered in Little Rock, Arkansas, is renowned for its information systems, which have allowed it to achieve sparkling financial performance while keeping its expenses low and its margins high. William H. Dillard (see A Profile in Excellence) has long championed the chain's investments in technology. All items in the store are bar coded so that management knows exactly what is selling. The result is that the stores are less likely than the competition to be out of fast-moving items and less likely to be stuck with unfashionable ones that have to be marked down. Fewer and smaller markdowns, faster turnover, tight control on expenses, and astute buying add up to a retail success story.[4]

The new retail technology, however, has a language all its own that anyone interested in retailing today must understand.

Understanding the Terminology. Retailers used mechanical cash registers for many years to ring up sales and make change. The original purpose of the cash register was to reduce employee theft by having cash under the control of one employee.

The first machines were really adding machines set on top of a cash drawer. A clerk pushed buttons and cranked an arm to enter information into the register. Later versions displayed the price of each item in large numbers for both the clerk and customer to read. Finally, mechanical registers printed a record of each sale and calculated the amount of change due.

Electronic Cash Register. The **electronic cash register** (ECR) was introduced in the 1960s. The ECR uses electric light beams to enter information at high speed. More and more ECRs are being used as part of a computer support system to provide management with up-to-date reports. The equipment has the ability to store data and transfer it from one location to another.

The new electronic technology has brought about changes in the way merchandise is marked, the way money and credit are handled, and the way the merchant works with financial institutions and vendors. ECRs produce increased savings through better inventory management, reduction of under-rings at the cash register, and higher labor productivity.

POS In-Store Technologies. A **point-of-sale (POS) cash register** is the input device for many retailing systems. A POS device scans and records a variety of information when a transaction occurs. The information is stored and can be called up whenever it is needed. The system can reveal which merchandise, styles, and colors are selling best.

Scanning and Wanding. Scanning and wanding are the most widely used methods of data entry at the POS terminal. More than 90 percent of the retailers in a recent Ernst & Young survey were scanning at the point of sale. In addition, more than 50 percent were scanning goods with hand-held scanners on the shelf or rack, and 25 percent were scanning goods as part of backroom inventory.[5]

Scanning began in supermarkets, where bar codes are read by a fixed slot scanner. Wanding has been used primarily in general merchandise retailing. Many items in general merchandise retailing, such as apparel, cannot easily be passed over a fixed slot scanner.

Hand-held scanning and slot scanning (fixed scanning) are now roughly comparable in cost. The result is a mixture of fixed and hand-held scanning in retail outlets. Fixed scanners are typically used in the front of the store. Hand-held scanners are more likely to be used in individual departments. A combination of fixed and hand-held scanners is typically used in the back areas for such functions as receiving and marking.

One factor fueling the drive for automation is the emergence of industry standard systems that allow retailers to create their own software. Such software can be developed by the vendor, the retailer, or an independent third party, who then offers it on a standard industry platform.

The Universal Product Code. The universal product code (UPC) is the marking standard in both food and general merchandise retailing. Most people are familiar with the small black-and-white bars on supermarket and general merchandise items. The bars are codes that contain information about the product and the manufacturer. The bar codes are passed over an electronic scanner, and the information is transferred into computer memory for later retrieval. Computers may then automatically update the store's inventory, look up the price of the item in question, print a receipt for the customer, or perform other functions. UPC scanner and marking systems offer the following benefits:

1. Improved accuracy.
2. Improved customer satisfaction. Speed, accuracy, quietness, and the detailed receipt are consumer pluses.
3. Time and labor savings. Some stores report productivity gains of up to 45 percent when item-price marking is eliminated.
4. Improved inventory and financial control.

Scanning's greatest long-term benefit is its ability to generate totally new marketing information:

1. Accurate readings, item by item, of actual item movement at the point of sale.
2. Daily store-by-store readings of consumer buying behavior.
3. Fast, accurate feedback on test-market experiments.
4. Measurement of the effects of marketing and promotional activity.

Most retailers thrive on the right assortment of merchandise, minimal inventory, and rapid turnover. The POS systems and scanner technology allow frequent and up-to-date information on product sales rates, stock outages, sales patterns, and similar information that can be grouped for buyers by department.

Universal Vendor Marking. **Universal vendor marking** (UVM) is a standard vendor-created merchandise identification system. The need to mark items at the store level can be eliminated largely by the use of such a standardized format. Indeed, much of the ticketing for Sears, Montgomery Ward, Toys 'R' Us, Wal-Mart, and J. C. Penney is now done at the vendor level.

Electronic Data Interchange. Retailers are increasingly using **electronic data interchange** (EDI) to communicate with vendors. (EDI is a computer-to-computer exchange of data.) Approximately 46 percent of retailers are using programs that electronically remit payments and invoice data directly to vendors.[6]

Price Chopper Supermarkets and Ralph's Grocery Company of Compton, California, among others, are using computerized direct store delivery systems requiring vendors to send invoice information electronically as part of a quick response (QR) partnership. *QR partnerships* require sharing of information between vendors and retailers to allow timely replenishment of inventory without the necessity of a large backroom inventory at the store level.

The systems use the *uniform communication standard* (UCS) codes developed by the Universal Code Council to allow direct exchange of information between the vendor and store computers. The generic standard in North America is ANSI X.12, and EDI FACT is the international standard.

Other common uses of EDI, in addition to processing payment, include order entry and materials management systems that keep track of shipments. Savings from EDI are of two kinds: the direct **mechanical benefits** and the indirect **strategic benefits.** The mechanical benefits include error reduction, the elimination of key entry, and reduced response time. The indirect benefits occur as a result of enhanced business systems capabilities.

J. C. Penney is a pioneer that has moved beyond the purchase order as the primary use of EDI. The company anticipates having 5,000 suppliers connected to its EDI system by 1995. In 1991, the company had 600 suppliers on EDI and was transmitting more than 200,000 documents a month.[7]

The Merchandise Information System. No single merchandise information system can apply to all types of retailing. However, the concepts underlying such systems are the same for all retailing sectors. They include establishing design objectives and developing the necessary system modules.

Establishing Merchandising Objectives. Agreeing on merchandising objectives is a first step in taking advantage of the retail technology and information base available to merchandise planners. A typical objective is to facilitate planning and decision making at all levels to increase gross margins, reduce markdown, and optimize inventory turnover. System design objectives logically flow from merchandising objectives.

Establishing System Design Objectives. Establishing system design objectives requires decisions about input, processing, and output design requirements.

Examples of **input requirements** include (1) the need to capture information for both units and dollars so that the financial and the unit control systems are in balance; (2) the need to capture information at an economically feasible level of detail; (3) system capability for both batch and on-line data entry functions; and (4) the ability to add classifications, departments, and merchandise divisions as needed.

Processing requirements include retention and maintenance of data files and security procedures so that information and data entry functions are provided only to authorized individuals.

Output requirements call for a system that limits the information provided on a regular basis, but that can provide additional information as needed.

Components. Agreeing on the components of the system is the final step. The components include a planning system, a processing system, and an information reporting system, as shown in Figure 5–2.

Planning system module. An on-line planning system allows merchandise planners to maintain an optimal inventory for meeting customer demand, keep purchases in line with the financial resources available, and provide the information needed at each selling location to meet merchandising objectives. The merchandise system works interactively, allowing executives to develop a seasonal merchandising plan for each merchandise classification. Modules of the system are designed to enable management to prepare seasonal plans in both units and dollars, monitor performance against the plan, and establish exception reporting and inquiry (results outside control limits).

Processing system module. A processing system includes all activities associated with the ordering, receiving, handling, and distribution of merchandise from the time the decision to buy is made until the items are available for sale in the store. The system requires five separate modules: order management, receiving and checking, marking, distribution, and systems control and monitoring, as shown in Figure 5–2.

Information reporting system module. An information reporting system allows merchandise planners to establish a record of sales and merchandise on hand and on order at multiple selling and nonselling locations. The information is available by store, merchandise, division, department, and class, as well as by vendor, style, color, size, price, and perhaps other merchandise assortment characteristics. This information often is organized into such reporting modules as style status and summary reporting, vendor analysis, price revisions, merchandise replacement, and sales promotion evaluation.

The Management Information System. A management information system provides two additional sources of information that aid in decision making: information on operating and macro environments and assessments of performance at the department and store levels.

Environmental Scanning. In addition to the data requirements just discussed, management also needs ways to identify long-term strategic problems and opportunities. Circuit City Stores, a consumer-electronics retailer, for example, decided to abandon the highly competitive New York market after identifying the likely future acceleration of competition in the sale of consumer electronics equipment. Management decided instead to concentrate on medium-sized markets in the Southeast, which offered higher growth opportunities because of less competition.

FIGURE 5–2

COMPONENTS OF A MERCHANDISE INFORMATION SYSTEM

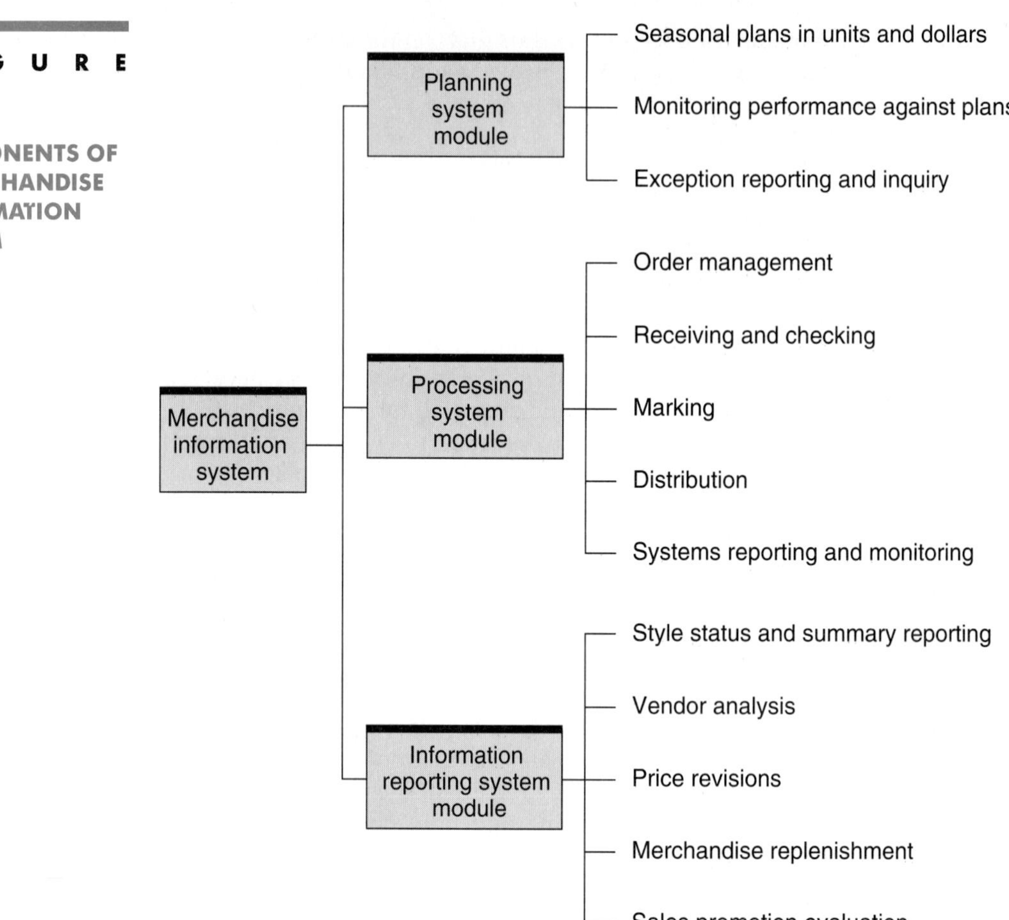

Critical environments to monitor for decision-making purposes are the operating environment and the macro environment. The **operating environment** consists of all organizations or groups that either directly affect or are affected by the retailer's competitive strategy. Examples include customers, competitors, suppliers, and shareholders. The **macro environment** includes the larger forces beyond the control of the firm, such as technology or social trends, that can affect its future. The key to success is to recognize the implications of the identified factors for retail strategy.

The operating environment audit. This is an important task for management to perform. Key issues for each constituency are shown in Table 5–2.

Important **customer issues** include size of and trends in the market, key customer shopping strategies, the nature of customer buying decisions, and factors affecting patronage.

Key **competitor issues** include trends in the market shares of primary competitors; the strength of the competition; positioning strategies of the

TABLE 5–2

KEY ISSUES IN AN OPERATING ENVIRONMENT AUDIT

Customers

1. Can you describe the customer base for the retail sector of interest in such terms as age, income, stage in life cycle, lifestyle, or similar dimensions?
2. What is the projected growth in the primary customer base over the next five years?
3. Do customers see the merchandise sold primarily as impulse, convenience, shopping, or specialty goods?
4. What are the key customer shopping strategies for the merchandise?
5. What is the purchase frequency?
6. Are brands important to the customers?
7. Are customers in this retail sector prone to shop by mail, by phone, or in person?
8. Are the customers likely to make purchases more on a rational, or utilitarian, basis or more on the basis of ego satisfaction?
9. How do customers view the offerings of the various competitors? Which firm seems to be most differentiated from the competition?
10. Do buying decisions vary by market segment?
11. What attributes appear to determine patronage (e.g., price, merchandise, quality, or location)?

Competitors

1. Which are the primary competitors, and what are their market shares?
2. What are the financial and other resources of the primary competitors?
3. Does entry appear readily possible for another competitor?
4. What are the marketing and positioning strategies of the various competitors?
5. Are the competitors part of a vertical marketing system? If so, what type of system?
6. Are any of the competitors especially innovative or aggressive?
7. Do any of the competitors appear to have unique cost advantages? If so, why?
8. Which competitors are leaders, and which are followers?

Suppliers

1. What is the power of key suppliers?
2. Are key suppliers likely to practice forward integration in the near future?
3. How important is the retailer to the supplier?
4. Are alternative sources of supply readily available?
5. How difficult would it be to switch suppliers?

Shareholders

1. Are shareholders satisfied with the dividend structure if the firm is publicly traded?
2. Is there any evidence of shareholder dissatisfaction about the social responsibility and environmental sensitivity policies of the firm?
3. Is the level of community involvement at the local level sufficiently strong?

competition; unique cost advantages, if any, of competitors; and which competitors are leaders and which are followers.

The behavior of **suppliers** must be carefully evaluated. Suppliers can become powerful competitors if they engage in a process of forward integration, for example, and establish retail outlets. They can also be of critical importance if only a few suppliers exist, giving them strong bargaining power with the retailer. Similarly, suppliers have substantial power if the retailer would encounter large switching costs in changing suppliers.

Shareholders can be important in determining both short-term and long-term marketing plans. Managers of publicly held companies must always keep the market value of the company stock in mind when developing corporate strategies. Concerns over social responsibility, environmental sensitivity, and similar issues can influence retail strategy, as we saw in Chapter 4.

The Macro-level audit. A macro-level assessment must include evaluation of economic and resource factors, technological factors, and social and legal environments, as discussed in Chapters 3 and 4. Key issues are highlighted in Table 5–3.

Changes in the macro environments are important because they are often accompanied by changes in customer preferences, which, in turn, may require major changes in the strategic priorities of the firm.

Scanning the **economic and resource environment** consists of an assessment of trends in inflation, the nature of the business cycle, import quotas and tariffs, and similar issues. For example, accelerating unemployment with an attendant drop in consumer purchasing power characterizes a recession. Consumers in such situations are less likely to spend resources on leisure activities but to accelerate do-it-yourself projects.

The **social and cultural environments** reflect the beliefs and values that guide the thoughts and actions of individuals and organizations. These beliefs and values change over time and can alter consumer preferences and marketing practices. Consumerism was a driving force in the 1970s, as was social activism. During the mid-to-late 1980s, concern over AIDS dramatically changed the patterns of sexual behavior for many people and the resulting marketing programs for some retailers. Environmental sensitivity is a driving force in the 1990s that is guiding the consumption patterns of many consumers.

The **legal and political environments** affect every dimension of the retail firm from merchandising to promotion to location. Regulations may prohibit or discourage certain practices, permit previously prohibited practices, or provide new and unique opportunities. The changes reflect society's changing expectations, which can significantly alter supplier or customer relationships.

Technological changes can significantly affect the relationship between customer and retailer. New and improved technologies can lead to dra-

TABLE 5–3

THE INGREDIENTS FOR A MACRO ENVIRONMENTAL AUDIT

Economic/Resource Environment

1. What are the current and forecasted rates of inflation?
2. What is the forecasted real growth in the economy for the next few years?
3. What are the likely influences of foreign competition?
4. Are raw materials essential to the products of the firm likely to be in short supply or to be available only at increasing prices?
5. Are growth rates for the offerings of the firm (if the firm is geographically dispersed) likely to vary widely by regions of the country over the next few years?
6. What are the trends in unemployment?
7. What are the trends in energy, construction, and rental costs?
8. What are the likely effects of import quota and tariff changes?

Technological Environment

1. Is new technology on the horizon that will require the firm to expend large sums of money to remain competitive?
2. Are electronic funds transfer, two-way interactive television, and similar advances likely to pose a challenge?
3. Are near-term product substitutes likely to be developed?

Social Environment

1. What are the current and likely future pressures from consumerism as they relate to the firm under analysis?
2. What are the current trends in consumer lifestyles, and how are these likely to affect the firm?
3. What are the population trends among the age groups that are primary markets for the firm?

Legal Environment

1. Are pending actions by the FTC or other regulatory agencies likely to affect the firm in the near future?
2. Is the firm likely to be vulnerable to affirmative action measures, equal credit opportunity regulations, or privacy regulations?
3. Are the firm's pricing, promotion, and product safety actions in compliance with existing regulations?

matic shifts in customer preferences. Technology can also affect every dimension of the marketing mix.

Assessing Performance. Assessing performance needs to occur throughout the organization as part of a retail decision support system. The measures may occur on a daily, weekly, monthly, quarterly, or annual basis, depending on the dimensions of performance being evaluated. Profitability analysis, for example, may be conducted quarterly, or even monthly, to measure the performance of various merchandise lines or departments. In contrast, the appropriateness of competitive strategy may be evaluated every three to five years.

A variety of control devices can be used to track performance and may be implemented at either the departmental level or the store level. Store level measures include customer feedback, market share analysis, and operating ratio analysis. Departmental level measures include analysis of sales variance and sales-to-expense ratios.

Store-level controls. Continuing **customer feedback** is necessary for sound management decisions. Customer surveys can be undertaken, for example, to establish the organization's actual image, compared with the one desired by management; customer perception of the friendliness and competence of the sales staff; and the level of customer satisfaction with after-sale service, the merchandise mix, and similar dimensions.

Management often focuses on sales growth as a measure of performance. Such an analysis is not sufficient unless it tells management how the firm is performing relative to its competition. If a firm's **market share** is increasing relative to its competitors', the organization probably is on firm ground. Still, care and attention are necessary in evaluating such information.

Early warning indicators of problems are important. Monitoring selected **financial ratios** can help determine whether problems are developing. The reason the ratios are important is that an organization is essentially a pool of cash, and the objective of the firm is to effectively manage cash flows.

Comparisons of ratios to similar stores as reflected in trade data such as that published by the National Retail Federation can alert management to problems. We advise managers to become familiar with industry-specific information for their line of retailing.

Department-level control measures. **Sales variance analysis** enables management to compare actual sales to sales goals. A variance analysis can then be conducted to determine why the firm is outside target limits. Assume the annual plan for a department called for management to sell 500 dresses at $40 each, or $20,000, as shown in Table 5–4. Suppose that management sold only 400 dresses at $35 each, or $14,000. The difference between planned and actual performance is $6,000. Management needs to know how much of the difference occurred because of the decline in price and how much occurred because of a decline in volume. As shown below, two-thirds of the difference occurred because of a decline in sales volume.

Price decline variance: ($40 − $35) × 400 =	$2,000
Volume decline variance: $40 × (500 − 400) =	4,000
Total variance	$6,000

The management's task at this point is to determine why the sales volume was not achieved and what steps are needed to correct the problem.

A periodic evaluation of the **sales-to-expense ratio** can also help management determine whether the firm is either overspending or underspending in its efforts to reach sales targets. Disaggregated ratios can

TABLE 5–4 OPERATING RESULTS FOR DEPARTMENT A (WOMEN'S DRESSES)

	Planned	*Actual*	*Variance*
Sales (number of dresses)	500	400	
Sales price ($)	40	35	
Revenue ($)	20,000	14,000	(6000)

include the ratio of sales force costs to sales, advertising to sales, sales promotion (such as displays and in-store sampling) to sales, and sales administration to sales. Such expense ratios should be charted, and upper and lower limits established. When a ratio exceeds either limit, management needs to determine why the deviation is occurring.

CHAPTER HIGHLIGHTS

- The cash register and the computer are two of the major electromechanical inventions that have occurred in the history of retailing. This technology is affecting almost every aspect of retailing, including merchandise management, buying, pricing, promotion, location, operations, and personnel.
- The point-of-sale (POS) terminal allows all sales data to be captured at the point of sale. The data can then be recalled for processing and analysis to give management timely, detailed information to aid in decision making.
- Scanning and wanding, electronic data interchange, and standardized communication technologies are among the newer technologies affecting retailing.
- A retail decision support system is useful in helping the retailer to plan and implement marketing strategy and to assess the success of the strategy implementation decisions.
- The data sources of a retail decision support system include internal data, external data, and primary data. Data generated as part of model building, a merchandise information system, and a management information system are also important.
- The new retail technology has allowed the development of merchandising information systems to assist in all dimensions of the merchandising process. Such systems typically include a planning system module, a processing system module, and an information reporting system module.
- Environmental scanning allows management to identify long-term strategic problems and opportunities. Retailers are usually interested in assessing trends in the operating and macro environments. Operating environment issues include customers, competitors, suppliers, and shareholders. Macro environment issues include the economic and resource environments, social environment, legal environment, and technological environment.
- Assessing performance is also an important dimension of the management information system. Performance is assessed through both store-level controls and departmental-level control measures. Examples of store-level controls include customer feedback, market share analysis, and operating ratios. Departmental-level control measures include sales variance analysis and analysis of sales-to-expense ratios.

STUDY QUESTIONS

1. What are the advantages of the electronic cash register over the mechanical cash register?
2. Describe database retailing as discussed in Focus 5–1. Why is database retailing becoming such an important element of competitive strategy today?
3. McDonald's in 1992 began inviting customers to join the McDonald's VIP Club by filling out a form listing name, address, home phone number, and sex. Customers receive special offers on their birthday, a newsletter, and McDonald's coupons by mail. McDonald's is now offering to rent the list to outside parties. Is McDonald's acting unethically? Should it obtain a customer's consent before including his or her name on the list rented to outside parties?
4. What are the benefits of UPC scanner systems to the retailer and the consumer?
5. What are the primary data sources available to aid retailers in decision making? What are the strengths and weaknesses of each type of data?
6. Describe the components of a retail information system and describe how they are important to the retail planning process.
7. Why is information on operating environments important to retailers?
8. Describe the components of the macro-level audit and the types of information important in it.
9. Review the types of measures and controls important in helping the retailer assess the performance of the organization.
10. The ABC Shoe Store sales plan called for the sale of 22,000 pairs of Nike Airliners at a selling price of $48 a pair. During 1993, however, the company managed to move only 20,000 pairs at a price of $39 per pair. What is the sales variance for the Nike Airliner, and what is the variance with respect to price and volume?

A P P L I C A T I O N S

CASE 1: Grass-Roots Marketing Yields Clients in Mexico City

Entrepreneur Peter Johns wanted to do business in Mexico but he couldn't buy the thing he needed most: information. So he dug it up himself.

In the process, he found that any entrepreneur hoping to do well in many foreign countries should gather grass-roots marketing intelligence.

Johns had a plan to distribute mail-order catalogs for upscale U.S. companies. He figured that with Mexico's economy on the mend, the rich were itching to buy more foreign-made luxuries. He knew that well-heeled Mexicans have long gone on shopping sprees across the border. But when he sought to test his theory against hard data, he could find none.

The 54-year-old Johns, who has spent 30 years in international marketing, couldn't find a marketing study for Mexico City that he considered up to snuff. Government census reports weren't much help, either; they stop breaking down income levels at about $35,000, and they give ranges, rather than precise numbers, on family size.

So Johns trooped into the neighborhoods and shopping areas of the affluent to take a look for himself. What he saw brightened his spirits: satellite dishes, imported sports cars, and women carrying Louis Vuitton handbags abounded. Drawing on those impressions, and on other information he gathered on his own, he came to his own conclusion: his target market is about 300,000 families. Assuming three people per family, that would be about 5 percent of the city residents.

"And there is no question there is a sense of consumer deprivation in the A-B [luxury] market of Mexico City," says Johns.

As Mexico opens up its economy to foreign capital, foreign capitalists are discovering that rudimentary market research is scant. Even if they have money to spend, as Johns does, they often can't find specialists to compile the information. So, like Johns, they are scrounging around on their own. It's a self-help exercise that is likely to be repeated all over the world in emerging market economies, not only in the Third World but also in former Communist nations.

"Mexico is really hot now," says Florence Leighton of Dillon, Agnew & Marton, an international list broker in New York. "There are relatively few consumer lists in Mexico, but how could there be since the Mexican consumer has just come into his own?"

Once he decided to take the plunge, Johns fell into a second information gap. His new enterprise, Choices Unlimited, had acquired rights from about 20 U.S. companies—from Gump's giftware to Hanna Anderson children's wear to Hammacher Schlemmer sportswear—to distribute their catalogs in Mexico City. Now, he needed mailing lists—and couldn't find them.

Owners of mailing lists in Mexico don't like to sell them because buyers tend to recycle them without authorization, says Leighton. One Mexican magazine did offer to sell its list to Johns, but the cost was too high. Besides, the addresses on the list didn't include zip codes, key factors in determining household wealth.

So Johns asked for the membership lists of the city's exclusive golf clubs. He got them—free. By asking around, he also landed directories of the parents of students at some of the city's exclusive private schools, also for free.

"That's called grass-roots marketing intelligence," says Johns, who was born in Namibia, carries a French passport, and has lived the past decade in San Francisco.

This intelligence allowed him to make a glitzy debut. Choices sponsored a fashion show at a packed, members-only nightclub called the Quetzal. After an indoor pyrotechnic show, models swished by prospective buyers as bartenders and sushi chefs plied the crowd with food and drink.

Shortly thereafter, 800 people plunked down $28 apiece in pesos to become charter members of Choices. They'll get catalogs, a promotional discount, and more fashion-show invitations. In mid-October, the company expanded its telephone operating hours.

Johns is optimistic. He thinks his business will get a big boost from the signing of a free-trade pact between the United States, Mexico, and Canada.

Johns hopes to have a Mexican customer base of 7,500 families spending an average of $600 a year, which means he should have another product to sell: his customer list.

Source: Reproduced with permission from Dianna Solis, "Grass-Roots Marketing Yields Clients in Mexico City," *The Wall Street Journal*, October 24, 1991, p. B2.

Applying Retailing Principles

1. Would survey research be a possibility for obtaining the types of data that Johns needs? What are potential problems?
2. How are firms such as Toys 'R' Us, Sears, Pizza Hut, and others able to enter the Mexican market without the types of problems encountered by this entrepreneur?
3. Are the problems Johns faces in Mexico different from the problems faced by entrepreneurs seeking to launch start-up ventures in the United States? If so, how?

CASE 2: Marketers Zero In on Their Customers

Shoppers in a big midwestern city early last year found extra rows of strawberry-flavored cream cheese at one supermarket. Just a mile away, another store had almost no strawberry but lots of the diet version. Still another had mostly 12-ounce cartons of Philadelphia cream cheese.

Staged by Kraft USA, the experiment combined a demographic profile of cream cheese buyers with data showing which supermarkets drew most of those shoppers. After that, Kraft pinpointed 30 stores where people frequently bought items from special displays and installed coolers in them, tailoring the types of cream cheese in each to the tastes of the store's shoppers. The result? Sales jumped 147 percent over the previous year's.

Welcome to the latest in micromarketing. These days, consumer product companies find focusing on a region or state or even a city is not enough. Increasingly, the target is narrowed to a bullseye no bigger than an individual neighborhood or a single store.

The trend is possible because of new insights provided by the spread of checkout scanners, which are generating more sophisticated data on consumers and buying habits. In addition, a few big food companies and boutique research firms have begun correlating data on individual stores and shoppers in ways that marketers could only dream of a few years ago. And the trend is gathering momentum now because market researchers are about to start digesting a demographic bonanza: the U.S. census data. Until now they have had to make do with old census data that were updated periodically.

The technique, still largely experimental, does have limits. The depth of statistics available can be overwhelming. A food company can get enough information, for example, to tailor dozens of in-store signs to different consumer lifestyles. But is that the best use of marketing dollars?

Another hurdle: grocery chain operators, the ultimate arbiters of what is allowed in their stores, have to sign off on the store-specific programs. And when grocery chains have centralized operations (as many do), with buying decisions and store formats largely directed from headquarters, this kind of marketing requires a difficult culture change. "It's definitely the right way to go, but you can only go as far as the retailer wants, and some won't hear of it because they're not in a data management mode," says Bob Schimtz, director of market research for Lever Brothers Co., which uses this approach for new soap products.

The latest research might sound like shopper espionage. But scanners don't identify specific people. The research examines tiny units of several hundred people—single neighborhoods and census block groups that are like gold nuggets in the hands of marketers.

The community data connect food companies with shoppers as never before. "The real key here is the ability to go out and locate those folks on a store-by-store basis that are the right customers for a product," says Doug Anderson, a vice-president of Spectra Marketing Systems Inc., a Chicago consulting firm.

Using a network of food brokers and store surveyors, Market Metrics of Lancaster, Pennsylvania, collects statistics on 30,000 supermarkets around the country. In addition to compiling economic, social, and ethnic shopper profiles for each store, Market Metrics tracks traffic patterns, per capita food expenditures, and neighborhood population density, as well as store size, sales volume, and even exact measurements of space devoted to health and beauty, dairy, meat, and other products.

Combining those statistics with consumption pattern studies—the demographic profiles of people who buy any of 1,300 goods—Market Metrics can rank specific stores on how well they should sell everything from strained baby food to upscale pasta sauce.

That helped Borden, which makes Classico pasta sauce. To increase sales, the company had Market Metrics generate a list of the best stores for Classico consumers—those who earn at least $35,000, live in dual-income households in metropolitan areas, and are interested in gourmet-style pasta sauces. It showed, among other things, that in West Coast markets Classico would sell strongly in about 75 percent or more of the stores, while in more rural areas the number was 50 percent or less.

"You can't ask the mass market to pay a premium price for pasta sauce when Ragu and Prego are selling at 40 cents less," says Ed Yuhas, a Borden product manager. "We have to spend our money more efficiently. We can't just chase consumers who might try us but might not come back."

With today's complex data, food brokers and manufacturers can allocate precise amounts of products. Based on profiles of breakfast food eaters, for example, Market Metrics found that some National Supermarkets stores in St. Louis were devoting the wrong amount of shelf space to breakfast items.

After scrutinizing data about the predominantly low-income, black shoppers at five National supermarkets, Market Metrics found that the stores needed to increase shelf space 24 percent for hot cereals and 22 percent for waffle and pancake mixes and decrease it 14 percent for toaster products and 52 percent for breakfast snack and nutritional bars.

Some marketers use this approach to cut costs. Last winter, ActMedia, the in-store marketing unit at Heritage Media Corp., ran a taste-sampling program for a frozen microwave food. The item had sold poorly to that point, the manufacturer discovered, because people didn't believe it would be tasty. Unwilling to pay $400 to $500 for taste demonstrations in each store, the company bought data showing which stores had the highest percentages of microwave-oven owners. Then it held the taste programs in these stores.

Some big beverage companies have also experimented with micromarketing. Pepsi-Cola tries to stock more flavored soft drinks in stores where there are lots of children, the biggest drinkers of these beverages. And Coors Brewing Co. recently ran a successful program with Dominick's Finer Foods in Chicago involving in-store sampling of its Killiams beer, focusing on the 25 stores with the greatest potential sales for the "super premium" beer.

Store-specific marketing can even reduce the risk of new product failure. When Frito-Lay introduced its lower-oil, light line of snack chips nationally last year, it first found those stores whose customers fit the products' demographic profile: white-collar workers, 35 to 54 years old, earning more than $35,000. By increasing promotional spending, running in-store taste programs, and lobbying retailers to give more space to the pricier chips in the selected stores, Frito-Lay got the line off to a running start.

Some companies use the technique to promote new uses of old products. Quaker Oats recently pinpointed stores with an above-average number of shoppers who bake from scratch. It then placed an offer for old-fashioned cookie tins next to the company's oatmeal package to reinforce the notion of baking oatmeal cookies. The company calls the reaction "very favorable."

Adds Anne Koehler, a consultant in Wilmette, Illinois, and a former Quaker marketer, "The overlying concept is to do things in such a way that when the consumer walks by, she says, 'Right, this is the product for me.' "

Source: Reproduced with permission from Michael McCarthy, "Marketers Zero in on Their Customers," *The Wall Street Journal*, March 18, 1991.

Applying Retailing Principles

1. What are the advantages to firms that implement micromarketing? Are there limitations? If so, what are they?
2. How can micromarketing be valuable to companies launching new products into the marketplace?

NOTES

1. Martin Mayer, "Scanning the Future," *Forbes*, October 15, 1990, pp. 114–17.
2. Richard Gibson, "Low-Fat Burger Being Tested by McDonald's," *The Wall Street Journal*, November 15, 1990, p. B1; Richard Gibson, "Two Giants Give Each Other the Works as They Fight to Slice Up Pizza Market," *The Wall Street Journal*, September 15, 1989, p. B1; Scott Hume, "Chains Launch New Food Fight," *Advertising Age*, March 30, 1992, p. 58; Cyndee Miller, "Fast-Food Marketers Try to Cure Consumer Blahs," *Marketing News*, June 10, 1991, p. 6.
3. "Amoco, Burger King Team Up in Cross-Selling Test," *Marketing News*, October 14, 1991, p. 1.
4. Gretchen Morgenson, "A Midas Touch," *Forbes*, February 4, 1991, p. 42.
5. Ernst & Young Survey of Retail Information Technology Expenses and Trends as reported in *Chain Store Age Executive*, September 1991, p. 42.
6. Ernst & Young survey.
7. Renae Rouland, "Fulfilling EDI's Promise," *Discount Merchandising*, June 1991, p. 65.

P A R T

3

Selecting Markets in Which to Compete

Chapters 3, 4, and 5 reviewed the factors that affect retail strategy development. Part 3, which consists of Chapters 6 and 7, evaluates consumer behavior and ways in which retailers can develop strategies compatible with that behavior. Consumers are problem solvers. As such, they must make decisions on when to buy, how to buy, where to buy, and how much to buy. Retailers must be aware of how consumers perceive their outlets in the context of these decisions, and of the factors that influence consumers' perception of those outlets.

The changing lifestyles of consumers also influence merchandising strategy. Consumers today place increasing emphasis on convenience over cost in buying decisions, no longer feel guilty about indulging themselves, and seem to be obsessed with health and fitness. Such trends present both challenges and opportunities to retailers.

C H A P T E R

6

Keys to Understanding the Consumer

THIS CHAPTER:

Introduces the consumer as a problem solver.

Explains motives for shopping other than buying.

Discusses where consumers buy, how they buy, what they buy, and when they buy.

Explains the role of image in affecting consumer buying decisions.

Emphasizes the importance of responding to dissatisfied consumers.

RETAILING CAPSULE

THE PIER'S EXPANSION INTO EUROPE REFLECTS AN UNDERSTANDING OF CULTURAL DIFFERENCES

The Pier, backed by Texas-based Pier 1 Imports, has made its debut in Europe by opening three stores in the United Kingdom. The stores will test the firm's merchandise mix and concept before expansion into other European countries.

Some U.S. firms that have entered the European market have not been successful. Lack of success often stems from management's belief that European consumers are the same as American consumers. Due to a lack of understanding of the highly regional shopping patterns in the United Kingdom alone, many U.S. retailers never get off the ground even though their concepts are readily translated in Europe.

The Pier's managment recognizes, however, that retailing's success factors in Europe are not the same as at home. Because of this, an understanding of cultural differences has affected The Pier's European retailing strategy. The English taste in home furnishings appears to lie somewhere between the more conservative American and less conservative French. Apparently, the French are more receptive to modern things.

As an example of the differences between American and European consumers, Europeans have a greater need for closet wardrobes than American since space for walk-in or built-in closets is almost nonexistent in European homes. Also, the smaller size of European homes means The Pier's U.S.-built bedside tables are too large.

Other differences affecting The Pier's product mix include the colors used inside the home. For example, British taste in interiors tends toward warm colors such as pale yellows, warm greens, and peaches. In contrast, in warmer climates such as Spain or Greece, the preferred colors are whites, azure blues, bright yellows, and reds.

Like the U.S. stores, much of the merchandise in The Pier is from India, whose trading history with Britain makes its sales in U.K. stores significant.

A growth vehicle for The Pier in Europe may be mail order. With the growth in Europe's mail-order industry, the high costs of land, and the increasing time constraints of dual-income families, mail order may be an effective way to sell home furnishings.

Source: Based on Allyson L. Stewart, "U.S. Puts Pier Pressure on Europe's Retailers," *Marketing News*. August 2, 1992, pp. 6–7.

Management of The Pier understands the benefits of developing retail strategy from the consumer's viewpoint. Many signs seem to indicate that The Pier's chances of long-term success in Europe are bright, provided management keeps close to its customers and its original concept.

An old saying is that nothing happens until a sale is made. Sales can only occur when the retailer understands and responds to how consumers buy, what they buy, where they buy, and when they buy. Retailers must also understand the consumer as a problem solver and seek to develop merchandise offerings to address unmet needs, as shown in the Retailing Capsule. An additional critical dimension is knowing how consumers form images of retail outlets and how to develop merchandising and marketing strategies compatible with the desired image.

Types of Consumer Decisions

Keep in mind the following points about consumers and their shopping behavior while you study this chapter:

1. Consumers are problem solvers. The role of the retailer is to help them solve their buying problems.
2. Consumers try to lower their risk when buying merchandise by seeking information. They also seek information for reasons other than risk reduction.
3. Store choice and merchandise choice depend on variables such as location, image, hours, and price, which are under the influence of the retailer.
4. Many other factors, such as store atmosphere and courtesy of sales clerks, affect the in-store behavior of consumers.

Motives for Shopping

Consumers shop for reasons other than buying. These reasons can be grouped into personal and social motives. **Personal motives** include role playing, diversion, sensory stimulation, physical activity, and self-gratification. **Social motives** include the desire for social experiences, peer group attraction, status and power needs, the pleasure of bargaining, and being with others of similar interests. An understanding of the reasons for shopping can help a retailer induce shoppers to make purchases even when the primary purpose of the trip is for social or personal reasons.

Personal Motives

Personal motives result from internal needs of the consumer, which are distinct from the needs fulfilled in purchasing a good or service.

Role Playing. Consumers often engage in activities that they perceive as associated with their role in life. Familiar roles include those of homemaker, student, husband, or father. For example, a husband may perceive that in his role he should purchase only high-quality gifts from prestigious outlets for his wife.

Diversion. Shopping often provides the opportunity to get a break from the daily routine. Walking through a shopping center can allow a person to keep up with the latest trends in fashion, styling, or innovation. Knowing this, mall managers often schedule antique or auto shows in an effort to attract consumers.

Regional shopping malls are popular browsing sites because of their comfortable surroundings and appealing ambience. Factors such as store variety, decorations, and decor affect activity levels in shopping malls. Stores that carry deep product assortments and unique brands are especially attractive to browsers because of the novelty and stimulation inherent in such outlets.

Physical Activity. Many people welcome the opportunity to walk for exercise in a safe, temperature-controlled environment. Some malls have thus organized walking and health clubs in response to such needs. The malls are opened for walking before the shops are opened for business.

Sensory Stimulation. Shoppers often respond favorably to background music, scents, and other types of sensory stimulation as part of the shopping process. Customers tend to feel more at ease, spend more time, and shop more often in a store that plays background music.[1]

Self-Gratification. Shopping can alleviate loneliness or other emotional stress. Some also enjoy people-watching while shopping. Self-gratification helps explain the development of family amusement centers in shopping malls.[2] Pier 39 in San Francisco is a renowned festival marketplace, as is West Edmonton Mall in Edmonton, Alberta, and the Mall of America in Bloomington, Minnesota. These attractions often blend an amusement park with a shopping complex (see Exhibit 6–1).

EXHIBIT 6–1

Courtesy Mall of America. Photo by Bob Perzel

Adding that extra touch of excitement can increase the shopper's stay.

Social Motives

Social motives result from the desire for group interaction of one sort or another.[3]

Social Experiences. For many people shopping has become a social activity. They take advantage of such opportunities to meet friends or to develop new acquaintances. Some malls feature special before-noon promotions especially designed to serve older people. Others arrange cooking demonstrations and similar activities.

Hobbies. Interest in a hobby may bring people together, as it is a common desire to meet people who are like oneself. Thus, retailers can provide a focal point for people with similar interests or backgrounds. Retail computer outlets sponsor hobbyist clubs for this reason.

Peer Group Attraction. Individuals may shop to be with a peer or reference group. Patronage of elite restaurants reflects such behavior. Similarly, one will often find teenagers at a record shop that offers music appealing to their tastes. Some outlets also have advisory boards composed of the most influential people in a city. In addition, local opinion leaders are often consulted about advertising and promotion programs.

Status and Power. Some consumers seek the opportunity to be served and catered to as part of the shopping experience. Such an activity may be one of their primary ways to get attention and respect.

The Pleasure of Bargaining. Some people enjoy the opportunity to negotiate over price. They get ego satisfaction as a result of bargaining.

The reasons for shopping other than buying, especially in a mall setting, help explain why many people today contend that malls have replaced the central business district as the center of social activity in a community.

Shopper Profiles

Consumer attitudes toward shopping, as distinct from motives for shopping, also affect shopping behavior. Understanding consumer attitudes, therefore, is also important in strategy development. For illustrative purposes, consumers can be categorized as follows based on their attitudes toward shopping:

The buy-for-one consumer

The stability-seeking consumer

The get-my-money's-worth consumer

The time-buying consumer

The **buy-for-one-consumer** represents the rapidly increasing number of single-person households, comprising divorced people and both young and elderly single people. These people seek food items packaged in single servings. They use utensils especially made for preparing meals for one person. They have more time for leisure and consequently spend more on entertainment and travel.

Many of these people are upwardly mobile professionals with high earning power but high expectations from the marketplace. They are good customers who expect quality products and quality salespeople to wait on them.

The **stability-seeking consumer** normally represents the blue-collar, middle-class household. Such people provide a good market for many products and services, including durables such as recreation equipment and equipment for various do-it-yourself activities, home satellite dishes, and high-definition TVs and VCRs.

Stability-seeking consumers are somewhat overwhelmed by the rapid changes occurring around them. They seek a return to yesterday (by watching *Lucy* on TV), a return to nature (by buying indoor plants), and life simplification (with hobbies and do-it-yourself activities that give them a sense of control over their destiny). This group of consumers readily responds to friendliness, personal attention, the work ethic, and the traditional American value and morality structure.

The **get-my-money's worth consumer** is something of a consumer activist, an admirer of Ralph Nader, and a supporter of various social activist causes. People in this category look for good values—though not always at the lowest price. They seek energy-efficient homes and appliances, and look for durability and retailers who are socially responsible and environmentally sensitive. They substitute consumer labor for consumer costs. This group uses self-service gasoline stations and is willing to use unbranded products. This group and the stability-seeking segment have fueled the growth of retailers such as Crate & Barrel, a retail chain that sells cooking items, kitchen accessories, and home furnishings and Lechter's, a retail chain specializing in household organization and storage items. Both chains have capitalized on the "back to basics" movement.

The **time-buying consumer** reflects the rapidly growing number of households with two or more incomes. The female often maintains the household in addition to a full-time job outside the home. Such households are prone to use telephone shopping services and catalogs, to purchase well-known national brands, and to be receptive to such appliances as microwave ovens. They are also prime markets for cellular telephones, fax machines, laptop computers, personal shopper services, lawn care, and home delivery of groceries.

A MODEL OF THE CONSUMER DECISION PROCESS

The decisions facing shoppers in making a buying decision depend on their past experiences with the merchandise and the outlet from which to make a purchase. Many decisions, such as buying a loaf of bread, are routine because consumers have made similar purchases many times before. Such activities are known as **low-involvement decisions** and require little thought by the shopper and no comparison shopping. Other decisions, however, such as buying an automobile, may be difficult for some consumers because of their lack of experience or the risk involved in making a wrong decision. Consumers exhibit **high involvement** in such situations as they actively compare merchandise and retail outlets before making a buying decision.

When making other than routine purchases, the consumer normally goes through five decision stages, shown in Figure 6–1. Retailers can influence consumer choices and actions at each stage of the decision process, as we will show in the following discussion.

Problem Recognition

The decision process begins when the consumer realizes that a difference exists between the present and preferred state of affairs. Sometimes, consumers may simply discover that they need to purchase gasoline for their automobile. Other things that may trigger problem recognition are a lack of satisfaction with an existing product or service; a raise; additional income from a spouse; the need to purchase a gift; or a change in dress fashions. Retailers can also trigger problem recognition through advertising; in-store displays; or the creative use of sight, sound, or smell (see Exhibit 6–2).

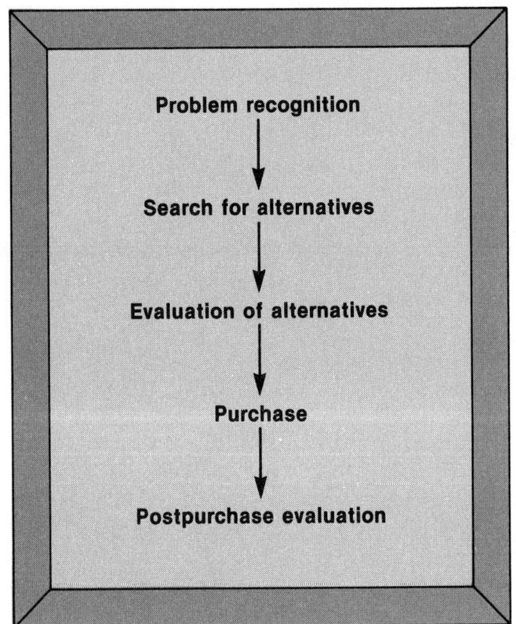

FIGURE 6–1

A MODEL OF THE CONSUMER DECISION PROCESS

Search for Alternatives

The consumer seeks and evaluates information after problem recognition occurs. The search may be physical or mental. Mental search means drawing on past experience. The consumer may need up-to-date information about products, prices, stores, or terms of sale. Physical or mental search may be required to obtain the needed information.[4]

Problem-Solving Behavior. Depending on the consumer's background and experience, he or she may exhibit extensive, limited, or routinized response behavior (Table 6–1). Each type of problem solving requires a different response by the retailer.

Extensive Problem Solving. Consumers engage in extensive problem solving when faced with a first-time purchase in an unfamiliar product category, perhaps during the introductory or early growth stages of the life cycle of the product or service class. Examples include cellular phones and personal computers. Retailers should provide consumers with information on uses of the product or service, reasons why they need it, and characteristics of the product or outlet important to consider in the purchase.

Limited Problem Solving. The consumer who is familiar with the class of product or service engages in limited problem solving; the decision becomes a choice between brands or outlets. An example for many of us

EXHIBIT 6–2

Courtesy FTD/Florists' Transworld Delivery Association

Retailers can trigger problem recognition by reminding consumers of the need to make purchases during special times of the year.

would be small appliances. Shoppers evaluate brands by comparing prices, warranties, after-sale service programs, knowledge and friendliness of salespeople, or similar features. At this stage, facilitating brand-to-brand comparisons is often a key element of the retail marketing plan. Marketing research, as discussed in Chapter 4, can help retailers discover which

TABLE 6–1

PROBLEM-SOLVING BEHAVIOR

Level Required	Typical Products	Retailer Response
Extensive	Personal computers Cellular phones	Provide information on the following: Uses of product or service Reasons why consumer needs product Important characteristics
Limited	Small appliances Clothes Breakfast cereal	Facilitate brand-to-brand comparisons Target features important to consumer
Routinized response	Health and grooming aids Food items Automobile gas	Convenience of location

features consumers find important. Marketing programs can then reflect that information.

Routinized Response Behavior. Many consumers reach a stage of routinized response behavior after they become familiar with a product class, the brands within the class, or an outlet. Such buyers tend not to engage in any kind of information search before a purchase. They exhibit **low-involvement behavior.** Low-involvement products are of limited interest to the consumer, carry little risk of a wrong choice, and are not socially visible. Low involvement typifies the purchase of a loaf of bread or a tank of gasoline at the most convenient outlet. Neither the brand nor the outlet is important to the customer.

Information Sources. The retailer can make information available to consumers in a variety of forms to help them in their search. Consumers are normally exposed to (1) marketer-dominated sources, (2) consumer-dominated sources, and (3) neutral sources of information, as shown in Figure 6–2.

Marketer-Dominated Sources. Marketer-dominated information sources are the promotional component of the retailing mix. They include advertising, personal selling, displays, and sales promotion. The retailer exercises control over the content of these sources. Typically, the retailer provides information on price, product features, and terms of sale.

Consumer-Dominated Sources. Consumer-dominated sources include friends, relatives, and acquaintances. Consumer-dominated information is normally perceived as trustworthy. Satisfied consumers are especially important because they tend to talk to others about their shopping experiences. Additional consumer-dominated sources of information are people who are known and respected by their peers. Word-of-mouth information from such people is likely to be received favorably. Dissatisfied

FIGURE 6–2

CONSUMER INFORMATION SOURCES

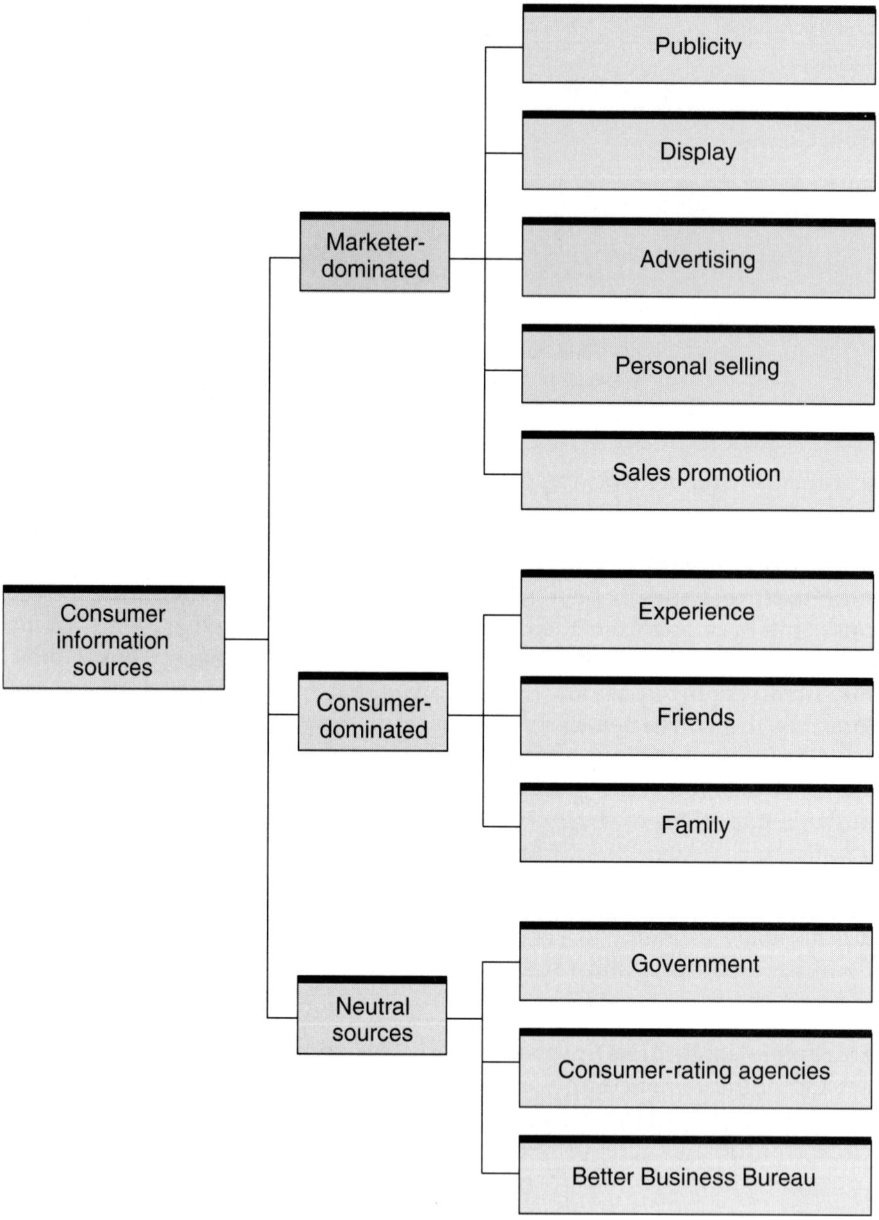

customers can have a negative impact on an outlet. They tend to talk more about their experience than do satisfied consumers.

Neutral Sources. Neutral sources of information tend to be perceived as accurate and trustworthy. Consumers Union and local Better Business

TABLE 6–2 FACTORS INFLUENCING THE CHOICE OF MERCHANDISE AND THE CHOICE OF RETAIL OUTLETS

Factors Affecting Merchandise Choice		Factors Affecting Store Choice	
Product Features	*Service Features*	*Store Characteristics*	*Employee Characteristics*
Fashion	Credit terms	Hours	Knowledge
Brands	Installation	Layout	Friendliness
Quality	Accessories	Cleanliness	Helpfulness
Styles	Delivery	Displays	Courteousness
Colors	Layaway	Decor	
		Image	

Bureaus are examples of agencies that provide neutral information. Government rating agencies and state and local consumer affairs agencies also are viewed as neutral information providers. Government agencies, for example, provide information on gasoline mileage for autos and energy efficiency ratings for appliances.

The most information is usually provided by marketer-dominated sources, although consumers are likely to rely more on personal sources. Marketer-dominated sources help to create initial awareness. Personal and neutral sources are then used to evaluate outlets or brands.

Evaluation of Alternatives

After background information is acquired, the consumer evaluates the outlet and product attribute alternatives. Examples of these attributes are shown in Table 6–2. Attribute importance varies among consumers. Product trial and demonstration is one way of assessing attribute alternatives. Research may be needed to determine the attribute importance in target market segments.

Table 6–3 lists the attributes important in choosing a store, based on analysis of nearly 178,000 shoppers in 27 markets. As shown, price ranked first overall, followed by selection, quality, location, and service. (The numbers do not add to 100 percent because only the top five reasons for store choice are listed.) The importance of these attributes varies by type of retailer, as shown.

Risk Reduction

A desire to reduce the risk of a poor decision influences the evaluation of alternatives. Six types of risk affect the choice of outlet and merchandise alternatives:

1. *Performance risk:* the chance that the merchandise purchased may not work properly.
2. *Financial risk:* the monetary loss from a wrong decision.

TABLE 6–3

WHY SHOPPERS CHOOSE STORES

The Myth of "Location, Location, Location"

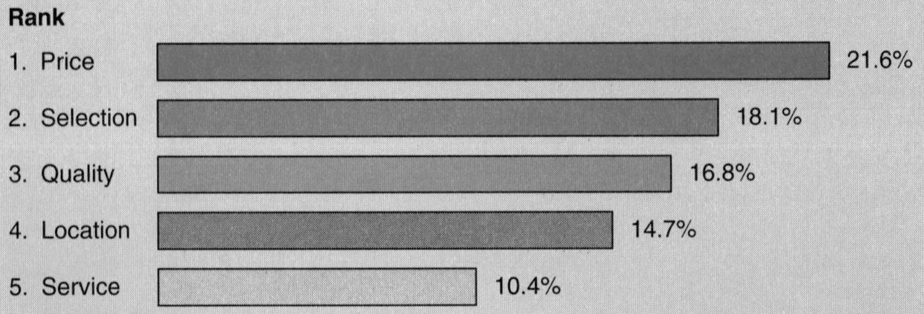

Rank	
1. Price	21.6%
2. Selection	18.1%
3. Quality	16.8%
4. Location	14.7%
5. Service	10.4%

Among 177,788 shoppers of all categories of stores in 27 markets nationwide, price was named the chief reason for choosing one store over another. Price is cited 21.6 percent of the time, compared to only 14.7 percent for store location.

1 Price	
Grocery retailers	33.1%
TV/VCR retailers	26.9
Department stores	23.5
Shoe retailers	22.1
Home improvement/hardware	16.7
Furniture retailers	15.5

Grocery stores are the most price sensitive and furniture is the least price sensitive. In the 27 markets measured, for example, 50 percent of grocers who ranked first, second or third in price also ranked first in the market area as the most preferred grocer.

2 Selection	
Department stores	26.4%
Grocery retailers	24.6
Shoe retailers	20.3
TV/VCR retailers	16.3
Home improvement/hardware	13.4
Furniture retailers	12.3

Selection as a motivator for choosing one store over another is about twice as frequent with department store and grocery shoppers as it is with furniture shoppers.

3 Quality	
Department stores	24.4%
Grocery retailers	22.8
Shoe retailers	18.7
TV/VCR retailers	16.3
Furniture retailers	13.0
Home improvement/hardware	10.8

Quality is expected by department store and grocery shoppers, but it is less important to furniture and home improvement/ hardware customers.

4 Location	
Grocery retailers	36.3%
Department stores	21.2
Shoe stores	13.3
Home improvement/hardware	12.0
TV/VCR retailers	11.2
Furniture retailers	7.4

Grocery shopping's frequency raises location to a high level of importance, but furniture stores are least affected by location because of infrequent purchases involving large amounts of money.

5 Service	
Grocery retailers	16.6%
Department stores	14.8
TV/VCR retailers	12.0
Shoe retailers	9.2
Furniture retailers	8.1
Home improvement/ hardware retailers	8.0

Although often considered a cure-all, service as a motivator for choosing a store ranks last among the five motivations.

Source: Robert E. O'Neill, "Price Drives Shopping Center Retailing," *Monitor,* September 1989, p. 23.

3. *Physical risk:* the likelihood that the decision will be injurious to one's health or cause physical injury.
4. *Psychological risk:* the probability that the merchandise or outlet will be compatible with the consumer's self-image.
5. *Social risk:* the likelihood that the merchandise or outlet will not meet with peer approval.
6. *Time loss risk:* the likelihood that the consumer will not be able to get the merchandise adjusted, replaced, or repaired without loss of time and effort.[5]

The task of the retailer is to minimize each of the risks for the consumer. For example, performance risk and financial risk can be addressed by guarantees or exchange privileges. Performance risk can also be addressed by offering instruction in training programs. Psychological and social risks can be minimized by focusing on the brands carried, national advertising programs that support the merchandise, and the individuals serving as advisors to the outlet. Time loss risk can be addressed by stressing the chainwide applicability of warranties for repair, availability of on-site repair or replacement, and similar services.

The Purchasing Decision

Choosing the outlet and the merchandise does not end the purchasing process. The consumer still has to decide on the method of payment, accessories (such as a camera lens with a camera purchase), an extended warranty, and method of delivery for bulky merchandise. Retailers have the opportunity for "plus" sales of merchandise and services at this point.

Post-Purchase Evaluation

Retailers need to reassure consumers after major purchases that they made the right decision. Consumers are often afraid that they may have spent their money foolishly. A follow-up letter or a phone call can help provide reassurance. Service providers such as walk-in medical clinics often call the day after seeing a patient as a way of showing concern for the patient's welfare.

The level of satisfaction influences whether a consumer will recommend an outlet or merchandise line to friends and family. Retailers need to be sensitive to consumer concerns, and then work to alleviate them.

UNDERSTANDING THE HOW, WHEN, WHERE, AND WHAT OF SHOPPING

Retailers probably can have the most influence on the behavior of consumers during the information search and evaluation stage of the decision process. An understanding of the **how, when, where,** and **what** of consumer shopping behavior can help retailers be responsive to consumer needs for information during their search and evaluation efforts.

The retailer needs to have the right merchandise at the right place, at the right time, and at the right price and quality to match consumer decisions on where to buy, what to buy, how to buy, and when to buy.

What includes consumer decisions on merchandise price and quality, brand, and criteria used in evaluating merchandise. **When** includes decisions on such issues as time of day and day of the week to shop. Similarly, **how** includes decisions on whether to engage in store or nonstore shopping. **Where** means the choice of the outlet at which to make the purchase.

Where Do Consumers Shop?

Shopping Centers. Consumers may choose shopping centers because of convenience, a controlled climate, and the merchandise assortments available. Others go to shopping centers because they can meet friends there, and shopping centers provide a festive atmosphere and a convenient way to keep up with the latest trends in fashion, as we discussed earlier in the chapter.[6]

Some people prefer shopping at strip shopping centers as opposed to the enclosed malls. Strip centers require less walking and generally involve less hassle in shopping. In addition, access is easier than to enclosed malls, but the merchandise selection is limited in comparison.

Downtown. Some people prefer to shop downtown because of convenient public transportation and the availability of nonshopping facilities, such as financial institutions. Others work downtown and find it convenient to shop there. Finally, some consumers, often those with lower incomes, live near the downtown area and have no other shopping alternative.

Outshopping. Some consumers shop out of town (outshopping) because (1) the selection may be better, (2) they may want to get out of town for a visit, and perhaps a good meal, (3) they may work out of town and do their shopping after work, and (4) store hours, store personnel, and services may be better.

Outshoppers tend to be younger and have higher incomes, more education, smaller families, and a shorter tenure in the community. They also tend to be dissatisfied with the selection, service, price, and quality of goods available at local retailers. Furthermore, "outshopping itself may provide a novel experience, new sensations, variety, and fun. For some people, outshopping may be a form of experience seeking."[7] Retailers can often thus expand their trading area by offering entertainment events, promoting the uniqueness of their merchandise offerings, or creating an image for the outlet as the "in" place to shop, which is generally attractive to outshoppers.

Nonstore Shopping. Catalog and telephone shopping are the primary types of nonstore shopping, although in-home or in-office selling by firms such as Avon or Tupperware still occurs. In addition, television channels such as Home Shopping Network and QVC (Quality, Value, Convenience) are attracting in-home shoppers.[8] Nonstore shopping allows consumers to make purchases at their leisure without leaving home. Nonstore shoppers tend to have higher incomes and higher education. Because they have more education, nonstore shoppers often see less risk than other consumers in buying in a nonstore setting.

Merchants can stress several factors in promoting nonstore purchases. Buying convenience is a primary advantage. Good product guarantees and exchange privileges are important, as is the ready availability of credit.

Specialty catalogs have become popular in recent years. Database marketing, as discussed in Chapter 5, has enabled catalog retailers to precisely define target markets for their merchandise. Catalogers such as Lands' End, L. L. Bean, and others are nationally known and offer complete satisfaction (see Exhibit 6–3). They will accept returns for just about any reason.[9]

Choosing a Store

Consumers make decisions about specific outlets at which to shop after deciding the general area in which they will shop (downtown, through mail-order outlets, or at a shopping center, for instance). The image of a retail outlet is important in such a decision. The store "has become the brand . . . in the current economic environment. The consumer's perception of the retailer and what a retailer stands for has become the single biggest reason for selecting to shop a particular store."[10] The major attraction characteristics include the merchandise, services offered, physical facilities, and employees. All of these characteristics are under the direct influence of retailers.

The multiattribute model of consumer choice is one that is frequently used to help retailers understand the importance of various outlet features to consumers. The model can be applied as follows:

$$As = \sum_{i=1}^{n} B_i \, W_i$$

As = Attitude toward the store

B_i = Belief of a consumer that a store possesses a particular attribute

W_i = The weight or importance of the attribute to consumers

n = Number of attributes important to consumers in their choice of a store

Example. Assume that the four attributes shown in Table 6–4 are important in the consumer's choice of a place at which to shop. The *belief*

EXHIBIT 6–3

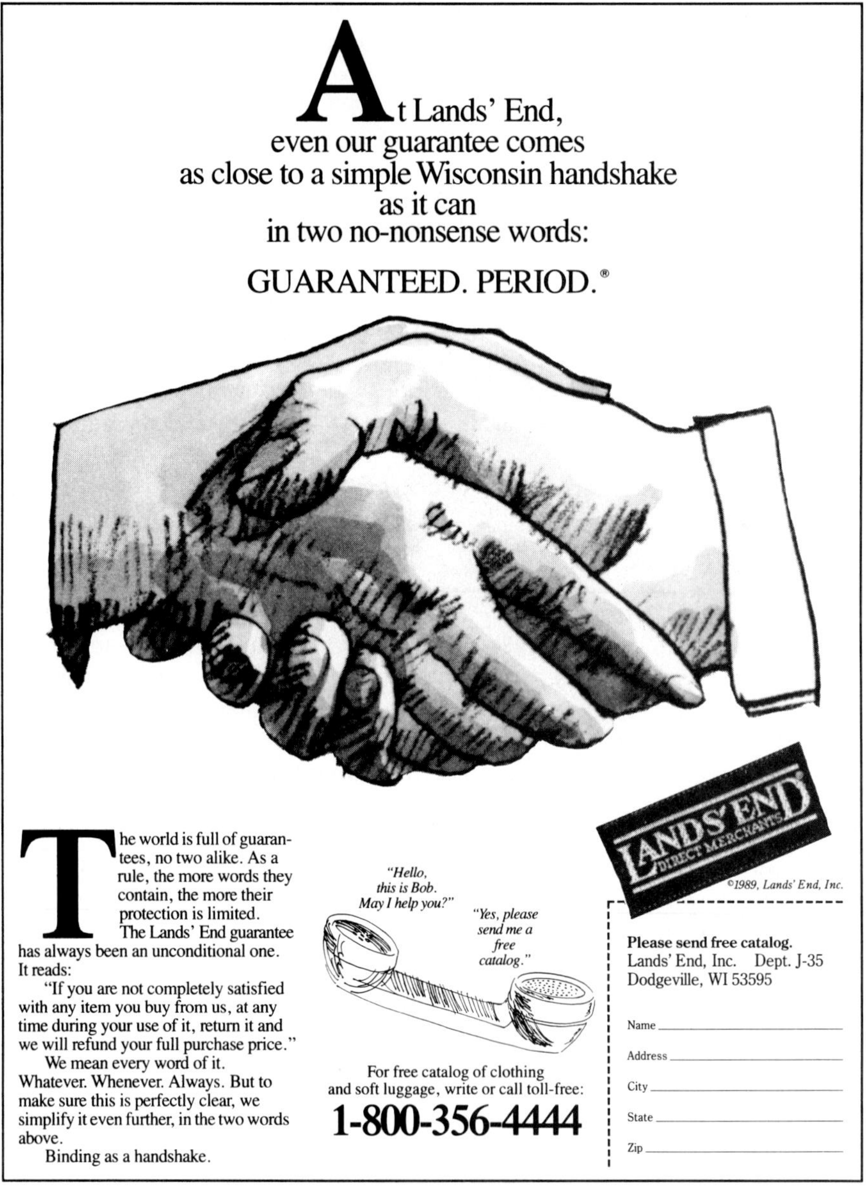

© Lands' End, Inc. Reprinted courtesy of Lands' End Catalog

Lands' End guarantee of 100 percent satisfaction

TABLE 6–4

THE MULTI-ATTRIBUTE MODEL OF OUTLET CHOICE

Attributes	*Belief Weight* (B_i)	*Importance Weight* (W_i)	*Sum* $(B_i \times W_i)$
Low price	2	3	6
Wide merchandise assortment	1	1	1
Courteous personnel	3	2	6
After-sale service	2	2	4
			17

$$As = \sum_{i=1}^{4} B_i W_i = 17$$

about the extent to which an outlet reflects each attribute is rated on a scale of 1 to 3, with a score of one indicating a strong belief. Consumers rate the *importance* of each attribute on a scale of 1 to 5, with one reflecting a high degree of importance.

As shown in Table 6–4, the importance and belief scores are multiplied for each attribute and summed to develop a measure of the consumer's attitude toward each store being evaluated. Scores could range from 4 $(1 \times 1 \times 4)$ to 60 $(3 \times 5 \times 4)$, with 4 being the most favorable score. Store attributes vary in importance by outlet type and consumer segment.

Understanding Store Image

The above model is one way to determine a consumer's image of a retail outlet.[11] **Image** is the way consumers "feel" about an outlet. The image is what people believe to be true about an outlet and how well those beliefs coincide with what they think it should be like. The image may be accurate, or it may be quite different from reality. Knowing how consumers feel about an outlet, however, is important in developing strategies for attracting them.

One of the nation's foremost retailers is Neiman-Marcus. The firm, under the legendary leadership of Stanley Marcus (see A Profile in Excellence), has developed a unique image in the minds of consumers. Some of the components of its store and nonstore mystique are shown in Focus 6–1.

Why Think about Image?[12] The retailer should be concerned about image because the flow of customer traffic depends on it. Management may have what they think is the right merchandise at the right price in the right style in the desired size, color, and quality. But it is what the customer *thinks* of the price, the quality, and the service that is important.

Also important is the customers' impression of the employees. If they like the employees, they are more apt to have favorable impressions of what the outlet offers.[13]

A Profile in Excellence

STANLEY MARCUS

Stanley Marcus spent his adult life looking for and selling the finest and most elegant products in the world. He fervently believes that there is a market for "the best," despite the consistent increase in the price of quality and the shift in industry to mass marketing.

When Herbert Marcus, Stanley's father, began promoting his new store in Dallas in 1907, he extolled the quality and beauty of his merchandise and the superiority of the service. He succeeded in establishing a fashion authority image for Neiman-Marcus. The store was a great success among affluent, fashion-conscious women in Dallas.

Herbert Marcus laid the groundwork for Stanley to add to the mystique that is associated with the Neiman-Marcus name to this day. When Stanley joined his father in the retail business, it was a small, family operation with a good local reputation for integrity, fashion leadership, and quality. However small, the Marcuses were rigorous in maintaining their standards of taste in the merchandise, advertising, and other activities in which the store participated. Stanley proceeded to build on those solid assets after the death of his father. He wanted his customers to be proud of the Neiman-Marcus label on their clothing. At every opportunity he hammered on the theme that his store had more high-quality merchandise than any other outlet between New York and California until he gained the satisfaction of hearing customers join in on his claims. He spanned the globe in a continual search for the finest and most elegant products available. Today, Neiman-Marcus has locations in virtually every major upscale market area in the United States.

How Are Images Formed? Outlet attributes collectively make up the elements that comprise its image. Each attribute should be aligned with management's positioning strategy for the outlet.

Price Policy. An outlet's prices influence the way people think about its other dimensions. Therefore, prices must be consistent with the other elements of the retailing mix. A supermarket learned this fact when it installed carpeting. The plush floor covering created a higher-priced image. Customers felt that prices had gone up even though they had not. Yet it isn't always desirable for an outlet to give the impression that it is a bargain center. A low-price policy can sometimes create an unfavorable image. Some customers believe that low quality goes with low prices. The importance of price varies with the type of product, family income, and competitive offerings, to name a few of the considerations.

Customers usually make up their mind about an outlet's prices based on its advertising, displays, merchandising practices (such as stocking national brands), and location. They also rely on their impression of the outlet's pricing policies rather than on actual knowledge.

Two questions that can be helpful in image-building efforts are these:

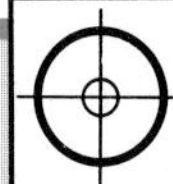

FOCUS 6–1

THE UNIQUENESS OF NEIMAN-MARCUS

The Neiman-Marcus Christmas Book has become one of the most popular and best-publicized Christmas books in the world. The catalogue is known for some of the most unusual and imaginative gifts, such as "His and Her" airplanes, Jaguars, and mummy cases. From the design of the cover to the originality of the merchandise, the Christmas book reflects the Neiman-Marcus belief in quality, good taste, and value.

Exclusivity ... never daring to conform, Neiman-Marcus takes great pride in the ability to offer exclusive merchandise in many areas of the store. Look for the "Made Exclusively for Neiman-Marcus" label. This ensures that the merchandise, whether it is a deck of cards displaying the Neiman-Marcus logo or an exclusively designed Russian lynx fur coat, will not be duplicated anywhere else in the world.

The precious jewelry department at Neiman-Marcus has been recognized as one of the largest and finest-quality jewelry operations in the world. Besides the fact that many of the jewelry pieces are one of a kind, Neiman-Marcus also designs in its own workroom. Other services offered include polishing, remounting, and jewelry appraisal. Expert guidance is offered with every purchase to ensure that each piece of jewelry will be enjoyed for years to come.

Many celebrities will frequent Neiman-Marcus, owing to its world-renowned reputation. We depend on our entire staff to extend a warm welcome. Employees should stay in their own department to allow the visitor time to shop without interference. In other words, let's extend the same courtesies to all our customers.

Source: Courtesy of Neiman-Marcus.

- What price do the customers expect to pay?
- Do the customers consider price as important as quality, convenience, dependability, and selection?

Merchandise Variety. Image improves when customers find a product that they like but cannot find in other outlets. Uniqueness is one of the appeals of specialty catalogs. On the other hand, a failure to stock certain expected items may give a retailer's entire product line a bad name. Similarly, when customers find one product that displeases them, they are apt to become more critical of the rest of the offerings. The key is to know consumer preferences.

Employees. Salespeople and other employees affect an outlet's image. Customers may react negatively if the educational level of an outlet's personnel is different from theirs. Whether an outlet appeals primarily to professional or working-class people, salespeople should dress and speak in such a way that the customers feel comfortable talking to them. Telephone personnel should be knowledgeable, friendly, and efficient, as should back-office personnel.

Outlet Appearance. What people see as they pass by an outlet is another important element in its image. Even people who never enter an outlet form an impression from its outside appearance. That impression may be the reason they don't break their stride when they go by the outlet. Consumers form images of nonstore retailers based on their reliability in filling orders, the knowledge of employees, the ease of resolving complaints, and similar attributes.

Inside an outlet, the layout and the decor reinforce customers' impressions about the products and salespeople. For example, classic design fixtures usually appeal to older and more conservative groups. Plain, inexpensive-appearing fixtures help to build a good image with young families whose incomes are limited. Low ceilings may make the store more personal, and indirect lighting usually makes the customer think of higher quality. Some color schemes are considered masculine, feminine, or neutral, which may be important in displaying certain types of merchandise.

Type of Clientele. The image that people have of an outlet is influenced by the type of people who shop there. Some people, for example, think of a shop as one where professional people usually shop. They think of other outlets as ones where blue-collar workers usually shop.

Advertising. Advertising tells people whether the outlet is modern or old-fashioned, low-price or high-price, small or large. It also communicates other things of both a physical and psychological nature.

For example, when printed ads are full of heavy black print, customers get an image of low prices. Conversely, white space often connotes quality. A food store could improve its image by including a personal interest feature in its weekly ad of special prices. The outlet could feature a recipe, perhaps with the picture of the chef who originated it. Catalog retailers are judged by the design and layout of the catalog, the quality of the paper, the use of color, the professionalism of the models, and similar variables.

Changing the Outlet's Image

An image is a complex affair, and managers should not try to change an outlet's image without careful thought and planning. However, if a retailer is dissatisfied with the image customers seem to have, it should ask three questions:

- What kind of image will serve best in the existing market?
- What kind of image does the store have now?
- What changes can be made to improve the image?

A store cannot be all things to all people (see Case 1 at the end of the chapter, featuring J. C. Penney's struggle to change its image). In fact, one of the competitive strengths in retailing is that each outlet can be different. Many outlets are successful because they specialize and their owners and managers build an image around that particular specialty. Some image changeovers are successful, however. Spiegel, a well-known catalog merchant, was able to shift its image from one of serving primarily lower-income, blue-collar families to that of a slick, upscale catalog merchant.

Keeping the Image Sharp

Like the human face, an outlet's image does not stay bright by itself. It requires care and regular maintenance. Maintaining an outlet's image—regardless of the type of outlet—can be handled in the same way as other management problems. Managers should review the image periodically just as they periodically review financial statements. They can then find potential trouble spots and correct them before they get out of hand.

Listen to Customers. Management can ask customers what they like about an outlet and why they prefer it to others. Their answers give an idea of the strong points in the firm's retailing mix and its image. They can also indicate what products and services should be advertised and promoted. A simple questionnaire such as that shown in Figure 6–3 for Bradlees can provide useful customer information.

All customers speak in sales. What they buy, or don't buy, speaks louder than words. Keeping track of sales by item can help to determine what customers like or don't like.

Management should also look at competitors. They can do some comparison shopping with the goal of trying to find out what strong points competitors use to create attractive images.

Listen to Noncustomers. Management often finds that there are more people in their neighborhood who don't patronize them than who do. Why? Often only one or two aspects of an operation irritate people and keep them from having a good image of it. A grouchy cashier, for example, can cause such potential customers to think poorly of the whole store.

How Do Consumers Shop?

The way in which consumers select products and services and the distance they will travel to shop also affect merchandising decisions.

The Costs of Shopping. Some consumers try to minimize the costs of shopping. The costs of shopping comprise money, time, and energy. **Money costs** are the cost of goods purchased and the cost of travel. **Time costs** include the time spent getting to and from the store or stores, time spent in getting to and from the car, and time spent paying for

FIGURE 6–3

QUESTIONNAIRE DESIGNED TO COLLECT IMAGE INFORMATION

Now It's Your Turn

We'd like to know what you think of our service, our merchandise, our personnel, and our appearance. We value your ideas and welcome your comments because we want to make Bradlees the kind of store you like to shop!

Please take a moment to rate us on each item indicated below. If there is anything else you'd like to add, we've included a space for your comments.

Rate Us

Please circle number that best applies to each category.

	Excellent	Very Good	Average	Below Average	Poor
Speedy Checkout	1	2	3	4	5
Availability of Sale Items	1	2	3	4	5
Raincheck Fulfillment	1	2	3	4	5
Employee Courtesy	1	2	3	4	5
Return Policy	1	2	3	4	5
Complaints Satisfactorily Resolved	1	2	3	4	5
Merchandise Quality	1	2	3	4	5
Regular (non-sale) Prices	1	2	3	4	5
Store Cleanliness	1	2	3	4	5
Restroom Facilities	1	2	3	4	5
Well Lit Parking Lot	1	2	3	4	5
Overall Rating of Bradlees	1	2	3	4	5
Compared to other Stores	1	2	3	4	5

Dear Karen: ____________

Name ____________

Street ____________

City ____________ State ____________

Zip ____________

Home Phone ____________ Work Phone ____________

Store Location ____________

Date and Time of Visit ____________

Source: Courtesy of Bradlees.

TABLE 6–5

COSTS IN SHOPPING AND BUYING

Cost of merchandise
Other monetary outlays
1. Parking fees.
2. Automobile gasoline and wear and tear.
3. Installation.
4. Credit.
5. Repairs.
6. Wrapping.
7. Babysitting fees.
8. Warranties.

Nonmonetary costs
1. Time away from other activities.
2. Waiting in line.
3. Comparison of merchandise between stores.
4. Comparison of alternative merchandise offerings.
5. Travel time.

Emotional costs
1. Frustration caused by out-of-stock items.
2. Dealing with surly or indifferent sales assistants.
3. Bargaining over price and terms of sale.
4. Concern over a wrong decision.
5. Effects of crowding.

merchandise. **Energy costs** include carrying packages, fighting traffic, parking, waiting in line, and various other psychological costs, as shown in Table 6–5.

Management can be responsive to these problems by having the proper store hours and by offering shoppers credit, delivery, and similar services. Nonstore retailers can offer 24-hour phone service, overnight expedited delivery (often for an extra charge), and customer service representatives to answer questions about complex product purchases.

Consumers are willing to travel farther for specialty goods than for either shopping or convenience goods because they believe the satisfaction they obtain from getting exactly what they want more than offsets the cost of the extra effort. **Convenience goods** are items for which consumers are indifferent to brand name and will purchase at the most accessible outlet. **Shopping goods** are products for which consumers make comparisons between various brands in a product class. A **specialty good** is one for which a consumer insists on a specific brand.

It is not possible to generalize about the types of merchandise that can be described as convenience, shopping, or specialty goods. Consumers view merchandise differently. What is a shopping good to one consumer may be a convenience good to another one. Typical examples of convenience, shopping goods, and specialty goods can be identified, however. Table salt is a convenience good for many shoppers. Household durables or appliances are shopping goods for many people. A Rolex watch may be regarded by many shoppers as a specialty good.

Overall, less time is spent today in shopping than in the past. The reasons include advertising, which makes information more easily available; less time available for shopping because most adults work outside the home; and increasing nonstore alternatives for purchases. Many shoppers do not visit more than two stores even when buying items such as television sets.

How Far Are Consumers Willing to Travel? Most shoppers at grocery stores live within a half-mile of the store. Shoppers usually will travel about 10 minutes to shop for higher-priced merchandise. Typically, 75 percent of the people who travel to a large shopping center live within 15 minutes of the center. However, shoppers will travel much farther to purchase specialty goods.

What Do Consumers Buy?

Price and brand are two major attributes that affect consumer purchases. Price is important because it is often a measure of worth. Brand is often relied on as a measure of quality. Other factors that are important in merchandise choice include open-code (freshness) dating, unit pricing, shelf displays, shelf location, and coupons.

Price. Consumers ordinarily do not know the exact price of an item of merchandise, but they usually know within well-defined ranges. The higher-income consumer usually is less price conscious than the lower-income consumer seeking the same merchandise. The greater the percentage of a shopper's income that is spent on an item, the greater price awareness he or she is likely to have. In general, price is not as important to the nondiscount shopper as it is to the discount shopper. Indeed, high price is considered by some shoppers as a signal of value.

Brands. Some consumers purchase only well-known national brands of manufacturers such as Del Monte to help avoid the risk of a bad purchase. But other consumers buy nonbranded items, or generics, such as paper products, drugs, and liquor to take advantage of 30 to 40 percent savings. They rely on the reputation of the outlet as an assurance of quality in buying the items. Some stores, such as Kroger, sell their own brands. These are known as **private brands.**

Private brands have become more important to department stores and specialty stores in recent years. They began developing their own private-label brands to maintain desired merchandise margins and to protect the integrity of their image as outlets such as Kmart began selling designer-label merchandise.

More and more supermarkets are also selling private-label merchandise, including colas and fruit juices. Sam's Choice, a cola drink, is now available in many Wal-Marts across the United States. Analysts expect that Wal-Mart will develop a wide array of private brands to compete head-to-head with national brands.

Open-Code Dating. Open-code dating, or freshness dating, means that the consumer can tell the date after which a product should not be purchased. The strongest users tend to be young consumers who have higher incomes and higher levels of education and live in the suburbs. The usage pattern for nutritional labeling is similar to that for open-code dating.

A Question of Ethics

The Center for Science in the Public Interest (CSPI) is a consumer advocacy group that monitors the food industry. Although most of their criticism is directed toward manufacturers and legislators, retailers recently came under attack.

"Supermarkets are pushing sugary cereals to kids," said the director of CSPI's Children's Nutrition Campaign. As proof of this contention, CSPI surveyed supermarkets across the country and found that sugary breakfast cereal was strategically placed at children's eye level, and healthy "adult" cereals are usually placed on higher shelves. Because these products are at their eye level, "children are attracted by the brand names and flashy packaging and then plead with their parents to buy them.

"It's bad enough that cereal companies bombard kids with thousands of ads for junky products. Supermarkets, which often brag about their nutrition efforts, compound the problem by using marketing tricks to tempt kids to grab the sugary cereals," says CSPI.

Are supermarkets taking unfair advantage of children's infatuation with unhealthy breakfast cereals? If you think this is true, do you think there should be regulations governing displays for children's products?

Unit Pricing. Unit pricing states price in such terms as price per pound or ounce. Shoppers use this information as a guide to the best buys. Again, younger, higher-income consumers are more likely to use these data. Brand switching occurs often when prices are stated on a per-unit basis.

Shelf Displays and Location. Retailers tend to give the most shelf space to merchandise with the highest profit margins, often their private labels. Profits tend to drop if managers shift store displays and layout too often. Point-of-sale materials, even simple signs, can increase item sales by as much as 100 percent. End-of-aisle and special displays can have even larger effects on consumer buying behavior (see A Question of Ethics).

Consumers are most prone to purchase merchandise displayed at eye level. Merchandise located on the lowest shelves may present difficulties for elderly or infirm customers, and merchandise on the higher shelves may be difficult for some individuals to reach. The ideal shelf location depends on the customer. For example, merchandise directed primarily at children should be on a lower shelf level to establish eye contact.

Shelf location becomes especially critical for low-involvement products because consumers are likely to purchase the first item to catch their attention. Examples include cleaning supplies or paper products. Conversely, consumers are likely to make brand comparisons in a high-involvement product class such as salad dressings. Shelf location may be a less critical factor in such situations since consumers will make a more concerted effort to compare alternative offerings.

Coupons. Coupons can be used to draw new customers to an outlet and to increase purchases made by regular customers. They can also be used to

EXHIBIT 6–4

24 reasons to shop at Safeway.

We're Open 7 a.m.
We're Open 8 a.m.
We're Open 9 a.m.
We're Open 10 a.m.
We're Open 11 a.m.
We're Open 12 p.m.
We're Open 1 p.m.
We're Open 2 p.m.
We're Open 3 p.m.
We're Open 4 p.m.
We're Open 5 p.m.
We're Open 6 p.m.
We're Open 7 p.m.
We're Open 8 p.m.
We're Open 9 p.m.
We're Open 10 p.m.
We're Open 11 p.m.
We're Open 12 a.m.
We're Open 1 a.m.
We're Open 2 a.m.
We're Open 3 a.m.
We're Open 4 a.m.
We're Open 5 a.m.
We're Open 6 a.m.
We're Open 7 a.m.

Now these Safeway locations are open to serve you 24 hours a day.

Evans & Downing, Denver • 1st & Steele Cherry Creek • 14th & Krameria, Denver • Parker & Dartmouth, Aurora • 80th & Wadsworth, Arvada • Arapahoe & Quebec, Englewood • Highway 285 & Logan, Englewood • Colfax & Garrison, Lakewood • 84th & Federal, Westminster • 28th & Arapahoe, Boulder • Washington & Malley Drive, Northglenn

Printed with Permission of Safeway Stores, Incorporated

Ad designed to appeal to the busy lifestyle of today's consumer

offset the negative features of a store by drawing customers to a poor location. Nine out of ten people redeem coupons during a year. The coupon users tend to have slightly higher incomes than the average household and usually have children. They are especially good customers for retailers. Trading stamps, rebate offers, and similar strategies also can be used to attract new customers and to retain the loyalty of current customers.

When Do Consumers Buy?

Sunday and continuous store hours are attractive to many shoppers. Sunday is often the only time some families can shop together, and working people are more likely to shop in the evenings and on Sunday. Ads such as that shown in Exhibit 6–4 for Safeway reflect the increasingly busy lifestyle of today's consumers.

Many retailers do not like Sunday openings or long hours because they believe that long hours drive up costs without helping profits. However, consumer preference for these hours and competitive pressures are making the openings increasingly common.

Consumers often turn to nonstore retail shopping options such as catalogs or interactive computer shopping because they allow flexibility concerning the time of day that purchases are made.

Many retailers experience wide seasonal variations in sales. Some retailers make one-third or more of their sales in November and December. Spring dresses sell well just prior to Easter. Picnic supplies sell best in the summer, and snow ski equipment during the winter.

RESPONDING TO CONSUMER DISSATISFACTION

Consumer complaints are a signal that not all is well in the business.[14] Retailers should not ignore people with complaints but should actively seek feedback—what they like and don't like, how they can be better served, their satisfaction with store policies, and so forth. Unfortunately, too few outlets do this.

It is too simple to say that the customer is always right. Some customers do not pay their bills. They shoplift, switch price tags, and so forth. Nor is the customer always wrong. Retailers sometimes use bad credit information, make errors in customers' accounts, and sell inferior merchandise.

How Do Consumers View Retailers?

Retailers rate weakest in communicating with consumers, in being interested in customers, in providing good value for money, and in honesty concerning what they say about merchandise. Chains tend to rate highest in the quality of the job they perform; appliance and automobile repair services often rank at the bottom of the list.

How Are Problems Being Solved?

Retailer Responses. reshness dates now appear on many products. Nutritional labeling is also being practiced and was mandated for many products in 1993. Unit pricing is another aid to the consumer.

Some stores provide in-store consumer consultants, consumer advisory panels, consumer affairs forums, buyer guides, employee training on consumer rights, and signs, sales notices, and applications in languages other than English when appropriate.

Voluntary Action Groups. Voluntary action groups are organizations sponsored by an industry and are designed to respond to consumer complaints about products or services. The groups also provide information to consumers to help them make important buying decisions. Such groups include the Major Appliance Consumer Action Panel, the

Automobile Consumer Action Panel, and the Furniture Industry Consumer Action Panel.

Consumers also need to act responsibly to avoid unnecessary problems. Consumers are likely to have fewer problems with merchandise when they understand how to operate the items they purchase, use proper care in handling the equipment, bring defective merchandise to the attention of retailers, are aware of their rights as consumers, and make comparisons before their purchases.

Better Business Bureaus. Better Business Bureaus serve a useful purpose in handling consumer problems at the local level. Complaints about false advertising and mislabeling of items are often taken to Better Business Bureaus. The bureau in each community is supported by dues from member firms. Membership is voluntary.

Many smaller communities do not have Better Business Bureaus. In such situations the function of monitoring business practices is usually carried out by local chambers of commerce. The chambers have codes of conduct that all ethical merchants are urged to follow, and chamber members work to help ensure that business licenses are not issued to firms engaging in questionable practices. They also sponsor seminars that are designed to alert members to questionable business practices that can alienate consumers.

A Philosophy of Action for Management

The demands of consumers normally are not unrealistic. They simply want more, better, and honest information. Most retailers do not want to make money by selling merchandise that may hurt customers or drive them away. Customers simply want such things as better labeling, honesty in advertising, and full information on credit terms.

Some retailers such as L. L. Bean, a well-known catalog retailer, make a special effort to advertise directly to consumers to tell them about their customer satisfaction programs. L. L. Bean guarantees 100 percent satisfaction and will accept returns at any time for any reason. Bean will either replace the purchase or refund the purchase price and will pay all regular postage and handling charges.

CHAPTER HIGHLIGHTS

- Consumers shop for reasons other than buying. These reasons can be grouped into personal and social motives. Personal motives include role playing, diversion, sensory stimulation, physical activity, and self-gratification. Social motives include the desire for social experiences, peer group attraction, status and power needs, the pleasure of bargaining, and the desire to be with others who have similar interests.
- Consumer attitudes toward shopping, as distinct from motives for shopping, also affect shopping behavior. For strategy purposes, consumers can be categorized based on their

shopping behavior. Typical categories include the buy-for-one shopper, stability-seeking shopper, get-my-money's-worth shopper, and the time-buying shopper.

- Consumers go through a series of stages in making a purchase decision. These stages, for other than routine purchases, include problem recognition, information search, evaluation, the purchase decision, and post-purchase evaluation. Retailers can influence consumer choices and actions at each stage of the decision process.
- Retailers can have the most influence on the behavior of consumers during the information search and evaluation stage. An understanding of the how, when, where, and what of consumer shopping and buying behavior can help retailers be responsive to consumers' needs for information.
- Consumers use marketer-dominated, consumer-dominated, and neutral sources of information in making store and product choices. Marketer-dominated sources include advertising, personal selling, displays, sales promotion, and publicity. Consumer-dominated sources include friends, relatives, acquaintances, and others. Neutral sources include government rating agencies and state and local consumer affairs agencies.
- Consumers try to minimize risks during the purchase evaluation stage. These risks include performance risk, financial risk, physical risk, psychological risk, social risk, and time loss risk.
- Many consumers try to minimize the costs of shopping when making purchase decisions. These costs include money, time, and energy. Actual purchases by consumers are influenced by many factors, including price and brand, shopping aids such as open-code dating and unit pricing, shelf displays and shelf locations, coupons, trading stamps, and rebates.
- Retailers also need to be sensitive to consumer concerns, which often take the form of consumerism. Efforts at solving consumer dissatisfaction usually start with the retailer from whom a purchase was made. In recent years, a variety of retailers have responded by providing in-store consumer consultants, consumer advisory panels, consumer affairs forums, buyer guides, and employee training on consumer rights.

Study Questions

1. Briefly describe each of the steps of the consumer decision process.
2. What are some reasons that consumers might prefer to shop downtown? Why do some people prefer to shop in shopping centers?
3. What is the importance of image to the retailer? How does it affect the shopping behavior of consumers? Think of the two largest department stores in your community. How would you describe their images?
4. How does open-code dating and unit pricing information aid consumers in making purchase decisions? Develop a profile of the consumers who are most likely to use these types of shopping information.
5. What are some of the things retailers can do to reduce each of the six types of purchase risk?
6. Provide an example of each of the personal and social motives discussed in the chapter as reasons for shopping but not buying.
7. What are some things that retailers can do to help consumers minimize the costs of shopping?
8. What steps can retailers take to lower the level of consumer dissatisfaction?
9. What are some retailers doing to help consumers buy more effectively?
10. What roles do voluntary action groups and Better Business Bureaus play in helping to resolve consumer dissatisfaction?

A P P L I C A T I O N S

CASE 1: J. C. Penney: Trapped between the Up and Down Escalators

In 1983 J. C. Penney stopped trying to be all things to all people. Management eliminated the automotive, hardware, electronics, and lawn and garden lines from its stores. They instead focused on apparel and home furnishings, key items for shoppers in malls.

Thus began Penny's process of transforming itself from a mass merchandiser into a fashion department store. Penney expanded its lines of brand-name clothes, cosmetics, and jewelry. Its stores now feature marble floors and fancy woodwork, reflecting the company's upscale aspirations. Its ads boasted of "Fashion Coming to Life." But the transition has been difficult for the firm. The fastest-growing retailers during the previous decade were at either end of the price scale—discount stores like Wal-Mart or upscale chains like Ann Taylor.

Penney's efforts at repositioning have also created a confusing image for many shoppers. One retail analyst observed that "they overstepped their customer. . . . Five years ago, a normal dress may have been $50 at Penney. Now it's more like $85, when they should have been around $70." Penney has begun offering more merchandise at lower prices, but still continues to target its overall product mix to women with middle and upper-middle incomes.

Penney's problem is that, although its image has improved from its days as a general retailer, it still hasn't attracted the elite cosmetic and apparel vendors. The inability to attract such vendors has made it difficult to appeal to upper-income customers.

Recently, Penney has been backing off from its emphasis on fashion and style and has pushed value more strongly. Management has also turned to more moderately priced merchandise in ads that are a harder sell than previous ones.

Source: Based on Evan Ramstad, "Recession Catches J. C. Penney in Mid-Stride," *Birmingham News,* August 25, 1991, p. 4D; "Trapped between the Up and Down Escalators," *Business Week,* August 26, 1991, pp. 49 and 50; Christie Fisher, "Penney's Pinching," *Advertising Age,* September 2, 1991, p. 42.

Applying Retailing Principles

1. Why does J. C. Penney have such a confusing image in consumers' minds today? What is its primary customer base?
2. What can Penney do to establish a clearer image with its target customers?
3. What is the image J. C. Penney should strive to project as a middle-of-the-road merchant positioned between low-end merchandisers such as Wal-Mart and upper-end merchandisers such as Ann Taylor? What other stores compete in the mid-market segment?

CASE 2: Toys 'R' Us Takes a "No Frills" Approach to Japan

Toys 'R' Us simply transplanted its American "no frills" sales approach to Japan (see Exhibit 6–5). For the consumer, the main advantage is the lower price tag. Most toys are sold 10 to 25 percent lower than the manufacturer's suggested price.

But the advantages in pricing may not compensate for the decline in service and showroom presentation, both extremely important for an affluent and demanding clientele. Many Japanese customers, who are conditioned to a much higher level of sales help, did not come away favorably impressed after their first visit to the American-style store.

The crowds may have looked great on television news, but many customers had a different reaction: "Shopping is difficult," or "Not as cheap as expected."

These sort of responses are a good example of the cultural differences that exist between Japan and the United States.

With shelves reaching up to the ceiling, some 4.3 meters (nearly 15 feet) high, and many products still in their boxes, the toys are not at a child's eye level—and are inaccessible for even the parents.

In the United States—perhaps because of the Santa Claus tradition—toys are for parents to give

EXHIBIT 6–5

Courtesy of Toys 'R' Us—Japan Ltd.

Toys 'R' Us' entry into Japan experienced some rough spots in responding to consumer needs.

their children. Parents choose what they think suitable, and that is what their children receive. But in Japan the privilege to choose lies almost exclusively with the child. The parent goes to the toy store with his or her child, but it is the boy or girl who decides what to buy.

And so in Japan toys are displayed, perhaps in a jumbled fashion, at the little ones' eye level. This gets their attention and invites them to play. Furthermore, in Japanese shops or department stores, toys are in motion everywhere. Toys that make sounds blare. The noisy racket may be harsh to Western ears, but for Japanese kids it's close to heaven.

Children and their parents will go to a toy store with nothing definite in mind, as a form of family leisure. Or even if they know what they want beforehand, they often leave the store with something else. Mom or Dad will take a toy, put it in the child's hand, get a reaction, and then buy it if it meets acceptance. There is no real hands-on experience at Toys 'R' Us.

In a Japanese store, a clerk will politely show how the toy works, and will explain if other parts are needed. If the toy needs batteries, these are automatically added to the bill, unless the buyer instructs otherwise. Gift-wrapping and free delivery of bulky items are also taken for granted.

But at a discount outfit, salespeople are generally too busy stocking shelves to stop for customers. Some customers complain they got home only to find that no one had informed them that batteries were not included. An American consumer would have known better, but Japanese consumers are used to that extra bit of service—and are ready to pay for it.

The entry of Toys 'R' Us will make Japanese retailers more competitive. But on the other hand, the American chain may eventually end up adapting to Japanese sales practices and consumers' tastes and modify its own policy. Like the hamburger chains that now offer Japanese dishes, its original strategy may prove short-lived.

Source: Reproduced with permission from Hitoshi Takahashi, "Making Child's Play," *Japan Today,* March 1992, p. 13.

Applying Retailing Principles

1. Describe the shopping behavior differences between American and Japanese consumers in making toy purchases.
2. What store design features need to be modified by U.S. retailers competing in Japanese markets?
3. What modifications in marketing plans and store policies may be necessary to respond to Japanese preferences and traditions in their in-store behavior?
4. Contrast the role of the child as the focus of toy buying behavior in Japan and the United States.

Notes

1. For further reading see Easwar S. Iyer, "Unplanned Purchasing: Knowledge of Shopping Environment and Time Pressure," *Journal of Retailing* 65 (Spring 1989), pp. 40–57; Dennis W. Rook, "The Buying Impulse," *Journal of Consumer Research* 14 (1987), pp. 189–99.
2. Jane A. Black, "Shoppers Just Wanna Have Fun," *Monitor,* October 1989, pp. 30–37; Jimmy Golen, "Biggest Mall in U.S. Will Open Soon," *The Birmingham News,* March 10, 1992, p. B1.
3. Andrew M. Forman and Ven Sriram, "The Depersonalization of Retailing: Its Impact on the 'Lonely Consumer,' " *Journal of Retailing* 67 (Summer 1991), pp. 152–53.
4. N. Srinivasan and Brian T. Ratchford, "An Empirical Test of a Model of External Search for Automobiles," *Journal of Consumer Research* 18 (September 1991), pp. 233–41.
5. For further reading see Mark Dunn, Patrick E. Murphy, and Gerald Skelly, "The Influence of Perceived Risk on Brand Preferences in Supermarket Products," *Journal of Retailing* 62 (Summer 1986), pp. 204–16.
6. "Shopping the Big Centers," *Monitor,* June 1990, pp. 13–14.
7. William C. LaFief and Paul J. Hensel, "Outshopping and Hedonic Consumption," in Mary Gilly, et al. (eds.), *Enhancing Knowledge Development in Marketing* (Chicago: American Marketing Association, 1991), p. 109.
8. Seth Lubove, "Don't Leave Home," *Forbes,* October 28, 1991, pp. 164–66.
9. Jeffery A. Trachtenberg, "Catalogs Help Avon Get a Foot in the Door," *The Wall Street Journal,* February 28, 1992, p. B1.
10. Cyndee Miller, "Study Says Consumers Perceive Stores As Brands," *Marketing News,* August 19, 1991, p. 25.
11. Jan Benedict, E. M. Steenkamp, and Michel Weedel, "Segmenting Retail Markets on Store Image Using a Consumer-Based Methodology," *Journal of Retailing* 67 (Fall 1991), pp. 269–70; Carol Motley, "Do You See What I See: A Conceptual Model for Analyzing the Congruousness between Retailers' and Customers' Retail Store Image Perceptions," in Robert L. King (ed.), *Retailing: Reflections, Insights and Forecasts* (Miami, Florida: Academy of Marketing Science and American Collegiate Retailing Association, 1991), pp. 33–37.
12. Reproduced with modification from Roger Blackwell, "Knowing Your Image," *Small Marketers Aids,* no. 124 (Washington, D.C.: U.S. Small Business Administration).
13. Toni Mack, "Caviar Yes, Chardonnay No," *Forbes,* October 28, 1991, pp. 152–53.
14. Cathy Goodwin and Ivan Ross, "Consumer Evaluations of Response to Complaints: What's Fair and Why," *Journal of Services Marketing* 4 (Summer 1990), pp. 53–61.

C H A P T E R

7

What Is Lifestyle Merchandising?

THIS CHAPTER:

Explains the techniques of lifestyle analysis.

Illustrates the benefits of lifestyle merchandising.

Shows the role of lifestyle merchandising in retail strategy.

RETAILING CAPSULE

THE GAP: READING THE CUSTOMER RIGHT

The Gap was born in the hippie and head shop days of 1969, the creation of Donald Fisher, a California real estate developer. Fisher opened his first outlet in San Francisco and offered "tons of Levis." Levi Strauss at the time would not allow discounts on its jeans, which allowed Fisher to achieve a 50 percent markup. The Federal Trade Commission in 1976, however, ruled that manufacturers could not set retail prices. Discounters flooded the market and The Gap suffered. Fisher then turned to higher-margin store-brand apparel sold under such labels as Foxtails. The merchandise was decidedly schlocky, however.

Fisher hired Millard Drexler in the early 1980s to structure a turn-around of The Gap as its core customers aged. He removed the pipe rack displays and strengthened The Gap's basic jeans and sweats assortments designed to appeal to an older audience. He also brought in all-cotton merchandise in a deep assortment of colors, which he displayed in attractive settings.

Drexler also introduced four cuts of jeans for women and three for men. The jeans feature names such as Relaxed Fit (loose-fitting, very relaxed leg) and Reverse Fit (full at the top, tapered at the bottom). Drexler recognized that the baby boomers can no longer fit into the slim-cut jeans they wore at Woodstock, but that they still want to wear jeans.

Levi jeans have been completely removed from The Gap stores. The Gap now sells only clothes under its own labels. Drexler also opened GapKids to sell T-shirts, jeans, and sweaters for the under-12 set. He added still another division when he opened babyGap boutiques, which sell simple, unfrilly dresses, overalls, and other basics in The Gap's array of colors for infants and toddlers. The Gap is also opening stores downtown to attract working parents and other shoppers too tired to make the trip to the mall after work or on the weekends.

Drexler did stumble in responding to what turned out to be a lifestyle fad. In 1983 Fisher bought Banana Republic, which was then two San Francisco–area stores and a catalog of safari-style clothes. The Indiana Jones series, *Romancing the Stone,* and *Out of Africa* triggered a khaki craze in the early and mid-1980s. But by 1988 consumers were no longer enamored with the safari look and the Banana Republic stores lost a lot of money. The store is now being repositioned as a sort of upscale Gap that offers more adventurous fashions. The safari theme has been removed from most of the stores.

Source: Based on Russell Mitchell, "The Gap," *Business Week,* March 9, 1992, pp. 58–64; Susan Carminiti, "Gap: Reading the Customer Right," *Fortune,* December 2, 1991, p. 106; Francine Schwadel, G. Christian Hill, and Jeffrey A. Trachtenberg, "Decline in March Sales Gives Investors Pause," *The Wall Street Journal,* April 10, 1992, p. B6.

The Retailing Capsule shows how changing demographics and lifestyles affect the strategies of retailers such as the babyGap (Exhibit 7–1). Demographics alone do not allow retailers to adequately understand and serve a market. Astute executives such as Drexler focus on the attitudes, interests, and opinions of consumers to supplement demographic data. Spiegel, for example, has redefined its customers by life stages in recognition that not all people at the same age are experiencing the same life events (Focus 7–1).[1]

Lifestyle concepts influence every dimension of retailing. The two key terms in this chapter are **lifestyle** and **psychographics.** Lifestyle is a customer's pattern of living and self-concept as reflected in his or her purchase and use of merchandise. Psychographics are the ways of defining and measuring the lifestyles of consumers.

Why has lifestyle merchandising become so important? We live in an age in which large differences exist in the behavior of people with similar demographic profiles. This diversity makes it hard to offer merchandise to consumers based only on an analysis of their age, income, and education. Instead, retailers need to know how people spend their time and their money, and what they value—so that retailers can serve customers better. Market segmentation based on lifestyle characteristics gives retailers a more realistic picture of the customers they want to serve.

EXHIBIT 7–1

© Lawrence Ivy

babyGap: The latest addition to the Gap portfolio is based on the theme "For Every Generation."

THE EVOLUTION OF LIFESTYLE MERCHANDISING

Lifestyle retailing has grown in importance over the past two decades. Until the mid-1960s, retailing was characterized by a sameness in operations. Dominant merchants included Sears, Woolworth, A&P, and other retailers that were different only in degree. Managers could be shifted from one store to another across the country and would find few differences between the stores. Changes began to occur with the acceptance of the marketing concept in the 1960s and the positioning concept in the 1970s, forerunners of lifestyle merchandising.

The Marketing Concept

The marketing concept was developed in the early 1960s by packaged goods firms such as Procter & Gamble in response to the lack of attention to the needs of consumers in merchandising decisions. The marketing concept involves focusing on consumer needs and integrating all activities of the enterprise to satisfy the needs identified. Earlier strategies focused

FOCUS 7–1

LIFESTAGES: NEW SPIEGEL STRATEGY

Rather than lump customers together by age, Spiegel has taken the approach of grouping them by lifestages—recognizing, for example, that one 40-year-old woman may be a new grandmother, another a new mother.

"The thing is, not all people at the same age are at the same point in their life," explains a spokeswoman. "And lifestage will be much more important in determining what merchandise a customer may need and want.

"And that's where our approach differs again from other retailers: rather than simply telling customers, 'Here's the merchandise we've got,' we find out what they want and then go out to find it for them," she adds.

In targeting specific segments of its customer base, Spiegel uses seven basic lifestages: starting out, career growth, family growth, starting out II, mid-life crisis, aging well, and mature.

The "broadcast" cross-section of customers is reached through the company's three "big books": spring and summer, fall and winter, and the holiday collection. These are split about half and half between fashion and home merchandise.

Then, different clusters of customers are targeted with specialty catalogs, most of which are produced in more than one edition each year. Among the titles are the following:

"For You," one of the first specialty books and "extremely successful," says a spokeswoman, featuring fashions for women in size 14 and up.

"RTW," for "ready to wind down," consisting of "stress-free," easy basics for men and women.

"In Home," a collection of bed and bath fashions.

"Together," featuring colorful and affordable exclusive designs for women with a focus on detailing.

"Agenda," consisting of "polished" styles, including easy knits for women and basics for building a wardrobe.

"Real Life Dressing," apparel that blurs the line between weekday and weekend clothing, for customers with a distinctive personal style.

Why has Spiegel developed and implemented the concept of lifestages as part of its competitive strategy?

Source: "Lifestages: New Spiegel Strategy," *Stores*, July 1990, p. 52.

primarily on operations efficiency and not on responding to the needs of unique market segments.

Retailers in the 1960s, even though they insisted that the customer is always right, often implemented the marketing concept only in the context of day-to-day operations, not in the context of the broader strategic dimensions of retailing. Policies relating to refunds, hours of operation, and customer service were developed with a consumer focus. However, such issues as product lines, store location, and merchandise lines still retained the sameness of earlier years.

A Profile in Excellence

LAURA ASHLEY

Welsh-born Laura Mountney was a member of the Women's Royal Navy Service in Europe during World War II. After the war, she was a secretary for the National Federation of Women's Institutes until her marriage to Bernard Ashley in 1949. Her fashion empire began with the sale of silk-screened scarves and tea towels that she created in her spare time at home. The demand for these articles quickly became so large that Bernard Ashley quit his day job and became his wife's business partner. In 1954, Laura Ashley as a retail outlet was born. Bernard Ashley handled the operational dimensions of the business and his wife concentrated on the creative side.

In the mid-1960s, Laura Ashley began designing dresses and blouses in addition to her earlier creations. Her designs appealed to young and old alike. The simplicity of design, natural fabrics, and flowery prints combined to create clothing that displayed the wholesome image that Laura Ashley herself conveyed.

Laura Ashley was a simple woman whose lifestyle did not change dramatically in spite of the wealth she accumulated. She maintained a "homely air about her." She preferred the country to the city and the past to the present. Her attitudes are evident in her designs, which are romantic and nostalgic.

Laura Ashley found her inspiration in museums and libraries, where she would spend hours examining old books and fabrics. She was particularly fond of pre-Raphaelite William Morris. His influence is evident in her home furnishings line. Laura Ashley believed that the past was more interesting than the present and that this philosophy was responsible for the appeal of her wares.

Laura Ashley stores exemplify the English lifestyle. The storefronts evoke images of Victorian England (Exhibit 7–2). Saleswomen wear the flower-print dresses, jumpers, and matched outfits they sell. Fabrics and sheets and wallpaper are also sold in the shops. The demand for frilly, flowery Laura Ashley clothing for children has continued to expand, making the Laura Ashley label popular in yet another segment of the retail market.

The Positioning Concept

The concept of *market positioning* emerged during the early 1970s as an extension of the marketing concept. Positioning was the forerunner of contemporary lifestyle merchandising as retailers sought to capitalize on the strategic implications of the marketing concept. Retailers began to tailor merchandising strategies to specific consumer segments. The segments to be served were defined, however, largely in terms of *demographics* such as age, income, and education.

Wal-Mart was an early leader in positioning. The company experienced rapid growth by serving small-town and rural markets. Each dimension of store operations was geared to serve these markets. Other chains, such as Toys 'R' Us, experienced equal success by using demographics-focused market positioning.

Lifestyle Merchandising. Astute retailers such as Laura Ashley (see A Profile in Excellence) and Les Wexler, founder of The Limited stores, quickly realized that defining consumers in terms of demographics alone

EXHIBIT 7–2

Courtesy Laura Ashley Inc.

Laura Ashley is a pioneer in lifestyle retailing.

was not sufficient for fast growth. The concept of lifestyle merchandising thus evolved. The new focus was on understanding and responding to the living patterns and self-concepts of customers rather than making merchandising decisions primarily on the basis of consumer demographics.

A portfolio of lifestyle-oriented outlets then emerged as the next evolutionary stage for some retailers. Management recognized that a portfolio of outlets is likely to be more profitable than focusing on only one or two target groups. Even such a traditional mass merchant as Kmart has opened a variety of lifestyle-oriented retailing specialty outlets such as Builders Square targeted to the do-it-yourself market, and Northern Reflections, launched in Canada as a faux-country chain stocked with casual clothes.

An example of a lifestyle portfolio is shown in Table 7–1 for The Limited. Victoria's Secret offers designer lingerie for the fashion-conscious contemporary woman 25 to 45 years of age. Sizes Unlimited features large-sized apparel for women ages 25 to 50. Lane Bryant is the nation's leading retailer of medium-priced basic and intimate apparel designed for larger women, especially those over 25 years of age. The Limited Express offers medium-priced sportswear and accessories to fashion-oriented women 15 to 25 years of age. The Limited stores, probably the most widely known firm in the portfolio, sells medium-priced fashion apparel to fashion-conscious contemporary women ages 20 to 40.

The Limited management often locates several of the different lifestyle stores side-by-side in shopping malls so that each is accessible to the others

TABLE 7–1 THE LIMITED—A PORTFOLIO OF LIFESTYLES

The Limited is a growing company whose business is to provide fashion, quality, and value to the American consumer through multiple retail formats:

The Limited Stores
The Limited Stores sell medium-priced fashion apparel tailored to the tastes and lifestyles of fashion-conscious contemporary women 20 to 40 years of age. The majority of Limited stores are located in regional shopping centers with the remainder in key downtown locations.

Limited Express
Distinguished by a unique store design and merchandise selection, Limited Express stores offer an exciting assortment of medium-priced sportswear and accessories designed to appeal primarily to fashion-forward women 15 to 25 years of age.

Lane Bryant
Lane Bryant is the nation's leading retailer of women's large-sized apparel. The Lane Bryant stores specialize in the sale of medium-priced fashion, basic, and intimate apparel designed to appeal to the large or tall woman, with particular emphasis on those over 25 years of age. The stores are located in regional shopping centers throughout the United States.

Brylane Mail Order
The nation's foremost catalog retailer of women's large-sized apparel and shoes, Brylane Mail Order publishes five catalogs, each directed to a specific type of special-sized customer. The catalogs include Lane Bryant, Roaman's Tall Collection, Lerner Woman, Sue Brett, and Lerner Sport.

Structure
Clothing for men who have a sense of style and are willing to experiment with fabrics and colors in seeking a sense of fashion uniqueness.

Bath & Body Works
Personal care products made from natural ingredients that offer healthful benefits. Developed in response to people's concerns about inadequate nutrition and artificial ingredients.

Penhaligon's
Fine scents, toilet waters, and pomades sold in shops in England as well as in selected stores around the world.

Victoria's Secret
Through retail stores and a nationally distributed mail-order catalog, Victoria's Secret offers European and American designer lingerie for the fashionable contemporary woman 25 to 45 years of age.

Sizes Unlimited
This division is an off-price retailer of women's special-size apparel. Composed of Sizes Unlimited and Smart Size stores, the division offers nationally known brand and private-label merchandise designed to appeal primarily to women 25 to 50 years of age. The stores are located in smaller shopping centers throughout the East and Midwest.

Henri Bendel
Merchandise targeted to upscale, sophisticated individualists with ahead-of-the-game taste in clothes and accessories. The international looks appeal to women who want sophisticated style and quality.

Abercrombie & Fitch
An upscale sporting goods retailer headquartered in Chicago, which in its glory days was the retailer of choice for some of the world's most famous outdoor sports fanatics. The enterprise fell on hard times during the early 1980s and was acquired by The Limited, which is restoring its former luster.

Lerner
Merchandise assortments emphasizing current fashion in sportswear, coats, dresses, and accessories at budget prices.

Limited Too
High-fashion, high-quality, moderately priced clothing for girls sized 4 to 14.

Cacique
Lingerie with a Parisian accent for the sophisticated woman seeking feminine, sensual, and fashioned-to-fit lingerie.

through inside doors. Newer additions to The Limited portfolio include Structure for men; Limited Too for girls; Bath & Body Works for the environmentally conscious market segment; Lingerie Cacique, offering French lingerie; and Penhaligon's, offering English toiletries.

WHY WORRY ABOUT LIFESTYLE MERCHANDISING?

Management is better able to describe and understand the behavior of consumers when it thinks in terms of lifestyle. Routinely thinking in terms of the activities, interests, needs, self-concepts, and values of customers can help retailers plan merchandise offerings, price lines, store layout, and promotion programs that are tightly targeted to core customer markets. However, lifestyle analysis only adds to the demographic, geographic, and socioeconomic information discussed in Chapter 4 that retailers need in serving markets effectively. Lifestyle analysis is not a substitute for this information. Rather, all the information sources taken together give retailers a richer view of their customers and help them recognize and serve consumer needs.

What Shapes Lifestyles?

We are all a product of the society in which we live. We learn very early concepts such as honesty and the value of money, and these values stay with us throughout our lives. Cultural influences, plus individual economic circumstances, produce consumer lifestyles—traits, activities, interests, and opinions reflected in shopping behavior. Individuals can be grouped into distinct market segments based on the similarities of their lifestyles.

Where Do Lifestyles Come From?

The lifestyles of consumers are rooted in their values. **Values** are beliefs or expectations about behavior shared by a number of individuals and learned from society. Some of these values do not change much over time, and others can change quite rapidly. The major forces shaping consumer values include family influence, religious institutions, schools, the media, and early life experiences.

Examples of changing household values in each decade since the 1950s are shown in Table 7–2. During the 1950s most women did not work outside the home. The primary household emphasis was on money, home ownership, and material possessions. Television was beginning to make people more aware of trends around the world.

During the 1960s the homogeneous value system of the United States began to fragment as the baby boom generation questioned the existing social norms. Divorce rates soared, and antiwar, antiestablishment, and antigovernment protests became commonplace.

During the 1970s personal fulfillment emerged as one of the primary values of society. The divorce rate continued to accelerate. Women increasingly entered the work force. Health foods, natural products, and handcrafted goods became popular with many segments of consumers, and retail outlets emerged to meet these needs. Inflation accelerated, as did advances in technology ranging from personal computers to videocassettes.

During the 1980s consumers reassessed their personal values and goals. They again became interested in solving problems at the grass-roots level. A greater personal tolerance across all segments of society allowed advances in women's rights, workers' rights, and racial justice. Individuals again focused on their responsibilities in addition to their rights, but material excesses were rampant.

The 1990s are also bringing a unique set of lifestyles to the marketplace.[2] Time-constrained consumers are finding shopping more of a chore and less of a pleasure than did their predecessors. Instead, they want convenience, as reflected in in-home shopping options, in-store personal shoppers, quality merchandise, knowledgeable salespeople, and products that are easy to care for.[3] Tradition, rather than change, characterizes many of the 1990s consumers. Many of the priorities for the 1990s are still being defined, which presents both challenges and opportunities for retailers.

A study of cultural and economic lifestyle influences offers some of the most important and interesting ways of understanding consumers. This information helps in serving them more effectively. The following examples of such analyses will help you understand the impact of lifestyles on consumer buying behavior.

Values and Lifestyles (VALS). Stanford Research International (SRI) has developed a trademarked program entitled VALS (values and lifestyles) that can help retailers understand the effect of consumer preferences and expectations on market planning decisions.[4] Their program is summarized in Figure 7–1. VALS was modified with the introduction of VALS 2, which places less emphasis on values and more emphasis on the psychological underpinnings of behavior.

The VALS program allows retailers to predict consumer responses to merchandise or to outlets based on the VALS categories established. For example, people who use yogurt regularly have been found to be societally conscious, as have the experiencers and achievers. Similarly, the experiencers are more likely to buy imported cheese than domestic cheese. Achievers, experiencers, and societally conscious individuals shop more frequently at supermarkets and convenience stores than other groups do, and they also buy more on each trip to the store.

Furthermore, VALS information can help retailers develop promotional campaigns targeted at specific groups. Societally conscious consumers read

TABLE 7–2 SHIFTING CONSUMER VALUES IN THE UNITED STATES

The 1950s

1. Money, home ownership, and material possessions became important signs of social status.
2. Most families consisted of a married couple with a "working" husband and a "nonworking" wife.
3. Upward mobility and economic self-sufficiency were major goals.
4. Television brought people, places, and ideas from around the globe into family living rooms.
5. People were better housed, fed, and educated than ever before.
6. General Eisenhower, a wartime symbol of freedom and victory, was elected president.
7. In the midst of postwar conformity the rebellious "beat generation" shocked the establishment late in the decade with unconventional lifestyles.
8. Fads, from hula hoops to pink bobby socks, were the norm. Everyone tried everything.

The 1960s

1. A once-homogeneous value system began to fragment.
2. The baby boom generation questioned traditional social norms.
3. Between 1930 and 1960 the divorce rate doubled.
4. Self-awareness and self-understanding became important personal goals.
5. John Kennedy moved into the White House and was assassinated almost three years later.

The 1970s

1. Personal goals of self-fulfillment became more entrenched.
2. "Me" values replaced traditional values.
3. Women began to reject traditional, stereotyped roles in the home. More women entered the work force while the divorce rate increased rapidly.
4. Upward mobility and materialism were rejected as desirable goals.
5. Health foods, natural products, and handcrafted goods flooded the marketplace.
6. The Watergate scandal made citizens question an already tenuous faith in "the American way."
7. Unemployment and inflation began to escalate.
8. Encounter groups and self-help books tried to explain America's social roller coaster.
9. Advances in technology transformed microcomputers, satellite dishes, videocassettes, and videodiscs into household items.

The 1980s

1. Unbridled materialism abounded.
2. Scandals over insider trading rocked Wall Street.
3. Massive failures of savings and loan associations funded by high-risk junk bonds occurred.
4. Environmental preservation, recycling, and environmentally friendly marketing became the cornerstones of competitor strategy.

magazines often but do not watch much television. When they do, it is often a cable channel. They listen to radio on an average basis but focus on news, soft rock, and classical music.

VALS's limitation was that it did not account for how well consumers' motivations matched with their ability to buy the goods and services they wanted. For this reason, SRI developed VALS 2, which explains not just what consumers buy, but why and how they make purchase decisions. The system introduces and defines the notions of psychological and material resources and describes the critical role they play in the translation of psychological motivation into purchasing behavior.[5]

TABLE 7–2 *continued*

6. War in Vietnam escalated.
7. Antiwar, antiestablishment, antigovernment protests echoed across the land.
8. Racial tension rocked inner cities from Detroit to Los Angeles.
9. The hippie movement and its philosophy of peace, love, and understanding was born in San Francisco.
10. The family seemed to be torn apart—both literally and figuratively.
11. Religious cults and spiritual movements promised asylum from troubled times.
12. Tolerance and freedom opened the door to women's rights, racial justice, worker rights, and social flexibility.

5. Massive debt brought about by mergers and acquisitions and financed by internal cash flow led to bankruptcy of many well-known American retailers.
6. The oldest of the Yuppies reached middle age.
7. Economic realities forced Americans to reassess personal values and goals.
8. Diversity in family forms became the norm.
9. Economic realities led to the return of do-it-yourself projects and bartering for goods and services.
10. Information became a powerful economic resource.
11. The "body beautiful" fueled the fitness craze.

The 1990s

1. Time is the currency of the 1990s. Convenience is paramount.
2. The demand for quality drives most buying decisions.
3. Consumers are questioning whether consumption is really the road to happiness.
4. The fitness craze of the 1980s is over but consumers remain preoccupied with health.
5. Most consumers label themselves environmentalists, and retailers are responding.
6. Technological innovations are making staying home fun.
7. The return to traditional values and the fear of AIDS is making casual and extramarital sex off limits.
8. A growing animal rights movement is slowing the demand for fur.
9. Neotraditionalism synthesizing the positive dimensions of traditional family values—family, home, stability—prevails, but in the context of personal freedoms resulting from the sexual revolution and the women's and civil rights movements.

Source: "New Values and Lifestyles," *J. C. Penney Forum*, September 1983, p. 10. Update by the authors.

The VALS 2 system divides consumers into eight groups, determined by their psychological makeup or self-orientation, and their financial resources. **Self-orientation** refers to the patterns of attitudes and activities that help people reinforce, sustain, or modify their social self-image.

For VALS 2 purposes, resources include education, income, self-confidence, health, eagerness to buy, intelligence, and energy level. Resources generally increase from adolescence through middle-age and decrease with extreme age, depression, financial reverses, and physical or psychological impairment.

VALS finds three patterns to be highly effective predictors of consumer behavior: principle, status, and action orientations.

Principle-oriented consumers are guided in their choices by their beliefs or principles, rather than by feelings, events, or desire for approval. **Status-oriented consumers** are heavily influenced by the actions, approval,

FIGURE 7–1

VALS AND VALS 2

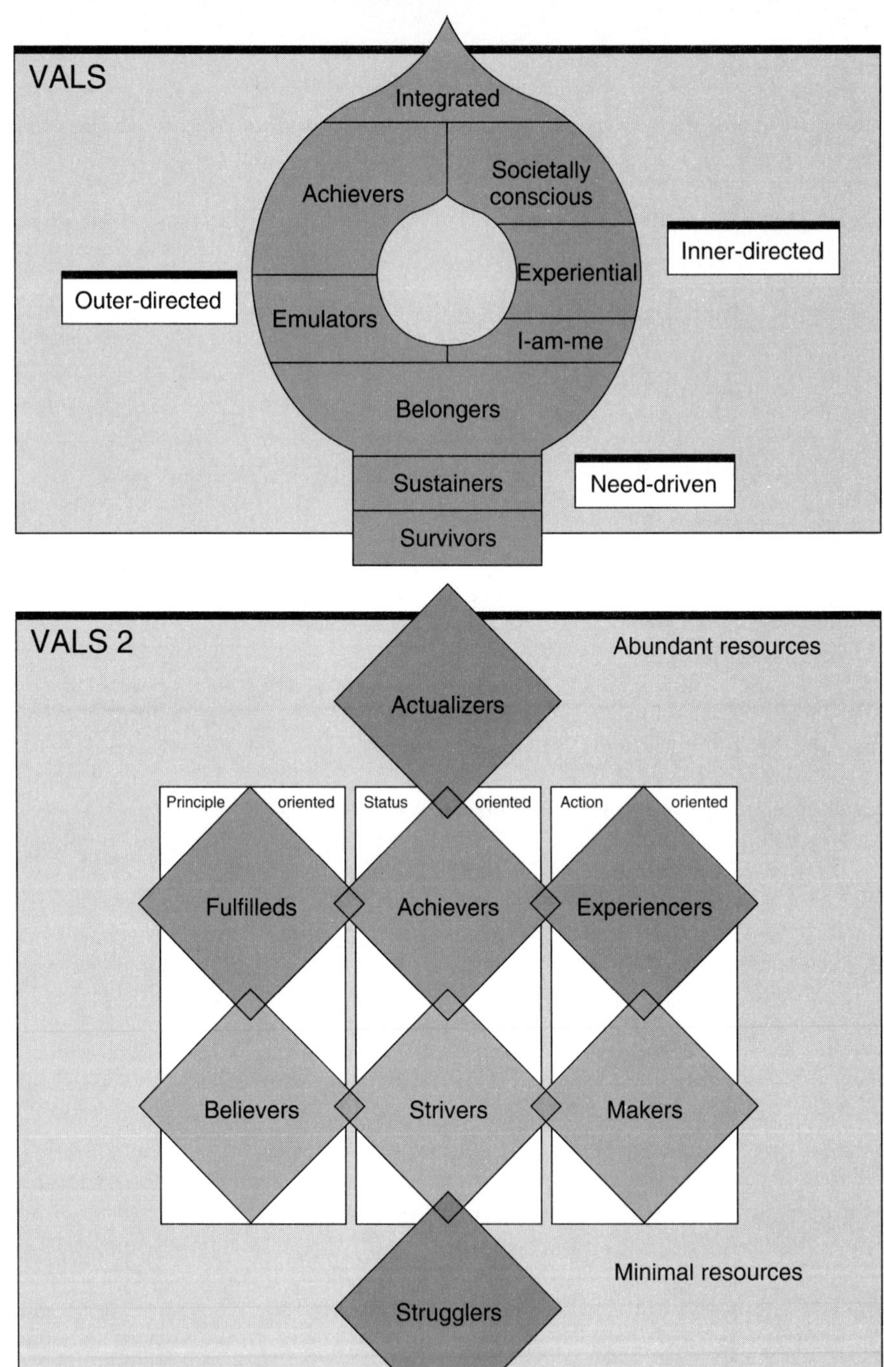

Source: Reprinted with permission from Marsha Farnsworth Riche, "Psychographics for the 1990s," *American Demographics*, July 1989, p. 26. For subscription information call (800) 828-1133.

and opinions of others. **Action-oriented consumers** are guided by a desire for social or physical activity, variety, and risk taking.

Each of the groups has distinctive attitudes, lifestyles, and life goals. Consumers within each group buy products and services and seek experiences characteristic of themselves.

With those factors as a foundation, a thumbnail sketch of the eight VALS 2 segments follows:[6]

- *Actualizers* are successful, sophisticated, active, take-charge people with high self-esteem and abundant resources. Their possessions and recreation reflect a cultivated taste for the finer things in life.
- *Fulfilleds* are mature, satisfied, comfortable, reflective people who value order, knowledge, and responsibility. Most are well educated, and in, or recently retired from, professional occupations. Although their income allows them many choices, they are conservative, practical consumers, concerned about functionality, value, and durability in the products they buy.
- *Believers* are conservative, conventional people with concrete beliefs and strong attachments to traditional institutions: family, church, community, and the nation. They follow established routines, organized in large part around their homes, families, and social or religious organizations. As consumers, they are conservative and predictable, favoring American products and established brands.
- *Achievers* are successful career-oriented people who like to, and generally do, feel in control of their lives. They value structure, predictability, and stability over risk, intimacy, and self-discovery. They are deeply committed to their work and their families. As consumers, they favor established products that demonstrate their success to their peers.
- *Strivers* seek motivation, self-definition, and approval from the world around them. They are striving to find a secure place in life. Unsure of themselves, and low on economic, social, and psychological resources, they are deeply concerned about the opinions and approval of others. They emulate those who own more impressive possessions, but what they wish to obtain is generally beyond their reach.
- *Experiencers* are young, vital, enthusiastic, impulsive, and rebellious. They seek variety and excitement, savoring the new, the offbeat, and the risky. Still in the process of formulating life values and patterns of behavior, they quickly become enthusiastic about new possibilities but are equally quick to cool. They are avid consumers and spend much of their income on clothing, fast food, music, movies, and videos.
- *Makers* are practical people who have constructive skills and value self-sufficiency. They live within a traditional context of family, practical work, and physical recreation and have little interest in what lies outside that context. They experience the world by working on it (for example, building a house or canning vegetables), and have sufficient skill, income, and energy to carry out their projects successfully. They are unimpressed by material possessions other than those with a practical or functional purpose.

A Question of Ethics

FREDERICK'S OF HOLLYWOOD TRADES ITS X-RATING FOR AN R

Frederick's of Hollywood, the primary seller of sexually explicit merchandise after World War II, in the late 1980s eliminated such lewd merchandise from its offering as "metal studded black vinyl body suits and whips, earthquake-proof ceiling mirrors, and bras with built-in nipples for that cold-weather look all year round." In management's words, they decided to "keep the naughty but lose the lewd." In so doing, management gave up the customer who was looking for sleazy, offensive products.

Frederick's lifestyle positioning strategy currently is one that is less traditional than Victoria's Secret, with more "today" merchandise targeted to customers averaging 23 to 25 years of age. For example, Frederick's eliminated wigs, costumes, dresses, and sportswear from all but its main store and the catalog. They replaced the revealing sketches of models in their catalog with photographs that conceal key anatomical details. The stores have been repainted in softer colors. Softer lighting has been installed, as have open, inviting fronts. Hard-edged mannequins have been replaced with less brassy versions.

Frederick's kept one of its best-known departments—bras (in push-up and padded styles)—but has also added fashion bras. The firm also concentrates on bustiers and other items that can be worn as underwear as well as outerwear. Management eliminated the explicit books, vibrators, and sex games.

Frederick's still features musical panties that play a variety of Christmas songs and thigh-high black boots with spike heels, as well as fancy G-strings, garters, and edible panties. They have retained their traditional sensual feeling throughout the stores and are still more direct in intent than Victoria's Secret in offering apparel with high-cut legs, low-cut backs, and plunging fronts. Management in 1989 also opened the Frederick's of Hollywood Lingerie Museum and the Celebrity Lingerie Hall of Fame (Exhibit 7–3) in the landmark flagship store on Hollywood Boulevard with its fuchsia awnings. The museum started as a display showing the history of the bra and also features undies worn by such celebrities as Madonna, Mae West, and Cher. Frederick's management says that sex still sells and that they are simply trying to be more contemporary in approach.

Is Frederick's of Hollywood overtly sexist in its basic merchandising strategy? Should retailers appeal to the baser instincts of society?

Source: Based on "Desleazification Pays Off," *Stores,* May 1991, pp. 44–47; Kathleen Kerwin, "Frederick's of Hollywood Trades Its X-Rating for an R," *Business Week,* December 11, 1989, p. 64.

- *Strugglers'* lives are constricted. Chronically poor, ill-educated, low-skilled, without strong social bonds, aging, and concerned about their health, they are often despairing and passive. Their chief concerns are for security and safety. They are cautious consumers, and although they represent a very modest market for most products and services, they are loyal to favorite brands.

According to SRI, the VALS 2 segments are balanced in size so that each truly represents a viable target for retailers. In addition, some of the

EXHIBIT 7–3

© Alan Levenson

Undies of the ages: Shoppers can view garments worn by Mae West, among others, at the Frederick's of Hollywood Lingerie Hall of Fame Museum.

segments with similar characteristics interconnect with one another, so they can be combined in various ways to suit particular retailing purposes.

What Else Do We Know about Changing Cultural Patterns?

1. Parents are spending less time with very young children. Today more than 30 percent of preschool children are in day-care centers, a segment of retailing that will continue to grow very rapidly. Kinder-Care is the nation's largest day-care chain.

2. The divorce rate remains high. As a result, the value patterns of today's children are shifting. More children are being raised with only one parent. Many children now learn some of their values from individuals other than family members. Trends indicate, however, that a shift to traditional values and family units is occurring, which may lead to a decline in the divorce rate.

3. People move more often than in the past. Thus, less influence comes from the extended family. Many of today's young people lack roots and a sense of traditional family values.

4. Religion is not important in many people's lives. As a consequence, the moral standards of previous years are changing. People are more prone to pursue pleasure and less likely to practice self-denial. Retailers are therefore likely to feature merchandise with a sexual orientation but to avoid the sleaze factor (see A Question of Ethics). Religion may again assume a more central life in the role of consumers, however, as part of the return to traditional values in the 1990s.

5. Schools are becoming more important in shaping values. More young people are staying in high school, and approximately half now go to college. Young people are being exposed to a larger number of different values than in the past and are more willing to experiment and try alternative lifestyles (including illegal drugs).

6. Individuals in each generation have different experiences. More than 80 percent of consumers today were not alive during the Depression. Many have little awareness of World War II. Today's middle-aged people grew up in an era of low-cost credit, plentiful jobs, job security, and loyalty to one's country and parents. These same people also grew up with the Vietnam War and an energy crisis and are unprepared for the downward mobility brought about by the restructured economy of the 1990s.[7]

7. Family size is decreasing and more single-person households are being formed, as discussed in Chapter 4. Single-person households reflect lifestyles for which "family norms" are irrelevant. Smaller family sizes and the lifestyles that accompany them are creating new merchandising opportunities. These householders have more discretionary income and spend more money on restaurant eating, educational products, and travel services. Their homes are typically smaller than in the past, as are their furnishings.

8. The decline in the number of children is being accompanied by an increase in adult-oriented lifestyles. More and more adult-oriented programming is available to households through cable television and the networks. The popularity of adult soap operas reflect this trend in society, as do restaurants such as TGI Friday's.

9. The yuppies (young urban professionals) are getting older. The number of people aged 35 to 44 increased approximately 37 percent during the 1980s. The number of people aged 25 to 34 increased almost as rapidly. These householders typically have two incomes, are well educated, and have the money to support their lifestyle preferences. Such households now account for one-third of the U.S. population and almost half of all household income.

The yuppies are placing more emphasis on their homes than they did when they were in their twenties (see Case 1 at the end of the chapter).

They are purchasing more expensive home furnishings and quality art, are major consumers of services, and engage in do-it-yourself projects.

A new phrase has entered our language to reflect the values of the aging yuppie. They are known as couch potatoes and practice what is popularly described as "cocooning." They are increasingly inclined to buy things that provide control, comfort, and security against what they perceive as a harsh outside world. Domino's Pizza, capitalizing on this lifestyle, became a national force in the pizza business by providing home delivery. The La-Z-Boy Showcase Shops have profited from this trend, which has also fueled retail markets for VCR ownership and video tape rentals.

10. Families earning more than $50,000 a year are rapidly increasing in number, although they still comprise no more than 5 percent of the population. Affluent buyers seek products and services that reflect their self-image and are interested in aesthetics as much as performance. From retailers, they seek the highest-quality merchandise that reflects prestige and fashion. They expect high-quality service and expert consultation.

Affluent dual-income households provide strong markets for luxury products such as satellite dishes, boats, and premium cars. Retailers such as Neiman-Marcus and Bloomingdale's are positioned to serve these markets.

11. The roles of the male and the female in the household are no longer as clearly defined as in the past. Women increasingly buy financial services and other previously male-oriented products. More and more men are becoming purchasers of household products, and young adults of both sexes are learning how to manage homes and cope with problems of school and education. Retail promotions increasingly are universal in content and not targeted specifically to either males or females.

12. One of the most dramatic changes has been the effect of technology on consumer lifestyles. The development of videocassette players led to the emergence of video outlets that specialize in renting movies and VCR equipment. Busy consumers are responding to the opportunity to view films at their convenience in the privacy of their homes rather than going to movie theaters. Microwave ovens have led to changes in the types of foods eaten, and in-home interactive shopping offered by the Home Shopping Network and other cable services is beginning to redefine how and when consumers shop.

13. Not all consumers are sharing in the affluence of some demographic segments. Some consumers, as part of their lifestyles, are very responsive to coupons and other promotions. They use generic products, buy at flea markets and garage sales, are willing to accept less service in return for lower prices, and actively seek goods that last longer and require less maintenance. Such consumers are responsible for the growth of warehouse outlets and off-price and outlet malls.

TABLE 7–3 ANALYSIS OF FASHION LIFESTYLES

Factor Number	*Factor Name*	*Representative Fashion Lifestyle Statement*
1	Fashion Consciousness	• I consider myself to be fashion/style conscious. • An important part of my life and activities is dressing smartly.
2	Price Consciousness	• I buy more clothing on sale than I do at regular prices. • I am very cost conscious when it comes to clothes.
3	Quality Consciousness	• For the amount of money, I will generally buy one good item rather than several of lower price and quality. • The quality of the merchandise I buy is more important to me than the price I have to pay.
4	Classic Tastes	• I prefer classic looks to more trendy looks in clothes. • I wait until new fashion looks have become well accepted before I buy them myself.
5	Fashion Disenchantment	• More and more, I find that no matter at which stores I shop, the fashions are all the same. • I'm finding it increasingly difficult to buy fashions that look good on me.
6	Advice-Seeking Tendency	• My apparel selections are strongly influenced by clothing worn by people I admire. • When shopping for a suit, I rely heavily on the advice of the salesperson.
7	Recreational Shopping (Shopping as fun)	• I love to shop for clothes. • I enjoy looking through fashion magazines.
8	Utilitarian Shopping (Shopping as a necessity)	• I make clothing purchases only when there is a need, not on impulse. • Because I have a very active lifestyle, I need clothes for many different kinds of occasions.

Source: Robert J. Kopp, Robert J. Eng, and Douglass J. Tigert, "A Competitive Structure and Segmentation Analysis of the Chicago Fashion Market," *Journal of Retailing*, 65 (Winter 1989), p. 507. Reproduced with permission.

14. Health awareness continues to be important in American society. Consumers are interested in being good to themselves. The result is a continuing growth in health club membership, the popularity of aerobics centers and diet centers, and restaurants featuring vegetarian cuisine.

15. The more money people have to spend, the less time they have to spend it. The most affluent households typically have two wage earners who have little time for shopping. As a result, they will gladly pay for time-saving goods and services ranging from lawn care to day care. They have also caused the rapid growth in deli operations, store-front medical clinics, and home-cleaning services. They demand convenience with accountability in the form of warranties and straight talk from retailers. Such consumers also seek high-quality recreation because of the limited amount of time available to them. They go to fashionable ski resorts, theme restaurants, and expensive golf and tennis resorts.

Segmenting Markets by Lifestyle

The information necessary to understanding lifestyle market segments is developed from consumer research. Marketing researchers question consumers about the merchandise they purchase; their media habits; and their activities, interests, and opinions.

Example. One study of 1,650 respondents yielded eight fashion segments (see Table 7–3) that can help you understand how **lifestyle segmentation** can be used in a retail setting.[8]

The eight segments are fashion consciousness, price consciousness, quality consciousness, classic taste, fashion disenchantment, advice-seeking tenancy, recreational shopping (shopping as fun), and utilitarian shopping (shopping as a necessity).

Lifestyle Merchandise Classifications

One of the trends in merchandising directed at males is selling to "the better young man," defined by the general merchandise manager of Saks Fifth Avenue as being 18 to 25 years of age and "a fashion-aware young man in a college or university, who doesn't have the budget yet for more expensive clothes." A representative of Carson Pirie Scott & Company says that this new category is an attitude—a lifestyle type of selling that borrows from the excitement of women's ready-to-wear merchandise.

Some stores have opened separate shops with an updated, traditional flair, giving fashion direction with designer jeans from such firms as Sasson. Levi Strauss's "Dockers" collection is also popular. Saks Fifth Avenue calls its better young man's shop the "Early On" and hopes to encourage its clientele to purchase designer collections, such as Geoffrey Beene and Calvin Klein.

Superspecialty Retailing

The superspecialists include such firms as Topps & Trousers, The Proving Ground, Sox Appeal, and County Seat. Their exceptional profitability and rapid growth have made them formidable competitors for department and general merchandise stores and small independent retail operations.

The stores offer a limited assortment of contemporary merchandise aimed at specific lifestyle segments, typically adults aged 18 to 35 with an interest in fashion.

Management is centralized, and the retailers are able to respond to market trends almost instantly. Personal service, breadth and depth in merchandise, and the ability to keep pace with fashion trends give these outlets a strong image relative to department stores and independent outlets.

The Role of Ambience

The essence of visual lifestyle retailing is reflected in the concept of **ambience** (or atmospherics). Ambience is a term loosely defined but critical to lifestyle merchandising. Adolph Novak, a leading store designer,

EXHIBIT 7–4

Courtesy Hard Rock Cafe

Hard Rock Cafe is an example of a store as theater.

defines ambience as "the general quality of design which expresses the character of a store, resulting in an institutional personality immediately recognized by the consumer public."

Ambience is a lifestyle reflection of two elements: (1) the interior decor, which includes everything within the store, such as walls, ceilings, floor, lighting fixtures, customer services, signing, and merchandise; and (2) exterior design. The interior and exterior designs should be in harmony. Exterior design often draws customers to the outlet by identifying the type or quality of the firm.

Considerable research has been done on ambience in the context of hedonic consumption as part of the overall lifestyle experience. **Hedonic consumption** has been defined as those facets of consumer behavior that relate to the multisensory and emotional aspects of the shopping experience and product consumption.[9] In other words, consumers may be attracted by sights, sounds, smells, color, and displays as part of the retailing experience.

An excellent example of store as theater is the Hard Rock Cafe in Los Angeles (Exhibit 7–4). The Cafe is a place that people do not easily forget.

Serving Customers with Unique Lifestyles

Continuing market fragmentation has made lifestyle sensitivity even more critical to retail success. Cultural differences require unique types of information for shoppers, as do pressures of time faced by professionals, exemplified by the need for longer store hours and personal shopping services. More knowledgeable salespeople are often required.

Information. Large retailers in such metropolitan markets as Miami, New York, and Los Angeles offer multilingual services to attract and serve foreign tourists. Many of these stores maintain lists of employees who speak foreign languages. Store directions and information pamphlets are sometimes printed in foreign languages. Saks Fifth Avenue has provided its international shopping service for more than 60 years. The service is offered free to make shopping easy for tourists.

Shopping Services. Shopping services are becoming increasingly popular with professionals. Customers make an initial visit to an outlet and provide retailers with essential measurements and other information needed to help make merchandise selection decisions. These customers can then call ahead and have several outfits assembled for their approval when they arrive at the store. Such services require creative talent of salespeople but can lead to significant plus sales for the outlet.

Store Hours. Longer shopping hours are especially common in suburban areas, where stores may be open late each night of the week and on Sunday to accommodate busy households. Sunday and evening hours are found less frequently in central business districts. Increasing numbers of two-income households will continue to demand that retail outlets remain open in the evenings and on Sundays.

Effects on Retail Salespeople. Retail salespeople have to identify with both the items being sold and the lifestyle of the customer buying the items. Department store branches also need to be merchandised to fit the lifestyles of the customers living in the local area. Scanning and information analysis technology is making such analysis and merchandising possible.

Better Promotion Efforts. Lifestyle merchandising is changing the media mix used by retailers. Various radio and television stations offer sports, "middle-of-the-road" music, ethnic programming, or all-news programs to reach audiences with specific lifestyles. Specialty catalogs and direct-mail promotions are targeted to specific lifestyles and customer interest groups, as we discussed in Focus 7–1.

Visual Merchandising. Creating the artistic environment that is essential to lifestyle merchandising requires a unique blend of lighting, background, and props. All visual merchandising themes should start with what the customer wants and should communicate important merchandise information. These points are discussed in further detail in Chapter 16.

UNDERSTANDING EMERGING GLOBAL LIFESTYLES

Global telecommunications, frequent cross-border travel, and a global economy are creating an international youth culture whereby fashion, music, and food are becoming part of a universal, international lifestyle that is essentially the same in Seattle, Madrid, and Osaka. "It is consumer-driven: drinking cappuccino and Perrier; furnishing the apartment with IKEA; eating sushi; dressing in the united colors of Benetton; listening to U.S.-British rock while driving the Hyundai over to McDonald's."[10] Groups of consumers in New York and Milan often have greater similarities than consumers do in Manhattan and the Bronx.

Television media deliver the same images around the world. McDonald's competes for the same expensive real estate whether in New York's Times Square, the Ginza in Japan, or the Champs-Elysées in Paris. Sushi bars have flooded the United States, Tex-Mex cuisine is served in Israel, and more than 25,000 oriental restaurants operate in the United States.

Fashion, especially, is becoming international in this era of global travel and telecommunications. Italian youths today tend to dress in blue denim, and Americans are switching to Italian suits. Fashion-conscious youth favor clothes from such international fashion retailers as Laura Ashley, Benetton, and Esprit, all outfitters of the global lifestyle. Benetton's "All the Colors of the World" oozes international flavor unmatched in history. Esprit, based in California, is also one of the world's leading sportswear merchants. Habitat, a British home furnishings merchant, operates its stores worldwide, as does IKEA, the Swedish unassembled furniture merchant, whose catalogs are published in 12 languages.

Global pricing is the result of global merchandising and global electronics. Prices are controlled electronically so that outlets around the world for any particular chain are largely immune to currency fluctuations. A Chanel suit sells for essentially the same price on Rodeo Drive, in Hong Kong, and in Paris.

The Wall Street Journal, the British-based *Economist,* and the *Financial Times* are transmitted around the world by satellite transmission. The *Economist* is read by people in more than 170 countries. Less than 25 percent of its readers live in Great Britain. Vast cultural exports from the United States essentially have conquered the world. The first all-American Disneyland outside the United States opened in Japan. EuroDisneyland opened in Paris in 1992.

English has emerged as a universal language as the cultures of English-speaking countries increasingly dominate world trends. More than 1 billion English speakers live in the world today. English is the language of the international youth culture, who are equally comfortable singing the lyrics of U2, Madonna, or Michael Jackson. Global lifestyles are slowly helping to overcome the cultural nationalism in Wales, Quebec, Iran, and Shanghai. No longer can progressive merchants think in terms of U.S. lifestyles only as nationalist borders become unimportant for other than political reasons.

Chapter Highlights

- Retailers can more readily meet the needs of customers if they understand how people spend their time and money and what they value. This type of information is called lifestyle analysis.
- Lifestyles are based on people's values. The forces affecting consumer values are the influence of family, religious institutions, schools, and early life experiences.
- Retail management philosophies concerning meeting the needs of consumers have evolved over time. Until the 1950s retailers were supply oriented. By the 1960s the marketing concept was widely accepted; it requires management to orient all activities of the firm toward the customer.
- Positioning, an extension of the marketing concept, emerged in the early 1970s. Management began to target their offerings to narrow groups of demographically defined consumers. By the mid-1970s, lifestyle merchandising emerged and emphasized the activities, interests, and opinions of consumers.
- The latest development in marketing strategy is a lifestyle portfolio of stores owned by a single organization with each store targeted toward the needs of a different group of consumers.
- The Stanford Research International VALS program offers retailers the opportunity to structure lifestyle-focused marketing programs. The SRI analysis combines the notions of psychological and material resources and shows the cultural role they play in the translation of psychological motivations into purchasing behavior.
- Society today is characterized by parents who spend less time with young children than in previous generations, high divorce rates, and the relative unimportance of religion. The increasing importance of schools in shaping the values of youth, decreasing family sizes, increasing number of single-person households, and the redefinition of the role of the male and female are affecting shopping behavior. Similarly, health awareness, poverty of time, and lifestyle changes brought about by dramatic changes in technology are redefining shopping behavior.
- Sensitivity to lifestyle differences affects the retailing strategist in various ways, including making him or her aware of the importance of lifestyle merchandise classifications, the psychological effects of design and layout on purchasing behavior, and ambience on targeted consumer markets.
- Retailers are offering personal shopper services in response to the expectations of certain lifestyle segments, seeking to match retail salespeople with the merchandise they are selling, and harmonizing visual merchandising displays with customer lifestyle segments.
- Understanding global lifestyles is becoming more important to the marketing strategy decisions of many retailers.

Study Questions

1. Define lifestyle and psychographics. What is the relationship of one to the other?
2. Summarize the changes occurring in society that are shaping consumer values. Discuss the resulting effects on retailer strategies.
3. Is demographic analysis as discussed in Chapter 4 less important when retailers become interested in understanding the influence of lifestyles on buying decisions?
4. Explain the role of in-store ambience in serving targeted lifestyle segments.
5. Why is it important for the backgrounds of salespeople to match the lifestyles of the customers they serve?
6. Why are the baby boomers such an important market segment for retailers? What are their most dominant lifestyle characteristics?

7. Are lifestyles becoming more global today or are they still primarily nation-specific?
8. Trace the differences in management philosophy between the homogeneous retailing philosophy of the 1950s, the marketing concept of the 1960s, the positioning philosophy of the 1970s, and lifestyle retailing in the 1990s.
9. How are analyses such as VALS valuable to retailers in planning their merchandising strategy?
10. Why are modern catalog and direct sales merchants prone to focus on lifestyle niches as opposed to the traditional broad-based catalogs that were used by firms such as Sears and J. C. Penney?

APPLICATIONS

CASE 1: GARDENING BLOOMS AS BABY BOOMERS DIG INTO AN ENVIRONMENTALLY CORRECT HOBBY

When Chicago ad executive Walter Radloff built a house recently, he made sure the lot was on the west side of the street. He wanted his new garden to catch the late afternoon sun.

Gardening is blossoming across the country as baby boomers discover this stay-at-home hobby. It can be either inexpensive or fashionably extravagant, and it is environmentally correct. Real estate brokers point out that it can increase the resale value of your house.

Baby boomers haven't had to abandon their trendy tastes either; they just grow their favorite variety of Italian lettuce themselves. Sales of fresh herbs—another yuppie favorite—doubled industry-wide in 1991 to $161 million, says the gardening association. Affluent gardeners don't even have to get too much dirt under their fingernails. Using bedding plants rather than seeds simplifies and speeds up the planting process. Much like cooking from prepared mixes, "there's no chance of failure," says Bruce Butterfield, the association's research director.

At White Flower Farm, a gardening catalog company in Litchfield, Connecticut, business is "definitely beginning to build," says Steve Frowine, a horticulturist. Yuppie gardeners want unusual, high-quality plants, he says, and White Flower Farms offers such prizes as a new day lily called Mallard in a "rich and strong" shade of red for $12.95. Also popular are certain European and Asian vegetables such as bok choy, for use in low-salt, low-cholesterol meals, Frowine says. "It's obsessive," he adds. "The boomers just keep acquiring things and buying the best."

Pricey gardening accessories are also big sellers. At Smith & Hawken mail-order company in Mill Valley, California, consumers are buying clothes for playing in the dirt. Popular items include baggy pants with insertable knee pads and seven roomy pockets for tools ($39), as well as plastic clogs with removable rubber insoles ($34 a pair).

Smith & Hawken says it can't keep enough of its hand tools—many of them imported from England—on the shelves. Also popular with environmentally conscious customers: its composter line and "beneficial bug lure." Teak benches for the garden, made from plantation wood so that they won't deplete the rain forest, are selling well despite price tags that range from $500 to $2,000. "They're expensive," the spokeswoman says, "but people are investing in their gardens."

Parents are also snapping up gardening paraphernalia for their children. Gardener's Supply Co., a mail-order firm in Burlington, Vermont, has experienced "very steady sales growth" since it opened in 1983, says spokesman Paul Conrad. But sales of child-size products like its $29 wheelbarrow and $24.95 hoe, rake, and shovel set surged in 1991, he says. "Gardening is a great family activity," Conrad says, "and a great antidote to Saturday morning cartoons." He adds that Gardener's Supply fields a steady string of requests for its "Kids and Compost—A Family Activity Guide."

Part of gardening's appeal is that it allows baby boomers to demonstrate how environmentally sensitive they are. Hot-selling items at Frank's Nursery & Crafts, the nation's largest lawn-and-garden retailer, include organic pesticides and bark mulches, which help conserve water and keep weeds under control, says a spokeswoman for the General Host Corp. unit.

Bricker's Organic Farm in Augusta, Georgia, has seen a "noticeable increase" in business in the past two years, says founder Bill Bricker. Its flagship product: Kricket Krap, a natural fertilizer made from cricket manure. The painted four-pound jars sell like hotcakes for $6.95 apiece through Bricker's mail-order service. "After they have a laugh, they come back for more," says Bricker.

Source: Portions reproduced with permission from Christina Duff, "Gardening Blooms As Baby Boomers Dig into an Environmentally Correct Hobby," *The Wall Street Journal*, March 11, 1992, p. B1. Reproduced with permission.

Applying Retailing Principles

1. Why are the baby boomers attracted to environmentally correct gardening as an increasingly popular hobby?
2. What attributes reflect the lifestyle merchandising strategies of White Flower Farm and Smith & Hawken?
3. Is gardening as a hobby likely to be faddish (as a result of the weak economy of the early 1990s) or is it likely to be a permanent trend as the baby boomers age?

CASE 2: TURNING CONSERVATIVE, BABY BOOMERS REDUCE THEIR FRIVOLOUS BUYING

The American middle class has been repeating the same cycle for decades. Wanting to feel prosperous and successful, it goes on a binge of conspicuous consumption. Then, debt-laden and disillusioned, it retreats to traditional values of financial security and a simpler life. Sometimes a recession acts as a catalyst.

The last retreat was the 1970s, amid overnight fascination with generic goods, home cooking, and self-service gas stations. E.F. Schumacher's "Small Is Beautiful" became a best seller. Now, it's happening again, as the shop-till-you-drop mentality of the 1980s fades away.

Yet this time, trend-watchers say, the swing of the pendulum could be more pronounced—and affect the economy far more deeply. The reason: it's happening just as baby boomers finally are starting to grow up. The generation that led the urge-to-splurge frenzy now finds itself up to its graying temples in responsibilities: children, mortgages, and retirement worries.

It doesn't take a psychologist to figure out that around age 40, which some baby boomers have already hit, is when youthful dreams yield to reality. And reality isn't always a party. Many baby boomers delayed childbearing so long that they now face the daunting task of saving simultaneously for college and retirement. Caring for aging parents, now living longer than previous generations, is another worry.

In addition, many boomers are realizing that their sheer numbers make it tough to get that next promotion. So they are hitting the inevitable career plateau—and earnings peak—relatively early.

Another change in many baby boomers is increased concern for matters beyond their own lives. Independent Sector Inc., a nonprofit coalition, reports big increases in their volunteerism and donations between 1988 and 1990.

But the transition to a more conservative lifestyle isn't always easy. In Evanston, Illinois, Steven Steiber and his wife, Deborah Silver, both 39, say that they are still adjusting to the pressures.

Much of Steiber's income, which exceeds $75,000 a year, is consumed by the big mortgage on their Cape Cod–style home and the monthly payment on a universal whole life insurance policy. Silver no longer has a paycheck because she is a stay-at-home mother to the couple's children, a four-year-old and infant twins.

They joke about their "Leave It to Beaver" lifestyle. But unlike Ward and June Cleaver, they worry—

and argue—about money. Steiber believes strongly that they should live within their means. Silver agrees in principle but feels frustrated by his insistence that they carry out their latest home-improvement project gradually instead of borrowing and doing everything at once.

Source: Portions reprinted with permission from Francine Schwadel, "Turning Conservative, Baby Boomers Reduce Their Frivolous Buying," *The Wall Street Journal*, June 19, 1991.

Applying Retailing Principles

1. Profile the lifestyle and buying behavior patterns of the baby boomers during the 1980s as contrasted to the 1990s.
2. What types of retailers are likely to benefit and what types are likely to lose as a result of changes in the lifestyles of the boomers?

Notes

1. "Lifestages: New Spiegel Strategy," *Stores*, July 1990, p. 52.
2. See John Huey, "What Pop Culture Is Telling Us," *Fortune*, June 17, 1991, pp. 89–92; Patricia Sellers, "Winning Over the New Consumer," *Fortune*, July 29, 1991, pp. 113–24; Susan G. Garland, Laura Zinn, Christopher Power, Maria Shao, and Julia F. Siler, "Those Aging Boomers," *BusinessWeek*, May 20, 1991, pp. 106–11; Thomas Palmer, "Americans Restitch the Family Fabric," *The Birmingham News*, March 1, 1992, p. C1.
3. Walter Salmon, "Backroom Keys to Profitability," paper presented at the January 1989 meeting of the National Retail Merchants Association in New York City.
4. John L. Lastovicka, John P. Murry, Jr., and Eric A. Joachimsthaler, "Evaluating the Measurement Validity of Life Style Typologies with Qualitative Measures and Multiplicative Factoring," *Journal of Marketing Research* 27 (February 1990), pp. 11–23.
5. Martha Farnsworth Riche, "Psychographics for the 1990s," *American Demographics*, July 1989, pp. 25–31.
6. Reproduced with permission from "New VALS 2 Values and Lifestyles Segmentation," *Stores*, 1989, p. 37. Copyright (c) The National Retail Federation. All rights reserved.
7. "Downward Mobility," *BusinessWeek*, March 23, 1992, pp. 56–63.
8. Robert J. Kopp, Robert J. Eng, and Douglass J. Tigert, "A Competitive Structure and Segmentation Analysis of the Chicago Fashion Market," *Journal of Retailing* 65 (Winter 1989), pp. 496–515.
9. Elizabeth Hirschman and Morris B. Holbrook, "Hedonic Consumption: Emerging Concepts, Methods and Propositions," *Journal of Marketing*, Summer 1982, pp. 92–101.
10. John Nesbitt and Patricia Aburdene, *Megatrends 2000* (New York: William Morrow and Company, 1990), p. 18.

PART 4

The Resources Needed to Compete

Thus far, the text has focused on the information that retailers need before they make decisions about competitive strategies. This part of the book, in contrast, addresses the resources needed to compete. Chapter 8 focuses on types of ownership, the sources of financing available, how changes occur in the organization of retail firms over time, issues in buying and selling a retail business, and problems in family-owned businesses. Chapter 9 discusses choosing the retail location. Location, site selection, and building decisions are important because these decisions have long-lasting effects on the retailer's profitability.

Finally, Chapter 10 provides a framework for understanding the personnel functions, including recruiting, training, and motivation of employees. Personnel costs are among the highest costs facing retailers.

C H A P T E R

8

Organizing and Financing the Retail Enterprise

THIS CHAPTER:

Explains the advantages and risks of ownership.

Reviews the legal forms of retail organization.

Highlights the problems and opportunities in buying and selling a retail business.

Explores the characteristics needed for success as an owner or manager.

Emphasizes the importance of planning in retail success.

Introduces the sources of operating capital available to retailers.

Explains the problems that can emerge in family-owned retail businesses.

RETAILING CAPSULE

CRATE & BARREL

Crate & Barrel Inc. is a privately held home furnishings chain based in Northbrook, Illinois, that in 1992 consisted of 36 outlets and a catalog operation. The owner, Gordon Segal, conceived the idea for Crate & Barrel in 1962 as a newlywed freshman out of Northwestern University working as a real estate agent. Late one night while washing the dishes with his wife, he began contemplating one of their plates, a German import purchased on a trip to New York City. He decided that "there must be other people in Chicago with good taste and no money."

Segal contacted European housewares manufacturers and negotiated shipments directly to Chicago, which allowed him to avoid markups by importers and wholesalers. He launched the business with $12,000 in savings and a $5,000 loan from his father. His first store, 1,600 square feet, was in a former grain elevator in the gentrifying section of Chicago called Old Town. Lacking money for fixtures, Segal displayed the merchandise, primarily plates, cookware, and glassware, on turned-over packing crates and barrels—hence the company name.

Segal over time used his cash flow to gradually start a second, then a third, and finally a fourth store. He then entered furniture retailing on a small scale, converting one of Crate & Barrel's smaller Boston stores into a furniture outlet. He used the store to test alternative types of furniture for sale and to establish relationships with suppliers. Segal then opened a second furniture store in 1989 and at the end of 1992 had five furniture locations. Segal is known as something of a trend setter for the "Crate look"—nothing too contemporary or too colonial with a little Shaker influence in the kitchen and a bit of a country look in the living room. Today, furniture accounts for 20 percent of Crate & Barrel revenues.

Segal's primary customers are women in their thirties, newlyweds, and older couples furnishing a second home. He offers these upwardly mobile

customers an assortment of home furnishings that is carefully selected and that costs roughly half what department stores charge.

Source: "Crate & Barrel Flagship Dazzles Chicago," *Chain Store Age Executive,* December 1990, pp. 114–55; Lisa Collins, "Crate Gets Report—A Customer at a Time," *Crain's Chicago Business,* November 26, 1990, p. 20; Lisa Collins, et al., "Recession, What Recession? Crate Can't Handle Crowds," *Crain's Chicago Business,* November 19, 1990, p. 8; Annemarie Mannion, "Crate & Barrel's New Store Reflects Its Image," *Chicago Tribune,* October 21, 1990, p. 14.

Many people share Gordon Segal's dream of owning their own business in spite of the long hours, the financial risks, and the fiercely competitive nature of retailing (Exhibit 8–1). One such person is Gary Comer, founder of Lands' End (see A Profile in Excellence).

More than 2 million retail businesses exist in the United States. Two-thirds of these firms have fewer than four employees, and 80 percent are single-unit establishments. Clearly, most retail businesses are small by any standard.[1]

THE REWARDS OF OWNERSHIP

The chance to do things *their way* is what makes most entrepreneurs tick. Freedom of action for retail entrepreneurs is more important than prestige, power, or money.[2] Making the rules, as opposed to working for a boss, is a common dream.

The retail owner's vision can be as idealistic as combating environmental deterioration or as trivial as establishing and enforcing a dress code. Regardless, the attraction is that the owner is establishing the values, setting the agenda, and defining the vision. Examples of such entrepreneurial visions are illustrated in Focus 8–1.

THE RISKS OF OWNERSHIP

The risks of ownership are high. Going-out-of-business signs are a part of every community. But aspiring entrepreneurs should not be discouraged from starting their own businesses if they are willing to take a risk because the rewards can be great.

Early Failure Is Likely

The first five years are the toughest for the business owner. Of the retailers who fail, almost 60 percent fail in the first five years.[3]

EXHIBIT 8–1

Courtesy Crate & Barrel

Crate & Barrel, the successful home furnishing chain, is a dream come true for entrepreneur and founder Gordon Segal.

One study of retail failures revealed the following facts: (1) the larger the size of the retail business, the greater the chances of survival; (2) the greater the degree of urbanization, the lower the rate of business survival; (3) retailers dealing in "big-ticket" items had a higher chance of survival than retailers dealing in "small-ticket" products; and (4) rates of survival were highest for corporations (50.8 percent), intermediate for partnerships (30.5 percent), and lowest for sole proprietorships (20.7 percent).[4]

The Causes of Failure

The most common reasons for failure are inadequate profits, unbalanced experience, poor sales, and unexpected expenses. Failure because of neglect, fraud, or disaster is unusual, as shown in Table 8–1.

Identifying growth opportunities can enhance the chances of success. For example, the number of appliance dealers, gas stations, and variety stores declined in the 1980s. The primary growth sectors, based on an increase in the number of stores, included fast-food outlets, bookstores, and consumer electronics stores, as shown in Table 8–2. The hot fields for

A Profile in Excellence

GARY COMER

Gary Comer, a member of the Forbes 400 since 1987, claims that Lands' End sprouted from his own personal experiences. Comer, a Chicago native who never attended college, started in the advertising business at Young & Rubicam upon graduation from high school. He worked there for 10 years and attained award-winning status as a copywriter. However, sailing was Comer's real love. The evolving changes in the sport that no company really understood bothered him. Thus, in 1963, Comer started Lands' End as a catalog supplier of sailboat hardware.

The early Lands' End catalogs were actually editorials written by Comer on the various aspects of sailing and the corresponding equipment. Soon readers started asking where foul-weather gear and duffel bags could be found. In response, Comer began a gradual expansion of his product lines. Primarily, he offered duffel bags, then sailing clothes, and eventually a more general line of casual clothing. By 1976 Comer realized that the casual lines of clothing and luggage were his most profitable items and discontinued sailing hardware and accessories.

Lands' End has a customer base of more than 4 million people, maintained by Comer's philosophy of customer service and loyalty to his company's casual and durable image. A typical customer is highly educated and professional, well-rounded both culturally and socially, and financially secure.

Despite his catering to the more prosperous section of American society, Comer remains relatively inconspicuous. In 1978 he relocated his company from Chicago to rural Dodgeville, Wisconsin. There he set up a 475,000-square-foot warehouse equipped with 575 phone lines.

Although Comer has begun to selectively expand his product lines at the request of his customers, he is wary of his products' becoming too upscale. Instead, he has chosen to focus on providing quality goods, getting them to the customer quickly, and providing the customer correct orders. This is all done while maintaining an atmosphere of friendly customer service.

the 90s, based on growth predicted by the U.S. Department of Labor, are restaurants and bars, employment agencies, grocery stores, computer services, hotels and motels, and management and consulting services.[5]

Systematic differences exist between businesses that survive and those that fail. The surviving retailers are more likely to use business plans, to get started with higher levels of operating capital, and to use professional advisors such as bankers, attorneys, and CPAs. Similarly, the owners are more likely to have a college degree, and to run the business full time as opposed to employing a professional manager.

STARTING A NEW RETAIL VENTURE

Would-be entrepreneurs interested in opening a new business can form a sole proprietorship, a partnership, or a corporation. The advantages and disadvantages of each form of business are shown in Table 8–3. Management may also decide to purchase an existing business instead of starting a new one. The forms of business are the same whether starting a new

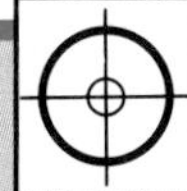

FOCUS 8–1

THE RETAIL ENTREPRENEUR'S VISION IS THE FOUNDATION FOR A NEW VENTURE

The Body Shop. Anita Roddick began with a vision in 1978. She wanted to create a company that would sell naturally based cosmetics that would never be tested on animals. Her company would fight to protect the environment and would commit itself to important social causes. It would avoid making miracle claims; in fact, it would shun all forms of advertising. (For further details, see the Retailing Capsule in Chapter 4.)

Ben & Jerry's. When Ben Cohen and Jerry Greenfield started their ice cream company in 1978 they were determined to establish a different kind of company: a portion of its profits would be plowed back into community projects, and a portion would be given to employees, suppliers, and others who made the business succeed. They also wanted to create a workplace that was productive, enjoyable, and equitable; among their most celebrated policies was one preventing the highest-paid worker from earning more than five times the lowest-paid worker. (The multiple is now seven.)

Just Desserts. Just Desserts, a San Francisco maker and retailer of bakery products, was founded by co-owner Elliott Hoffman on the belief that employees were typically not involved enough in business decisions.

So Hoffman introduced a unique participation plan for his 250 employees. Under the plan, employees in each of the company's seven stores write their own monthly business plans, including sales targets, budgets, and marketing strategies. If the seven stores together reach 95 percent of projected profits during any given month or quarter, a portion of the profits is distributed among all employees.

What common threads, if any, do you see in the visions behind the retail startups mentioned here?

Source: Portions reproduced with permission from Udayan Gupta, "Keeping the Faith," *The Wall Street Journal*, November 22, 1991, p. R16.

business or buying an existing firm. Franchising is also a popular option and is discussed in detail in Chapter 20.

The Sole Proprietorship

The sole proprietorship is usually defined as a business that is owned by one person. To establish a sole proprietorship, management need only obtain the necessary licenses and begin operations. It is therefore the most widespread form of retail organization.

Advantages. Less formality and fewer legal restrictions are associated with a sole proprietorship. It needs little or no governmental approval and is usually less expensive than a partnership or corporation. Furthermore, the proprietor is not required to share profits with anyone, and there are no co-owners or partners to consult (except possibly one's spouse). The

TABLE 8–1

COMMON REASONS FOR FAILURE

Underlying Causes	*Percentage**
Neglect	2.0
Fraud	0.9
Inadequate profits	22.2
Inexperience	12.0
Poor sales	19.8
Heavy expenses	11.7
Capital problems	14.7
Industry weakness	10.5
Other (poor location, high interest rates, competition)	5.3

*Because some failures are attributed to causes not shown, the total of major categories is less than 100%.

Source: Dun & Bradstreet Corporation.

TABLE 8–2

THE FASTEST-GROWING RETAILERS DURING THE PERIOD FROM 1980 TO 1990

	Percentage Increase in Number of Outlets
Fast-food outlets	78
Bookstores	76
Consumer-electronics stores	54
Newsstands	51
Chain drugstores	36
Jewelers	33
Chain supermarkets	32

Source: Based on *U.S. News and World Report,* July 8, 1991, p. 57.

TABLE 8–3 THE ADVANTAGES AND DISADVANTAGES OF EACH FORM OF OWNERSHIP

	Sole Proprietorship	*Partnership*	*Corporation*
Advantages	Easy to organize Easy to dissolve Owner keeps all profits	Easy to organize Greater capital availability Combined management experience	Limited financial liability Easier to raise capital Specialized management skills
Disadvantages	Unlimited financial liability Difficult to raise capital Limited life of firm The business is based on the heartbeat of one individual	Unlimited liability Divided authority Hard to dissolve	Complex government regulations Expensive to organize Various tax disadvantages

manager is thus able to respond quickly to business needs in his or her daily management decisions governed by various laws and good sense.

Disadvantages. The individual proprietor is responsible for the full amount of business debts, which may exceed his or her total investment. The liability extends to all the owner's assets, such as house and car. Additional problems of liability, such as physical loss or personal injury, may be lessened by obtaining proper insurance coverage.

The enterprise also has an unstable business life. It may be crippled or terminated upon illness or death of the owner. Less capital is usually available to a sole proprietorship than to other types of business organizations. Long-term financing is especially difficult to arrange.

A small business owner might select the sole proprietorship to begin with. Later, if he or she succeeds and wishes to expand, the owner can form a partnership or corporation.

The Partnership

The Uniform Partnership Act, adopted by many states, defines a partnership as "an association of two or more persons to carry on as co-owners of a business for profit." Although not specifically required by the act, written articles of partnership are customarily executed. These articles outline the contributions of each partner to the business (whether financial or managerial) and generally delineate the roles of the partners in the business relationship.

Some of the characteristics that distinguish a partnership from the sole proprietorship are the limited life of the partnership, unlimited liability of at least one partner, co-ownership of the assets, shared management responsibility, and shared partnership profits.

Advantages. Legal formalities and expenses are few compared with the requirements for creation of a corporation. Partners are usually motivated to apply their best abilities by direct sharing of the profits. Furthermore, in a partnership, it is often possible to obtain more capital and a better range of skills than in a sole proprietorship.

A partnership typically has a more flexible decision-making process than a corporation does. But it is less flexible than a sole proprietorship. The partnership, as with a sole proprietorship, is relatively free from government control and special taxation.

Disadvantages. A primary disadvantage is the unlimited liability of at least one partner. In addition, elimination of any partner constitutes automatic dissolution of partnership. However, the business can continue operations based on the right of survivorship and possible creation of a new partnership. Partnership insurance might be considered.

The partnership, as the sole proprietorship, is likely to have difficulty in obtaining large sums of capital compared to a corporation. This is particularly true of long-term financing. However, by using individual partners' assets, opportunities are probably greater than in a sole proprietorship.

The Corporation

The corporation is the most complex of the three types of business structures. We shall discuss only the general characteristics of the corporation. As defined by Chief Justice Marshall's famous decision in 1819, a corporation "is an artificial being, invisible, intangible, and existing only in contemplation of the law." In other words, a corporation is a legal entity distinct from the individuals who own it.

Formation. A corporation usually is formed by the authority of a state government. Corporations that do business in more than one state must comply with federal laws regarding interstate commerce as well as with state laws, which may vary considerably.

The procedure required to form a corporation is that subscriptions for capital stock must first be taken and a tentative organization created. Then, approval must be obtained from the Secretary of State in the state in which the corporation is to be formed. The approval is given in the form of a charter for the corporation, stating the powers and limitations of the enterprise.

Advantages. A key advantage to the corporation is the limitation of each stockholder's liability to a fixed amount of investment. In the case of illness, death, or other cause that results in the loss of a principal (an officer or owner), the corporation continues to exist and do business.

It is also relatively easy to secure long-term financing from lending institutions by taking advantage of corporate assets and the personal assets of principals as guarantors. (Personal guarantees are often required by lenders).

Disadvantages. A disadvantage is that the corporation's activities are limited by the charter and by various laws. However, some states do allow very broad charters. In addition, extensive government regulations and reporting requirements are imposed. Furthermore, less incentive often exists if the manager does not share in profits. Finally, the corporation faces double taxation—both on income from corporate profits and on individual salaries and dividends.

Subchapter S

The purpose of Subchapter S is to permit a retail business to have its income taxed to the shareholders as if the corporation were a partnership. This arrangement avoids the double tax. Another advantage is that shareholders can offset business losses incurred by the corporation against their income. The partners' loss exposure is limited to the amount of their investment.

The Limited Liability Company

Limited liability companies (LLCs) are emerging as attractive start-up vehicles in some states. LLCs offer the tax advantages of a partnership and the legal safeguards of a corporation. Chapter S corporations, for example, cannot have corporate shareholders, but shareholders are allowed under an LLC.

Corporations cannot juggle income and deductions. In contrast, LLC partnership members can divide income and tax liability in the most advantageous way. The allocation of profits and losses among partners, for example, may change from year to year to fit the individual tax needs of the partners. An additional benefit is that only the LLC's assets, not an individual's personal assets, are at risk. The LLCs do not limit partner activity, nor do they limit the number or types of owners, as S corporations do.[6]

Buying a Retail Business[7]

The retail entrepreneur often gets started by buying an existing business instead of starting a new one. Buying a retail business is a complex process. The potential buyer needs professional help from accountants, bankers, brokers, and attorneys on specific issues.

Decide on the Type of Retailing

The first thing to do is to think through the motives for wanting to purchase a business and the criteria in selecting one. The would-be entrepreneur needs to reflect on his or her experience, both vocational and avocational—what he or she is good at and enjoys.

Finding Sellers

Sellers are easy to find. Indeed, potential buyers can be overwhelmed by the options available.

Print Advertising. Business opportunity classified ads often contain descriptions of retail businesses for sale. Many ads are placed by intermediaries (business brokers), but some are placed directly by the owners. The larger local newspapers are the best source of ads for smaller privately held retail firms.

Business opportunity ads usually describe the business in several short phrases, keeping its identity anonymous, and list a phone number or post office box for reply. The ads are worded to demonstrate the business's best qualities, both financial and nonfinancial, and many include a qualifying statement describing the kind of cash investment or experience required.

Trade Sources. Trade sources can be a viable source of information on businesses for sale. Key people within an industry or in companies on the periphery of the industry, such as suppliers, often know when businesses come up for sale. Every retail sector has a trade association, and trade association publications can also do a good job of advertising a business for sale.

Evaluating the Business

The buyer needs to begin by reviewing the history of the business and its operating procedures. Find out how the business was started, how its mission may have changed since its inception, and what past events have occurred to shape its current form. The potential buyer needs to understand the retailer's methods of acquiring and serving customers and how the functions of sales, marketing, finance, and operations interrelate.

The business' financial statements, operating documents, and practices should also be reviewed.

Income Statement. The potential earning power of the business should be analyzed by reviewing profit and loss statements for the past three to five years. It is important to substantiate financial information by reviewing the business's federal and state tax returns. The business's earning power is a function of more than bottom-line profits or losses. The owner's salary and fringe benefits, noncash expenses, and nonrecurring expenses should also be calculated.

Financial Ratios. Sales and operating ratios should be calculated to identify areas requiring further study. Key ratios are the current ratio, quick ratio, accounts receivable turnover, and inventory turnover. Terms defined in basic finance and accounting classes. The significance of these ratios, the methods for calculating them, and industry averages are available through sources such as Dun & Bradstreet, Robert Morris Associates, and the small business reports produced by the Bank of America. Look for trends in the firm's ratios over the past three to five years. Chapter 12 contains a detailed discussion of ratios and other measures of performance evaluation.

Financing the Business

A buyer's source of financing depends in part on the size of the business being purchased. The majority of retail firms (particularly the smaller ones) are purchased with a significant portion of the purchase price financed by the owner. The buyer, however, still must make a down payment on the remainder and have adequate working capital sources available.

If the funds needed for the down payment are not readily available, the buyer must look for financing from an outside source. To grant such financing, the lender is almost certain to require personal collateral for the loan as well as a compendium of financial and operating data on the business to be acquired.

Pricing the Retail Enterprise

Buyers and sellers usually do not share the same perspective about the worth of a retail enterprise. Each has a distinct rationale, and that rationale is usually based on a combination of logic and emotion. For the transaction to succeed, both parties must be satisfied with the price and understand how it was determined.

Factors That Determine Value. The topic of business evaluation is so complex that any explanation short of an entire book does not do it justice. The process takes into account many variables and requires that a number of assumptions be made. The most important factors include the following:

- Recent profit history.
- General condition of the firm, including condition of facilities, completeness and accuracy of books and records, morale, and so on.
- Market demand for the type of retail operation.
- Economic conditions, especially cost and availability of capital and any economic factors that directly affect the business.
- Ability to transfer goodwill or other intangible values to a new owner.
- Future profit potential.

Rule-of-Thumb Formulas. Rule-of-thumb formulas do provide a quick means of establishing whether a price for a certain business is in the ballpark. Formulas are normally calculated as a percentage of either sales or asset values, or a combination of both.

Typical formulas are as follows: beauty salon, .25 to .75 times gross income, plus equipment and inventory; gas station, $1.25 to $2.00 per gallon pumped per month; grocery store, .25 to .33 times gross income, plus inventories; restaurants, .25 to .50 times gross income; car dealership, 1.25 to 2.0 times net income, plus equipment and inventory.[8]

Comparables. Using comparable sales as a means of valuing a firm has the same inherent flaw as rule-of-thumb formulas. Rarely, if ever, are two businesses truly comparable. However, businesses in the same industry do have some characteristics in common, and a careful comparison may allow conclusions to be drawn.

Balance Sheet Methods of Valuation. This approach calls for the assets of the business to be valued. It is most often used when the business being valued generates earnings primarily from its assets rather than from the contributions of its employees, or when the cost of starting a business and getting revenues past the break-even point doesn't greatly exceed the value of the firm's assets.

Income Statement Methods of Valuation. Although a balance sheet formula is sometimes the most accurate method to value a retail business, it is more common to examine an income statement. Income statement methods are most concerned with the profits or cash flow produced by the business' assets.

The Role of Advisors

A variety of resources are available for buyers who want to obtain professional advice. These resources include business owners in the industry, Small Business Administration counselors, industry consultants, business valuation experts, accountants, and attorneys. Each of these resources can be of assistance, and each has its limitations.

Business owners, SBA counselors, consultants, and intermediaries are the best source of industry information and operating suggestions. SBA, SCORE (Service Corps of Retired Executives), and ACE (Active Corps of Executives) counselors provide their service free of charge and can be reached through local SBA offices. Business owners may be willing to give free advice, and they are often the best source of information. No one knows more about an industry than someone who is successfully running a business in it.

Accountants are best used to perform an audit (if one is needed), to help interpret financial statements, or to provide advice in structuring the transaction to minimize tax consequences for the buyer and seller.

Probably the most often consulted advisor is an attorney. Attorneys are asked to do everything from assessing the viability of the business and appraising its value to negotiating the purchase price and preparing the necessary documents. Attorneys, however, cannot assess the viability of a business. That is something only the buyer can do. Attorneys also generally cannot value a business, but they can occasionally help negotiate a price between buyer and seller.

Structuring the Transaction

Taxes and other factors have an important effect on the overall value of the transaction to the principals. Each type of structure carries with it different tax consequences for the buyer and seller.

Asset Versus Stock Transactions. The purchase of a business can be structured in either of two basic formats: the purchase of the stock or the purchase of the assets.

Asset Transactions. In an asset transaction, the assets to be acquired are specified in the contract. Practices vary from industry to industry but, in general, all the assets of the business except cash, accounts receivable, and liabilities are transferred to the buyer.

Stock Transactions. Stock transactions generally call for all of the assets, liabilities, and stock to be transferred to the buyer. In some cases, the buyer may choose not to accept certain assets or liabilities.

Installment Sales. It is rare for privately held retail firms to change hands for all cash prices. Almost all transactions are structured as installment contracts that provide for the seller to receive some cash, but that require the new owner to finance the bulk of the purchase price. For smaller privately held retail firms, the down payment often ranges from 10 to 40 percent of the selling price, and the buyer executes a promissory note (secured by the assets of the business) for the balance.

THE IMPORTANCE OF PLANNING[9]

In beginning the new business, proper planning is the most important ingredient in success. Effective planning will do more than anything else to help avoid failure. Success and planning go together.

The new owner or manager should take the following steps in beginning the planning process:

1. Plan together with partners or associates.
2. Make performance expectations clear to everyone.
3. Provide for feedback on progress to keep plans on track.
4. Make plans goal oriented rather than activity oriented.
5. Remember that hard work is vital to success but that this should be accompanied by efficient work.

There are no set requirements for the contents of a business plan. The most important consideration is the quality of the plan, not its length. Suggested contents for a business plan follow. Each plan will be different and subject to variations on this list, but these suggestions will at least help the owner to get started.

1. Summary of the mission of the retail firm—just a few paragraphs on what the owner is doing and his or her plans for the future.
2. A paragraph each on the retail industry in the community as a whole, the company, and its products or services.
3. Market research and analysis:
   a. Consumers.
   b. Market size and trends.
   c. Competition.
   d. Estimated market share and sales.
4. Marketing plan:
   a. Overall marketing strategy.
   b. Pricing.

TABLE 8–4 OPERATING COSTS AND OPERATING EXPENSES FOR A TYPICAL RETAIL BUSINESS

Opening Costs	*Operating Expenses*
Inventory	Rent (including one month's deposit)
Fixtures and equipment	Taxes, licenses, and permits
Leasehold improvements (wiring, plumbing, lighting, air conditioning)	Advertising and promotion
Security system	Legal and accounting fees
Exterior sign	Wages (including owner's)

- *c.* Sales tactics.
- *d.* Service.
- *e.* Advertising and promotion.

5. Management team:
   - *a.* Organization.
   - *b.* Key management personnel—who are they and what will they do?
   - *c.* Ownership and compensation.
   - *d.* Board of directors.
   - *e.* Any supporting services.
6. The financial plan (the owner may need accounting help):
   - *a.* Profit and loss forecasts.
   - *b.* Pro forma cash flow analysis.
   - *c.* Pro forma balance sheets.
7. Proposed company offering:
   - *a.* Desired financing.
   - *b.* Capitalization.
   - *c.* Use of funds.
8. Overall schedule of activities for the next three years.

OPERATING CAPITAL NEEDED

After the business plan is developed, sources of capital must be obtained. The main thing to do is avoid an early shortage of funds. Retailers therefore need to begin by estimating the capital needed to open and operate a business. Many have a tendency to underestimate starting capital.

Overall, 18 percent of small businesses are launched with capital of less than $5,000. More than 73 percent are launched with capital of $50,000 or less.[10]

Retailers need to plan for two categories of costs: (1) **opening costs,** which are one-time costs such as the cost of fixturing and decorating, and (2) **operating expenses,** which are the estimated ongoing expenses of running the business for a designated time period. Examples of these costs are shown in Table 8–4. Operating expenses are shown in more detail in Table 8–5. Most retail businesses have the same expense categories.

TABLE 8–5

TYPICAL EXPENSE CATEGORIES

Expenses
Wages (including owner's salary and payroll taxes)
Rent
Utilities
Advertising and promotion
Supplies
Depreciation
Insurance
Legal and accounting fees
Maintenance and repairs
Auto expenses
Taxes, licenses, and permits
Miscellaneous

Developing a Cash Flow Forecast

Cash flow projections are helpful in planning for the opening and for unforeseen difficulties. They are necessary when approaching a bank about loans.

A cash flow forecast is designed to predict when the firm will receive cash and when it must make payments. Cash inflow and outflow vary by type of retailer, especially for firms that experience highly seasonal sales.

Management can use a cash budget, as shown in Table 8–6, to help estimate cash flow. **Negative cash flow** (which occurs when outlays exceed income) should be funded with the initial capital developed for the new venture. Retailers can base the projections on experience or on trade association statistics, from trade magazines, and from bankers. A retailer should know approximately what the operating costs and the cash inflow will be before opening the business. Enough money to cover all expenses for about six months is needed. Management should be conservative if it is uncertain about how much money is needed. It should borrow too much rather than too little, in order to avoid having to come back later for additional funds.

As shown in Table 8–6, anticipated cash sales for a hypothetical retail jewelry store in the first three months of operation are $53,000, $58,000, and $66,000 per month. Average monthly sales based on a yearly sales forecast of $750,000 are $62,500 ($750,000 divided by 12). Management expects to lose $200 at the end of the first month, to break even at the end of the second month, and to show a profit at the end of December. December is traditionally a very strong month for jewelry sales. Conceivably, the business could lose funds during the early part of the following year because 50 percent or more of jewelry sales typically are made in the last three months of the year.

Sources of Funds

We will illustrate how merchants can get the capital they need. Suppose that a son of the owner of Stein's jewelry store decides to go into business. He has worked for the family business for 10 years, in addition to part-time

TABLE 8–6 PROJECTED CASH FLOW BUDGET FOR THREE MONTHS ENDING DECEMBER 19——

	October	*November*	*December*
Anticipated cash receipts			
Cash sales	$53,000	$58,000	$66,000
Payment for credit sales	2,000	4,000	4,500
Other income			
Total receipts	55,000	62,000	70,500
Anticipated payments			
Cost of merchandise	27,500	31,000	32,250
Payroll	20,000	21,000	21,500
Promotion	4,000	4,500	6,000
Sales commissions	1,200	1,300	1,600
Loans to be repaid	1,500	1,500	1,500
Maintenance	—	100	300
Utilities	600	600	700
Outside accounting and legal fees	400	2,000	1,300
Total	55,200	62,000	65,150
Expected surplus at end of month	(200)	—	5,350
Desired cash operating balance	2,000	2,000	—
Short-term loan needed	2,000	2,000	—
Cash available	—	—	5,350

and summer work. He wants to be on his own, and his family has given its blessing.

Using the logic suggested earlier in the chapter, young Stein computes that he will need the following capital:

Operating expenses for six months	$175,000
Opening costs (fixtures, equipment, leasehold improvements)	50,000
	$225,000

Equity. Over the years Stein has saved and inherited enough to "comfortably" cover 45 percent of his capital needs. Thus, he needs an additional $123,750 ($225,000 × .55).

Suppliers. Stein's projected annual sales are $750,000. Assume a markup of 50 percent on retail, and two merchandise turns per year. **Retail markup** is the difference between the invoice cost and the retail price. **Merchandise turns** are the number of times the average inventory is sold and replaced in a given time period. On the basis of our assumptions, Stein can probably receive financing from suppliers of $31,875 based on the terms of sale of net 30 (invoice must be paid within 30 days to maintain a good credit rating) with no discount for early payment. The computations are as follows:

$$\frac{\text{Projected annual sales} \times \text{percentage markup}}{\text{Number of turns}} = \frac{\$750{,}000 \times .50}{2}$$
$$= \$187{,}500 \text{ total cost of inventory for 6 months}$$

Therefore, $187,500 must be financed. With terms of 30 days to pay, Stein can probably get financing for one-sixth (or 17 percent) of the inventory needed for one turnover period, which is six months (30 days is one-sixth of the six-month turnover period based on two turns per year). Thus, the amount financed by suppliers should be calculated as follows:

$$\$187{,}500 \times .17 = \$31{,}875$$

Stein still needs $91,875 additional capital ($123,750 − 31,875 = 91,875).

Financial Institutions and Government. With his relatively healthy equity investment, Stein would probably be successful in securing loans from banks to assist in financing inventory and accounts receivable as well as some fixed assets, although inner-city retailers are likely to have problems—see A Question of Ethics. The Small Business Administration, though often considered a difficult avenue because of the complexity of its process, is a source of help. The agency can guarantee a percentage of the loan made by a commercial bank to the new venture.

To continue the scenario, assume that Stein has secured his permanent capital needs. His jewelry store has been in operation for some time. He has brought in additional partners as owners; he has increased his sales; his receivables have grown; and he needs more financing.

Stein can generate his capital needs to meet these new obligations from either internal or external sources. The major way to generate capital inside the firm is from profitable operations. His external sources of capital have been discussed previously, but once the business is profitable, he may be able to issue stock or bonds if the business is a corporation or sell a part of the interest to a partner.

PROBLEMS IN THE FAMILY-OWNED RETAIL BUSINESS[11]

More than three-fourths of the firms in America are family owned or controlled. So chances are good that many aspiring retail owners will go into the family business.

Whenever people put up money and operate a business, they prize their independence. "It's my business," they tell themselves, in good times and in bad times.

However, it's "our" business in a family retail company. Conflicts sometimes abound because relatives look upon the business from different viewpoints.

A Question of Ethics

INNER-CITY RETAILERS ARE STARVED FOR CAPITAL

Corporate America has wailed about a credit crunch restraining it in recent years, but it has gone through nothing like the credit starvation that is a governing condition of inner-city retailers. Here one can see all the usual worries that go with running any business, plus the myriad woes of the ghetto.

During the 1970s, banks began an exodus from neighborhoods like these, says John Caskey, a Swarthmore College economist who has researched patterns of bank branch closings. In five cities that Caskey studied, the total number of bank branches rose to 447 in 1989 from 302 in 1970, but banks pulled out of poor neighborhoods as they opened branches in wealthier communities. He found that 23 percent of richer neighborhoods had bank branches in 1970, and that figure rose to 43 percent in 1989. But only 18 percent of the poorer areas had branches in 1970, and that fell to 14 percent in 1989. "There is a clear avoidance of minority neighborhoods," he says, "that shows up even after adjusting for income."

"You don't want to have 18 or 20 percent money," says Emmanuel Dickey, who employs four people in his hardware store. "That's the financial woe for a small-businessman." Yet the alternative usually is to have no money at all. Many business owners in Dickey's neighborhood have stories about being denied needed capital, or getting it only at a rate that can kill a business.

A few doors away, at Gifts By Gail, owner Gail Oliver says the cost of simply putting together the documentation for a loan has always deterred her from dealing with banks. In the past, she says, "I've been to the high-interest boys," and she paid an annualized rate of well over 100 percent.

The proliferation of such high-cost competitors, from pawn shops to fly-by-night lenders to high-priced finance companies, provides another indirect indicator of the retreat of banks from the inner city.

Of course, there is an array of government programs, federal, state, and local. But in many cases, the experiences of inner-city business owners with those programs have been "horrific," says Michael Crescenzo, vice-president for Arch Development Corp., a nonprofit development company funded by a local utility company.

In the rare instances when loans are approved, they are usually the result of assiduous efforts by local, private, nonprofit community development corporations. Using private resources, unencumbered by the red tape that entangles government lenders, they improve the odds for getting a local business loan approved.

Are banks justified in their tendency to avoid making loans to inner-city merchants?

Source: Portions reproduced with permission from Jonathan Moses, "Credit Where Due? Small Businesses, Key to Urban Recovery, Are Starved for Capital," *The Wall Street Journal,* June 11, 1992, p. 1.

Relatives who are inactive partners, stockholders, and directors see only dollar signs when judging capital expenditures, growth, and other major matters. Relatives who are engaged in daily operations judge matters from the viewpoint of the things necessary to make the firm successful. Obviously, these two viewpoints may conflict.

Basically, the problems facing the manager of a family-owned business are the same as those confronting the owner-manager of any retail firm. But the job of the "family manager" is complicated because of the relatives who must be reconciled to the facts of the marketplace and the counting house.

When the Sparks Fly

Different opinions do not always produce discord, but sometimes they cause sparks to fly. Emotion is an added dimension as brothers and sisters, uncles and aunts, nephews and nieces, and parents and children work together in a small business.

Another aspect of the emotional atmosphere is that nonfamily employees often tend to base their decisions on family tensions. They know how their bosses react and are influenced by this knowledge.

Is the Manager Really in Control?

In many family-owned retail businesses, the elder statesman of the family becomes president or chairman of the board of directors. But day-to-day management is in the hands of other members of the family.

One way to obtain objective control in a family-owned business is to hire an outsider to manage the day-to-day operations, when the company can afford it. Any manager may become as biased as any other family member. With a hired manager, the family members will have their hands full in setting policies and in planning for growth. An efficient hired manager will see to it that all employees—family and nonfamily alike—know whom to report to at all times.

The manager's authority to suspend or discharge flagrant violators of company rules should also be spelled out. Management control is weakened if special allowances are made for family employees.

An important question connected with authority is this: who takes over when something happens to the family member who heads the business? A position may be up for grabs if the family hasn't provided for an orderly succession. This need is especially critical when the top family member is approaching retirement age or is in poor health.

Your Brother-in-Law Needs a Job?

One of the most common problems in a family retail business is the unavoidable request to hire relatives who do not have talent. But what is a person to do when a sister or another close relative says, "Bob really needs a job"? The emotional aspect of such family relationships is hard to fight. But relatives should try to go into it with their eyes open. It will be hard to fire Bob if he turns out to cost more money than his presence is worth.

The key is to see that the nontalented relative does not affect the relationship the owner or manager has with other members of the staff. Other employees will respect a determination to keep relatives in line.

Is Nonfamily Turnover High?

Some family-owned retail companies are plagued with high turnover among their nonfamily managers. Sometimes relatives are responsible. They resent outside talent and, at best, make things unpleasant for nonfamily executives. In other cases, top-notch managers and workers leave because promotions are closed to them. They see the relatives being pushed into executive offices. The exit interview is a useful device for getting at the root of this type of turnover.

Spending to Save Money?

The owner-manager may feel the need to make an expenditure to improve efficiency, and other family members might oppose this expenditure. They view it as an expense rather than an investment. They believe that funds spent for items such as more efficient equipment encroach on their year-end dividends.

One way to help these relatives see that you have to spend money to make money is to base the arguments for the expenditures on facts and figures that nonfamily employees have gathered. If the opposing relatives refuse to accept internally generated projections, call in outside business advisors. Relatives will sometimes believe advisors such as a banker, accountant, or attorney when they won't accept a relative's judgment.

Status Quo Blocks Growth

When some of the relatives in a family-owned retail business grow older, they tend to become attached to the status quo. They don't want things to change and are afraid of risk. With this attitude, they can, and often do, block growth in the family business.

The solution to such a problem is to urge or suggest that the status quo members slowly disappear from the scene of operation. One way is to dilute their influence in management decisions. For example, the status quo relatives might sell some of their stock to younger relatives. Status quo relatives might also be persuaded to consider gradual retirement.

How Is the Pie Divided?

Paying family members and dividing profits among them can also be a difficult affair. Many people believe that they are underpaid, but relatives who comment as follows generally feel an unusual amount of resentment:

"Uncle Jack sits around and gets more than I do."

"Aunt Sue goes to Europe on the returns of money her husband put into the business before he died 10 years ago."

"Your brother goofs off and rakes in more than you do."

How can these complaints be resolved? They can't be, entirely. But if the business is a small corporation, certain equalizing factors can be accomplished through stock dividends.

Salaries are best handled by paying amounts competitive with those paid in the area. Find out what local salary ranges are for various management jobs and use these ranges as a guide for paying both family and nonfamily personnel. When you tie pay to the type of work that the individual does, it is possible to show disgruntled relatives the value that the industry puts on their jobs.

Fringe benefits can also be useful in dividing profits equitably among family members. Benefits such as deferred profit sharing plans, pension plans, insurance programs, and stock purchase programs offer excellent ways to placate disgruntled members of the family and at the same time help them to build their personal assets.

SELLING THE RETAIL BUSINESS

The Decision to Sell

Retailers choose to sell for a variety of reasons:

- Retirement.
- Partnership dispute.
- Diminished interest in the business caused by boredom or frustration.
- Illness or death of one of the principals.
- Sales and earnings have plateaued because the company lacks the working capital or management resources to grow.
- Losing money.

Selling a retail business is different from selling any other asset one owns because a business is more than an income-earning asset. It is a lifestyle as well. The decision to part with it can be an emotional one. Personal ambitions should be weighed against economic consequences to achieve a properly balanced decision to sell or not.

It is said that timing is everything, and certainly that old axiom is true as applied to the decision to sell a business. Intelligent retailers carefully plan the decision to sell. They recognize that a business should be sold only after proper preparation and not because of sudden personal frustration or a short-term downturn in sales.

Preparing the Business for Sale[12]

Nearly every privately held retail firm is operated in a manner that minimizes the seller's tax liability. Unfortunately, the same operating techniques and accounting practices that minimize tax liability also minimize the value of a business. As a result, there is often a conflict between running a retail business the way an owner wants and preparing the business for sale.

Although it is possible to reconstruct financial statements to reflect the actual operating performance of the business, this process may also force the owner to pay back income taxes and penalties. Therefore, plans to sell a business should be made years in advance of the actual sale. This will permit the time required to make necessary changes in accounting practices that demonstrate a three- to five-year track record of maximum profits.

Audited statements are the best type of financial statements because they are most easily verified by the buyer. Good financial statements don't eliminate the need to make the business aesthetically pleasing. The business should be clean, the inventory current, and the equipment in good working order. Next, a valuation report should be prepared. The valuation report eliminates guesswork and the painful trial-and-error method of pricing that so many owners rely on. Finally, a business presentation package should be prepared. All facets of the business should be addressed in this document.

Chapter Highlights

- The most common reasons for failure in retailing are management incompetence, unbalanced experience, and lack of experience in the line of trade. Failure caused by neglect, fraud, or disaster is unusual.
- Many people enter retailing by buying an existing business. Such people have to decide on the type of business they want to buy based on their interests, skills, and experience, as well as the financing they can arrange.
- Opportunities to buy a business can be discovered by working with business brokers, studying newspaper ads, and contacting trade sources.
- In deciding whether to buy a business, the potential buyer should determine why the business is for sale, whether a profit is being earned, what the operating ratios of the business are as compared to industry averages, and what the worth of the business assets is.
- Capital is needed for two categories of cost in starting a business: opening costs, which are one-time costs, and operating expenses, which are the estimated ongoing expenses of running the business.
- Sources of cash include owner's equity, the credit available from suppliers, loans from financial institutions, government agencies, and the sale of stock.
- Retailers have the choice of forming a new business as a sole proprietorship, a partnership, or a corporation. Alternatively, they can operate as an independent firm or become part of a marketing system.
- Many retail organizations operate as family-owned businesses. Problems can abound in such situations because of emotional conflicts, conflicts over who is really in control, different goals for the rate and amount of growth, and ways that profits will be shared.

Study Questions

1. Why are the risks of business ownership so high?
2. What are the major causes of retail business failure?

3. Evaluate the strengths and weaknesses of each of the three forms of private business ownership (sole proprietorship, partnership, and corporation).
4. What are the advantages of a Subchapter S corporation arrangement?
5. How does a retailer determine the amount of capital needed?
6. Describe the various sources of capital that are available to a new retailer.
7. What problems are likely to be encountered in a family-owned retail business?
8. What are the key financial ratios a retailer needs to examine in deciding whether to buy a business? What do each of these ratios measure?
9. What factors determine the value of a retail business?
10. What does the retailer need to do in preparing a business for sale?

APPLICATIONS

CASE 1: Spaghetti Warehouse

Robert Hawk opened the Spaghetti Warehouse in 1970 in an abandoned pillow factory on the west side of downtown Dallas. He turned it into a family-style Italian restaurant offering basic pasta dishes at prices that college students and young families could afford. The business was so successful that he quit his full-time job after six months. At the end of 1991, the Spaghetti Warehouse had restaurants in some 20 cities and $43 million in annual sales with an average five-year return on equity of 14.5 percent.

The basic fare is simple: 11 different made-from-scratch pasta sauces as well as lasagna, manicotti, cannelloni, and chicken parmigiana. The restaurants are about 15,500 square feet with 450 seats. Lunch is less than $6, and the average dinner bill, minus alcoholic beverages and tip, is around $8. The firm has continued to prosper, even in the recent difficult economic times, because people do not stop eating out in bad times. They simply shift to less expensive options.

The Spaghetti Warehouse pursues a strategy that allows it to keep prices low and profits high. Management picks up old factories and warehouses in run-down areas of inner cities as a source of inexpensive real estate. An example is the purchase of an abandoned furniture warehouse in Oklahoma City in 1989 for $187,000. Management received a $100,000 tax credit for renovating the building because it was in a historic area. The company was then able to spend around $2 million in refurbishing the building.

The furnishings, typically picked up at auctions and junk shops, add to the entertainment value of each Spaghetti Warehouse. Restaurants are filled with mismatched tables and chairs, brass beds converted into seating, chandeliers, stained glass windows, eat-in trolley cars, and church confessionals turned into phone booths.

The basic pasta menu is inexpensive to prepare. Costs are minimized still further by centrally buying such staples as cheese, tomato sauce, and spaghetti directly from manufacturers. The service is kept high and costs low by paying managers year-end bonuses that range between 30 and 50 percent of their base pay. The bonuses are tied to the restaurant's profitability and sales growth. The result is that a typical Spaghetti Warehouse manager will earn almost $70,000, and the kitchen manager will earn at least $45,000. Hawk recently signed his first franchise agreements to locate Spaghetti Warehouses in Kansas, Tennessee, and southern California.

Source: Based on Claire Poole, "Crazy Like a Hawk," *Forbes*, November 11, 1991, pp. 248–49.

Applying Retailing Principles

1. Outline the ingredients of Hawk's competitive strategy.

2. How does Spaghetti Warehouse manage to maintain tight cost control while still providing customers with a high level of service?
3. Speculate on the reasons that Hawk has decided to franchise the Spaghetti Warehouse concept.

CASE 2: Small Retail Chain Switches Directions amid Changes Sweeping PC Industry

There was a time when being a computer dealer was practically a license to print money.

The computer revolution was new, and novice buyers relied on such dealers as Walter F. Manley III to steer them to reliable machines, even if it meant paying a little more. Corporate and individual customers flocked to the five First Step Computer stores Manley owned in the Richmond, Virginia, area because they were among the privileged few that carried Apple computers. The stores' annual sales grew to $20 million, and Manley grew comfortable.

But the changes sweeping the computer industry haven't spared anyone, least of all such midsized dealers as Manley. Many of his blue-chip brands, including Apple, Compaq, and IBM have been reduced virtually to commodities by a flood of low-cost clones. And new retail competitors are pouring into the market, turning the PC business into a seemingly endless round of price cutting.

Now, in a fight to save his business, the 36-year-old Manley is remaking First Step, concentrating on providing high-quality service to corporate clients while essentially writing off individual customers. "I don't pick fights with Arnold Schwarzenegger, and I don't compete with CompUSA in retail," he says.

For Manley, the most crippling blow came early in 1991, when Apple announced plans to sell its business computers to consumers in mass-market discount outlets. Manley and other long-time dealers fought the move, arguing that the computer maker would lose its cachet in the corporate world. "We'd spent years trying to convince businesspeople that Apple computers were more than high-tech Etch-a-Sketches," he says.

As First Step slipped into the red, Manley reassessed his strategy. His salespeople told him in no uncertain terms that they weren't making money on in-store sales to individuals; they needed to sell to big business. He agreed, even though giving up most of his walk-in traffic went against old habits; in the mid-1980s, the peak walk-in years, Manley estimates, about 60 percent of his business came from individuals. Now, they constitute less than 5 percent of his volume.

Adopting as his motto a phrase from an old-time baseball star—"Hit 'em where they ain't"—Manley closed his retail store closest to a CompUSA superstore and turned the rest of his shops into showrooms where his technically adept salespeople could pitch a range of computer products to corporate buyers, acting more as consultants than product pushers.

The new strategy seems to be working. Morale among the salespeople is high because they can use their expertise to win high-commission sales instead of working a sales floor filled with tire-kickers.

But First Step isn't out of the woods, and the strain is wearing on Manley and his family, says his wife, Lindsay Manley, who runs a decorating business from their home. Lindsay Manley says goodbye to her husband at 8 A.M. and usually doesn't see him again until 10 P.M. "Every day is a stress day," she says. "I ask, 'How was your day?' and he just says, 'Ohhh.' "

Manley is nagged by the fear that the computer manufacturers he considers his business partners will again shift their distribution strategies. An Apple representative was quoted in the trade press recently as saying that Apple hadn't ruled out selling its PCs by mail, which would cost Manley hundreds of thousands of dollars in sales.

"He said he won't sell mail-order, but that could change at a moment's notice," Manley says. He asks incredulously, "I've got millions of dollars invested in selling Apple computers, and his position could change at a moment's notice?"

Source: Portions reproduced from Jim Bartimo, "Retail Chain Switches Directions, Forced by Changes in PC Market," *The Wall Street Journal,* November 29, 1991, pp. B1–B2.

Applying Retailing Principles

1. Outline the stages in the evolution of retail computer stores.
2. Did Manley take the right steps in responding to the changing economic conditions in the PC industry?
3. What options are available to Manley if suppliers such as Apple Computer begin to aggressively sell by direct mail?
4. How can Manley determine when it is time to sell his business?

Notes

1. *Statistical Abstract of the United States,* U.S. Department of Commerce, 1991, p. 767.
2. Brent Bowers and Jeffrey A. Tannenbaum, "More Important than Money," *The Wall Street Journal,* November 22, 1991, p. R6; Bill Schwartz, "Twenty Reasons Why I Envy the Entrepreneur," *The Wall Street Journal,* November 22, 1991, p. R12.
3. "Least Likely to Succeed," *U.S. News and World Report,* October 23, 1989, p. 80.
4. Alvin Starr and Michael Massell, "Survival Rates for Retailers," *Journal of Retailing* (Summer 1981), p. 93.
5. "Hot Fields of the 90s," *U.S. News and World Report,* October 23, 1989, p. 80.
6. Jeffrey A. Tannenbaum, "Partnership, Corporation Aren't Only Ways to Start Out," *The Wall Street Journal,* May 14, 1991, p. B2.
7. Portions reproduced with modification from John A. Johansen, *Buying or Selling a Business,* Management Aid no. 2.029, U.S. Small Business Administration.
8. Teri Thompson, "When It's Time to Sell Out," *U.S. News and World Report,* June 26, 1989, p. 64.
9. Adapted with permission from Mark Weaver, "The Importance of Planning," in *How to Start a Successful New Business,* Tuscaloosa, Alabama, Chamber of Commerce.
10. "Start-Ups on a Shoe String," *U.S. News and World Report,* October 23, 1989, p. 78.
11. Portions reproduced with modification from Robert E. Levinson, *Problems in Managing a Family-Owned Business,* Management Aid no. 2.004, U.S. Small Business Administration, Washington, D.C.
12. For further reading see Jeffrey Tannenbaum, "How to Make the Most out of Selling a Small Business," *The Wall Street Journal,* February 22, 1990, p. B2.

C H A P T E R

9

Making the Location and Site Decision

THIS CHAPTER:

Explores the influence of shopper behavior on site and location decisions.

Explains the importance of competitive strategy in the location decision.

Emphasizes factors important in market area choice.

Addresses the importance of area analysis in site selection.

Reviews frequently used techniques in trading area estimation and sales forecasting.

Illustrates techniques for estimating the amount of business that can be done in a given area.

Highlights factors to consider in the decision to build, lease, or buy.

RETAILING CAPSULE

GEOGRAPHICS: KNOWING WHERE YOUR CUSTOMERS AND COMPETITORS ARE

Geographics (geographic information systems) became widely known during Operation Desert Storm. The new geographic software technology allows retailers to put stores and distribution centers on a map, overlay them with census data, track income areas, and determine where to open the next store. The power of the digitized maps becomes evident when they are displayed on a color graphics terminal.

Several factors are accelerating the explosive growth of geographics. First, the U.S. Bureau of the Census now sells street maps and economic and population data down to city blocks on compact discs. A 44-disc set of street maps that covers the entire United States is available for $11,000; national economic data on 17 discs cost an additional $1,700. Second, programmers have determined how to combine the census data with traditional retail databases such as lists of customers, mortgages, and registered car owners.

Third, the U.S. Supreme Court has ruled that phone directories are not covered by copyright. Thus, researchers can now buy compact discs of phone listings and merge the data with more traditional information found in retailers' files. A typical geographics assignment would be to produce a retail gravity model weighing demographic data based on the needs of a particular retailer. An auto parts retailer, for example, would weigh an analysis toward owners of foreign cars based on disks bought at the motor vehicle department.

Source: Based on David Cheerbrick, "Geographics," *Forbes,* January 6, 1992, pp. 262–67.

EXHIBIT 9–1

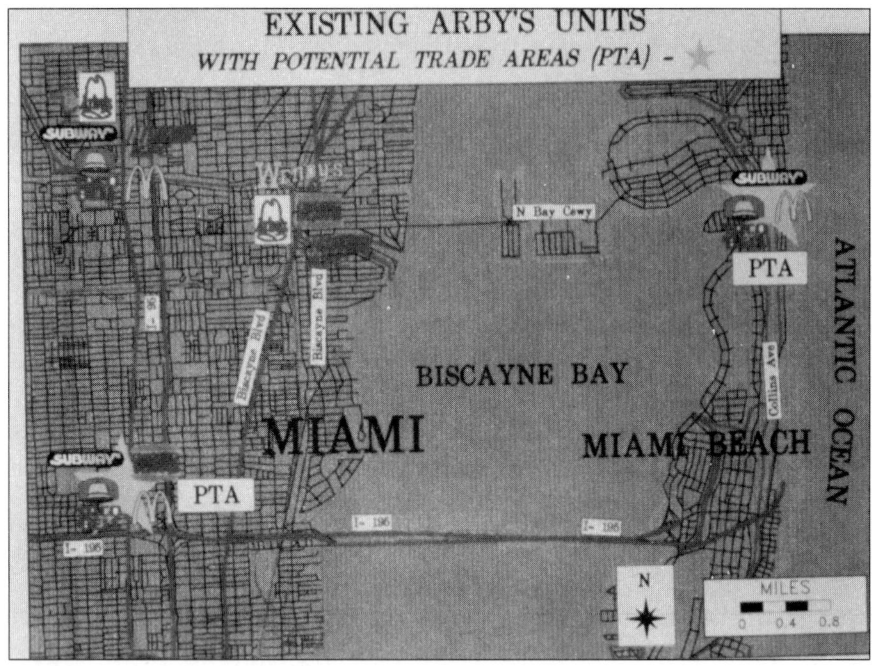

Courtesy Arby's, Inc.

A geographic information system helps Arby's rank neighborhoods and households by their potential expenditure on fast food and compare potential store sites on exposure to competition.
Source: Based on David Cheerbrick, "Geographics," *Forbes*, January 6, 1992, pp. 262–67.

Location decisions begin with an assessment of the retailer's strategy, followed by market selection decisions, analysis of various urban areas, and site selection. For example, Arby's, the roast beef chain, uses geographics in locating new stores (Exhibit 9–1). Choice of location determines how goods and services are made available to the customer. Even small differences in location can significantly affect profitability and market share because location affects both the number of customers attracted to the outlet and the resulting levels of retail sales.

The following examples help illustrate the importance of location in retailers' competitive strategy.

Dillard's, a department store chain headquartered in Arkansas, has a goal of being the number one or number two store in market share in all communities where it is located. The result is that the chain continues to locate primarily in second-tier cities such as Wichita, Oklahoma City, and Memphis. Such locations tend to be ignored by the more glamorous chains.[1]

Dairy Queen has mainly located in small-town America and in so doing has been among the most successful in the fast-food industry. It has

TABLE 9–1 MATRIX OF CONSUMER GOODS AND STORES

		Stores: *Convenience*	Stores: *Shopping*	Stores: *Specialty*
Goods	Convenience	Consumers prefer to buy the most readily available brand and product at the most accessible store.	Consumers are indifferent to the brand or product they buy, but shop among different stores in order to secure better retail service or lower retail prices.	Consumers prefer to buy at a specific store but are indifferent to the brand or product purchased.
Goods	Shopping	Consumers select a brand from the assortment carried by the most accessible store.	Consumers make comparisons among both retail-controlled factors and factors associated with the product or brand.	Consumers prefer to trade at a certain store, but are uncertain as to which product they wish to buy and examine the store's assortment for the best purchase.
Goods	Specialty	Consumers purchase their favored brand from the most accessible store that has the item in stock.	Consumers have strong preference with respect to the brand, but shop among a number of stores to secure the best retail service or price for this brand.	Consumers have preference for both a particular store and a specific brand.

Source: Yoram Wind, *Product Policy: Concepts, Methods, and Strategy* (Reading, Mass.: Addison-Wesley Publishing, 1982), p. 71.

produced double-digit sales and profit gains year after year. Dairy Queen officials suggest that promoting their restaurants as the local hangout—the place to go after a high school football game—will continue to give it an edge.[2]

Crate & Barrel, based in Northbrook, Illinois, is a home furnishings chain (featured in the Retailing Capsule for Chapter 8) that locates mostly in upscale malls in such cities as Boston, Dallas, Washington, D.C., and San Francisco.

THE INFLUENCE OF SHOPPER BEHAVIOR ON LOCATION DECISIONS

Merchandise can be classified as convenience, shopping, or specialty goods based on customer buying habits. Stores can be classified in the same way, as shown in Table 9–1. Understanding how consumers perceive merchandise and stores can help in making location decisions.

Convenience Goods. Convenience goods are often purchased on impulse at outlets such as 7-Eleven. Accessibility and the volume of traffic passing a site are the most important factors in selecting a site to sell convenience goods. Some convenience goods outlets such as card shops are often located close to major department stores in shopping malls and depend on them to attract traffic. Such outlets are known as parasite stores.

Shopping Goods. Consumers purchasing shopping goods prefer to compare the offerings of several stores before deciding what to buy. The Gap and The Limited Stores are examples of shopping goods outlets. Consumers may shop at each of these stores, and even a few department stores, before purchasing anything. Consumers will travel farther to purchase shopping goods than to purchase convenience goods but will not make a special effort to reach a particular outlet if others offering similar merchandise are more easily accessible.

Specialty Goods. Specialty goods are items for which consumers will make a special effort to purchase a particular brand. Outlets featuring such merchandise generate their own traffic. Examples include Waterford crystal and exclusive designer clothing from Valentino, Claude Montana, and Givenchy.

In summary, if management offers "shopping goods," the best location is near other stores offering similar merchandise. Locating a shopping goods store in a convenience goods center is not recommended. Take a look at shopping centers in your area. Invariably, you'll find a clothing or shoe store—in trouble—in a shopping center that carries mainly convenience goods.

Stores that carry shopping goods and those that offer convenience goods often locate in the same regional shopping center. But it is still important to locate in the section of the center that is compatible with the retailer's product lines. For example, a pet store should not be located adjacent to a restaurant or a dress shop. Management would, however, want to locate a gift shop near theaters or restaurants—in short, any place where lines of patrons may form, giving potential customers several minutes to look at the display windows.

Stores and merchandise cannot always be classified as neatly as this discussion suggests. Stereo shops, for example, sell blank tapes, and beauty salons sell shampoo, conditioners, brushes, and so forth for the convenience of their customers. Still, for strategy purposes, focusing on the core strategy implied by the type of merchandise and the store is important in targeting customers.

COMPETITIVE STRATEGY AND LOCATION DECISIONS

Differences in competitive strategy can result in different location objectives, even for retailers offering similar types of merchandise.

Regional Dominance

Management may decide to become regionally dominant rather than locate the same number of outlets over a much wider area. (Of course, over time some retailers expand nationwide or even globally.) An example of a regionally dominant retailer is Nordstrom in the Northwest, although the

A Profile in Excellence

SAM WALTON

Sam Walton believed the keys to his success were his "associates" (employees) and his willingness to change with the market. He realized that every day presents a different situation in the retail business.

During his youth, Walton exhibited ambition and a joy for work. After working several jobs and earning a degree in economics from the University of Missouri, he started his career in retailing as a management trainee at J. C. Penney. After marrying and serving in the Army, he decided to purchase his own store with the money he had saved.

His quest began in Newport, Arkansas, where he leased a Ben Franklin store. Forced to relocate his business, Walton moved to Bentonville, Arkansas. By 1962, he had opened 15 Ben Franklin stores under the name Walton's 5&10. But his real dream lay in the idea of a discount store, and he tried to convince Ben Franklin executives of the validity of the concept. His theory was to operate a discount store in a small community and, in that setting, offer brand-name merchandise at low prices with friendly service. Even though the Ben Franklin executives showed no interest, Walton opened the first Wal-Mart in Rogers, Arkansas.

In 1970 Walton's company went public. Equipped with 41 stores, sales of $72 million, and fewer than 3,000 employees, Wal-Mart stock was listed on the New York Stock Exchange. In recent years, Walton ventured into deep discount warehouse stores by offering goods in bulk. Today, the company operates Wal-Mart stores, Sam's Wholesale Clubs, and Hypermart USA stores, which combine a Wal-Mart discount department store with a warehouse-style supermarket and several other retail concepts. New formats are continually being tested.

firm is now starting to expand into other regions of the country. Similarly, Kroger is focusing on maintaining its competitive health by "filling in" its store density in and around its existing market strongholds.

The advantages of regional dominance include the following:

- Lower costs of distribution because merchandise can be shipped to all the stores from a central warehouse.
- Easier personnel supervision.
- The ability to better understand customer needs.
- The likelihood of a strong reputation in the area.
- Better economies in sales promotion because the outlets are concentrated in one region.

Sam Walton (see A Profile in Excellence) pioneered bringing sophisticated retailing strategies to small towns in the Southeast. In so doing, he became the largest retailer in the United States, as measured by sales, in less than 30 years.

Retailers practicing regional dominance can offset their high fixed costs by high market share. Typically, the retailers, measured on a city-by-city basis, that have the leading market shares have the highest profits.[3] In addition, high market share increases the number of stores in an area, which in turn improves customer convenience.

Market Saturation

This strategy is similar to regional dominance. However, saturation is often limited to a single metropolitan market. The advantages are the same in both instances. Dominance simply occurs on a larger scale.

All markets in retailing are local. Astute retailers therefore often concentrate on local markets in which they have a good chance of becoming the dominant player rather than spreading themselves across the regional or national scene.

Au Bon Pain (a Boston based fast-food retailer) practices market saturation and has several locations within a few blocks. Some cannibalization occurs, but the incremental increases in sales and profitability more than offset the cannibalization and discourage competitors from entering the market. In 1990 Au Bon Pain had 16 locations within a five-mile area of downtown Boston.

Smaller Communities

Why are smaller communities becoming such popular places to locate? One reason is that building codes make it more difficult to build in large cities. Costs are also higher and competition is tougher in larger markets. Each of the 300 largest metropolitan areas is now served by at least one of the nation's 11 largest merchants.

For several reasons, secondary markets, communities of 50,000 to 200,000, have become attractive targets for national chains. These communities often welcome new business. The quality of life may be higher even though wage rates are lower. Unions are often less of an issue. The markets are easier to serve, and competition is often less intense.

But national chains are also locating in communities of 2,500 or fewer. Hampton Inns is building scaled-down motels in small towns. McDonald's is testing three café concepts designed for small towns. And Target stores have begun opening stores in towns of 3,500 to 15,000.[4]

THE CHOICE OF REGION OR METROPOLITAN AREA

As noted previously, the retailer's location strategy ultimately reflects both growth and expansion objectives. Developing the location plan after making strategic decisions about growth requires a careful study of potential markets based on preestablished criteria. The stages in the location decision are shown in Figure 9–1.

Assessment of markets compatible with the firm's competitive strategy begins with choices among regions or metropolitan areas that appear to offer the greatest market potential for meeting the firm's growth objectives.

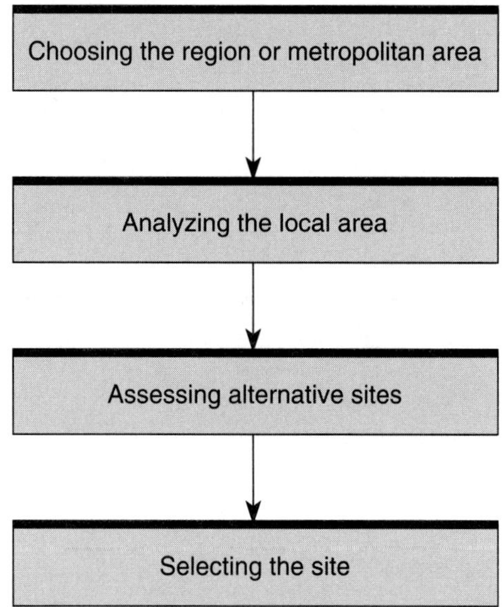

FIGURE 9–1

STAGES IN THE LOCATION DECISION

Management evaluates the economic base of targeted regions, the intensity of competition, size and socioeconomic characteristics of the population, and the overall aggregate potential of each area, as shown on Table 9–2.

Analysis of different potential sites within the region or metropolitan area selected is known as **local area analysis.** Finally, the **site selection** decision must be made from among the site alternatives.

Data Sources

Management typically relies on secondary data in evaluating the attractiveness of market areas. Publications from the U.S. Bureau of the Census, as noted in the Retailing Capsule and discussed in Chapter 5, provide useful information on population and housing. The Survey of Buying Power data is published annually by *Sales and Marketing Management* magazine. Data are also made available by private firms through the use of computerized databases.

The Survey of Buying Power combined with Census of Population data is the source of information most frequently used in evaluating the attractiveness of alternative regions and metropolitan areas. The Survey reports the Buying Power Index (BPI) of different cities, states, and metropolitan areas. The index is a measure of relative purchasing power and is a weighted average of income, population, and total retail sales for the preceding year. The Survey also provides Graduated Buying Power Indices by market area. Such data reflect the buying power of households with different income levels.

TABLE 9–2

FACTORS TO CONSIDER IN AREA SELECTION

Population characteristics
- Total size
- Age and income distributions
- Growth trends
- Education levels
- Occupation distribution and trends

Competitive characteristics
- Saturation level
- Number and size of competitors
- Geographic coverage
- Competitive growth trends

Labor characteristics
- Availability of personnel
  - Management
  - Clerical
  - Skilled
- Wage levels
- Unions
- Training

Economic characteristics
- Number and type of industries
- Dominant industry
- Growth projections
- Financial base

Supply source characteristics
- Delivery time
- Delivery costs
- Availability and reliability
- Storage facilities

Location characteristics
- Number and type of locations
- Costs
- Accessibility to customers
- Accessibility to transportation
- Owning and leasing options
- Utility adequacy

Promotion characteristics
- Type of media coverage
- Media overlap
- Costs

Regulation characteristics
- Taxes
- Licensing
- Zoning restrictions
- Local ordinances

Index of Retail Saturation

Survey of Buying Power data and census data need to be supplemented with an analysis of the competition. One of the most commonly used measures of competitive intensity is the Index of Retail Saturation (IRS). The lower the level of market saturation, the higher the likelihood of success. The formal relationships are as follows:

$$IRS_1 = \frac{C_1 \times RE_1}{RF_1}$$

where

IRS_1 = Index of Retail Saturation for area 1
C_1 = Number of customers in area 1
RE_1 = Retail expenditures per consumer in area 1
RF_1 = Retail facilities in area 1

The data utilized in the formula are readily available. Census data can be used to determine the number of customers within the market areas being studied. Expenditure data from the U.S. Bureau of Labor Statistics can be used to develop retail expenditure information per consumer by product type. The number and square footage of facilities within each market area can be determined by observation. Consider the following example in analyzing supermarket potential in hypothetical market A. The 100,000 consumers in market A spend an average of $25 per week in food stores. There are 15 supermarkets serving market A, with a total of 144,000 square feet of selling area.

$$IRS = \frac{100{,}000 \times \$25.00}{144{,}000} = \frac{\$2{,}500{,}000}{144{,}000} = \$17.36$$

The $17.36 per square foot of selling area measured against the dollar amount of sales per square foot necessary to break even provides a measure of saturation in market A. The $17.36 figure is also useful in evaluating relative opportunity in different market areas. The results are counter intuitive. Specifically, the higher the Index of Retail Saturation, the lower the level of competition.

LOCAL AREA ANALYSIS

The next step is to assess the nature of the local retailing structure in the promising areas and to conduct a more intense analysis of the competition after the application of the previously described market screening criteria.

Understanding the Dynamics of the Local Retail Structure

The urban business pattern is constantly changing as new retail outlets are built, inner cities decay and are rebuilt, and central business districts lose their attraction as magnets for major retailers. Understanding the shopping center structure, the dynamics of central business districts, and the nature of stand-alone sites available is important at this stage of the analysis.

Shopping Centers. The shopping center's effect on retailing has been profound. Indeed, planned suburban shopping centers are one of the most visible aspects of retail restructuring after World War II. Growing suburbanization forced retailers to shift from downtown retail areas to suburban locations. The expansion made it possible for many retail firms to achieve, for the first time, a high level of regional penetration as larger regional markets were opened to chain retailers.

The traditional reliance of larger centers on department stores and mass merchandisers as their primary strengths is now becoming a liability, however. Consumer patronage is shifting from department stores to specialty outlets and specialized shopping centers. The more familiar types of specialized centers are shown in Figure 9–2.

Traditional shopping centers still dominate the retailing scene in sheer numbers, although their relative importance is declining.[5] By far the largest number of traditional centers are neighborhood outlets, as seen in Figure 9–3. The differences between neighborhood centers, community centers,

FIGURE 9–2 SHARE OF SHOPPING CENTERS BY MARKET POSITIONING

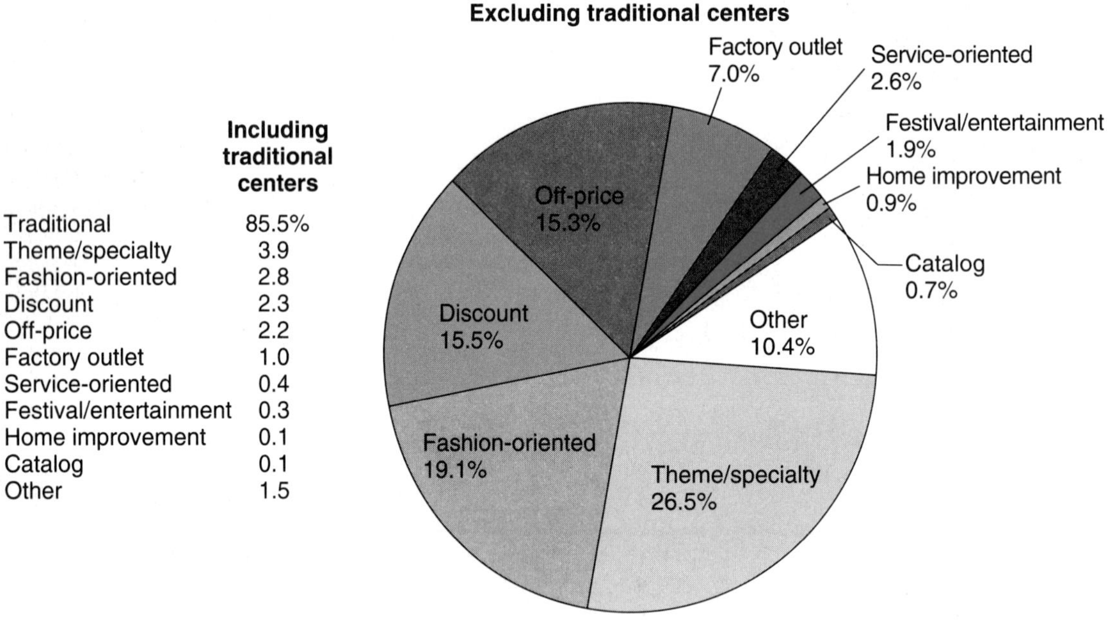

	Including traditional centers
Traditional	85.5%
Theme/specialty	3.9
Fashion-oriented	2.8
Discount	2.3
Off-price	2.2
Factory outlet	1.0
Service-oriented	0.4
Festival/entertainment	0.3
Home improvement	0.1
Catalog	0.1
Other	1.5

Source: *Monitor,* May 1990, p. 74. Reproduced by permission.

and regional or super-regional centers are explained in Exhibit 9–2. The various types of specialized centers are described next.

Theme or Specialty.[6] Developers and managers classify about 4 percent of their properties as theme or specialty centers. These can be quite diverse in thematic format, size, and market orientation, but all share features that distinguish them from other centers: a common architectural theme that unites a wide range of retailers who repeat the theme in their spaces; tenants who offer unusual merchandise; restaurants and entertainment that serve as anchors, rather than supermarkets or department stores; and a strong appeal made to tourists as well as local shoppers.

Fashion Oriented. These centers consist mainly of apparel shops, boutiques, and craft shops carrying selected merchandise of high quality and price. They appeal to high-income shoppers. Growth was strongest for fashion-oriented centers in the mid-1980s but has slowed recently. Their share is almost 3 percent of the total number of centers.

Discount. A discount center is usually anchored by one or more discount stores with a strong representation of discount merchants. The centers appeal mainly to lower-income groups, as compared to off-price centers.

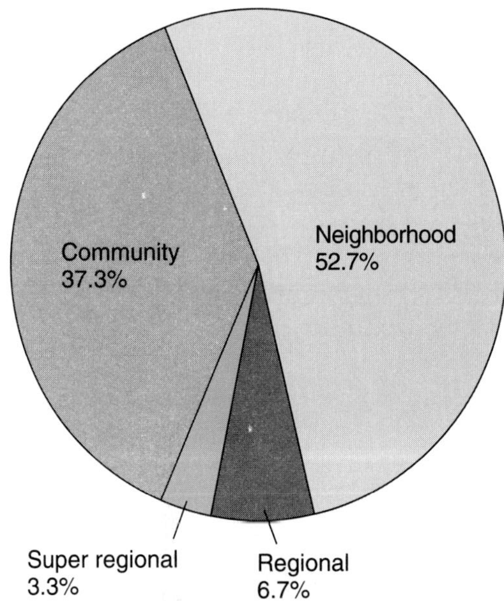

FIGURE 9–3

CATEGORY SHARE OF TRADITIONAL SHOPPING CENTERS

Source: *Monitor,* May 1990, p. 64. Reproduced by permission.

Discount centers are just ahead of off-price centers in number, accounting for more than 2 percent of the total number of centers.

Off-Price. These are centers with a heavy concentration of specialty and department stores selling brand-name goods at 20 to 70 percent off manufacturers' suggested retail prices. The quality of goods is higher than in discount stores, so off-price centers draw upon middle- and upper-middle-income shoppers. The share of total centers is slightly over 2 percent.

Factory Outlet. In contrast to factory outlets of the past, typically found at the factory site, these centers consist of retail outlets owned and operated by manufacturers where goods are sold directly to the public (see Exhibit 9–3). Factory outlet malls draw a combination of middle- and lower-income customers and often include some off-price stores. (Some researchers combine off-price centers with factory outlet centers.)[7] By themselves, factory outlet centers comprise 1 percent of the total number of centers.

Festival or Entertainment. With a strong representation of restaurants, fast food, specialty retailers, and entertainment facilities, festival or entertainment centers tend to be large. Frequently, they spring from adaptive reuse of older buildings or are connected with mixed-use projects. Their share of the total is under 1 percent of centers, and opportunities for new growth are considered limited.

EXHIBIT 9–2 **DIFFERENCES BY TYPE OF SHOPPING CENTER**

In a neighborhood shopping center, the leading tenant is a supermarket or drugstore. The typical leasable space is 50,000 square feet, and the typical site area is 4 acres. The minimum trade population is 7,500 to 40,000.

In a community shopping center, the leading tenant is a variety or junior department store. The typical leasable space is 150,000 square feet, and the typical site area is 10 acres. The minimum trade population is 40,000 to 150,000.

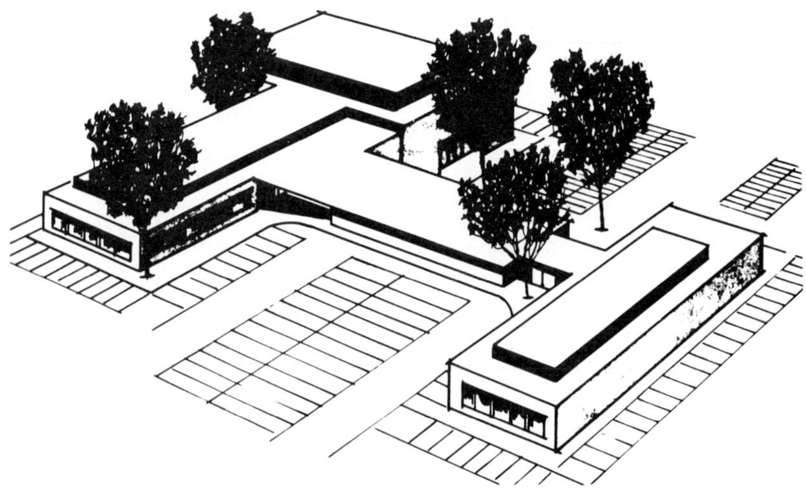

In a regional shopping center, the leading tenant is one or more full-line department stores. The typical leasable space is a minimum of 400,000 square feet, and the typical site area is 30 acres. The minimum trade population is 150,000 or more.

EXHIBIT 9–3

Courtesy Festival Management Corporation

Escondido Promenade is part of the next generation of factory outlet discount malls.

Catalog. These are centers anchored by one or more catalog showroom stores. This category experienced strong growth in the 1970s and virtual disappearance in the 1980s. Their share of the total number of centers is about 0.1 percent.

Service Oriented. These centers depend heavily upon service-oriented retailers, such as opticians, dentists, repair services, health clinics, legal services, and so forth. Their present share is expected to grow in strip centers, the largest industry component and one with much space to fill.

Home Improvement. These centers are anchored by a large home improvement retailer or feature a concentration of home improvement and hardware specialty retailers. As yet, numbers are not significant, but this concept is expected to grow.

Single Theme. Zeroing in on consumer needs in a narrow range such as auto care, home decorating and design, or weddings, this new approach calls for tenanting the center solely with retailers and services that match the theme.

EXHIBIT 9–4

Courtesy HomeBase

HomeBase is one of the leading chains of home improvement warehouses in the nation. The outlets are located in 13 Western and Midwestern states and are typical examples of free-standing destination outlets.

Other categories of centers have continued to appear in recent years as location options for retailers. Among them are **power centers,** which combine the off-price or home improvement center with several anchors.

The various shopping center types are at different stages of their life cycles. Discount centers flourished in the late 1960s through the mid-1970s, followed by a decline in the 1980s. Catalog centers spurted in the 1970s but had virtually disappeared by the end of the 1980s. The theme and specialty fashion-oriented centers experienced strong growth in the mid-1980s. Off-price and factory outlets surged between 1983 and 1988 as retailers became interested in locations that reflected strong price and value relationships. Locating in a type of center that appears to be out of favor with shoppers can be risky.

Stand-Alone Locations. Today's most rapidly expanding retailers, including Toys 'R' Us, Wal-Mart, IKEA, and HomeBase (Exhibit 9–4), often do not locate in shopping centers. Historically, such developers were excluded from regional and super-regional centers as undesirable tenants. They thus built free-standing sites on major traffic arteries. Free-standing locations offer a variety of advantages including no common area maintenance charges, and no loss of individual store identity.

Not surprisingly, retailers preferring free-standing locations are those requiring the highest average gross leasable area. That is why these locations are favored by destination retailers such as warehouse clubs, category-dominant specialty stores, and hypermarts. They require large volumes to be economically successful and huge amounts of parking space.[8]

Costs are becoming so high, primarily because of the cost of raw land, that going it alone may be more difficult in the future. Destination retailers are therefore beginning to choose locations in strip centers.

Central Business District Locations. The high concentration of commercial buildings makes the central business district (CBD) one of the important components of urban structure. The CBD attracts people from throughout the metropolitan area, often including visitors. Mass transit also brings people into the CBD in many metropolitan areas. Such areas contain a wide variety of stores and often include the flagship of one of the leading department store chains. Examples include Bloomingdale's in New York, Filenes in Boston, and Dayton's in Minneapolis.

Downtown locations, however, are increasingly unattractive as a location option. The central cities have lost not only population but also income. Retailers have had to shift from downtown areas to suburban locations to follow their customers. Lack of space for expansion, lack of parking space, the absence of evening and weekend shoppers, and traffic congestion also contribute to making downtowns unattractive options for many firms. Especially for large retailers, the CBD is just one of many "regional" shopping centers. Downtown areas today contain less retail activity than their populations would suggest. Furthermore, retail and service activity has virtually disappeared from the low-income areas bordering many CBDs.

The strengths and weaknesses of shopping center, stand-alone, and CBD locations are summarized in Table 9–3.

The Competition

Assessing the competition is also necessary in local area analysis. Various measures of competition can be used, including number of stores per capita, number of stores overall, and per capita selling space. A primary difficulty, however, is defining the nature of competition. A complete competitive inventory can be developed based on publications by local chambers of commerce, physical surveys of the area, and personal observation. The data developed should include information on the physical characteristics of the competing outlets, the level of services provided, the size and overall condition of the outlets, merchandising policies, and target market segments.

TABLE 9–3 STRENGTHS AND WEAKNESSES OF SELECTED LOCATION ALTERNATIVES

Type of Location	*Strengths*	*Weaknesses*
Regional shopping center	Large number of stores Drawing power of large anchor stores Parking availability Balanced tenant mix	Occupancy costs Some inflexibility (e.g., store hours, merchandise sold)
Community shopping center	Operating costs Shopping convenience Shared promotions	Poor tenant mix Facility condition High vacancy rate
Neighborhood shopping center	Shopping convenience Very low operating costs Distance from customer	Few tenants Susceptible to competition Facility condition
Central business district	Mass transit Urban redevelopment Business/work traffic generates exposure	Parking Limited shopping hours Facility condition Suburban shift Rent costs
Solo location	Lack of close competition Lower rent More space for expansion Greater flexibility	Harder to attract customers Probably have to build instead of rent Higher promotion costs

ASSESSING ALTERNATIVE SITES

The amount of sales that can be generated at alternative sites is also a crucial factor in site selection. Developing an estimate of the trading area for each site and forecasting sales is important in determining whether the sites produce the minimum revenue needed to cover expenses and create the desired profit.

Estimating the Trade Area[9]

Retail sales forecast accuracy depends on the retailer's ability to estimate the trade areas for alternative sites. The **trade area** is the geographic region that comprises the primary customer base.

A variety of factors influence the size of the trade area:

1. The price of a good at one place compared to its price at another place.
2. The number of inhabitants within easy access of the site.
3. The density and distribution of population.
4. The income and social structure of the population.
5. The proximity of other shopping opportunities.

Retailers differ from manufacturers because they have to be close to their target market; consumers typically shop at the nearest retail outlet that will meet their needs. Techniques for measuring a trading area range from simple seat-of-the-pants descriptive approaches to complex mathematical models.

Descriptive Techniques. *Watch the "big boys."* Some stores watch what the "big boys" do and then follow them. For example, specialty outlets such as County Seat tend to locate in the regional shopping centers where mass merchandisers such as Sears and J. C. Penney serve as anchors. The smaller specialty stores know that the major outlets have done their homework and will draw customers to the center.

Information from Existing Stores. Retailers with existing stores have an advantage over people opening an outlet for the first time. The experienced retailers can use information about their existing store or stores in deciding the new location. But management needs to be sure that the stores are alike in all key respects; otherwise, relying on the track history of the existing store is risky business.

License Plate Analysis. One of the more common methods of measuring trading areas for comparable stores is auto license plate analysis. The retailer determines the addresses from public records (often at the county courthouse) of the vehicles in the parking lot of an existing store or one similar to a planned outlet. By plotting these locations on a map, the retailer can get a feel for the general nature of the trading area.

Check Clearance Data. Check clearance data can also be used to determine a store's trading area. However, such data is based on the assumption that the geographic distribution of cash customers and charge customers is the same. Plotting the addresses allows management to determine the size and shape of the primary trading area. Secondary data can then be used to determine the characteristics of the trading area.

Credit Records. Credit records can also be analyzed to determine the trading area of an existing store as a model for a new one. A sample of charge accounts is selected, and customer addresses are plotted on a map. This method has the same weakness as an analysis of check clearance data.

Customer Spotting. Customer spotting is a frequently used technique for determining the location of target customers for a new outlet. The home addresses of all customers of an existing store are spotted on a map and a circle is drawn to define the primary trading area in the outlet. This information can be used to determine likely trading areas for other potential sites.

Driving Time Analysis. Driving time analysis helps define a trading area by determining how far customers are willing to travel to reach an outlet. Trading areas typically are measured in terms of time instead of distance because of the problems of congestion and physical barriers. A rule of thumb is that customers will travel no more than five minutes to reach a convenience outlet. Three-fourths of the customers of a large regional shopping center will normally drive 15 minutes to reach the center.

Customer Survey. A good way to determine a trading area is to conduct or sponsor a customer survey. The survey can be done by mail, telephone, or personal interview. Retailers may also be able to participate in surveys sponsored by the local chamber of commerce or a similar organization.

A customer survey can provide other useful information as well. Such information might include demographics (such as age, occupation, number of children); shopping habits (for example, type of store preferred, frequency of shopping, area of town preferred); purchasing patterns (for instance, who does the family buying); and media habits (radio, television, and newspaper habits).

Mathematical Models.

Reilly's Law. Reilly's "Law" is often used in calculating the trade area breakpoint between two or more small retail communities. It is less useful for calculating intracity trading areas. Reilly's Law states that the amount of retail trade attracted from an intermediate area between two competing communities is directly proportional to the population of the two communities and inversely proportional to the square of the distances from the two communities to intermediate areas. Reilly's Law is often expressed in the context of the breakpoint formula developed by Paul Converse:

$$D_B = \frac{D}{1 + \sqrt{\frac{B_A}{B_B}}}$$

where

B_A, B_B = Population sizes of centers A and B (B is the smaller community)

D_B = Breakpoint distance of trade to center B

D = Distance between centers A and B

In applying the formula, assume the following information:

B_A = 200,000 population

B_B = 50,000 population

D = 25 miles

The breakpoint, or the point at which residents are indifferent to the two trade centers, between city A and city B is thus 8.3 miles. These breakpoints can be calculated between several cities and joined together to form a set of trading area boundaries for a community, as shown below.

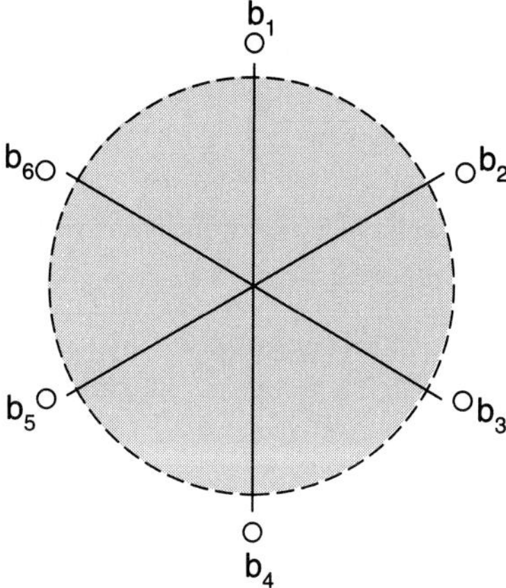

The formula can be modified in several ways, including the substitution of driving time for distance and square footage of retail floor space for population.

In essence, Reilly's Law states that the size of a trading area increases as population density decreases. For example, people may travel several miles to shop at a small rural village because there are no other alternatives. However, the same people would be willing to travel only a few blocks in a major metropolitan area because of the presence of a variety of stores. Reilly's Law applies only to communities of similar size. In addition, trade areas vary by type of goods sought, a reality not reflected in Reilly's model. Patronage is also assumed to be linearly related to time or distance from the consumer's household. Again, physical barriers and congestion, among other factors, can make that assumption unrealistic.

The Huff Model. David Huff, a marketing geographer, developed an intracity trading area model that overcomes many of the limitations of Reilly's model. For example, Huff's models assume that the likelihood of consumer patronage increases with the size of a center. Consumers are willing to travel greater distances as additional merchandise is available at a central location. The probability of patronage is also assumed to be linearly related to time or distance from the consumer's household. The formal expression of the model is as follows:

$$P(C_{ij}) = \frac{\dfrac{S_j}{T_{ij}\lambda}}{\displaystyle\sum_{j=1}^{n} \frac{S_j}{T_{ij}\lambda}}$$

where

$P(C_{ij})$ = Probability of a consumer at a given point of origin i traveling to a given shopping center j

S_j = Square footage of selling space devoted by shopping center j to the sale of a particular class of goods

T_{ij} = Travel time involved in getting from a consumer's travel base i to shopping center j

λ = An empirically estimated parameter that reflects the effect of travel time on various kinds of shopping trips.

The most frequently used method of estimating λ is a computer program developed by Huff and Blue.[10] After estimating λ, management can determine the trading area of a shopping center for any product class. The steps involved in using the Huff model are as follows:

1. Divide the area surrounding a shopping center into small statistical units within a constructed grid. Such units represent the i's in the model.
2. Determine the square footage of retail selling space of all shopping centers (the j's) included within the area of analysis.
3. Ascertain the travel time involved in getting from each statistical unit i to each of the specified shopping centers, j.
4. Calculate the probability of consumers in each of the statistical units going to each shopping center for a given product purchase. That is,

$$P(C_{ij}) = \frac{\dfrac{S_{ij}}{T_{ij}\lambda}}{\displaystyle\sum_{j=1}^{n} \frac{S_j}{T_{ij}\lambda}}$$

where

$P(C_{ij})$ = Probability of consumers from *each* of the statistical units going to a specific shopping center

λ = Parameter estimate appropriate to the type of product class

5. Map the trading area for the shopping center by drawing lines connecting all statistical units having similar probabilities. For illustration, assume the following information for three shopping centers in an area of interest, with $\lambda = 2$. Using Huff's notation,

$$S_{j_1} = 10{,}000 \text{ sq. ft.}$$

$$S_{j_2} = 15{,}000 \text{ sq. ft.}$$

$$S_{j_3} = 20{,}000 \text{ sq. ft.}$$

$$T_{ij_1} = 2 \text{ miles}$$

$$T_{ij_2} = 3 \text{ miles}$$

$$T_{ij_3} = 4 \text{ miles}$$

$$P(C_{ij}) = \frac{\dfrac{10{,}000}{2^2}}{\dfrac{10{,}000}{2^2} + \dfrac{15{,}000}{3^2} + \dfrac{20{,}000}{4^2}} = 0.46$$

Thus, the probability of consumers traveling from statistical unit i to shopping center j_1 is 0.46. The probabilities for each statistical unit would have to be calculated to yield a complete trade area map. Connecting the various lines would show the trade area. The trade area of center j_1 would not be a fixed line but a series of zonal probability contours radiating from the shopping center.

Various studies support the model for use in forecasting patronage decisions for retail shopping centers. Significant support has also been found for incorporating measures of consumer images of competing retail chains into forecasting models for site selection decisions.

The advantage of Huff's model is that it includes two variables: selling space and travel time. Another strength is that it includes the effects of competition on shoppers' behavior. The probability contours of the Huff model also allow for the irregularity of trading areas.

Still, the Huff model has its weaknesses. It assumes that consumers with comparable demographic characteristics will exhibit similar retail patronage behavior. In addition, Huff's model includes all potential retail centers in the system, although not all centers might be patronized. Finally, research has shown that using a consumer-specified set of shopping centers as opposed to an arbitrarily imposed set in the traditional Huff model improves the performance of the model.

Forecasting Sales

The next step after estimating the size of the trade areas of alternative sites is to determine the amount of business that can be done in each.

Descriptive Assessment. Retailers need five sets of data to help estimate the amount of sales available in a trading area: number of people in the trading area; average household income; amount of money spent each year by each household on the type of goods sold by the firm, for example, groceries, drugs, or apparel; the total market potential; and the share of the total market potential management can expect to get.

The number of people in a trading area can be obtained from an analysis of U.S. census data. Data are reported by census tracts (small areas with 4,000 to 9,000 people) for all cities with a population of 50,000 or more. County data are reported in the Survey of Buying Power. The average household income in each census tract is published by the U.S. Bureau of the Census every 10 years. The Survey of Buying Power, as noted earlier, also reports data annually on effective buying income (EBI) by county and metropolitan area. Information about the amount of money spent each year on various types of merchandise can be found in several places. Data published by the U.S. Department of Labor is probably the best source.

Multiplying average annual household income by the number of families in the trading area yields **total sales potential.** Multiplying total sales potential by the percentage of the average annual household income spent on each type of good (for example, groceries) yields **total sales potential by type of good.**

Retailers then decide on the amount of the available sales potential they can get. One way is to plot competitors in each trading area on a map and estimate the sales levels of each one. Indicators may be the number of checkouts, number of employees, square footage, or industry trade averages for sales per square foot as reported by the Urban Land Institute publication entitled *Dollars and Cents of Shopping Centers.* Retailers must also decide on the amount of business they need to make a profit. Then, they decide on how much business they can take from the competition. Table 9–4 shows this five-step process.

Other Factors to Consider

Numerous other factors also affect the choice among alternative sites. A merchant's association can be vitally important, for example, as can the responsiveness of the landlord, and the nature of the lease. Local community leaders sometimes can be violently opposed to a location they consider incompatible with the area. Locations in historic areas are particularly sensitive issues (see A Question of Ethics). Finally, some communities have no-growth or anti-growth policies that make it difficult to secure needed permits and licenses.

Responsiveness of the Landlord. The responsiveness of the landlord to the merchant's needs is important. Some landlords actually hinder the operation of their tenants' businesses.

By restricting the placement and size of signs, foregoing or ignoring needed maintenance and repairs, and renting adjacent retail spaces to incompatible—or worse, directly competing—businesses, landlords may cripple a retailer's attempts to increase business.

Sometimes landlords lack the funds to maintain their properties. Rather than continuing to invest in their holdings by maintaining a proper

TABLE 9–4 ESTIMATING ANNUAL SALES IN A RETAIL STORE'S TRADING AREA

Factor:	*A*		*B*		*C*		*D*		
Method:	Number of households in a census tract in retail trading area	×	Median annual income of the households in the census tract	×	Proportion of a household's annual income spent on items sold by store	×	Proportion of money spent on item that will be spent in store	=	Proposed store sales revenue from census tract
Census tracts in trading area:									
354XX	6,500	×	$10,000	×	.20*	×	.10†	=	$1,300,000
354XY	8,500	×	8,000	×	.15	×	.15	=	1,530,000
Total projected annual sales									$2,830,000

* The proportion of .20 means that 20 percent of the typical household's annual income of $10,000 is spent on merchandise sold by this store.

† The proportion of .10 means that management anticipates that 10 percent of the total merchandise purchased in this census tract will be purchased at this specific store.

A Question of Ethics

McDONALD'S MOVES INTO HISTORIC BOSTON DISTRICT

McDonald's wanted to open a restaurant on one of the most historic streets in Boston. Neighbors and community organizations objected, and the fast-food giant was unanimously turned down.

Then came the Big Mac attack.

To counter its 400 opponents, McDonald's enlisted its own community groups and gathered a petition signed by 500 supporters. It doled out goodies to the neighborhood. It hired well-connected consultants. And when the new restaurant came up for a second vote before the Zoning Appeals Board, the same body voted in favor of McDonald's.

"McDonald's hired guns worked on this for a long time. They did what they had to do—outreach and political networking," laments Joseph Milano, co-owner of the Union Oyster House restaurant, a Boston landmark that dates back to the early 1800s.

The controversial victory shows how some companies are using savvy marketing and financial clout to disarm community opposition and get what they want.

The dispute over McDonald's new franchise restaurant provoked strong passions because of its proposed location in the city's cobble-stoned Blackstone Block District.

The district is listed in the National Register of Historic Places because it contains the last surviving 17th-century street pattern in town. Across the street stands Faneuil Hall, where colonists once met to protest British taxes and where tourists now roam among dozens of shops and restaurants. Benjamin Franklin spent his childhood near the Blackstone District and John Hancock once owned land there. Nearby are Paul Revere's house and the Old North Church in the North End community.

Was McDonald's justified in its actions? Should a retailer locate in an area where there is significant opposition?

Source: Suzanne Alexander, "McDonald's Moves into Historic Boston District Using Grass-Roots Lobby to Reverse the Zoning Vote," reproduced with permission from *The Wall Street Journal*, October 28, 1991, p. B6.

appearance for their buildings and supporting their tenants, they try to squeeze the property for whatever they can get.

In addition to speaking with current tenants, management should talk to previous tenants in the general area. They should find out what businesses they were in and why they left. Did they fail or just move? If the opportunity presented itself, would they be retail tenants of this landlord again?

Zoning and Planning. The town's zoning commission can provide the appropriate zoning maps for the retail locations being evaluated. Here are some points to consider:

1. Are there restrictions that will limit or hamper operations?
2. Will construction or changes in city traffic or new highways present barriers to the store?

3. Will any competitive advantages currently found at the location being considered be diminished by zoning changes that would be advantageous for competitors or even allow new competitors to enter the trade area?
4. Most zoning boards, along with economic and regional development committees, plan several years in advance. They can probably provide valuable insights to help decide among tentative retail locations.

Leases. Directly related to zoning is the intended length of stay and the lease agreement. Before entering into any rigid lease agreement, management should get information on future zoning plans and decide how long to remain at the location under consideration:

1. Do managers plan to operate the business in the first location indefinitely, or have they set a given number of years as a limit?
2. If the business is successful, will management be able to expand at this location?
3. Is the lease flexible, so that management has an option to renew after a specified number of years? On the other hand, is the lease of limited duration so, if need be, management may seek another location?

Management should study the proposed lease agreement carefully and get advice from a lawyer or other experts. Check the following points about the lease:

- Does it peg rent to sales volume (with a definite ceiling), or is it fixed?
- Does it protect the outlet as well as the property owner?
- Will the landlord put in writing the promises he or she has made about repairs, construction and reconstruction, decorating, alteration, and maintenance?
- Does the agreement contain prohibitions against subleasing?

A host of other considerations vary in importance, depending on the line of business. The following questions do not exhaust all possibilities, but they may help decide among alternative retail locations:

- How much retail, office storage, or workroom space is needed?
- Is parking space available and adequate?
- Is there adequate fire and police protection?
- Will sanitation or utilities be a problem?
- Is exterior lighting in the area adequate to attract evening shoppers and make them feel safe?
- Is the store easily accessible?
- Will crime insurance be prohibitively expensive?
- Will space be needed for pickup or delivery?
- Is the trade area heavily dependent on seasonal business?

- Is the location convenient to where the employees live?
- Do the target customers live nearby?
- Is the population density of the area sufficient?

Getting Help in Choosing a Location. Choosing a retail location is, at best, a risky undertaking. Considering the consequences of choosing a location that proves to be unsuitable, it pays to get as much assistance as possible.

Local chambers of commerce in cities of more than 125,000 usually have a division devoted primarily to assisting budding owners or managers in finding suitable locations for their businesses. This is a free service that surprisingly few people take advantage of.

The U.S. Small Business Administration (SBA) has field offices located throughout the country. SBA field offices can provide free counseling assistance, literature, and information to help in selecting a retail site.

Management may wish to hire a consultant to analyze two or three top location alternatives. It costs less to provide the consultant with preselected potential locations than to initiate an open-ended search for a location. The business school of a nearby college or university may also be able to provide help.

Other sources of information on potential locations include bankers, lawyers, and realtors. However, keep in mind that realtors' compensation is based on commissions for renting property.

Selection of a retail location requires time and careful consideration. It should not be done in haste just to coincide, say, with a loan approval. If management has not found a suitable location, it should not plan to open until it is sure it has what it wants. A few months' delay is only a minor setback compared to the massive—often fatal—problems that occur from operating a retail business in a poor location.

Overemphasized Factors

When making decisions, many retailers overemphasize certain considerations. One is the initial cost of the property. This is a one-time charge, and if a retailer is buying a site, an additional $1,000 or so may not be significant when it is amortized over the number of years the business plans to remain at that site. A lower-priced property is not a bargain if the costs of operation on that site are higher than on a more expensive property.

Another overemphasized factor is tax considerations. Between communities, tax differences have tended to level off. Although some areas have gross volume taxes and others income taxes, the net collected from most businesses tends to be the same. On rare occasions, some significant differences occur because of peculiarities of some companies, but these are not necessarily permanent.

TABLE 9–5

RATING SHEET FOR SITES

Factor	Importance to Management*	×	Management Attractiveness Ranking of Each Factor Considered†	=	Total Score
Future growth potential	2		1		2
Present size	6		4		24
Investment required	5		6		30
Strength of competition	4		5		20
Ability to meet the needs of the segment	1		3		3
Profit potential	3		2		6
Total					85

* 1 is most important.
† 1 is most attractive to management.

SELECTING THE SITE

A perfect location rarely exists. Ideally, management would like to find a location with easy accessibility and high traffic flow at a reasonable price in a desirable shopping environment.

The final choice among alternative sites can be made after management decides on the *importance* of selected factors in choosing a site and the *attractiveness* of the sites based on these factors. Multiplying importance by attractiveness, as shown in Table 9–5, yields a score for each factor. Summing the scores for each factor allows management to compare alternative sites more objectively in making the final choice.

CHAPTER HIGHLIGHTS

- Location is a key factor in the retailing mix. Retailers should consider such a decision as carefully as pricing, promotion, and other elements of the retailing mix.
- Key factors in choosing a region in which to locate include its size, composition of its population, labor market, closeness to the source of merchandise supply, media mix available, economic base, existing and probable future competition, availability of store sites, and legal restrictions.
- Choosing a location within a community is also important. Retailers can decide on a shopping center, downtown, or stand-alone location. Shopping centers may be either planned or unplanned.
- Shopping center developers are becoming astute positioning strategists. The newer types of centers include theme and specialty centers, discount centers, off-price centers, factory outlet centers, festival and entertainment centers, catalog centers, service-oriented centers, and home improvement centers.
- Retailers can employ a variety of techniques in assessing the probable size of a trade area. These techniques include a study of existing stores, license plate analysis, check clearance analysis, analysis of credit records, mathematical models, and customer surveys.
- After establishing the size of the trade area, management must then determine the amount of business that can be done there. The

amount of business is a function of the number of people in the trade area, the average household income, the amount of money spent each year by each household on the type of goods sold by the firm, the market potential, and the share of the market that management expects to attract.

- Choosing a specific site involves assessing the size and mix of vehicular or foot traffic passing a site, the ability of the site to intercept traffic enroute from one place to another, the nature of adjacent stores, type of goods sold, and adequacy of parking.

Study Questions

1. Explain why regional dominance and market saturation are viewed as desirable location strategies.
2. What do you consider to be the important factors in selecting a site for a fast-food outlet? How do these contrast, if at all, with your notion of the key factors for the location of an outlet selling stereo components?
3. In deciding whether to locate in a particular shopping center, what are the factors the retailer needs to consider?
4. Distinguish among neighborhood, community, and regional shopping centers.
5. What are the advantages and disadvantages of a free-standing location?
6. What factors have led to the decline of downtown areas as desirable locations for many retail outlets? What can downtown areas do to better compete with suburban shopping centers?
7. Distinguish among the following techniques that retailers use to determine the size of a trading area: license plate analysis, check clearance analysis, credit record analysis, and customer surveys.
8. What are the various types of information a retailer needs in estimating the likely amount of sales within a trading area? What are some sources from which this information can be obtained?
9. What factors account for the newest trends in shopping center positioning strategies? What types of centers are in the declining phase of their life cycle and which types of centers appear to be in the growth phase?
10. Why are some communities opposed to development of additional local retail facilities? Are such trends likely to increase or decrease during the decade of the 1990s?

Problems

1. The distance between the community of Macon, with a population of 151,000, and the community of Milledgeville with a population of 13,600, is 31 miles. Using Reilly's Law, calculate the break point between the two cities. What does the break point imply in retail location decisions?
2. The driving time between city A and city B is approximately 75 minutes. Retail store A in city A has 240,000 square feet of floor space, and retail store B in city B has 150,000 square feet of floor space. Using Reilly's Law, calculate the point at which residents of either community are indifferent relative to the two retail stores.
3. Huff's model assumes that the likelihood of consumer patronage increases with the size of a retail center. Suppose $\lambda = 2$ and the consumers can shop at two retail centers where the square footage of the first retail center devoted to the sale of a particular class of goods is 50,000 square feet and that of the second retail center is 35,000 square feet. Furthermore, the distance from the first retail center to the consumer's home is 2 miles and the second is 3 miles. What is the probability

of the consumers traveling from origin i to shop in either retail center?

4. There are about 125,000 consumers in Meriden who spent an average of $150 per year in shoe stores. There are approximately 17 stores selling footwear in this area. Their combined square feet of selling area is 76,500. Calculate the Index of Retail Saturation for Meriden.

A P P L I C A T I O N S

CASE 1: Developers of Big Shopping Malls Tutor Faltering Tenants in Retail Techniques

With retailing in a slump, many shopping center developers are doing more than just collecting rent: they are trying to teach faltering tenants how to survive.

A growing number of landlords are offering workshops on retailing techniques. Some are even hiring consultants to help individual stores. Although benevolent, these actions are accounted for by a considerable element of self-interest. The landlords hope their programs will help stem rent concessions and forestall vacancies in their malls.

In addition, developers benefit directly from tenants' success because of leases that link rents to stores' gross sales. Landlords typically get a percentage of any sales above a threshold level set out in the leasing contract.

Tenant aid programs respond to a glut in shopping centers after the building boom of the 1980s. New mall construction has slowed to a crawl, so developers are left with two main ways of boosting profit: luring new customers from other malls or getting existing customers to spend more. "Now the most important thing is making the most out of what you've got," says Mary Rutkoski, director of mall marketing at Edward J. DeBartolo Corp., a Youngstown, Ohio, developer.

"Rather than hand out rent abatements when times are tough, [developers] have come to the realization that they would rather lend assistance" to bolster tenant sales, says Dana Dekker, senior marketing director at Richmond Center in Vancouver, British Columbia, commenting on alternatives to rent relief.

"There was a time when [tenant] vacancies were almost an unheard of thing. Now I think it's a fact of life for most centers. With economic conditions the way they are, we all know it looms in the background," Rutkoski says.

Tim Gonerka, manager of the Rouse Co.'s Tabor Center, a 65-store complex in Denver, says that his mall's counseling program has kept two or three retailers from going under.

Libby Smith runs the Positively Wild novelty item store at the Tabor Center. She says the mall's advisors told her that her main problem was a failure to focus her line of merchandise. "We just showed up every day and sold stuff," she says. "One month we'd have a lot of blow-up palm trees, the next month T-shirts. There wasn't a lot of cohesiveness about it."

After prodding from mall management, Smith decided that all her merchandise would have an animal theme. Then she added a jungle motif for the "tropical shopping experience." The result: sales at Positively Wild jumped 33 percent, putting the store "on the borderline" of paying percentage rent, Smith says. Any rise in sales this year will mean increased income for the Tabor Center.

Gloria Martin, owner of Keepsakes Too at the Tabor Center, asked the mall for help after the last Christmas season turned into a disaster. On management's advice, she has begun changing her window displays more frequently and added some $10 to $15 impulse items to her line of more expensive home furnishings. "If we don't turn the store around with what their advice has been, we shouldn't be in business," she says.

Source: Portions reproduced with permission from Larry M. Greenberg, "Developers of Big Shopping Malls Tutor Tenants in Retail Techniques," *The Wall Street Journal*, April 24, 1991, p. B1.

Applying Retailing Principles

1. How important should the availability of tutorial assistance programs for retailers be in choosing a retail site? What types of retail firms are most likely to take advantage of such assistance?
2. Should developers tell their tenants how to run their businesses? What can developers do besides offer tutorial assistance to stimulate sales?
3. Speculate on the types of shopping centers that are experiencing vacancies and the types of tenants who are likely to have difficulty meeting target sales levels. What are the alternatives for such centers? (You may want to refer to Case 2 in Chapter 4 as one example of efforts to reposition faltering shopping centers.)

CASE 2: The Gap Opens the Door to New Mall Concept

Town Square in Wheaton, Illinois (a suburb roughly 25 miles west of downtown Chicago), is part of a new trend—major shopping malls without department store anchors. Town Square is anchored by The Gap instead of a department store. The Gap, Gap Kids, Banana Republic, and Gap Outlet will be in the mall. All the remaining space is to be leased to specialty stores.

Anchorless malls are but one trend that is beginning to reshape the retail structure. Too much competition exists in shopping malls, especially for a population that is shopping less often.

Analysts predict that the retailing structure will look markedly different by the year 2000. For example, Management Horizons predicts that half of all retailers will be out of business by that time and that new retail construction will be moving at a snail's pace. Overstoring, overmalling, and changing demographics are likely to reduce the demand for goods and services available from traditional shopping centers.

Malls are responding to these changes in various ways. Some are offering valet parking, early-morning mall walks, and seniors-only shopping hours to benefit America's aging population. Still others are responding to the needs of busy parents. Malls are leasing space to child-care facilities to ease shopping trips. American Cartoon Theaters, for example, is opening kids-only cartoon theaters in numerous malls.

Experts contend that many shopping center developers still do not pay sufficient attention to population demographics. They note that there is "a market that doesn't want noise, bright lights, or lots of action. But stores are being created as if the entire population is between 14 and 35 years old."

The experts also forecast that malls of the future will have to rely on entirely different chains. One strong candidate is category killer stores such as Toys 'R' Us and Circuit City, which today are seldom found in large, enclosed malls. Still others argue that mall owners will begin to lease empty department store space to grocery outlets. Such a trend is underway in France, where the hypermarket Euromarche is entering malls in the Paris area. Increasing numbers of service operations will also find malls attractive outlets. Examples include health care facilities, day-care centers, multiuse centers that will house retail and entertainment facilities, and office space.

Experts also contend that malls will become more reflective of the diverse markets they serve, and they predict that current heavy dependence on apparel will lessen.

Source: Based on Adrienne Ward, "The Gap Opens Door to New Mall Concept," *Advertising Age,* January 21, 1991, p. 39.

Applying Retailing Principles

1. Why aren't traditional shopping malls as attractive to retailers as they were in earlier years?
2. Were shopping centers during the 1980s targeted primarily to teens and young adults? If so, why?
3. What shifts in the mix of mall tenants is likely to occur? Speculate about whether we are likely to see malls targeted primarily at senior citizens, ethnic groups, and similar market segments.

Notes

1. Gretchen Morgenson, "A Midas Touch," *Forbes*, February 1991, p. 42.
2. "Will the Big Mac Melt Dillybars?" *The Tuscaloosa News*, November 25, 1990, p. 11E.
3. Gary L. Crittenden, "Retailing's Critical Link: Market Share and Profitability," *Retail Control*, October 1990, p. 10.
4. Bruce Hager and Julia Flynn, "Podunk Is Beckoning," *Business Week*, December 23, 1991, p. 76.
5. Avijit Ghosh and Sara McLafferty, "The Shopping Center: A Restructuring of Postwar Retailing," *Journal of Retailing* 67 (Fall 1991), pp. 253–67.
6. Based on Robert O'Neill, "What's New in Shopping Center Positioning," *Monitor*, May 1990, pp. 68–70.
7. Howard Schlossberg, "Factory Outlets 'Mills' Growing but Long-Term Success Questioned," *Marketing News*, September 30, 1991, p. 1.
8. Jane A. Black, "Anchorless Centers," *Monitor*, September 1989, pp. 28–29; see also Howard Rudnitsky, "Battle of the Malls," *Forbes*, March 30, 1992, pp. 46–47.
9. For further reading, see Stephen Brown, "Retail Location Theory: Retrospect and Prospect," *Irish Marketing Review* 5, no. 2, 1990–91, pp. 52–60.
10. David L. Huff and Larry Blue, *A Programmed Solution for Estimating Retail Sales Potential* (Lawrence, Kansas: Center for Regional Studies, 1966).

C H A P T E R

10

Developing the Human Resources Plan

THIS CHAPTER:

Emphasizes the importance of formal personnel policies.

Explains how to determine needed job skills and how to recruit applicants.

Discusses how to select employees.

Reviews the essentials of an employee pay plan.

Shows how to plan employee benefits.

Defines the role of an employee performance appraisal system.

Outlines the issues involved in employee motivation and job enrichment.

Explores how to organize for profits.

RETAILING CAPSULE

ITO YOKADO AND NORDSTROM: PIONEERS IN EMPLOYEE ENFRANCHISEMENT

New ways of doing things are necessary to retail success in the 1990s. One idea that is working is enfranchisement—granting freedom and responsibility to employees in carrying out their job responsibilities. Enfranchisement comes about by a combination of pay for performance and empowering employees to make on-the-spot decisions supportive of a high level of customer service. The concept is an outgrowth of total quality management programs in retailing.

The Ito Yokado Group and Nordstrom are two retail organizations with vastly different cultures, but each has experienced remarkable success in pioneering the concept of employee enfranchisement. The Ito Yokado Group is a Japanese chain of department stores, restaurants, convenience stores, and other retail shops. Nordstrom is a chain of fashion department stores headquartered on the U.S. West Coast.

Sales at both Ito Yokado and Nordstrom, as shown in Table 10–1, are more than twice the average of their major competitors. The differences in return on assets are even more astounding.

Ito Yokado launched its program in 1982 with an emphasis on strengthening in-stock inventory and better understanding customer needs, and it redesigned and remerchandised outlets to reflect a renewed goal to provide value to customers. The program is consistent with Ito Yokado's traditional emphasis on seniority and job flexibility as part of a culture grounded in the delegation of decision making to a large number of people and in the heavy use of part-time employees. Management provided the employees with the latest information technology, complete current information, responsibility for decision making, and pay levels above the market rate based on the overall performance of the organization.

Nordstrom is known for its unusually wide selection of merchandise combined with a high level of service and competitive prices. Nordstrom employees are told that their sole responsibility is to satisfy customers. Such a message is reflective of the attitude expected of Nordstrom employees at all levels of the organization. Nordstrom pays its salespeople a commission on sales based on the extent to which they exceed their supervisors' projected forecasts. Strong merchandise depth, good store ambience, excellent locations, a primary emphasis on customer satisfaction, and strong monetary incentives have produced sales per square foot more than twice the industry average. The Nordstrom and Ito Yokado successes are strong evidence that empowerment as a human resources principle can serve an important role in retailing strategy during the 1990s.

Source: Based on Leonard A. Schlesinger and James Heskett, "Enfranchisement of Service Workers," *California Management Review* 33, no. 4, Summer 1991, pp. 83–100. Copyright 1991 by the Regents of the University of California. By permission of the Regents.

The new breed of retailer understands that employees want to work at a company that they can be proud of, that has values compatible with their own, that is focused on the long term, and that cares about morals and ethics and about the organization's effect on the environment.[1] Consider the following companies in addition to those mentioned in the Retailing Capsule:

Wal-Mart. Sam Walton realized from the beginning that a strong human resources base is at the heart of any organization committed to satisfying customer needs. He developed an organization that includes such programs as stock ownership and profit sharing to encourage employees to be more responsive to customers.[2]

Au Bon Pain. Management empowered its employees by implementing a partner/manager program in its stores. This is a profit-sharing program whereby the manager and associate manager of each unit share in the profits of that unit. Management also implemented a mystery shopper program (see Chapter 5) as an organized customer feedback project. Sales

TABLE 10–1

COMPARATIVE DATA FOR ITO YOKADO AND NORDSTROM

	*Ito Yokado**	*Nordstrom*†
Annual sales volume	$14.9 billion	$ 2.7 billion
Annual growth rate in the past five years:		
Subject company	8.0%	24.2%
Major competitors	5.1%	8.3%
Return on sales:		
Subject company	2.8%	4.5%
Major competitors	1.1%	2.1%
Return on assets:		
Subject company	3.4%	8.4%
Major competitors	1.9%	3.5%
Degree of empowerment	Extensive	Extensive
Amount of incentive, as percentage of total compensation	Up to 33%	Up to 100%
Nature of incentive	Group	Individual
Levels enfranchised	Managers and employees	Managers and employees
Employees included	All full-time and ⅓ of part-time	All full-time
Primary concentration	Buying, inventory control	Sales
Role of management	"Teachers & advisors"	"Satisfying customers"
Results	Fewer stockouts, lower inventory levels, less inventory loss, higher merchandise quality, employee commitment	Sales per sales hour and sales per square foot of selling space roughly double industry averages, low recruiting and advertising costs, average costs for sales labor and real estate in relation to sales, high employee and customer loyalty

*Operating data are for 1983 to 1988, and exclude franchised operations.
†Operating data are for 1983 to 1988.

Source: Leonard A. Schlesinger and James Heskett, "Enfranchisement of Service Workers," *California Management Review,* 3, no. 4, Summer 1991, p. 86. Reproduced by permission.

increased by more than 60 percent and controllable profits for the company, after salaries, nearly tripled over those from the previous year.[3]

Avon. At the New York headquarters office, all minority employees belong to in-house race-based networks. The networks serve as advocacy groups that have become an integral part of minority relations in the firm (see Exhibit 10–1). The Black Professionals Association, Avon Hispanic Network, and Avon Asian Network developed independently of one another as social groups but soon developed into self-help organizations devoted to encouraging minority recruiting and career development. The

EXHIBIT 10–1

© Steven Hill

Avon minority networks pave the way.

network heads meet directly with the Avon CEO in addressing issues important to the organization.[4]

Human resources staffs as never before are looking for ways to motivate and empower employees. The challenges are numerous:

- A labor shortage of 18 to 24-year-olds, who normally are the front line in the battle for retail sales.
- Training a nontraditional work force consisting increasingly of immigrants, Hispanics, Asians, blacks, and older people.
- Competing against other industries that normally pay more for entry-level and mid-level management employees.
- Identifying innovative approaches to finding and keeping good employees.
- Meeting expectations for sales increases, productivity, and customer satisfaction.
- Finding ways to remain competitive as mid-level managers and top-level executives continue to be eliminated in downsizing programs.[5]

The U.S. Bureau of Labor Statistics reports that between now and the year 2000 the service sector will create 20 million new jobs, 75 percent of them in retailing. The pool of entry-level workers, however, is dropping at the very time the number of entry-level jobs is increasing.[6]

Employees should not be regarded as throwaway assets. All dimensions of the human resources plan ranging from selection and placement to pay and performance appraisal should be structured to allow employees to feel as though they are a vital part of the organization.

The focus should always be on achievement-producing results. Intense people orientation, constantly reinforced, is the key to getting everyone committed to the goals to be achieved. The key element is making champions out of the people who give winning performances. The Disney Store, discussed in Focus 10–1, refers to employees as "cast members." McDonald's uses the term "crew members," and J. C. Penney refers to its employees as "associates." They all seek out reasons and opportunities to reward good performance.

The remaining portions of this chapter focus on three things: what employees are expected to do for the company, what the company can do for the employee, and how the two can work together to accomplish organizational objectives.

What the Employees Are Expected to Do for the Company

1. Job description and job analysis.
2. Recruit applicants.
3. Select employees.

What the Company Can Do for the Employee

1. Develop an employee pay plan.
2. Plan employee benefits.
3. Employee performance appraisal.

How the Company and Employees Can Work Together to Accomplish Organizational Objectives

1. Employee relations and personnel policies.
2. Job enrichment.
3. Organizing.

THE JOB ANALYSIS AND JOB DESCRIPTION[7]

A manager looking for someone to fill a job should begin by spelling out its requirements in a job description. Retailers should determine what skills are desirable, what skills an applicant can get by with, and what kind of training the employee needs.

If good job descriptions and clear job specifications exist, selection, training, and salary decisions will be much easier.[8] Job descriptions and job specifications are written from a job analysis.

FOCUS 10–1

"DISNEYESE"—A TOTAL CUSTOMER FOCUS

Everyone who is "employed" by Disney, from dishwasher to monorail operator, begins with three days of training and indoctrination at Disney University.

Disney never hires an employee for a job. The "actors" are "cast" in a "role" to perform in a "show." Sometimes the show is called Walt Disney World, sometimes Disneyland, sometimes The Disney Store, and so forth. Their main purpose is to look after the "guests." Disney has never had customers.

Every "cast member" is provided with a "costume," not a "uniform." That way a guest doesn't have to ask "Do you work here?" Each cast member is told not to hesitate to get a new costume if the old one gets dirty. Cast members do not work the floor; they are "on stage." The stock rooms and other nonpublic areas are "backstage."

One cast member is always designated to be the "greeter." The greeter position is a very important one. The role is to greet all guests as they enter and as they leave, and to thank them for "visiting our store," not for shopping. The greeter sets the tone for the guests' visit and also acts as a small deterrent to shoplifting because people are less likely to shoplift if they have been recognized by someone when they entered the store.

The words *no* and *I don't know* are not part of the Disney script. Everything is positive. Instead of "I don't know," cast members say, "I'll find out." Instead of, "We don't have any," cast members say, "We are out of," and instead of saying, "That item won't be available until," they say, "That item will be available on." Any response to the guest is phrased in a positive manner.

The Disney Store does not have stuffed animals; it has "plush" animals. A Disney Store cast member always points with an open palm, not the index finger. When you point with the index finger, four fingers are pointing back at you. Besides, when you were younger and your parents pointed at you, you knew you were in trouble.

The Disney show is several things. It's the entire experience that is created by the environment, the merchandise, the attractions, the music, and so forth, but, most importantly, it is the people. The cast members have a certain look that includes style of hair, makeup, name tags, and so on, all of which are a part of the Disney script.

What dimensions of the Disney employee culture appear to set the firm apart from other retailers?

Source: Prepared by Donald Smith, a cast member at The Disney Store, a Division of Walt Disney Enterprises.

Job Analysis

Job analysis is a method for obtaining important facts about a job. The job analysis obtains answers to four questions that the job description and job specification require:

1. **What** physical and mental tasks does the worker accomplish?
2. **How** does the person do the job? Here management describes the methods used and the equipment involved.
3. **Why** is the job done? This is a brief explanation of the purpose and responsibilities of the job that helps to relate it to other jobs.

4. **What qualifications** are needed for this job? Here the manager lists the knowledge, skills, and personal characteristics required.

A job analysis thus provides a summary of the following job elements:

- Duties and responsibilities.
- Relationships to other jobs.
- Knowledge and skills.
- Working conditions.

Conducting the Analysis. An easy way to begin a job analysis is to think about the various duties, responsibilities, and qualifications required for the position and jot them down on a notepad. The ingredients of a job analysis outline are shown in Table 10–2. Management should talk with the supervisor or the person who now holds the job to fill in the details about it.

When conducting a job analysis, describe the job and its requirements rather than the employee performing it. (The present employee may be overqualified or underqualified for the job or may simply have characteristics irrelevant to the job.)

Also keep in mind the ultimate goals of job analysis: to simplify and improve employee recruitment, training, and development, and to evaluate jobs for determination of salary and wage rates.

Using the Job Analysis. The job description and job specification can be written from the analysis. A **job description** describes the content and responsibilities of the job and the way it ties in with other jobs in the retail firm. The **job specification** describes the personal qualifications required to do the job.

The diagram below demonstrates the relationship of job analysis to job description and job specification.

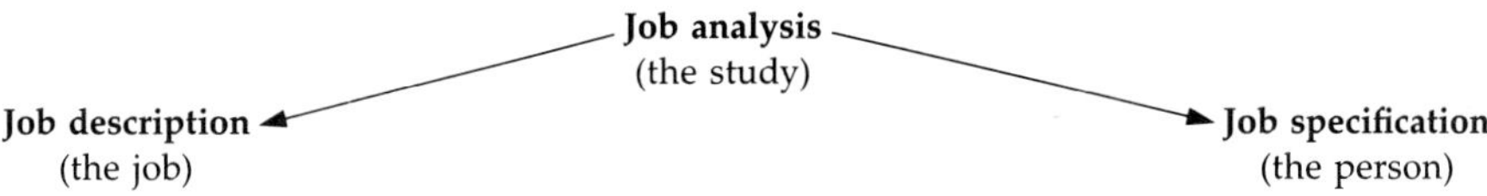

In addition to their usefulness in explaining duties and responsibilities to the applicants, job descriptions and specifications can help with the following processes:

- **Recruiting.** Job descriptions and specifications make it easier to write advertisements or notices announcing the job opening or to explain the job to an employment agency.
- **Interviewing applicants.** Because a job description provides a written record of the duties and requirements of a particular job, and a specification provides the qualifications needed for the job, they can be helpful in

TABLE 10–2

JOB ANALYSIS OUTLINE

Full-Service Gas Station Attendant

Duties

- Operates gasoline pump.
- Cleans windshields.
- Assists mechanics when requested.
- Takes end-of-day meter readings.
- Looks at tires.
- Cleans wrecker.
- Checks credit card list.
- Provides correct change to customer.
- Enforces no-smoking rule near gas pumps.

Education/experience

- Read, write, add, subtract, give change.

Relationships

- Reports to manager every morning and at the end of the shift.

Knowledge/skills

- Operate gas pump.
- Check oil and fluids.
- Add oil and fluids.
- Operate cash register.
- Bill customer using credit card.
- Operate emergency safety equipment.
- Change a flat tire and check air.
- Replace windshield wiper blades.

Physical Requirements

- Capable of basic manual skills.
- Able to work on feet all day.

On-the-job hazards/working conditions

- Minimal danger of equipment-related hazards if safety rules and regulations are followed.

---

planning an interview, especially as guidelines for asking the applicant key questions.

- **Training and development of new employees.** Having the duties of each job clearly defined can provide a basis for determining what knowledge and skills have to be taught to new employees and helps to plan training so that important skills are learned first and the training is comprehensive.
- **Coordination.** Job descriptions, when they are available, can help ensure that people know what is expected of them and that their activities are better coordinated.
- **Setting wage rates and salaries of employees.** By providing a better perspective of the relative amounts of work required and qualifications needed for different positions, fairer wage rates and salaries may be established.

TABLE 10–3

SAMPLE JOB DESCRIPTION FORM

JOB DESCRIPTION

Job Title: Department Manager Date: ________

Statement of the Job

Supervises retail sales personnel, maintains merchandise displays, orders merchandise for the department, and provides training for sales staff.

Major Duties

1. Plans merchandise assortments and selection.
2. Works with merchandise vendors in planning the following:
   a. Delivery dates for merchandise assortments.
   b. Prices to be paid, including discounts and allowances.
3. Supervises and supports departmental retail sales staff as follows:
   a. Provides up-to-date information on merchandise assortments and selection.
   b. Maintains and coordinates work schedules.
4. Provides continuing training in customer relations, sales skills, store policies, and advancement opportunities.
5. Sees to proper care and display of merchandise assortments.

Relationships

The department manager supervises the department's retail sales staff and the assistant department manager. The department manager reports to the store manager in planning programs to meet department sales and profitability goals.

- **Employee relations.** The information about the job in the description can ensure that fewer misunderstandings will occur about the respective duties and responsibilities of various jobs.

Job Description

A fully adequate job description should fit on one piece of paper. For instance, a job description for a department manager might look like Table 10–3.

Job Specification

A job specification describes the type of employee required for successful performance of the job. One way to prepare a job specification is shown in Table 10–4.

RECRUITING APPLICANTS[9]

The steps just discussed allow the retailer to answer inquiries concerning the position and save the trouble of interviewing applicants who do not meet minimum standards for the job.

Selecting the Right Recruiting Methods

The recruiting methods used depend upon what type of employee is sought and how hard the retailer wants to search for the best available candidate.

TABLE 10–4

SAMPLE JOB SPECIFICATION FORM

JOB SPECIFICATION

Job Title: Visual Merchandiser — Date: ________

Education (List only that which is really necessary for the job, e.g., high school, college, trade school, or other special training.)

Bachelor's degree in fashion merchandising or related field.

Experience (The amount of previous and related experience a new employee should have.)

1 year experience in a similar department.

Knowledge/Skills (List the specific knowledge and skills the job may require.)

Must know how to perform the following tasks:

- Develop attractive seasonal displays of merchandise.
- Creatively use lighting and visual effects in merchandise display.
- Work with vendors on special merchandise displays.
- Negotiate display allowances.
- Select fabrics, colors, and other display materials.
- Work with department managers in planning special sales and promotional events.

Physical and Mental Requirements (Mention any special physical or mental abilities required for the job, e.g., 20/20 eyesight, availability for irregular work hours, ability to work under time pressure, etc.)

Must have a pleasant personality and clean appearance. Must be well mannered and able to stand on feet all day.

Each recruiting method has its advantages and disadvantages. Some may be time-consuming, such as direct newspaper ads, which require screening of all who apply, or notices on college bulletin boards, which may be very slow in bringing in an adequate number of applicants. Others can be fairly costly, such as employment agencies, where competent applicants often expect the retailers to pick up the fee. Some can be used concurrently, but it would be inefficient to use others in such a way. Various possibilities are suggested in Table 10–5.

Reviewing Recruiting Practices

It is useful to review the firm's recruiting practices from time to time to see how they can be improved. The retailer may wish to simply note what brought success, as well as the methods that did not seem to work well. For example, it may turn out that the store's employees have often been able to refer better applicants than the employment agencies. Or it could be that advertising in the local newspaper seems to bring better applicants than posting notices on college bulletin boards. A summary and checklist for recruiting practices is shown in Table 10–6.

Star Wars Technology Affects All Retailing Functions

(Courtesy Arthur Andersen & Co.)

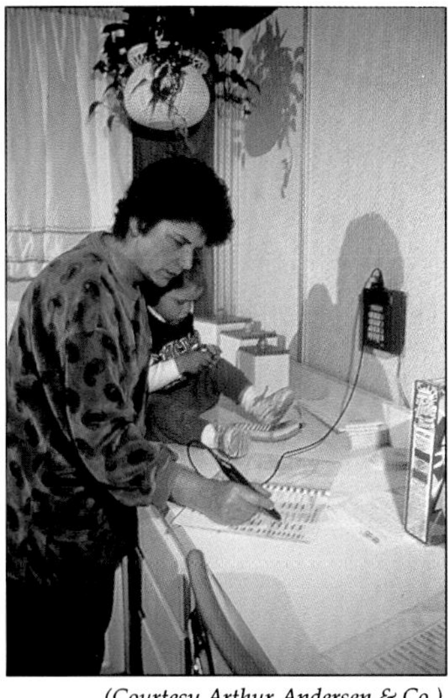

(Courtesy Arthur Andersen & Co.)

AT THE STORE WHERE YOU CAN'T BUY ANYTHING, ANDERSEN CONSULTING SMARTSTORE 2000 IN CHICAGO PRESENTS A CROSS SECTION AND BREEDING GROUND FOR TECHNOLOGICAL ADVANCES DESIGNED TO ADDRESS CONSUMER, MANUFACTURER, AND RETAILER PRIORITIES

(Courtesy Arthur Andersen & Co.)

KMART'S AUTOMATED DISTRIBUTION CENTER – THE PICTURES TELL THE STORY

(Courtesy of Kmart Corporation)

(Courtesy of Kmart Corporation)

(Courtesy of Kmart Corporation)

IT MAY LOOK LIKE NBC, CBS, OR EVEN CNN, BUT IT'S J. C. PENNEY'S IN-HOUSE TV STATION FOR INTRACOMPANY MERCHANDISE COMMUNICATION

(Courtesy of J. C. Penney Company, Inc.)

(Courtesy of J. C. Penney Company, Inc.)

(Courtesy of J. C. Penney Company, Inc.)

The Year 2000 Is Closer Than You Think

(Courtesy Walgreens)

Cashier-assisted scanning at Walgreens.

(Courtesy Walgreens)

Walgreens' satellite dish will become commonplace on the retailing scene as the year 2000 approaches.

(Courtesy of American Greetings Corporation)

An exciting innovation–Computerized/personalized greetings, the CreataCard.

TABLE 10–5

SOURCES OF EMPLOYEE RECRUITS

- Recruiting through an employment agency
- Recruiting through the local Chamber of Commerce
- Advertising in local magazines or newspapers
- Advertising in the specialized magazines and journals of your trade
- Informing friends and acquaintances of the position
- Asking business associates to refer individuals who might be interested and qualified
- Recruiting through a state employment service
- Recruiting through CETA and county agencies
- Stealing employees from competition
- Recruiting through specialized trade schools
- Advertising in local shopper-type newspapers

Selecting Employees

After recruiting a number of job candidates, the retailer has to weed out the unqualified ones and then select the best remaining candidate for the job. The main tools will be the questions asked and perhaps pre-employment tests. Answers to some questions may be obtained through a résumé, but by far the most informative answers come from a job interview and the job application form.

Many different selection methods are available. These include personal interviews, tests, and recommendations from various people who had

TABLE 10–6 SUMMARY AND CHECKLIST FOR REVIEWING AND IMPROVING RECRUITING PRACTICES

Know the job and the skills required for the job, and the kind of person you are looking for (a job description and job specification can help you here).
Give the people who answer the telephone an adequate description of the job so that they can answer inquiries without referring them to you.
Give a brief job description to employees, school personnel, and businesspeople you know to help you with recruiting so that they can inform prospective applicants of the specific nature of the position you want to fill.
Set minimum standards for applicants so that others can screen inquiries for you.
Use all potential sources for bringing in applicants that are appropriate for the respective positions.
Run an ad under several different headings or titles whenever an initial ad does not supply an adequate number of qualified applicants.
Visit employment agencies to check the quality of screening personnel, and ask them to visit your operation with you so that they understand your needs more clearly.
Conduct a follow-up of your recruiting practices from time to time.
Review, from time to time, what attempts brought you good candidates and what attempts were less successful.
Review periodically, how successful various types of applicants are.
Thank employees, businesspeople, school officials, or others who have helped by sending you candidates.
Review, from time to time, the cost of your recruiting practices in terms of actual money spent, time used by others, and your own time.
Try different approaches if you find that your recruiting cost is high.

contact with the candidates. The personnel office seeks to develop objective criteria in screening applicants to achieve the best match of person and position. One frequent approach to this problem is the development of performance criteria. Such an approach involves identifying the characteristics of those who perform the job in a superior manner. These characteristics are then sought in potential new employees. Ideally, a limited number of characteristics can be isolated. Executives can use the performance criteria in predicting which applicants will perform most satisfactorily. Such predictors may include intelligence scores, tests of manual dexterity, formal education, or past related job experiences.

One potential problem, however, is bias against some applicants because of the measures being used. Federal, state, and local governments actively challenge selection tools that can lead to bias in hiring. Companies can use employment tests if they can show that the tests are valid and reliable in predicting job success and that no better way exists to make such evaluations. This process is difficult and requires the use of statistics, including coefficients of correlation and other measures. Tests may also be biased because of cultural or language problems for some applicants.

The burden of proof rests with the employer. The employer must be able to show that the procedure utilized is capable of predicting job performance and does not systematically discriminate against any one group of applicants. Arbitrary job descriptions that specify minimum education levels, age, sex, marital status, or similar requirements are open to challenge. Management cannot use that "gut" feeling any more, because a rejected applicant may sue, charging unlawful discrimination on a variety of grounds.

Preliminary Screening of Applicants. It is wise to ask applicants to send résumés before scheduling appointments for interviews. This has two advantages:

- Reviewing résumés will enable the retailer to screen out some unacceptable job candidates. Priorities can also be assigned to the résumés so that the most promising candidates are seen first. In this way, the retailer will run less risk of losing the best ones to job openings in other firms while going through the selection procedure.
- When the retailer decides to interview a candidate, some background information on the person will be available from the résumé and thus will enable the retailer to ask better questions and conduct a better interview.

Equal Employment Opportunity Laws. In trying to obtain answers to key questions, the retailer must keep the laws of the land in mind. Questions that have no bearing to the job are discriminatory. That is, the applicant may gain the impression that the decision to hire is based on something other than the ability to perform the job. If this is the case, the

TABLE 10–7 MAJOR FEDERAL FAIR EMPLOYMENT PRACTICES REGULATIONS

Regulation	*General Coverage*	*Private Employer Jurisdiction*	*Basic Requirements*
Title VII of the Civil Rights Act of 1964, as amended in 1972 (Equal Employment Opportunity Commission).	Discrimination in employment on the basis of race, color, sex, national origin, or religion.	Employers with 15 or more employees.	Affirmative action may be included in a conciliation agreement or by court order.
Age Discrimination in Employment Act of 1967, as amended.	Age discrimination in employment of persons between the ages of 40 and 70.	Employers with 20 or more employees.	Affirmative action may be required after discrimination is found to exist.
Equal Pay Act of 1963, as amended in 1974 (Equal Employment Opportunity Commission).	Discrimination in compensation on the basis of sex.	Employers under coverage of the Fair Labor Standards Acts.	Affirmative action other than salary adjustment and back pay is not required.
Executive Orders 11246, 11375, and 11141.	Discrimination in employment on the basis of race, color, age, religion, or sex.	Employers holding federal contracts or subcontracts in excess of $10,000.	Written affirmative action plans are required of federal contractors and subcontractors with contracts in excess of $50,000 and 50 or more employees.
Vocational Rehabilitation Act Amendments of 1973 and Executive Order 11914.	Discrimination in employment on the basis of physical or mental handicap.	Employers holding federal contracts or subcontracts in excess of $2,500.	Same as above.
Vietnam Era Veterans Readjustment Act of 1974.	Discrimination against disabled veterans and Vietnam War veterans, but more of an affirmative action order than antidiscrimination policy.	Employers holding federal contracts or subcontracts in excess of $10,000.	Same as above.
Pregnancy Discrimination Act of 1978, amending the Civil Rights Act of 1964.	Discrimination against pregnant women in hiring, promoting, or giving a wage increase.	Any firm with 15 or more employees.	Women affected by pregnancy-related conditions must be treated in the same way as people who have other disabilities.

retailer may be breaking one or several of the equal employment opportunity laws, summarized in Table 10–7, and be sued for damages.

Equal employment opportunity laws state that the retailer may not discriminate against an applicant on the basis of the applicant's race, religion, sex, national origin, or age. Affirmative action programs can help ensure that the employer is sensitive to the need for racial, cultural, sexual, and demographic diversity.

In addition to these federal laws, there are many state laws that are intended to accomplish essentially the same purpose.

Interviewing Promising Applicants

After preliminary screening, it is necessary to interview the remaining job candidates.

Planning the Interview. Before the interview, review the candidate's application form and résumé. Reviewing the candidate's background against a job specification is a quick way to check for completeness of information, and it often brings to mind additional questions to ask.

Confirming Initial Impressions. Experienced interviewers agree that they gain greater insight into the potential of an applicant during a second interview several days, or possibly weeks, after the first one. Some people ask applicants to plan to spend several hours at a second interview.

Checking References. The final step in the selection procedure is the reference check. References need to be checked for only the one or two applicants best qualified for the job. It is best to contact references on the telephone, or in person. Here, open questions should be used to bring out the most information about an applicant.

Checking the accuracy of information the applicant has given is generally easy. The reference can be asked the dates the employee worked for the organization, the salary level, and the reasons for separation.

The failure to adequately check references and background can be costly. McDonald's, for example, was ordered to pay over $200,000 in a negligent hiring case when an ex-convict guilty of child molestation attacked a woman and her young son. The company had argued that it didn't know the employee had a previous conviction for child molestation.[10]

Executive Development Programs

Thus far, we have focused on the issues of hiring entry-level employees. Executive development and training programs, often of primary interest to college graduates, are covered in the appendix at the end of the text. Executive training programs involve rotation among various departments to allow a junior executive to become familiar with all operations. The programs vary in content and are designed to provide a springboard to senior management positions. Such programs provide extensive on-the-job training assignments to allow employees to develop an understanding of both merchandising and operations management procedures. The completion of the program typically involves a promotion to a position of greater responsibility in a retail store.

DEVELOPING THE PAY PLAN[11]

A formal pay plan, one that lets employees understand not only their current salary but also where they can go as far as salary is concerned, will not solve all employee relations problems. It will, however, remove one of those areas of doubt and rumor that may keep the work force anxious, unhappy, less loyal, and more mobile.

Types of Salary Plans

A formal pay plan does not have to cost a lot of time and money. Formal does not mean complex. In fact, the more elaborate the plan, the more difficult it is to put into practice.

The foremost concern in setting up a formal pay plan is to get the acceptance, understanding, and support of management and supervisory employees. A well-defined, thoroughly discussed, and properly understood plan is a prerequisite for success.[12]

Job Evaluation and Compensation. The question of how much to pay an employee in a particular position is a complicated matter. If management offers too little pay, a good employee will leave. Only a less motivated, less able employee will remain. On the other hand, management has little to gain by paying an employee more than what is being paid elsewhere for a comparable job.

Job evaluation is a method of ranking jobs to help establish compensation levels. The diagram that appeared earlier can now be used to demonstrate the relationship of these four basic personnel management tools.

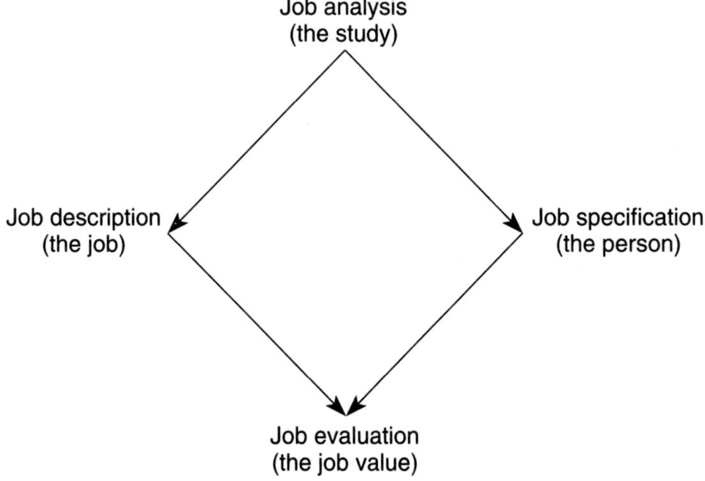

A job evaluation is developed by evaluating the responsibilities from the job description and the items on the job specification. The reason for job evaluation is to establish a fair level of employee compensation.

In determining pay rates, it is important to keep several principles in mind:

- Equal pay for equal work.
- Higher pay for work requiring more knowledge, skill, or physical exertion.
- Reasonable pay in comparison to pay for similar work in other organizations.
- Overqualified employees are not paid more (or much more) than other employees in the same position.
- Very little or no extra pay for the length of time an employee has remained with the firm in the same position.
- Total earnings reflect, in some way, the employee's contribution to the organization.
- As much as possible, pay scales are known to employees.
- Fairness in application of these principles.

One rule of thumb is to pay the most important nonsupervisory job at least as well as other firms pay for the same job and to do the same for the least important nonsupervisory job. Rates for all other jobs can then be set in between.

The Rank Method. A simple way to evaluate jobs is to rank them, possibly with the aid of job descriptions. The most valuable and complex job is assigned a '1'; the job that is second in complexity and importance, a '2'; and so on, until all jobs have been assigned a number. (Jobs that are equal in importance may be assigned the same number.) In creating new jobs, management can then place them into their proper places in the ranking.

For example, suppose a restaurant manager who is looking for an assistant manager, a cook's helper, and a dishwasher has created the following ranking list:

Job Rank	*Job Title*	*Salary or Wage Rate*
1	Manager	$25,000.00–$30,000.00
2	Assistant Manager	
3	Cook 1	$15,000.00–$17,000.00
4	Cook 2	$6.00–$6.50/hour
5	Head Waiter/Waitress	$5.50–$6.00/hour
6	Cook's Helper	
7	Waiter/Waitress	Min. wage and tips averaging $5.00/hour
8	Dishwasher	

In this case, then, the assistant manager should be paid more than a cook, but less than a manager, somewhere between $15,000 and $25,000 per year. A cook's helper seems to fit in the range of less than $6.00 per hour, but more than $5.00 per hour. The dishwasher, being the "least important" job, would receive minimum wage or only a little above it.

The Classification Method. In this method, jobs are evaluated and rated on two scales:

- **Complexity.** The responsibilities and qualifications required and their importance to good performance.
- **Length of time.** The extent to which the responsibility and qualification is utilized during a typical day.

For example, if knowledge of computer programming is required, it may receive a 7 for responsibility and qualification, but if that knowledge is required only a few hours out of each week, it may receive a 2 for length of time. These two numbers can then be multiplied and averaged with all other qualifications and responsibilities of that job to provide a classification number. Large numbers indicate the more difficult and important positions. The method of evaluating jobs based on classification is a complex one and cannot be adequately described in this book. (For further reading, see textbooks on compensation management.)

Planned Pay Structure. In general, a planned pay structure makes it possible to tie individual rates of pay to job performance and contribution to company goals. Table 10–8 shows the most frequently used retail sales pay plans.

Straight Salary. A straight salary is most likely to be paid in a small store in which employees have a variety of responsibilities other than selling. This plan also avoids the temptation for employees to engage in "pressure" selling. The drawback is that the plan does not provide an incentive for extra effort, which may lower employee motivation.

Salary Plus Commission. A salary plus commission is the most frequently used plan in retailing, primarily because it emphasizes both selling and customer service. It provides an extra financial incentive for "plus sales" and also provides a stable income for employees.

Quota Plus Bonus. The quota plus bonus plan provides, in addition to a base salary, for the payment of a bonus as a varying percentage of sales achieved above a quota established for each category of merchandise. The program allows unique sales incentives to be established by category of merchandise or tasks, does not encourage overly aggressive selling, and does provide a stable income during periods of slow sales. The disadvantages are that the plan can be misunderstood by employees and that it must be changed to reflect changes in the merchandise mix by season.

TABLE 10–8 STRENGTHS AND WEAKNESSES OF SELECTED FORMS OF RETAIL SALESPERSON COMPENSATION

Method of Payment	*Formula*	*Advantages*	*Disadvantages*
Straight salary	Amount of pay established in advance for a defined pay period	Definite and easy for employees to understand Generally best for smaller stores Minimizes temptation to use "pressure" selling Encourages more conscientious and careful work Provides easier managerial control Good for inexperienced/new employees Simplifies payroll Provides a definite income to employees Fair	Inflexible Provides no financial incentive for extra effort Compensation does not fluctuate in proportion to sales volume Lack of incentives could promote laziness Strong supervision often required No opportunity to earn extra income
Example: Calculate the earnings of a salesperson who worked 40 hours during a week at the rate of $6 per hour. *Solution:* 40 × $6 = $240			
Salary plus commission	Guaranteed minimum salary plus a small additional percentage based on amount of sales	Easy for employees to understand Emphasizes selling and customer service Stable income guaranteed when volume is low Provides financial incentive for extra effort Incentives easily controlled by management Good opportunity to earn extra income Less managerial supervision necessary	Small incentives could be ineffective Even ineffective salespeople receive commissions Increases departmental selling costs Poor salespeople could lose customers with "pressure" selling
Example: A salesperson who earns $6 per hour plus 2 percent commission on sales worked 39 hours during the week and had sales of $2,400 for that period. *Solution:* (39 × $6) + ($2,400 × 2%) = $234 + $48 = $282			
Quota bonus plan	Various percentages of sales are paid for different levels of sales achieved above the quotas set for each category of merchandise	Effective in smaller establishments Good incentives for special sales or tasks Encourages competitive spirit Stable income guaranteed when volume is low Does not overly promote "pressure" selling Very flexible for managerial use Automatic check against excess personnel Ensures prompt service to customers Less managerial supervision necessary	Not as easily understood by employees Sales returns could cause withheld bonuses and thus ill feelings Setting rates for quota bonuses is a delicate task Quota could be difficult to set from past sales Bonuses must be changed often for seasonal goods Unattainable bonuses destroy incentive

Example: A salesperson earns an 8 percent commission on sales made in excess of $2,000. Calculate the weekly earnings for an employee whose sales equaled $4,000, assuming the salesperson earns a weekly base salary of $200.
Solution: ($4,000 − $2,000) × 8% = $160 + $200 = $360

Method of Payment	*Formula*	*Advantages*	*Disadvantages*
Straight commission	Salary is based entirely on a percentage of sales. The percentage is typically higher for the most profitable merchandise.	Provides strong incentives to salespeople Easy for employees to understand Attracts better salespeople Guarantees planned selling cost for store Easy for management to operate Drawing account to ensure a definite income per pay period could be established by management to offset some disadvantages of this method (When necessary, pay is charged against future commissions)	Employees must be well trained and supervised No guaranteed income Factors beyond salesperson's control could substantially diminish earnings Too uncertain for average retail salesperson "Pressure" selling strongly encouraged Customers could be antagonized Focus generally on high-cost goods Senior salespeople take high-cost goods, leaving juniors with low-cost goods Ill will and tension level between salespeople

Example: Calculate the earnings of a salesperson whose sales for the week were $5,200 at the commission rate of 7 percent.
Solution: $5,200 × 7% = $364

Drawing account	Cash advance to a salesperson against future sales	Provides security Guarantees regular income Stabilizes income when sales are highly seasonal Discourages overly aggressive selling	Employee may view the draw as a salary, not a loan Employees in arrears may quit

Example: A retail salesperson draws $1,000 at the beginning of each month, and she earns a commission of 10 percent on sales volume. Her monthly sales during this period are $40,000, then $15,000, and finally $30,000.
Solution

Month	*Draw*	*Sales volume*	*Commission earned*	*End-of-month payment*
December	$1,000	$30,000	$3,000	$2,000
January	$1,000	$ 5,000	$ 500	0 (rep owes $500)
February	$1,000	$20,000	$2,000	$500, computed as follows: Commission = $2,000 Less draw − $1,000 Less February debt −$500 Net $500

Straight Commission. The straight commission plan provides a strong incentive for outstanding salespeople and thus is likely to attract talented sales personnel. The disadvantage is that the arrangement can promote overly aggressive "pressure" selling which can antagonize customers. Employees may also be prone to focus excessive attention on high-cost goods, thereby creating ill will and tension between salespeople.

Drawing Account. A drawing account is a cash advance paid to retail salespeople. The account is established as a "draw" for the employee as needed. The amount withdrawn is repaid to the company out of the sales commissions earned during each period. A drawing account may or may not be guaranteed. Under a **nonguaranteed** plan, the advance is a loan. The balance of the debt is carried over to the next period if the salesperson does not earn a sufficient amount in commissions to pay back the advance in a single period. A **guaranteed** draw account is one in which the loan debt is cancelled if the salesperson's commissions are less than the draw. In effect, a guaranteed draw is much like a salary. For that reason, the nonguaranteed draw is more widely used because it is less of a financial burden on the retailer.

Drawing accounts are designed to offset some of the disadvantages of the straight commission plan. They provide both security and regularity of income. The accounts are subject to abuse, however. Salespeople may view the draw as salary rather than a loan. In addition, employees in arrears may simply quit. Drawing accounts are declining in popularity because of the problems involved in administering them. Retailers instead are more prone to supplement a commission with a salary.

Installing the Plan

At this point, employers have a general pay plan, but they do not, of course, pay in general. They pay each employee individually. They must now consider how the plan will be administered to provide for individual pay increases.

There are several approaches for administering the pay increase feature of the plan:

- **Merit increases,** granted to recognize performance and contribution.
- **Promotional increases,** given to employees assigned different jobs in higher pay levels.
- **Tenure increases,** given to employees for time worked with the company.
- **General increases,** granted to employees to maintain real earnings as required by economic factors and to keep pay competitive.

These approaches are the most common, but there are many variations. Most annual increases are made for cost of living, tenure, or employment market reasons. Obviously, employers might use several, all, or combinations of the various increase methods. Whichever they choose, employers should document salary increases for each employee and record the reasons for them.

Updating the Plan

To keep the pay administration plan updated, the employer should review it at least annually. Adjustments should be made where necessary. This is not the kind of plan that can be set up and then forgotten.

During the annual review, the managers should ask themselves these important questions: Is the plan working? Are we getting the kind of employees we want or are we just making do? What is the turnover rate? Do employees seem to care about the business? What matters is how the plan helps employers achieve the objectives of the business.

PLANNING EMPLOYEE BENEFITS[13]

Employee benefits costs have continued to accelerate since the enactment of the first state law requiring workers' compensation around 1900 and passage of the Social Security Act of 1935.

Benefits include holidays and paid vacations, insurance, health care, pensions, social security, disability payments, and services such as credit unions, product or service discounts, legal assistance, travel clubs, and food services.

Social security, workers' compensation, and unemployment compensation—which are the only legally required benefits—can be managed with minimal difficulty by keeping records, submitting forms to the proper authorities, and paying for the required coverage. But when choosing and managing other types of benefits, employers should get professional advice in planning and setting up a program.

Many employers now pay for most, if not all, of the employees' life, medical, and disability insurance. The rapid escalation of benefits cost, as compared to direct pay compensation, has caused managers to become more diligent in controlling these costs.

The benefits plan should be sufficiently flexible to meet the varying needs of employees. For example, employees who are older and no longer have children at home have different needs from employees with young children. Some employees may prefer more dental coverage, or still others with a spouse employed elsewhere may prefer limited medical coverage but higher life insurance coverage.

EMPLOYEE PERFORMANCE APPRAISAL

Many retail employees are under a merit pay system. This approach involves a periodic review and appraisal of how well they are doing. An effective plan does the following:

- Establishes good two-way communication between the manager and the employee.
- Relates pay to results.
- Provides a standardized approach to evaluation.
- Helps employees see how they can improve by better understanding their job responsibilities and management's expectations.

Performance reviews also help the manager doing the appraising to gain insight into the organization. An open exchange between employee and employer can show the manager where improvements in equipment, procedures, or other factors might improve employee performance. Managers should try to foster a climate in which employees can discuss progress and problems informally at any time.

Again, to get the best results, it helps to use a standardized form of appraisal. A typical form focuses attention on results achieved; quality of performance; volume of work; effectiveness in working with others; effectiveness in dealing with customers, suppliers, and other employees; initiative; job knowledge; and dependability.

EMPLOYEE RELATIONS AND PERSONNEL POLICIES

There are many ways to manage people. The manager can be strict or rigidly enforce rules. Communications can be one-way from boss to employee. The job might get done, but with fairly high turnover, absenteeism, and low morale.

Or the owner can make an extra effort to be a "nice guy" to everyone on the payroll. Controlling the daily operation will become more and more difficult. But there is another way in which employees can feel as though they are a part of the firm, manager and employees can communicate effectively with each other, and rules are fair and flexible, yet enforced with positive discipline. The job gets done efficiently and profitably, and the business does well.[14] Fairness and credibility start with top management and establish the value system of the organization, as illustrated in A Question of Ethics.

Developing Job Commitment[15]

The key point is that when a job satisfies basic needs, the employee may bring greater commitment to the job.

Five factors generally cause a deep commitment by most employees:

1. **The work itself.** To what extent does the employee see the work as meaningful and worthwhile?
2. **Achievement.** How much opportunity is there for the employee to accomplish tasks that are seen as a reasonable challenge?

A Question of Ethics

THE RISE AND FALL OF A RETAIL KING—THE JOE BROOKS SAGA AT ANN TAYLOR

Joe Zatz (who changed his name to Joe Brooks) created one of retailing's most potent myths. He zoomed through the ranks of Federated Department Stores, moved to become President of Filene's, and then joined Lord & Taylor as its chairman. He made it the crown jewel of its corporate parent, Associated Dry Goods (ADG), before being forced out in 1986 by the May Company when it took over ADG. He then bought Ann Taylor, a chain of sophisticated fashion stores, in 1989 with the aid of Merrill Lynch Capital Partners before being forced out two years later as the firm went into a tailspin. Brooks's behavior provides insight into the power of top retailing executives and the potential for its abuse.

Brooks employed his three children at Ann Taylor: Victoria as a fashion designer, Elizabeth in public relations, and Thomas, who at age 38 was made president and chief operating officer. In 1991, Thomas was caught smuggling watches worth about $140,000 through the U.S. Customs Office at Kennedy Airport. (In 1984 he had been caught with about $7,000 in undeclared goods at the Los Angeles International Airport.) Brooks sought to downplay his son's mistake, calling it stupid but noting that other people do it. Pressure from executives with Merrill Lynch forced Thomas Brooks to resign.

Joe Brooks has a love for the good life. He earned $250,000 in 1975, $400,000 in 1980, $679,000 in 1986, and $1,952,000 in 1990. The manager in one of Ann Taylor's Florida stores reports that a bathroom was set aside for Brooks whenever he visited. Security guards were posted. "He had a special toilet seat, special colognes. The whole store was painted before he came. I guess he was a clean freak." He apparently believed that he was royalty and expected to be treated as such.

Various other allegations that he took advantage of his position emerged. One fashion executive, for example, said that his firm provided tens of thousands of dollars' worth of clothing to the Brooks family, for which he was never paid. He points out that no bill was sent. "He asked me to make special dresses for his wife many times ... they were free of charge. Remember, this store has hundreds of branches. The orders are so large. They have got you by the short hairs. Don't say no. The question is, at what point does it become questionable?"

What ethical problems, if any, do you see in Brooks's behavior?

Based on Michael Gross, "The Great Zatzby: The Rise and Fall of a Retail King," *New York*, January 20, 1992, pp. 34–43.

3. **Responsibility.** To what extent does the employee have assignments and the authority necessary to take care of a significant function of the organization?
4. **Recognition.** To what extent is the employee aware of how highly other people value the contributions he or she makes?
5. **Advancement.** How much opportunity exists for the employee to assume greater responsibilities in the firm?

These five factors tend to satisfy certain critical needs of individuals:

- The feeling of *being accepted* as part of the firm's workteam.
- *Feeling important*—that the employee's strengths, capabilities and contributions are known and valued highly.
- The chance to *continue to grow* and become a more fully functioning person.

If these needs are met, management will have taken significant steps toward gaining the full commitment of employees.

Positive Discipline

The word *discipline* carries with it many negative meanings. It is often used as a synonym for punishment. Yet discipline is also used to refer to the spirit that exists in a successful sports team for which team members are willing to consider the needs of the team as more important than their own.

Positive discipline in a retail firm creates an atmosphere of mutual trust and common purpose in which all employees understand the company rules as well as the objectives and do everything possible to support them.

Any disciplinary program has, as its base, the premise that all employees clearly understand exactly what is expected of them. This is why a concise set of rules and standards must exist that are fair, clear, realistic, and communicated. Once the standards and rules are known, discipline can be enforced equitably.

Corrective Action. No matter how good the atmosphere is in a business, rules are bound to be broken from time to time. In those situations, corrective action is sometimes necessary. In some rare cases, the violation may be so severe that serious penalties are necessary. If an employee is caught in the act of stealing or deliberately destroys company property, summary dismissal may be called for. In other cases, a corrective interview may be needed to determine the reasons for the problem and to establish what penalty, if any, is appropriate. Such an interview should include all, or most, of the following steps:

1. Outlining the problem to the employee, including an explanation of the rule or procedure that was broken.
2. Allowing the employee to explain his or her side of the story. (This step will often bring out problems that need to be resolved to avoid rule violations in the future.)
3. Exploring with the employee what should be done to prevent a recurrence of the problem.
4. Reaching agreement with the employee on the corrective action that should be taken.

A written grievance procedure that is known to employees can be very helpful in creating a positive atmosphere. It informs employees how they

A Profile in Excellence

MARY KAY ASH

Mary Kay Ash has not always been the glamorous "pink" lady and executive of a top cosmetic company, but she has always been a person who put forth her best effort.

Mary Kay was forced into working when her husband of 11 years abandoned her with three children. She took a job with a direct sales company, Stanley Home Products, specializing in housewares. After 13 years and numerous awards, she became affiliated with World Gift, a direct sales firm involved in decorative accessories. For health reasons, Mary Kay retired from World Gift. She married but became bored with retirement. During her period of retirement, Mary Kay thought about "what was wrong with male-run companies" and decided to do something about it.

In 1963, she paid $5,000 for a tanning solution formula that she had first noticed at a Stanley party in 1953. That was the beginning of the Mary Kay empire.

Mary Kay has a unique ability to motivate people. She promotes sisterhood within the company. The beauty consultants see her as the "ultimate" in beauty, both physical and mental. She builds up excitement and enthusiasm in encouraging each beauty consultant to strive for personal goals. Mary Kay's theme "You Can Do It" encourages her beauty consultants not to quit, not to give up, but to keep on selling. She continually praises and rewards. She gives cars for reaching predetermined, attainable goals, and other prizes such as diamond pendants, telephone answering machines, leather briefcases, and rings. She also offers her beauty consultants the ability to be their own boss, paying a 50 percent commission on retail sales and allowing the consultants to set their own work hours.

can obtain a hearing on their problems and it assures them that the owner or manager becomes aware that the problem exists. When employees know that someone will listen to them, grievances are less serious, and hearing a complaint carefully often is half the job of resolving it.

A good grievance procedure begins with the manager making it a point to be actively looking for signs of possible sources of dissatisfaction, and by noticing changes in employee behavior that signal that a problem may exist. This often makes it possible to handle a situation when it is still easy to resolve.

JOB ENRICHMENT

Too many companies today still treat employees as throwaway assets. The average annual turnover rate among hourly restaurant employees, for example, is 300 percent. Many employees leave within 30 days of employment, wasting whatever training they've been given. The retail investment is too high to allow such problems to occur.

Forward-thinking managers view the employee as a total person (see A Profile in Excellence). They are concerned with what the employee does during working hours and during time off the job. They try to help

10–9 MOST FREQUENTLY OFFERED MOTIVATION AND ENRICHMENT PROGRAMS

	Have Such a Practice	*Favor Such a Practice*
Flexible working hours	59%	71%
Maternity benefits	91	84
Paternity benefits	37	49
Adoption benefits	49	69
Flexible workplaces	37	51
Sick leave for family illness	59	61
Leave without pay, position assured	75	69
On-site child care	6	22
Subsidies for child care	22	33
Monetary support of community-based child-care facilities	27	41
Resource referral directory for child-care facilities	47	73
Flexible employee benefits	30	69
Part-time work for managers and professionals with proportional benefits	49	63

Source: "Family Benefits: What Companies Are Providing." Reprinted from *Stores,* Magazine © National Retail Federation Enterprises, Inc. November 1990, p. 66. Reproduced by permission. The data are derived from Barbara Zeitz and Lorraine Dusky, *The Best Companies for Women,* Simon & Schuster, 1988.

employees get more education, sharpen job skills, and participate in worthwhile nonjob activities.

Keeping employees satisfied at work is more than a matter of salary. Employees want to feel that they belong and that the company cares about them as total human beings.

Programs such as flex time, job sharing, on-site day care, and total quality management have emerged in retailing in recent years as management has sought to increase productivity and enrich the job by reducing worker stress at home and at work. The most popular programs are shown in Table 10–9.

Typical Programs

Flex Time. Flex time is a system by which workers can arrive and depart on a variable schedule. Flex time programs contribute to improved employee morale, a greater sense of employee responsibility, less stress, and reduced turnover. Retailers with flex time programs include J. C. Penney, Dayton Hudson, and Sears Roebuck.

Job Sharing. Job sharing occurs when two workers voluntarily hold what was formerly one position. In effect, two permanent part-time positions result from one full-time position. Job sharing differs from work sharing. **Work sharing** usually occurs in organizations during economic recessions, when all employees are required to cut back on their work hours and are paid accordingly. Job-sharing programs are in place at such retailers as B. Dalton Booksellers and Walgreen's drugstores. Job sharing is a way to retain valuable employees who no longer want to work full time. Management has found that enthusiasm and productivity in such programs is high.

Child-Care Programs. Young children pose a special problem for working parents. More than half of all single mothers with preschool children are now in the work force. Increasing numbers of large retailers such as Zale's (Exhibit 10–2) are responding to this trend with their own child-care centers at corporate headquarters. Patogonia runs its own on-site centers, and Rich's splits costs for day-care facilities. County Seat and Toys 'R' Us have voucher programs, which let employees set aside pre-tax dollars to pay for child care, and Kmart and Dayton Hudson offer child-care referral lists.[16]

Employee Assistance Programs. Drug and alcohol abuse are two of the most obvious areas in which employers can provide counseling and assistance. Other programs include giving scholarships to children of employees and encouraging community volunteer work. Many retail firms such as Montgomery Ward, Saks, and Gimbels participate in the National Merit Scholarship Program.

Total Quality Management (TQM). TQM programs create situations in which employees at all levels have input into decisions that affect the retail organization. Employees gain an increased sense of self-worth by taking part in the process. Management also benefits from the ideas of dedicated workers at all levels in the organization. Managers and workers seek consensus on company operations instead of having orders simply passed down from above. The total quality concept was initially started in the United States, popularized in Japan, and then imported back into the United States. The benefits from such programs include higher productivity, less turnover, and less absenteeism.

Improved Communications. Mechanisms should be in place for regular communication between managers and hourly employees. Opportunities should be provided for the employees to communicate their concerns to management.

ORGANIZING

Decisions must also be made on how the retail firm will be organized. Most merchants are all-arounders. They do all jobs as the need arises, or assign tasks to employees on a random, nonspecialized basis. Employees are extensions of the managers to carry out the tasks they lack time to do

EXHIBIT 10–2

Courtesy Zale Corporation

Zale's started its on-site day-care center at its Dallas headquarters. The 5,500-square-foot center is licensed to accommodate 85 children aged six weeks to five-and-a-half years.

themselves. Small merchants don't think of setting up distinct functions and lines for the flow of authority, nor do they select specialists to handle each function. As a store grows, however, specialization becomes necessary. The primary purpose of organizational structure is to "support market-driven values and behavior and reinforce desired behavior across the business."[17]

Basic Organization Principles

Certain management principles need to be considered in organizing the firm.

- The principle of specialization of labor.
- The principle of departmentalization.
- The span-of-control principle.
- The unity-of-command principle.

Specialization. Modern organizations are built on the concept of specialization. More and better work is performed at less cost when it is done by specialists than when it is done by employees who shift from one job to another and who continually improvise.

Specialization is of two kinds: **tasks** and **people.** Specialization of tasks narrows a person's activities to simple, repetitive routines. Thus, a relatively untrained employee can quickly become proficient at a narrow specialty.

Specialization of people involves not simplifying the job, but developing a person to perform a certain job better than someone else can. Training and experience improve the quality and quantity of the work.

In the smaller retail store, most of the specialization is of the second type; but in larger stores there is more need for narrow task specialization. For example, certain special records must be kept, and certain phases of merchandise handling must be done by a well-trained person.

Departmentalization. Management will probably find that it can group jobs into classes such as the following (each demanding a certain combination of skills for good performance):

- **Merchandising;** buying and managing inventory for different groups of merchandise.
- **Direct and general selling and adjustments;** customer contact.
- **Sales promotion;** largely concerning advertising and display.
- **Accounting and finance;** records, correspondence, cash handling, insurance, and sometimes credit.
- **Store operation;** building, equipment, and safety measures.
- **Merchandise handling;** receiving, marking, storing, and delivering.
- **Personnel;** employment, training, employee benefits, and personnel records.

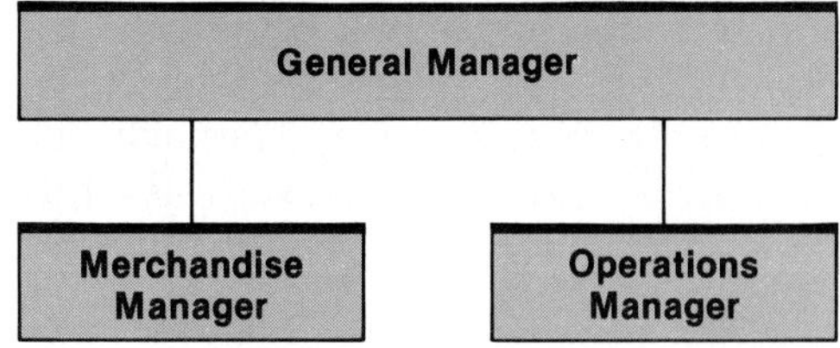

FIGURE 10–1

THE SIMPLEST ORGANIZATION

Recognizing the many functions to be performed doesn't mean that a specialist is necessary for each of them. Management can combine some functions. But management should look ahead and have an organization plan that provides for various specialized positions when they are needed.

Span of Control. Span of control addresses the question of how many subordinates should report to a supervisor. Generally, a supervisor's span of control should be small because an individual can work effectively with only a limited number of people at one time. Span of control, however, depends on factors such as the competence of the supervisor and subordinates, the similarity of the functions to be performed, and the physical location of people.

Unity of Command. The unity of command concept involves a series of superior-subordinate relationships. This concept states that no person should be under the direct control of more than one supervisor in performing job tasks. Thus, an employee should receive decision-making power from and report to only one supervisor. An unbroken chain of command should exist from top to bottom. Otherwise, frustration and confusion will occur.

How to Organize for Profitable Operations

The two functions that probably will be organized first are **merchandising** and **operations,** or store management, as noted by Paul Mazur, the father of modern retailing organization principles. Such an organization would look like the one illustrated in Figure 10–1.

The **merchandise manager** has other functions in addition to being responsible for buying and selling. The person supervises or prepares merchandise budgets (or both); handles advertising, displays, and other promotions; and is responsible for inventory planning and control.

The **operations manager** is responsible for building upkeep, delivery, stockrooms, service, supplies, equipment purchasing, and similar activities.

As a store continues to grow in size, specialization of labor occurs. The organization structure may begin to look like the one in Figure 10–2.

As shown in Figure 10–2, the next managers who should be added are financial, promotion, and personnel managers. The financial manager, or controller, handles the finances of the firm and probably has an accounting

FIGURE 10–2 FIVE-FUNCTION ORGANIZATIONAL PLAN

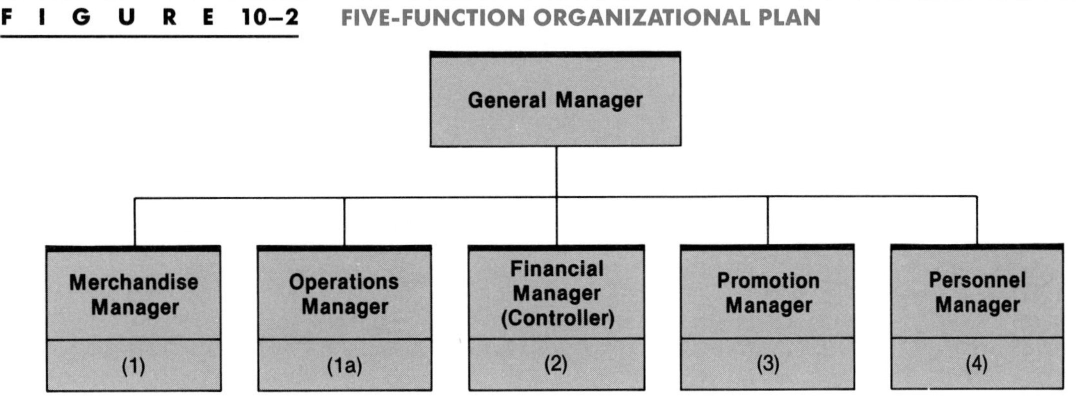

background. The organization structure in the figure is typical of most department stores. A food operation, however, performs the same functions, as do all retail firms.

Trends in Organizing

Prior to World War II, the typical organization plan gave the merchandising manager responsibility for *both* buying and selling. But after World War II, shopping centers were developed, and downtown stores "branched" to the shopping centers. The merchandise manager became responsible not only for buying and selling merchandise in the downtown (main) store, but also in the branches. This situation proved to be impossible. One merchandise manager could not be responsible for buying, supervising sales, and general management of both the main store and the branch stores. So a trend developed during this "branching" era to separate the buying and selling functions.

Separation of Buying and Selling. There are arguments for and against the separation of the buying and selling responsibilities in the organization.

Those **opposing** the separation of the two functions pose the following arguments:

- The buyer must have contact with consumers to be able to understand their needs.
- Those who buy merchandise should also be responsible for selling it.
- It is easier to pinpoint merchandising successes and failures when the two functions are combined.

Those who **favor** the separation of the two functions counter their opposition as follows:

- If the two functions are combined, buying is likely to have more importance than selling.
- Buying and selling require two different types of job skills.
- With technology, reports, and so forth, it is not necessary for the two functions to be combined.
- Salespeople can be shifted more easily under this arrangement.

The arguments against separating the buying and selling functions do not seem as strong as the counterarguments. The branch store problem seems to demand separation. Thus, the trend is to separate the two. Figure 10–3 shows a department store that is organized for the separation of buying and selling. The general merchandise manager is responsible for buying, and the vice-president of branch stores is responsible for selling.

Food stores could have faced the same conflict, but their expansion history actually solved their problems. Rather than branching, these companies expanded as chain-store organizations. No main stores exist in a chain organization. Buying and selling are always separated.

Centralization versus Decentralization[18]

Specialty Stores. Specialty stores historically have been highly centralized. The Limited, until around 1990, for example, consisted of roughly a dozen major fashion divisions controlled by the chairman. The organizational philosophy was that synergies between the divisions in distribution, real estate and legal departments, and so forth could be achieved by centralization. The firm has moved since 1990 to aggressively decentralize its business. Each division now has autonomy in merchandising and operations. The only issues controlled centrally are finances and reporting relationships.

Home Depot, in a similar move away from centralization, has created three divisions—west, northeast and southeast. Management decided that the separate divisions could more effectively merchandise to regional customers with different needs and tastes. Toys 'R' Us also made the decision to operate its Kids 'R' Us and its international divisions as separate, autonomous units.

Department Stores. Department stores are exhibiting a countertrend to the decentralization trend among specialty stores. Traditionally, each department store division in a multidivision holding company was allowed to operate independently and to compete not only with other department stores but also with other divisions of the parent organization. Bloomingdale's for example, competed not only with Neiman-Marcus and Macy's but also with Abraham and Strauss, another division of Federated Department Stores.

FIGURE 10–3 ORGANIZATION FOR SEPARATION OF BUYING AND SELLING

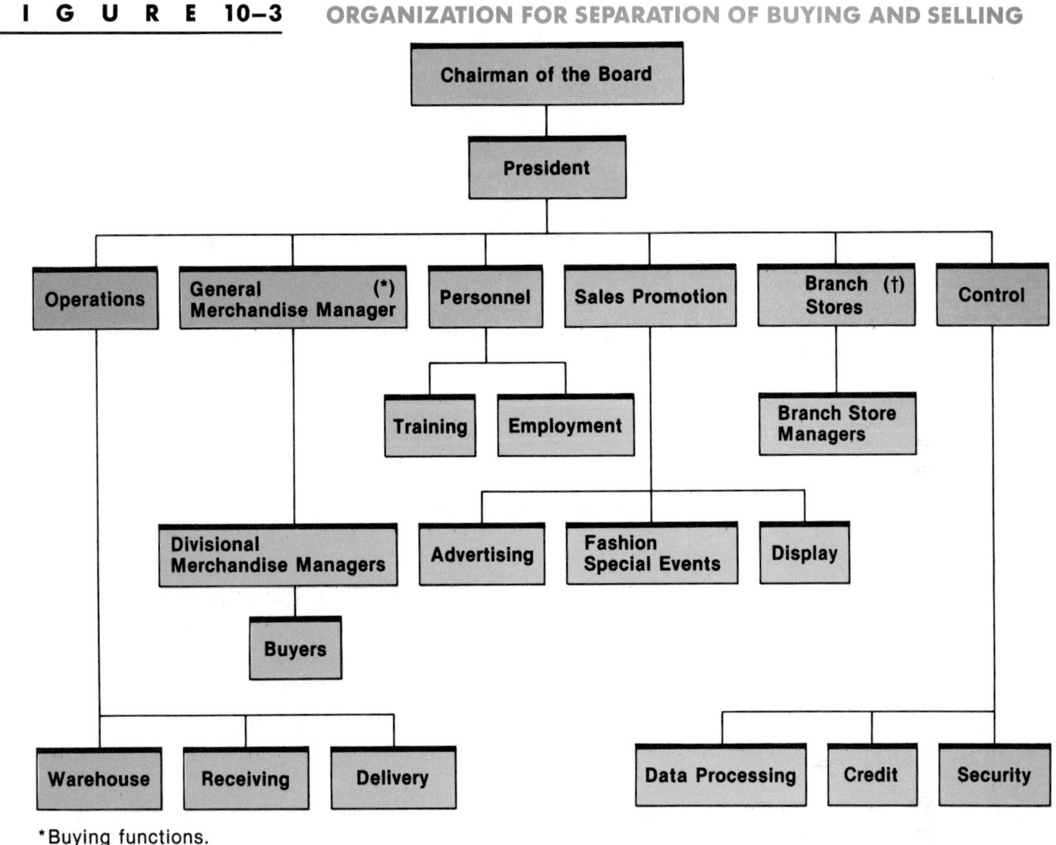

*Buying functions.
†Selling functions.

Federated, as have other department stores, has recently determined that perhaps department stores can be operated more efficiently by a higher degree of centralization. Dillard's pioneered the concept of centralized buying practices and exercises control over all major activities without delegating them to the field.

In essence, department stores have recognized that they do not need a buyer for each classification in every division to be efficient. Rather, operating information systems and electronic merchandising have made it possible for the buyers to make chainwide decisions. May department stores, for example, has merged divisions in Ohio and Washington. Finally, in addition to merging several divisions, Federated Department Stores has centralized buying in its New York office.

Chapter Highlights

- Staffing a store with the right people is a critical part of a retailer's strategic plan. Staffing needs vary depending on the type of merchandise carried, services the store will offer, the image management wants to project to customers, and the way in which the firm wants to compete.
- The initial step in developing a human resources plan is to develop descriptions of the jobs to be filled. Then, job analysis is undertaken to determine the skills needed for the jobs.
- Recruiting to attract the right people is a critical element of the plan. Recruits may be sought either inside or outside the firm. Specific federal guidelines exist for administering selection tests and in otherwise screening employees, and management must follow these guidelines.
- An equitable employee pay plan is another important component of a personnel plan and it can contribute to higher employee productivity and satisfaction. Retailers should make sure that employees understand how the pay plan was developed, how it will be administered, and how they will be evaluated for pay increases or promotions. Closely related to the pay plan is establishing the level and type of employee benefits.
- Employee performance appraisal also needs to occur on a regular basis; normally employees are appraised annually. Standardized forms should be developed for this purpose. Supervisors should discuss their ratings with the employees and give suggestions for performance improvement.
- Employee motivation and job enrichment are also important elements of the personnel plan. Management must recognize that employees have such needs as the desire for recognition and achievement, which cannot be satisfied by money alone.
- Basic organizational principles are specialization of labor, departmentalization, span of control, and unit of command.
- The two functions that probably will first be organized in a retail store are merchandising and operations (store management).

Study Questions

1. What are the key laws that affect recruiting, selection, and compensation of employees?
2. What are the relationships among a job analysis, a job description, and a job specification?
3. Briefly describe the steps for developing a formal compensation plan.
4. What is likely to be the most effective method for compensating (a) a retail salesperson, (b) an accountant, and (c) a department buyer?
5. Why should management establish an employee performance appraisal plan? What are some of the performance factors that might be evaluated?
6. Why should procedures for handling disciplinary matters and employee grievances be established, even in the absence of a union?
7. What are some of the things retailers can do to help motivate employees?
8. What are the ingredients of the empowerment concept, which is emerging as an important human resources principle in the 1990s?
9. Describe the human resources environment of the 1990s.
10. How do department stores and chain stores differ in their organizational structure? Why are they different?

A P P L I C A T I O N S

CASE 1: The Service-Driven Service Company for the 1990s: Taco Bell

Ray Kroc founded McDonald's in 1955. Nothing was left to chance in store operations. Everything was totally uniform, almost down to the number of french fries in a scoop. The success of McDonald's was enormous. By the end of the 1980s, however, revenue began to stagnate. McDonald's has been working harder than ever to regain its premier status, but has continued its traditional production-line thinking.

Taco Bell, in contrast, experienced sales growth exceeding 60 percent annually in the period from 1989 to 1991, even though the overall fast-food market was flat. Profits increased by over 25 percent annually, compared to less than 6 percent for McDonald's. This surge in profitability occurred at the same time Taco Bell cut the prices on its core menu by 25 percent.

Taco Bell represents the new model of customer service that has human resources at the center of a total quality management program. The core elements of the new model, compared to the old industrial assembly-line approach of McDonald's, recognizes that investments in people are as valuable as investments in machines. Technology is harnessed to support people, not simply to monitor their actions. Recruiting and training personnel such as sales clerks is as important as training for management. Compensation is linked to performance at every level of the organization.

The premise of Taco Bell is everything the company does should be focused on helping employees deliver value to customers along dimensions important to them. Taco Bell believes that customers value service, physical appearance, and food, and nothing more.

Taco Bell management began its turnaround by empowering its people, by getting rid of its seven-layer organization, and by eliminating many supervisors. Today, one supervisor has responsibility for at least 20 stores compared to one for about every 5 stores in 1988. The role of the district managers has shifted from directing and controlling to coaching and supporting, backed by state-of-the-art information systems designed to help employees raise quality and productivity.

Sophisticated technology has also freed Taco Bell restaurant managers from 15 hours per week of nonproductive paperwork by providing real-time data on customer satisfaction, employees, and costs. Taco Bell also outsources some of its ingredients such as shredded lettuce and chopped tomatoes so that stores today resemble assembly lines as opposed to manufacturing operations. The result was the elimination of more than 15 hours of backroom labor per day from the typical store. Employees and managers now focus on customer service, not manufacturing meals. The ratio of front-line personnel to backroom workers has been reversed. More employees are focusing on providing service and on factors important to the bottom line.

Taco Bell management carefully selects employees who reflect attitudes supportive of teamwork and responsibility. They then provide these employees with continual training. The restaurant managers' job descriptions require that half their time must be spent on developing employees. Taco Bell managers are eligible for bonuses of up to 225 percent of the industry average based on the performance of their outlets.

McDonald's, in contrast, continues to focus on more of the same: advertising, a continuous stream of new products, and more locations. Taco Bell has shown that more of the same no longer works in today's economic environment.

*Based on Leonard A. Schlesinger and James L. Heskett, "The Service-Driven Service Company," *Harvard Business Review,* September–October 1991, pp. 71–81; "McDonalds May Change Menu Board and Seating," *The Wall Street Journal,* April 19, 1992, p. B5.

Applying Retailing Principles

1. Contrast the ingredients of McDonald's and Taco Bell's competitive strategies in the 1990s.
2. List the human resources dimensions of Taco Bell that contribute to its record of success. What other retailers come to mind that seem to follow the principles of Taco Bell? What retailers appear to be following the McDonald's model?

CASE 2: Managing Diversity: Retailing's Next Strategic Challenge

Toys 'R' Us. Toys 'R' Us experienced dramatic sales and profitability improvements when management implemented a diversity program. Their program is based on the new golden rule: "Do unto others as they want to be done unto." The focus is on recognizing employees' individual needs. The critical issue is not treating all employees equally, but on treating them equitably. After implementing a program consisting of 24 hours of instruction and discussion, Toys 'R' Us has reduced turnover by as much as 50 percent in some difficult labor markets such as Philadelphia and Detroit. Managing diversity is becoming an even more critical issue as the firm expands into Europe and Japan.

J. C. Penney. In 1990, the chairman of J. C. Penney established a women's advisory team. The women's program goes beyond an affirmative action program. It focuses on what women bring to the business in terms of meeting the needs of the customer. Penney's long-term goal is to have women in at least 45 percent of all management positions.

The team's first action was to establish a mission statement: "In support of our company's business objective of becoming a national department store, the women's advisory team is dedicated to fostering and promoting the advancement and career development of women at all levels, and, specifically, to facilitating upward mobility to senior management."

The next action of the women's team was to hold a number of focus groups representing associates at all management levels to identify some of the issues and roadblocks that inhibit the advancement of women at Penney. They found concern among women that their upward mobility was affected by their family status as wives or mothers. There was a belief that networking—an important part of the corporate promotion and decision-making system—often excluded women unintentionally. It was perceived that male managers tended to feel more comfortable with men and inadvertently excluded women in decision-making or mentoring. With respect to job assignments, certain positions appeared to be stereotyped as "male" or "female" jobs, creating a barrier for women who wished to gain experience in key areas of the business.

To address these issues, Penney management suggests that progressive companies must do four things. First, they must learn the issues and roadblocks preventing women from gaining advancement. Second, a formal plan for advancing women should be established. Third, the plan must be communicated and implemented, and fourth, management must demand results. If goals are not achieved, those accountable should be asked why.

Source: Portions reprinted with permission from "Managing Diversity: Retailing's Next Strategic Challenge," *The Retail Report* 5, no. 4 (1992), pp. 1–2. Published by the Center for Retailing Education and Research, the University of Florida.

Applying Retailing Principles

1. What are the common threads in the programs of Toys 'R' Us and J. C. Penney?
2. What is meant by the statement that the critical issue is not treating employees equally, but treating them equitably?
3. Do you believe the barriers perceived to be hindering the progress of women in retailing management positions are similar to, or different from, the barriers often experienced by ethnic minorities? Are the barriers real? If so, what can be done to lower them?

NOTES

1. Frank N. Sonnennberg, "A Strategic Approach to Employing Motivation," *Journal of Business Strategy,* May/June 1991, p. 41.
2. George Stalk, Philip Evans, and Lawrence E. Shulman, "Competing on Capabilities: The New Rules of Corporate Strategy," *Harvard Business Review,* March–April 1992, pp. 57–59.
3. Earl Hart, James Heskett, and Earl Sasser, *Service Breakthroughs* (New York: The Free Press, 1990), p. 203.

4. "Avon Calling—On Its Troops," *BusinessWeek*, July 8, 1991, p. 53.
5. Jules Abend, "Personnel Strategies," *Stores*, September 1990, p. 42.
6. Sandra M. Hutton, "Help Wanted!" *Monitor*, May 1990, p. 193.
7. The material on job analysis, job descriptions, and job specifications is reproduced, with modifications, from *Job Analysis, Job Specifications, and Job Descriptions*, Self-instructional booklet no. 1020, Washington, D.C., U.S. Small Business Administration.
8. This material is reproduced, with modifications, from Walter E. Green, "Staffing Your Store," Management aid no. 5.007, Washington, D.C., U.S. Small Business Administration.
9. Based on *Recruiting and Selecting Employees*, Booklet no. 1021, Washington, D.C., U.S. Small Business Administration.
10. Marj Charlier and Wade Lambert, "McDonald's Told to Pay $210,000 in Damages in Negligent Hiring Case," *The Wall Street Journal*, March 15, 1991, p. B3.
11. Based on Jean F. Scolland, "Setting Up a Pay System," Management aid no. 5.006, Washington, D.C., U.S. Small Business Administration; see also "Help Wanted," *The Retailing Strategist* 2, 1991, pp. 20–23.
12. Alan J. Dubinsky and Michael Levy, "Influence of Organizational Fairness on Work Outcomes of Retail Salespeople," *Journal of Retailing* 65, Summer 1989, p. 148.
13. Based on John B. Hannah, "Changing Employee Benefits," Management aid no. 5.008, Washington, D.C., U.S. Small Business Administration.
14. Robert F. Lusch and Ray R. Serpkenci, "Personal Differences, Job Tension, Job Outcomes, and Store Performance: A Study of Retail Store Managers," *Journal of Marketing* 54, January 1990, p. 85.
15. For further reading, see Leonard Berry and Parsu Parsuraman, *Marketing Services: Competing Through Quality* (New York: The Free Press, 1991), pp. 167–69.
16. For further reading, see "Support for Child Care," *Stores*, November 1990, pp. 64–65; Penny Gill, "Child Care: Growing Ground," *Stores*, November 1990, pp. 52–53; "Zale's: Leader in DayCare," *Stores*, November 1990, pp. 57–62; "County Seat: Vouchers," *Stores*, November 1990, p. 63.
17. George S. Day, *Market Driven Strategy* (New York: The Free Press, 1990), pp. 360–61.
18. Based on Walter F. Loeb, "Unbundle or Centralize: What Is the Answer?" *Retailing Issues Letter* 4, no. 3, May 1992, pp. 1–4.

P A R T

5

Positioning for Competitive Advantage—The Marketing Plan

We have reviewed the retailing structural dynamics, outlined the essence of strategic planning, highlighted environments affecting retail strategy development, focused on the consumer dynamics of the market, and identified the resources needed to compete. Now it is time to focus on the issues involved in developing the retailing plan to help implement competitive strategy. Chapters 11 through 19 cover such topics as merchandise and expense planning and control, buying and inventory management, and pricing. Other retailing plan components addressed are physically handling and securing merchandise; store design, layout, and merchandise presentation; selling; promotion; and, finally, customer support functions.

The way in which the marketing decisions are addressed within individual firms depends largely on their positioning strategy, the resources available, and the behavior of competitors. In other words the retailing plan is what differentiates Neiman-Marcus from Kmart.

CHAPTER

11

Merchandise Planning and Control

THIS CHAPTER:

Emphasizes the need to make merchandise management decisions that support the overall competitive strategy of the firm.

Illustrates a variety of merchandising philosophies that help a firm gain a competitive advantage.

Describes the process of developing a merchandise budget to make inventory investment decisions.

Focuses on issues to consider in making merchandise width and support decisions.

Discusses how to establish inventory control systems to control both dollar inventory investment and merchandise items.

RETAILING CAPSULE

SHARPER IMAGE REVAMPS PRODUCT LINE

Sharper Image is trying to change its image from a company offering "pricey playthings for yuppie boys and girls." Whereas the company's strategy was successful in the 1980s, when conspicuous spending was something to which younger, affluent consumers aspired, that strategy is not proving to be successful in the 1990s—an age in which conspicuous consumption is passé.

To overcome the image of the yuppie toy store, Sharper Image is completely revamping its product line. For example, the company that made its name selling such items as a $649 model of a Ferrari Testarossa is now adding more lower-priced items. So right next to the $249.95 "paper chain you can wear" is a $29.95 pair of aviator sunglasses. Even though the company still carries some extravagant items, it now has over 200 products under $50, up fourfold from last year.

Management has also decided to get out of the name-brand electronics business because price wars made margins too slim. Instead, more emphasis will be given to apparel and footwear. Furthermore, the company will add to its line of private-brand goods. Management is also recruiting manufacturers for a new licensing program. Manufacturers of exercise equipment, consumer electronics, jewelry, fragrances, cutlery, sunglasses, small leather goods, activewear, exercisewear, and active footwear are being targeted.

Some market analysts believe that Sharper Image "stands for something that's not easy to translate to today's New Traditionalism." However, company management believes that even though the 1990s may not be the era of conspicuous consumption, it isn't going to be the Middle Ages either. Maybe somewhere between the extremes there is a strategy for the firm.

Source: Based on Carrie Dolan, "Sharper Image Is Beefing Up Earnings by Adding More Items Priced under $50," *The Wall Street Journal,* February 6, 1991, p. B6; Cyndee Miller, "Sharper Image Revamps Product Line, Sells Items Consumers Can Actually Buy," *Marketing News,* May 11, 1992, p. 2.

The Retailing Capsule illustrates the importance of providing a merchandise offering consistent with the needs of the store's target market and the need to change the offering mix as the needs of that target market change over time. It also underscores the important role that merchandise management plays in the overall competitive strategy of a firm.

Merchandise Management

Development of the merchandise plan is the logical place to begin a discussion about competitive advantage in the marketplace because without merchandise (or some offering) a retail establishment cannot exist. **Merchandise planning** includes all the activities needed to balance inventory and sales. The major portion of this chapter is directed toward the merchandise plan at the department or classification level. Although each type of retailing has unique procedures for merchandise planning, our examples from the general merchandise sector apply to virtually any setting.

If the function of merchandise planning is somewhat technical, the concept of merchandising is not. Traditionally, **merchandising** has been defined as offering the right merchandise at the right price at the right place in the right quantities at the right time. We support these "rights," but we see merchandising in the 1990s as much more. We see merchandising as a part of the strategic plan—the creative positioning tactics that support the long-run mission and objectives of a firm. Merchandising today must include short-term creative tactics based on management philosophies that can provide the firm with a differential advantage.

Merchandise management is the management of the product component of the retailing mix; it comprises planning and control activities. Its purpose is to ensure that the inventory component of the mix supports the overall merchandising philosophy of the firm and meets the needs of target customers. A retailer who is well known for developing a merchandising strategy designed to achieve these objectives is L. L. Bean, highlighted in A Profile in Excellence. The following sections provide examples of merchandising philosophies that illustrate how strategists strive to create a competitive advantage for their firms.

Merchandising Philosophies

The following examples illustrate the diversity of applications of merchandising techniques as part of marketing strategy. In each case, merchandising was used to help create a sustainable competitive advantage for the firm.

Merchandising Changes That Support Changes in Competitive Strategy[1]

In its mass-merchandising heyday, J. C. Penney focused on middle-income Americans whose choices were determined by price and reliability. But

A Profile in Excellence

L. L. BEAN

Leon Leonwood Bean grew up in the hill country of western Maine during the late 1800s. Orphaned at the age of 12, he had to make his own way working on the farms of friends and relatives. He once wrote, "My life up to the age of 40 years was most uneventful, with a few exceptions."

One of these exceptions occurred at the age of 13 when he went on his first deer hunting trip, which was a success. From the experience, he developed a life-long passion for hunting and fishing. His working career, however, was not so successful. He was never content to stay in one place long enough to really get established.

In 1907 Bean began working at his brother Ervin's haberdashery store in Freeport, Maine, where he earned $12 a week. His salary was not his main concern—he was more concerned about keeping his feet dry and comfortable on hunting trips. Thus, he fashioned some lightweight leather uppers on rubber overshoe bottoms and added other refinements. He wore them afield and was delighted with the results. He made several more pairs for his hunting companions. They, too, liked the boot's dry, lightweight comfort and encouraged Bean to sell them to the public.

In 1912 he obtained a mailing list of Maine hunting license holders, set up shop in Ervin's basement, and prepared a three-page brochure that proclaimed, "You cannot expect to successfully hunt deer or moose if your feet are not properly dressed. The Maine Hunting Shoe is designed by a hunter who has tramped the Maine woods for the past 18 years. We guarantee them to give you perfect satisfaction in every way." When the rubber bottoms separated from the leather tops on 90 of the first 100 pairs of boots, Bean kept his word and refunded the purchase price. He borrowed more money, perfected the bottoms, and with undiminished confidence mailed more brochures.

Bean considered word-of-mouth advertising and customer satisfaction critical. He stated in his catalog, "We consider our customers a part of the organization and want them to feel free to make any criticism they see fit in regard to our merchandise or service." To hear that one of his products failed was a genuine shock to him. He'd charge around the factory trying to find an explanation. Then he'd write the customer, return his money, enclose a gift, invite her fishing, or do anything to make the matter right. In his own words, Bean's business philosophy was this: "Sell good merchandise at a reasonable profit, treat your customers like human beings, and they'll always come back for more."

Source: Leon A. Gorman, *L. L. Bean, Inc.: Outdoor Specialties by Mail from Maine,* Company brochure, 1981.

discounters stole away many of the price-conscious, and regional malls gave the quality-conscious more, and more fashionable, alternatives. While Penney spent the 1950s and 1960s snapping up choice locations in the new regional shopping malls, shoppers coming to the malls did so to buy clothes and accessories, not car batteries, refrigerators, or lawn mowers. They also wanted brand names, which Penney had booted out years before in favor of higher-margin private labels.

Thus, in the 1980s, Penney make a bold strategic move to upgrade its image and become a fashionable national department store for middle-income and upper-middle-income consumers. To support this strategy, major changes were made in the firm's merchandise mix. Penney closed down its appliance, lawn and garden, paint, hardware, and automobile lines in 1983 and its home electronics and sporting goods lines in 1988, surrendering more than $1.5 billion in annual sales. In expanded men's and women's fashion departments, $7.99 polyester ties and $29.99 women's shifts gave way to $22 silk neckwear and $80 career dresses.

In spite of all of the changes, Penney's sales per square foot lag behind many of its rivals. Market analysts believe that one thing Penney needs to do is to continue to improve its merchandise mix and exploit fashion trends—especially by carrying more "coveted" brand names. As one industry analyst commented, "It's difficult to categorize yourself as a department store when you don't have Clinique makeup."

However, Penney has encountered problems in getting big-name suppliers to sell their lines in Penney stores. It took three years of negotiation to convince Levi Strauss & Co. to sell its jeans through Penney. Only after years of lobbying does it now carry Haggar and Van Heusen brands in the men's department, Oshkosh B'Gosh in children's, and Maidenform and Warner's in lingerie. Some manufacturers such as Elizabeth Arden, Estée Lauder, Liz Claiborne, and Evan-Picone still won't sell to Penney. Company officials, especially those who have worked hard to upgrade the firm's merchandise, believe that cosmetics and women's apparel makers fear that their image will be negatively affected if they sell to Penney and that other stores might drop their lines. For example, some industry analysts believe that the designer Halston lost some of his prestige after marketing clothing through Penney stores in the mid-1980s. Company officials are optimistic, however, and believe that the years of change will eventually produce a breakthrough. As stated by Penney Chairman William R. Howell, "I'm confident that there will be a day when all of these options will be at our disposal. Just as the Berlin Wall came down very quickly, I'm very optimistic."

Adding and Deleting Merchandise

Retailers must constantly evaluate their merchandise mix to determine whether they need to add or delete merchandise lines. Additions may be needed as a result of factors such as a change in the firm's competitive strategy, customer needs, or competitive conditions. For example, five of The Limited's divisions added beauty products to their traditional apparel and accessories offerings. The decision to add this line was a major merchandising change but one that management believed it needed for the company to meet the needs of its customers and to be more competitive.[2] Furthermore, Eddie Bauer, after years of selling jackets, sweaters, and outdoor goods, is, on an experimental basis, offering furniture, housewares, and fashionable career wear for women. Some industry analysts say these additions are a gamble, but company officials are optimistic. The firm undertook a survey to check whether consumers would buy furniture and found that the Eddie Bauer name is very credible in home furnishings.[3]

Service firms likewise often add to their offering mix in an attempt to better meet needs and compete effectively. For example, United Parcel Service (UPS) has over time added to its service offerings. In 1982 the firm added next-day air service; in 1986 the company allocated $1.5 billion a year for information technology to provide computerized billing and package tracking information; in 1990, it began offering guaranteed 10:30 A.M. delivery; and in 1991 UPS initiated Saturday delivery and international service.

Conversely, sometimes retailers delete merchandise lines. Many department stores are reducing the number of lines carried and are dropping such lines as appliances, toys, sporting goods, and health and beauty aids so that they can focus on fashion items. Their managers have realized that they cannot compete effectively in these lines. Similarly, many jewelry stores that once carried crystal stemware, china, and flatware have dropped these lines as department stores and catalog showrooms have proved to be formidable competitors for these offerings.

In some instances, retailers have removed specific items of merchandise from their merchandise offerings in response to consumer concerns, as illustrated in A Question of Ethics.

Private Brands as a Merchandising Issue

One of the most perplexing problems facing retailers today is the optimal balance between private (store or dealer) brands and manufacturer (national) brands. **Private brands** are owned by a retailer and sold only by that owner. **Manufacturer brands** are owned by a manufacturer and can be sold by whomever the owner desires. For example, Ralph Lauren and Calvin Klein are manufacturer brands, whereas Charter Club is one of Macy's private labels.

Several factors explain the shift among many retailers to strong private-label programs. Popular manufacturer brands have become so pervasive that virtually all competitors have the same merchandise. Off-price stores get designer merchandise; consequently, consumers do not want to pay full price in conventional stores. Private-label goods have moved into upscale merchandise and often display excellent quality. Finally, private brands give a retailer distinction and offer higher margins than manufacturer brands (see Chapter 14 for a discussion of price strategy differences between private and manufacturer brands). In addition, consumer acceptance of private brands is high. A 1991 Gallup Poll for the Private Label Manufacturers Association found consumer acceptance of store brands at a record high, with nearly 90 percent of those surveyed having bought them.[4]

Hence, in all sectors of retailing—from upscale fashion retailers to discount operations—management is adding private brands. The nation's largest retailer, Wal-Mart, is adding to its line of private brands. In addition to its store brands in staples such as paper towels and bathroom tissue, the

A Question of Ethics

Many Stores Not Selling *Body Count* Album

In June 1992 then-vice-president Dan Quayle added his name to the list of people opposed to the song "Cop Killer" included in the album *Body Count* by Ice-T and Body Count, produced by Time-Warner Inc. Mac Mackay, Quayle's assistant press secretary, says that, although Quayle recognizes Time-Warner's first-amendment right to release the song, he is opposed to it on moral grounds, stating, "It could be inciteful."

Protests by individuals and many law enforcement agencies and groups were successful insofar as some music stores removed the album from their shelves. Kimberly Garwood, spokesperson for Super Club Music Corporation, released the following statement: "The *Body Count* album has been removed from all Super Club Music stores.... We have decided that until such time as a legal decision about the alleged obscene lyrics may be reached, it is our preference to respond in this way." Super Club Music owns over 300 Turtle's, Record Bar, and Tracks music stores.

Some music stores, however, are continuing to stock the album or to take special orders for it if it is not available in the store. A manager of one of the stores said that he is opposed to censorship in any form. He also stated that sales of the album have probably been greater than normal because of the publicity that it has received, and that many people are buying the album, whether they like the music or not, on the free-speech principle it represents. He added, "When you tell somebody they can't have something, that's when they want it the most."

Do you believe that the retailers who pulled the album from their shelves acted responsibly and ethically? Why would retailers continue to carry the tapes in the face of controversy? Do you think that retailers have an ethical responsibility not to stock merchandise that could incite improper behavior from those who buy the product?

Source: Based on Louis Cooper, "Many Stores Not Selling *Body Count* Album," *The Crimson White*, June 24, 1992, pp. 1–2.

firm has introduced Sam's American Choice, a private brand that includes such products as colas, cookies, and fruit drinks. The line plays off several Wal-Mart themes—value, patriotism, and innovation. The packaging has red, white, and blue graphics and carries the following message: "At Wal-Mart, we're searching the USA to create something special." Furthermore, Wal-Mart apparently learned a lesson from some retailers that stumbled when they offered customers low-priced store brands of low quality. Wal-Mart does not believe that customers will accept a lower-quality product and therefore has developed the Sam's line with quality in mind.[5] The status of private branding in the retail food industry is discussed in a later section of this chapter.

Even though more and more retailers are introducing private brands and many others are adding to their line of private brands, some retailers have reduced the ratio of private to manufacturer brands in their stores.

Examples include J. C. Penney (as discussed earlier) and Sears. Sears' dramatic shift from private labels to a strong manufacturer brand statement has been attributed largely to its new philosophy of appealing to a broader range of consumers by offering more choices to more people. Some market analysts believe that part of Macy's problems today stem from the firm's heavy emphasis on private brands. The private brands crowded out some of the better-known manufacturer brands; and many of Macy's loyal customers, unable to find the manufacturer brands they had grown up with, began shopping elsewhere.[6]

Licensing as a Merchandising Issue

Licensing is an arrangement in which the licenser or owner of a "property" (the concept to be marketed) joins with a licensee (the manufacturer of the licensed product) to sell retail buyers the licensed merchandise. Licensing is a key merchandise issue today because it provides the opportunity to capture a market whose customer is younger, richer, better educated, and willing to pay more than the average consumer for what he or she wants. When considering licensing as a merchandising tactic, retailers must evaluate the opportunity in terms of the partnership that must evolve. The licensee who offers the property must be strong, have a good product, and provide sufficient marketing support for the offering. Care Bears is an example of a licensing success which was adequately supported over time.

Stores devoted exclusively to licensed merchandise are now an established part of the retailing scene. For example, some entertainment companies are opening their own retail operations to carry their licensed properties. Until Disney Stores came along, no one paid much attention to the idea of retail outlets that sold only merchandise related to one entertainment entity, be it a Hollywood studio, a cartoon production house, or a television network. Now, Warner Brothers, the Hanna-Barbera cartoon studio, Turner Broadcasting, Ringling Bros., and the National Broadcasting Company (NBC) all have retail stores. Warner Brothers, for instance, has opened 4 stores and is adding 15 more. The most popular line of merchandise is "Looney Tunes," featuring characters such as Bugs Bunny, Porky Pig, and Daffy Duck. Disney is clearly the leader in the field, however (see Exhibit 11–1). The chain has grown to more than 200 stores, including units in Canada, Puerto Rico, Japan, the United Kingdom, Germany, and France.[7]

Merchandising in the Retail Food Industry

Managers in the retail food industry are responding positively to consumer lifestyles and demands for convenience items. "Hot" merchandising tactics include placing more and more emphasis on perishables; offering more and better prepared foods; and offering more nonfood merchandise. In addition, food retailers are practicing micromarketing and are working with manufacturers to help tailor the store's merchandise offerings to the tastes and needs of the specific consumers who primarily shop in the store.

EXHIBIT 11–1

Courtesy The Disney Store, Inc.

DISNEY STORES operates more than 130 units, and plans to open stores in Canada, Puerto Rico, Japan, the U.K., and France.

Another trend is an increasing emphasis on private labels. Although food retailers have long offered private brands, stores today are offering private labels in an increasing number of merchandise lines and are also improving the quality of their private brands. For example, A&P's latest generation of private brands is a far cry from their plain, and now defunct, Ann Page bargain line of grocery items. The company is now pushing a fancy new line of olive oil laced with garlic essence, champagne mustard packaged in handsome ceramic pots, and blue corn tortilla chips with sesame seeds. Likewise, Kroger, Safeway, and Von's are improving the quality and packaging of their store brands as a way of cementing customer loyalty and increasing profits.[8]

International Dimensions

As retailers move into international markets, they must decide whether their merchandise offering must be modified to appeal to foreign consumers and to compete effectively. Although making no changes is the most cost-efficient approach, modifications are often needed to tailor the offerings to consumers' needs and to adjust to other environmental conditions. For example, when fast-food operations initially moved into international markets, many of their offerings were the same as those sold in the domestic market, with some minor variations and additions, such as including wine as a beverage choice in units located in France. Now, however, because of intensifying competition, many of these fast-food operations are adding to their menus and offering more "local" items. For example, rising competition in Japan is forcing McDonald's to go beyond the Egg McMuffin and the Big Mac. In some of its units, it is now offering rice balls, Chinese dumplings, curry with rice, and fried rice. More along the "burger" line, McDonald's launched the Teriyaki McBurger and the Cheese Katsyu Burger, which is a pork-cutlet burger covered with melted cheese, drenched in katsu sauce, and topped with shredded cabbage. PepsiCo Inc.'s Kentucky Fried Chicken, Japan's second-biggest fast-food chain, has also added some local items to accompany its fried chicken. It introduced grilled rice balls and a fried salmon sandwich. Industry analysts believe that competition will intensify as Japan's fast-food industry, now totaling about $31 million in sales annually, starts to mature. Such competition will require even more innovative menu offerings.[9]

MERCHANDISE PLANNING

As defined earlier, merchandise planning includes those activities needed to ensure a balance between inventory and sales. This section of the chapter focuses on a variety of issues related to merchandise planning, with emphasis on the development of the merchandise budget. Before proceeding with this discussion, however, some terms must be defined.

Basic Terms

A retailer's **product line** consists of all of the products or services that his or her firm offers. Product lines are typically defined in terms of variety and assortment.

Variety (also known as the number of classifications or categories) refers to the number of different lines of merchandise (or services) in a product line. For example, the product line of a superstore would include such varieties as meat, bakery goods, dry groceries, and frozen foods. No natural relationship necessarily exists among the classifications.

Assortment means the range of choices (selections) available for any given classification in a product line. Assortment can also be defined as the number of *stockkeeping units* (SKUs) in a category. For example, a one-pound can of Maxwell House coffee is one SKU; a two-pound pack of Chock Full O'Nuts coffee is another SKU. However, do not confuse the number of items with an SKU. In other words, a food store might have 100 cans of the one-pound Maxwell House coffee, but this represents only one SKU.

Stock Balance

The purpose of merchandise planning is to maintain **stock balance**—a balance between inventory and sales. Figure 11–1 is a diagram of the merchandise-planning process. We will refer to this diagram through most of the chapter (note that points 2 and 3 have already been defined).

FIGURE 11–1 THE MERCHANDISE-PLANNING PROCESS

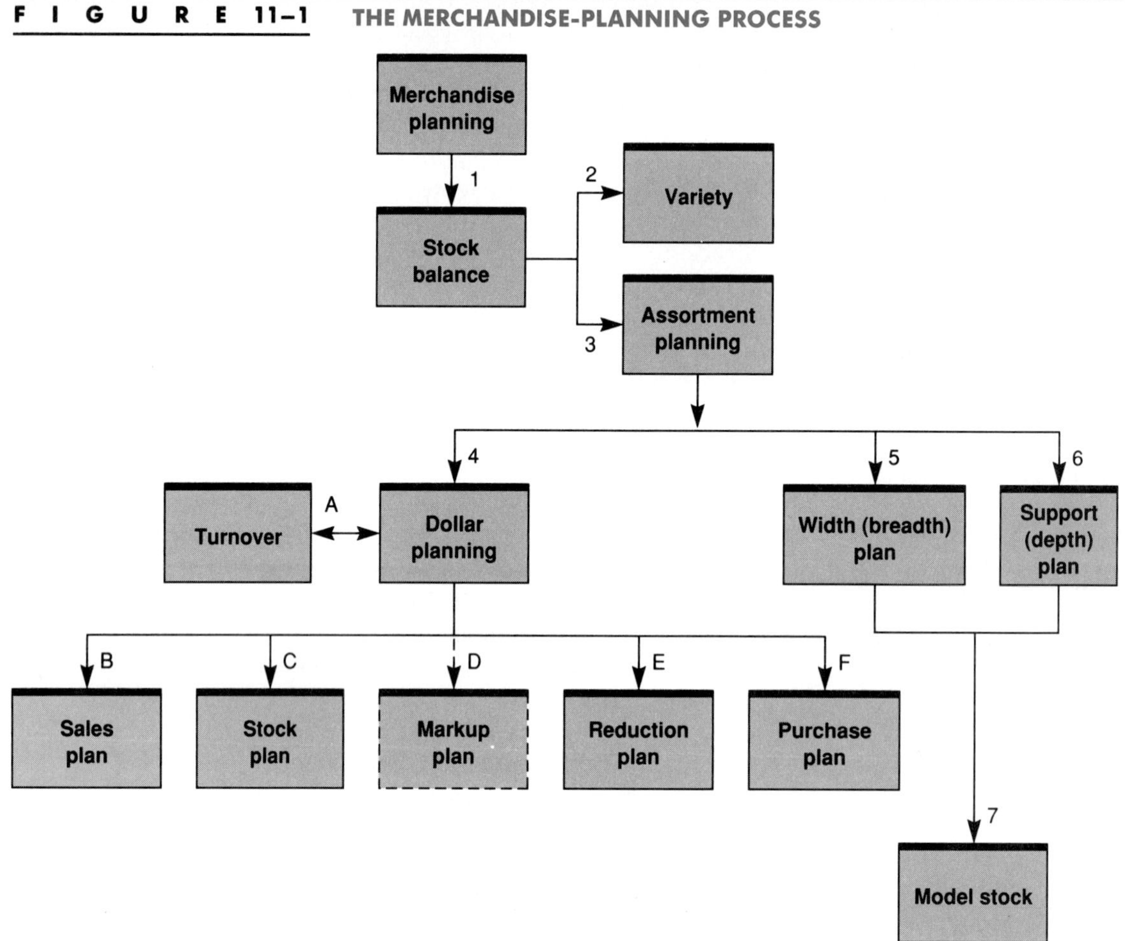

As shown in Figure 11–1, the three aspects of stock balance are width (or breadth), point 5; support (or depth), point 6; and total dollars, point 4.

Width. **Width** (or breadth) refers to the assortment factors necessary to meet the demands of customers and to meet competition. Referring to the coffee example used earlier, the following might be a width plan:

Brand		Types		Sizes
(Folger's Maxwell House, private)	×	(regular, instant, freeze-dried)	×	(3 in each kind of coffee)
3 SKUs		3		3 = 27 SKUs

Thus, 27 SKUs are needed to meet customer wants and to compete effectively.

Support. **Support** (or depth) refers to the number of units of merchandise needed to support expected sales of each assortment factor. For example, the retailer needs to know how many one-pound cans of Folger's regular-grind coffee versus one-pound cans of instant coffee cans are needed. This information depends on the sales importance of each factor. If, for example, 10 percent of sales are in Folger's one-pound regular grind, the retailer may want 10 percent of support to be in that SKU. The decision process sounds simple, but the "art" of merchandising enters here. Knowledge of the customer market, the image of the store or department, and other factors all enter into this decision. Only expertise in planning the composition of stock will give retailers confidence in this activity.

Dollars Invested. Width and support decisions do not tell the retailer how much money needs to be invested in inventory at any one time. Thus, the total dollar investment in inventory is the final way to look at stock balance. Here, the concept of merchandise turnover comes into play.

Merchandise **turnover** is the number of times the average inventory of an item (or SKU) is sold, usually in annual terms. As shown in Figure 11–2, turnover can be computed in units or on a dollar basis in either cost or retail terms.

For turnover goals to be meaningful, they must be based on merchandise groupings that are as alike as possible. Planning on the basis of large, diverse merchandising groupings is unwise. For example, a storewide turnover rate for a full-line department store would be meaningless because the store might carry products as diverse as furniture and health and beauty aids. The turnover rate for furniture would be lower than for health and beauty aids simply because of the nature of the product and the rate at which consumers purchase and repurchase these two product categories.

Furthermore, it is impossible to tell whether a particular turnover rate is good or bad unless it is compared to something. The retailer can compare turnover rates to average industry rates for similar types of retail operations, to past years' turnover rates, or to established goals.

The objective is to have a turnover rate that is fast enough to give the retailer a good return on money invested in inventory, but not so fast that the retailer is always out of stock. The benefits of a "healthy" turnover rate include a higher sales volume owing to fresher stock. The morale of salespeople may be better because they are not continuously being urged to move "old" stock. Higher prices may result from fewer markdowns. A healthy turnover rate may enable retailers to take advantage of special buys offered by manufacturers, such as close-outs, that lead to reduced cost of goods. Finally, certain operating expenses associated with carrying inventory, such as insurance, are reduced when the retailer has a healthy turnover rate.

FIGURE 11–2 STOCK TURNOVER COMPUTATION

Based on dollars

Turnover at retail

How to calculate turnover:

$$\text{Turnover} = \frac{\text{Retail sales } (\$100{,}000)}{\text{Average inventory in retail dollars } (\$25{,}000)} = 4 \text{ times}$$

How to calculate average retail inventory

Add together all available inventory figures and divide by the number of counts, e.g.

Beginning of year	$30,000
Midyear	20,000
End of year	25,000
Total	$75,000
Average = $75,000 ÷ 3 = $25,000	

or

Turnover at cost

$$\text{Turnover} = \frac{\text{Cost of sales } (\$60{,}000)}{\text{Average inventory at cost } (\$15{,}000)} = 4 \text{ times}$$

Calculate what was available; subtract what is left; then calculate what moved out, all at cost

How to calculate cost of sales

Beginning inventory	$18,000
+Purchases	57,000
=Total dollars available	$75,000
−Ending inventory	15,000
=Cost of goods sold	$60,000

Based on units

$$\text{Turnover} = \frac{\text{Number of units sold } (3{,}200)}{\text{Average inventory in units } (800)} = 4 \text{ times}$$

Too low a turnover rate signals that a problem exists. The retailer should try to determine why the turnover rate is low and take corrective action. To improve a turnover rate that is too low, retailers can try to increase sales, reduce the size of average inventory, or both.

As suggested earlier, retailers should avoid having too high a turnover rate. Too rapid a turnover may indicate that the retailer is subject to stockouts (not having an item available when the customer wants it) or that too small an assortment is being offered to customers. Too high a rate may also suggest that the retailer is not ordering in large enough quantities to take advantage of quantity discounts, an action that increases the cost of goods. Too high a turnover rate may also lead to increased costs associated with acquiring and ordering merchandise. In general, too high a rate suggests that the retailer is not investing enough in average inventory and thus needs to increase average inventory.

Developing the Merchandise Budget

This section of the chapter focuses on merchandise planning in total dollars, or the development of a merchandise budget. A **merchandise budget** is a plan of the dollar amount of merchandise to buy, usually set up by merchandise classification and by month and based on sales and profitability goals. Later sections look at planning in terms of width and support. Before discussing the budgeting process, however, let's look at the various approaches to preparing the budget.

Approaches to Preparing the Merchandise Budget

Traditionally, merchandise planning has been structured around either a bottom-up or a top-down approach. The bottom-up approach starts with estimates at the classification level. These estimates are then combined into a departmental merchandise budget and finally into a total company plan. The top-down approach starts with a total dollar figure established by top management. This dollar figure is then allocated to the various merchandise classifications. A third method, which probably results in the most accurate merchandise plan, is the interactive approach. Here management sets broad guidelines and the buying staff then follows the bottom-up approach with management review.

The Merchandise Budgeting Process

The following items affect profit return and are included in the merchandise budget (refer to Figure 11–1):

1. Sales.
2. Stock (inventory).
3. Reductions.
4. Purchases.

Table 11–1 presents a diagram of these profit factors. We will refer to this diagram as each factor is discussed in greater detail.

Sales Planning. The starting point in developing a merchandise budget is the sales plan. Note from Table 11–1 that sales are first planned by season and then by month. To illustrate sales planning, we will use a sport shirt classification to plan a merchandise budget.

TABLE 11–1

SCHEMATIC DIAGRAM OF MERCHANDISE BUDGET

	Components to Be Budgeted					
	Sales		Stock	Reductions		Purchases
	Season	*Month*		*Season*	*Month*	
Quantitative (factual) data						
Qualitative (subjective) data: trends and environmental factors						

Sales Planning by Season. A season is the typical planning period in retailing, especially for fashion merchandise. Assume that the merchandise budget is being planned for the 1994 spring season (February through July, since in retailing, a season is six months). The retailer would start planning in November 1993.

In planning seasonal sales, retailers often begin by looking at last year's sales for the same period. Rather than merely using the past period's figure as their sales forecast, retailers need to evaluate the factors that affect sales to determine whether they need to modify their sales forecast. For example, recent sales trends should be considered; retailers must determine whether these trends are likely to continue. Furthermore, forces outside the firm that would affect the sales forecast need to be evaluated. For example, a retailer's projections would be affected if a new apparel store opened in the community that carried similar assortments. Similarly, adverse economic conditions in the community caused by plant closings might also affect the forecast. Next, retailers must look at internal conditions that might affect the sales forecast. Moving the sport shirt classification to a more valuable location within the store is an example of an internal condition.

Exact numbers cannot be placed on all of these external and internal factors. Retailers must, however, use judgment and incorporate all relevant factors into the sales forecast. Assume that sales for the spring of 1993 totaled $15,000. If the retailer believes that sales will increase by 10 percent, the forecast for the spring 1994 season would be $16,500 ($15,000 × 1.10 = $16,500).

Sales Planning by Month. The planned seasonal sales must now be divided into monthly sales. Again, the starting point is spring 1993. Assume the following sales distribution by month for this season: February, 10 percent; March, 20 percent; April, 15 percent; May, 15 percent; June, 30 percent; and July, 10 percent. Furthermore, assume the retailer has considered trends and all internal and external factors that would affect this distribution and has decided that no adjustments need to be made. Based on this analysis, the season's planned sales by month for spring 1994 would equal the figures shown in Table 11–2.

TABLE 11–2

SPRING SALES PLAN, 1994

Month	Percentage of Total Season's Business in 1993	×	Season's Sales Forecast	=	Planned Sales for Months of 1994 Season
February	10		$16,500		$ 1,650
March	20		16,500		3,300
April	15		16,500		2,475
May	15		16,500		2,475
June	30		16,500		4,950
July	10		16,500		1,650
Total	100				$16,500

Stock Planning. The next step in developing the merchandise budget is to plan stock (inventory) levels by month. Several different techniques can be used to find the amount of monthly stock that is needed to support monthly sales. Because the **stock-to-sales ratio** is often used to plan monthly stock levels for fashion merchandise and for highly seasonal merchandise, we will discuss it here to illustrate the concept of stock planning.

The stock-to-sales ratio reflects the relationship between the dollar amount needed in inventory at the beginning of a month to support planned sales for that month. For example, if $30,000 in inventory is needed at the beginning of a month to support sales of $10,000, the stock-to-sales ratio would be 3 ($30,000/$10,000 = 3).[10]

The retailer multiplies the month's planned sales figure by the month's stock-to-sales ratio to determine beginning-of-month (BOM) inventory. For example, as shown in Table 11–3, planned sales for the month of February are $1,650. Multiplying $1,650 by the month's stock-to-sales ratio of 4.7 yields a BOM inventory for February of $7,755.[11]

In determining monthly stock-sales ratios, retailers can use existing stock-sales ratios from past performance. However, retailers must judge whether the prior periods' stock-to-sales figures need to be adjusted. Trade data may also be used. Even if retailers use their own information, they should still compare it with trade statistics. Stock-to-sales ratios can also be calculated directly from the turnover goal set for the line of merchandise. To do this, the retailer simply divides the desired annual turnover figure into 12 (the number of months in a year). For example, if the turnover goal is 2.5, the average monthly stock-to-sales ratio for the year would be 4.8 (12/2.5 = 4.8). If the desired turnover rate were 4, the average monthly stock-to-sales ratio for the year would be 3 (12/4 = 3). As one can see, the lower the turnover rate, the higher the average monthly stock-to-sales ratio.

Table 11–3 provides information on needed monthly BOM stock for spring 1994. We will make one additional point about BOM inventory. The

TABLE 11–3

BOM STOCK, SPRING 1994

Month	*Planned Sales*	×	*Stock-to-Sales Ratio*	=	*Planned BOM Stock*
February	$ 1,650		4.7		$ 7,755
March	3,300		4.2		13,860
April	2,475		4.3		10,640
May	2,475		4.4		10,890
June	4,950		3.4		16,830
July	1,650		6.9		11,385
Total	$16,500				$71,360

end-of-month (EOM) inventory for a particular month equals the BOM inventory for the following month. For example, in Table 11–3, the BOM inventory for February is $7,755. The EOM inventory for February would be $13,860, the BOM inventory for March.

Reductions Planning. **Reductions** are anything other than sales that reduce inventory value. Reductions include employee discounts. If an item sells for $100 and employees receive a 20 percent discount, the employee pays $80. The $80 is recorded as a sale. The $20 reduces the inventory dollar amount but is *not* a sale—it is a reduction.

Shortages (shrinkage) are also reductions. A shoplifter takes a $500 watch from a jewelry department. Inventory is reduced by $500 just as if it were a sale. But no revenues come from shoplifting. If a salesperson steals another watch (internal pilferage), the results are the same. If a $1,000 watch is received into stock but is marked $500 by clerical error, fewer inventory dollars are in stock than the retailer thinks.

Finally, markdowns are reductions. If a $25 tennis racket is not selling and is marked down to $15, the $10 markdown is counted as a reduction of inventory and only $15 is counted as a sale.

Why must reductions be planned as a part of the merchandise budget? Note from Table 11–3 that a planned BOM stock of $13,860 for March is needed to support March sales of $3,300 (with a 4.2 stock-to-sales ratio). However, suppose that the retailer's reductions during February amount to approximately $5,000. The EOM inventory in February (BOM for March) is $5,000 less than it would have been if no reductions had been taken. So reductions must be planned and accounted for so that the retailer will have sufficient BOM inventory to make planned sales.

Assume that reductions for the spring season in the department are planned at 8 percent of seasonal sales, or $1,320 ($16,500 × .08). Assume that the same percentages used to allocate the season's sales to each month are used to allocate the $1,320 in reductions to each month. The planned monthly reductions for the 1994 spring season would thus appear as in Table 11–4.

TABLE 11–4

PLANNED REDUCTIONS, SPRING 1994

Month	*Planned Percentage of Business*	×	*Total Reductions*	=	*Amount of Reductions*
February	20		$1,320		$ 264
March	10		1,320		132
April	10		1,320		132
May	10		1,320		132
June	20		1,320		264
July	30		1,320		396
Total	100				$1,320

Planned Purchases. Up to this point, the retailer has determined planned sales, stock, and reductions. The next step in developing the merchandise budget is to plan the dollar amount of purchases on a monthly basis. Planned purchases are figured as follows:

Planned purchases = Planned sales + Planned reductions +
Planned EOM stock − Planned BOM stock

We need dollars of purchases to make sure we have enough inventory to cover our sales plan, to take care of our planned reductions, and to make sure we have enough retail EOM inventory to be in business the following month. We already have dollars to contribute to these needs in the form of BOM inventory.

As an illustration, assume that the retailer wants to calculate planned purchases for March. Look at Tables 11–3 and 11–4 to get the needed information:

Planned purchases =	$ 3,330	(planned sales for March, Table 11–3)
	+ 132	(planned reductions for March, Table 11–4)
	+ 10,640	(EOM March or BOM April, Table 11–3)
=	$ 14,102	(Dollar needs for March)
	− 13,860	(BOM March—existing inventory, Table 11–3)
=	$ 242	(planned purchases)

An important point is that purchases are planned in terms of *retail* dollars. However, when buying merchandise, the buyer must think in terms of the *cost* of merchandise. Thus, it is necessary to convert the planned purchases figure at retail to a cost figure. This conversion process will be explained in detail in Chapter 14, but, for now, simply remember this: to convert retail dollars to cost dollars, multiply retail dollars by the complement of the initial retail markup. For example, assume that planned purchases for a given month are $1,000 at retail, and that the planned initial markup is 40 percent of retail. To convert retail dollars to cost dollars, multiply $1,000 by 60 percent, the complement of the planned initial markup (100% − 40% = 60%). Thus, planned purchases at cost would be $600 ($1,000 × 60% = $600).

We have now worked through the dollar merchandise planning process. However, as Figure 11–1 shows, the retailer also needs to plan the width and support factors of stock balance (points 5 and 6). The following sections of the chapter focus on these issues.

PLANNING WIDTH AND SUPPORT OF ASSORTMENTS

Now that the retailer knows how much to spend for stock, he or she must still decide what to spend the dollars for (width) and in what amounts (support). The goal here is to set up a **model stock plan** (Figure 11–1, point 7), which is the retailer's prediction of demand at specific times of the year, expressed in unit terms.

The Width Plan

Figure 11–3 is a model stock plan for our sport shirt classification. Assume that the primary customer-attracting features are knit and cut-and-sewn shirts. Even though the illustration is simple, it shows that to offer customers only one sport shirt in each width (or assortment) factor for both knit and cut-and-sewn, 270 shirts (2 × 5 × 3 × 3 × 3) are needed (Column 1 of Figure 11–3).

The Support Plan

The support (or depth) plan involves deciding how many sport shirts are needed in each of the five assortment factors (see Figure 11–3). Assume that 800 sport shirts are needed for one turnover period. Also assume that turnover is 3; then 800 sport shirts are needed for 4 months (12 months divided by 3 = 4). Remember that the retailer is planning dollars at the same time as assortments, so the amount of dollars will affect support.

If the retailer believes that 90 percent of sales will be in cut-and-sewn shirts, then 720 shirts will be needed (800 × .90 = 720). Following Figure 11–3, one can see that the retailer will have 144 of size A, 58 in color A, 29 at price point A, and 12 in design A.

The Art of Planning

The foregoing discussion of the formulation of the width and support stock appears to be a rather routine approach to planning. In fact, the decisions about the percentage relationships among the various assortment factors are based on many complex factors relating to store objectives and to the "art" of retailing. In planning the assortment width factors, the entire merchandising philosophy and strategic posture of management are of critical importance. The factors would be significantly different for a classification in a Neiman-Marcus store than for the same classification in a Kmart outlet. The Neiman-Marcus merchandiser would consider the most unusual styles and fashion colors. Price points would also greatly exceed those of Kmart.

FIGURE 11–3 MODEL STOCK OF SPORT SHIRTS

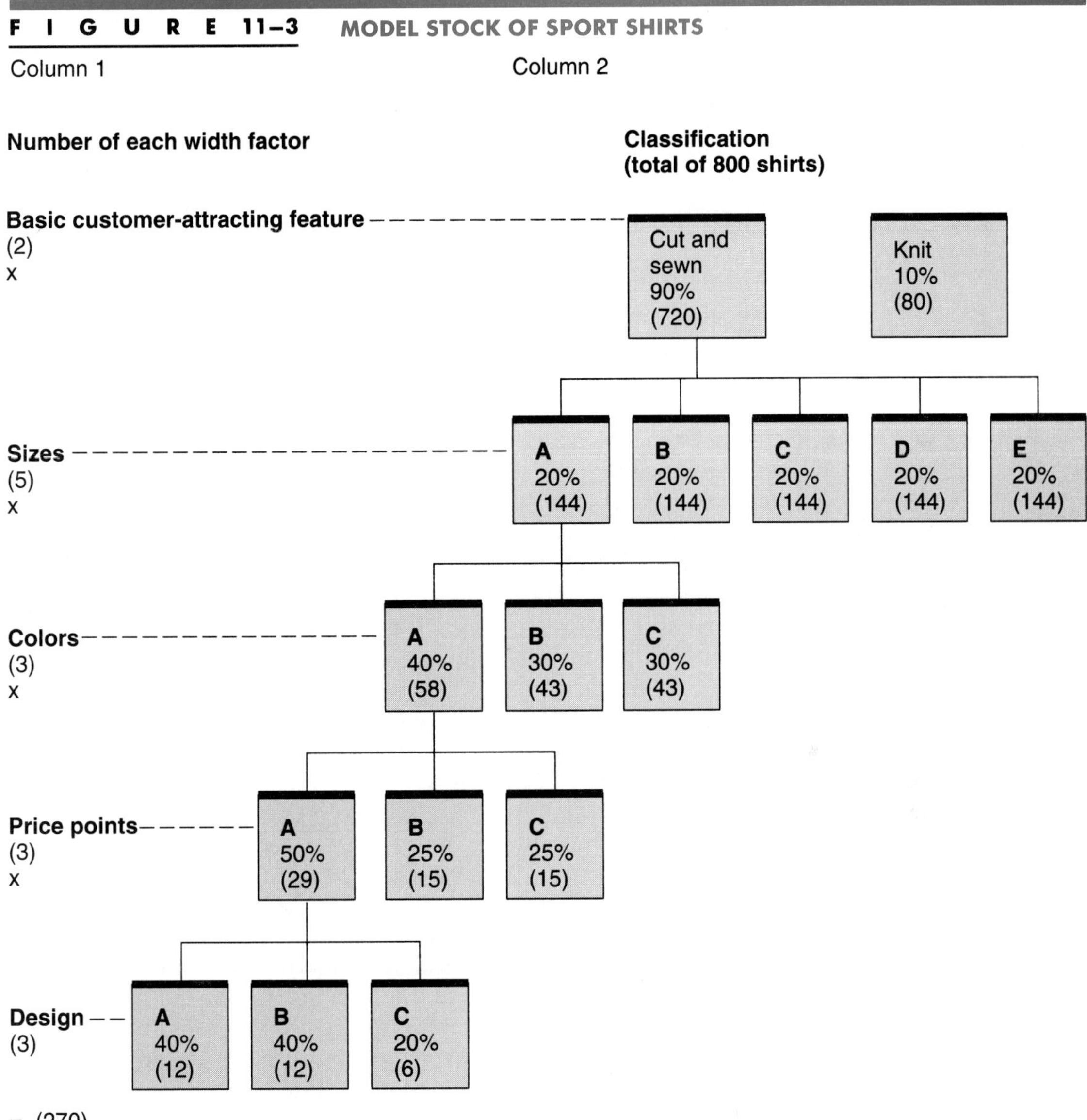

Note: The percentage in each factor is the expected importance of that assortment factor. Numbers in parentheses represent the share of the 800-shirt total; for example, 90% × 800 = 720, 20% × 720 = 144, and so on.

In other words, the total image management wants the store to project and the strategy implemented to accomplish its objectives affect decisions on individual width factors and their relative importance. Certainly the target market of the store affects planning decisions. Environmental

FIGURE 11–4 THE RELATIONSHIP BETWEEN PLANNING AND CONTROL

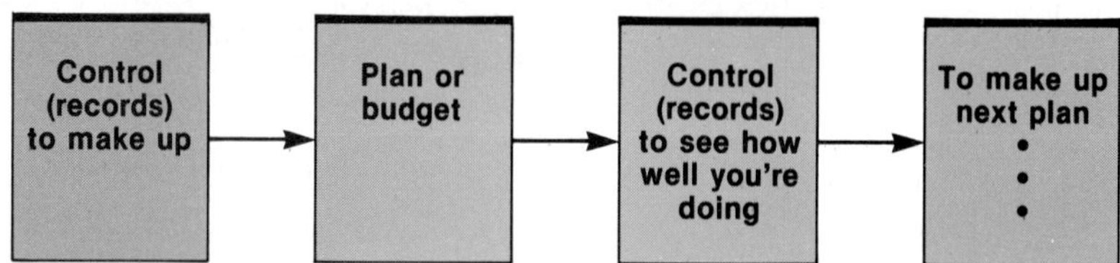

conditions of the planning period will also affect the factors. For example, as technological advances in textile fibers allowed more vibrant colorfast materials to enter the menswear industry, the width of offerings was expanded. The technology was a response to changing lifestyles, which dictated a more fashion-conscious male market for sportswear in general. In addition, changing styles of living and utilization of time for such activities as tennis and golf are reflected in current sportswear offerings.

We have focused on the "how to" rather than the "what" and "why" because of the artistic and creative nature of merchandising, the variability among different types of merchandise classifications, and especially the virtual impossibility of teaching the *art* of merchandising. Our major concern is that you appreciate how the operating and the creative aspects of merchandise planning are related.

THE MECHANICS OF MERCHANDISE CONTROL

The relationship between planning and control is essential, direct, and reciprocal. As shown in Figure 11–4, control records are needed to develop plans. Once a plan is developed, control records are needed to determine the retailer's success.

Earlier in this chapter we discussed the development of a merchandise budget in dollars and a model stock for width and support factors. In the following section, we will discuss the systems used to control the merchandise budget. Figure 11–5 illustrates the relationship between merchandise planning and control systems. Note from the figure that two systems are used for controlling the merchandise plan. **Dollar control** is the way of controlling dollar investment in inventory. **Unit control** is used to control the width and support aspects of stock balance. Figure 11–6 shows how these two types of control work together.

Dollar Merchandise Inventory Control

To control dollar inventory investments, the retailer must know the following:

1. The beginning dollar inventory.
2. What has been added to stock.

FIGURE 11–5 FROM PLANNING TO CONTROL

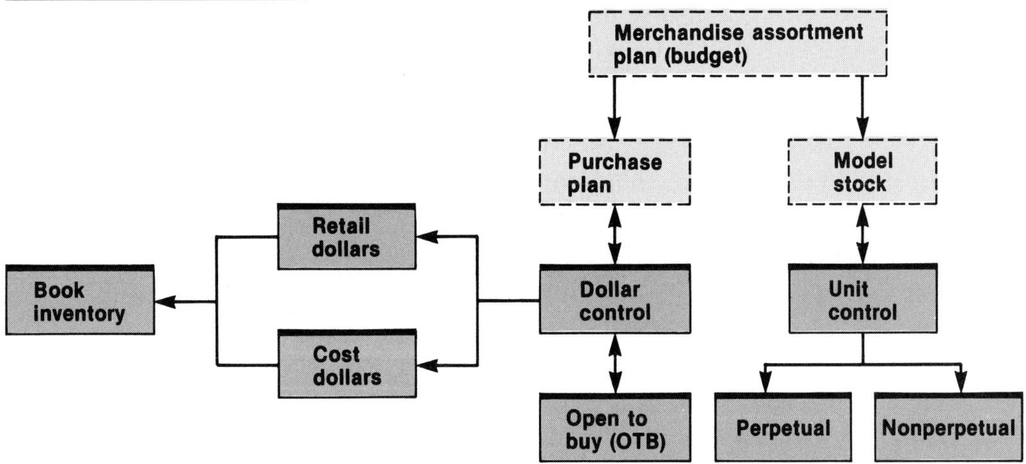

3. How much inventory has moved out of stock.
4. How much inventory is now on hand.

A more detailed statement appears later in this section, but the following illustration shows the basic facts the retailer must know to control dollar inventory investments:

1. Inventory at beginning of period	\$10,000
+2. Total additions to stock	2,000
= Stock available for sale during period	\$12,000
−3. Total deductions	2,500
=4. Inventory at end of period	\$ 9,500

To determine the value of inventory at the end of the period (4 in the illustration above), the retailer may take a **physical inventory** (actually

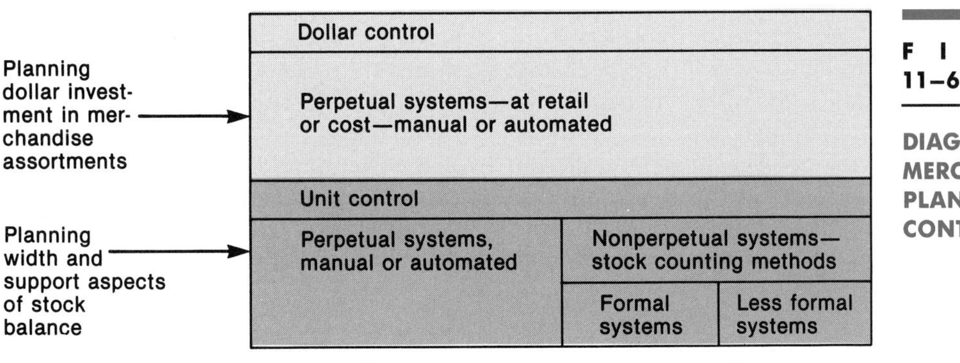

FIGURE 11–6

DIAGRAM OF MERCHANDISE PLANNING AND CONTROL

count all of the inventory on hand) or set up a book inventory, or **perpetual inventory,** system. It is impractical to take a physical inventory every time the manager wants to know how much inventory is on hand. Thus, retailers set up a book inventory system. This enables them to know the dollar value of inventory on hand without having to take a physical inventory.

A book inventory system is necessary for efficient dollar control. Information must be collected and recorded continually; it can be recorded in retail dollars or in cost dollars, manually or by computer.

Retail Dollar Control. Table 11–5 shows the items typically included in a retail dollar control system. The system provides answers to the following questions:

1. What dollar inventory did the retailer start with? The BOM inventory dated 3/1 gives the answer to this question. This figure is the EOM February figure.
2. What has been added to stock? The additions to stock are purchases, transfers, and additional markups that add dollar value to the beginning inventory.
3. How much inventory has moved out of stock? The deductions from stock are sales, markdowns, and employee discounts, which reduce the total dollar value of inventory available for sale.
4. How much inventory is on hand now? The EOM inventory, dated 3/31, is the difference between what was available and what moved out of stock. This is the book inventory figure.

The explanations in Table 11–5 should be studied carefully because they are important to a full understanding of the items that affect retail book inventory. The information in Table 11–5, however, should not be confused with an accounting statement (discussed in Chapter 12); it comes from accounting data, but it is for control purposes only.

Examine in Table 11–5 the notation "including shortages" on the EOM line. Because these are "book" figures, a chance for error exists. The only way to determine the accuracy of the book figure is by taking a physical inventory.

As shown in Table 11–5, the retail book figures indicate the value of on-hand inventory to be $9,300. Assume that when a physical inventory is taken, the retail value of on-hand stock is $9,000. This situation represents a **shortage** of $300. Shoplifting, internal theft, short shipments from vendors, breakage, and clerical error are common causes of shortages. If, on the other hand, the physical inventory had indicated the value of stock on hand to be $10,000, then the retail classification has incurred an **overage** of $700. An overage situation is usually caused by clerical errors or miscounts.

TABLE 11–5 ILLUSTRATION OF BOOK (PERPETUAL) INVENTORY—SPORT SHIRTS—FOR MARCH

Items Affecting Dollar Value of Inventory during Month				*Necessary Explanations of Certain Items*	*Where the Information Comes From*
BOM inventory, 3/1			$10,000		EOM February inventory
Additions to stock:					
Purchases	$2,000				Purchase records or invoices
Less—vendor returns	(100)			Goods go back to resource	Vendor return records
Net purchases		$1,900			
Transfers in	$ 200			In multistore firm goods transfer from one store to another	Interstore transfer forms in multistore firm
Less—transfers out	(100)				
Net transfers in		100			
Additional markups		300		Price increase after goods in stock	Price change forms
Total additions			2,300		
Total available for sale			$12,300		
Deductions from stock:					
Gross sales	$2,500				Daily sales report
Less—customer returns	(100)				Return forms
Net sales		$2,400			
Gross markdowns	$ 500			Reduction from original price	Price change forms at start of a sale
Less—markdown cancellations	(100)				Price change cancellation at end of sale to bring prices back to regular
Net markdowns		400			
Employee discounts		200		Employee pays less than merchandise price	Form completed at sale
Total deductions from stock			$ 3,000		
EOM inventory, 3/31 (including shortages)			$ 9,300	A book inventory figure so actual amount is somewhat different (physical inventory necessary for actual)	Derived figure from additions and deductions from BOM inventory

TABLE 11–6

DETERMINING OPEN TO BUY (OTB)

Planned purchases		= 25,000	(EOM inventory or BOM March)
		+ 2,500	(Planned sales—February)
		+ 600	(Planned reductions—February)
		=$28,100	(Dollars needed)
		− 24,000	(BOM February at retail) (EOM January)
		=$ 4,100	(Planned purchases)
Commitments against planned purchases during the month of February:			
On order to be delivered in February:	$1,000		
Merchandise received as of February 15:	$1,500	− 2,500	(Commitments against planned purchases)
OTB as of February 15		=$ 1,600	(Note: The $1,600 figure is in retail dollars and must be converted to cost to use as a buying guide in the market.)

Open to Buy. One of the most valuable outputs of a retail dollar control system is **open to buy** (OTB), which exists to "control" the merchant's utilization of the planned purchases figure. Dollar control provides the essential information to set up an OTB system.

Table 11–6 illustrates how OTB as of February 15 can be calculated. As shown in the table, OTB is determined by deducting from planned purchases *commitments* that have been made. The two commitments are merchandise on order that has not been delivered and merchandise that has been delivered. Remember, planned purchases relate only to one month (in the example, the month of February). OTB also relates to only one month. If, for example, merchandise was ordered in January to be delivered in March, that amount would not be a February commitment and would not affect OTB for February. Table 11–6 shows that, as of February 15, the retailer has $1,600 (in retail dollars) to spend for merchandise to be delivered in February. At the beginning of any month with no commitments, planned purchases and OTB are equal. Assume, however, that by February 20 all of the OTB has been used and that, in fact, the buyer has overcommitted by $100. This situation is called *overbought* and is not a good position to be in. This leads to another point that must be made about OTB.

OTB must be used only as a guide and must not be allowed to actually dictate decisions. A retailer, however, always wants to have OTB to take advantage of unique market situations. The system must also allow for budget adjustments. If the buyer needs more OTB, he or she must convince management of the importance of a contemplated purchase and obtain a budget increase for planned sales. Alternatively, the buyer can

TABLE 11–7

PERPETUAL COST DOLLAR CONTROL

Date	BOM Inventory	Cost of Items Received	Cost of Items Sold	Net Change
March 1	$15,000	$1,500	$1,000	+$ 500 ($1,500 – $1,000)
March 2	15,500	—	2,000	– 2,000
March 3	13,500	400	1,200	– 800 (+ $400 – $1,200)
March 4	12,700			

increase planned reductions, take more markdowns than have been budgeted, or increase the planned EOM inventory in anticipation of an upswing in the market. Each of these is a legitimate merchandising option and indicates that the OTB control system is flexible, as any budget control system should be.

Cost Dollar Control. Retail dollar control is used more often than cost dollar control. The major problem in using cost instead of retail control is *costing* each sale. Costing means converting retail dollars to cost dollars after each sale is made. Because of this costing problem, a cost dollar control system is used only when merchandise has an unusually high unit value and when there are relatively few transactions. With merchandise such as furniture or automobiles, cost dollar control is practical. However, for merchandise classifications such as our sport shirt illustration, retail dollar control is used. Table 11–7 shows the kind of information needed for a perpetual cost control system. When using a cost dollar control system, it is not possible to record additional markups and reductions such as markdowns and employee discounts because all the figures are in cost dollars.

Unit Merchandise Inventory Control

Unit control is the system used to control the width and support aspects of stock balance (see Figures 11–5 and 11–6). Unit control is simpler than dollar control because fewer factors affect units than affect dollars invested. The difference is that the price changes do not affect units carried. As Figures 11–5 and 11–6 indicate, the two types of unit control are perpetual and nonperpetual (or stock-counting) systems.

Perpetual Unit Control. Perpetual unit control, like perpetual dollar control, is a book inventory. Table 11–8 provides an illustration of perpetual unit control.

A perpetual book inventory for unit control is the most sophisticated of the unit systems. Because perpetual book systems require continuous recording of additions and deductions from stock, they are more expensive to operate. However, use of point-of-sale systems reduces costs and saves time in collecting the information needed. If the system is manually maintained, sales information can be recorded by writing on a sales check

TABLE 11–8 ILLUSTRATION OF PERPETUAL UNIT CONTROL—SPORT SHIRTS—FOR MONTH OF MARCH

BOM inventory			1,000
Additions to stock:			
Purchases	250		
Less vendor returns	(40)		
Net purchases		210	
Transfers in	41		
Less transfers out	(20)		
Net transfers		21	
Total additions			231
Total available for sale			1,231
Deductions from stock:			
Gross sales	225		
Less customer returns	(8)		
Net sales		217	
Total deductions from stock			217
EOM inventory, 3/31 (including shortages)			1,014

and having the information recorded in the office, detaching a part of a sales ticket to be counted later, or deducting items sold from a tag on a floor sample.

Note in Table 11–8 the notation "including shortages," which appears on the EOM line. As with dollar control, this is a book figure; thus, there is chance for error. Again, the only way to determine the accuracy of the book figure is to take a physical inventory. The concepts of shortages and overages apply here just as they do in dollar control. The only difference is that shortages and overages are expressed in terms of number of units rather than in dollars.

Nonperpetual Unit Control. Nonperpetual unit control systems are also called stock-counting systems. These systems are not book inventory methods. Therefore, the retailer will not be able to determine shortages or overages because there is no book inventory against which to compare a physical inventory.

Nonperpetual systems are a compromise. Perpetual control is better, and the retailer gets more and better information. But sometimes the benefits simply do not justify the cost. Nonperpetual unit control systems include formal and less formal systems.

Formal Systems. The requirements of formal, nonperpetual systems are as follows: (1) a planned model stock, (2) a periodic counting schedule, and (3) definite, assigned responsibility for counting.

Department:__________Classification:__________Stock number:__________

Item description:__________Fabric:__________Style:__________

Design:__________Cost:__________Retail:__________Vendor number:__________

Miscellaneous:__________

Date of count:__________On hand:__________On order:__________

Received:__________Sold:__________

FIGURE 11–7

FORMAL UNIT CONTROL SHEET

Let's use a tie classification as an example. Every tie in stock might be counted once a month. The retailer might select the first Tuesday of each month for the count schedule. Based on the stock on hand, the stock on order, and the stock sold, the buyer will place a reorder as the information is reviewed each count period. Figure 11–7 is an example of a count sheet.

For formal, nonperpetual systems to be used effectively, the rate of sale of the items being controlled must be predictable. Furthermore, the items controlled by formal systems should not be so fast moving and fashionable that the retailer needs to know the status of stock more often than the periodic count schedule will permit. The alert merchant will spot-check between count dates to catch any out-of-stocks that might occur. Formal systems do account for items on order (which less formal systems do not).

Less Formal Systems. Some kinds of merchandise can be controlled with a less formal system. If immediate delivery of goods is possible, there is no need to account for merchandise on order. However, the retailer still must have a planned model stock and a specific time for visually inspecting the stock.

Under a less formal system, there will be a minimum stock level (for instance, shelf level or number of cases in the stockroom). When the stock reaches that level, a reorder is placed. This system might be used quite effectively in the canned goods department in a supermarket.

CHAPTER HIGHLIGHTS

- Merchandising plans must be developed to support the firm's overall competitive strategy. Merchandising should be viewed as a component of the retailing plan that can create a competitive advantage for the firm.
- The purpose of merchandise planning is to maintain stock balance—a balance between inventory and sales. The three aspects of stock balance are width (or breadth), support (or depth), and total dollars invested.

- Merchandise planning (budgeting) can be structured around either a bottom-up or a top-down approach. Perhaps the best approach is an interactive one.
- The following items affect profitability and are included in the merchandise budget: (1) sales, (2) inventory or stock, (3) reductions, and (4) purchases.
- In addition to knowing how much money to spend for stock, the retailer must also decide what to spend the money on (width) and in what amounts (support).
- Planning is useless unless retailers monitor results to determine whether goals are being met. This monitoring process is the control element of merchandise management. Retailers need both dollar and unit control systems.
- Dollar control is used to control dollar investment in stock. To do this, the retailer must know what the beginning dollar inventory is, what has been added to stock, how much inventory has moved out of stock, and how much inventory is now on hand. Dollar control systems can be maintained on a cost basis, but retail dollar control is more often used.
- One of the most valuable outputs of a retail dollar control system is open to buy (OTB), which exists to control the retailer's utilization of the planned purchases figure. As with all budgets, flexibility is essential.
- Unit control is simpler than dollar control because price changes do not affect units. The two types of unit control are perpetual and nonperpetual (or stock-counting) systems; the latter can be either formal or less formal.

Study Questions

1. Explain the relationship between merchandising and merchandise management.
2. Speculate on the future of private versus manufacturer brands in various types of retailing operations (for instance, food retailing, department stores, specialty operations).
3. Define and explain the relationships among the following terms: product line, variety, and assortment.
4. Describe the three aspects of stock balance.
5. What is meant by the term *merchandise turnover?* What are the benefits of having a healthy turnover rate? What are the problems of having too high a turnover rate? If a turnover rate is too low, what can the retailer do to improve the rate?
6. Discuss the components of the merchandise budget (sales, stock, reductions, and purchases). Indicate the elements to be considered in each.
7. Explain open to buy (OTB). Why would a retailer attempt to have OTB always available? How can a retailer who has overbought make adjustments to get more open to buy?
8. What is the difference between a retail dollar control system and a cost dollar control system? Under what conditions might a cost dollar control system be used effectively?
9. What is the difference between a shortage and an overage? How are they determined? What are causes of each?
10. What is the purpose of unit control? What is the difference between perpetual and nonperpetual unit control systems? What is the difference between formal and less formal nonperpetual unit control systems?

PROBLEMS

1. If net sales for the first four months of operation are $50,000 and the average retail stock for the same period is $25,000, what is the annual stock turnover rate?
2. Given the following figures, what is the stock turnover rate for the season?

	Retail Stock on Hand	*Monthly Net Sales*
Opening inventory	$16,500	
End of: 1st month	16,450	$7,500
2nd month	16,000	6,900
3rd month	17,260	7,250
4th month	16,690	6,840
5th month	15,980	6,620
6th month	16,620	7,180

3. What is average stock if the stock turnover rate is 4 and net sales are $36,000?
4. What is cost of goods sold if the stock turnover rate is 3.5 and the average stock at cost is $7,800?
5. A new department shows the following figures for the first three months of operation: net sales, $160,000; and average retail stock, $180,000. If business continues at the same rate, what will the stock turnover rate be for the year?
6. Last year a certain department had net sales of $21,000 and a stock turnover rate of 2.5. A stock turnover rate of 3 is desired for the year ahead. If sales volume remains the same, how much must the average inventory be reduced (*a*) in dollar amount and (*b*) in percentage?
7. A certain department has net sales for the year of $71,250. The stock at the beginning of the year is $22,500 at cost and $37,500 at retail. A stock count in July showed the inventory at cost as $23,750 and at retail as $36,250. End-of-year inventories are $25,000 at cost and $38,750 at retail. Purchases at cost during the year amounted to $48,750. What is the stock turnover rate (*a*) at cost and (*b*) at retail?
8. Given the following information for the month of September, calculate (*a*) planned purchases and (*b*) open to buy:

Planned sales for the month	$ 9,200
Planned reductions for the month	100
Planned BOM inventory	14,600
Planned EOM inventory	15,500
Merchandise received to date for September	9,800
Merchandise on order, September delivery	500

9. Given the following information for the month of July, calculate (*a*) planned purchases and (*b*) open to buy:

Planned sales for the month	$27,000
Planned reductions for the month	650
Planned EOM inventory	36,000
Stock-to-sales ratio for July	1.5
Merchandise received to date for July	13,800
Merchandise on order, July delivery	5,250

10. Given the following information for May, calculate open to buy (*a*) at retail and (*b*) at cost:

Planned sales for the month	$57,000
Planned reductions for the month	1,200
Planned EOM retail stock	72,000
Stock-to-sales ratio for May	1.2
Planned initial markup at retail	42%
Merchandise received for the month of May	35,000
Merchandise on order, May delivery	16,400
Merchandise on order, June delivery	100

A P P L I C A T I O N S

CASE 1: We Have No Open to Buy

George Barker had the opportunity of a lifetime in his estimation. Here he was, an assistant buyer in the home store of a major full-line department store in the Southeast, and his boss, Clarence Adams, senior buyer of home goods, was en route to the Orient for an extended buying trip. Adams had left George in charge—up to a point. George knew that if any really difficult problem arose, he should consult with Finus Cooke, the division's merchandise manager for the hard lines and all home store goods.

George was quite comfortable working with dollar control and open to buy data, as he and Adams discussed their position weekly. Thus George knew, as of October 15, that the department was virtually overbought for the month. He also knew that it was important to keep some OTB available for fill-ins for the remainder of the month.

On October 18, a sales representative from one of the major suppliers of table linens called George to offer a remarkable lot of goods amounting to approximately $50,000 at retail. The merchandise could be sold, with a full markup, at half price. It would be a terrific promotion, George was sure. He had to let the sales representative know by the end of the day, as the offer would then be made to a competitor.

George went to his CRT to recheck the store's OTB. No change—no dollars available to spend. The promotion had not been planned, but George knew the linens would walk out of the stores, and a real profit would be made.

Applying Retailing Principles

1. Should George go to the divisional merchandise manager and try to get more open to buy? Why or why not?
2. Assuming that George does go to the divisional merchandise manager to try to get more open to buy, what arguments could he present?

CASE 2: Auto Dealers Attract Shoppers by Providing a Bumper Crop of Cars under One Roof

In the beginning of auto retailing, there were single-brand dealers in isolated locations. Then, dealers began to locate closer to each other, usually on commercial arteries, forming a car dealer strip. Then dealers began to carry competing brands, but generally no more than two or three. The latest step in this evolutionary process—a step that promises to revolutionize auto retailing—is a dealership carrying a dozen or more brands.

One such dealership is Motor Werks of Barrington Inc., located in Barrington, Illinois. The company offers 10 brands (including Porsche, Cadillac, Honda, Sterling, Suzuki, and BMW), plus a used-car franchise, under one roof. Six showrooms line a wide hallway that also contains cars on display. Space is allocated to the various brands on a performance basis. For example, Hondas are the biggest seller, so they get the biggest showroom. On the other side of the hall is a large service department containing 48 service bays.

Source: Adapted from Gregory A. Patterson, "Auto Malls Lure Shoppers by Providing a Bumper Crop of Cars under One Roof," *The Wall Street Journal*, June 14, 1991, pp. B1, B3.

Applying Retailing Principles

1. From the consumer's perspective, what are the advantages of an automobile dealership carrying many brands?
2. From the dealer's perspective, what are the advantages of carrying many brands?
3. What concerns might automobile manufacturers have about this concept?

Notes

1. The material in this section is based on Karen Blumenthal, "Penney Moves Upscale in Merchandise but Still Has to Convince Public," *The Wall Street Journal,* June 7, 1990, pp. A1, A6.
2. Pat Sloan, "No Longer Limited," *Advertising Age,* November 20, 1989, p. 40.
3. "Eddie Bauer Moves Indoors, but Will Consumers Buy It?" *Marketing News,* January 20, 1992, p. 14.
4. Wendy Zellner, "The Sam's Generation?" *BusinessWeek,* November 25, 1991, p. 36.
5. Jennifer Lawrence, "Wal-Mart Puts Its Own Spin on Private Label," *Advertising Age,* December 16, 1991, p. 26; Wendy Zellner, "The Sam's Generation?" *BusinessWeek,* November 25, 1991, pp. 36–38.
6. Jeffrey A. Trachtenberg, "How Four Loyal Managers Invested in Macy—And Watched It Sink," *The Wall Street Journal,* April 24, 1992, p. B1.
7. David P. Schulz, "Entertainment Goes Retail," *Stores,* June 1992, pp. 46–48.
8. "Groceries Fight Recession by Offering Store Brand," *The Tuscaloosa News,* January 19, 1992, p. 7E.
9. Yomiko Ono, "Japan's Fast-Food Companies Cook Up Local Platters to Tempt Local Palate," *The Wall Street Journal,* May 29, 1992, p. B1.
10. This discussion assumes an ongoing concern with last year's figures available. In a budget process for a new store, estimates and projections based on trade figures and experience are particularly valuable.
11. Readers may wonder why 4.7 times more dollars' worth of inventory than sales are needed. The width and support factors explain this. An example can help illustrate this point. If retailers needed only one jacket to satisfy each customer's demand, they might get by with a one-to-one ratio. But people want to select from many choices. Thus, retailers need many more SKUs to support planned sales.

CHAPTER

12

Performance Evaluation

THIS CHAPTER:

Provides an understanding of the components of the balance sheet and the income statement.

Indicates the importance of ratio analysis as a means of analyzing retail performance.

Focuses on the strategic profit model (SPM) as a framework for monitoring performance results.

Explains the concept of gross margin return on inventory investment.

Examines approaches to determining the cost and value of inventory.

Describes the accounting practices that help management decide on inventory value and appraise profitability and performance.

Presents alternative approaches to departmental performance evaluation.

Discusses concepts related to evaluation of space utilization.

RETAILING CAPSULE

WALGREENS' WINNING STRATEGY

Walgreens is the largest drugstore chain in the United States and one of the longest-running successes in retailing. While recession and debt have hurt many venerable merchants, Walgreens, based in Deerfield, Illinois, is overflowing with cash. It has 1,678 stores in 29 states and Puerto Rico and plans to add 1,300 by the end of the 1990s. In terms of financial performance, sales in 1991 were $6.9 billion, an increase of 11.2 percent from the previous year. In 1991 net profits were $198.3 million, up 11.4 percent from 1990.

Walgreens prospers even in the face of increasing competition from deep-discount chains such as F&M, as well as from discount department stores and supermarkets that have pharmacies. What are the secrets to Walgreens' success? Walgreens thrives by paying attention to customers, sticking to a simple business plan, and investing heavily in technology.

What Walgreens may lack in price, they make up for in convenience. The company picks locations with extreme care. The typical Walgreens is not located in a megamall at the end of a huge parking lot. Rather, it is a midsize store on a main street in a big city or suburb.

The company's major money-maker is its pharmacy division. Because Walgreens' prescription profits are being squeezed by insurance companies, HMOs, and Medicaid programs, the company has used technology to enhance productivity. Walgreens was one of the first drugstore chains to link all its pharmacies electronically to third-party payment plans, eliminating the need for pharmacists and customers to fill out time-consuming claim forms. It has installed scanners in all stores and has developed an inventory control system that tracks demand and automatically reorders merchandise. The chain's satellite communications network ties every pharmacy to a mainframe computer in Des Plaines, Illinois. This investment in technology is

also beneficial to customers; a customer can get a refill of his or her medication at any store, many of which are open 24 hours.

Source: Adapted from Ronald Henkoff "A High-Tech Rx for Profits," *Fortune,* March 23, 1992, p. 106.

Firms such as Walgreens are successful not only because they devise effective strategies to attract customers and to compete, but also because they monitor and evaluate performance to determine whether their strategies are being implemented effectively and whether changes in strategy and operations are needed (also see A Profile in Excellence). Walgreens' measures of performance are clear evidence of excellent results.

This chapter focuses on monitoring and evaluating performance. The tools presented in the chapter help retailers assess their effectiveness in implementing strategy and provide a framework for determining shortcomings and identifying areas that need improvement.

KEY FINANCIAL STATEMENTS AND RATIOS

The balance sheet, the income statement, and various ratios derived from them give management the information it needs to evaluate the effectiveness of strategy in financial terms.

The Balance Sheet

The **balance sheet** is a snapshot of a firm's financial health on a specific date. Table 12–1 lists the components of the balance sheet: **assets** (current and fixed), **liabilities** (current and long term), and **net worth** (the owners' claim on the assets of the business—that is, the owners' investment or equity). The simplest expression of the balance sheet equation is this: assets = liabilities + net worth.

The Income Statement

The **income statement** shows operating results over a period of time and indicates whether investments in assets and strategy have been successful and profitable (see Table 12–2). The income statement indicates net sales, **gross margin** (the difference between net sales and cost of goods sold), total expenses, and after-tax profit. Recall from Chapter 11 that cost of goods sold is computed as follows:

  Beginning inventory
+ Purchases

A Profile in Excellence

WALLY AMOS

In 1975, Wally Amos founded the Famous Amos Chocolate Chip Cookie Company. In the beginning, Amos was involved in all aspects of company operations. However, as time passed, he became increasingly bored with the day-to-day operations of the company and was more concerned with promoting his cookies. Amos was a consummate salesman, and his knack for promotions led to company sales of $7 million in 1981.

In spite of the growth of sales, little was being done to handle the everyday operations of the organization. As cash flow continued to decrease, Amos remembered that the reason he had started the company was to make money. Thus, in 1985 he sought professional assistance and found a group of investors willing to supply the company with the cash needed to get back on track. Amos, in turn, granted them majority stock ownership. Even though Amos was left with only 8 percent ownership in the company, he believed the business still reflected his personality and continued to promote the cookies.

Amos is now contemplating other entrepreneurial endeavors, including plans to start a shoe company, author a book, and write a screenplay for a PBS series. Regardless of the final outcome of these ventures, Amos vows not to involve himself in the day-to-day dimensions of company operations.

= Goods available for sale
− Ending inventory
= Cost of goods sold

Information from the income statement assists management in making any necessary adjustments. For example, if expenses are higher than in the past and higher than in similar stores, management may decide that corrective action is needed. In general, the income statement is a valuable tool for measuring the results of operations.

Ratio Analysis

Retailers establish ratio goals as part of their financial plan. They can then compare performance with objectives. Comparison over time is valuable, as is comparison of performance ratios with trade data for similar firms. Monitoring selected financial ratios can help determine whether problems are developing.

Table 12–3 presents a summary of key financial ratios, their methods of calculation, and the information they show. One study found that two of the ratios appearing in the figure—**return on assets** (net profit after taxes divided by total assets) and the **current ratio** (current assets divided by current liabilities) effectively discriminated between failed and successful retailing firms.[1] Too high a current ratio and the inability to make a profit, as reflected by return on assets, were among the major symptoms of failure

TABLE 12–1

BALANCE SHEET DECEMBER 31, 19___

Assets			
Current assets:			
Cash	$15,000		
Accounts receivable	24,000		
Merchandise inventory	84,000		
Prepaid expenses	10,000		
Total current assets		$133,000	
Fixed assets:			
Building	$85,000		
Furniture and fixtures	23,000		
Total fixed assets		108,000	
Total assets			$241,000
Liabilities and Net Worth			
Current liabilities:			
Accounts payable	$20,000		
Wages payable	18,000		
Notes payable	32,000		
Taxes payable	5,000		
Interest payable	3,000		
Total current liabilities		$ 78,000	
Fixed liabilities:			
Mortgage payable	$75,000		
Total fixed liabilities		75,000	
Total liabilities		$153,000	
Net worth:			
Capital surplus	$80,000		
Retained earnings	8,000		
Total net worth		88,000	
Total liabilities and net worth			$241,000

in the retail firms studied. We also call your attention to leverage ratios. **Leverage** is a situation in which a business unit acquires assets worth more than the amount of capital invested by the owners; the higher the ratio, the higher the amount of borrowed funds in the business. As shown in Table 12–3, leverage can be measured in various ways. Regardless of how it is measured, however, too high a leverage ratio can be dangerous, especially in periods of economic instability and high interest rates. The problems surrounding many leveraged buyouts in retailing in recent years illustrate the danger. Bankruptcy and massive sell-offs of assets occurred as expectations about profitability, growth, and the ability to service debt never materialized (see A Question of Ethics). Several other ratios presented in Table 12–3 will be discussed in later sections of the chapter.

TABLE 12–2

INCOME STATEMENT YEAR ENDING DECEMBER 31, 19___

Gross sales	$208,600			
Less returns and allowances	16,300			
Net sales			$192,300	100%
Cost of goods sold:				
Opening inventory	$ 21,650			
Net purchases	113,500			
Goods available for sale		$135,150		
Less closing inventory		28,495		
Cost of goods sold			106,655	55.46
Gross margin			$ 85,645	44.54
Expenses:				
Rent	$ 19,400			
Payroll	32,950			
Advertising	8,825			
Insurance	1,475			
Travel	2,160			
Utilities	5,265			
Miscellaneous	580			
Total expenses			70,655	36.74
Profit before taxes			$ 14,990	7.80
Income tax			4,950	2.57
Net profit after taxes			$ 10,040	5.22%

THE STRATEGIC PROFIT MODEL

The objective for all retailing is to make a profit, but exactly what does "making a profit" mean? Perhaps the most common way to describe profit is net profit after taxes—the bottom line on the income statement. Profit performance is often evaluated in terms of sales volume—that is, profit as a percentage of sales. For strategic purposes, the most valuable way to view profit is in terms of a return on investment (ROI). However, return on investment can be viewed two ways: return on assets (ROA) and return on net worth (RONW). The ROA reflects all funds invested in a business, whether they come from owners or creditors. The RONW is a measure of profitability for those who have provided the net worth funds—that is, the owners.

The strategic profit model (SPM) is a framework for monitoring retail performance results. The SPM, derived from information obtained in the balance sheet and the income statement, provides the essential ratios for evaluating performance, as illustrated in Figure 12–1. Figure 12–2

TABLE 12–3 A SUMMARY OF KEY FINANCIAL RATIOS, HOW THEY ARE CALCULATED, AND WHAT THEY SHOW

Ratio	*How Calculated*	*What It Shows*
Profitability ratios:		
1. Gross profit margin	$\frac{\text{Sales} - \text{Cost of goods sold}}{\text{Sales}}$	An indication of the total margin available to cover operating expenses and yield a profit.
2. Operating profit margin (or return on sales)	$\frac{\text{Profits before taxes and before interest}}{\text{Sales}}$	An indication of the firm's profitability from current operations without regard to the interest charges accruing from the capital structure.
3. Net profit margin (or net return on sales)	$\frac{\text{Profits after taxes}}{\text{Sales}}$	Shows aftertax profits per dollar of sales. Subpar profit margins indicate that the firm's sales prices are relatively low or that its costs are relatively high, or both.
4. Return on total assets	$\frac{\text{Profits after taxes}}{\text{Total assets}}$ or $\frac{\text{Profits after taxes} + \text{Interest}}{\text{Total assets}}$	A measure of the return on total investment in the enterprise. It is sometimes desirable to add interest to after-tax profits to form the numerator of the ratio because total assets are financed by creditors as well as by stockholders; hence, it is accurate to measure the productivity of assets by the returns provided to both classes of investors.
5. Return on stockholders' equity (or return on net worth)	$\frac{\text{Profits after taxes}}{\text{Total stockholders' equity}}$	A measure of the rate of return on stockholders' investment in the enterprise.
6. Return on common equity	$\frac{\text{Profits after taxes} - \text{Preferred stock dividends}}{\text{Total stockholders' equity} - \text{Par value of preferred stock}}$	A measure of the rate of return on the investment the owners of the common stock have made in the enterprise.
7. Earnings per share	$\frac{\text{Profits after taxes} - \text{Preferred stock dividends}}{\text{Number of shares of common stock outstanding}}$	Shows the earnings available to the owners of each share of common stock.
Liquidity ratios:		
1. Current ratio	$\frac{\text{Current assets}}{\text{Current liabilities}}$	Indicates the extent to which the claims of short-term creditors are covered by assets that are expected to be converted to cash in a period roughly corresponding to the maturity of the liabilities.
2. Quick ratio (or acid-test ratio)	$\frac{\text{Current assets} - \text{Inventory}}{\text{Current liabilities}}$	A measure of the firm's ability to pay off short-term obligations without relying on the sale of its inventories.
3. Inventory to net working capital	$\frac{\text{Inventory}}{\text{Current assets} - \text{Current liabilities}}$	A measure of the extent to which the firm's working capital is tied up in inventory.

Note: Industry average ratios against which a particular company's ratios may be judged are available in *Modern Industry* and *Dun's Reviews* published by Dun & Bradstreet (14 ratios for 125 lines of business activities), Robert Morris Associates' *Annual Statement Studies* (11 ratios for 156 lines of business), and the FTC-SEC's *Quarterly Financial Report* for manufacturing corporations.

Source: Arthur A. Thompson and A. J. Strickland III, *Strategic Management: Concepts and Cases,* 6th ed. (Homewood, IL: Richard D. Irwin Co., 1992), pp. 282–83. Adapted with permission. Copyright © Richard D. Irwin, Inc.

Ratio	*How Calculated*	*What It Shows*
Leverage ratios:		
1. Debt-to-assets ratio	$\frac{\text{Total debt}}{\text{Total assets}}$	Measures the extent to which borrowed funds have been used to finance the firm's operations.
2. Debt-to-equity ratio	$\frac{\text{Total debt}}{\text{Total stockholders' equity}}$	Provides another measure of the funds provided by creditors versus the funds provided by owners.
3. Long-term debt-to-equity ratio	$\frac{\text{Long-term debt}}{\text{Total stockholders' equity}}$	A widely used measure of the balance between debt and equity in the firm's long-term capital structure.
4. Times-interest-earned (or coverage) ratio	$\frac{\text{Profits before interest and taxes}}{\text{Total interest charges}}$	Measures the extent to which earnings can decline without the firm becoming unable to meet its annual interest costs.
5. Fixed-charge coverage	$\frac{\text{Profits before taxes and interest} + \text{Lease obligations}}{\text{Total interest charges} + \text{Lease obligations}}$	A more inclusive indication of the firm's ability to meet all of its fixed-charge obligations.
Activity ratios:		
1. Inventory turnover	$\frac{\text{Sales}}{\text{Avg. inventory (in retail dollars)}}$	When compared to industry averages, it provides an indication of whether a company has excessive or inadequate inventory.
2. Fixed assets turnover	$\frac{\text{Sales}}{\text{Fixed assets}}$	A measure of the sales productivity and utilization of plant and equipment.
3. Total assets turnover	$\frac{\text{Sales}}{\text{Total assets}}$	A measure of the utilization of all the firm's assets; a ratio below the industry average indicates the company is not generating a sufficient volume of business, given the size of its asset investment.
4. Accounts receivable turnover	$\frac{\text{Annual credit sales}}{\text{Accounts receivable}}$	A measure of the average length of time it takes the firm to collect the sales made on credit.
5. Average collection period	$\frac{\text{Accounts receivable}}{\text{Total sales} \div 365}$ or $\frac{\text{Accounts receivable}}{\text{Average daily sales}}$	Indicates the average length of time the firm must wait after making a sale before it receives payment.
Other ratios:		
1. Dividend yield on common stock	$\frac{\text{Annual dividends per share}}{\text{Current market price per share}}$	A measure of the return to owners received in the form of dividends.
2. Price-to-earnings ratio	$\frac{\text{Current market price per share}}{\text{After-tax earnings per share}}$	Faster growing or less risky firms tend to have higher price-to-earnings ratios than slower-growing or more risky firms.
3. Dividend payout ratio	$\frac{\text{Annual dividends per share}}{\text{After-tax earnings per share}}$	Indicates the percentage of profits paid out as dividends.
4. Cash flow per share	$\frac{\text{After-tax profits} + \text{Depreciation}}{\text{Number of common shares outstanding}}$	A measure of the discretionary funds exceeding expenses that are available to the firm.

A Question of Ethics

PROBLEMS RELATED TO LEVERAGED BUYOUTS

January 15, 1990, marked an important day in the saga of retail leveraged buyouts (LBOs). On that day Campeau Corporation's giant U.S. retail companies, Allied Stores Corporation and Federated Department Stores, Inc., filed for Chapter 11 protection. It was the largest retailing bankruptcy in history.

In 1988 Campeau paid more than 12 times earnings before interest and taxes to acquire Federated. He used cash from Allied Stores to finance the takeover and gave Allied half of the stock in Federated in return. Allied sold two valuable properties, Brooks Brothers and Ann Taylor clothing chains, for the $693 million needed to repay the $500 million loan provided by Bank of Montreal and the French-based Bank Paribas to acquire Federated. The money drained from Allied to finance the Federated takeover left Allied financially crippled—some Allied stores didn't have the resources to stock shirts and other items for the 1989 Christmas season. Allied also couldn't pay interest to a large group of investors holding bonds that matured in 1997.

Creditors also looked hard at First Boston Corporation's role. The firm, along with Wasserstein, Parella & Co., acted as investment bankers in the Federated takeover. First Boston supplied Campeau with a $257 million bridge loan, but the firm also issued an opinion supporting the $500 million loan withdrawal by the other banks. Bondholders questioned First Boston's objectivity because of its dual role as advisor and lender.

Who loses when situations such as this occur? Many people—banks, bondholders, investment firms, vendors, and the employees and customers of the retail firms—are affected.

Is it wrong for "conglomerateurs" to overleverage companies that must weather industry cycles and volatile markets? Should investors be allowed to finance retail buyouts with a small amount of equity but huge amounts of junk bonds? Should Allied's money have been used to finance the Federated deal? Was this a fraudulent transfer of assets?

Source: Based on Todd Mason, Amy Dunkin, Michele Galen, Leah J. Nathans, and Stephen Phillips, "It'll Be a Hard Sell," *BusinessWeek*, January 29, 1990, p. 26; Robert J. McCartney, "A Move toward Reparations for Losers in Empire's Demise," *The Washington Post*, August 18, 1991, pp. H1, H5.

diagrams the SPM. Boxes 1 through 5 provide the basic ratios that comprise the model. A simple algebraic representation of the model would look like this:

$$\overset{(1)}{\frac{\text{Net profit}}{\text{Net sales}}} \times \overset{(2)}{\frac{\text{Net sales}}{\text{Total assets}}} = \overset{(3)}{\frac{\text{Net profit}}{\text{Total assets}}} \times \overset{(4)}{\frac{\text{Total assets}}{\text{Net worth}}} = \overset{(5)}{\frac{\text{Net profit}}{\text{Net worth}}}$$

Specifically, the purposes of the SPM are as follows:

1. To emphasize that a firm's principal financial objective is to earn an adequate or target rate of return on net worth (RONW).

FIGURE 12–1 THE STRATEGIC PROFIT MODEL PROCESS

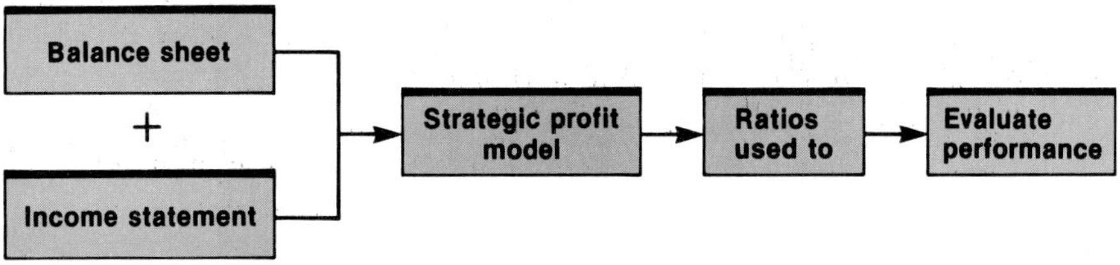

Balance sheet
+
Income statement
→ Strategic profit model → Ratios used to → Evaluate performance

FIGURE 12–2 THE STRATEGIC PROFIT MODEL

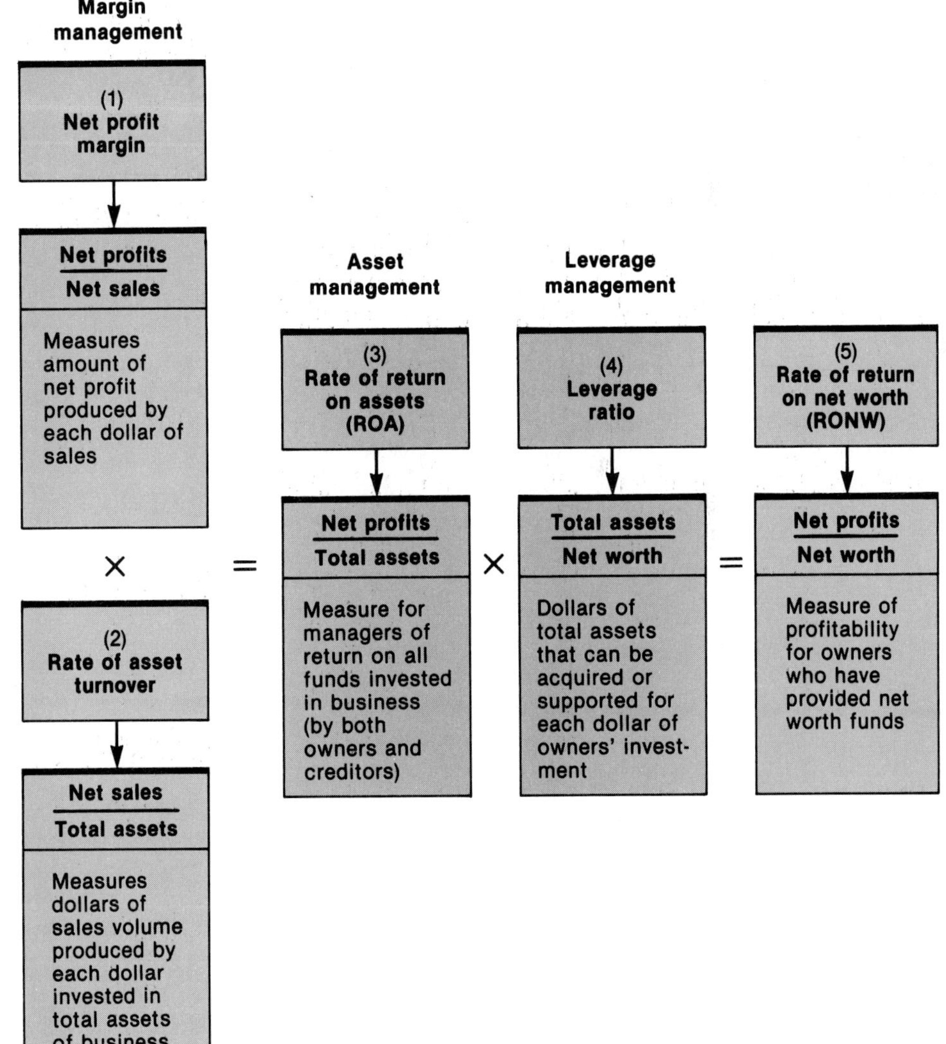

2. To provide an excellent management tool for evaluating performance against the target RONW and high-performance trade leaders.
3. To dramatize three principal areas of decision making—margin management, asset management, and leverage management. A firm can improve its rate of RONW by increasing its profit margin, raising its rate of asset turnover, or leveraging its operations more highly.

Please note that in the SPM, leverage is calculated differently than the methods shown in Table 12–3 and is probably different from methods you learned in any accounting or finance courses you have taken. The ratio in the SPM is another way of calculating leverage; this ratio enables management to determine the extent to which debt is being used to support the asset base of the firm.

Gross Margin Return on Inventory Investment

Gross margin return on inventory investment (GMROI), another performance evaluation indicator, is stated as follows:

$$\text{GMROI} = \frac{\text{Gross margin dollars}}{\text{Average inventory investment (expressed in retail dollars)}}$$

This single ratio, however, does not indicate clearly the focus we want to emphasize—the important relationship between profit return (margin) and sales-to-retail stock (which is inventory turnover, discussed in Chapter 11). Consequently, a more useful way to express GMROI is as follows:

$$\text{GMROI} = \frac{\text{Gross margin dollars}}{\text{Total sales}} \times \frac{\text{Total sales}}{\text{Average inventory investment (expressed in retail dollars)}}$$

We must emphasize that gross margin return on retail inventory investment is not a real measure of return on investment because investment is in cost dollars. But many retail managers with a planning focus maintain retail book inventory figures. Thus, retail value GMROI can be calculated more frequently using the more common and more easily obtainable turnover component. Sales-to-cost inventory ratios are more accurately return-on-investment ratios. In this particular discussion, however, the value of utilizing retail GMROI outweighs the somewhat different terminology. Our intent is to focus on the effect of turnover on profitability; retail value is therefore important.

The value of the turnover and margin components of the GMROI concept can be seen in Table 12–4. Three hypothetical retail classifications each produce the same GMROI, although they have differing gross margin percentages and turnover components. This table illustrates that management can focus on either turnover or gross margin in strategic planning to obtain identical GMROI results.

TABLE 12–4 EXAMPLES OF DIFFERING RETAIL OPERATIONS, MARGINS, AND TURNOVERS RESULTING IN IDENTICAL GMROI

Type of Store	*Gross Margin (percent)*	×	*Turnover Ratio*	=	*GMROI (percent) (retail)*
Discount store sport shirt classification	25.0		4.0		100.0
Specialty store sport shirt classification	40.0		2.5		100.0
Department store sport shirt classification	33.3		3.0		100.0

DETERMINING COST AND VALUE OF INVENTORY

This section focuses on the importance of merchandise inventory in performance evaluation and the problems that arise in determining its cost and value. The importance of merchandise inventory is reflected in several ways. Merchandise inventory is typically the largest current asset on the balance sheet. The value of ending inventory is also used to calculate cost of goods sold—a figure reported on the income statement. An error in determining the inventory figure will cause an equal misstatement of gross profit and net income in the income statement. The amount of assets noted on the balance sheet will also be incorrect by the same amount. The effects of understatements and overstatements of inventory at the end of a period are demonstrated in Table 12–5, which includes an abbreviated income statement and balance sheet.

Determining Inventory Cost

A major problem in determining inventory cost arises when identical units of a product are acquired over a period of time at various unit cost prices. When items are sold, in some departments or classifications it may be possible to identify those units with specific purchases. This can occur when assortments and varieties of merchandise carried, sales volume, and transactions are relatively small. More often, however, specific identification procedures are too complex to justify their use. Consequently, one of two accepted costing methods, each approved for income determination by the Internal Revenue Service, may be adopted to determine the cost value of ending inventory.

The assumption of the **first in, first out** (FIFO) method of costing inventory is that costs should be charged against revenue in the order in which they were incurred—that is, the first shirts purchased are the first ones sold. Thus, the inventory remaining at the end of the accounting period is assumed to be of the most recent purchases. Assume the following represents purchases of sport shirts for the year:

TABLE 12–5 EFFECTS OF CORRECT STATEMENT, UNDERSTATEMENT, AND OVERSTATEMENT OF ENDING INVENTORY ON NET PROFITS

Income Statement—19—			*Balance Sheet—19—*	
Net sales		$200,000	Merchandise inventory	$20,000*
Beginning inventory	$ 30,000		Other assets	80,000
+ Purchases	110,000		Total	$100,000
= Available for sale	140,000		Liabilities	30,000
− Ending inventory	20,000*		Net worth	70,000
= Cost of goods sold		120,000	Total	$100,000
Gross profit		80,000		
− Expenses		55,000		
= Net profit		$ 25,000		
Net sales		$200,000	Merchandise inventory	$12,000†
Beginning inventory	$ 30,000		Other assets	80,000
+ Purchases	110,000		Total	$ 92,000
= Available for sale	140,000		Liabilities	30,000
− Ending inventory	12,000†		Net worth	62,000
= Cost of goods sold		128,000	Total	$ 92,000
Gross profit		72,000		
− Expenses		55,000		
= Net profit		$ 17,000		
Net sales		$200,000	Merchandise inventory	$27,000‡
Beginning inventory	$ 30,000		Other assets	80,000
+ Purchases	110,00		Total	$107,000
= Available for sale	140,000		Liabilities	30,000
− Ending inventory	27,000‡		Net worth	77,000
= Cost of goods sold		113,000	Total	$107,000
Gross profit		87,000		
− Expenses		55,000		
= Net profit		$ 32,000		

*Ending inventory correctly stated.
†Ending inventory understated $8,000 (thus income, assets, capital also).
‡Ending inventory overstated $7,000 (thus income, assets, capital also).

	Units	*Unit Cost*	*Total Cost*
February 1 (Beginning inventory)	50	$ 9	$ 450
April 15 (Purchases)	40	13	520
May 1 (Purchases)	30	14	420
October 1 (Purchases)	100	16	1,600
Available for sale during year	220		$2,990

Further assume that 90 shirts were sold; thus, the physical inventory at the end of the fiscal year (January 31) is 130 shirts. Based on FIFO and the assumption that the inventory is composed of the most recent purchases, the cost of the 130 shirts is as follows:

October 1 (most recent purchases)	100 shirts	@	$16	=	$1,600
May 1 (next most recent)	30 shirts	@	14	=	420
Inventory, January 31	130 shirts				$2,020

If we deduct the end-of-period inventory of $2,020 from the $2,990 available for sale during the period, we get $970 as the cost of merchandise sold. FIFO is generally in harmony with the actual physical movement of goods in a retail firm. Thus, FIFO best represents the results that are directly tied to merchandise costs.

The costing method known as **last in, first out** (LIFO) assumes that the most recent cost of merchandise should be charged against revenue. Thus, the ending inventory under LIFO is assumed to be made up of earliest costs. Refer to the previous example:

February 1	50 shirts	@	$9	=	$ 450
April 15	40 shirts	@	13	=	520
May 1	30 shirts	@	14	=	420
October 1	10 shirts	@	16	=	160
Inventory, January 31	130 shirts				$1,550

If we deduct the end-of-period inventory of $1,550 from the $2,990 available for sale during the period, we get $1,440 as the cost of merchandise sold.

We can now compare FIFO and LIFO:

	FIFO	*LIFO*
Merchandise available for sale	$2,990	$2,990
Inventory, January 31	2,020	1,550
Cost of merchandise sold	$ 970	$1,440

FIFO yields the lower cost of merchandise sold and thus yields higher gross margin and net income as well as higher inventory figures on the balance sheet. On the other hand, LIFO yields a higher figure for cost of goods sold and lower figures for gross margin, net income, and inventory.

In periods of inflation, most companies experience increases in inventory investment. Companies that value inventories at current costs (using FIFO) will have high inventory valuation and thus higher taxable income and

TABLE 12–6 THE EFFECT ON PROFITS OF VALUATION OF ENDING INVENTORY AT ACTUAL COST, DEPRECIATED, OR APPRECIATED MARKET VALUE

	(1) Actual cost		(2) Depreciation		(3) Appreciation	
Net sales		$100,000		$100,000		$100,000
Merchandise available for sale	$70,000		$70,000		$70,000	
Ending inventory	10,000		4,000		12,000	
Cost of goods sold		60,000		66,000		58,000
Gross profit		$ 40,000		$ 34,000		$ 42,000
Expenses		35,000		35,000		35,000
Net profit		$ 5,000		$ (1,000)		$ 7,000

income taxes. Increased taxes require almost immediate cash outlays, and "inventory paper profits" tied up in inventory are not available for investment in other assets or for the payment of dividends. LIFO will usually give an ongoing firm a financial statement showing a lower income before taxes and lower inventory values. This lower income will also result in lower tax payments and increased cash flow. LIFO is inflation oriented.

Given the technicality of LIFO/FIFO issues, retailers need qualified advisors to help them know when to stay with FIFO or change to the LIFO method of valuing inventories.

Conservative Valuation of Inventory

Another problem in determining the value of merchandise inventory is placing a conservative value on the inventory—that is, at cost or market, whichever is lower. This approach is an alternative to valuing inventory at cost.

In using the conservative method, the retailer must first determine the cost of inventory. Cost refers to the actual price of merchandise at the time of its purchase. Market means the cost required to replace the merchandise at the time of the inventory. Table 12–6 demonstrates the effect on profits of valuing the ending inventory at actual cost, a depreciated value, and an appreciated value. In addition, it provides a rationale for the acceptance of the conservative practice of valuation.

At any given time, merchandise in stock may not be valued at the amount originally paid for it. Let us first consider the situation in which the merchandise has declined in value because of obsolescence, deterioration, or decreases in wholesale market prices. The first column in Table 12–6 indicates the value of inventory at its actual cost ($10,000). The second column indicates that, if the retailer were to replace the same inventory at the time of valuation, it would be depreciated to $4,000 (a $6,000 decline in the value from actual cost). In this situation, because the market value is lower than the original cost of the inventory, the retailer would use the $4,000 market figure in developing financial statements. Thus, instead of a $5,000 profit on the income statement, a $1,000 loss would be incurred. By valuing the ending inventory at $4,000 rather than at the cost of $10,000, management will be taking its losses in the period in which they are incurred. This is logical, because the ending inventory of one period becomes the beginning inventory of the next. Thus, by placing a realistic depreciated market value on ending inventory, the lower figure (which will be the next beginning inventory value) will give the merchant the opportunity to reflect a proper beginning inventory cost in the next period. This lets the merchant show realistic, and perhaps profitable, performance in the next period. This $4,000 ending inventory figure also becomes an asset item on the balance sheet. A realistic valuation reflecting declining value is wise because otherwise the assets, and consequently the net worth of the firm, would be overstated.

Now let us consider a situation in which merchandise in stock has increased in value because of inflation or scarcity of materials. Here, we must compare columns 1 and 3. The third column indicates that, if the retailer were to replace the inventory at the time of valuation, it would be appreciated to $12,000 (a $2,000 increase in value from the actual cost). In this situation, because the original cost of the inventory is lower than the market value, the retailer would use the $10,000 cost figure in developing financial statements. Thus, instead of a $7,000 profit, a profit of $5,000 would be realized. The $2,000 difference represents "paper profits," or anticipated profits on merchandise that has not been sold and, thus, should not be reported.

In summary, retailers' inventories should be valued at cost or market, whichever is lower. As with the method chosen for the determination of inventory cost (LIFO or FIFO), the method selected for inventory valuation (cost, or lower of cost or market) must be consistent from year to year. The Internal Revenue Service accepts either method. However, if LIFO is adopted by a firm, the inventory must, for tax purposes, be based on cost. A LIFO inventory cannot be valued at the lower of cost or market for tax purposes. On the other hand, it is important that a cost or market valuation method be used for financial reporting purposes.

METHODS OF INVENTORY VALUATION

An objective of this chapter is to introduce the accounting practices that assist management in inventory valuation decisions. Retailers invest large sums of money in merchandise and must know at all times the value of this inventory investment. The information is needed for tax reasons, for computing various measures of performance, and for making day-to-day decisions. How is value placed on inventory? The two main ways are the cost method and the retail method.

The Cost Method

The cost method provides a book evaluation of inventory in which only cost figures are used. All inventory records are maintained at cost. When a physical inventory is taken, all items are recorded at actual cost, including freight. The cost of sales and cost of markdowns (depreciation) are deducted from the total merchandise available to provide the book inventory at the lower of cost or market value, which can be checked by means of a physical inventory. The limitations of the cost method are as follows: difficulty in determining depreciation; difficulty for large retailers with many classifications and price lines; the impracticality of daily inventory; and the difficulty of costing out each sale, allocating transportation charges to the cost of the sales, and reducing markdowns to cost. However, the cost method is appropriate in operations with big-ticket items, where there are few lines and few price changes, where the rate of sale is rapid, and where management has very sophisticated computer expertise.

The Retail Method

Because of the limitations of the cost method, the retail method of inventory costing is more widely used. The retail method is a logical extension of a retail book (perpetual) inventory utilized for dollar control (see Chapter 11). The retail method is, in actuality, an income statement that follows certain programmed steps in the final determination of net profits. These steps, illustrated in Table 12–7, are described in the following section.

Steps of the Retail Method

1. Determine the total dollars of merchandise handled at cost and retail. As indicated in Table 12–7, we start with a beginning inventory that, we assume, is an actual, physical inventory from the end of the previous period. To this figure we add purchases (minus vendor returns and allowances), any interstore or departmental transfers, and transportation charges (at cost only). A price change, which is a part of step 1, is additional markups. Suppose the retailer has a group of sport shirts in stock that were recently received. They are carried in stock at $14.95. Wholesale costs have increased since the delivery, and the wholesaler suggests that an additional markup of $3.00 per unit be taken, bringing the retail price to $17.95. We take a physical count and find that we have 700 shirts in stock; thus, we take an additional markup of $2,100 to accommodate the price increase. Immediately after processing the price change, suppose we find that the count was incorrect, or the amount of the additional markup was too high due to a misunderstanding. At any rate, the retailer wants to cancel $600 of the additional markup so that the mistake can be corrected (see step 1 in the statement for the handling of this situation). Cancellation of an additional markup is not a markdown,

TABLE 12–7 STATEMENT OF RETAIL METHOD OF INVENTORY

Calculations	*Step*	*Items*	*Cost*	*Retail*	*Cost*	*Retail*	*Percent*
	1	Beginning inventory			$ 60,000	$105,000	
		Gross purchases	$216,000	$345,000			
		Less returns to vendor	(9,000)	(14,100)	207,000	330,900	
		Transfers in	3,000	4,800			
		Less transfers out	(4,500)	(7,200)	(1,500)	(2,400)	
		Transportation charges			4,500		
		Additional markups		2,100			
		Less cancellations		(600)		1,500	
		Total merchandise handled			270,000	435,000	
($270,000 ÷ $435,000)	2	Cost multiplier/cumulative markon					62.069/37.9
	3	Sales, gross		309,000			
		Less customer returns		(9,000)		300,000	
		Gross markdowns		12,000			
		Less cancellations		(1,500)		10,500	
		Employee discounts				1,500	
		Total retail deductions				312,000	
($435,000 − $312,000)	4	Closing book inventory @ retail				123,000	
		Closing physical inventory @ retail				120,750	
($123,000 − $120,750)		Shortages				2,250	0.75
($120,750 × 0.62069)		Closing physical inventory @ cost			74,949		
($270,000 − $74,949)	5	Gross cost of goods sold			195,051		
($300,000 − $195,051)	6	Maintained markup			104,949		34.9
		Less alteration costs			(3,000)		
		Plus cash discounts			6,000		
($104,949 + $3,000)		Gross margin			107,949		35.9
		Less operating expenses			75,000		25.0
		Net profit			32,949		10.9
	5	Gross cost of goods sold			195,051		
		Less cash discounts			(6,000)		
		Net costs of goods sold			189,051		
		Plus alteration costs			3,000		
		Total cost of goods sold			192,051		
($300,000 − $192,051)	6	Gross margin			107,949		35.9
		Less operating expenses			75,000		
		Net profit			32,949		10.9

which reflects market depreciation. Instead, cancellation is a procedure for adjusting an error in the original additional markup. Summing all the items that increase the dollar investment in inventory provides the total merchandise handled at cost and retail ($270,000 and $435,000, respectively).

2. Calculate the cost multiplier and the cumulative markon. As indicated in Table 12–7, the computation of the cost multiplier (sometimes called the cost percentage or the cost complement) is derived by dividing the total dollars handled at cost by the total at retail (that is, $270,000/$435,000 = 62%). This is a key figure in the retail method and, in fact, involves the major assumption of the system. The cost multiplier assumes that, for every retail dollar in inventory, 62 percent (or 62+ cents) is in terms of cost. The assumption of the retail method is that if cost and retail have this relationship in goods handled during a period, then that same relationship exists for all the merchandise remaining in stock (that is, the ending inventory at retail).

The cumulative markon is the complement of the cost multiplier (that is, 100.00 − 62.069 = 37.931) and is the control figure to compare against the planned initial markup (see Chapter 14, where this planned figure is discussed). Let's assume that the planned initial markup is 37 percent. If our interim accounting statement shows, as ours does, that our cumulative markon is 37+ percent, then management will consider that operations are effective, at least as they relate to the planned markup percentage. The initial markup is planned to cover reductions (markdowns, employee discounts, and shortages) and to provide a maintained markup (or gross profit or margin) at a level sufficient to cover operating expenses and to ensure a target rate of profit return.

3. Compute the retail deductions from stock. Step 3 includes all the retail deductions from the total retail merchandise dollars handled during the period. Sales are recorded and adjusted by customer returns to determine net sales.

Markdowns are recorded as they are taken. For example, let's assume that during this period a group of 1,200 sport shirts retailing for $25.95 are put on sale at a price of $15.95. We would thus take a markdown of $12,000 before the sale. After the sale, we want to bring the unsold merchandise back to the regular price (an additional markup is not appropriate because we are merely cancelling an original markdown). Consequently, we put a markdown cancellation through the system for the remaining shirts. Assume that 150 shirts were not sold, making a cancellation of $1,500 and reestablishing the original retail price of $25.95.

Employee discounts are included as deductions because employees often receive a discount on items purchased for personal use. Assume that employees are given a 20 percent discount. If a shirt retails for $19.95, the employee would pay $15.96. If the discount were not entered as a separate item in the system, the difference between the retail price and the employee's price would cause a shortage. Recording employee discounts as a separate item also gives management a good picture of employee business obtained and affords a measure of control over use of the discount. Summing all the items in step 3 results in total retail deductions from stock ($312,000).

4. Calculate the closing book (or physical) inventory at cost and retail. The statement thus far has afforded us a figure for the dollars at retail that we have available for sale ($435,000) and that we have deducted from that amount ($312,000). Thus, we can compute what we have left ($435,000 – $312,000), or the ending book inventory at retail ($123,000). We are assuming that this is a year-end statement and that we have an audited, physical inventory of $120,750. Consequently, we can now determine our shortages by deducing the amount of the physical inventory from the book inventory ($123,000 – $120,750 = $2,210, which is 0.75 percent of sales).

Let's assume, however, that we were working with an interim statement rather than a fiscal-year statement. If this had been the case, we would include in our retail deductions from stock (step 3) an estimated shortages figure, which would give us as accurate a figure as possible for total deductions, and thus a figure for closing book inventory at retail. If we have an interim statement, then the cost multiplier is applied to the book inventory at retail to determine the cost value. If there is a physical retail inventory figure, as in Table 12–7, then we use that figure for cost conversion because the physical inventory figure is accurate.

The key to the retail method, as noted earlier, is the conversion of the retail inventory to cost by multiplying the retail value by the cost multiplier ($120,750 × 0.62069). In our illustration, the cost value of ending inventory is $74,949.

5. Determine gross cost of goods sold. Because we know the amount of merchandise handled at cost ($270,000) and we know what we have left at cost ($74,949), we can determine the cost dollars that have moved out of stock ($270,000 – $74,949 = $195,051).

6. Determine maintained markup, gross margin, and net profit. Two procedures may be followed at this step. We prefer the first method because of the emphasis given to the concept of maintained markup in Chapter 14. The gross margin and net profit figures in either case are identical; slightly different accounting philosophies are the determining factor. We show you both ways to let you see the differences between them.

In the first method, gross cost of goods sold is deducted from net sales to determine maintained markup ($300,000 – $195,051 = $104,949). Alteration costs (or workroom expenses) are traditionally considered in retailing as merchandising, nonoperating expenses and are offset by cash discounts earned (nonoperating income). The net difference between the two is added or subtracted from maintained markup to derive gross margin ($104,949 – $3,000 + $6,000 = $107,949), from which operating expenses are deducted to calculate net profits before taxes ($107,949 – $75,000 = $32,949). The various percentages appearing on the statement (with the exception of the cost multiplier and the cumulative markon) are all based on net sales.

The second method for determining gross margin and net profit differs in that cash discounts earned are deducted from gross cost of goods sold to derive net cost of goods sold ($195,051 – $6,000 = $189,051). Alteration costs are added to that figure to obtain total cost of goods sold ($189,051 + $3,000 = $192,051). Total cost of goods sold is deducted from net sales ($300,000 − $192,051) to obtain the gross margin figure of $107,949. As in the first method, expenses are deducted from gross margin to determine net profit.

Evaluation of the Retail Method. The retail method of inventory valuation offers the retailer many advantages:

1. The method is easily programmed for computer systems, and accounting statements can be drawn up at any time. Income statements and balance sheets are normally available once a month.
2. Shortages can be determined. The retail method is a book inventory, and this figure can be compared to the physical inventory. Only with a book inventory can shortages (or overages) be determined.
3. The retail method, through its book inventory, serves as an excellent basis for insurance claims. In case of loss, the book inventory is good evidence of what should have been in stock. This point, as well as the two previously mentioned, are advantages because the retail method is a perpetual, book inventory method. The following two advantages are uniquely related to the system of the retail method of inventory.
4. The physical taking of inventory is easier with the retail method. The items are recorded on the inventory sheets only at their selling prices, instead of their cost and retail prices.
5. The retail method gives an automatic, conservative valuation of ending inventory because of the way the system is programmed. Thus, the retail method provides a valuation of ending inventory at cost or market, whichever is lower.

Even though there are many advantages to using the retail method, it has been criticized. A major complaint is that it is a "method of averages." This refers to the determination of the cost multiplier as the average relationship between all the merchandise handled at cost and retail, and the application of this average percentage to the closing inventory at retail to determine the cost figure. Such a disadvantage, more real in the past than today, can be largely overcome by classification merchandising or dissection accounting—that is, breaking departments into small subgroups with homogeneity in terms of margin and turnover. The new technology in point-of-sale systems affords unlimited classifications and thus allows the homogeneity necessary for implementation of the retail method, giving management a good measure of the actual effectiveness of operations.

The retail method of inventory is not applicable to all departments within a store. For example, unless the purchases can be retailed at the time of receipt of the goods, the system cannot be used. A drapery workroom could not use the method, for example. Consequently, there are certain cost departments within some retail establishments. However, such a condition does not lessen the value of the system where it can appropriately be used.

Departmental Performance Evaluation

Individual departments within a retail firm must be analyzed to evaluate performance and to determine whether changes need to be made in any aspect of the departments' operations. An important component of departmental evaluation is the assignment of costs to the individual departments. But before discussing approaches that may be used to assign costs to departments, we direct your attention to the nature of costs in a retail operation.

Types of Costs

Direct costs are costs directly associated with a department. Such costs would cease to exist if the department were eliminated. An example of a direct cost is advertising in support of products sold in a given department. **Indirect costs** are costs that cannot be tied directly to a department. An example is the store manager's salary.

In conducting a departmental performance evaluation, management must first redefine costs from natural accounts to functional accounts. **Natural accounts** are companywide accounts defined by the accounting department and include such categories as salaries, rent, promotion, and cost of supplies. **Functional accounts** reflect the retailing function involved. An example would be the allocation of salaries to administrative support, sales personnel, and so forth. Management must then determine which of two approaches (the contribution margin approach or the full costing approach) will be used to assign costs to individual departments.

Cost Allocation Approaches

In the **full costing approach,** both direct and indirect costs are assigned to departments (see Table 12–8). Each department's direct costs and its allocation of indirect costs are deducted from the department's gross margin to determine its net profit or loss. The store's indirect costs can be allocated to departments in several ways, including equal allocation to all departments or allocation based on the sales volume of each department. Advocates for the full costing approach argue that all the costs of operating a department should be included so that management has an accurate picture of how each department contributes to the overall profitability of the firm. However, the approach has been criticized because of the arbitrary bases sometimes used to assign indirect costs to departments and because it can lead managers to erroneous conclusions about whether a department should be abandoned or deleted. Let's look at the issue of deleting a department in more detail.

TABLE 12–8 EXAMPLE OF THE FULL COSTING APPROACH

	Department					
		A		*B*		*C*
Sales		$20,000		$10,000		$15,000
Cost of goods sold		5,000		5,000		3,000
Gross margin		$15,000		$ 5,000		$12,000
Expenses						
Direct	$5,000		3,000		5,000	
Indirect	6,000		5,000		3,000	
Total expenses		11,000		8,000		8,000
Net profit (loss)		$ 4,000		($ 3,000)		$ 4,000

As shown in Table 12–8, the full costing approach shows that Department B is operating at a loss. Management's initial reaction might be to delete the department. However, several factors should be considered before making such a decision. First, Department B is covering all of its direct costs and is contributing $2,000 toward the coverage of store indirect costs. If Department B were deleted, the indirect costs currently being allocated to the department would have to be reallocated between Departments A and C, which would negatively affect their profit pictures. Thus, management might want to consider to what extent equitable bases are being used to allocate indirect costs to the departments. For example, Department B may be receiving a disproportionate share of indirect expenses. Several others factors should be considered in deciding to delete a department. For example, some departments are important because of their traffic-drawing ability. Their profit performance may be poor but they are important in drawing customers who then make purchases in other departments. Furthermore, sales in one department often affect sales in some other department. Thus, if management were to delete a department, the action could negatively affect sales in other departments. Before deleting a department, management should carefully consider not only the accounting data but also these other factors.

In the **contribution margin** approach only direct costs are assigned to departments. The department's direct costs are deducted from its gross margin to determine its contribution to the store's indirect costs. Advocates of this approach argue that, even if a department is showing a loss under the full costing approach, it may still be making some contribution toward indirect costs and thus should not be abandoned or deleted. Advocates also argue that focusing only on direct costs in evaluating departmental performance is logical because indirect costs will continue even in the absence of the department.

TABLE 12–9

EXAMPLE OF THE CONTRIBUTION MARGIN APPROACH

Sales (millions)	
Department 1	$16.2
Department 2	12.4
Department 3	11.6
	$40.2
Merchandise costs	31.0
Gross margin	$ 9.2
Expenses	
Promotion	$ 2.6
Sales salaries	3.0
Overhead	1.2
Net profit before taxes	$ 2.4

Let's look more closely at the process of departmental evaluation, using the contribution margin approach. Assume that sales in Departments 1, 2, and 3 of a retail store are as shown in Table 12–9. Total store sales for the three departments are $40.2 million, and the cost of merchandise is $31.0 million. Storewide net profit before taxes is $2.4 million. The natural accounts of merchandise costs, promotion costs, and sales salaries (all of which are direct costs) must be transformed into functional accounts in order to assign the costs on a departmental basis. All costs except overhead, which is an indirect cost and thus not assignable to the departments, are assigned to the three departments, as shown in Table 12–10.

A departmental performance evaluation can now be conducted for each department, as shown in Table 12–11. Department 1 contributes $4.3 million towards coverage of indirect costs and thus is responsible for the majority of the contribution margin. Even though Department 3 contributes $800,000, it is not a strong department in comparison to Department 1 and may need an evaluation to check where improvements could be made. Department 2 is showing a negative contribution margin and, thus, is in serious need of a detailed evaluation. Salespeople might need retraining, advertising and sales promotion efforts and expenditures may need to be reevaluated, and alternative vendor relationships may need to be established. Management may even consider deleting Department 2; however, before doing so, it should carefully consider the issues discussed earlier in this section.

SPACE EVALUATION

The final performance evaluation issue we will discuss is that of space use within the store. Effective use of space translates into additional dollars of profit. Retailers must therefore evaluate whether store space is being used in the most effective way. Management can use a variety of measures to

TABLE 12–10 TRANSFORMATION OF NATURAL ACCOUNTS TO FUNCTIONAL ACCOUNTS ($ MILLIONS)

			Functional Accounts		
Natural Accounts	*Total*		*Dept. 1*	*Dept. 2*	*Dept. 3*
Merchandise costs	31.0		10.0	11.3	9.7
Salaries	3.0				
		Sales personnel	0.8	1.0	0.6
		Administrative	0.2	0.3	0.1
Promotion	2.6				
		Department signing	0.1	0.2	0.1
		Newspapers	0.8	0.9	0.2
		Radio	—	0.2	0.1

evaluate space utilization, but we will discuss the gross-margin-per-square foot method to illustrate one method retailers can employ.

Table 12–12 shows the calculations involved in evaluating space utilization by the gross margin per square foot method. Sales per square foot less cost of merchandise sold per square foot yield the gross margin per square foot figure.

With this figure, management can compare departments of various sizes selling different types of goods. Such an analysis can show management which departments are doing well, which are not, which might improve if expanded, and which can be reduced in space allotment.

For example, based on the calculations shown in Table 12–12, management might be tempted to decrease the selling space allocated to Department A in order to increase the selling space devoted to Department B. However, the decision to reallocate space is not a simple one. Advertising and selling costs for a department may rise when its selling space is increased. After the reallocation, the merchandise mix may change, which can result in either higher or lower gross margins. Management thus needs to simulate the likely changes in the variables used in the calculations as a result of possible shifts in space allocation and determine whether reallocations are likely to increase the overall profitability of the firm.

CHAPTER HIGHLIGHTS

- The balance sheet, the income statement, and various ratios derived from them give management information needed to evaluate the effectiveness of strategy in financial terms.
- The strategic profit model (SPM) emphasizes that a firm's principal financial objective is to earn an adequate or target rate of return on net worth (RONW) and dramatizes three areas of decision making (margin management, asset management, and leverage management) for improving RONW.

TABLE 12–11

CONTRIBUTION MARGIN ANALYSIS BY DEPARTMENT ($ MILLIONS)

Department 1	
Sales	$16.2
Merchandise costs	10.0
Gross margin	6.2
Direct expenses	
Salaries	1.0
Promotion	.9
Contribution to indirect costs	$ 4.3
Department 2	
Sales	$12.4
Merchandise costs	11.3
Gross margin	1.1
Direct expenses	
Salaries	1.3
Promotion	1.3
Contribution to indirect costs	($ 1.5)
Department 3	
Sales	$11.6
Merchandise costs	9.7
Gross margin	1.9
Direct expenses	
Salaries	0.7
Promotion	0.4
Contribution to indirect costs	$ 0.8
Summary	
Contribution	
Department 1 contribution to indirect costs	4.3
Department 2 contribution to indirect costs	(1.5)
Department 3 contribution to indirect costs	0.8
Less overhead (shown in Table 12–9)	(1.2)
Net profits before taxes (as shown in Table 12–9)	$ 2.4

- Gross margin return on inventory investment (GMROI) is a performance evaluation indicator that focuses on turnover and gross margin percentage.
- Merchandise valuation is an important factor in performance evaluation. One of two methods—first in, first out (FIFO) and last in, first out (LIFO)—may be adopted to determine the cost value of inventory. According to the conservative rule, however, inventories should be valued at the lower of cost or market.
- In terms of accounting practices that assist management in inventory valuation decisions, retailers may use the cost method or the retail method. The cost method provides a book evaluation of inventory in which only cost figures are used. However, because of the limitations of the cost method, the retail method is more widely used.

TABLE 12–12

CALCULATING GROSS MARGIN PER SQUARE FOOT

Three calculations are involved in figuring gross margin per square foot:

1. $\frac{\text{Total sales}}{\text{Total square feet}} = \text{Sales per square foot}$

2. $\frac{\text{Cost of merchandise sold}}{\text{Total square feet}} = \text{Cost of merchandise sold per square foot}$

3. $\text{Sales per square foot} - \text{Cost of merchandise sold per square foot} = \text{Gross margin per square foot}$

Example

	Department A	*Department B*
Sales	$50,000	$70,000
Cost of merchandise sold	$30,000	$35,000
Square feet of space	500 square feet	700 square feet
Sales per square foot	$100	$100
− Cost of merchandise sold per square foot	60	50
= Gross margin per square foot	$ 40	$ 50

- Individual departments within a retail firm must be analyzed to evaluate performance and to determine whether changes are needed in any aspect of the departments' operations. In evaluating departments, management may use either the contribution margin approach or the full costing approach.
- Effective use of space can translate into additional dollars of profit. Thus, retailers must evaluate whether store space is being used in the most effective way. The gross margin per square foot method is one method retailers may use.

STUDY QUESTIONS

1. Distinguish between the balance sheet and the income statement. Illustrate an advocated format for each.
2. Explain the problems related to defining the terms profit and investment.
3. What are the purposes of the strategic profit model (SPM)?
4. Discuss the effects of turnover and margin planning on the return of each dollar invested in inventory using a GMROI format.
5. Why is it difficult to determine cost of ending inventories? How do FIFO and LIFO relate to this problem? Explain the assumptions of and compare the two methods.
6. Explain the conservative method of inventory valuation and discuss the rationale of accountants who support this method.
7. Describe the cost method of inventory valuation. What are the limitations of the cost method? Under what conditions would this method be appropriately used?
8. Explain in simple terms what the retail method of inventory is. Briefly describe the steps of the retail method. What are its advantages and disadvantages?
9. What is the difference between direct costs and indirect costs? What is the difference between natural accounts and functional accounts? Explain and evaluate the full costing approach and the contribution margin approach as alternative methods for assigning costs to individual departments within a retail store.
10. Discuss the factors management should consider in deciding whether to eliminate a department within the store. Likewise, discuss the factors management should consider in making space reallocation decisions.

APPLICATIONS

CASE 1: Ratios and Decision Making

Bobbie's Fashiontique is a small, family-operated store staffed by Mr. and Mrs. Townsend (in their late fifties) and their daughter Bobbie. Bobbie's parents started the business for her when she left her job as an elementary school teacher. The Townsends had been employed by a large department store throughout their careers until opening Bobbie's. Mr. Townsend was the manager of warehouse and traffic and delivery at the department store when he left. Previously, he had been in charge of receiving and marking. Mrs. Townsend had been in charge of alterations and fur storage. At one time she also ran a customer adjustment department.

The Townsend family had no real merchandising or control background. Consequently, whenever they faced an accounting problem, they either ignored it or turned it over to the accounting firm that did their routine bookkeeping and tax returns.

Realizing that the family's management sophistication was limited, Bobbie joined the state retail association and went to a seminar on financial management. After the conference, she was confused and frustrated. She didn't even know whether the store was making any money. She was certain the family had to obtain more information, especially about operating ratios. Bobbie called her accounting firm and talked to Tom Maden. She asked him to calculate key ratios and to tell her what they meant. Tom took the latest balance sheet and income statement of the Fashiontique and came up with these figures for Bobbie's firm and similar companies:

Ratio	*Bobbie's Fashiontique*	*Trade*
Net profit margin	4.8%	10.2%
Rate of asset turnover	1.7×	1.5×
Return on assets	8.16%	15.3%
Leverage ratio	4.0×	2.8×
RONW	32.64%	42.84%

Applying Retailing Principles

1. You are Tom Maden. Use the concept of the strategic profit model and interpret the data for Bobbie.
2. Point out the strengths and weaknesses of Bobbie's Fashiontique and the areas that need particular attention.

CASE 2: Inventory Cost Determination in a Volatile Market

Mr. Richard Edwards, who worked for many years for Zale's Jewelry Company, has taken a lease in a new regional mall in his hometown. He plans to open a fine, guild-type jewelry store with approximately 1,000 square feet of space and a very limited merchandise mix compared with some of the competitors in his market. He has learned, however, from his Zale's experience that the action is in gold jewelry and diamonds. "No table-top goods for me," Dick told a friend. "Every discount house and catalog showroom carries silver flatware, china, and crystal. I can't compete with them with the service I'll give and the rent I have to pay in the mall."

When Edwards was with Zale's, they changed from FIFO to LIFO. He was a store manager and knew how to perform under the new method, but didn't feel comfortable deciding which was best for him. He was watching prices of gold and diamonds skyrocket (with some sharp drops now and again, too) and knew that LIFO had great advantages in periods of rising prices. But he really didn't understand the logic.

Applying Retailing Principles

1. Assume you are Richard Edwards. Prepare questions and answers that must be examined before a sound decision can be made.
2. Assume Richard is making his decision at the time you are preparing this case. What would you recommend he do?

PROBLEMS

For Problems 1 through 3, use the retail method of accounting and prepare a well-organized statement to determine the following sets of figures: (a) cumulative markon percentage, (b) ending inventory at retail, (c) ending inventory at cost, (d) maintained markup in dollars and percentage, (e) gross margin of profit in dollars and percentage, and (f) net profit in dollars and percentage.

1.

Item	*Cost*	*Retail*
Beginning inventory	$20,000	$ 35,000
Gross purchases	72,000	115,000
Purchase returns and allowances	3,000	4,700
Transfers in	1,000	1,600
Transfers out	200	400
Transportation charges	1,216	
Additional markups		700
Additional markup cancellations		400
Gross sales		111,000
Customer returns and allowances		11,000
Gross markdowns		4,500
Markdown cancellations		1,000
Employee discounts		500
Estimated shortages, 0.4 percent of net sales		
Cash discounts on purchases	1,600	
Workroom costs	800	
Operating expenses	16,000	

2.

Item	*Cost*	*Retail*
Additional markup cancellations		$ 620
Estimated shortages, 0.05 percent of net sales		
Gross markdowns		8,000
Workroom costs	$ 500	
Sales returns and allowances		12,000
Transportation charges	2,094	
Beginning inventory	44,000	64,000
Purchase returns and allowances	2,200	5,200
Markdown cancellations		1,200
Gross purchases	65,600	105,240
Gross additional markups		2,480
Gross sales		102,000
Employee discounts		1,400
Cash discounts on purchases	1,500	
Operating expenses	11,000	

3. Item	Cost	Retail
Gross sales		$27,200
Beginning inventory	$14,300	20,100
Sales returns and allowances		200
Gross markdowns		2,200
Gross additional markups		650
Transportation charges	418	
Purchase returns and allowances	830	1,720
Employee discounts		500
Gross purchases	17,200	27,520
Markdown cancellations		300
Operating expenses	3,800	
Cash discounts on purchases	200	
Additional markups cancelled		150
Alteration and workroom costs	300	
Ending physical inventory		16,500

Given below are the balance sheet and the income statement for a retail firm. Use this information to work Problems 4 and 5.

Balance Sheet

Assets		Liabilities and net worth	
Current assets	$342,000	Current liabilities	$252,000
Fixed assets	300,000	Long-term liabilities	170,000
Total assets	$642,000	Total liabilities	$422,000
		Net worth	$220,000
		Total	$642,000

Income Statement

Net sales	$752,000
Cost of goods sold	480,000
Gross margin	$272,000
Operating expenses	182,000
Profit before taxes	$ 90,000
Taxes	30,000
Profit after taxes	$ 60,000

4. Calculate the current ratio.
5. Using the strategic profit model (SPM) format, calculate the (a) net profit margin, (b) rate of asset turnover, (c) rate of return on assets (ROA), (d) leverage ratio, and (e) rate of return on net worth (RONW).
6. Given the following information, calculate each department's gross margin per square foot:

	Department A	*Department B*
Sales	$56,000	$43,800
Cost of goods sold	39,200	31,200
Selling space	540 square feet	300 square feet

7. Given the following information for a department in a retail store, calculate gross margin return on inventory investment (GMROI):

Net sales	$246,000
Cost of goods sold	98,400
Retail inventory (beginning of year)	120,000
Retail inventory (mid-year)	126,000
Retail inventory (end of year)	123,000

8. You are given the following information (for shirts) concerning beginning inventory and purchases during the year:

	Number of Shirts	*Cost per Shirt*	*Total Cost*
Beginning inventory	60	$ 6	$ 360
May purchases	70	8	560
September purchases	80	10	800

Assume that, during the year, 110 shirts were sold and that you want to determine the value of ending inventory. Calculate the cost dollar value of ending inventory using (a) the FIFO method and (b) the LIFO method.

9. The XYZ Store consists of two departments. In one department, TV sets are sold; stereos are sold in the other department. For last year, TV set sales were $100,000; for stereos, $80,000. Cost of goods sold for TV sets was $50,000; for stereos, $30,000. Direct expenses related to the sale of TV sets were $25,000; for stereos, $30,000. Total store indirect expenses were $30,000. Store policy is to allocate 60 percent of indirect expenses to TV sets and 40 percent to stereos. (a) Assuming that management uses the contribution margin approach to evaluate departments, determine each product line's contribution margin. (b) Assuming that management uses the full costing approach to evaluate departments, determine each product line's profit. (c) What if the retailer had sold only stereos and no TV sets? What would have been the store's profit or loss situation for the year?

Notes

1. Subhash Sharma and Vijay Mahajan, "Early Warning Indicators of Business Failure," *Journal of Marketing* 44 (Fall 1980), pp. 80–89.

C H A P T E R

13

Buying and Inventory Management

THIS CHAPTER:

Explores the personal traits needed for buying.

Explains the ingredients of information partnerships between retailers and vendors.

Outlines the sources of merchandise for retailers.

Identifies the factors influencing the buying cycle.

Shows how to calculate desired inventory levels.

Reviews alternatives in the selection of merchandise suppliers.

Illustrates how retailers negotiate price, discounts, datings, and transportation charges.

RETAILING CAPSULE

WAL-MART SET TO ELIMINATE REPS AND BROKERS

Wal-Mart, flexing its enormous marketplace muscle, is trying to squeeze the independent sales representative out of the product buying process.

In a letter to manufacturers, David D. Glass, Wal-Mart's chairman and chief executive officer, said that the discount retailer has decided it should deal only with "principals," or employees of its suppliers. People who represent more than one company, such as a broker or manufacturer's representative, won't qualify, he said.

Wal-Mart's distaste for sales representatives isn't new; some brokers already have lost some lines they used to sell to the retail chain. But that was comparable to losing "a finger or a toe," says Jack Springer, executive director of a trade group for general merchandise reps. Now, he says, "They're going for the jugular."

The installation of an advanced computer system that allows manufacturers to peek into Wal-Mart's store and warehouse inventories has given Wal-Mart a new reason to renew its assault on manufacturers' representatives. In his letter, Mr. Glass cited the system, along with the need for "improved communication and increased reaction time," as the rationale for eliminating third parties.

Some industry participants see this as an attempt by Wal-Mart to eliminate a layer of costs, a logical desire for a retailer that brags about its everyday low prices. But manufacturers are forbidden by federal antitrust laws from offering discounts in place of commissions or brokerage fees. And some manufacturers aren't overjoyed at the big retailer's attempt to influence the way they do business.

The brokers and manufacturers' reps stand to lose most. Because Wal-Mart can easily account for half of a rep firm's commissions, some could be forced out of business.

With so much at stake, some rep firms have decided to fight back by raising money for a public relations campaign to spotlight Wal-Mart's actions. Others are vowing to sue if Wal-Mart forces a manufacturer to cut them off.

Source: Karen Blumenthal, "Wal-Mart Set to Eliminate Reps, Brokers," *The Wall Street Journal,* December 2, 1991, p. A3. Reproduced with permission. Copyright © 1991 Dow Jones & Company, Inc. All rights reserved worldwide; see also Michael Selz, "Independent Sales Reps Are Squeezed by the Recession," *The Wall Street Journal,* December 27, 1991, p. B1.

The buying function is critical to the success of any retail firm. Buyers can be viewed as investment specialists and can be responsible for millions of dollars in merchandise. They must forecast demand for the merchandise, negotiate with vendors on a variety of issues such as price and transportation, and work as a partner with the vendor in the sale of the merchandise.

As shown in the Retailing Capsule, the roles of the retailer, manufacturer, and vendor in the buying process are changing. Power is shifting to large retailers such as Wal-Mart who deal directly with the manufacturer, cutting out vendors such as wholesalers, and translating savings into lower prices for consumers and healthier bottom lines.[1]

Still, most retailers, especially smaller ones, continue to make purchases through wholesalers and manufacturers' representatives. Buying relationships will continue to change and evolve, over time, however, as new technology makes more and better information available to retailers and allows them to work with manufacturers and wholesalers in new and creative ways.

GOALS OF GOOD BUYING[2]

For people not acquainted with retailing, the work of a buyer may seem relatively simple—finding and purchasing needed merchandise at a good price. But there is more to buying than bargaining with vendors.[3] Not only are there other functions to consider, but good buying also involves buying the right merchandise for customers at the best price in the right quantity of the right quality from vendors who will be reliable and provide other valuable services. A thorough and competent buyer must consider many factors. These comprise the buying process, which involves four main steps:

The Buying Cycle

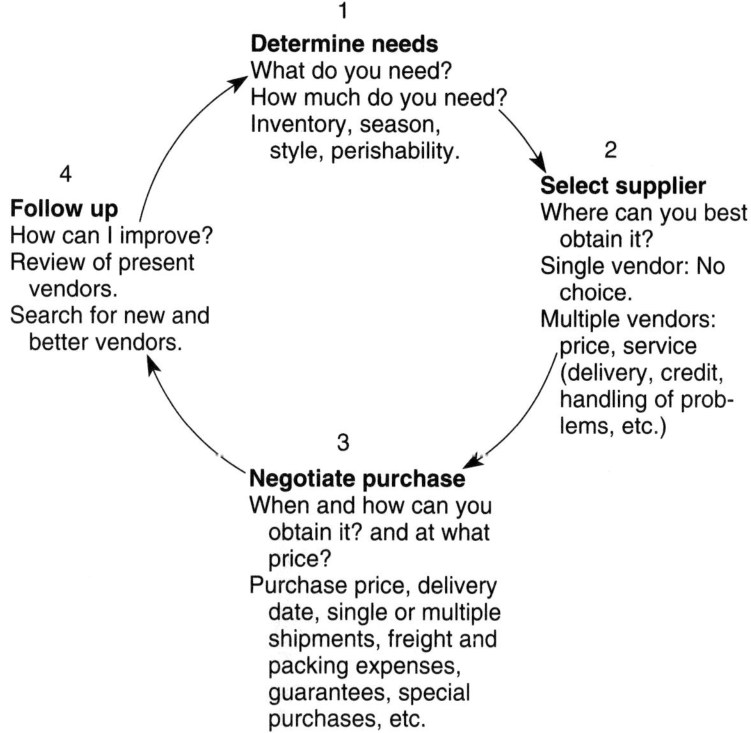

1. Determining needs. For each line of merchandise, the buyer must determine what will be needed until the next time the line is reviewed. Determining what is needed involves, for some items, merely looking at inventory and past sales. For other lines, it involves risky decisions—which styles to select and how much of each to buy. One thing management does not want is a lot of merchandise in stock when a style is outmoded or the season is past.

2. Selecting the supplier. After determining the merchandise needs, the buyer must find one or more vendors who can supply the merchandise. Some merchandise can be bought only from one vendor; in this case, the only decision to be made is whether to carry the line. For most merchandise, several suppliers are available. In these instances the buyer must evaluate price as well as service in terms of reasonable and reliable delivery; adjustment of problems; and help in emergencies and other matters such as credit terms, spaced deliveries, and inventory management assistance.

3. **Negotiating the purchase.** This crucial third step involves not only the purchase price but also quantities, delivery dates, single- or multiple-shipment deliveries, freight and packing expenses, guarantees on the quality of the merchandise, promotion and advertising allowances, special offers on slightly damaged materials or sell-outs, and so forth.

4. **Following up.** Finally, to improve service, the buyer must review the relationship with each vendor from time to time to determine whether changes should be made. As necessary, the buyer should search for alternate or new suppliers.

DETERMINING NEEDS

Different types of merchandise require different techniques to determine what is needed. It is therefore important to recognize, for various merchandise lines, whether they are primarily **staples, seasonal items,** or **style** or **perishable items.**

The goal in each case, whether the merchandise is primarily staple, seasonal, style oriented, or perishable, is to establish or maintain inventory at the lowest possible level and still have a sufficient variety of colors, sizes, or models available from which customers can choose. Such a practice will minimize losses caused by obsolescence and spoilage and free capital for other uses.

Timeliness

Progressive retailers continue to refine the buying process, shorten lead times in ordering merchandise, maintain the minimum inventory level needed to meet customer needs, and have sufficient flexibility to quickly respond to changing customer tastes. Such retailers include Benneton and The Limited.[4] The Limited's apparel acquisition system works four to five times faster than the systems used by most other retailers. Management is thus able to maintain less inventory than competitors, be more responsive to customer needs, and maintain higher gross margin than the norm. Benneton manufactures to match the orders from its stores and has a responsive distribution system.

Forecasting Sales

The issues involved in sales forecasting vary, depending on whether the merchandise is primarily staples, seasonal items, or style or perishable items. The issues to be considered and the complexity of the buying decision are different in each instance.

Staples. Staple or semi-staple merchandise is generally in demand year round, with little change in model or style. Basic appliances, hardware, housewares, books, domestics, and basic clothing items such as underwear and pajamas fall into this category. Staples, even if the store is primarily focused on seasonal fashion, generate extra profit and bring customers into the store who may then purchase some of the primary merchandise.

The important characteristic of staples is steady usage. Deciding how much to buy, therefore, depends primarily on the following factors:

- **Sales trends,** taken from records showing how much of each staple sold during the past two or three months, and also how much sold during the same period in the previous year. The buyer thus can tell whether the item has increased or decreased in popularity or has remained the same. The buyer then decides, if the trend is up, whether to increase average inventory, or whether to assume the same sales trend without running out of stock.
- **Profitability**—items that bring a better return on investment in space and capital are the more desirable items to buy.
- **Discounts,** which are usually available for large-quantity purchases.

The combination of these factors provides a general indicator of needs in staple merchandise.

Seasonal Merchandise. Seasonal merchandise, as implied, is in demand only at certain times of the year. Examples include sleds, snow tires, bathing suits, sun glasses, lawn equipment, and patio furniture. Although some seasonal items can be reordered during peak demand to replenish inventory, many items are unavailable or cannot be obtained quickly enough to meet demand. Therefore, sufficient levels of the merchandise is bought well in advance of the season.

Forecasting needs for seasonal items depends primarily on knowing the past customer demand for the item or merchandise line. One method is to maintain a month-by-month tally of units sold, either by dollar value or quantity. These records can then be examined on a yearly basis, enabling the buyer to identify selling trends and make the correct buying decisions.

One method of maintaining records is to use a separate sheet, index card, or computer record for each merchandise item, group of items, or line. In the following example, note that in 1994 the greatest number of widgets were sold in April, and at the end of the season, 20 remaining items in inventory had to be sold below cost.

Merchandise item: Widget

	Sales record				
	1994	1995	1996	1997	1998
January	-0-				
February	$ 50.				
March	$ 700.				
April	$2,200.				
May	$1,000.				
June	$ 300.				
July through December	-0-				
Total units bought	300				
Sold below cost	20				

For the novice buyer who has no previous sales records to rely on, suppliers and their salespeople can serve as a good source of information for predictions. No foolproof method exists for accurately predicting future sales. Usually, though, a good prediction of future sales can be made by considering these factors:

- Past experience with the merchandise.
- Records of previous sales.
- Length of the season.
- Planned selling price.
- Planned advertising and promotion support.
- Changes in competitive intensity.
- Predictions of consumer buying from trade journals.

These factors together can give the buyer a fairly good idea of the quantity of each item likely to sell during the upcoming season.

Style and Perishable Items. Items of style or fashion include such merchandise as fur coats, apparel, and sportswear. Stylish items are usually more expensive than staples and seasonals. Because the demand for any particular style tends to increase rapidly and then drop off just as quickly, overbuying can have a disastrous effect on profits. Once a style is "out," it is often difficult to sell it at a profit.

Perishable merchandise has similar characteristics. If management buys more than can be sold, some of it will begin to spoil and bring only a fraction of the normal price.

Wet Seal, the trendy juniors' apparel chain specializes in the sale of stylish items. Management has succeeded in the fashion industry because of savvy merchandising. Wet Seal's reliance on local suppliers allows it to respond quickly to the fickle demands of fashion-conscious teens. Indeed, the chain needs less than six weeks to get a new design into stores, compared with four months for companies that use Asian suppliers.[5]

Faddish items present similar difficulties. An example is Teenage Mutant Ninja Turtles. Hong Kong–based Playmates International Holdings Ltd. owns the license to produce Ninja Turtle toys. Its management vigilantly guards against the boom and bust scenarios that characterized Cabbage Patch dolls and Teddy Ruxpin, the talking teddy bear. For example, Playmates consistently undersupplies the market. Executives believe that keeping the Turtles in tight supply helps keep up demand as kids fight in the aisles for them.[6]

Management can plot the progress of different styles to see how they usually behave. A few examples of such graphs appear in Figure 13–1. They can help predict how much and when to buy.

When plotting graphs, it is important to note all special, significant events such as sales, including those of major competitors. These events

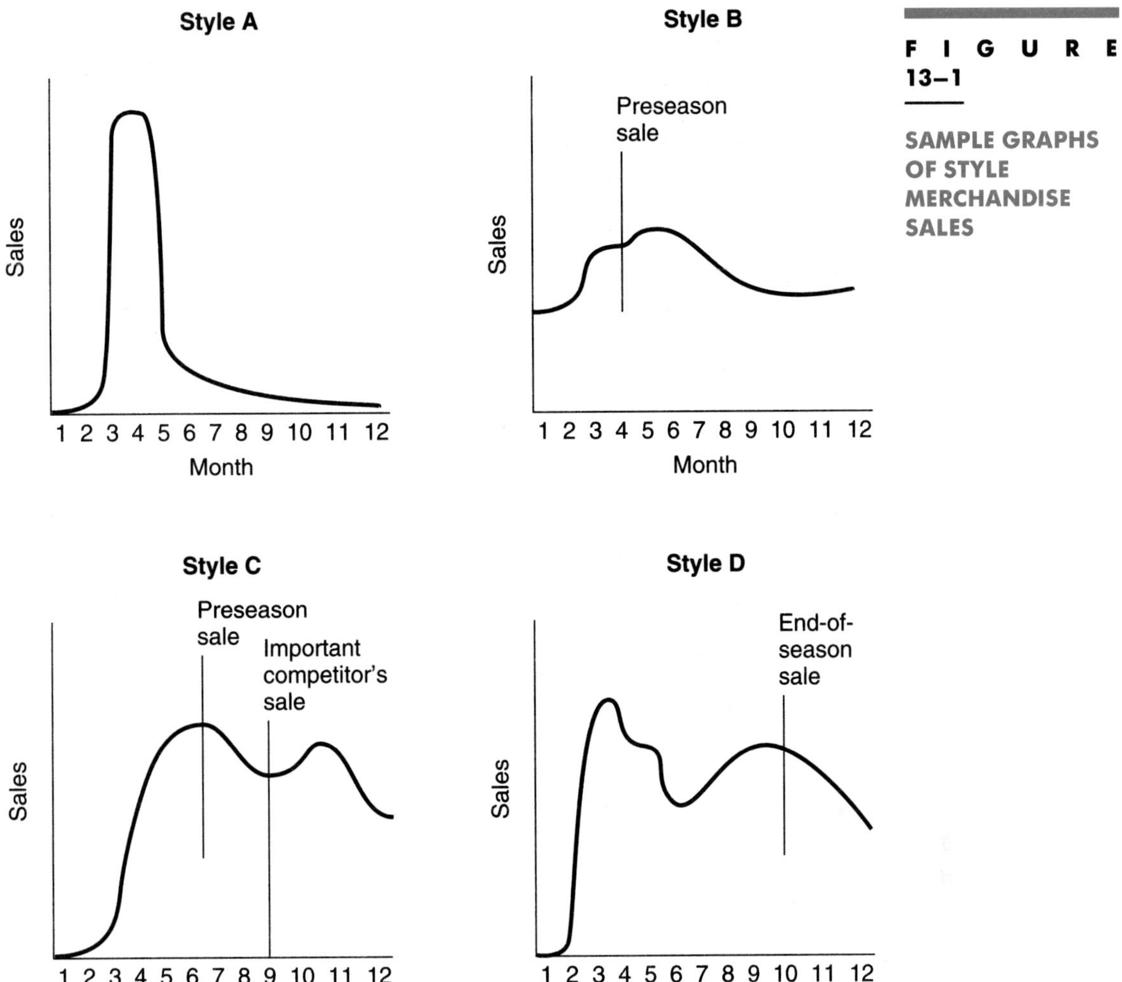

FIGURE 13–1

SAMPLE GRAPHS OF STYLE MERCHANDISE SALES

also have to be planned or predicted, and kept in mind when forecasting merchandise needs.

Although graphs may not predict sales very accurately, they usually will narrow the amount of buying error. Sometimes, however, an overstock of nonseasonal goods occurs because of overbuying or because the items are either unstylish or of poor quality. In such a case, the stock should be reduced as soon as possible to minimize losses.

Establishing Buying Guidelines

How much stock should be ordered? Why not enough merchandise for one month, or two months, or even six months?

In some cases, product shelf life may be the determining factor. If a grocer stocked more than two days' supply of muffins, they would lose their freshness and the grocer would lose customers. Delivery is immediate. The grocer gives the order directly to the bakery truck driver and the driver fills the order in minutes.

More often, there are many other factors to consider. Take the case of the retailer who may require two weeks to receive delivery from suppliers on some items. On an emergency basis, the retailer may be able to replenish inventory more promptly, but only by forfeiting quantity discounts or incurring extra delivery charges. For most items, it is better to accept normal delivery, taking full advantage of all available discounts and minimizing freight charges. Lead time and needed levels of safety stock influence the amount and frequency of purchases.

Lead Time. The length of time between order placement and receipt of goods is called **lead time.** If the lead time is two weeks, would it be sufficient to establish a minimum inventory level of two weeks' supply? Probably not. If an item was not reordered until only two weeks' supply remained, there would probably be just enough stock on hand to cover expected sales until the order arrived. However, if anything went wrong (and it usually does), a stockout would occur before the order was received. An unexpectedly large request from a customer might not be filled, for example, because of insufficient inventory. A strike, shipping delays, manufacturing problems, or unforeseen weather conditions could seriously delay the arrival of the merchandise. The stockout could continue for several weeks. Therefore, most businesses maintain a **safety,** or cushion, stock as protection against unexpected occurrences.

Safety Stock. The size of the safety stock depends on the factors that could interrupt deliveries. Suitable guidelines can be developed based on experience in the industry. In addition, many items require a **basic stock,** an amount sufficient to accommodate regular sales, offering customers a reasonable assortment of merchandise from which to select.

Assume that the lead time for a particular item is two weeks. The safety stock that the business wishes to maintain is four weeks' supply. Additionally, a one-week basic stock is required. The desired inventory level would be established as the sum of these factors:

Lead Time	2 weeks
+ Safety Stock	4 weeks
+ Basic Stock	1 week
= Inventory Level	7 weeks

How Much to Buy. The desired inventory level should be considered an **order point.** Whenever the stock of an item falls below this point, it should be ordered.

For example, if a camera shop wishes to maintain a 10-week supply of film in inventory and average sales of a particular film type are 50 rolls per week, the order point would be 500 (50 × 10) rolls. When inventory drops below 500 rolls, more film should be ordered.

The quantity of film purchased depends on the usual time between orders, called the **ordering interval.** Sufficient supplies need to be maintained so that inventories between orders average out to the desired level.

A stock equal to expected sales during the camera shop's two-week order interval should be added to the order point to determine the **order ceiling.**

Order ceiling = Order point + Order interval sales
Order ceiling = 500 + (50 × 2)
Order ceiling = 600

An order quantity could then be determined as follows, assuming 450 rolls are on hand:

Order quantity = Order ceiling − Stock on hand
Order quantity = 600 − 450 = 150 rolls

If an order for 50 rolls had already been placed, but not yet received, the present order should be reduced by the 50 rolls on order. The new order would then be 100 (150 − 50) rolls.

Review. Let us review the steps involved in establishing order quantities using a hardware store as an example. The store desires to maintain a basic tool stock equal to one week's sales and a safety stock of one week's sales for saws. Average weekly sales are three saws. Lead time for order placement and delivery is two weeks. Orders are placed every four weeks.

A desirable inventory level, or order point, is then calculated as follows:

Lead time	2 weeks
+ Basic stock	1 week
+ Safety stock	1 week
= Order point	4 weeks or 12 (4 × 3) saws

Whenever the supply of any saw drops to a four weeks' supply or below, an order should be placed.

To determine the order quantity, management must first calculate the order ceiling:

Order point	4 weeks
+ Order interval	4 weeks
= Order ceiling	8 weeks or 24 (8 × 3) saws

Assume that an order is being prepared for saws. Average weekly sales are 3 saws and the stock on hand is 10 saws. This is below the order point of 12 (4 × 3) saws. The order quantity would be calculated as follows:

	Order ceiling	24
−	Stock on hand	10
=	Order quantity	14

The hardware store should order 14 saws. If any are already on order, the outstanding order quantity should be subtracted.

The Economic Order Quantity Model. The economic order quantity (EOQ) model is another method for calculating order quantity. It is most applicable when demand is known, continuous, and constant, as in the case of staple merchandise. The model reflects both the variable costs of ordering inventory and inventory carrying costs. Variable costs decrease with larger orders because the costs of ordering are spread over more units. However, carrying costs such as insurance go up as the order quantity goes up. Management thus seeks an order quantity where the combination of inventory ordering costs and carrying costs are at a minimum. The formula is shown below:

$$Q = \sqrt{\frac{2SO}{IC}}$$

where

Q = Economic order quantity
S = Estimated annual unit sales
O = Variable costs per order placed
I = Inventory carrying costs as a percentage of item's unit cost
C = Unit cost of item

If $S = 4$ per week (208 per year), $I = 0.1872$, $O = \$0.90$ per order, and $C = \$5$ per unit, Q would be 20 units:

$$Q = \sqrt{\frac{2 \times 208 \times 0.90}{0.1872 \times 5}} = \sqrt{\frac{374.40}{0.9360}} = \sqrt{400} = 20$$

Therefore, the economic order quantity is 20 units, or a five-week supply.[7]

Replenishment Systems Assistance. Most computer manufacturers provide information on the inventory management systems available for their computers. In addition, computer service companies often have material available describing the use of their computer software programs for inventory management. These companies are a good source of information on inventory management techniques, as well as help on specific inventory management problems.

Last, maintaining good merchandise control practices, as described in the following section, will help ensure successful buying.

Merchandise Control Systems. To manage inventory successfully, management should maintain accurate and up-to-date records of sales and stock on hand for every item. Inventory records tell you what you *have*. Sales records tell you what you *need*. Inventory records are used for making the following decisions:

- Purchasing items to replenish inventory.
- Clearing out obsolete items that are no longer in demand.
- Adding new items to inventory.

The best control system depends largely on the number of different items in inventory. A bicycle shop might carry 40 or 50 items in inventory, and a supermarket or pharmacy may carry several thousand items.

Every retailer should at least have a manual inventory control system. Manual systems generally are based on an inventory control card similar to that shown below.

Inventory Control Card

3648 Toaster			
Date	*On Hand*	*In*	*Out*
8/1	27		
8/2	26		1
8/4	38	12	
8/6	36		2
8/8	35		1
8/10	32		3

A separate record is maintained for each item in inventory. The stock status is shown for the end of each day. All changes in inventory are shown as "in" or "out." In the "in" column, management lists all orders received from suppliers, returns from customers, and so forth. In the "out" column, management identifies all sales, returns to suppliers, and similar changes.

When many items are maintained in inventory, electronic data processing services may be necessary. These are available through local service bureaus. On a specified schedule, the business submits records of sales, receipts, and orders for the previous period so that the service bureau can update the inventory records. Depending on the type of business and the programs available from the service bureau, it might provide a sales analysis for each item, which can guide the business inventory replenishment. Many retailers today handle such an analysis on their own computer system.

Information Partnerships

Electronic data interchange (EDI), quick response (QR), and just-in-time (JIT) delivery are changing the way merchandise is ordered and shipped (see Exhibit 13–1). New partnerships are emerging between retailers and

EXHIBIT 13–1

Courtesy Vanity Fair Mills, Inc.

A cosmetic retailer's inventory is evaluated and a reorder created before uploading to a supplier using an electronic data interchange system.

vendors that are making the buying and replenishment process more timely and cost effective, as we discussed in the Retailing Capsule.

Ingredients. The ingredients of these emerging partnerships include the following:

- **Electronic data interchange.** EDI consists of software systems that allow for direct communication of standard business documents between retailers and vendors. Electronic sharing of information enables retailers and vendors to reduce reorder cycle times and speed delivery of replenishing inventory.
- **Just-in-time.** JIT systems are designed to allow delivery of only the quantity of a specific product needed at the precise time it is needed. Firms such as Dayton Hudson, for example, will provide manufacturers with a six-month forecast of demand but a one-week lead time forecast of sizes, designs, and colors.
- **Quick response.** This is an information-sharing partnership between retailers and vendors (often manufacturers) that provides retailers with timely replenishment of inventory sufficient to meet customer demand without the necessity of carrying high levels of inventory in anticipation of customer demand. These partnerships will not work without a strong alliance between the vendor and the retailer. The level of trust and information sharing required in such relationships is unprecedented.

QR consists of several interrelated technologies and partner initiatives. Six factors are considered essential:[8]

- Sharing inventory data among trading partners.
- Sharing sales and marketing data among trading partners.
- Using bar coding on packaging to track sales and inventory.
- Enabling customers to order through EDI.
- Managing stock replenishment for key customers.
- Using automated stock replenishment systems.

Although national retailers such as Sears and Kmart have used it for several years, the system is becoming affordable and cost effective for small and medium-sized retailers and manufacturers.

Quick delivery and rapid merchandise turns deliver several benefits. They can ensure both a high level of profitability and a low level of stockout, the most desirable dimensions of an inventory strategy. Short lead times can also ensure that the merchandise is more likely to be fashionable and, for perishables, fresh. Shorter lead times can help the retailer influence the size, color, and style mix closer to the fashion season.

Large companies such as Wal-Mart link their databases directly to the manufacturers of the merchandise, as noted in the Retailing Capsule. Small manufacturers and independent and regional retailers typically link through third-party providers, such as Geisco, CompuServe, and Prodigy. Either way, the results are improved efficiency, stronger relationships, and higher profits for suppliers and retailers alike.

For suppliers, EDI provides added service to retailers—a step beyond the usual merchandising, order-taking, shipping, and billing process. It strengthens the bonds between the companies as the suppliers become more important players in the retailers' merchandising plans.

For sales reps, it eliminates the tedium of frequent order taking and paper shuffling, which in turn enables them to focus on presenting new and special products and promotions, learn more about their customers by developing stronger interpersonal relationships, meet each customer's special needs, and call on more customers.

For retailers, it provides added efficiency and effectiveness. It enables them to serve their customers better by ensuring adequate, reliable stock. It also improves profitability by increasing stock turns and minimizing stock of slow items. For small retailers, the system relieves the mathematical drudgery of estimating turnover, forecasting demand, and determining economic order quantities.

Finally, it frees everyone to concentrate on business activities other than inventory maintenance. It clearly shows how improved marketing improves other business functions.

Lingerie manufacturer Vanity Fair, of Monroeville, Alabama, for example, offers its customers a combined merchandising, stock replenishment,

A Profile in Excellence

CHARLES LAZARUS

Charles Lazarus is regarded as the developer of the one-stop shopping supermarket for toys. He opened the first Toys 'R' Us outlet in 1957. His stores have become a dominant force in the toy industry with stores throughout North America, Europe, and the Far East.

Lazarus relies heavily on computer databases to spot trends in consumer demand for products and to flash early warnings when toy fads are beginning to fade. Within the industry, it is relatively simple to introduce a new product line. The expertise lies in knowing when to drop it.

Under Lazarus's direction, Toys 'R' Us was one of the first retailers to implement QR and EDI technology in establishing vendor partnerships. Management can pull sales information from individual stores, transmit it back to the distribution centers for inventory replenishment, and then send the information back to headquarters. Within 15 minutes to half an hour, management knows how a particular store was doing 30 minutes earlier. The ability to manage merchandise ordering and replenishment from a total systems perspective gives Toys 'R' Us an important advantage over the competition.

prompt delivery, and EDI program. It provides retailers detailed data on their inventory trends, stock turns, and sales volumes on weekly, monthly, quarterly, and annual bases.

Data can be transferred by electronic mail, floppy disk, or hard copy. Standard electronic transactions include price and sales catalogues, purchase orders, advance shipping notices, order status, invoices, and remittance advice.[9]

As an additional example, the Toys 'R' Us information system is so effective that management knows more about toy sales than any of its manufacturer suppliers. Indeed, the Toys 'R' Us vendor partners often rely on spring and summer Toys 'R' Us sales in establishing production levels and in redesigning products for their Christmas lines.

Many experts view Toys 'R' Us as a circus with Charles Lazarus (the CEO and founder) as the ring master (see A Profile in Excellence). Efficient operating systems, huge buying volume, and unprecedented breadth and depth has allowed Lazarus to virtually dominate the competitive arena for toys.

SELECTING SUPPLIERS

Some suppliers may be excellent, and some less than desirable (even those offering quick response options). The first step toward replacing undesirable ones or selecting suppliers for new merchandise is to obtain a list of those to consider. Awareness of available suppliers and their services will place the buyer in a position to choose the best one.

Information Sources

Information about merchandise lines can be developed in a variety of ways:

1. **Salespeople.** Vendor salespeople can provide excellent information about sources of supply. Many are well informed about alternative sources of noncompeting lines and can often suggest new services and products. Salespeople are also a good source of information about the merchandise selection practices of similar stores in different parts of their territories.
2. **Trade magazines.** General and specialized trade journals often contain advertisements placed by suppliers and articles that provide clues to desirable new sources.
3. **Business contacts.** Customers or other business contacts may be able to provide useful information about potential suppliers.
4. **Trade exhibits.** These provide an excellent opportunity to see a variety of new products and compare similar products of different manufacturers.
5. **Yellow pages.** The yellow pages in the telephone directory contain listings of local suppliers.

How to Make Vendor Contacts

Vendors can be contacted in a variety of ways. Each source of contact offers advantages and disadvantages to the retailer. Furthermore, buyers can choose from several options for purchasing merchandise. Examples include various forms of group or central buying, arranging for merchandise to be placed in the outlet on consignment, or leasing some departments to outside sources with unique expertise.

Sales Representatives. A traditional source of vendor contact is the sales representative, although, as seen in the Retailing Capsule, large retailers sometimes prefer to deal directly with the manufacturer. In such lines as groceries and drugs, where item turnover is very fast, salespeople may call on the retailer almost weekly. For fashion lines, the representative will usually call on a seasonal basis. Vendor contact may also begin through catalogs and price lists for some types of retailers.

The Central Market. A **central market** is a place where a large number of suppliers concentrate. It may be a large, single building such as the Merchandise Mart in Chicago. New York City is still the primary central market for many types of merchandise, especially women's fashions. Chicago and High Point, North Carolina, are well known for furniture.

Not all central markets are permanent. For example, the fine-jewelry central market is held in New York periodically, in January and July. Such central market events are called **trade shows.**

Resident Buying Offices. Resident buying offices are located in central markets. Large retailers maintain their own offices, and others will contract for specified services. Resident buyers are experts in market information

TABLE 13–1

TYPES OF RESIDENT BUYING OFFICES

Type of Office	*Characteristics*	*Example*
Cooperatively owned office	An office owned by the stores it serves with directors chosen from member firms	Frederick Atkins
Independent buying office	An office not owned by any retail store or group. It sets its own operating policies and often handles hard and soft goods	Felix Lilienthal & Co.
Divisional resident office	An office owned and operated by a retail chain or similar multi-unit retailer	Associated Dry Goods Corporation

and typically represent many retailers. They remain in constant contact with suppliers and know what is new, what is "hot," and when prices are changing. They have market clout because they represent many different retailers. The most common types of resident buying offices are shown in Table 13–1.

The key role of resident buying offices is to provide advice and information, not only when the retail buyer is in the market, but also when the buyer cannot be present. The offices range from one-person operations to large firms that may provide space and secretarial help for the retail buyer.

Wholesalers. Wholesalers are a major source of supply in many sectors of retailing, including food, hardware, and drugs. Wholesalers can be classified as those who take title to goods—**merchant wholesalers**—and those who do not take title—known as **functional middlemen.** Functional middlemen include **brokers,** who receive a commission to bring manufacturers and retailers together, and **manufacturers' agents,** who sell the merchandise lines of several different suppliers. Various types of wholesalers are shown in Table 13–2. Such wholesalers normally supply staple, nonfashion merchandise.

Manufacturers. Some merchandise, as noted elsewhere, may be purchased directly from the manufacturer. National chains such as J. C. Penney and Sears are larger than most wholesalers. Thus, they are able to purchase more cheaply by buying directly from the manufacturer. Manufacturers will tailor-make merchandise for large national chains. Many such items are sold under the retailer's private label, such as Penney's Fox shirts and Plain Pocket jeans.

Voluntaries and Cooperatives. Independent retailers sometimes strengthen their competitive positions by working together to secure greater strength in buying merchandise. These arrangements are known as buying groups. A **cooperative** arrangement exists when independent retailers organize a wholesale firm. A **voluntary** is created when a wholesaler arranges to handle the buying function for a collection of retailers.

TABLE 13–2

TYPES OF WHOLESALERS

Type	Description
Merchant wholesalers	
Full service	Perform a wide array of functions including delivery, credit, selling, management assistance, and risk taking.
Specialty	Carry only one part of a product line but do so in depth.
Limited line	Carry great depth of assortment in one or two product lines.
General merchandise	Carry several merchandise lines.
Limited service	Offer restricted number of functions for their suppliers and customers.
Rack jobber	Operate primarily in grocery and food trades and handle mostly nonfood items such as health and beauty aids, paperback books, and hardware items. Take title and handle all marketing functions.
Truck	Active in perishables and semiperishables such as milk and bread. Primary functions are selling and delivery and serving needs of hotels, supermarkets, and restaurants.
Cash and carry	Sell limited lines of high-turnover items to small retailers. Neither deliver nor provide credit.
Functional middlemen	
Agents	Represent either buyers or sellers on permanent basis. Have written agreement with management that specifies territory they will cover, price at which goods or services will be sold, and terms of sale.
Brokers	Carry no inventory, do no financing, and normally do not represent management on a continuing basis. Only role is to negotiate exchanges. Paid a commission fee by organization that uses their services.
Commission merchants	Agents that take physical possession, negotiate sales for management, arrange for delivery, and provide for transportation. Arrangements with management normally not long term. Tend to specialize in marketing of agricultural products for farmers who own output but who do not belong to cooperatives that could arrange for sale of their output.

Retail buying groups are prominent in hardware, furniture, appliances, home renovation products, groceries, and electronic equipment. Nearly half of retail hardware sales in the United States are made by the members of buying groups. The services offered include support in pricing, logistics, promotion, private-label products, and integrated marketing strategies.

Retailers also have a variety of other options in their choice of merchandise sources. Some are quite unorthodox, as shown in A Question of Ethics.

Supplier Evaluation Criteria

Factors to consider in determining the best supplier are discussed in this section.

A Question of Ethics

CHILD WORLD SAYS RIVAL CHEATS

Where does Toys 'R' Us Inc., the giant toy retailer, buy some of the goods that line its shelves? Down the street at Child World Inc. stores, one of its biggest rivals.

Strange as it seems, that's what Child World claims—and Toys 'R' Us isn't denying it.

Child World contends that Toys 'R' Us is "systematically abusing" Child World promotions that specifically exclude dealers, wholesalers, and retailers. The promotion gives customers gift certificates valued at $25 on purchases when they buy $100 of products, with smaller certificates given for smaller purchases.

Child World, based in Avon, Massachusetts, alleges that Toys 'R' Us managers and employees, under the guise of being regular customers, "make large purchases of items that Child World sells at close to cost—particularly diapers, baby food, and formula—receiving the dollars-off coupons and reselling the Child World goods as Toys 'R' Us inventory."

Toys 'R' Us wouldn't dispute the allegations and said that the practice is common in the industry. "It's not an unusual thing for one retailer to buy merchandise from another. I'm sure that we have. We know that [Child World] has done it to us," said Angela Bourdon, a spokesperson for the Rochelle Park, New Jersey, retailer. A spokesperson for Child World denied that it has purchased goods in bulk from Toys 'R' Us.

Do you see anything unethical in this alleged practice of Toys 'R' Us?

Source: Susan Alexander, "Child World Says Rival Cheats; Toys 'R' Us Answers: 'Grow Up.' " Portions reproduced with permission from *The Wall Street Journal*, September 19, 1991, p. B1, B4.

Price and Discounts. Price, overall, is the most important supplier evaluation criterion, although criteria vary by type of merchandise. As shown in Table 13–3, for example, price is the most important item for general merchandisers, but ranks behind on-time delivery in importance for apparel and accessory retailers.[10] Price has many dimensions because it includes quantity discounts; special allowances; the chance to buy special lots, seconds, or sell-outs; and dating of invoices.

Reliability. Reliable delivery is important. Unreliable delivery can create problems of stockout, which result in sales loss. In addition, slow or unreliable delivery also requires the buyer to maintain larger average inventories, which result in increased carrying costs. A good supplier will respond when the store has a sudden emergency and will also protect the store when shortages of merchandise exist because of a strike or disaster.

Quality. Quality, and assurance that quality is always the same, is almost as important as price and closely linked to it. Obviously, in selecting a supplier, buyers want to be certain that they will rarely, if ever, receive a poor-quality shipment.

TABLE 13–3 SUPPLIER EVALUATION CRITERIA: OVERALL AND RETAIL SUBGROUP MEANS

		Means for Industry Subgroups*		
Supplier Evaluation Criteria (listed in descending order)	*Overall Mean*	*General Merchandiser*	*Apparel and Accessories*	*All Others*
Price	4.46	4.55	4.25	4.48
On-time delivery	4.12	3.85	4.57	4.10
Service quality	4.00	3.90	3.77	4.13
Good communication	3.89	3.62	4.17	3.95
Easy to work with	3.81	3.76	3.75	3.85
Percentage shipped complete	3.70	3.65	3.85	3.67
Flexibility	3.69	3.58	3.75	3.72
Maintains short order cycle	3.68	3.74	3.90	3.59
Willingness to customize service	3.68	3.58	3.85	3.67
Consistency of order cycle	3.64	3.95	3.22	3.57
Customer support	3.63	3.71	3.22	3.69
Early notification of disruption	3.42	3.47	3.36	3.41
Positive attitude	3.42	3.32	3.36	3.49
Management quality	3.36	3.05	3.20	3.55
Master carton packaging quality	3.27	3.63	3.92	2.82
Shelf unit packaging quality	3.13	3.50	2.90	3.00
Automatic substitution rates	2.53	3.17	2.78	2.04

*Calculated on a one to five scale with one labeled as of no importance and five as very important.

Source: Cornelia Dronga, Richard Germain, and James R. Stock, "Dimensions Underlying Retail Logistics and Their Relationship to Supplier Evaluation Criteria," *The International Journal of Logistics Management* 2, no. 1 (1991), p. 22.

Services. Suppliers can provide many services, including spacing of deliveries, which allows the buyer to purchase a larger quantity than the store may immediately handle, thus giving the advantage of quantity discounts; recycling of packaging to reduce overall freight and packing expenses (and to help protect the environment); providing advertising and promotional materials and displays to help promote merchandise; and giving away free supplies such as literature and bags for the customers. In some industries, suppliers offer inventory services to retailers. Usually these are provided for a small fee but they can be quite valuable in helping the retailer manage inventory with greater efficiency.

Accessibility. Accessibility is another factor on which suppliers should be judged. It is often important to contact the supplier about special problems that may arise. A supplier who is difficult to contact is not as desirable as one easy to reach.

Brand Name Recognition. National brand names are important for some lines of merchandise. Some retailers, especially in department and specialty store retailing, have succeeded in establishing strong name recognition for private brands as a way of protecting the merchandise from excessive price competition and of providing an advantage in the marketplace. For fashion merchandise, color, position on the fashion cycle, styling, and distinctiveness are also important factors in the vendor selection decision.[11]

Psychosocial Factors. Psychosocial factors can also be important in vendor selection. Personal friendships can play a role. Such relationships are especially prevalent with small, family-owned retailers, where price concessions often are not a part of negotiations.

Methods of Buying

Group Buying. Group, or cooperative, buying is the joint purchasing of goods by a number of noncompeting, nonaligned stores such as independent department stores. By combining their orders into one large order, the stores hope to get lower prices. These group arrangements can be beneficial in other ways, too, because the noncompeting buyers can share knowledge about markets, fashion trends, and so forth. Group buying can be arranged through resident buying offices.

Some buyers have difficulty entering into group buying. They give up some of their individuality, and that hurts. Fashion merchants particularly find cooperative buying difficult because they believe their customers are unique.

Central Buying. Central buying is most often practiced by chains. As branch-store organizations grow in size, central buying is also logical for them. Central buying means that one person handles the buying of goods for all stores in the firm.

In firms where central buying occurs, most of the authority for buying lies outside any one retail outlet. In some supermarkets, store managers are given authority to purchase locally produced items, and the remaining merchandise stock is centrally purchased.

Because they order in such large quantities, central buyers hope to get favorable prices. Technology is important in central buying, as the buyer must have adequate and rapid information from individual stores. Such information is necessary to make effective buying decisions.

Overall, 85 percent of the warehouse grocery products are purchased centrally for A&P, Waldbaum, Food Emporium, Super Fresh, Farmer Jack, and Kohl's. Publix Supermarkets in Lakeland, Florida, has added grocery products to the list of items purchased centrally. Lucky Stores, Dublin, California, has moved health and beauty care, general merchandise, and liquor to centralized buying.[12]

Committee Buying. Committee buying is a version of central buying. It is a way to achieve the savings of central buying while having more than one person share the buying responsibility. This type of buying is common in firms selling staples, such as hardware stores.

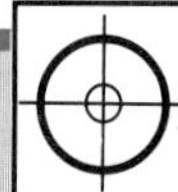

FOCUS 13–1

JAPANESE VERSUS AMERICAN RETAILING
Culture is not the only difference; buying methods vary, too

Because of the dramatic differences between the cultures of the United States and Japan, it should not be surprising that there are differences between the two countries' methods of retailing.

According to Kan Yamanaka, president of Tobu Department Store Co., "The major difference between the American retail system and that of the Japanese is in the purchasing of merchandise. In the American retail system, merchandise is purchased based on buyers' responsibility. The primary goal is to maximize gross margin by taking a higher degree of risk.

"Contrary to that, in the Japanese retail system, merchandise is traditionally traded on a consignment basis. This system brings a risk-free advantage to the buyers' responsibility, but it lowers the gross margin figure. If there is any system or technique applicable to Tobu, the American purchasing system would be the most beneficial example.

"There are many other rationales in the American system that the Japanese could apply to their retail organizations. However, the most important idea here is that any retail business must be closely fitted into the local lifestyle of consumers and their culture. Without understanding these two important factors, a retail business cannot meet with success. Simple economics or marketing theory cannot always be a determinant for a successful retail business."

Source: Reprinted with permission from *Stores* magazine, June 1992, p. 29.

Consignment. In consignment, suppliers guarantee the sale of items and will take merchandise back if it does not sell. Therefore, the retailer assumes no risk in such an arrangement (other than the possibility of nonproductive shelf space). Merchandise from an unknown supplier or a high-risk item might require such an arrangement. If a buyer has overspent the assigned budget, consignment can also be attractive. But the buyer must be aware that most vendors do not offer consignment if the goods can be sold any other way. In contrast to American practices, most merchandise in Japan is acquired on a consignment basis, as noted in Focus 13–1.

Leased Departments. If retailers do not have the skills to operate a specialized department, they may choose to lease it. Shoe, camera, jewelry, and optical departments, as well as beauty salons and restaurants, are often operated under lease arrangements. By leasing to an expert, the retailer can provide customers with specialized items without fear of failure caused by inexperience.

Leased departments are common in mass-merchandise stores. However, after mass merchandisers learn how to run a department, they often take it over as a company-operated department.

NEGOTIATING THE PURCHASE

The buyer should be prepared to sacrifice something during the negotiation. Then he or she can ask the supplier, "What are you willing to give up?" Remember, the retail buyer is trying to get the best deal, and the vendor is trying to hold the price up to protect profits. Buyers usually attempt to negotiate on the following elements:

1. Cost.
2. Discounts.
3. Datings.
4. Transportation charges.

Cost Price. One area of negotiation is the cost, or list, price of the merchandise. Certain laws, however, affect the amount of dealing that can be done to get a good price from a vendor, as discussed in Chapter 3. Some vendors will not negotiate price.

After the gross wholesale list price has been negotiated and established, the buyer must turn to other areas for negotiation.

Discounts. Even though identical list prices may be offered by various vendors, they may offer different discounts. An understanding of these purchase terms is necessary to negotiate the best price.

Trade. A trade discount is a reduction off the seller's list price and is granted to a retailer who performs functions that are normally the responsibility of the seller. A trade discount may be offered as a single percentage or as a series of percentages off list price. If the list price on a sport shirt is \$14.95, with a trade discount of 40 percent, the retailer will pay \$8.97 (\$14.95 − \$5.98). The \$5.98 (\$14.95 × .40) is the trade discount. The same buyer might be offered an identical sport shirt from another manufacturer at a list price of \$14.95 less 30 percent, 10 percent, and 5 percent. The net price in this case would be computed as follows:

List price	=	\$14.95	
	−	4.48	(\$14.95 × 0.30)
	=	10.47	
	−	1.05	(\$10.47 × 0.10)
	=	9.42	
	−	0.47	(\$9.42 × 0.05)
Net price	=	\$ 8.95	

An alternative way of calculating the net price in this example is to use the complement of the discount percentages. In this case, the net price would be calculated thus: \$14.95 × .70 × .90 × .95 = \$8.95.

Quantity. A quantity discount is a reduction in unit cost based on the size of the order. Such discounts may be **noncumulative,** meaning the reduction is based on one order, or **cumulative,** meaning the reduction is computed over purchases for a specified period of time.

When deciding whether a quantity discount is worthwhile, the buyer must compare the money saved with the extra inventory carrying cost.

To determine the value of a quantity discount, use the following steps:

1. Determine the savings from the quantity discount.
2. Determine how much extra merchandise the store would have to carry in inventory, and for how long.
3. Multiply the average extra stock by the carrying charge (which is usually 20 to 25 percent) to obtain the additional cost of carrying the extra stock for a year.
4. Determine the additional carrying costs for the period of time it will take to work off the extra stock.
5. Compare the savings from the quantity discount with the cost of carrying the extra inventory and decide whether it is worthwhile to buy the larger quantity.

For example, if the buyer can save $500 by taking an extra $6,000 of merchandise into stock, and if it will take six months to work off the extra stock, the buyer would perform the following calculations:

$$\text{Cost savings (discount)} = \$500$$

Extra inventory would be $6,000 in the beginning and zero six months later; therefore

$$\text{average extra inventory} = \$3{,}000$$

$$\text{Carrying costs of average extra inventory} =$$

$$\$3{,}000 \times 25\% \times \tfrac{1}{2}\text{ year} = \$750 \times \tfrac{1}{2} = \$375$$

$$\text{Actual savings} = \text{cost savings} - \text{carrying costs} = \$500 - \$375 = \$125$$

The real savings from taking the discount would be only $125, so this deal would be worthwhile only if the store can work the extra inventory off in six months without getting stuck with any hard-to-sell merchandise.

Seasonal. A seasonal discount is a special discount given to retailers who place orders in advance of the normal buying period.

Promotional Allowance. Vendors offer this type of discount to retailers as compensation for money spent in advertising particular items. This discount may also be given for preferred window and interior display space for the vendor's products.

Cash. A premium is often granted by the vendor for cash payment prior to the time that the entire bill must be paid. The three components of the cash discount terms are a percentage discount; a period in which the discount may be taken; and the net credit period, which indicates when the full amount of the invoice is due. A cash discount stated as 2/10, n/30, means that the retailer must pay the invoice within 10 days to take advantage of the discount of 2 percent. The full amount is due in 30 days.

A cash discount may be taken in addition to a trade or another type of discount. Returning to the previously discussed example, the $8.95 net bill for the sport shirt, assume that the invoice is dated May 22. The retailer has 10 days to take the discount. Payment is due June 1 (nine days in May and one in June). If the invoice is paid within this time, the retailer will remit $8.77 instead of $8.95 ($8.95 × .02 = $.18; $8.95 − .18 = $8.77). If the retailer does not discount the invoice, then the bill must be paid in full by June 21.

The 2 percent in the example represents an annual interest rate of 36 percent. Why? The full invoice payment is due in 30 days. Since the 2 percent cash discount can be taken if the invoice is paid within 10 days, the discount is allowed for paying the bill 20 days earlier than necessary. There are 18 twenty-day periods in the year (figuring 360 days in a year), so this comes to 36 percent annually (18 × 2 percent).

Datings. The agreement between the vendor and the retailer as to the time the discount date will begin is known as **dating.**

Cash Datings. Technically, if the terms call for immediate payment, the process is known as cash dating and includes COD (cash on delivery) or CWO (cash with order). Cash datings do not involve discounts.

Two reasons may cause a negotiation to include cash terms. First, the seller may have a cash-flow problem and insist on cash on delivery (or with the order) to meet the bills incurred in the processing or distribution of the goods. Second, the retail buyer's credit rating may be such that the only way a seller will deal with the firm is on a cash basis.

Future Datings. Future datings include end of month, date of invoice, receipt of goods, and extra dating.

End-of-month (EOM). If an invoice carries EOM dating, the cash and net discount periods begin on the first day of the following month rather than on the invoice date. To allow for goods shipped late in the month, an invoice dated on or after the 25th of the month may be considered dated on the 1st of the following month. Thus, on a 2/10, n/30 EOM billing dated May 26, the 10-day discount period begins on July 1, not June 1. As a result, dating is further extended.

For example, if the $8.95 invoice for the sport shirt reads "2/10, n/30 EOM," and is dated May 22, the retailer has until June 10 to pay the invoice and take the 2 percent discount (that is, pay $8.77). If, on the other hand, the invoice is dated May 26 (within the same EOM terms), then the retailer has until July 10 to take the 2 percent discount.

Date of invoice (DOI). Date-of-invoice, or ordinary, dating, is self-explanatory. Prepayments begin with the invoice date, and both the cash discount and the net amount are due within the specified number of days from the invoice date. The DOI method is not particularly favorable to the retailer. If the vendor is slow in shipping the merchandise, payment may actually be due before the merchandise arrives.

Receipt of goods (ROG). Certain vendors are more distant from their customers than their competitors are. Rather than be at a competitive disadvantage with ordinary datings, they may offer receipt-of-goods (ROG) datings. With ROG datings, the time allowed for discounts and for payment of the net amount of the invoice begins with the date the goods are received at the buyer's place of business.

Extra. Extra datings allow the retailer extra time to take the cash discount. For example, 2/10-60 extra, n/90 means that the buyer has 70 days to take the cash discount and the net amount is due in 90 days. Returning to the example of the sport shirt, if the invoice is dated May 22 with ordinary dating, payment is due (assuming 2/10, n/30) on June 1. However, with 2/10-60 extra, n/90, the retailer can take the 2 percent cash discount through August 1 (10-day discount period through June 1, 29 additional days in June, and 31 days in July).

Transportation Charges

The final aspect of negotiation relates to who will bear the responsibility for shipping costs. The most favorable arrangement for the retailer is **FOB (free-on-board) destination,** in which the seller pays the freight to the destination and is responsible for damage or loss in transit. A more common shipping arrangement is **FOB origin,** which means that the vendor delivers the merchandise to the carrier and the retailer pays for the freight.

Small retailers typically do not have the power to bargain with a vendor on the discount or the transportation charges. On the other hand, large retailers may be able to obtain price concessions from the supplier by bargaining on discounts even though the list price of the merchandise does not change.

Follow-up

The last step in the buying cycle is follow-up. Follow-up consists of continuous checking to find more desirable suppliers, merchandise, and buying and merchandise control practices. Finding better suppliers can be accomplished only by getting to know existing suppliers and being alert to information sources on new ones who may come into the market. Improving merchandise selection is a matter of merchandise management, as discussed in Chapter 11. Better buying practices evolve from experimentation with improved methods whenever a problem appears.

CHAPTER HIGHLIGHTS

- Information partnerships, rather than adversarial relationships, are beginning to characterize the interaction between retailers and vendors. Large retailers have been especially assertive in establishing long-term partnerships with vendors.
- Electronic data interchange (EDI) and quick response (QR) mechanisms are at the heart of the emerging retailer-vendor relationships today. The application of such techniques has led to shorter lead times in merchandise delivery, and less on-hand inventory because of rapid replenishment schedules, especially for staples.
- Tensions inevitably emerge as a result of retailers bypassing such middlemen as wholesalers and independent sales representatives.
- The buying cycle consists of determining needs, selecting suppliers, negotiating purchases, and following up after the purchase.
- Buyers face different problems depending on whether the merchandise bought is primarily a staple, a seasonal item, or style or perishable merchandise. The goal in each instance is to establish or maintain inventory at the lowest level and still have a sufficient assortment from which customers can choose.
- The primary factors influencing the level of staples to be purchased include sales trends, profitability on various items, and discounts available.
- One way to establish buying levels for style and perishable items is to plot the progress of past styles to see how they typically behave and use the resulting information as a guide in future purchasing decisions.
- A variety of factors determine what stock should be ordered. Product shelf life may be the determining factor for some items. The length of time between order placement and receipt of goods is also important. Most businesses maintain a safety, or cushion, stock as a protection against variation in demand and delivery.
- Sources of information on suppliers include salespeople, business contacts, trade registers and directories, trade exhibits, and the yellow pages.
- Suppliers can be contacted in a variety of ways, including making purchases in a central market and using resident buying offices.
- Successful inventory management requires retailers to maintain an accurate and up-to-date record of sales and stock on hand for every item they sell. Inventory systems may be either manual or computer based.
- Factors to be considered in determining the best supplier include prices and discounts, quality, reliability, services, and accessibility.
- Group, or cooperative, buying entails joint purchasing of goods by a number of noncompeting, nonaligned stores. Other forms of buying include central buying and committee buying.
- Buyers normally attempt to negotiate on the following elements of the purchase price: cost price of the item, discounts, datings, and transportation charges.

STUDY QUESTIONS

1. Discuss the roles and responsibilities of a buyer.
2. In what ways can a buyer make market contacts?
3. What is a resident buying office? What are its functions? What are the various types of resident buying offices?
4. Describe the different methods of buying.

5. Explain the types of discounts available to retailers.
6. Explain the types of datings available to retailers.
7. Discuss each element of the buying cycle.
8. How have electronic data interchange and quick response programs changed the nature of the relationships between retailers and vendors?
9. What factors are leading to a shift of power in buying from the manufacturer to the retailer?
10. Under what circumstances are personal relationships likely to be important in negotiations with vendors?

PROBLEMS

1. A manufacturer offers terms of 2/20, n/60. The cash discount is equivalent to what annual rate of interest? (Use 360 days as a year.)
2. A lamp manufacturer offers terms of 2/10, n/40. The cash discount is equivalent to what annual rate of interest? (Use 360 days as a year.)
3. An invoice for a billed amount of $620 with terms of 3/10, n/30 ROG also shows a trade discount of 20 percent. If the invoice is paid before the end of the discount period, what is the amount the retailer must pay?
4. A manufacturer of hats quotes terms of 2/10, n/30 and grants retailers trade discounts of 20 percent and 10 percent. The list price of the hats is $480 per dozen. A retailer receives an invoice dated April 2 for eight dozen of these hats. The invoice is paid April 8. What is (a) the net cost to the retail store per hat and (b) the net amount of the cash discount taken?
5. An invoice dated March 5 in the amount of $2,800 with terms of 3/10, n/30, EOM and a trade discount to retailers of 10 percent, 5 percent, and 2 percent arrives with the merchandise on March 7. The invoice is paid May 2. What amount is due the vendor?
6. A manufacturer of women's blouses quoted terms of 3/10, n/30, EOM and grants retailers trade discounts of 15 percent, 10 percent, and 4 percent. The list price of the blouses is $300 per dozen. A retailer receives an invoice dated October 29 for nine dozen of these blouses. The invoice is paid December 2. What is the net cost to the retailer per blouse?
7. A manufacturer offers terms of 3/10, n/30, EOM. An invoice for a billed amount of $480 is dated July 29 and is to be paid August 5. What amount will the retailer pay the manufacturer?
8. A university supply store sells 1,000 mugs per year. The unit cost of each mug is $1. Variable costs per order placed are $5 and the inventory carrying cost percentage is 25 percent. What is the economic order quantity for this merchandise?
9. A retailer sells 10,000 widgets per year. The unit cost of each widget is $5. Variable costs per order are $25 and the inventory carrying cost percentage is 10 percent. What is the economic order quantity for this merchandise?
10. A retailer sells 120,000 gallons of premium gasoline a year to its customers. He orders 12,000 gallons at a time. Lead time for the orders is five days and the safety stock is a three-day supply. Sales are assumed to be constant over a 365-day year. Calculate the order point.
11. Using the information in question 10, and given that the order cycle is 14 days, determine the maximum to be maintained in inventory and the stock on hand.

APPLICATIONS

CASE 1: The Lyon's Den

The Lyon's Den had been a winner ever since Jane and Jim Lyon opened their gift shop in an old renovated home and moved in over it. The business was started in 1950. Over the years it had become "the" place for gifts and, eventually, decorating services in a city of some 70,000 and a trading area at least twice that size. Jane said on occasion that it was fashionable to live over the store. Their apartment was a virtual showcase for the many lines of fine silver, china, crystal, and decorator furniture items that were carried in the shop. The Lyons made no pretense of using their home to display their wares—they believed that such items in use were virtually presold.

Over the years, their lines expanded. To the traditional gift lines they added cosmetics and linens. Nothing in the shop was carried anywhere else in the trade area. Jane and Jim felt that exclusivity was a major advantage for The Lyon's Den.

Several years ago, Jane, who does the bulk of the buying (Jim is the decorator and accountant), believed that she had secured a market first for the area. She was able to acquire the finest and most prestigious lines of stainless Hensen. The name was not known in the market, but the quality was unsurpassed. Jane knew that, given an exclusive, she could develop a demand for the line that would make her a leading outlet for the merchandise. She had done this before; she knew merchandise and was a merchant with foresight—an entrepreneur who liked a challenge. The salesperson, whom she met at a regional trade show, assured her of market protection, and thus she set out to launch the new line.

She ran ads and invited special customers to attend a reception to meet the manufacturer. The market had probably never had such a dramatic introduction and perhaps never would again. After a year and a half, the line was one of the most profitable in the shop. Some brides were convinced that, without Hensen from The Lyon's Den, marriage was out of the question. Jane had done what she set out to do—create a market demand for the line and bring in new customers because of it.

Just this morning, Jane got a phone call from the New York office of Hensen's. The national sales manager was on the phone with some distressing news for The Lyon's Den. Lucille's Table Top, a new market entrant carrying medium- to high-priced table accessories, had just been into the New York showroom and had bought the Hensen line. The sales manager believed that, because Lucille's was in a shopping center some distance from The Lyon's Den, the competition would be negligible. In addition, the sales manager said that company policy was actually not to give exclusives in a market. The salesperson who originally opened the Lyons' account had not been aware of the policy.

Applying Retailing Principles

1. What options are available to Jane?
2. What are the advantages and disadvantages to a supplier of granting a retailer the exclusive right to sell a line of merchandise?

CASE 2: Quick Response at Sears

(Tim Troy, national logistics manager for Sears Roebuck, discussed his company in a retailing magazine; his comments are adapted for this case study.)

As Sears remodels all of its apparel floors to our new power format, we are reclaiming much of the old stockroom space and turning it into valuable selling space. The luxury we had in the past of 50 percent of our available square footage as backstock is no longer possible. As we remodel to an 80/20 ratio of selling to stock space, we have a strategic mandate to flow product more often and in smaller shipments.

The Sears of old carried a huge assortment of product on the floor with backstock in the store to ensure we were always at a 98 percent plus level of service. Obviously, this is no longer a profitable way to do business.

Quick response gave us a way to maintain these broad assortments, maintain a good level of service, and add thousands of square feet to our selling floors without major construction. At the per square foot cost of prime mall real estate, we see a huge profit potential in this strategy. This potential is only as great as our vendors' willingness to convert rapidly to EDI and quick response. To date, we have had excellent cooperation from all our partners.

The desire to be a true quick response retailer and the ability to execute that desire in a large corporate structure are sometimes very difficult. Step one is a full and complete upper management buy-in of the need for these new technologies and the need to form a true open partnership with our vendors. We were fortunate to have this kind of support since 1984.

Step two for Sears was naming a corporate EDI director with a support staff of four highly qualified executives with a mission statement to have all our vendors on the major EDI transaction sets by a specified date.

Strategies and Priorities. EDI supports three of our key business strategies:

- Increased focus on customer service.
- Reduced cost of operations.
- Enhanced relationship with our trading partners.

We view EDI as more than the transmission of purchase orders; it is also a process involving more and more transaction sets that will benefit both our vendors and Sears. We will use EDI to enhance the important relationships that we have with our trading partners.

In essence, I have the luxury of being able to tie all the pieces together from the initial writing of an order, dynamic routing of the trucks, expediting "hot products" through the fashion centers, to delivery to the stores. The key to all of this is the new Sears apparel merchandising system, which we implemented after three years of development to make this entire logistics effort flow easy, trackable, and on-line for all users. We've succeeded in incorporating all the separate systems of the past into one master system with one administrative group overseeing its proper training and use. We believe this will be a key to our success in the future. EDI and QR are obviously elements of our new system. It all starts with the transmission of that purchase order and ends when the salesperson scans the ticket at the register.

We created a systems manager position within each of the placement or distribution groups that works within each buying division with the charter of implementing EDI and QR. These groups work closely with the corporate EDI director to make the transition as painless as possible for all parties. These are the people who perform the following duties:

- Provide the vendors with unit plans by stockkeeping unit (SKU) or by store from sales history to start the program.
- Plan each item's promotional calendar and supply this data to our vendors.
- Supervise and coordinate the weekly transmission of sales and inventory data to our QR partners.

We have installed over 38,000 cash registers in all major stores. The point here is that accurately capturing POS information from bar-coded tickets is the heart of the VICS quick response system.

Sears has been actively pursuing quick response for many years. Since the mid-1970s we have been sharing sales and inventory data to improve production planning and reduce order lead time. Currently, we are transmitting sales and inventory information to 94 vendors across 138 softline and hardline product lines.

For example, we send weekly unit sales at the item level to Amory Garment so that they can react to sales and adjust production accordingly. For Levi Strauss, we're transmitting weekly and monthly sales data and generating orders on a weekly basis.

For Diehard batteries, mufflers, and shocks, we transmit actual point-of-sale data directly to the manufacturers. These vendors maintain a model stock by SKU by store, and automatically replenish the merchandise based on sales activity.

In men's workwear, we're on a full quick response program with three suppliers with their commitment to ship merchandise within 72 hours after receiving our electronic purchase orders.

We are actively pursuing quick response relationships with additional sources and will continue to increase our efforts in this important area.

Adapted with permission from Tim Troy, "Quick Response at Sears," *Discount Merchandiser,* October 1990, pp. 66–67.

Applying Retailing Principles

1. What advantages did the quick-response system achieve for Sears and its vendors?
2. What changes are likely to occur in inventory planning and merchandising strategies as a result of the implementation of the QR and EDI technologies?

NOTES

1. Michael Selz, "Independent Sales Reps Are Squeezed by the Recession," *The Wall Street Journal,* December 27, 1991, p. B1.
2. The material on the buying function is based on *Business Basics: Retail Buying Function,* Self Instructional Booklet 1010, Washington, D.C., U.S. Small Business Administration; for further reading, see Daniel Bello, "Retailer Buying Strategies at Merchandise Marts," in Terry Shimp et al. (eds.), *American Marketing Association Educators Proceedings* (Chicago: American Marketing Association 1986), pp. 178–81.
3. Ralph D. Skipp, Jr., *Retail Merchandising: Principles and Application* (Boston: Houghton Mifflin, 1976), pp. 12–14.
4. George Stalk, Jr. and Thomas M. Hout, *Competing Against Time* (New York: The Free Press, 1990), p. 110.
5. Kathleen Kerwin, "Stamped with Teen Seal of Approval," *BusinessWeek,* May 27, 1991, p. 83.
6. Andrew Tanzer, "Heroes in a Half-Shell," *Forbes,* October 28, 1991, p. 50.
7. Patrick Cash, *The Buyers Manual* (New York: National Retail Merchants Association, 1979), p. 388.
8. "Competing for the American Consumer: Partnering for Quick Response," *Coopers & Lybrand Executive Briefing,* April 1992, p. 2.
9. This material is reproduced, with permission, from Bill Stack, "Small Firms Can Reap Huge Gains with Electronic Data Interchange," *Marketing News,* April 1, 1991, p. 14.
10. For further reading see Susan S. Fiorito, "Testing a Portion of Sheth's Theory of Merchandise Buying Behavior with Small Apparel Retail Firms," *Entrepreneurship Theory and Practice,* Summer 1990, pp. 19–34.
11. Fiorito, "Testing a Portion."
12. "Centralized Buying: Wave of the Future?" *Supermarket News,* January 20, 1992, pp. 14–15.

C H A P T E R

14

Determining Retail Prices

THIS CHAPTER:

Relates the role of price to the retailer's competitive strategy.

Discusses store policies, consumer issues, and external factors that affect retail pricing.

Presents mathematical computations related to pricing.

Describes the kinds of price changes that may be made after the original pricing decision.

RETAILING CAPSULE

FAST-FOOD CHAINS HOPE DINERS SWALLOW NEW "VALUE" MENU OF HIGHER-PRICED ITEMS

"Reeling from brutal price wars, fast-food chains are redefining what's a bargain. . . . The slew of sandwiches that let people eat lunch for a dollar and change last year are barely mentioned in ads. And some of the cheapest items on the menus have been dropped altogether." For many chains, out-and-out discounting has run its course.

Restaurant analysts see companies keeping their discounted "come-ons" but repackaging them as only one of many ingredients in the value equation. Thus, many chains are expanding the concept of "value" to include the quality of the food, service, and ambience, in addition to price. Some chains are pushing the more expensive items on their menus and are featuring combination, or "combo," meals that allow the counter employees to steer customers toward items with higher profit margins. One McDonald's franchisee has added service to his value equation by offering patrons of his stores a free lunch if they are dissatisfied with their overall dining experience. McDonald's advertising campaign "What you want is what you get" focuses on image and reflects the idea that value is more than price.

Many franchisees believe that these changes have occurred none too soon. For example, at discount-leader Taco Bell, many independent franchisees rebelled against the company's pricing strategy and even formed an independent group, in part because of their dissatisfaction with what they regard as overly zealous pricing. In fact, the president of the franchisee group has indicated that many group members are ignoring Taco Bell's guidelines and are raising prices slightly on some items normally costing 59, 79, or 99 cents. The franchisees say the price increases have not negatively affected business and were necessary to revive profits. Even though Taco Bell has introduced a $1.99 Steak Burrito Bel Grande and offers a few other items priced above $1, company officials say they are sticking with the low-

price strategy that ignited the industry's price war. Industry analysts are watching the company closely to see how their low-price strategy fares in the long run. Although the chain has rung up big sales gains, in recent months its profit growth has slowed sharply. Furthermore, after establishing itself as the discount leader, many believe that the chain would have difficulty abandoning that image if inflation and other economic factors led to the need to increased prices.

Source: Based on Richard Gibson and Laurie M. Grossman, "Fast-Food Chains Hope Diners Swallow New 'Value' Menu of Higher-Priced Items," *The Wall Street Journal,* March 12, 1992, p. B1; Bradley Johnson, "Taco Bell Bucks Trend," *Advertising Age,* March 16, 1992, p. 4.

The Retailing Capsule illustrates the complexity of issues involved in price setting. It suggests that in setting prices management must consider competitors' prices, the effect of pricing decisions on channel partners, the relationship between pricing decisions and promotion campaigns, the need to look at the entire product line when making price decisions on individual products, and the effect of pricing on consumers' perceptions and image of the firm. Of particular significance, the capsule underscores management's need to understand the important role price can play in a firm's competitive strategy and the need to make price decisions that support that strategy.

Relating Price to Competitive Strategy

A retail pricing plan should start from explicitly defined objectives. For example, management must decide whether financial goals will be achieved by higher margins on merchandise and thus perhaps lower turnover, or lower margins and higher turnover. Various trade-offs must be made in such decisions. For instance, if management's objectives are short-run profit maximization, pricing should maximize cash flow. A policy of strengthening market position, on the other hand, probably would call for prices that are not above those of the market leader.

The absence of a distinct pricing policy often reflects a lack of strategic focus. For example, traditional department stores are being squeezed from both above and below their traditional market segments. Many have failed to develop a viable pricing strategy for the 1990s. They are being squeezed on the lower end by the value merchants such as Kmart and Wal-Mart, and on the higher end by style merchants such as I. Magnin and Saks and the specialty chains such as Benneton and the various Limited stores.[1] Similarly, traditional supermarkets are feeling the squeeze from gourmet and convenience stores on the one hand and superstores and warehouse stores on the other.[2]

One way of relating price to competitive strategy is to differentiate among retailers that price **above** the market level, **at** the market level, and **below** the market level.

Pricing above the Market Level

Some firms price above the competition. Reasons that stores are able to follow this strategy include the following: they carry unique or exclusive merchandise; they cater to customers who are not price conscious and who want the highest-quality and style goods; they provide unusual services; they have a prestigious image customers are willing to pay for; they create professional salespeople who are customer oriented and knowledgeable and who wish to develop long-term customer relationships; and they offer conveniences such as location and time.

West Point Market in Akron, Ohio, is an example of a merchant with above-the-market pricing. The firm caters to affluent shoppers who want quality merchandise and personal attention. The store stocks an extensive selection of gourmet and specialty foods, employs more people than the average supermarket, and has used color, lighting, artwork, flowers, and other design components to create an atmosphere unusual for a food store. Other well-known examples of above-the-market retailers include Neiman-Marcus, Haagen-Dazs, Tiffany, Gucci, and Bergdorf's Men's.

Pricing at the Market Level

At-the-market pricers offer prices roughly the same as their competitors. When following such a strategy, the retailer tries to make the store different in ways other than price and thus competes on a nonprice basis. Department stores such as Bloomingdale's, Marshall Field, and J. C. Penney are examples of middle-of-the-road pricers. Penney's goal, for example, is to offer merchandise which accounts for 80 percent of the total transactions in a regional shopping center. Management is willing to give up the top and bottom price points. The top price points would require a level of expertise and acceptance of risks in high fashion that Penney management does not wish to pursue. The lower price points reflect merchandise quality levels below Penney standards and would require them to compete directly with discount stores. Penney management believes that the store has no distinctive competencies at the top and bottom price points; thus, the store is positioned as a middle-of-the-road fashion retailer offering strong price-to-value relationships. Other examples of at-the-market pricers are supermarkets such as Kroger and Publix, Western Auto stores, and Rexall drugstores.

Pricing below the Market Level

Below-the-market pricers offer acceptable-quality merchandise at low prices. Examples include off-price retailers, warehouse grocery firms, warehouse clubs, factory outlet stores, and discount houses. Competition in these operations is almost entirely on a price basis. Specific retail firms that are successfully emphasizing consistently low prices are Wal-Mart, Home Depot, Toys 'R' Us, Staples in office products, IKEA in contemporary furniture, and Paperama in paper goods.

Below-the-market pricing is a difficult pricing strategy to carry out and maintain. To successfully implement such a strategy, the firm must focus on lowering the cost position of the firm. Many retailers have failed using this strategy because they have been unable to constantly monitor and adjust their cost components. To reduce costs, firms attempt to obtain the best prices possible for their merchandise; locate the business in an inexpensive location or facility; closely control inventory and limit the lines to fast-moving items; offer no or limited services; and, in general, monitor all cost components on a continuous basis to determine where cost savings can be realized. IKEA has even been highly successful in shifting a variety of cost burdens onto the consumer and actually getting him to like it. When a shopper selects, for example a bookcase, she pays for it at a central location and then picks up the merchandise from a separate distribution area or selects it from warehouse shelves. Once the consumer is home, he must assemble the bookcase himself (only one tool—an Allen wrench—is needed, and it comes with the purchase).[3]

We cannot emphasize enough the danger of price competition to retailers whose cost structure makes it impossible for them to compete on the basis of price in the long run—for instance, department stores attempting to match prices with warehouse clubs. Department stores and specialty stores must compete on a nonprice basis. Otherwise, the margins on their merchandise would be reduced to such a level that the future of the firm would be in doubt. These outlets have found that a more viable competitive strategy includes offering high-quality private brands and excellent service in an exciting, vibrant, upscale atmosphere.

A variety of other factors affect retail price setting, in addition to the overall competitive strategy of the firm. The following sections focus on store policies, consumer issues, and external factors that affect price decision making.

STORE POLICIES AFFECTING RETAIL PRICING

All stores have pricing policies that are often based on industry practice. Some of these policies are discussed in the following sections.

A One-Price versus a Flexible-Price Policy

The majority of retail firms in the United States offer goods at one take-it-or-leave-it price. Bargaining with customers is unusual. In other countries, however, such as Mexico or Italy, varying prices and haggling are common practice. In the United States, some stores selling big-ticket items such as automobiles, appliances, and furniture follow a variable-price policy and bargaining occurs over the price paid for the product. However, some automobile dealers today are adopting a one-policy policy and are refusing to negotiate price (see Case 1 at the end of the chapter).

In some product categories (for example, automobiles, tires, and batteries) the variable price may be due to trade-ins. If customers are good bargainers, the retailer may actually take a lower price than desired. Thus, retailers who have a trade-in policy should plan their original prices very carefully.

Retailers can follow a variable price policy even when they do not negotiate with consumers on the price of the product itself. Negotiating over whether to charge for delivery and installation and varying the price of warranties can all result in a variable price policy.

Certain advantages exist in a store with a one-price policy. Customers do not expect to bargain, so salespeople and customers can save time. Furthermore, salespeople are not under pressure to reduce prices.

Price-Line Policy

Retailers practicing a **price-lining** strategy feature products at a limited number of prices, reflecting varying merchandise quality. A price-lining strategy can be implemented with either rigid **price points** or more flexible **price zones.** Using suits as an example, a merchant might establish a limited number of price points to indicate quality differences between merchandise. The "good" suits might be priced at $175, the "better" suits at $225, and the "best" suits at $300. Alternatively, the retailer may decide to use price zones instead of rigid price points. For example, prices for good suits might fall between $175 and $200.

Price lining offers certain advantages. For example, some customers become confused and cannot make up their minds when they see too many prices. Price lining makes shopping easier for consumers because there are fewer prices to consider. Furthermore, inventories can be controlled more easily. The salespeople can learn the stock more easily with price lining. And it is much easier to explain differences between the merchandise when it is carefully planned and priced to show differences. In addition, the buyer may not have to shop as many vendors if specific retail prices are sought.

Certain problems exist in price lining, however. The retailer may feel hemmed in by the price line and lose some of his or her flexibility. Also, selection may be limited. If wholesale prices rise and fall rapidly, it may be difficult to maintain rigid price points. This is a reason for the use of price zones.

Leader Pricing Policy

In **leader pricing,** the retailer takes a less-than-normal markup or margin on an item to increase store traffic. (Some call this loss-leader pricing, implying a loss of the normal amount of markup or margin.) In using leader pricing, the retailer is trying to attract customers to the store who will also purchase items carrying normal profit margins. However, if customers only buy the leaders, the retailer is in trouble. Thus, in selecting the leader item, retailers should choose products that will stimulate purchases of other, perhaps complementary, goods. For example, a food retailer may lower the price of ribs, which, in turn, might stimulate the sale of barbecue sauce, charcoal, starter fluid, and food products typically eaten with barbecued ribs. In a department store, using dresses as leaders might stimulate the sale of shoes, jewelry, and other accessories. Other characteristics of good price leader products are as follows:

- They are well-known and widely used items.
- They are items that are not usually bought in large quantities and stored.
- Such items have a high price elasticity of demand.
- They are priced low enough to attract many buyers.

Single-Price Policy

One of the fastest-growing trends in retailing today is the **single-price policy,** in which retailers sell all merchandise in the store at the same price. The single-price store is a retailing concept that goes back a century to Frank W. Woolworth's first five-and-ten store (see A Profile in Excellence).

An example of a single-price retail chain is Everything's $1.00 (see Exhibit 14–1). The Milwaukee-based chain has over 200 outlets and plans to add more. The latest trend in single-price retailing is specialization in clothing. The man often credited with bringing the single-price concept to clothing is Henry Jacobs, chairman of One Price Clothing Stores, an operation based in Duncan, South Carolina, that does $110 million in sales. Jacobs's 365 stores offer in-season, first-quality goods at the set price of $7 per item.[4]

Single-price retailers must maintain a low cost structure. Smart buying is a must. They seek out odd lots, closeout items, and factory overruns. Advertising costs are kept low, with the chains relying on word of mouth to promote their deals. In addition, capital costs for such stores are generally low.

Market analysts say that single-price stores such as those mentioned above are here to stay. They believe that, regardless of economic conditions, people of all walks of life are interested in getting good deals.

Price Discount Policy

Retailers may offer a variety of discounts, such as cash discounts, frequent shopper discounts, and discounts for specific segments of consumers.

Cash Discounts. Some retailers give a discount to customers who pay by check or cash rather than credit. The Cash Discount Act, passed in 1981, allows retailers to offer unlimited discounts to encourage cash payments. The discounts do not have to be offered to all customers and they do not

A Profile in Excellence

FRANK W. WOOLWORTH

At the time of Frank W. Woolworth's death in 1919, he had won fortune not in showing how little could be sold for much, but how much could be sold for little.

F. W. Woolworth was born in 1852. He received a public school education in a small town near Watertown, New York. At the age of 21, his dream of working in retailing became a reality when he took a job as a stockboy in the town's leading store. It was here that he developed the new idea of the five-cent counter, where every item held the same price. In 1879, he ventured to Utica, New York, and opened a five-cent store of his own, which was later relocated to Lancaster. This was the location of the first F. W. Woolworth.

With the new store, Woolworth developed three revolutionary practices that have become commonplace today. The first and second were that all merchandise was to be sold at a single price with spot cash transactions only. The third was that all goods were to be arranged on the counter so that customers could hold them. In 16 months' time, Woolworth opened four stores, closed three, paid all his debts, and had a net worth of $2,037.60.

After opening hundreds of successful five-and-dime stores, Woolworth formed F. W. Woolworth and Company in 1905. In 1912, he merged with five other corporations. At the same time, Woolworth became responsible for the world's first modern skyscraper, the Woolworth Building in New York City. Even though the idea of the five-and-dime has virtually disappeared, many Woolworth stores remain in operation.

have to be clearly and conspicuously made known to all customers. Thus, retailers can make such decisions on a customer-by-customer basis. Also, the discount can be based on a total amount of purchase or on one specific purchase.

Cash discounts can be profitable if retailers have a high proportion of credit sales, a high proportion of credit customers who are willing to pay by cash or check as a result of a discount, and large-ticket items or large-volume purchases.

Frequent Shopper Discounts. Some retailers are experimenting with frequent shopper discounts, such as the frequent flyer programs offered by the airlines, to generate greater sales volume and customer loyalty. Shoppers' cumulative purchases are tracked throughout the year, and bonuses are offered after shoppers reach a specified dollar volume of purchase. Additional bonuses are sometimes given to stimulate shopping on slow days or to clear out slow-moving merchandise.

Discounts to Specific Customer Segments. Increasing numbers of retailers are giving discounts to certain segments of consumers. For example, many retailers offer discounts to senior citizens. In addition, some retailers offer discounts to students and military personnel.

EXHIBIT 14–1

Courtesy Everything's $1.00

One of retailing's fastest-growing trends is the single-price retailer, such as Everything's $1.00.

Consumer Rebates

A **consumer rebate** is a sum of money given to the consumer by the manufacturer after, and thus separate from, the original purchase. Rebates are commonly used by manufacturers wanting to increase the sale of slow-moving merchandise. For example, in recent years, rebates of $500 to $1,500 on automobiles have been common.

Technically, rebates do not affect the retailer's initial pricing decisions because they are given by the manufacturer. However, retailers may lower their markups to further stimulate sales. Furthermore, rebates, if sizable, are often accepted as a down payment by retailers on the item to be purchased.

In some merchandise lines such as small appliances, retailers are increasingly resisting consumer rebates. Many retailers contend that customers are being trained to wait for rebates before making a purchase. Retailers fear that such programs will permanently lower their price structure. As a result, Kmart advised its small-appliance vendors that it would no longer advertise products carrying rebates. Similarly, Cotter and Company, a Chicago-based dealer cooperative, advised its resources that it would no longer accept rebates or feature them in its True Value direct-mail advertising programs.

Product and Service Issues

Retailers' pricing decisions are affected by type of products carried, brands carried, and services offered.

Type of Products. One product issue affecting pricing decisions relates to whether the products offered by the retailer are primarily convenience, shopping, or specialty goods. The nature of the product carried especially affects the extent to which a retailer has flexibility in establishing prices that are different from those of other retailers carrying the same goods. If products are viewed by consumers as convenience goods, prices do not vary greatly from store to store. Consumers do not believe it is worth their time to shop around for a better price (or quality) for convenience items because the savings are not likely to be worth the extra effort of comparison shopping. Thus, the retailer has only a little latitude in the pricing of these goods. A retailer has more leeway in setting prices for shopping goods. These are items for which consumers carefully compare price and quality differences before making a purchase decision. The retailer has the greatest latitude in pricing specialty goods in comparison to convenience and shopping goods. Specialty items are products consumers know they want and are willing to make an effort to acquire because they will not accept a substitute. To them, price is not particularly important.

Type of Brands. Another product-related issue concerns the extent to which a retailer carries private brands and generics in addition to manufacturer brands. Many retailers, such as The Limited, J. C. Penney, and Safeway, have their own private brands—brands owned by a retail or wholesale firm rather than by a manufacturer. Such brands are also referred to as dealer brands. A manufacturer brand, often referred to as a national brand, is owned by a manufacturer. A comparison of private and manufacturer brands is illustrated in Exhibit 14–2. A private brand may be carried only by the owner or the owner's designee. A manufacturer brand may be carried by anyone who buys from the manufacturer of the brand. Bokar is a private brand of coffee owned by A&P; Maxwell House is a manufacturer brand owned by General Foods Corp.

If private brands are featured, the retailer may offer them at prices lower than manufacturer brands and still make a good profit. This is possible because the retailer can pay less for the private-brand merchandise than for comparable manufacturer brands. Consequently, the merchant has more freedom in pricing private-brand items.

Department stores and general merchandise retailers are increasingly turning to private-brand merchandise as a source of competitive advantage, especially in the face of the challenges posed by off-price retailers. Designer labels such as Calvin Klein at one time were available exclusively in better department stores. Over time, the manufacturers of some

EXHIBIT 14–2

Courtesy Walgreens Company

Private brand (Walgreens) and manufacturer's brand (Kodak)

designer labels have broadened their distribution base to include off-price retailers as well as discount stores. The result was that the labels lost their exclusivity and became price "footballs" for the discounters. The department stores, because of their overhead, could not meet the prices of the off-pricers and discounters. As a result, they turned to private labels as a way of maintaining greater control over their merchandise lines and protecting their store image.

The question of generic merchandise and pricing is also important. **Generics** are "no-brand-name" goods, as shown in Exhibit 14–3. In buying generics, consumers are accepting lower quality in return for lower prices. Although generics contain lower-quality ingredients, consumers can save an average of 30 percent over manufacturer brands and 15 percent over private brands when buying generics. And generics are appealing to retailers because higher profits may be made on generics than on branded goods, even though generics are priced lower. Sales of generics appear strongest in low-ego-involved merchandise such as paper products and other staples. In general, however, generics appear to have peaked in popularity.

Variations in the Service Mix. Increasingly, retailers are competing in certain lines of business on a price and nonprice basis at the same time by varying the service mix. For example, gasoline service stations have full-service pumps that sell gasoline for a higher price per gallon than their

EXHIBIT 14–3

Courtesy of Delchamps

No-brand generics afford customers price advantages.

self-service pumps. Arco has gone one step farther and eliminated its service of in-house credit. The cost savings experienced by dropping credit cards has been passed on to consumers in the form of lower prices. Some furniture outlets are following a similar approach by charging for delivery and installation.

CONSUMER ISSUES AFFECTING RETAIL PRICING

A variety of consumer issues affect price decision making in retail operations. The following sections will focus on the issues of consumer demand and price sensitivity, price perceptions, psychological pricing, and consumer pressures.

Consumer Demand and Price Sensitivity

The level of consumer demand for a particular product or service affects price setting. Higher prices can be set for items for which consumer demand is strong. Lower prices may be required for products with less consumer demand.

A related issue is **price elasticity** of demand, or the extent to which consumer demand is responsive to price changes. Price elasticity is the ratio of the percentage change in the quantity demand to a percentage change in price:

$$e = \frac{Q_2 - Q_1/\frac{1}{2}(Q_2 + Q_1)}{P_2 - P_1/\frac{1}{2}(P_2 + P_1)}$$

The coefficient of price elasticity is usually negative because price and quantity demanded tend to be inversely related; that is, when the price

FIGURE 14–1

ELASTICITY OF DEMAND

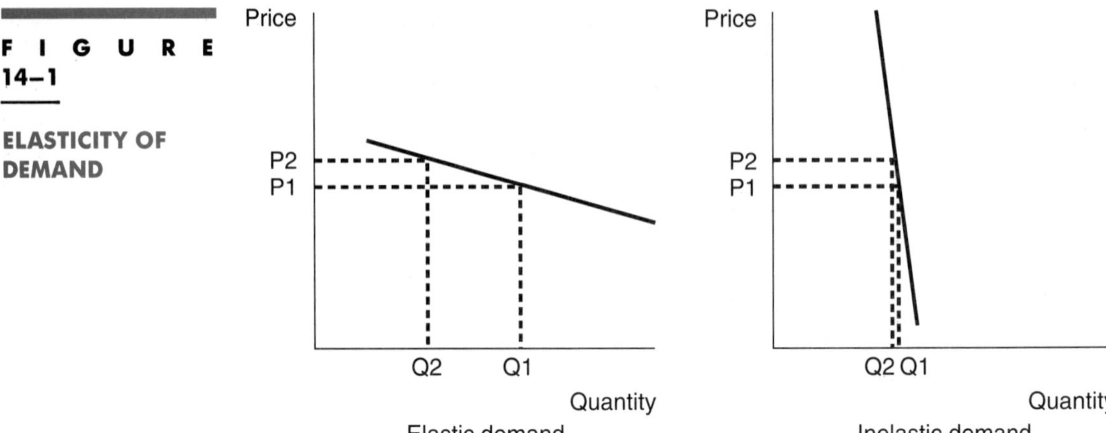

falls, the quantity demanded tends to rise, and when the price rises, the demand tends to fall. Thus, retail managers are more concerned with the size of the coefficient. A coefficient of more than one indicates that demand is elastic; a coefficient of less than one indicates that demand is inelastic. The percentage change in quantity demanded as a result of a percentage change in price is much greater for elastic than for inelastic demand. The demand curve on the left in Figure 14–1 illustrates elastic demand. A price increase from P_1 to P_2 results in a greater than proportionate decrease in quantity demanded (from Q_1 to Q_2). The demand curve on the right in Figure 14–1 illustrates inelastic demand—a price increase from P_1 to P_2 leads to a less than proportionate change in quantity demanded (from Q_1 to Q_2).

Retailers can determine whether demand is elastic or inelastic by analyzing how total revenue changes with respect to a price change. If demand is elastic, total revenue changes in the opposite direction of the price change. Thus, if price declines, total revenue increases; if price increases, total revenue decreases. If demand is inelastic, total revenue and price change in the same direction. If price declines, total revenue declines; if price increases, total revenue increases. The following example illustrates these relationships:

Price	×	Units demanded	=	Total revenue
$ 9		200 units		$1,800
10		150 units		1,500
11		140 units		1,540

With a price increase from $9 to $10, total revenue decreased from $1,800 to $1,500. Demand is elastic because price and total revenue changed in opposite directions. However, with a price increase from $10 to $11, total revenue likewise increased from $1,500 to $1,540. Demand is thus inelastic because price and total revenue changed in the same direction.

Understanding price elasticity of demand can help retailers make price change decisions for specific items of merchandise. For example, if a retailer is facing an elastic demand situation, a price reduction may be a viable strategic move because the result would be an increase in total revenue. Of course, before reducing price, the retailer would want to consider other factors, in addition to elasticity, such as the probable reaction of competitors. On the other hand, if demand is inelastic (such as the demand for specialty items such as antiques or original art works), reducing price would not be a good decision because a price reduction leads to a reduction in total revenue. The retailer might consider a price increase because such an action would lead to an increase in total revenue. However, retailers must be concerned about the magnitude of a price change, as demand tends to be more elastic for large price changes than for small price increases.

Price Perceptions

Consumer perceptions are important factors in establishing prices. For example, consumers have ranges of acceptable prices for products, and prices outside the acceptable ranges—whether too high or too low—are objectionable. Demand provides not only an upper constraint on pricing decisions—pricing what the market will bear—but also a lower constraint. Below certain price points, which vary widely from category to category, there is no elasticity of demand and lowering prices further does not have the classic effect of adding sales.

Research has also shown that, when buyers are given a range of prices, they are likely to choose the middle-priced item. Therefore, retailers can influence the choice of products that are perceived as middle priced. In particular, retailers who use price lists or price catalogs can influence consumers' price perceptions this way.

In judging prices, customers who find it difficult to compare the prices of individual items generalize from the overall price image of the store. Price images tend to be relatively stable, even in the face of special promotions. Management should thus consider not only the pricing of individual items but also the need for a favorable overall price image. A store may not need to place low prices on every item to have a low-price image; only certain key items need to be priced lower than expected.

Finally, consumer price perceptions tend to be imprecise about exact amounts, although reliable within well-defined ranges. Price-conscious shoppers perceive prices more accurately than less price-conscious shoppers. The number of stores shopped and the frequency of shopping trips also affect price perception accuracy.

Psychological Pricing

Certain types of prices have long been held to have special psychological effects on consumers. Odd-ending prices are set just below the dollar figure, such as $1.99 instead of $2.00. Legend has it that retailer Rowland

FIGURE 14–2

ODD PRICING

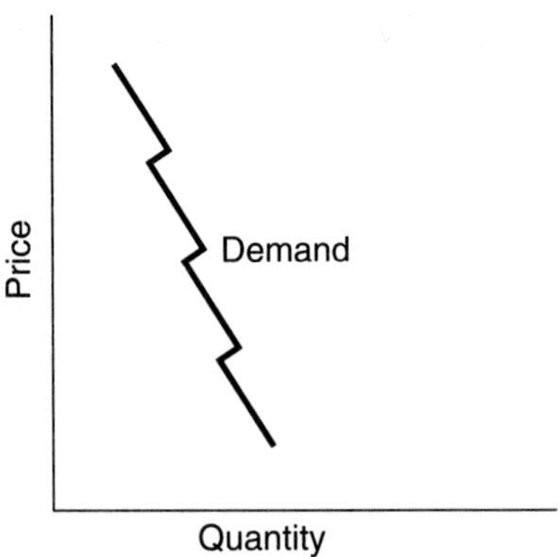

Macy instituted odd digits in the 1890s to keep employees honest. With odd prices, clerks had to make change and account for the transaction on a cash register. The wait also may have encouraged impulse purchases.

Although the phenomenon is not verified, retailers practicing odd pricing believe that consumers perceive odd-ending prices to be substantially lower than prices with even endings, despite the fact that the prices are only slightly lower in actual dollar terms. Although odd price endings are believed by many to have psychological value, some retailers prefer the even endings, wanting the extra markup, even if it is only a few pennies. Many transactions of a few cents could be important over time.

Odd pricing often suggests that the price has been established at the lowest level possible. Thus, consumers may actually buy less when the price is lowered from the appropriate odd price to the next lower even-numbered price. This behavior by consumers is contrary to economists' law of demand and results in a jagged demand curve for the product, as illustrated in Figure 14–2.

Consumer Pressures

Consumer pressures for unit pricing information, individual item price marking, and similar shopping aids also affect retail pricing practices. For example, some states now require retailers to price mark individual items instead of shelf marking only. Such a requirement adds to the retailer's cost. Similarly, activist consumer groups often publish prices of merchandise (especially food products) sold in competing stores in efforts to force prices down.

External Factors Affecting Retail Prices

A variety of external (environmental) factors affect retail price setting. The following sections focus on the issues of supplier policies, economic conditions, and the market structure in which the retailer operates.

FOCUS 14–1

PRICING BELOW SUGGESTED RETAIL

Randy Kramer, owner of the Racket Doctor tennis shop in Los Angeles, shaved a few dollars off the price of prestigious Prince rackets. Other retailers complained to Prince Manufacturing Inc. that Kramer had violated the company's price rules. A sales representative informed Kramer that because of the complaints Prince had no choice but to cut him off. Prince did and Kramer lost his most popular line. When Gorilla Bicycle Company in Salt Lake City threatened to sell popular Specialized mountain bikes at discount prices, the manufacturer refused to supply Gorilla not only with bikes but also tires and accessories.

The practice known as resale price maintenance is generally prohibited by federal antitrust laws. Over the years, however, the Supreme Court has carved out numerous exceptions, giving manufacturers considerable latitude to dictate higher retail prices. In fact, according to antitrust experts, practices that might appear to dampen competition aren't necessarily illegal. For example, the Supreme Court has ruled that manufacturers may impose prices unilaterally, although they may not do so in league with retailers.

Thus, one critical question is whether manufacturers conspire with some retailers to eliminate others. This issue becomes relevant when one retailer notifies the manufacturer that another retailer has engaged in price cutting. For example, what about the rivals' complaints to Prince about the Racket Doctor? Prince says that it does receive complaints about discounters from other retailers, but that it does not discuss one retailer's business with another. It also says that it does not seek complaints from a dealer about the actions of another retailer; it merely accepts complaints.

What are the justifications for manufacturers' suggesting minimum retail prices and refusing to sell to those who price below suggested retail? Are there any negative implications? If so, what are they?

Source: Based on Paul M. Barrett, "Anti-Discount Policies of Manufacturers Are Penalizing Certain Cut-Price Stores," *The Wall Street Journal,* June 18, 1991, p. B1.

Supplier Policies

Suppliers will often suggest prices to retailers. If the retailer depends heavily on a particular supplier, then the retailer will price at the suggested price. In such cases, the retailer gives up pricing flexibility in order to carry the brand. See Focus 14–1 for a more detailed look at the issue of suggested retail prices and the possible repercussions for retailers who price below suggested retail.

Often manufacturers will offer retailers **distributor allowances,** which are discounts or extended payment terms or a combination designed to encourage them to purchase additional merchandise. Such discounts enable retailers, in turn, to lower their prices to stimulate sales. For example, Zenith Radio Corporation has given distributor allowances to help expand the sales of its television sets. Similarly, as the stereo equipment and VCR business has entered the maturity stage of the product life cycle, firms such as Sony, JVC, Hitachi, and others have offered

TABLE 14–1

PRICE CONCEPTS

Original retail price	$1,000
Less reductions	−200
Sales retail price	$ 800

distributor discounts of 15 to 20 percent and extended payment plans to encourage dealers to buy more stock.

Economic Conditions

Retailers must be conscious of economic conditions and their effect on pricing decisions. During periods of inflation, consumers expect (but do not welcome) price increases. In times of recession, prices may go down. Retailers must be sensitive to economic changes because they often require price adjustments.

In addition, retailers must be aware of any voluntary or required government price controls that can limit price decisions. Clearly, changing and uncertain economic conditions make pricing complex.

Market Structure

The degree of competition in the market will greatly affect pricing decisions. If little competition exists, the retailer has greater leeway and flexibility in setting prices than in situations with a great deal of competition.[5] For example, a retailer with an exclusive on a brand in a market can price with greater freedom than retailers whose products are carried by many retailers in the market.

In addition, competitors' actions in the pricing area must be monitored. A good retailer is aware of prices being charged by competitive outlets. Furthermore, in making initial price decisions and price change decisions, a retailer must consider competitors' probable reactions.

THE ARITHMETIC OF RETAIL PRICING

This section presents information to aid your understanding of the arithmetic of pricing. Every retailer is faced with the issues explained in this section.

Concepts of Price and Markup

As a beginning point, several terms need to be defined. First, as shown in Table 14–1, price can be looked at in two ways. The **original retail price** ($1,000) is the first price at which an item (or a group of items) is offered for sale. The **sales retail price** ($800) is the final selling price, or the actual amount the customer paid. Thus, before the item was sold, a $200 reduction or markdown occurred. (Reductions can also include employee discounts and shortages or shrinkage.)

Table 14–2 shows that markup can be viewed in two ways. **Initial markup** is the difference between the cost of merchandise and the original

TABLE 14–2

MARKUP CONCEPTS

The Concept of Initial Markup	
Original retail price	$102,000
Less invoice cost	80,000
Initial markup	$ 22,000
The Concept of Maintained Markup	
Original retail price	$102,000
Less planned reductions	2,000
Sales retail	100,000
Less invoice cost	80,000
Maintained markup	$ 20,000

retail price, or $22,000 ($102,000 − $80,000 = $22,000). The initial markup percentage is the initial markup expressed as a percentage of the original retail price, in this case 21.6 percent ($22,000/$102,000). **Maintained markup** is the difference between invoice cost and the sales retail price, or $20,000 ($100,000 − $80,000 = $20,000). The maintained markup percentage is the maintained markup expressed as a percentage of sales retail, in this case 20 percent ($20,000/$100,000). Maintained markup covers operating expenses and provides the retailer with a profit. Maintained markup and initial markup differ by the $2,000 reductions. For purposes of this discussion, maintained markup can be considered the same as gross margin.

Planning Markup Goals

Retailers must determine the initial markup to be placed on merchandise as it goes on the sales floor. Some retailers do not use a planning process to establish initial markup percentages. They simply add a fixed percentage to wholesale prices. Many retailers, for example, first set prices merely by more or less doubling the price they pay wholesalers. If the goods do not sell at that price, the retailer marks them down. Suppliers understand this system and often establish their prices so that, when increased by the typical markup, the result is the retail selling price they want for their merchandise.

Other retailers use a planning process to establish initial and maintained markup goals. As part of this planning procedure, the retailer must develop projected figures for sales, operating expenses, reductions, and profits for the operating period. These figures can then be used in the following formula to calculate the initial markup percentage that should be placed on merchandise as it comes into the store:

$$\text{Initial markup percentage} = \frac{\text{Expenses} + \text{Profit} + \text{Reductions}}{\text{Sales retail} + \text{Reductions}}$$

Assume that management has forecast sales of a merchandise line at $100,000, expenses of $15,000, a profit return of 5 percent of sales ($5,000),

TABLE 14–3

PLANNING MARKUP GOALS

$$\text{Initial markup percentage} = \frac{\textit{Expenses + Profit + Reductions}}{\textit{Sales retail + Reductions}} = \frac{\$15{,}000 + \$5{,}000 + \$2{,}000}{\$100{,}000 + \$2{,}000} = 21.6\%$$

$$\text{Maintained markup percentage} = \frac{\textit{Expenses + Profit}}{\textit{Sales retail}} = \frac{\$15{,}000 + \$5{,}000}{\$100{,}000} = 20 \text{ percent}$$

and reductions as 2 percent of sales ($2,000). As shown in Table 14–3, a planned initial markup of $22,000, or 21.6 percent, is necessary to maintain a markup of $20,000, or 20 percent.

Of course, a retailer cannot expect to have a uniform initial markup policy. That kind of policy would suggest that every item brought into a department would carry the same initial markup. Too many store policies and external factors exist for a uniform markup to make sense.

Planned markup figures become a good check. Actual performance in markup during an operating period can be checked against what has been planned.

Pricing Computations

Every retailer needs practice in computing some routine relationships among cost, initial markup, and the original retail price. There is no need to memorize formulas, although we will present formulas for those who like them. Simply remember that Cost + Initial markup = Original retail price. Before working specific pricing problems, let's first look at the ways markup percentages can be expressed.

Expressing Markup Percentages. The initial markup percentage can be expressed as a percentage of the cost of the item or as a percentage of the retail selling price. To illustrate, assume that a color television set costs the retailer $500. The original retail selling price is set at $800. The dollar amount of the markup is $300. The initial markup percentage based on cost is 60 percent ($300/$500). Based on retail, the markup is 37.5 percent ($300/$800). Remember that the markup percentage on cost = $ markup/$ cost, and the markup percentage on retail = $ markup/$ retail.

In working with pricing, the buyer is often confronted with the need to convert a markup on retail to a markup on cost or vice versa.

Conversion of Markup—Retail to Cost. Assume that a supplier quotes an initial markup of 42 percent on retail. What is the equivalent markup on cost? The formula is shown below:

$$\text{Markup percentage on cost} = \frac{\text{Markup percentage on retail}}{100\% - \text{Markup percentage on retail}}$$

If the retail markup is 42 percent, then retail is 100 percent, and cost must be 58 percent. So markup as a percentage of cost is .42/.58 = .724, or 72.4 percent. In other words, a 42 percent markup on retail is the same thing as a 72.4 percent markup on cost. Clearly, markup on cost will always be larger than markup on retail because the cost base is smaller than the retail base.

Conversion of Markup–Cost to Retail. Suppose that a vendor quotes an initial markup of 60 percent on cost. What is the equivalent markup on retail? Use the following formula:

$$\text{Markup percentage on retail} = \frac{\text{Markup percentage on cost}}{100\% + \text{Markup percentage on cost}}$$

If the cost markup is 60 percent, then cost must be 100 percent, and retail 160 percent. So markup on a retail base is .60/1.60 = .375, or 37.5 percent. In other words, a 60 percent markup on cost is the same as a 37.5 percent markup on retail.

Pricing Problems. The following problems illustrate the various types of pricing decisions made by retailers.

1. A chair costs a retailer $420. If a markup of 40 percent of retail is desired, what should the retail price be?

If 60 percent = $420, then 100 percent = $420/.60, or $700, the retail price needed to achieve the desired markup of 40 percent on retail.

Formula: Whenever the retail price is to be calculated and the dollar cost and markup percent on retail are known, the problem can be solved with the following equation:

$$\$\ \text{Retail} = \frac{\$\ \text{Cost}}{100\% - \text{Retail markup percentage}}$$

2. A dryer retails for $300. The markup is 28 percent of cost. What was the cost of the dryer?

If 128 percent = $300, then 100 percent = $300/1.28, or $234.37, the retailer's cost.

Formula: Whenever the cost is to be calculated and the retail price and markup percentage on cost are known, the problem can be solved as follows:

$$\$\ \text{Cost} = \frac{\$\ \text{Retail}}{100\% + \text{Cost markup percentage}}$$

3. A retailer prices a jacket so that the markup amounts to $36. This is 45 percent of retail. What is the cost of the item and its retail selling price?

If 45 percent = \$36, then 100 percent = \$36/.45, or \$80. If the retail price is \$80 and markup is \$36, cost is \$80 − \$36 = \$44.

Formula: Whenever the dollar markup and the retail markup percentage are known, the retail price can be determined as follows:

$$\$\text{ Retail} = \frac{\$\text{ Retail markup}}{\text{Retail markup percentage}}$$

PRICING ADJUSTMENTS

In practice, retailers may raise or lower prices after the original pricing decisions have been made. These pricing adjustments may be additional markups or markdowns.

Additional Markups

During inflationary periods, additional **markups** may be needed. Such adjustments are made when the retailer's costs are increasing. Some consumers resent such adjustments; they view price increases as unjustified because the initial price was established based on a given cost structure.

Markdowns

A **markdown** is a reduction in the original selling price of a product. As shown in an earlier section of the chapter, markdowns are a part of a planned pricing strategy and affect decisions on initial markups.

Markdowns are probably the most widely used way of moving items that do not sell at the original retail price. One of the most famous retail department store organizations in the United States is Filene's Basement in Boston. This firm made its name through its widely known "automatic markdown policy." The policy operates as follows: When an item has been in the store for 12 days, it is marked down to 75 percent of list; after 6 more days, it is reduced to 50 percent; when 6 more days pass, it is reduced to 25 percent; and after 30 days, it is given to charity. Very little merchandise is given to charity.

Markdowns may also be used for promotional reasons. The goods may not be slow moving, but markdowns create more activity.

Markdowns, however, should be handled with care. Consumers normally do not expect large markdowns on luxury items, for example. Customers may question product quality if prices are slashed too much. Seasonal, perishable, and obsolete stock are exceptions. Furthermore, excessive markdowns should be avoided. If markdowns are too common, the retailer should find out the reason. They can be caused by buying, selling, or pricing errors. A plan should be worked out to correct these errors once they have been determined.

Increasingly retailers are using markdowns to move merchandise and generate sales. Even some of the most expensive department stores are

A Question of Ethics

EXCESSIVE USE OF MARKDOWNS LEADS TO QUESTIONABLE BEHAVIORS

The number of retail sales and markdowns has exploded in recent years, leaving many consumers perplexed about pricing tactics and wondering whether they are really getting bargains. The key issue is how a consumer should judge whether a sale price has market validity.

For example, all the price cutting has made some people anxious that they aren't getting the best price. A consultant interviewing 300 Chicago-area shoppers after Christmas found that 82 percent of those interviewed believed they could probably have found even better deals if they had looked around just a little harder.

Some believe that retailers are manipulating prices by elevating the "original price" to an unreal level, and then announcing what appears to be a dramatic discount. Especially problematic is private-label merchandise. With private-label sales, comparison shopping is impossible and consumers therefore have no standard by which to judge price validity. A similar problem, especially in the sale of electronic goods such as stereos and VCRs, is an advertising tactic daring customers to find lower prices on comparable merchandise, when in fact the goods were specifically made for the store, so identical items don't exist elsewhere.

Market analysts also believe that some retailers mislead consumers by saying that they are offering sale prices for a limited time only, when they offer such prices continuously through most calendar periods.

What are the various ways in which retailers may engage in questionable practices regarding sales and markdowns? What do you think has motivated such actions? What do you think will be the long-run implications of firms' attempting to attract consumers primarily through deep discounting?

Source: Based on Leslie N. Vreeland, "Sorting Out a Sale from a Scam," *Money,* April 1991, pp. 138–40.

resorting frequently to markdowns. The extensive use of markdowns is evidenced by research conducted by a retail consultant who estimates that 75 percent of all department store items are being sold at markdown prices, compared with 40 percent a decade ago.[6] Some analysts believe that retailers have created a promotional monster from which they will have difficulty retreating. Others believe that excessive use of markdowns has also led to some retailers engaging in questionable behaviors (see A Question of Ethics).

CHAPTER HIGHLIGHTS

- Price must be set to support the retailer's competitive strategy. As such, retailers may price above the market level, at the market level, or below the market level. In pricing above the competition, retailers must offer the consumer some benefit (for example, services, knowledgeable salespeople, or unique merchandise) to justify above-the-market prices. At-the-market pricers offer prices roughly the same as their competitors and attempt to make the store different in ways other than price. Below-the-market pricers offer acceptable quality merchandise at low prices. To effectively execute such a strategy, the firm must focus on lowering its cost structure.

- All stores have pricing policies that are often based on industry practices. Examples include a one-price versus a flexible-price policy, a price-line policy, a leader pricing policy, a single-price policy, a price discount policy, consumer rebates, and product and service issues.
- A variety of consumer issues affect price decisions in retail operations. Such issues include consumer demand and price sensitivity, price perceptions, psychological pricing, and consumer pressures.
- A variety of external (environmental) factors affect retail price setting. Examples include supplier policies, economic conditions, and the market (competitive) structure in which the retailer operates.
- Retailers must understand the arithmetic of pricing. In addition to planning markup goals, they must be able to perform a variety of mathematical calculations involved in making pricing decisions.
- In practice, retailers may raise or lower their prices after they have made the original pricing decisions. These pricing adjustments may be in the form of additional markups or markdowns.

Study Questions

1. Discuss the possible price level strategies available to the retailer. Give an example of a type of retail organization that follows each of the strategy options.
2. What are the advantages of instituting a one-price policy? What are the various ways a flexible-price policy can be achieved?
3. Illustrate price lining and evaluate the concept.
4. Discuss the concept of leader pricing. What are the characteristics of products that are good price leaders?
5. Describe and evaluate the concept of a single-price policy.
6. Because consumer rebates are given by a manufacturer rather than a retailer, how might they affect a retailer's pricing decisions?
7. How does a retailer's flexibility in setting prices depend on the extent to which he or she is selling primarily convenience, shopping, or specialty goods? How can a retailer offer private brands and generics at prices below manufacturer brands and still make a good profit?
8. What is meant by the concept of price elasticity of demand? Explain how a retailer can determine whether demand is elastic or inelastic by studying the directional changes in price and total revenue. How does the nature of demand elasticity affect retailers' pricing decisions?
9. Summarize the information presented in the text concerning external factors affecting retail price setting.
10. Define the following terms: original retail price, sales retail price, initial markup, and maintained markup.

Problems

1. If markup on cost is 38 percent, what is the equivalent markup on retail?
2. If markup on retail is 16 percent, what is the equivalent markup on cost?

3. A suit costs a retailer $58.80. If a markup of 45 percent on cost is required, what must the retail price be?
4. A lamp is marked up $180. This is a 60 percent markup on retail. What are (a) the cost and (b) the retail price?
5. The retail price of a ring is $8,500. If the markup on retail is 78 percent, what was the retailer's cost of the ring?
6. The retail price of a picture is $45.00. If the markup on cost is 40 percent, what was the retailer's cost of the picture?
7. Men's wallets may be purchased from a manufacturer for $400 per dozen. If the wallets are marked up 30 percent on cost, what retail price will be set per wallet?
8. Women's scarves may be purchased from a manufacturer at $82.50 per dozen. If the scarves are marked up 28 percent on retail, what is the retail price of each scarf?
9. What are (a) the initial markup percentage and (b) the maintained markup percentage in a department that has the following planned figures: expenses, $7,500; profit, $4,600; sales, $30,000; employee discounts, $500; markdowns, $1,500; and shortages, $250?
10. Sales of $90,000 were planned in a department in which expenses were established at $25,000; shortages, $3,000; and employee discounts, $1,000. If a profit of 6 percent of sales is desired, what initial markup percent should be planned?

A P P L I C A T I O N S

CASE 1: The No-Dicker Sticker

In buying automobiles, consumers generally expect to negotiate price. However, when Saturn, a new division of General Motors, introduced its first models in 1990, it announced its one-price policy. Combined with a reputation for quality and service, the strategy of setting sticker prices of its compact sedans and coupes below those of competitors and then sticking to those prices is paying off. In 1991, its first full year, Saturn sold more cars per dealer than any other car maker, an honor held by Honda the previous two years.

Of course, fixed pricing in the automobile industry isn't new. Over the last 20 years, popular imports and a few domestic models such as the Corvette have been able to command inflexible top dollar. The question is whether bargaining can be taken out of the picture for "bread-and-butter" cars. Apparently, more and more car dealers believe it can. For example, a Pontiac dealer in West Palm Beach, Florida, replaced his commissioned sales staff with salaried "sales consultants" who show cars and take orders. He posted low, nonnegotiable prices and canceled most of his advertising. Since he made these changes, his business dollar volume has tripled. He plans to convert his Toyota and Mazda dealerships into no-haggle emporiums also.

Source: Adapted from Steven D. Kaye, "The No-Dicker Sticker," *U.S. News and World Report*, April 27, 1992, pp. 74–76.

Applying Retailing Principles

1. What would motivate a car dealer to adopt a one-price policy? What benefits would likely result from adopting such a policy?
2. Even though most consumers are probably accustomed to negotiating price when buying an automobile, why might some consumers find a one-price policy appealing?

CASE 2: A New Way to Say Low Price

In Kansas City, Kansas, a market dominated by deep-discounting warehouse grocery stores, an independent grocer, Frank Hopfinger, operating nine conventional stores under the name of Frank's Food Mart, decided there had to be a way to compete with the discounters. His solution? The Cost Plus Food Outlet.

The Cost Plus Food Outlet is a 51,000 square-foot store making the unusual claim that every item on the shelves is sold at cost plus a 10 percent surcharge. For every item sold, the shelf is marked with a tag indicating a dollar figure. That dollar figure represents the retailer's cost—that is, what was actually paid for the item including freight and handling charges. When the customer gets to the checkout stand, a 10 percent surcharge is added to the total. To allay any confusion about the surcharge, customers are given a flier explaining how to read the register tape.

To ensure credibility, Cost Plus backs up its claim by freely acknowledging that it doesn't offer customers the lowest prices in town on high-visibility items such as Miracle Whip, Bounty paper towels, or Tide detergent—which many competitors use as loss leaders. In fact, there are even shelf "talkers" (labels) under some items that state; "We can't save you money on this item. We only carry it for your convenience."

Source: Adapted from "In Kansas City, a New Way to Say Low Prices," *Chain Store Age Executive,* October 1991, p. 29.

Applying Retailing Principles

1. Cost Plus' success depends on whether it can persuade customers that it offers a real savings on the majority of items. Do you think Cost Plus will be able to do this and thus compete effectively against the discounters? Explain your response.
2. Is there any way that Cost Plus' claims could be confusing to consumers?
3. Rather than competing against the discounters on a price basis, what alternative strategies could Hopfinger have adopted?

NOTES

1. R. Fulton Macdonald, "Shake, Rattle & Roll: The Coming Retail Revolution," *Retail Control,* April–May 1992, pp. 21–22.
2. Richard A. Rauch, "Retailing's Dinosaurs: Department Stores and Supermarkets," *Business Horizons* 34 (September–October 1991), p. 22.
3. Bill Saporito, "IKEA's Got 'Em Lining Up," *Fortune,* March 11, 1991, p. 72.
4. Kate Fitzgerald, "$1 Store Fills the Bill," *Advertising Age,* December 16, 1991, p. 26; Gretchen Morgenson, "Shades of Frank W. Woolworth," *Forbes,* December 9, 1991, pp. 41–43.
5. For further reading, see Judith Graham, "Retailers Seek to End Era of Price Cuts," *Advertising Age,* February 6, 1989, p. 57; Francine Schwadel, "The 'Sale' Is Fading as a Retailing Tactic," *The Wall Street Journal,* March 1, 1989, p. B1.
6. Leslie N. Vreeland, "Sorting Out a Sale from a Scam," *Money,* April 1991, pp. 138–40.

C H A P T E R

15

Physically Handling and Securing Merchandise

THIS CHAPTER:

Explains how multiunit retail organizations manage the movement of merchandise from consolidation warehouses or distribution centers to individual stores.

Focuses on issues related to the management of physical handling activities.

Describes activities involved in receiving, checking, and marking merchandise.

Presents procedures for controlling internal theft.

Discusses problems associated with shoplifting and measures retailers can take to detect and prevent such behavior.

RETAILING CAPSULE

EFFECTIVE MERCHANDISE DISTRIBUTION CITED AS A MAJOR FACTOR IN WAL-MART'S SUCCESS

Why does Wal-Mart have a cost structure low enough to accommodate everyday low prices and greeters? What has enabled the company to continue to grow far beyond the direct reach of Sam Walton's magnetic personality? The secret of Wal-Mart's success lies in a set of strategic business decisions—one key ingredient of which is the company's distribution and inventory replenishment system.

This system reached its fullest expression in the implementation of a technique known as "cross-docking." In this system, goods are continuously delivered to Wal-Mart's distribution centers, where they are selected, repacked, and then dispatched to stores, often without ever sitting in inventory. Instead of spending valuable time in the warehouse, merchandise crosses from one loading dock to another in 48 hours or less.

Wal-Mart runs 85 percent of its goods through its distribution system. Cross-docking enables Wal-Mart to achieve the economies that come with purchasing full truckloads of goods while avoiding the usual inventory and handling costs. This reduces Wal-Mart's costs of sales by 2 to 3 percent compared with the industry average.

Why don't all retailers use cross-docking? It is difficult to manage. To make cross-docking work, Wal-Mart has made strategic investments in a variety of interlocking support systems. For example, cross-docking requires continuous contact among Wal-Mart's distribution centers, suppliers, and every point of sale in every store to ensure that orders can flow in and be consolidated and executed within a matter of hours. Wal-Mart therefore installed a private satellite communication system that daily sends point-of-sale data directly to Wal-Mart's 4,000 vendors. In addition, Wal-Mart places a premium on frequent, informal cooperation among stores, distribution centers, and suppliers with far less centralized control than many retailers.

Another key component of the company's logistics structure is its fast and responsive transportation system. The company's 19 distribution centers are serviced by nearly 2,000 company-owned trucks. This truck fleet enables Wal-Mart to ship goods from warehouse to store in less than 48 hours and to replenish store shelves twice a week on average (in contrast, the industry average is once every two weeks).

Cross-docking is not the cheapest or the easiest way to run a distribution center. However, seen in the broader context of Wal-Mart's inventory replenishment capability, it is an essential part of the overall process of keeping shelves filled while minimizing inventory and purchasing in truckload quantities.

Source: Adapted from George Stalk, Philip Evans, and Lawrence E. Shuman, "Competing on Capabilities: The New Rules of Corporate Strategy," *Harvard Business Review*, March–April 1992, pp. 58–59.

The Wal-Mart example illustrates how an effective merchandise distribution system in a multiunit retail organization can be an important element of competitive strategy and can positively influence profitability.

MERCHANDISE DISTRIBUTION IN MULTIUNIT FIRMS

Some multiunit retailers operate under a system of direct store delivery (DSD), whereby merchandise is shipped from vendors directly to the individual stores in the chain. The possibilities of direct store deliveries have received increasing attention among multiunit retailers as a result of the efficiencies of vendor marking and electronic data interchange (EDI) between vendors and retailers. With EDI and vendor marking in place, stores would not have to do any checking or ticketing of goods. Shipments would arrive in floor-ready condition, so goods could flow directly from the receiving dock to the selling floor. Some retailers, however, believe that additional payroll costs, increased transportation costs, and lack of receiving facilities at the stores serve as barriers to significant increases in DSD implementation in the short term.[1]

Rather, many chain operations employ a merchandise distribution system involving the use of consolidation warehouses or distribution

EXHIBIT 15–1

Courtesy Mathews Conveyor Division

Conveyor systems move merchandise into the distribution center.

centers. Merchandise is shipped from vendors to the retail chain's distribution centers and from there is redirected to the individual store units.

Many distribution centers today are computerized and highly automated, using the most recent innovations in merchandise handling and moving equipment. Automatic guided vehicles, automated storage and retrieval systems, PC-controlled inventory management, computerized sorting systems, and automatic SKU picking are found in some of the larger distribution centers. Some industry analysts see as a very real possibility the use of robots to pick, pack, and deliver merchandise to outbound freight docks. Exhibit 15–1 shows a scene from a distribution center.

Advantages of Distribution Centers

Advantages of using highly automated, computerized distribution systems include more effective inventory control and merchandise reordering, more rapid movement of merchandise to increase turnover and margins at the stores, and cost efficiencies. Let's look more closely at specific advantages resulting from retailers' implementation of distribution technology.

Operating Efficiencies and Cost Reduction. Developing effective distribution systems can be an important factor in helping a retail firm lower its cost structure, which, in turn, leads to lower prices and higher levels of profitability. For example, Food Lion is among the fastest-growing firms in

A Profile in Excellence

JOSEPH E. ANTONINI

Joseph E. Antonini, sometimes referred to as the Iacocca of retailing, wants to boost his Kmart chain to the top. Living in Detroit with his wife and two children, Antonini has been striving to rid Kmart of its "polyester palace" image.

Upon graduating from West Virginia University with a B.S. degree, Antonini joined the S.S. Kresge Company (now Kmart Corporation) as a management trainee. By 1970 he had worked in eight different Kresge stores and had been a manager of three. After a diverse career path, he became chairman of the board, president, and CEO of Kmart Corporation. In this position, Antonini has brought about significant changes.

In addition to implementing advanced distribution technology, he has been adding more expensive merchandise to low-priced lines and recruiting celebrities to sell the goods. Race car driver Mario Andretti endorses Kmart's automotive products, and golfer Fuzzy Zoeller praises its sporting goods. To complement the merchandising changes, store design and merchandise layout modifications have also been made. All of these changes are being made in support of Antonini's desire to upgrade the Kmart image from a no-frills discounter to a discount retailer of quality, brand-name merchandise displayed in modern and attractive fixtures.

the supermarket industry. One way it keeps its prices low (but its profit margins high) is centralized buying and distribution. The company purchases merchandise for all stores from headquarters, getting huge volume discounts. The orders are then shipped to one of Food Lion's nine distribution centers to be delivered by company trucks to each of the chain's stores.[2]

Likewise, Circuit City has designed a low-cost distribution system that adds as much as one percentage point to its pretax margin of 4.5 percent—which is spectacular, considering that many firms in consumer electronics retailing are barely breaking even. Its computerized, highly automated distribution system enables more than $350 million in goods a year to move through its Atlanta warehouse with just 13 floor workers.[3]

Believing that improvement in distribution is "the last best profit frontier for retailers," Kmart developed a new information system and distribution program. As a result of the new system, the company has been able to reduce the inventory carried in its distribution centers by 20 percent and increase sales by 15 percent. The result has been an enormous savings in inventory carrying costs and a big reason for Kmart's improved performance (see A Profile in Excellence).[4]

Faster Movement of Merchandise. Retailers are finding that the speed with which they respond to change in the market—the **cycle time**—is a critical element in being more competitive. Highly automated, computerized distribution centers enable faster movement of merchandise to the individual stores, which results in higher sales and margins.

EXHIBIT 15–2

Courtesy Mathews Conveyer Division

Use of hanging garment monorail in distribution center speeds movement of merchandise to stores.

Such advantages were apparent to Decelle, a seven-unit off-price retailer based in Braintree, Massachusetts, after moving into a new, automated merchandise-handling facility. Before moving into the new facility, the chain was often backlogged up to four weeks in deliveries of merchandise from its warehouse to stores. The situation was so bad that the company was forced to mark down $200,000 worth of merchandise to $150,000 because it could not get the merchandise into the stores fast enough. Now, turnover time has been reduced to as little as two days from distribution center to store rack, and company executives believe that the quicker turnover has resulted in a 20 percent increase in store sales. A major component of the new distribution center is the way in which hanging garments are handled. Previously, the garments had to be unpacked from cartons, checked, ticketed, and repacked in cartons, only to be unpacked again later in the store. The new facility has a 26-line monorail system for handling hanging garments. A similar system is shown in Exhibit 15–2. The merchandise arrives hanging and remains hanging as it moves through the distribution center to the stores.[5]

Another firm that has benefited from reworking its logistics and distribution system is Mervyn's, the $4 billion division of Dayton Hudson that is headquartered in Hayward, California, and has 233 stores. Spending $80 million on improving its distribution system, the company has cut the average time merchandise spends moving between vendor and store from 14 days to less than 9. Whereas in 1986 it took five days for merchandise to move through one of its distribution centers, in 1992 merchandise was processed within 24 hours. Mervyn's has also worked with its over 1,000 vendors to ensure that merchandise arrives at the distribution centers in floor-ready condition. Currently, 90 percent of the merchandise arrives preticketed and 93 percent of all hanging garments arrive on hangers. The results? Mervyn's sales have increased by 50 percent, whereas inventory carrying costs have remained the same as five years ago.[6]

Greater Accuracy.[7] Common errors in multiunit organizations include individual stores' receiving the wrong merchandise from the distribution center, or receiving the right goods but in the wrong quantities. Rich's Department Stores, based in Salem, Massachusetts, dealt with this problem by using a computerized out-bound system that allows stores to know exactly what is on the way from the distribution center before it arrives at the stores.

When a store is scheduled to receive a shipment of merchandise from the distribution center, information concerning the shipment is put into a computer at the headquarters office. A printer generates peel-off bar code labels that are attached to the shipping cartons. Each bar code identifies a unique store, department, and warehouse transfer order. The cartons are moved through a wanding station, where an employee "reads" the bar codes with hand-held Telxon wands that have been programmed to accept only bar codes for a particular store. If an employee tries to scan a carton that has been mixed in with another store's shipment, a warning signal is emitted. Information concerning the shipment is then electronically communicated to the store. The system not only provides greater accuracy in the movement of goods to individual stores but also has led to reduced paperwork and labor savings at the store level.

Refined Merchandising Strategy.[8] Adding sophistication to its merchandising distribution process enabled closeout retailer Ira Watson to refine its merchandising strategy by expanding assortments. Watson, headquartered in Knoxville, Tennessee, has many stores located in rural areas. The chain used to ship only full case-loads of merchandise to its stores. This system limited each store's merchandise mix, but the firm did not want to load stores with large quantities of slower-moving items.

Watson then improved its distribution system to handle less than case quantities. The chain immediately began increasing assortments, filling in its existing merchandise mix with lines that had not sold quickly enough to be included when the distribution center shipped only full cases. The change enabled the company to give its customers more merchandise choices without having to handle more merchandise through its distribution system.

Regionalized versus Centralized Distribution[9]

The question of whether to have multiple distribution centers in regional locations versus a single distribution center is one that individual retailers must answer. There is no single answer to the question—it must be dealt with on a business-by-business basis. In making the decision, management must weigh trade-offs between such factors as warehousing, transportation, inventory-carrying, and administrative costs. However, the decision cannot be made by looking at distribution costs alone. Management must also consider the overall competitive strategy of the firm, especially with respect to the level of customer service the firm wishes to provide.

County Seat at one time had three distribution centers but now only operates one. Even though the firm has stores coast to coast, management believes that the economies of scale of having one center in Minneapolis justified closing the other two centers. It benefited from savings in several areas. In the past, goods brought in from overseas were divided among the distribution centers. Now only one shipment is needed. The elimination of shuttle trucks running between the distribution centers was another savings. Furthermore, with only one distribution center, management believes that the firm has been able to better standardize merchandise assortments nationwide.

A firm that has made a move in the opposite direction is Saks Fifth Avenue. Getting merchandise to the stores more quickly is what motivated management to open an additional distribution center in California. Part of Saks' decision was based on geographic factors, part on transportation, and part on vendor concentration. Rather than shipping products to Saks' main facility in Yonkers, New York, and then back to the West coast, it made more sense to receive goods from California vendors right in California and then distribute to the Western stores from there. In addition to saving time, servicing from a regional center gives the stores greater customized attention. Saks also has a center in the Miami area that has been in operation for many years.

Future Developments

Because of the dramatic changes occurring in retailing, changes are also likely to occur in the management and operation of distribution centers. For example, retail chains operating their own distribution centers are increasingly combining those centers with service features. Many activities carried out at the store level (such as hanger changes, merchandise marking, and Sensormatic tagging) are being moved from the stores into the distribution center.

As retailers gain greater control over their inventories and operate using quick response and just-in-time methods, some retailers are cutting back on the number of their distribution centers. In addition, some retailers are planning to decrease their square footage in distribution centers.[10]

Another possibility for the future is greater use of contract distribution services. The contract service processes merchandise according to the retailer's requirements. The service usually checks the merchandise, tickets it, repacks the goods by store, and sends the goods to the retailer's distribution center. At the retailer's center, the merchandise can be unloaded off one truck and right onto the store delivery truck.[11]

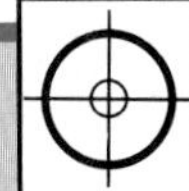

FOCUS 15–1

THE SUPER DISTRIBUTION CENTERS OF THE FUTURE

Marvin Glass, head of a distribution consulting firm, has developed his own distribution center concept for the year 2000. According to his plan, there would be huge regional distribution centers all over the country, each on the scale of a huge domed sports arena between 2 and 3 million square feet. These centers will not be operated by vendors or retailers but by a third party such as Federal Express or United Parcel Service. Instead of receiving merchandise for a single retailer, the center will be accepting huge volumes of inventory involving as many as 20 chains with thousands of stores. Here's how the super distribution center concept would work. A vendor accepts orders from retailers, packs the merchandise, and sends the orders to a consolidator in the same geographic region who then transports them to the huge regional distribution center. At the distribution center, merchandise would be assigned to the retail chain that owns it, processed (checked, marked, packed), and shipped to individual stores within the chain. Direct video communications between the chain's headquarters and the distribution center would enable buyers to check merchandise quality while it is in the distribution center. Because of economies of scale, these centers would be able to afford the latest in technology, including robots, automated equipment, and video telecommunications. Distribution costs under such a concept would be cut dramatically. For example, one cost-saving factor would be transporting goods to the stores. A bar code system would enable the center to assign all the cartons going to stores in the same shopping center to be delivered on the same truck.

SOURCE: "Future Stock: How Will It Be Moved?" *Chain Store Age Executive,* May 1987, pp. 242–44.

Probably the most imaginative picture of the distribution concept for the future is that envisioned by Marvin Glass, head of a distribution consulting firm that bears his name. See Focus 15–1 for a description of his concept of the super distribution center of the future.

International Dimensions

International expansion is an appealing, but sometimes logistically challenging, concept for retailers. Building a retail base in a foreign land can be realized in two ways: either stocking the store with locally sourced goods or stocking with the same sources as the stores in the retailer's home country. Looking at foreign retailers who have come to the United States, Carrefour is an example of the former and IKEA of the latter.

An example of a U.S. retailer moving into international markets is Talbots, which opened its first overseas store in Japan in February 1990. Talbots is taking the logistically more challenging route of not changing its sourcing. How does it handle foreign distribution? Talbots, whose domestic product line is 70 percent private label, simply considers Japan as another shipping destination. Merchandise made for Talbots, for example in Hong Kong, is handled as usual, except that the portion intended for

Retailing around the World – The Internationalization of the Marketing Mix

International Classics

(Dave Jacobs/Nawrocki)

London's treasure trove of retailing, Harrod's.

(Sipa -Press)

Galleries Lafayette is a Parisian classic.

(Courtesy The Postcard Factory)

Europa Boulevard at Canada's West Edmonton Mall – classic European specialty stores assembled on one "street" of the famous megamall in Alberta, offering North America a touch of the European continent.

The United States goes abroad

(Courtesy of Toys 'R' Us)

Toys 'R' Us has become extremely international, as the ad notes.

(Courtesy The Direct Selling Education Foundation)

Direct selling is one of the most important channels of distribution in Japan – Avon is calling on the Japanese.

McDonald's in Moscow – one of the big news stories in internationalization.

(Sipa-Press)

THE WORLD COMES TO THE UNITED STATES

(Courtesy United Colors of Benetton)

Benetton from Italy.

(Courtesy Miller/Zell, Inc.)

Infiniti automobile dealerships from Japan.

(Courtesy Laura Ashley)

Laura Ashley from England.

J. C. PENNEY'S CLASSIC PRESENTATION "FESTIVAL OF THE PHILIPPINES," THE KIND OF EVENT THAT RECOGNIZES AND HONORS A FOREIGN COUNTRY AND ITS PRODUCTS

(Courtesy J. C. Penney Company, Inc.)

(Courtesy J. C. Penney Company, Inc.)

(Courtesy J. C. Penney Company, Inc.)

Japan will be split out and shipped to Tokyo, and the remainder will be shipped to the U.S. After merchandise enters Japan, merchandise moves into a distribution center that Talbots shares with JUSCO Co., Ltd., one of Japan's largest retail conglomerates and Talbot's parent company. The company plans to add additional stores in Japan. As this is done, merchandise distribution may need to be changed.[12]

Some retailers who are having less than optimal results managing their overseas logistical operations are turning to third-party logistics management firms, such as INTRAL Corporation. Such firms manage goods from origin to destination and do so in such a way as to reduce the in-transit time and, thus, the in-transit inventory.

Domestic firms importing merchandise likewise face distribution decisions and issues. A study conducted in 1992 revealed that about 20 percent of retailers' stockkeeping units are sourced from foreign vendors, and that this percentage is relatively steady between different types of retailers, with the exception of home centers, which report only 6 percent of their stockkeeping units are sourced outside the United States.[13] A firm that has built a highly sophisticated network of systems to support its import merchandising is Pier 1 Imports, which carries goods from 44 countries. Goods arrive in North America at four convenient deep-water ports, where they are then transferred to six major regional distribution centers. The merchandise then moves by truck from the distribution centers to the company's 458 stores on a carefully scheduled basis. Each store orders its requirements through a data system that is part of a major POS installation completed in 1988.

PHYSICAL HANDLING ACTIVITIES

Physical handling involves receiving, checking, and marking merchandise. Although these activities are often performed in distribution centers in multiunit organizations, the following sections focus on these activities being performed in the retail store. Before discussing each of the activities, however, let's talk about several issues related to managing the physical handling process.

Managing the Physical Handling Activities

Several issues are related to managing physical handling activities. One is the question of who is responsible for carrying out the activities. A second issue involves the location of physical handling within the store. Finally, procedures for controlling the process must be established.

Assigning Responsibility. In a small retail store, the entire physical handling process is simple. A single individual such as a buyer or salesperson probably performs all the functions.

In a large retail firm, where the volume of goods handled may be quite large, specialized personnel perform the physical handling functions.

These personnel are included under the operating division rather than the merchandising division of the retail firm. There are several reasons for having the physical handling performed by specialists rather than by buyers or salespeople. Salespeople may resent having to do jobs other than selling and thus may be careless and negligent. In addition, salespeople are likely to be more efficient at selling if they do not have additional nonselling responsibilities. Specialized personnel, on the other hand, do a better job of performing operational functions; controls are better, and specialization normally results in a better, more efficient job.

Location. Except in a very small store, physical handling activities are normally located in a part of the store that is not used for selling. Even though the structure of the building affects the placement, several factors should be kept in mind when deciding the location of the physical handling activities:

1. The merchandise must be received from transportation carriers, so the receiving area needs to be easily accessible to delivery trucks.
2. The value of the space should be low in terms of traffic generated. "Expensive" space should be used for selling. An upper floor is sometimes used in a large store; however, vertical movement facilities are then needed to move the goods to the receiving, checking, and marking stations.
3. Depending on the kind of goods, the retailer may want to locate the receiving, checking, and marking area close to the sales floor or the stockrooms. Handling costs are high, so retailers must consider ways to keep these costs to a minimum.

One merchant opened a ready-to-wear boutique and allocated no space to physical handling when planning the store's layout. The washroom was soon being utilized for these activities. Even though the store was small, moving goods from the remote washroom to the selling floor was inefficient. This example illustrates that planning and organizing are essential management functions, regardless of the size of the business.

Controlling Physical Handling Activities. Every company strives to select the best method for controlling the physical handling functions. There are many variations, but the essential information must be collected by all retail managers. The J. C. Penney purchase order form is presented in Figure 15–1 for illustrative purposes.

Every retail company should have its own purchase order form. Using a supplier's form will diminish the control of physical handling functions. The simplest control feature of the purchase order is a discrete number—in this case, 02973, as shown in Figure 15–1.

This form contains important information. Above the supplier's name and address the buyer will place the supplier's number—another control feature, as each supplier has a specific number. The terms of sale (payment period and credit terms) are specified in the box labeled "terms." The box

F I G U R E 15–1 J. C. PENNEY PURCHASE ORDER FORM

JCPenney
JCP-9017 (REV. 4/80)

SUPPLIER NO.	TERMS	SHIP ONLY TO: J.C. PENNEY COMPANY, INC. STORE NO. 1786-3 UNIVERSITY MALL 1701 MCFARLAND EAST	BILL TO AND SEND DUPLICATE INVOICE TO STORE NO. 1786-3	J.C. PENNEY COMPANY, INC. UNIVERSITY MALL 1701 MCFARLAND EAST	ORIGINAL INVOICE TO DISBURS. OFFICE AT DALLAS, TEXAS
—					

SUPPLIER: SUPPLIER NAME / ADDRESS / CITY / STATE / ZIP CODE

IMPORTANT: ORDER NO., SUBDIVISION NO., OR EXPENSE CLASSIFICATION NO. MUST APPEAR ON ALL PACKAGES, INVOICES AND CORRESPONDENCE.
THIS ORDER IS MADE UPON THE EXPRESS TERMS AND CONDITIONS AS SET FORTH HEREIN AND ON THE BACK OF THIS ORDER FORM.

ORIGINAL

MAIL: ORIG TO / DUP TO — SUPPLIER | N.Y. | DAL | L.A. | MIA. | WAREHOUSE | EST. WT. | HOW SHIP

USE TRAFFIC DIV. INSTRUCTIONS UNLESS OTHERWISE SPECIFIED

SHIP BETWEEN THESE DATES: ORDER MAIL DATE / / | EARLIEST SHIP DATE / / | CANCEL DATE / / | ORDER NUMBER 02973

UNIT CONTROL: SK. NO. | PG. NO. | SUBDIVISION | ACCOUNT CODE | ACTIVITY NO. (N.F.R. ONLY)

RMM-4 ORDERS / / RECEIPTS / /

WRITE A SEPARATE ORDER FOR EACH SUBDIVISION OR EXPENSE CLASSIFICATION

LOT NO. OR ITEM	ORDERED QTY.	ORDERED UNIT	QTY. SHIPPED	WIDTH, COLOR PATTERN, ETC.	QUANTITIES BY SIZES • LIST SIZES ON FIRST LINE	COST PRICE	COMPANY RETAIL

FOLD

WRITE SPECIAL INSTRUCTIONS HERE:

MANAGER

DATE BILLED | TAG AND PRICE | FILLED | CHECKED | NO. PIECES | TOTAL COST | TOTAL RETAIL

MANAGER DO NOT WRITE IN THESE SPACES

labeled "mail" tells the mailroom whether the original or duplicate (or both) should be sent to the supplier or to a distribution point within the company. The remainder of the form is fairly clear. The "company retail" price will not be filled in on the original, which goes to the supplier. The office copy is for accounts payable. The receiving copy is utilized in the receiving, checking, and marketing activities. If back orders or incomplete shipments exist, the purchase order will be kept open. If the shipment is complete, the receiving copy of the purchase order is sent to the office for payment.

Physical Handling Activities

The issues just discussed relate to managing the physical handling process. Let's turn our attention now to a discussion of each of the activities comprising the process.

Receiving. **Receiving** is that phase of physical handling in which the retailer takes possession of the goods and then moves them to the next phase of the process. When the goods reach the store, packing cartons are inspected for damage. After the cartons are opened, individual packages in the cartons must also be inspected for damage. A receiving record must also be prepared. This record normally includes date and hour of arrival, weight, form of transportation, number of cartons, receiving number, invoice number, condition of packages, delivery charges, name of deliverer, amount of invoice, and department ordering the goods.

To ensure the effectiveness of the receiving department, the retailer must determine the most efficient methods for performing specific operations and then standardize these methods. In determining layout, management should plan for the straight-line movement of materials with as little backtracking as possible and the shortest distance possible. An attempt should be made to maximize machine operations and minimize hand operations. Sufficient equipment and standby equipment must therefore be purchased. Personnel working in the receiving area should be carefully selected, trained, and provided with adequate supervision. Finally, enough records must be maintained for control purposes.

Checking. **Checking** involves matching the store buyer's purchase order with the supplier's invoice (bill), opening the packages, removing and sorting the items, and comparing the quality and quantity of the shipment with what was ordered. Let's focus on the activities of quality and quantity checking.

Quality Checking. The decision "to check or not to check" for quality resides with the buyer. When quality checking is considered to be important, the responsibility is assumed by the buying staff. Remember—buyers are merchandise specialists; checkers are not.

Quantity Checking. Four accepted methods of quantity checking are:

- The **direct check.** The shipment is checked against the vendor's invoice. Goods under this system cannot be checked until the invoice arrives, so items might accumulate in the checking area if invoices have not arrived.
- The **blind check.** The checker lists the items and quantities received without the invoice in hand. This system is designed to avoid the merchandise accumulation problems associated with the direct check. The system is slower, however, because the list prepared by the checker must later be compared to the invoice.
- The **semiblind check.** The checker is given a list of the items in a shipment, but the quantity is omitted. The checker's job is to indicate quantities on the prepared list. The time saved in the checking process may be offset somewhat by the time required to prepare the list.

- The **combination check.** This system is a combination of the blind and direct checks. If the invoices are available when the goods arrive, the direct check is used; if the invoices have not come in, the blind check is used.

Marking. **Marking** is putting information on the goods or on merchandise containers to assist customers and to aid the store in the control functions.

Goods can be marked either within the store or by a vendor. Because we discussed vendor marking in previous chapters, we will not discuss it here. Instead, we will focus your attention on marking within the store.

Various methods are used for establishing the price information to be marked on the goods. One common method is **preretailing.** Under this system, the buyer places the retail price on the store's copy of the purchase order at the time it is written. The buyer may also **retail the invoice,** or place a retail price on the copy of the invoice in the receiving room.

In addition to marking individual items of merchandise in the workroom, retailers may use a number of other marking practices. For example, in **bulk marking,** items are not price marked until they reach the selling floor. Products that sell at very low prices and are subject to rapidly changing prices are typically bulk marked. The shipping carton is marked when the goods arrive; prices are placed on individual items when they are moved to the sales floor. This system is sometimes referred to as "delayed marking." In **nonmarking,** individual items of merchandise are not price marked. Usually the display fixture will indicate prices. In some instances, the person at the checkout counter is supplied with the prices of the goods. Nails, for example, are rarely, if ever, individually price marked.

Remarking is the practice of changing the price marked on merchandise to reflect price changes. The retailer must consider store image when deciding how this practice will be handled. Some store managers, for example, insist on new price tickets rather than merely marking through the old prices.

CONTROLLING EMPLOYEE THEFT AND SHOPLIFTING

An important part of merchandise management is controlling merchandise shortages. Merchandise shortages are caused by a variety of factors, such as poor paperwork controls, human error, computer glitches, vendor theft, shoplifters, and dishonest employees. Annually, the average shrinkage for retailers is around 2 percent of sales.

Because the greatest percentage of merchandise losses are due to employee theft and shoplifting, we will focus our attention on these two causes of merchandise shortage. Retailers in 1992 were estimated to have lost $12.6 billion to pilferage and shoplifting.[14]

Employee Theft

Employee theft is a bigger problem than shoplifting. Of the estimated $12.6 billion that retailers lose to pilferage and shoplifting each year, roughly 60 percent stems from employee theft.[15] The data shown in Table 15–1 lend

TABLE 15–1

LOSS PREVENTION STATS AT A GLANCE

	Average Shrinkage as a Percentage of Sales	Average Value of Merchandise Recovered at Retail per Apprehension	
		Employees	*Customers*
All participants	1.91%	$1,350	$196
Department stores	2.18	650	165
Drug chains	2.33	349	48
General merchandise/ mass merchants	1.82	801	87
Specialty apparel	1.84	3,044	225
Specialty hardlines	1.98	2,378	375
Supermarkets	0.93	592	107

Source: *Chain Store Age Executive,* January 1991, p. 5. Reproduced with permission.

further evidence. As shown, the average employee theft is $1,350, compared to $196 for shoplifters.

A study by a sociology professor at the University of Florida revealed that over one-third of the retail employees interviewed admitted that they stole property, merchandise, or money. The study found that apprehensions of female employees are slightly more prevalent than those of male employees and that young-adult employees are apprehended more frequently than other age groups.[16]

How Do Employees Steal? Discount abuse is the leading form of retail theft by employees. Most frequently, employees will purchase merchandise for friends and relatives who are not eligible for a discount. The amounts of merchandise purchased often exceed limits set by company policy. Employees may purchase merchandise at a discount and then have a friend return it for full value.

Some employee theft is carried out in collusion with customers. A Midwest supermarket chain discovered that a cashier was paying off her baby-sitter by undercharging her for groceries. Instead of running all the items over the scanner, the cashier lifted most of the items over the scanner so that they wouldn't register.

Working in collusion with a vendor is another way employees steal. The receiving clerk for one East Coast chain was signing for many more cases of cookies than were actually being delivered. The phantom cases added up to $15,000 before the employee was caught. (See Case 2 at the end of the chapter for other examples of theft occurring in a distribution center.)

Theft of merchandise and cash also occurs. Sales personnel who work directly with merchandise and cash may steal. However, one retailer discovered that the cleaning crew was stealing merchandise. The employees were caught stuffing merchandise into their cleaning buckets and vacuum cleaners.

Even though this is not a comprehensive treatment of the topic, these examples show that employee theft can occur in a variety of ways. Because of the magnitude of the problem, retailers must establish prevention and detection procedures for controlling internal theft.

Controlling Employee Theft.[17] There are numerous things retailers can do to control employee theft. The following sections focus on several ideas.

Improving the Quality of Personnel. Obviously, the greatest deterrent to internal theft is to hire honest people. Upgrading the level of retail personnel is largely a matter of careful personnel screening and selection, including careful reference checks, credit checks, and personal character examinations. Some retailers are also using written honesty tests such as the Reed report, which consists of psychologically oriented questions whose yes/no answers classify a person as prone or not prone to theft. Security experts stress that retailers should also implement drug testing because there has been a growing incidence of internal theft resulting from drug use.

Awareness Programs. Loss prevention personnel should be brought into pre-employment and post-employment training sessions to discuss the issue of employee theft. Such awareness programs show how employees can hurt themselves by stealing. Through awareness programs, management points out the store's policy on dealing with employee theft and the importance of honesty to job security and a good reference when an employee changes jobs. Because of the high turnover rate in retailing, management must constantly repeat its message regarding its stand on employee theft.

Awareness is continually emphasized when managers set good examples for their employees. When asked why they steal, employees often say that their supervisors do it, so they believe that their actions are justified. Thus, managers who understand that their own behavior sets the ethical tone in the workplace employ symbolic examples that illustrate highly ethical behavior.

Participatory Management and Profit Sharing. The ideas of participatory management and profit sharing stem from the premise that people do not steal from themselves. For example, in Japan, where an emphasis is placed on participatory management, many decisions are shaped by the workers themselves. Managers routinely mingle with employees to get their thoughts and ideas on how work can be done better. As a result, workers become emotionally involved with the success of the company. To steal from the company in Japan is unthinkable because the workers *are* the company.

Profit sharing likewise links the employee with the success of the company. A growing number of retailers now recognize that workers at all levels deserve to share in the success of the business, and employees are allowed to purchase stock in the company. Other firms routinely distribute profits as bonuses to employees in addition to paying dividends to stockholders.

Establish Reward Systems. Peer pressure and use of a reward system can be effective. For such a system to work, however, management must assure employees that confidence will be respected and anonymity ensured—that their efforts to help catch employee thieves will not place them in danger of termination, retaliation, lawsuits, or reputation as a "snitch." The number of stores training employees to look for internal theft and rewarding them for doing so is growing, and the rewards are sometimes significant.

Cash Register Controls. Because such a large percentage of employee theft occurs at the cash register, companies are instituting a variety of controls in this area. J. C. Penney, for example, uses a PC to help it chart register variances and cash refund fraud. Some retailers have been able to reduce cash register shortages and increase apprehensions of dishonest employees with a programmable computerized video recording system that watches POS. This video interface software product, known as POS/EM (point-of-sale exception monitoring) was designed by Data Based Security.

Other Control Measures. Other deterrents to internal thievery include use of employee identification badges; restriction of employee movement within the store before, during, and after selling hours; regular internal audits; surprise internal audits; and tight controls over petty cash, accounts receivable, payroll, and inventory.

Shoplifting

According to the FBI, shoplifting has increased 35 percent since 1987 and now represents the fastest-growing form of larceny in the United States.[18] But what does a shoplifter look like? The following section provides a description.

Who Are Shoplifters? Shoplifters are male or female, any race or color, as young as 5 or well into their 80s. Fortunately for retailers, many shoplifters are amateurs rather than professionals. Therefore, they are not difficult to spot, and with the right kind of handling, they may never try petty thievery again. Let's look at the various types of shoplifters.

Juvenile Offenders. Several studies have revealed that juveniles make up the largest percentage of shoplifters, accounting for approximately 50 percent of all shoplifting. Motives for shoplifting are primarily social rather than economic, especially among girls. Furthermore, shoplifting by juveniles is primarily unplanned; four times out of five it is done on impulse. Some juveniles will enter stores in gangs in an attempt to further intimidate management.

Impulse Shoplifters. Many "respectable" people fall into this category. Their thefts are not premeditated, but a sudden chance (such as an unattended dressing room or a blind aisle in a supermarket) presents itself, and the shopper succumbs to temptation. The shoplifting usually occurs while purchasing other merchandise. Items taken are generally for personal use.

Kleptomaniacs. Kleptomaniacs are motivated by a compulsion to steal. They usually have little or no actual use for the items they steal and in many cases could afford to pay for them. Experts believe that there are few real kleptomaniacs.

Professionals. Because the professional shoplifter is in the business of theft, he or she is usually skilled and hard to spot. Professionals generally steal items that can be quickly resold to an established "fence." The pro may case a store well in advance of the actual theft. They take no unnecessary chances and often work in pairs or organized teams. They seldom hit the same store twice.

Alcoholics, Vagrants, and Drug Addicts. Abnormal physical needs can drive people to theft. These criminals are often clumsy or erratic in their behavior and may be easier to detect than other types of shoplifters. The store owner should remember, however, that people under the influence of drugs or alcohol with an obsessive physical need may be violent and armed.

Theft resulting from drug use is increasing and is becoming a major problem for retailers. In fact, one New York company closed the doors of a store because of the crack problem. Today, many drug suppliers accept merchandise as an alternative to cash. Dealers rent small storage buildings, and, as they acquire quantities of merchandise, they send the goods overseas. Bartering for drugs is extremely profitable for drug dealers.[19]

Controlling Shoplifting. Time and money are better spent preventing shoplifting than prosecuting the offenders. Retailers can take action in several areas to control shoplifting.

Educate Employees. Retailers know that salespeople are the first line of defense against shoplifting. However, some salespeople hesitate to get involved because of fear of a possible confrontation. However, management can do a number of things to use salespeople more effectively as a way of controlling shoplifting:

TABLE 15–2

HOW TO RECOGNIZE SHOPLIFTERS

- Be on the lookout for customers carrying concealment devices such as bulky packages, large pocketbooks, baby carriages, or an oversized arm sling.
- Watch for shoppers walking with unnatural steps—they may be concealing items between their legs.
- Employees should be alert to groups of shoppers who enter the store together and then break up and go in different directions. A customer who attempts to monopolize a salesperson's time may be covering for an associate stealing elsewhere in the store. A gang member may start an argument with store personnel or other gang members or may feign a fainting spell to draw attention, giving a cohort the opportunity to steal merchandise from another part of the store.
- Shoplifters do not like crowds. They keep a sharp eye out for other customers or store personnel. Quick, nervous glances may be a giveaway.
- Sales help should remember that ordinary customers want attention; shoplifters do not. When busy with one customer, the salesperson should acknowledge waiting customers with polite remarks such as, "I'll be with you in a minute." This pleases legitimate customers—and makes a shoplifter feel uneasy.
- Salespeople should watch for a customer who handles a lot of merchandise but takes an unusually long time to make a decision. They should watch for customers lingering in one area, loitering near stockrooms or other restricted areas, or wandering aimlessly through the store. They should try to be alert to customers who consistently shop during hours when staff is low.

- Create awareness and concern. Managers must communicate their concern about shoplifting and keep employees constantly aware of the problem. Shoplifting and its effects should be discussed periodically at staff meetings. Salespeople should be reminded that shoplifting makes their job more difficult and diverts time from customers who are buying merchandise.
- Provide employee training and support. Salespeople should be taught how to recognize shoplifters and how to respond to the situation. Table 15–2 presents some points on how to recognize shoplifters. Management also needs to support the salespeople's efforts by giving them the tools and devices they need to detect shoplifters.
- Show appreciation. Salespeople need positive feedback; they need to know that their efforts are meaningful and recognized by management. They should be provided with periodic information on progress toward controlling shoplifting. Individual performance should be recognized by certificates of merit, monetary awards, notations on personnel evaluations, and similar means.

Plan Store Layout with Deterrence in Mind. Retailers should maintain adequate lighting in all areas of the store and keep protruding wings and end displays low. In addition, display cases should be set in broken sequences and, if possible, run for short lengths with spaces in between. Small items of high value (film, cigarettes, small appliances) should be kept behind a counter or in a locked case with a salesclerk on duty. Display counters should be kept neat; it is easier to determine whether an item is

TABLE 15–3 HOW LOSS PREVENTION EXECUTIVES AND SHOPLIFTERS RATE THE EFFECTIVENESS OF SOME SECURITY TOOLS

Type of Measure	*Retailers*	*Shoplifters*
EAS tags	2	1
Trained, aware personnel	1	2
POS systems	3	—
Guards, detectives	4	6
Concealed CCTV	5	4
Fitting room staff	6	5
Mirrors	7	3

Source: Jules Abend "EAS: Prime Deterrent to Thieves." Reprinted from *Stores,* © National Retail Federation Enterprises, 1989.

missing if the display area is orderly. If fire regulations permit, all exits not to be used by customers should be locked. Noisy alarms should be attached to unlocked exits. Unused checkout aisles should be closed and blocked off.

Use Audible Messages. Some stores have developed announcements that are broadcast over their internal public address systems. An announcement may say, "Security, please respond to section D3." The store may not actually have a security staff, but such a statement may very well deter a prospective shoplifter.

Use Protective Personnel and Equipment. Protective devices may be expensive, but shoplifting is more expensive. As shown in Table 15–3, shoplifters consider electronic tags as being the most effective protective device (retailers rate electronic article surveillance (EAS) tags as second most effective, behind trained, aware personnel). Some retailers are using an advanced EAS device referred to as the "tell tag." The tell tag is different from other EAS equipment because it actually alarms directly from the tag on the sales floor if a tampering attempt is made. The tell tag will also remind the sales associate to remove the tag by transmitting three short beeps when it comes in contact with equipment at POS.[20]

Apprehending, Arresting, and Prosecuting Shoplifters. To make legal charges stick, retailers must be able to (1) see the person take or conceal the merchandise; (2) identify the merchandise as belonging to the store; (3) testify that it was taken with the intent to steal; and (4) prove the merchandise was not paid for. If retailers are unable to meet all four criteria, they leave themselves open to countercharges of false arrest. False arrest need not mean police arrest; simply preventing a person from conducting normal activities can be deemed false arrest. Furthermore, any physical contact, even a light touch on the arm, may be considered unnecessary and used against the retailer in court.

In general, store personnel should never accuse customers of stealing, nor should they try to apprehend suspected shoplifters. If they observe suspicious behavior or an apparent theft in progress, they should alert store management, the store detective, or the police.

It is wisest to apprehend shoplifters outside the store. The retailer has a better case if it can be demonstrated that the shoplifter left the store with stolen merchandise. However, retailers may prefer to apprehend a shoplifter inside the store if the merchandise involved is of considerable value or if the thief is likely to elude store personnel outside the store premises. In either case, verbal accusation of the suspect should be avoided. One recommended procedure is for store employees to identify themselves and say, "I believe you have some merchandise you have forgotten to pay for. Would you mind coming with me to straighten things out?"

Some organizations have control files on shoplifters who have been caught. The local retail merchants' association can supply information about such services available in the area. These files can be checked for prior records. Unless the retailer gets positive identification and files the shoplifter's name with the police and local retail merchants' association, the "first-time offender" may claim this status each time he or she is caught shoplifting.

Each situation must be handled individually, and good judgment is required. For example, retailers may wish to release elderly or senile shoplifters and not press charges if there is some indication that the person could honestly have forgotten to pay for the merchandise. Juvenile shoplifters require special handling. A strict, no-nonsense attitude often makes a lasting impression on the young offender and may deter future theft. Prosecution is in order if the shoplifter is violent, lacks proper identification, appears to be under the influence of alcohol or other drugs, or appears to be a professional. If the theft involves merchandise of great value or management suspects a prior record, prosecution is essential.

Civil Recovery Procedures.[21] Some retailers are beginning to use civil recovery laws to get recourse from shoplifters. Civil recovery is a noncriminal court procedure, much like taking someone to small claims court. It can be used as an alternative or in addition to traditional criminal prosecution.

The laws give retailers the right to collect a certain amount of money from someone caught shoplifting. The maximum amount that can be collected varies by state. The procedure, however, can be complicated and time-consuming. As a result, some retailers choose to do civil recovery in-house, but many retailers prefer to work with an outside firm that specializes in civil restitution. Use of these statutes can be effective not only in collecting money from shoplifters but also in cutting down on repeat offenders.

A Question of Ethics

ENSURING THE SAFETY OF CUSTOMERS

There are no statistics available on the level of crime in shopping centers. No federal, state, or local law enforcement agency tracks it. Nor do any trade associations have reliable numbers. Yet despite the absence of hard figures, industry observers believe that shopping centers are not as safe as they used to be.

Although the majority of shopping centers remain safer than many city streets, retailers and consumers alike are concerned over the increasing level of crime in shopping centers. In addition, industry analysts believe that the violence of the crimes has also increased. What was purse-snatching before may now involve hitting or stabbing. Car theft in parking lots is also on the rise. Some mall developers have even reported drug dealers organizing their transactions (though not actually dealing) at center telephones and warring gangs strolling the centers (though fights are rare in the centers).

Is it realistic for customers to expect a location that attracts thousands of people a day to be any freer from crime than the average city street? To what extent do retailers and mall developers have an ethical and moral responsibility to ensure the safety of their customers? What are some specific courses of action that could be taken to ensure their safety?

Source: Adapted from Debra Hazel, "Crime in the Malls," *Chain Store Age Executive,* February 1991, pp. 27–29.

These sections have provided information on actions that retailers can take to secure their merchandise from shoplifting and employee theft. An important question is this: In addition to securing their merchandise, should retailers also be concerned with securing the safety of their customers? This question has become more and more relevant as retailers and consumers alike have become increasingly concerned over the growing level of crime, especially in shopping centers. This issue is addressed in greater detail in A Question of Ethics.

CHAPTER HIGHLIGHTS

- Many chain operations have merchandise distribution systems that involve the use of consolidation warehouses or distribution centers. Merchandise is shipped from vendors to the retail chain's distribution centers and from there is redirected to individual store units. Many of these centers are highly automated and computerized. Distribution centers provide several advantages and, when used effectively, can enhance retail productivity and efficiency.
- The physical handling process involves receiving, checking, and marking merchandise. Issues related to managing the physical handling process include assigning responsibility for carrying out the activities, locating the activities within the store, and establishing control procedures.
- Receiving is the phase of the physical handling process that involves taking possession of the goods and then moving them to the next phase of the process. Packing cartons and

individual packages must be inspected for damages. A receiving record should also be prepared.

- Checking involves matching the store buyer's purchase order with the supplier's invoice, opening the packaging and removing the items, sorting them, and comparing the quality and quantity of the shipment with what was ordered. Quality checking, if done, should be performed by the buying staff. Four accepted methods of quantity checking are the direct check, the blind check, the semiblind check, and the combination check.
- Marking is putting information on the goods or on merchandise containers. Goods can be marked either by vendors or by the retailer. Various methods may be used for establishing the price information to be marked on the goods. Retailers may use several different marking practices.
- Of the estimated $12.6 billion that retailers lose to pilferage and shoplifting each year, roughly 60 percent stems from employee theft. Because of the magnitude of the problem, retailers must establish prevention and detection procedures for controlling internal theft.
- Shoplifting is also a major problem retailers face. However, retailers can take several actions to detect and prevent shoplifting.

STUDY QUESTIONS

1. Describe the advantages of a multiunit retail organization employing a distribution system involving the use of consolidation warehouses or distribution centers.
2. What are the specific dimensions of the physical handling process? Briefly describe each.
3. Comment on the validity of the following statement: The buyer should always be responsible for the physical handling functions.
4. Discuss the factors a retailer should consider in deciding on the location of the physical handling activities within the store.
5. Comment on the validity of the following statement: Physical handling specialists should assume the responsibility of merchandise quality checking.
6. Explain the four accepted methods of quantity checking.
7. Define the following terms: preretailing, retail the invoice, bulk marking, nonmarking, and remarking.
8. What things can retailers do to control employee theft?
9. What are the various types of shoplifters? What can retail managers do to control shoplifting?
10. What are some points retailers must remember regarding the apprehension, arrest, and prosecution of shoplifters?

A P P L I C A T I O N S

CASE 1: Merchandising Decisions Affect Distribution Costs

Sometimes the activities of buyers are at cross-purposes with those performing the firm's merchandise distribution functions. One reason for this is the lack of understanding of how distribution adds to or subtracts from profitability. Another reason stems from the intensive nature of competition in retailing, especially among hard goods retailers.

Buyers, for example, are often unwilling to pull back on promotions even when the constant promotional emphasis at some chains exhausts distribution systems and creates increases in distribution expenses that offset profit gains.

In an attempt to deal with this problem, some retailers use a series of matrixes to measure increases in distribution costs that can be expected from merchandising strategies designed to generate added sales. Of course, some products can bear a larger percentage increase in distribution costs than can other products. For example, for a product that has a gross margin of only 5 percent, a 1 percent increase in distribution costs may be too high. However, for a product with a 35 percent gross margin, a 3 percent increase in distribution costs may not be too much.

The use of such matrixes helps retailers do a better job of judging how a buyer's merchandising decisions add to distribution costs, but the difficulty of using such matrixes requires a staff to work them out. And the increased staff adds to the costs of the firm.

Applying Retailing Principles

1. Explain how merchandising activities designed to increase sales can lead to an increase in merchandise distribution costs.
2. What are some things retailers can do to provide greater coordination between the merchandising and distribution functions and personnel?

CASE 2: Employee Theft at a Distribution Center

The loss prevention director of a chain in the Southwest began to think that employee theft might be the problem in its distribution center when merchandise transfers to the chain's 11 stores began turning up short. An outside security consultant was called in to study the situation.

The consultant noticed several things. Employees were entering and leaving the center through the loading dock door instead of the employee entrance. Employees at the center were allowed to buy damaged merchandise, but no one checked packages as employees left the building. In addition, employees were carrying out the trash with no one checking it. Employees were allowed to park their cars and trucks close to the loading docks. The distribution center had no security fence, so there was no way of controlling who entered or left the area around the center.

Based on investigations, it was discovered that about three-fourths of the center's 45 employees had engaged in thievery by some means. One supervisor, for example, led a group of six or seven employees in hiding merchandise in empty packing cases and trash bags. They carried them out with broken pallets to a truck waiting to carry trash to a dump. The truck driver dropped off the merchandise at an employee's home on the way to the dump.

Applying Retailing Principles

1. Summarize the company's security system problems that enabled employees to steal from the firm.
2. Recommend some things the company should change or initiate to prevent employee theft.

Notes

1. Gary Robins, "New Role for the DC?" *Stores,* April 1989, p. 30.
2. Walecia Konrad, "Food Lion: Still Stalking in Tough Times," *BusinessWeek,* June 22, 1992, p. 70.
3. Dean Fourt, "Circuit City: Wires Are Sizzling," *BusinessWeek,* April 27, 1992, p. 76.
4. Rita Koselka, "Distribution Revolution," *Forbes,* May 25, 1992, p. 60.

5. "Junking the Model T," *Chain Store Age Executive,* January 1986, p. 75.

6. See Koselka, "Distribution Revolution," pp. 54–58; "Mervyn's Cuts DC Time," *Chain Store Age Executive,* April 1992, pp. 26A–27A.

7. "What You See Is What You Get," *Chain Store Age Executive,* February 1986, p. 43.

8. "The Same Company, Different Goals," *Chain Store Age Executive,* February 1986, p. 24.

9. The material in this section is based on Gary Robins, "Logistics and the DC," *Stores,* April 1990, pp. 19–22.

10. "Distribution Centers . . . The Future," *Chain Store Age Executive,* April 1992, p. 11A.

11. Gary Robins, "New Role," p. 31.

12. Gary Robins, "The Logistics of Overseas Expansion," *Stores,* April 1990, pp. 22–23.

13. "Retail Distribution and Logistics," *Chain Store Age Executive,* April 1992, p. 15A.

14. Terri Thompson, David Hage, and Robert F. Black, "Crime and the Bottom Line," *U.S. News & World Report,* April 13, 1992, p. 58.

15. "Employee Theft in the Workplace: A Sociological Perspective," *Retailing Review* 1, no. 2 (Gainesville, Florida: Center for Retailing Education and Research, University of Florida, 1992), p. 1.

16. "Employee Theft in the Workplace."

17. The material in this section is based on Richard C. Hollinger and John W. Jones, *Dishonesty in the Workplace: A Manager's Guide to Preventing Employee Theft* (Park Ridge, Illinois: London House Press, 1989), pp. 39–44.

18. Terri Thompson, David Hage, and Robert F. Black, "Crime and the Bottom Line," p. 58.

19. Jules Abend, "Ex–NY Cop Cites New Popular Scams," *Stores,* June 1989, p. 63.

20. Jules Abend, "More Deterrents to Theft," *Stores,* June 1989, p. 63.

21. Based on "Loss Prevention Can Be Profitable," *Chain Store Age Executive,* December 1988, pp. 72–73.

C H A P T E R

16

Store Design and Layout and Merchandise Presentation

THIS CHAPTER:

Discusses aspects of exterior and interior store design.

Describes typical store arrangements.

Explains how to allocate space to selling departments and nonselling activities.

Presents factors to consider in locating selling departments and sales-supporting activities within the store.

Indicates the essentials of merchandise display.

RETAILING CAPSULE

NIKE TOWN COMBINES THEATER WITH SERVICE TO GET CUSTOMERS TO PAY FULL PRICE

When customers walk into Nike Town, located in downtown Portland, Oregon, they see plaster casts of Andre Agassi and Bo Jackson and, suspended from the ceiling, a statue of Michael Jordan going up for a slam dunk. The 20,000-square-foot store (which stocks every one of Nike's products—more than 1,000 new products each year) includes 14 shops featuring products for 25 sports.

The store appeals to every one of a customer's senses. Sounds, temperature, and lights are manipulated in each of the 14 shops. Each one, for example, plays a new age sound track of soothing mantras that hum louder when a customer pulls merchandise off a shelf. In the Aqua Gear shop, the temperature is warmer than in the Town Square outside. Customers hear surf crashing and seagulls squawking. In the All-Conditions Gear room, where biking and hiking goods are displayed, customers hear the sound of wind and feel a breeze from strategically placed fans. The temperature is 15 degrees cooler than in the Town Square outside. In the International running pavilion, the sound of a runner pounds out first on a surface that sounds like pavement, then gravel, then dirt. The basketball shop (The Force) looks like a gym, complete with a wooden floor and girders. Customers hear the sound of a ball dribbling and the squeak of sneakers on a wooden floor. Scattered throughout the store are autographed memorabilia such as Nolan Ryan's baseballs, Michael Jordan's first pair of Nikes, John McEnroe's busted racquets, and Bo Jackson's dirty cleats.

Source: Adapted from Kerry Hannon, "The 1992 Store of the Year," *Money,* December 1991, pp. 156–60.

The Retailing Capsule illustrates retailers' growing awareness that the environment in which merchandise is sold is as important as what is being sold. In many instances, identical merchandise can be found in directly competing stores. Thus, it is critically important for any given store to create a general atmosphere and specific presentations that will trigger buying decisions on its own sales floor rather than that of competitors.

STORE DESIGN

Store design refers to the style or atmosphere of a store that helps project an image to the market. Store design elements include such exterior factors as the storefront and window displays and such interior factors as colors, lighting, flooring, and fixtures.

Store design is an important image-creating element and should begin with an understanding of preferences, desires, and expectations of the store's target market. For example, store design for warehouse food stores and other stores whose target market is price-conscious shoppers features tile floors, harsh lighting, and limited in-store signing. Compare this design to that of a store whose target market is a more affluent clientele—for example, Marshall Field's. Its spacious, elegant store in Columbus, Ohio, exemplifies the attention to design that is as important today as it was to the founder, Marshall Field, when he created Marshall Field & Company in 1881 (see A Profile in Excellence). The store, designed to be a "cultural and social destination," incorporates many of the historical features of the company's 100-year-old flagship store in Chicago. One of the most distinguishing features of the new store is an expansive and panoramic well through which the escalators ascend (see Exhibit 16–1). The atrium's most distinguishing feature is a large bronze and stainless steel clock, which rests on a 38-foot pedestal on the lower floor. Design materials enhance the store theme and elegant ambience. For example, over 20 different types of wood are used for decorative purposes. Each merchandise grouping has its own environment and identity.[1]

Retailers must constantly monitor changes occurring in the external environments and alter store design to be responsive to these changes. For example, retail store design is being affected by the changing buying roles of men and women. With women becoming bigger buyers of automotive products, some auto-parts stores are changing their store design to shed their "macho" image. A Bumper-to-Bumper auto parts store in Fort Worth, Texas, decorates its walls with portraits of women working on their cars.

When a store changes its target market, repositioning often requires changes in store design. Recall from Chapter 2 that Frederick's of Hollywood, the world-famous lingerie chain, has refocused its attention on the mainstream mall shopper. As a result, the company's new image is more refined and less risqué. To complement the company's new image, Frederick's has embarked on an extensive store-redesigning program. In

A Profile in Excellence

MARSHALL FIELD

Marshall Field, reared in a strict New England farm family, arrived in Chicago in 1856 at the age of 21 with slightly under $1,000. With the help of his brother, he got a job as a clerk in the largest wholesale dry good firm in the city. Two years later, Field bought into the dry goods store of P. Palmer & Company with Levi Z. Leiter, forming Field, Leiter & Company. Despite two devastating fires and a serious depression, the company not only survived the 1870s, but in 1880 was a flourishing and highly profitable business. In 1881, Field purchased Leiter's partnership and created Marshall Field & Company.

With the company creation emerged the principles and policies that Field applied to his business. He would tolerate no deception of any kind in his relationships with customers and employees. His liberal treatment of customers is reflected in the well-known phrases "Give the lady what she wants" and "The customer is always right."

He believed in integrity of the highest order. In this, his main function was to assemble the widest possible assortments of quality merchandise not only from domestic sources, but from countries around the world. He believed in the fair and generous treatment of his employees. As a matter of policy, he paid higher wages and granted more liberal benefits than the average firm in the industry. He was among the first to make available to his customers such services as tea rooms; waiting, writing, and rest rooms; nurseries; information desks; theater ticket offices; and travel bureaus. He believed in operating only full-line quality stores so designed and equipped as to achieve the maximum in beauty and good taste. He believed that people responded to these qualities in the design of buildings and interiors just as they admired beauty and good quality in merchandise.

an effort to achieve a more sleek, contemporary image, every detail of the store has been changed. The new store features floor-to-ceiling glass windows, marble entrances, and mauve carpeting. Lighting is subdued and the color scheme muted. Chrome fixtures replaced brass ones. The end result is a more romantic, softer look.[2]

Creating the appropriate store design requires consideration of both the exterior and interior design of the store. Let's take a closer look at both of these elements.

Exterior Design

Store designers indicate that many retailers make the mistake of concentrating only on the inside of the store and fail to give adequate attention to the exterior of the building. However, a store's exterior is a most important aspect of image creation. The building's architecture and entrances, display windows, and signs are some of the image-creating elements related to exterior design.

Architecture and Entrances. A store's architecture can create image impressions in a number of ways. The architectural design may reflect the nature of the products sold in the store. A restaurant emphasizing Cajun

EXHIBIT 16–1

Store design: HTI/Space Design International. Photo by Don DuBroff.

Marshall Field's Columbus, Ohio, store pays tribute to classic flagship.

dishes may choose a New Orleans style with wrought iron balconies and stairs. A restaurant specializing in Southern cuisine may design the building to look like a Southern plantation. Crate & Barrel, with its flagship store in Chicago, illustrates well how store design is coordinated with merchandise. The architectural image of the store, like its merchandise, is derived from ordinary and natural materials used in a creative way. The building's modern shape and open design is reminiscent of Crate & Barrel merchandise.[3]

A store's entrance is important for several reasons. Gingiss Formalwear redesigned its stores in the St. Paul–Minneapolis area to enhance store visibility and to better communicate the kind of merchandise sold. The entrance to the stores attracts attention by presenting two life-size silhouette cutouts of men dressed in traditional formal wear. As seen in Exhibit 16–2, the cutouts, which are illuminated, flank the store's entrance.

Some designers see entrances as a transition zone, which suggests that entrances should provide for easy entry into the store. This idea is evident in the design of a supermarket chain in Austin, Texas. The designer created a 24-foot-high curved wall that "undulates across the exterior." The wall has six 10-foot-high openings through which shoppers pass, leading them

EXHIBIT 16–2

Courtesy Mark Morrow/Gingiss Formalwear Franchisee

A store's entrance enhances visibility and communicates merchandise sold.

into a courtyard. The courtyard serves as the transition zone. The effect is to make customers feel as though they have bypassed the hustle and bustle of the walk areas and the parking lot.[4]

Designers also emphasize the importance or consistency between the exterior and interior design elements. In designing Bloomingdale's 227,000-square-foot store in Boca Raton, Florida, the designer worked closely with the store's architect to ensure that the theme of the store's exterior was carried into the store's interior. The designer used stepping on the outside and copied the effect on the inside to make it look like art deco. In addition, the same creamy, peachy beige color was used both outside and on the inside.[5]

Display Windows. Window displays were downplayed during the 1970s and early 1980s because of increased cost cutting and energy consciousness among retailers. In addition, with emphasis placed on building stores in malls, more attention was given to merchandise presentation than to window displays.

Today, however, there is a renewed interest in store window displays, especially among department stores and higher-priced retailers and especially in cities where walking and window shopping are still in style.

Window displays may be used to enhance store image, to expose would-be shoppers to new products, or to introduce a new season. Much artistry is involved in developing effective window displays. Principles of good design—balance, proportion, and harmony—are all essential. Errors retailers sometimes make are using too much or too little merchandise, inappropriate props and lighting, or simply not changing a display frequently enough, with the result that it loses its significance.

Signs. Store signs not only identify the store and provide some information about it but also can be an important factor in creating a favorable image for the store. Some retailers have developed distinctive, widely recognized signs. An example is McDonald's with its golden arches. Many cities, however, have zoning laws that require both sign permits and design approval.

A store for which signage has taken on increased importance is Accessory Lady, a national chain consisting of over 100 stores. A key component of the store's design is the arch-shaped sign, measuring nearly 4 feet high and 10.5 feet long. Made from all-formed aluminum, the sign sits on top of two columns that are placed on either side of the framed-glass storefront entry. The sign is unusual in that it actually sits on the storefront. The sign and supporting columns are entirely freestanding, at least in those locations where mall guidelines allow. Management decided not to use neon, believing it inappropriate to the image of the store. Instead, internally lit channel letters fashioned from white acrylic ensure maximum visibility. Mirrored polished brass on the sides of each letter provides accent detail. The background is a dark, rich green with speckles of black. The sign, with its contrasting colors and arched shape, provides maximum visibility. Scaled-down versions of the sign are featured on custom-designed mirrors inside the store. Repeating the signage on the interior adds to the cohesiveness of the store.[6]

Interior Design

As indicated earlier, consumers respond not only to the products or services being offered but also to their surroundings. Environmental factors affect a shopper's desire to shop at the store and the amount of time spent in the store. The internal environment can also influence the customer's willingness to explore the environment and to communicate with salespeople. Thus, retailers must consider the psychological effects of their outlets on consumer purchasing behavior.

Increasingly, as suggested by the Retailing Capsule, retailers are combining theater and entertainment with interior store design. Two retailers, one on each U.S. coast, that illustrate how engaging and unusual stores can be are the Disney Store in Glendale, California, and F.A.O. Schwarz in New York. The Disney Store is like a small piece of Disneyland. It is entirely fashioned after a movie set populated by Disney characters. Even the display cases look as if they were created from giant rolls of film. At F.A.O. Schwarz, doormen, dressed as Nutcracker soldiers, welcome customers to the store. Inside, 20 costumed entertainers wander, juggling stuffed-cotton vegetables and demonstrating the season's hottest toys. Customers go to F.A.O. to have fun—it's theater.

In-store environments affect consumers' perceptions and image of the store. For example, Ralph Lauren's Madison Avenue store reflects a life of gentility, style, and romance. Old tapestries have been remade into cushions that fill the store. The stereo plays Vivaldi and jazz in the morning and Frank Sinatra at 5:00 P.M. Banana Republic is a plantation with ceiling fans.[7] Victoria's Secret has a distinctive personality—that of an English lady. "Although it is a traditional English-looking store, it is sensuous, feminine, but *not* a Victorian store by any means. That's the secret. It is her inner sanctum. Everything in these stores speaks of that culture."[8] The L. L. Bean store in Freeport, Maine, has created an image of the outdoors. Large windows and skylights contribute to the out of doors feeling as do the stuffed black bear and the duck decoys. The store contains an 8,500-gallon trout pond. As shown in Exhibit 16–3, the pond uses unmerchandisable space under the circular stairs and provides a focal point for the store.

A store's design should be based on an understanding of the target market and the contribution of design to the strategy for reaching and meeting the needs of that market. In designing its store at Southdale Center in Edina, Minnesota, Dayton Hudson stressed input it received in talking with customers about things they would like to see in the store. The designers incorporated more restrooms (with baby-changing facilities in both men's and women's lounges), larger fitting rooms, more three-way mirrors, wider aisles, and additional seating. The customer-oriented design is also evident in the layout. Instead of the traditional racetrack pattern, the aisles follow a crossed design and intersect at the centrally located elevators and escalators. All vertical transportation is located together to make it easier on the customer. Traffic flow is enhanced by the main aisles, which are 18 feet wide and extend the 400-foot length of the store. The aisles allow for uncomplicated and unencumbered circulation—customers can walk from one end of the store to the other without bumping into each other.[9]

One store that undertook what it thought were customer-friendly design changes found that some customers did not approve of all of the changes. Brooks Brothers, considered by many as the venerable bastion of traditional men's tailoring, spent $7 million renovating its flagship store on Madison Avenue in New York. Since the firm's founding in 1818, company management as well as its clientele have not had a high regard for change. Even though the renovated store has the same dark mahogany–paneled men's club decor and atmosphere, management installed escalators between the first three of its six floors. Old-line customers were shaken by the

EXHIBIT 16–3

Courtesy L.L. Bean, Inc.

L. L. Bean—interior design imparts a sense of the outdoors

new moving stairways. Many wrote William Roberti, Brooks Brothers' president, to say they found the escalators "jarring" and wanted things back the way they used to be.[10]

A store's interior design includes everything within the store walls that can be used to create atmosphere. These elements include floor, wall, and ceiling materials; lighting; fixtures; colors; scents; and sounds. The following sections focus on color, lighting, sound, and scents as store image-creating variables.

Color. Researchers have determined that color can affect store and merchandise image and shopping behavior. Studies have shown that people are physically drawn to warm colors such as red and yellow. Thus, warm colors (particularly yellow) are good color choices for drawing customers into a retail store, department, or display area. Warm colors are appropriate for store windows and entrances as well as for buying situations associated with impulse purchases. Cool colors (such as blue and green) are appropriate where customers must deliberate over the purchase decision.[11]

Background colors for product presentations are also a major concern for retailers. For example, the colors white, pink, yellow, and blue should not be used in the toddler department. Those are the colors of most of the merchandise; thus the garments would merely fade into the walls. Sometimes, the color that is used to show off the product should be related to the final use of the product. Fine jewelry, for example, may look dramatic against bold color backgrounds, but the color fine jewelry is most often seen against is flesh. On the other hand, costume jewelry is best presented against vivid tones.

Lighting. Lighting can be used to spotlight merchandise, to affect shopping behavior, and to lower operating costs. Office Depot, for example, switched from a fluorescent system to high-intensity discharge (HID) fixtures, which resulted in better visibility and reduced energy costs. With HID fixtures, the light goes up and then is redistributed down at different angles. Thus, the fixtures direct the light to the ceiling and walls in addition to illuminating the merchandise on display. Improved light distribution is important because Office Depot stacks its merchandise 16 feet high in a warehouse-style setting. Shoppers now have an easier time reading package labels. The HID units are also well suited for Office Depot, which uses up to three times more in-store signage than other retailers. Finally, management believes that the new lighting system adds to the overall appearance of the store, enhancing the store's color scheme and making the grey flooring and its patterns more attractive.[12]

Sound. Music affects shopping behavior. Some research has found that shoppers spend less time in a store when music is played loudly. One researcher discovered a 30 percent increase in supermarket sales when the store played slow music compared to fast music. The same researcher found that a restaurant's customers spent more time at their tables and consumed more alcoholic beverages but ate no more food when slow music was played compared to fast music. In all these studies, the improvement in sales was attributed to customers spending more time in the outlet, usually because they moved at a slower pace. Of interest is the fact that a significant number of customers surveyed after leaving a store did not recall that music was being played. This implies that shopping behavior was altered by a stimulus without shoppers' awareness.[13]

Scents. Research has shown that scents can affect consumer behavior; for example, if a grocery store pumps in the smell of baked goods, sales in that department will increase. Some department stores pump fragrances, carefully choosing them to match their target audience.

Interestingly, scents can affect the perception of products that don't naturally smell—such as shoes. In a study sponsored by Nike, participants examined a pair of Nike gym shoes in two separate rooms. One room was completely odor free; the other was filtered with a pleasing floral scent. The scent had a direct positive effect on the desirability of the sneakers on 84 percent of the participants. The results of the study suggest that stores could boost sales by releasing scents that appeal specifically to targeted audiences. For example, retailers might use a spicy odor if they are targeting men in their thirties; a mixed floral scent would be more

TABLE 16–1 ADVANTAGES AND DISADVANTAGES OF GRID, FREE-FLOW, AND BOUTIQUE LAYOUTS

Type	*Advantages*	*Disadvantages*
Grid	Inexpensive	Not visually exciting
	Simplifies security	Doesn't encourage browsing
	Easy to maintain	Limits creativity
	Conducive to self-service	Hinders customer movement
Free-flow	Flexible	Inefficient use of space
	Encourages impulse purchasing	Complicates security
	Visually attractive	More expensive than grid
	Allows browsing	May create customer confusion
Boutique	Flexible	Expensive
	Ability to target specific lifestyle customers	Complicates security
	Visually exciting	Inefficient use of space

appropriate for females in their sixties. Furthermore, retailers should choose scents to suit the area of the store and the time of the day.[14]

Store Layout

Store layout involves planning the internal arrangement of departments—both selling and sales supporting—and deciding on the amount of space for each department. Store layout is a very important element of store planning. Layout not only affects customer movement in the store but also influences the way merchandise is displayed. The following elements of layout planning will be discussed: (1) the overall arrangement of the store, (2) store size and the allocation of space to selling departments and sales support activities, and (3) location of selling departments and sales support activities within the store.

Arrangement of the Store

Typical layout arrangements are the grid, the free-flow, and the boutique concepts. Table 16–1 presents advantages and disadvantages of each layout alternative.

Grid Layout. In a **grid layout,** merchandise is displayed in straight, parallel lines, with secondary aisles at right angles to these. A supermarket typically uses a grid layout, as shown in Figure 16–1.

The grid layout is used more for store efficiency than customer convenience because it tends to hinder movement. Customer flow is guided more by the layout of the aisles and fixtures than by his or her desire for merchandise. For example, 80 to 90 percent of all customers in a supermarket with a grid layout pass the produce, meat, and dairy counters.

FIGURE 16–1 GRID LAYOUT

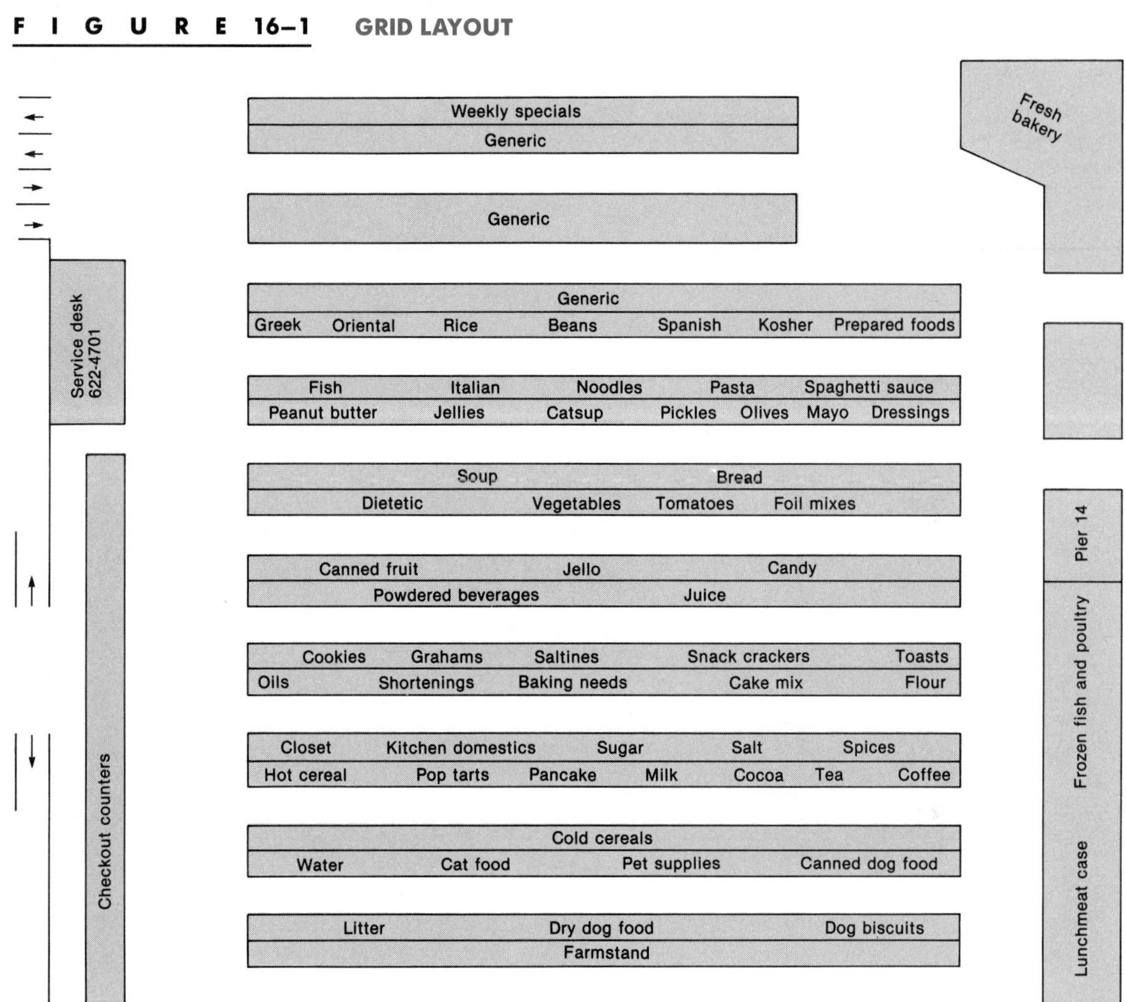

Fewer shoppers pass other displays, because the grid forces the customers to the sides and back of the supermarket.

In department stores, a grid layout on the main floor usually forces traffic down the main aisles. Shoppers are therefore less likely to be exposed to items along the walls, so demand (highly sought) merchandise should be placed along the walls instead of the main part of the store so that customer traffic is drawn to these normally slow-moving areas. (**Demand merchandise** is purchased as a result of a customer's coming into the store to buy that particular item.) Convenience goods and impulse merchandise should

FIGURE 16–2

FREE-FLOW LAYOUT

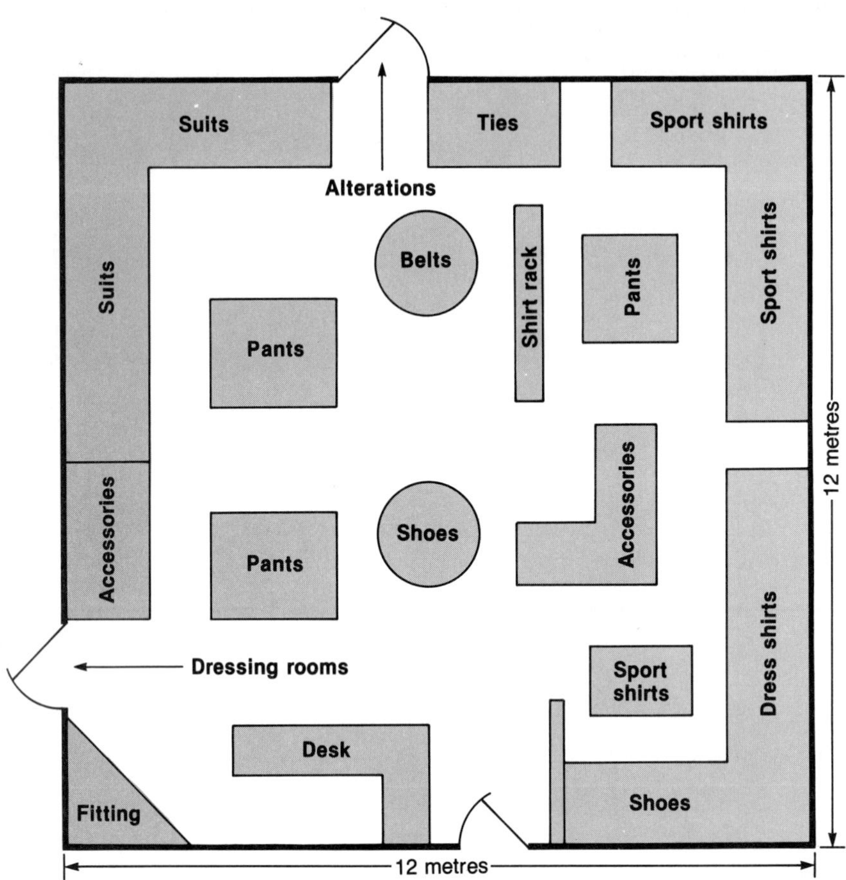

be displayed in the main part of the store. (**Impulse merchandise** is bought on the basis of unplanned, spur-of-the-moment decisions.)

Free-Flow Layout. In a **free-flow layout,** merchandise and fixtures are grouped into patterns that allow an unstructured flow of customer traffic, as shown in Figure 16–2. The free-flow pattern is designed for customer convenience and exposure to merchandise. Free-flow designs let customers move in any direction and wander freely, thus encouraging browsing and impulse buying. Merchandise divisions are generally made on the basis of low fixtures and signing. The visibility of all departments is possible from any point in the store, which allows for better departmental interselling. The layout, however, is more costly and uses space less efficiently than the grid layout. A free-flow arrangement is often used in specialty stores, boutiques, and apparel stores.

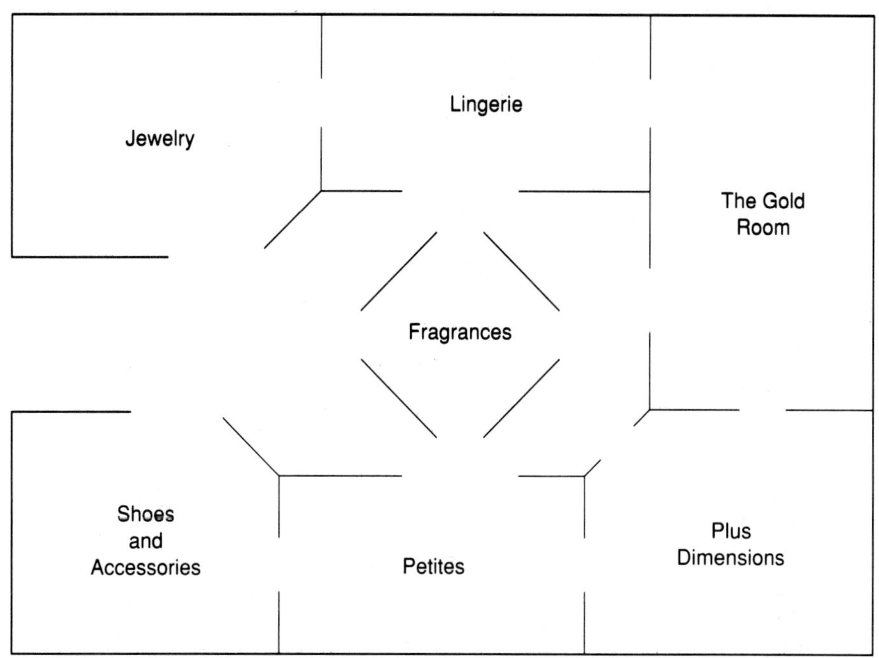

FIGURE 16–3

BOUTIQUE LAYOUT

Boutique Layout. A variation of the free-flow layout is the **boutique layout,** shown in Figure 16–3, where merchandise classifications are grouped so that each classification has its own "shop" within the store. Each shop has its own identity, including color scheme, style, and atmosphere. A shop may be aimed at a specific lifestyle segment and often features merchandise from a single designer or company.

Because of its higher construction and security costs, the boutique layout is primarily used in high-status department stores and other outlets where the sale of higher-priced merchandise allows absorption of the increased costs. However, some discounters are experimenting with the store-within-a-store concept. For example, Caldor, a Northeastern chain, devotes space exclusively to merchandise from Gitano. The "Gitano store" has entrances but no walls—its boundaries are marked by mannequins and double-sided light boxes featuring Gitano merchandise.

Store Size and the Allocation of Space

Store Size. For a variety of reasons, some retailers are reducing store size. Downsizing is becoming increasingly important, for example, as the cost per square footage of retail space soars. However, retailers who are reducing the sizes of their stores are attempting to maximize space productivity so that merchandise presentation and sales will not be

EXHIBIT 16–4

Collar Bar illustrates the concept of maximizing the cube.

negatively affected by the smaller store size. Industry analysts refer to this concept as "maximizing the cube." The concept requires maximum utilization of space, especially the walls of the store. A good example of this is the design of the 1,500-square-foot Collar Bar (see Exhibit 16–4). With the exception of some free-standing fixtures and some glass display counters, nearly all the merchandise is displayed on two-tiered hangrods or on shelves that have been built into the walls. Because the store is only 15 feet wide, a vaulted ceiling provides the illusion of space. In addition, the rear wall is mirrored, another technique used to make the small space appear larger. Another firm with a similar concept is Field's Hosiery. By maximizing the cube, the 50-unit chain, which once leased 2,000 square feet for a single unit, has been able to reduce the size of its per store space to 1,000 square feet without sacrificing merchandise flexibility.

Overseas expansion may lead to smaller stores. For example, when Talbots opened its first store in Japan the store was 2,100 square feet, about half the size of one of its U.S. stores. Two factors were at work here. One was the high cost of retail space; the other was a smaller inventory requirement owing to a smaller range of sizes. Whereas in the United States the company would have a size run starting at size 4 and go up to 18 or 20, in Japan the stores have a size run of only three or four sizes.[15]

As firms move into smaller markets, smaller outlets may be needed. For example, McDonald's wants to add stores, but major markets already are at or near saturation. Thus, a key to growth is entering smaller markets, and McDonald's see towns with populations of up to 4,000 as a revenue source it wants to tap. The company has learned, however, that its traditional outlets can't produce enough volume from smaller, rural markets to make profitable franchises. Thus, in these smaller markets, McDonald's is opening units about half the size of standard McDonald's restaurants that seat 50, including counter seating.[16]

One reason that the concept of hypermarkets has been unsuccessful in this country is their size. Wal-Mart, for example, built only four Hypermarket USA stores before canning its program. Kmart stopped at just three American Fare stores. According to industry analysts, customers think these stores are just too big. The Wal-Mart store in Garland, Texas, for example is 225,000 square feet (as big as five football fields). Not only do customers object to the size, but hypermarkets have to cope with the high cost of running such vast operations, including high air conditioning and heating costs and the hiring of 400 to 600 workers. Wal-Mart scratched its plans for a St. Louis hypermarket partly because it could not find a piece of land big enough for the store and its parking lot. Thus, rather than continuing with hypermarkets, these retailers are concentrating on supercenters—combinations of discount department stores and grocery stores—that average around 150,000 square feet.[17]

A retailer that is moving in the opposite direction and expanding the size of some of its stores is The Limited. Unlike its competitors such as Casual Corner and Foxmorr, The Limited is tripling and quadrupling the size of some of its stores and spending millions on a fresh look. For example, The Limited Express store in Northland Mall in Columbus, Ohio, is now 20,000 square feet—four times the size of the old store. Management expects to continue this expansion of superstores in order to accommodate expanded merchandise lines, including a children's collection, lingerie, and men's sportswear. When asked about the reason for the change, Leslie H. Wexner, The Limited's chairman and founder, responded, "Fifteen years ago people went to malls because there were 20 different shoe or apparel stores. But now no one wants to muddle through that many. Customers today want one-stop shopping and greater individuality, so they feel more secure when they see a broader assortment in one place."[18] Apparently, the expansion idea is paying off. Management says the larger stores are achieving the same sales per square foot as smaller outlets—some $350 per square foot annually, which is about $60 higher than the industry average.

Allocation of Space. Dividing total space between selling and sales support areas is an element of store layout planning. As a general rule, retailers other than specialty or fashion outlets devote as much space to the sales area as possible. However, the amount of sales space varies by size and type of store. In a very large department store, selling space may account for roughly 65 percent of total space. Jewelry stores need almost no sales support space. A home improvement center, however, may use more space for warehousing and storage than for selling. In general, the larger a store, the higher its ratio of sales support space to selling space.

The amount of space allocated to nonselling areas is being affected by greater vendor marking and the advent of electronic data interchange and quick response. These concepts enable merchandise to move more quickly and accurately through the distribution channel, with smaller quantities arriving at the store more frequently. Because large cushion stocks are not required, back rooms can be greatly reduced in size, and more store space can be used for merchandising. Montgomery Ward, as a result of changing its entire logistical network, no longer needs the large back rooms it had when its stores were originally built. One move to utilize this excess space has been to sublease space in some of its stores to other retailers.

Management can use three basic methods for allocating selling space: industry averages by type of merchandise, sales productivity of product lines, and the build-up (model stock) method.

Industry Averages. Management can use the national average percentage of selling space that a particular merchandise line occupies in a certain type of store. For example, assume that the health and beauty aids department accounts for 4 percent of total selling space on average in a superstore. Thus, in a superstore with 36,000 square feet of selling space, management would set aside 1,400 square feet for the health and beauty aids department (36,000 × .04 = 1,440).

Sales Productivity Method. Sales productivity is measured by sales per square foot of selling space. Assume that the planned sales for health and beauty aids is $144,000. If the national average sales per square foot for this department is $100, then management would allocate 1,440 square feet to the department ($144,000/$100 = 1,440).

Build-Up (Model Stock) Method. Let's use a ladies' blouse department to illustrate this space allocation method. The build-up method would proceed as follows:

1. Determine the ideal stock balance necessary to achieve expected sales volume. The merchant, based on past experience, may believe that sales of $30,000 per year are obtainable. Trade sources indicate that in the price line planned, three turns per year are realistic. Within the price-line structure, the average price of a blouse is $15. Given these assumptions, approxi-

mately 666 blouses will be needed as a normal offering during each turnover period ($30,000/3 = $10,000 in merchandise; $10,000/$15 = 666 blouses). Normally, 666 blouses must be in stock. However, the merchandise planner may vary from this number during months of high and low sales volume. In this method, planning ties merchandise needs to actual seasonal variations rather than to yearly averages. For example, Mother's Day might be the yearly peak sales period and should be considered in layout planning.

2. Decide how much merchandise should be kept on display and how much should be kept in reserve stock. How many of the 666 blouses should actually be displayed? Ideally, 100 percent should be on display because goods do not sell if they are not seen. This may not be realistic, so let's assume that two-thirds of the stock, approximately 444 blouses, will be displayed, and one-third will be in reserve.

3. Determine the best method of displaying the merchandise. This decision depends on the merchandise display equipment available and the affordable opportunities for display. Let's decide that we will hang the less expensive blouses on circular racks that have a glass top for display purposes. The most expensive blouses will be displayed in glass cases, where they can be accessorized with jewelry, scarves, and other small items. Reserve stock will be stored in drawers beneath the display cases.

4. Decide how many display racks and cases are necessary to display the items. The physical size and capacity of fixtures must be determined to answer this question. Scale models of fixtures are often placed on floor plans to assist in the layout planning process.

5. Determine the best way to handle the reserve stock. We have already decided that the reserve stock for the expensive blouses will be maintained under the display cases. Space can be allocated for the remaining items in special storage fixtures on the selling floor or in a stock area as close to the selling floor as possible.

6. Decide what service requirements are necessary for the department. Fitting rooms and a point-of-sale terminal or register will be needed. Likewise, depending on the nature of the operation, space for packaging may be required. Finally, all departments need aisles.

7. The total space needs can be determined by summing the space requirements found in steps 4, 5, and 6.

Locating Departments and Activities

Management must decide where to locate selling and sales support activities within the store. Several guidelines are available to retailers to help them make these decisions.

Locating Selling Departments. Convenience for customers and the effect on profitability are management's primary concerns in locating selling departments within the store. With these points in mind, the following suggestions are offered:

1. **Rent-paying capacity.** The department with the highest sales per square foot is best able to pay a high rent. Thus, this department should be placed in the most valuable, high-traffic areas of the store. If several departments are equally good, the decision may be made based on some financial indicator such as the gross margins of the merchandise.

2. **Impulse versus demand shopping.** Departments containing impulse merchandise normally get the best locations in the store. Departments carrying demand merchandise can be located in less valuable space because customers will hunt for these items.

3. **Replacement frequency.** Certain goods, such as health and beauty aids, are frequently purchased, low-cost items. Customers want to buy them as conveniently as possible, so the department should be placed in an easily accessible location.

4. **Proximity of related departments.** Similar items of merchandise should be displayed close together. In a superstore, for example, all household items—such as paper products, detergents, and kitchen gadgets—should be placed together so that customers will make combination purchases. Similarly, the men's accessories department—shirts, ties, and underwear—should be placed near the suit department in a department store. A customer wanting a new suit often needs a matching shirt and tie as well. Combination selling is easier when related items are close together. Location of related goods is even more important in a self-service store because no salesperson is around to help the customer.

5. **Seasonal variations.** Items in some departments are big sellers only a few months or weeks of the year. Toys and outdoor furniture are examples. Management might decide to place these departments next to each other. When toys expand at Christmas, extra space temporarily can be taken from outdoor furniture. During the spring and summer, the amount of space used for toys would be reduced to make more room for the outdoor furniture.

6. **Size of departments.** Management may want to place very small departments in some of the more valuable spaces to increase their visibility. A very large department could use a less desirable location in the store because its size will contribute to its visibility.

7. **Merchandise characteristics.** In a supermarket, bakery products (especially bread) should be near the checkout. Customers avoid crushing

these items in their carts by selecting bakery products at the end of their shopping. Products such as fruits and vegetables are usually displayed along a wall to allow more space and to better handle wiring for cooling.

8. Shopping considerations. Items such as suits and dresses are often tried on and fitted. They can be placed in less valuable locations away from heavy traffic. In addition, they are demand, not impulse, items and can be placed in out-of-the-way areas because shoppers will make an effort to find them.

9. New, developing, or underdeveloped departments. Assume that management has added a new department, such as more nonfoods in a superstore. Management may want to give more valuable space to the new department to increase sales by exposing more customers to the items.

Locating Sales Support Activities. Sales support activities, such as a credit department, can be thought of in several ways:

1. Activities that must be located in a specific area of the store. Receiving and marking areas should be located near the dock area, usually at the back of the store.
2. Activities that serve the store only. Such activities as office space and employee services can be located in the least valuable, most out-of-the way places.
3. Activities that relate directly to selling. Cutting areas for fresh meat need to be close to the refrigerators. Both refrigeration and cutting need to be close to the display cases. Drapery workrooms in department stores need to be close to the drapery department.
4. Activities with direct customer contact. In a supermarket, customers often want to check parcels or ask for information about an item. Credit departments and layaway services are needed in department stores. Such activities can be located in out-of-the way places to help increase customer movement in the store.

MERCHANDISE PRESENTATION

Merchandise displays can be used to excite, entertain, and educate consumers. If effectively used, they can have a profound influence on consumer behavior. For example, Rich's in Atlanta was selling only two pink Sony television sets a week. A designer then set up an elaborate display of pink cameras, televisions, tape players, and telephones held aloft by pink robots with whirring lights for eyes. Thanks to the merchandise display, the stock of pink equipment sold out in five days.

Often entire courses are devoted to the technical aspects of merchandise display. Because of space limitations, however, we must limit our discussion and will provide a brief overview of the following topics: the principles of display, interior displays, use of manufacturer-supplied display fixtures, and shelf space allocation.

Principles of Display

Managers need to be clever and creative enough to affect behavior through merchandise display. Displays should attract attention and excite and stimulate customers. In spite of the basically artistic and creative flair needed for display, some principles do exist:

1. Displays should be built around fast-moving, "hot" items.
2. Goods purchased largely on impulse should be given ample amounts of display space.
3. Displays should be kept simple. Management should not try to cram them with too many items.
4. Displays should be timely and feature seasonal goods.
5. Color attracts attention, sets the right tone, and affects the very sense of the display.
6. Use motion. It attracts attention.
7. Most good displays have a theme or story to tell.
8. Show goods in use.
9. Proper lighting and props are essential to an effective display.
10. Guide the shopper's eye where you want it to go.

Interior Displays

Interior displays can take a variety of forms, depending on the type of merchandise and image to be projected by the firm. The following are some guidelines for planning the effective arrangement of merchandise in departments. Also see Chapter 22 for a discussion of future trends in interior merchandise display.

1. Place items so that choices can readily be made by customers. For example, group merchandise by size.
2. Place items in such a way that "ensemble" (or related item) selling is easy. For example, in a gourmet food department, all Chinese food components should be together. In a women's accessories department, handbags, gloves, and neckwear should be together to help the customer complete an outfit.
3. Place items in a department so that trading up or getting the customer to want better-quality, higher-priced items is possible. For example, place the good, better, and best brands of coffee next to each other so that customers can compare them.
4. Place merchandise in such a way that it stresses the wide assortments (choices of sizes, brands, colors, and prices) available.
5. Place larger sizes and heavy, bulky goods near the floor.

EXHIBIT 16–5

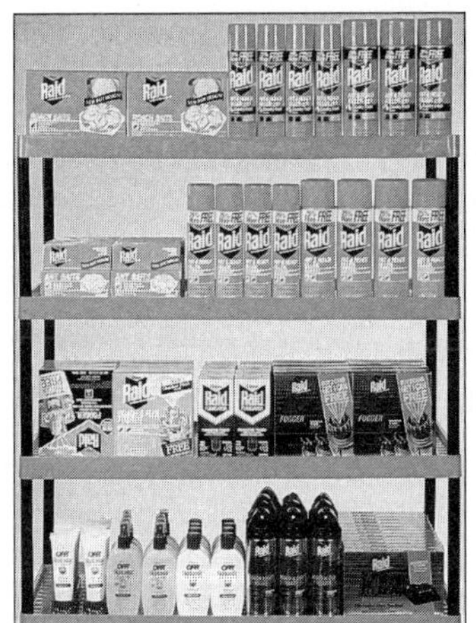

Courtesy S.C. Johnson & Son, Inc.

Manufacturer-supplied display fixture

6. If the firm carries competing brands in various sizes, give relatively little horizontal space to each item and make use of vertical space for the different sizes. This arrangement exposes customers to a greater variety of products as they move through the store.
7. Avoid locating impulse goods directly across the aisle from demand items. The impulse items may not be seen at all.
8. Use vertical space through tiers and step-ups, but be careful to avoid displays much above eye level or at floor level. The area of vertical vision is limited.
9. Place items in a department so that inventory counting (control) and general stockkeeping is easier.

Use of Manufacturer-Supplied Display Fixtures

Retailers are reacting more positively to the use of manufacturer-supplied display fixtures—one reason being that manufacturers are attempting to be more sensitive to the retailers' needs when designing such fixtures. In the past, retailers complained that many displays were ineffective for inventory control, used space poorly, and did not aid consumers in shopping. Retailers also felt many of the racks were unattractive and did not fit in with their store's decor.

Today, manufacturers are attempting to design display fixtures that overcome these problems. An example, as shown in Exhibit 16–5, is the display fixture for Raid insecticides. The in-store display features various Raid products arranged under a color code to help consumers pick the right spray for the right bug. A flip chart gives information on the habits of insects and suggests ways to "knock 'em dead." The unit can be arranged in various configurations to accommodate various store sizes.

In the self-service environment of mass marketing, manufacturer-provided displays can be used effectively as a selling tool. In the late 1980s Noxell launched Clarion makeup with a computer that is attached to the gondola. The computer allows customers to punch in their skin and coloring types, which then are used to make suggestions about which merchandise to buy.[19]

Shelf Space Allocation

A very important merchandise presentation issue is determining the amount of shelf space that should be allocated to individual brands or items in a product category. A number of rules have been devised for allocating facings to competing brands. One rule frequently stressed by manufacturers is that shelf space should equal market share. Thus, a brand with 20 percent market share in a category takes 20 percent of shelf space.

For a retailer, however, this rule makes little sense. It takes no account of the profit margins or direct costs associated with each item. Some retailers thus allocate space according to gross margin. Other retailers apply the concept of **direct product profitability** (DPP). Direct product profitability equals a product's gross margin (selling price minus cost of goods sold) plus discounts and allowances, less direct handling costs (see Table 16–2). More space should be allocated to brands or items with greater DPP. The use of DPP was limited until the development of the personal computer and spreadsheet programs such as Lotus 1-2-3, which have made the calculations much easier. DPP is actually a better measure of a product's performance than the product's gross margin and is thus replacing gross margin in merchandising decisions. The greater accuracy of DPP is shown in Table 16–2, which indicates that gross margin overstated the product's financial performance by \$1.36 (\$2.20 − 0.84 = \$1.36). As shown in Table 16–3, item A initially appeared to be more profitable than item B based on gross margin. However, in using DPP, discounts and allowances for item B were found to be higher and handling costs to be lower. The result is that DPP is higher for item B than item A.

Computer applications for shelf-space allocations are becoming more widespread. With the aid of software such as Superman III and AccuSpace, retailers can develop complete categories of products (planograms or shelf layouts) and experiment with efficient space use based on financial evaluation, product movement, profit yields, and other information. One area of great interest among chains is store-specific systems, whereby a retailer can identify the categories and products that best fit a specific store's customers. Retailers input information on package size, past sales history, projected sales, store deliveries, and other relevant data, and out comes an exact representation of the planogram schematic. The computer works to establish merchandising placement based on products that have

TABLE 16–2

COMPUTING DIRECT PRODUCT PROFITABILITY

Retail price	$9.50
Less cost of goods sold	7.30
Equals gross margin	$2.20
Plus discounts and allowances	
Merchandise allowance	.25
Payment discount	.10
Less direct handling costs	
Warehouse direct labor	.20
Retail direct labor	.75
Warehouse inventory expense	.05
Retail inventory expense	.06
Warehouse operating expense	.10
Retail operating expense	.50
Transportation to stores	.05
Equals direct product profitability	$ .84

the highest turnover or gross margins or other criteria that will allocate shelf space to best influence the consumer's behavior. During the planogram simulation, adjustments can be made to the database or planogram to best serve the retailer. For example, products tied to seasonal movement can be adjusted to reflect a temporary space allocation, or several planograms can be generated revealing layouts of different heights or widths.[20]

A particularly thorny problem is assigning space to new products. Some manufacturers, having conducted marketing tests, are able to recommend facing levels. The new item problem is simpler for a line extension. A new flavor of potato chips, for example, is invariably located with existing products in single-carton quantities until increased sales demand otherwise. In the case of a completely new category, facings can be provided only by creating new space or by destocking one or more lines from another category. Some firms tackle the new item problem by placing it in a special display until demand has stabilized at a predictable level of trial and repurchase. Because of the numbers of new products manufacturers attempt to introduce into the market each year and because of limited shelf space, some retailers (especially food retailers) are requiring manufacturers to pay slotting fees in order to gain shelf space for new products. These

TABLE 16–3

DIRECT PRODUCT PROFITABILITY COMPARISON

	Item A	*Item B*
Retail price	$19.00	$18.00
Less cost of goods sold	7.25	8.20
Equals gross margin	$11.75	$ 9.80
Plus discounts and allowances	.60	1.80
Less direct handling costs	3.50	1.70
Equals direct product profitability	$ 8.85	$ 9.90

A Question of Ethics

SUPERMARKETS DEMAND SLOTTING FEES

Increasingly, food retailers are demanding that manufacturers wishing to gain shelf space for new products pay a slotting fee. The practice is widespread: one manufacturer found that 69 percent of its major retail accounts wouldn't introduce new products without a fee. A big retail chain indicates that the $15 per store it charges to shelve a new item brings in $50 million a year.

The trend reflects a shift in the balance of power between food retailers and manufacturers. In the past, big food companies dictated to retailers the products they would carry and at what price. Now, because of size and because of the vast amount of information available from scanning systems, retailers are calling the shots.

Retailers contend the slotting fees are justified. With more than 10,000 new food products being introduced annually, there isn't enough room on the shelves to stock all the goods. They see it as a form of insurance—a way of guaranteeing at least some profit, or reduced risk, in taking on a new product.

Others see the issue otherwise. First, retailers do not require slotting fees for all new products. If a new product is going to be heavily advertised by the manufacturer, the retailers often do not require the fee. Furthermore, the practice may be keeping off the shelves products that are innovative and that may better meet consumers' needs than existing products. It is often the small and entrepreneurial food concerns that can't get shelf space because they can't afford to pay the slotting fees. And it is generally small and medium-sized producers that account for much of the innovation in the food industry. In addition, some question whether the amount of the slotting fees isn't simply passed on by the manufacturer to the consumer in the form of higher prices. The creator of a new line of cookies said that to pay one grocery chain's fee of $1,000 per store, a package of cookies that would have sold for $1.79 to $1.89 would have jumped to $2.29 to $2.39.

Do you think retailers are justified in requiring slotting fees? Why or why not? Are there any ethical issues involved in charging slotting fees? If so, what are they?

Source: Based on Lois Therrein, "Want Shelf Space at the Supermarket? Ante Up," *BusinessWeek*, August 7, 1989, p. 60; Richard Gibson, "Supermarkets Demand Food Firms' Payments Just to Get on the Shelf," *The Wall Street Journal*, September 12, 1988, p. B1.

fees range from $250 to $3,000 per store.[21] However, as illustrated in A Question of Ethics, some market analysts are concerned about the implications of retailers' requiring slotting fees.

CHAPTER HIGHLIGHTS

- Store design is a reflection of two elements: the interior design and the exterior design. Both should be in harmony with the store's merchandise and customers.
- Store layout is a very important part of store planning. One aspect of store layout is the arrangement of the store. Typical arrangements are the grid, free-flow, and boutique concepts.

- Another aspect of store layout is store size and the allocation of space to selling and sales support areas. Management can use three basic methods for allocating selling space: industry averages by type of merchandise, sales productivity of product lines, and the build-up (model stock) method.
- Management must decide where to locate selling departments and sales support activities within the store. Several guidelines are available to aid in making these decisions.
- Guidelines are also available to help management develop merchandise displays that attract attention and stimulate customers to purchase. Retailers often use manufacturer-provided display fixtures as manufacturers are increasingly trying to develop fixtures that specifically meet retailers' and customers' needs.
- An important aspect of merchandise display is determining the amount of space that should be allocated to individual brands in a product category. A number of concepts are useful in making this decision, and retailers are increasingly using planograms that have been computer generated.

Study Questions

1. What is meant by the term *store design*? What factors should a retailer consider when making store design decisions?
2. How can retailers use color, lighting, sound, and scents as image-creating variables?
3. Compare and evaluate the grid, free-flow, and boutique layouts.
4. Why are some retailers reducing the size of their stores?
5. Describe the three methods retailers can use for allocating selling space among the various departments in a store.
6. Summarize the guidelines retailers may use in deciding where to locate selling departments within the store.
7. What are the factors management should consider when deciding where to locate sales support activities within the store?
8. Discuss the guidelines retailers can use in planning interior display of merchandise.
9. What have been retailers' complaints regarding manufacturer-provided display fixtures? Why are retailers today often using manufacturer-provided displays?
10. What information can retailers use in allocating shelf space?

Problems

1. Assume a retailer is building a store that contains 40,000 square feet of selling space and is trying to decide how much space to allocate to health and beauty aids. Assume such a department accounts for 5 percent of total selling space on average. Use the industry average method to determine how many square feet should be allocated to the department.
2. Assume that the planned sales for a men's apparel department is $150,000 and the national average sales per square foot for this department is $60. Using the sales productivity method, determine how many square feet should be allocated to the department.
3. The owner of a shoe store is interested in finding the amount of space that should be allocated to the sale of children's shoes. Average annual store sales are $500,000 and approximately 12 percent of total sales is generated from children's shoes. Assume that the national average sales per square foot for this line of merchandise is $75. Using the sales

productivity method, determine how many square feet should be allocated to children's shoes.

4. A retailer is using the build-up (model stock) method to determine the amount of space to allocate to the budget apparel department. The clothes are to be displayed on circular racks, shelves, and flat cases and take up 1,200, 1,500, and 800 square feet, respectively. Space for reserve stock is to be maintained in an adjacent room containing 500 square feet. Fitting rooms and other service requirements, as well as aisles, will require 150 square feet of space. What total selling space is required?

5. Use the following information and calculate the product's direct product profitability (DPP):

Selling price	$20.00
Cost of product	14.50
Payment discount	.40
Merchandise discount	.25
Warehouse direct labor	.10
Warehouse inventory expense	.05
Warehouse operating expense	.08
Transportation to stores	.60
Retail direct labor	.88
Retail inventory expense	.05
Retail operating expense	.20

APPLICATIONS

CASE 1: Baby Boomers Seek Age-Friendly Stores

By the end of the decade, people 35 to 54 years old will be the dominant and fastest-growing segment of the U.S. population, with $280 billion more in spendable income than the segment had just two years ago.

To accommodate an aging population, many retailers are trying to create a more convenient shopping environment. Specific actions include easier-to-read labels, comfortable seating throughout the store, and shelving arranged so that customers don't need to bend over. Don't be surprised if some merchants attach magnifying glasses to shopping carts. Safety concerns may result in fewer free-standing displays around blind corners and more well-lit parking lots.

Source: Adapted from "Baby Boomers May Seek Age-Friendly Stores," *The Wall Street Journal*, July 1, 1991, p. B1.

Applying Retailing Principles

1. Why are retailers so interested in attracting and meeting the needs of consumers in the 35 to 54 age bracket?
2. In addition to the actions cited in the case, what are some additional things retailers could do in terms of store layout and merchandise presentation that would meet the needs of an aging population?
3. Could there be any negative repercussions to a retailer's implementing the types of changes addressed in the case? Explain your response.

CASE 2: Multiple Varieties of Established Brands Muddle Consumers

An increasingly attractive strategy for manufacturers is to introduce extensions of existing brands. The popularity of the strategy is evidenced by the fact that in 1991, 81 percent of new products introduced to the marketplace were extensions of existing brands, up from 70 percent in 1988.

Many consumers, however, find the number of options bewildering. Disposable diapers are a good example. For shoppers, the consequences of purchasing the wrong diaper—particularly one that's too big—can be dire. As new varieties of diapers continue to multiply, however, shoppers end up spending a lot of time in the aisle confused about what to buy. Shoppers face the same confusion in the food aisles. Campbell Soup, for example, at one time had a one-size staple packaged in uniform red-and-white cans. Today, the company offers regular Campbell's soup, home-cooking style, chunky, and "healthy request" varieties—and more than 100 flavors.

Retailers, likewise, are presented with the problem of trying to find shelf space for all these new products. If the new products are heavily promoted by the manufacturer and consumers ask for the product and expect to find it on the shelf, retailers find themselves in the position of deciding that they had better carry the product. To do so, many supermarket managers are discontinuing store-brand items that they would prefer to promote.

Retailers also realize that consumers get upset when they can't find certain products on crowded store shelves and often blame the store manager rather than the retailer. As one young mother whose newborn spent his first week in oversized Pampers because the supermarket was out of the tiniest size put it, "I don't blame the manufacturer. I blame the store."

Source: Adapted from Gabriella Stern, "Multiple Varieties of Established Brands Muddle Consumers, Make Retailers Mad," *The Wall Street Journal,* January 24, 1992, p. B1.

Applying Retailing Principles

1. What suggestions can you offer retailers for dealing with the shelf space problems that result as manufacturers increasingly engage in new product development through a line extension strategy?
2. What are the implications for retailers and consumers as retailers remove private brands from their shelves to make room for manufacturer brands?
3. Do you think consumers are justified in blaming retailers rather than manufacturers for the problems described? Explain your response.

Notes

1. "Grand Tradition Continues in Columbus," *Chain Store Age Executive,* October 1989, pp. 100–101.
2. Marianne Wilson, "The De-Sleazification of Frederick's," *Chain Store Age Executive,* September 1989, pp. 94–95.
3. "Crate & Barrel Flagship Dazzles Chicago," *Chain Store Age Executive,* December 1990, pp. 114–15.
4. "Design Sets the Stage for Products," *Chain Store Age Executive,* February 1988, pp. 13–14.
5. "Design Sets the Stage."
6. "Signage Enhances Image of Accessory Lady," *Chain Store Age Executive,* June 1991, p. 60.
7. Walter K. Levy, "Making a Difference," *Retail Control,* January 1992, pp. 8–9.
8. Marita Thomas, "Design for a New Retail World," *Stores,* January 1990, p. 159.
9. "Dayton's Design Is Customer Friendly," *Chain Store Age Executive,* October 1990, pp. 104–7.
10. Joshua Levine, "An Escalator? In Brooks Brothers?" *Forbes,* July 9, 1990, pp. 76–77.
11. Carlton Wagner, "Color Cues," *Marketing Insights,* Spring 1990, pp. 42–46.
12. "Office Depot Puts Spotlight on Its Goods," *Chain Store Age Executive,* September 1991, p. 94.
13. Ronald E. Millian, "Using Background Music to Affect the Behavior of Supermarket Shoppers," *Journal of Marketing* 46 (Summer 1982), pp. 86–91; Ronald E. Millian, "The Influence of Background Music on the

Behavior of Restaurant Patrons," *Journal of Consumer Research* 13 (September 1986), pp. 186–89.

14. Cyndee Miller, "Research Reveals How Marketers Can Win by a Nose," *Marketing News,* February 4, 1991, pp. 1–2.
15. Gary Robins, "The Logistics of Overseas Expansion," *Stores,* April 1990, p. 22.
16. Alan Salomon and Scott Hume, "Hot Fast-Food Ideas Cool Off," *Advertising Age,* September 30, 1991, p. 42.
17. Laurie M. Grossman, "Hypermarkets: A Sure-Fire Hit Bombs," *The Wall Street Journal,* June 25, 1992, p. B1.
18. Carol Hymowitz, "Upscale Look for Limited Puts Retailer Back on Track," *The Wall Street Journal,* February 24, 1991, p. B1.
19. Faye Brookman, "Fixtures Add Flexibility to Product Display," *Stores,* May 1992, pp. 84–85.
20. See Tom Steinhagen, "Space Management Shapes Up with Planograms," *Marketing News,* November 12, 1990, p. 7; Bob Cohen, "How Micromerchandising Can Work for Big Chains," *Chain Store Age Executive,* February 1992, p. 58; Dan Raftery, "The Interest Behind Space Management," *Distribution Management,* November 1990, pp. 76–77.
21. Lois Therrein, "Want Shelf Space at the Supermarket? Ante Up," *BusinessWeek,* August 7, 1989, p. 60.

C H A P T E R

17

Keys to Successful Selling

THIS CHAPTER:

Presents the types of retail selling.

Discusses the steps in the selling process.

Presents ways to increase sales force productivity.

RETAILING CAPSULE

BOOKS & CO.

Annye Camara and her husband Jo Neri cofounded Books & Co., in Dayton, Ohio, in 1978. Today, the firm is the largest independent bookstore in Ohio. In 1988, the store won the Charles Haslem Award for Bookselling Excellence, a national award given to only one company each year. The store's success is attributed to its focus on customers as well as its focus on its salespeople (the booksellers).

First of all, the owners devote time, concentration, creativity, and money to training. Everyone is trained in the same way, and management is clear and specific about expectations. The comprehensive training program emphasizes that the company's goal is great customer service.

The owners also encourage collegiality among the salespeople. For example, if a bookseller is not doing a good job, management examines the person's training and takes a team approach in trying to improve his or her performance. Those who need coaching are drawn more deeply into the circle, rather than being pushed out. Each bookseller's job description includes mentoring, coaching, and working respectfully with other booksellers, and this responsibility is viewed as a major part of everyone's performance reviews.

Finally, and most importantly, the owners listen to their salespeople. Staff are encouraged to share ideas and creative solutions. Management listens to each idea carefully, and booksellers whose ideas are implemented are rewarded.

Books & Co. has been able to create a sales staff that is committed and customer oriented. In fact, when customers are asked what they like best about Books & Co., their first responses are most often, "The wonderful people who help me."

Source: Adapted from Mervin Morris, Alan Gold, and Annye Camara, "Creating a Company," *Retailing Issues Letter* 4 (March 1992), pp. 1, 3–4.

The Retailing Capsule illustrates the strategic role that salespeople can play in the success of a retail operation. To the customer, the salesperson often *is* the business. The salesperson is the only person with whom the customer has contact. The salesperson encourages the customer to buy or, through a hostile or indifferent attitude, drives the customer away—sometimes forever.

BUILDING SALES AND PROFIT

Salespeople can play a significant part in generating greater sales and profits for a retailer for the following reasons:

- They can sell skillfully to realize maximum sales and profit from each customer attracted to the firm.
- They can provide customers with useful selling suggestions that will build sales and improve customer satisfaction.
- Salespeople can ensure that customers' needs are met so that returns are held to a minimum.
- They can develop a loyal following of customers who will return to the store and send their friends.
- Salespeople who follow store policies and procedures ensure that losses through billing oversights, failure to secure credit approvals, and acceptance of bad checks are held to a minimum.

Personal selling in retailing is essentially matching customers' needs with the retailer's merchandise and services. In general, the more skillfully this match is made, the better the personal selling. If salespeople make a good match, not only is a sale made, but a satisfied customer is created or maintained. Thus, a long-term, profitable relationship can be established.

In retailing, the top producers far outsell the average ones. The more top producers in a store, the more profitable it will be. Retailers cannot expect salespeople to become top producers by accident. There is no magic wand to wave or button to push to make this happen. However, there are a number of positive actions retailers can take to attract people with potential and, once hired, develop that potential to achieve maximum performance.

BASIC ISSUES

When Are Salespeople Needed?

The nature of the merchandise sold in the store is a factor affecting the extent to which salespeople are needed. For example, stores selling primarily convenience goods emphasize self-service. However, if the merchandise is expensive (such as furs) or technically complex (such as personal computers) and customers have little knowledge about the product, salespeople are needed. In such cases, consumers generally

EXHIBIT 17–1

Courtesy Symbol Technologies

Transaction processing

desire detailed information before making a purchase decision and expect to find knowledgeable salespeople to provide that information. Salespeople are also needed when negotiation over price is likely, as in car buying.

The overall strategy of the store affects the role assigned to salespeople. For example, in discount operations customers do not expect a fully staffed store. Of course, even discounters will assign salespeople to certain departments, such as those carrying more expensive, technically complex products (such as stereos and cameras) and merchandise that must be displayed in locked cabinets (such as guns). On the other hand, customers shopping in upscale, above-the-market retail stores expect high levels of customer service and expect personal selling to be emphasized.

What Are the Types of Retail Selling?

Several types of selling occur in retailing. A different type of person and different skill levels are needed for each type.[1]

Transaction Processing. The easiest selling task is **transaction processing**—a situation in which employees serve as checkout clerks or cashiers and do little, if any, actual selling (see Exhibit 17–1). Even though such employees do not sell in the sense of presenting merchandise and relating how merchandise can fill needs, transaction processors can affect consumers' perceptions of a store and their eagerness to shop in that store.

As a result, transaction processors should be trained to smile and pleasantly greet customers as they go through the checkout line, to ask whether they found everything they were looking for, and to thank them for shopping in the store. Such simple actions as these can do much to create a positive attitude among customers.

Routine Selling. **Routine selling** is a type of selling that involves the sale of nontechnical items. Salespeople selling clothing, for example, are engaged in routine selling. Such selling involves greater product knowledge and a better understanding of the selling process than transaction processing. Such salespeople assist the shopper in buying by giving them confidence, helping them locate merchandise, and answering simple questions. Those involved in routine selling often employ the technique of **suggestion selling** and use the customer's initial purchase to sell additional or related merchandise. This selling technique will be discussed in greater detail later in the chapter.

Creative Selling. **Creative selling** is a type of higher-level selling in which the salespeople need complete information about product lines, product uses, and the technical features of products. They are often called sales consultants and may, for example, work as interior designers in a furniture store. Creative selling occurs when the product is highly personalized, and the primary selling activities revolve around determining customers' needs or problems and creatively helping them meet those needs.

AN OVERVIEW OF PERSONAL SELLING

A basic concept in retail sales is that a sale must first occur in the mind of the buyer. The job of the salesperson is to lead the customer to a buying decision. A successful salesperson should think of selling as a process consisting of the steps shown in Table 17–1.

Understanding Target Customers

Salespeople should try to know as much about the store's customers as possible before approaching them. This may seem difficult at first, but the concept of market segmentation discussed in Chapter 2 may aid in identifying customers. The type of promotion featured by the store is also a key. For example, most customers shopping at Wal-Mart expect good price-to-value relationships and normally buy on the basis of price. These customers are often presold on products through manufacturer brand advertising and do not expect many services. On the other hand, the customers of an exclusive dress shop expect personalized attention, a high level of product knowledge from the salesperson, and a wide variety of services.

TABLE 17–1

STAGES IN THE SELLING PROCESS

Stage	*Purpose*	*Key*
Understanding target customers	Understand store's customer base	Store mission statement and promotion programs
Approaching	Stimulate interest	Offer merchandising assistance
Determining needs and wants	Decide how to meet customer needs	Ask questions, listen, and show or demonstrate a variety of merchandise choices
Demonstrating and handling merchandise	Create a desire for the product or service	Involve the customer
Answering questions and meeting objections	Overcome objections	Determine whether the problem is price, quality, service, or other features
Closing the sale	Obtain a purchase commitment	Ask for the purchase by use of proper closing techniques
Following up	Ensure continuing satisfaction	Call or write customer and resolve any problems

Salespeople can also play an important role in getting customers into the store. Some firms keep lists of their good customers' likes and dislikes. Salespeople should call these customers when new shipments of merchandise arrive. Some salespeople, however, dislike using the telephone to call customers and worry that they will be bothering their customers or that the customers will think they are being too pushy. Management should teach salespeople the proper techniques of telephoning customers and encourage and reward them for doing so.

Approaching the Customer

A recent survey revealed that more than three-fourths of the 800 salespeople surveyed said that what they disliked most about their job was approaching strangers.[2] Even though many salespeople may feel negatively about this aspect of the selling process, the initial approach is a crucial variable affecting a sale. Research has shown that salespeople who exhibit poor approach skills also perform poorly on subsequent selling tasks. Similarly, those exhibiting excellent approach skills also perform well on the selling tasks that follow.[3]

The approach is designed to gain the customer's attention, create interest, and make a smooth transition into a presentation. Various approaches to customers are possible, but the most commonly used approaches are the service approach and the merchandise approach.

With a **service approach,** the salesperson simply asks whether he or she can be of assistance to a potential customer by asking a question such as "Can I help you?" The greeting is especially useful if the customer has apparently made a selection and simply needs someone to ring up the sale. However, such an approach is weak because the customer is given the

TABLE 17–2 FREQUENCY OF INTRODUCTORY APPROACHES USED BY SALESPEOPLE

Approach	Specialty Store	Department Store
Verbal		
"Can I help you?"	52	83
"How are you doing?"	22	14
"Are you looking for something special?"	18	9
"What size do you need?"	5	0
"If you need help, let me know."	3	8
Product presentation	2	0
"We are having a sale"	1	0
"Are you finding everything you need?"		10
"Hello!"		3
"Do you like that?"		2
"Can I get a price for you?"		1
Personal introduction		1
"Yes?"		1
Behavioral		
Initial offer of a product demonstration	5	9
Smile	2	0
Interviewer had to seek out salesperson	12	21
Rep hovered	—	—
Total	122	164

Source: Lawrence B. Chonko, Marjorie J. Caballero, and James R. Lumpkin, "Do Retail Salespeople Use Selling Skills?" *Review of Business and Economic Research* 25 (Spring 1990), p. 41.

opportunity to quickly say "no." Even though it is weak, as shown in Table 17–2, the "Can I help you?" approach was found to be the most frequently used approach based on observations of salespeople in both specialty and department stores.

The **merchandise approach** begins with a statement about the merchandise or an open-ended statement related to the merchandise. Questions such as "The style you are looking at is very popular this year," or "For this style blouse, what size do you need?" The salesperson begins talking to the customer about the merchandise without asking whether he or she would like to be waited on. Such an approach is especially effective in making a smooth transition to the next stage of the selling process—determining customers' needs and wants.

Determining Customers' Needs and Wants

Salespeople should quickly discover the customers' needs and wants after the greeting. Good questioning and listening skills are the key. Once the salesperson has the customer's attention and understands his or her needs, the salesperson can quickly move the customer into the interest and desire stage and on to the buying stage.

Getting a customer to talk is important because it is the only way to find out his or her special problems, interests, and needs. Then, when making the sales presentation, the salesperson is in a position to stress the things that are important to the customer and to talk specifically about the situation. One way to develop information on customer needs and desires is to ask the customer about his or her planned use for the merchandise. This knowledge will help the salesperson better understand what the buying problem is and how the merchandise can help solve it. Such information can also provide insight into the price, styles, and colors a customer may prefer.

Salespeople must know not only the art of asking questions to discover needs but also that of listening. Knowing the importance of listening and actually doing it are two different things. Many salespeople keep planning what to say next instead of listening. As we will discuss later, a retailer's training program should stress techniques of effective listening.

Presenting and Demonstrating Merchandise

Effective questioning and listening helps determine which merchandise to show the customer and which features of the merchandise will help solve the buying problems he or she faces. For example, if a salesperson discovers that a customer is buying apparel for a trip abroad, the salesperson might point out items that are lightweight, that do not wrinkle easily, and that are most appropriate for the area of the world where the customer will be traveling.

Good salespeople have a mental outline they follow when presenting merchandise. This outline differs from a canned sales presentation in which the salesperson repeats exactly the same statements to each customer. The salesperson is free to deviate from a fixed statement but will still keep key points from the outline in mind as a checklist. A mental guide should include the following points:

1. Begin with the strongest features of the product. These features might be price, durability, or performance.
2. Obtain agreement on small points. This helps the salesperson establish rapport with the customer.
3. Point out the benefits of ownership to the customer. Salespeople should try to identify with the customer in making these points.
4. Demonstrate the product. A demonstration helps the customer make a decision based on seeing the product in action.
5. Let the customer try the product. Good salespeople get the customer involved as much as possible. The involvement pushes the customer toward the sale.

Other useful techniques include using solid, legitimate testimonials of customers who have used the product; discussing research results concerning the product; and providing information on product warranties and guarantees.

There are also certain things that salespeople should avoid doing. For example, they should not make exaggerated claims, make promises that they cannot keep, disparage competitors and their products, or misrepresent their own firm's offerings by citing inaccurate facts and figures.

Answering Questions and Meeting Objections

Customers may object to a point during the sales process. When that occurs, the salesperson should try to find the real reason for the objection, such as the price or quality of the product. The salesperson should try to get the customer to see the situation differently. He should acknowledge that he can understand why the customer holds a particular view, but he also should try to provide information that can overcome the objection. For example, an objection to a high price might be overcome by pointing out that the purchase is really an investment. The salesperson might also point out that the price of the product has not gone up any more than other items the customer has recently purchased. Above all, the salesperson should consider a customer's question as an opportunity to provide more information about the product or service. She should welcome objections as providing a way for overcoming obstacles to a sale.

Of course, the salesperson must realize that the customer's objection may be himself or herself rather than the product or its price. For example, the customer may find the salesperson too aggressive or may believe that he or she is engaging in questionable behaviors just to make a sale (see A Question of Ethics).

Closing the Sale[4]

Salespeople often have a problem with the close. Based on observation of 122 salespeople in specialty stores and 164 in department stores, a researcher discovered that only 24 percent of the specialty store salespeople and only 32 percent of the department store salespeople attempted to close the sale.[5] These findings support the commonly held perception that few retail salespeople attempt to close the sale. They would rather wait passively for the customer to volunteer to purchase.

Customers, however, often give signals to alert salespeople that a buying decision is at hand. Such signals may include questions about the use of the item, delivery, or payment. Facial expressions may also indicate that the customer is close to the buying stage. More frequently, it is up to the salesperson to bring up the closing question. An easy way to approach the close is through use of a trial close.

Trial Closes. A trial close is used to determine the prospect's readiness to buy. Trial closes occur either by asking questions to which the salesperson seeks agreement from the customer or by summarizing product benefits.

A Question of Ethics

CAR BUYERS FIND SOME SELLING TACTICS UNETHICAL

Some car buyers dread the thought of shopping for an automobile, primarily because of salespeople who use hard-sell tactics to make a sale. Use of these tactics often annoys customers to such an extent that they do not buy. Such tactics include the following:

- **Selling the Payments.** Focusing discussions on the monthly payments to divert the shopper's attention from the total price of the car.
- **The Slam Dunk.** Negotiating a price that earns a huge profit on a sale to an unsophisticated and unsuspecting buyer.
- **The Heavy Turnover System.** The customer is placed in a small, windowless room where a succession of salespeople wear down his or her resistance.
- **Low-Balling.** A comparison shopper is quoted an absurdly low price. After finding only higher prices elsewhere, the customer returns only to find that the sales manager won't approve the quote price and the salesperson then negotiates a higher price.
- **The Hull-Dobbs Technique.** Named after two salesmen reputed to be quite adept at this tactic, the goal is to make the shopper feel trapped until a sale is closed by holding on to a big deposit, or obtaining and refusing to return the keys to the customer's present car.
- **Stealing the Trade-In.** Offering an extremely low price on the new car, but buying the customer's old car for a ridiculously low price; the trade-in then yields a big profit.
- **The Puppy Dog.** The salesperson lets the customer take the car home thinking that the deal is closed except for minor details. The customer, already attached to the car, returns the next day to find the "details" may include a jump in interest or other costs.

What are some conditions in the retail car industry today that suggest that use of these tactics is going to be less successful in getting consumers to buy than in the past? If a dealer whose salespeople engaged in such techniques as these wanted to change the manner in which customers are treated, what specific actions would the dealer need to take?

Source: Adapted from David Woodruff, "What's This—Car Dealers with Souls?" *BusinessWeek*, April 6, 1992, pp. 66–67.

For example, if the prospect agrees with the salesperson on a series of questions (such as "Don't you think the self-defrosting feature of this refrigerator is a real convenience?" and "You probably need a larger refrigerator than your present one, don't you?"), it becomes difficult to say no when the salesperson asks for the order. In formulating the questions, the salesperson should focus on the points on which the prospect will likely agree. Questions should be asked consecutively to establish a pattern of agreement.

Another effective trial close is the benefit summary, which is a statement that summarizes product benefits, such as the following:

> Ms. Perkins, I think you'll find that the Brand X washer has everything you're looking for. A partial load cycle saves you water, energy, and money. Temperature controls protect your fabrics. And Brand X's reputation for quality assures you that this machine will operate dependably for a long time with little or no maintenance.

Closing Techniques. Now let's look at the most vital factor in the selling process—actually closing the sale. All previous steps have been taken with one purpose in mind: to close the sale and to get the customer to buy.

A variety of techniques can be used to close the sale. Let's look more closely at some of these techniques.

Direct Close. The direct close assumes that the prospect is ready to buy. In closing, the salesperson asks a direct question such as "Will this be cash or charge?" or "Would you like to put this on a budget plan?"

Assumptive Close. The assumptive close is a modification of the direct close. The salesperson assumes that the prospect is ready to buy but asks less direct questions, such as "Shall I call an electrician to arrange the installation?" or "Have you decided where you want the machine installed?"

Open-Ended Close. In the open-ended close, the salesperson asks open-ended questions that imply readiness to buy, such as "How soon will you need this sofa?" or "When should I arrange for installation?"

Action Close. The salesperson engages in some activity toward closing the sale, such as handing the customer a pen and saying "I'll write up the order right now and as soon as you sign it, we can deliver."

Urgency Close. The salesperson advises the prospect of some compelling reason for ordering immediately. Example statements are "That item has been very popular, and right now our inventory is running pretty low." or "Our special price on this product ends the 15th of the month."

Not all closing attempts are immediately successful. The customer may delay or may be unable to make a decision. If so, the salesperson should determine the reason for the delay. The reason will help the salesperson plan the next course of action in reestablishing the presentation of the product. For example, the customer might say, "I think I'll stick with my present car a while longer." If the salesperson has properly determined the customer's needs or problem, he or she might respond, "But didn't you say that repair costs were running very high? Isn't it worth a few dollars to know that you will save on repair costs and not have to worry about a breakdown at a critical time?"

The best closing approach depends on a variety of factors, such as the salesperson's individual selling style, the customer, and the product or service being sold. Regardless of the technique chosen, the most important thing to remember is to pursue some closing technique and not avoid this critical step.

Following Up

A note or telephone call to a customer after the sale is an important part of the selling process. Through such communications, the salesperson can again thank the customers for their patronage. They can provide additional information on the product purchased and assure the customers they have made wise product choices. For certain kinds of merchandise, such as major appliances and furniture, salespeople should make sure that the merchandise is delivered on time, that it arrived in good condition, and that installation, if needed, was satisfactory. Such communications can also be used to suggest other merchandise in which the customer might be interested and to invite him or her to visit the store again soon.

INCREASING SALES FORCE PRODUCTIVITY

The cost of retail selling is high, in spite of the low wages sometimes paid to sales personnel. However, these costs can be offset by developing a quality sales force and increasing its productivity.

For example, management should know how many salespeople are needed at a given time and avoid overscheduling. They should avoid having too few personnel available at periods such as lunch time and think about split schedules to cover these busy periods. Management should consider having less overtime and hiring more part-time personnel. Keep in mind that salespeople should be used for selling; such tasks as gift wrapping and shelf stocking should be done by nonselling personnel. The following sections discuss how better employee selection, effective training programs, appropriate compensation, and effective performance evaluation lead to increased sales force productivity.

Employee Selection

Finding good salespeople is a problem for large and small retailers alike. What retailers fail to realize is that much of the problem is of their own making. They may not define clearly what they mean by "good" salespeople or specify what qualities they are seeking. Therefore, to do a better job in finding and hiring salespeople, firms are doing several things.

First, many retailers are realizing that customers have more confidence in salespeople who are like themselves. As a result, some firms are attempting to hire salespeople that parallel as much as possible the firm's target customer. Firms that are doing so find that the result often leads to a rather diverse sales force. As an example, initially Home Depot was more concerned about moving inventory than providing customer service, so it hired young, strong males as floor employees. Management discovered, however, that these floor employees did not satisfy the needs of the firm's diverse customer base. Most customers were middle-aged men and women who had greater confidence in information provided by more mature, experienced salespeople. Don McKenna, vice-president of human resources at Home Depot, therefore developed a program to hire a diversity of salespeople. In addition to hiring more mature floor employees, the firm strives to employ more ethnic minorities and women to reflect the diversity in its customer base.[6]

Retailers should also develop job descriptions (discussed in Chapter 10) for their sales personnel. For example, a job description for a sales position in a sporting goods store might appear as follows:

> This job involves in-store sales of a full line of sporting goods ranging from items of low unit value (such as golf balls) up to higher-priced merchandise (such as complete sets of golf clubs and skiing equipment). The emphasis is on big-ticket items. Telephone follow-up selling is expected.

The job description forces the retailer to be more explicit about what a job requires and provides a guide for appraising the capabilities of prospective employees. For example, because the job discussed here emphasizes big-ticket items, the retailer should look for people who have this kind of experience. Many salespeople can do an excellent selling job on low–unit value merchandise but have trouble closing sales on big-ticket items.

Sales Training Programs

Many people wonder why training salespeople is necessary because their turnover is usually high. But effective training can increase employee sales levels, lead to better morale, produce higher job satisfaction, and lower job turnover. Training makes salespeople more knowledgeable and may make them feel more a part of the firm.

Unfortunately, when the word *training* is mentioned, the retailer typically associates it with formalized programs conducted by large department stores and national chains. However, sales training by smaller retailers does not have to be a formal and structured program. Actually, any conscious effort the retailer makes to improve the basic skills needed for effective retail selling is a form of sales training. The following sections focus on content areas typically included in sales training programs.

Job Orientation. The purpose of job orientation is to introduce the new salesperson to the business. An orientation will make the new employee feel at ease and better able to begin work. As part of the orientation process, salespeople should be given information about the company itself, such as who started the company and how long it has been in business. The company's promotion and personnel policies should also be explained. Information should also be provided on management expectations such as dress codes, goals, and performance evaluation. These and other issues that are part of a job orientation program are shown in Table 17–3.

Neiman-Marcus, as part of its job orientation program, provides each new salesperson with a handbook entitled "You're What We're Famous For" that includes rules, policies, and standards of conduct. All employees

TABLE 17–3

JOB ORIENTATION CHECKLIST

- Explain background:
  Company purpose
  Company image
  Kind of clients catered to
- Introduce to other employees and positions
- Explain relationship between new employee's position and other positions
- Tour the building:
  Working areas
  Management office
  Rest facilities
  Records
  Employee locker room or closet
  Other relevant areas
- Explain facilities and equipment
- Review the duties and responsibilities of the job from the job description
- Introduce to emergency equipment and safety procedures
- Questions and answers

must sign a statement indicating that they have read the booklet and understand its contents. This example is representative of information given to new salespeople in many stores.

Product Information. Salespeople should be knowledgeable about the products carried by the store. In-depth product information is especially needed in the sale of more technically complex merchandise. However, even if the merchandise is not technical, salespeople should be trained on how to present the product in the most effective way and how to respond to customer questions about the product. Some manufacturers send representatives into retail stores to provide salespeople with product information and to train them to present the merchandise effectively. Retailers should take advantage of this service if it is available.

A point that should be stressed in product training is that customers are not so much interested in the technical features of a product as they are in the benefits or problem-solving capabilities the product will offer. For example, a salesperson selling hiking boots could describe the product as being all leather and having waterproof seams. However, the customer is probably much more interested in the benefits he or she can expect to derive from these features. Hence, rather than simply focusing on the characteristics of the boots, the salesperson should point out that the all-leather composition makes the boots long lasting, and the waterproof seams enable the hiker to stay dry even on wet trails.

Customer Relations.[7] Sales personnel must understand that their role is to create satisfied customers, not just to make a sale. Retailers must teach salespeople that when customers enter the store, they are first a visitor, then a customer, and finally a client. Visitors may buy, customers buy, but a client returns to buy again. What can management do to ensure that salespeople are creating clients, not just customers?

Some retail training programs are showing salespeople how to develop "bonding" relationships with customers. Sales associates are thus being trained to greet customers by introducing themselves and offering a handshake, to maintain eye contact, and to ask the customer for his or her name. At Halls' and Swansons (divisions of Hallmark Cards) a "handshake campaign" was launched after a training session focusing on relationship building and bonding. Sales associates greeted customers with a handshake and implemented other techniques such as those cited above. The results were positive—management claimed that the number of customers saying "I'm just looking" decreased dramatically. When follow-up calls were made, customers remembered the sales associate. Furthermore, sales associates obtained and retained more useful information about the customer without the usual resistance.

Training should also focus on communication skills. Salespeople should be able to determine their own communication style as well as the communication style of each customer in order to discover unique ways to sell to each customer. They must learn the skills of observing and adapting. They need to learn how to watch the customer's actions, movements, and manner of speaking. Such signs reveal the customer's preferred communication style. Associates can then adapt their style to that of the customer's.

Salespeople also need to develop effective listening skills. As mentioned earlier, customers aren't interested in hearing about product features—they want to know about product benefits and problem-solving capabilities. To be able to decide which benefits to stress, salespeople must be adept at getting customers to talk and must also be good at listening. Good listening, however, is more than giving the other person a chance to talk. It means giving the person one's undivided attention. A good listener concentrates on what is being said and doesn't let his or her mind wander to other subjects. Good listeners also maintain eye contact. Asking a question now and then also helps. In addition, to keep the customer talking, salespeople should acknowledge that they are listening by prompting with nods, or commenting with "I see" or "I understand." Sales associates should not worry about what to say next. If they listen carefully, their next move will usually be obvious. It is not easy to be a good listener, but it is important.

Suggestion Selling. As described in an earlier section, in suggestion selling the salesperson tries to build upon the customer's initial request in order to sell additional or related merchandise (see Exhibit 17–2). In many cases, sales associates are so happy to make an initial sale that they fail to see the opportunity for add-on sales. But imagine what would happen if every associate sold an additional item to every customer buying just one item. There would be no additional expenses (except possibly for commission) and no additional advertising—nothing but additional sales.

The opportunities for suggestion selling are endless. For example, if a man buys a suit, the salesperson should suggest a complementary shirt and tie. For a tablecloth, a salesperson might suggest matching napkins. For an appliance, the salesperson might suggest an extended warranty. In

Courtesy The Parisian Company

EXHIBIT 17–2

Suggestion selling requires product knowledge and good selling skills.

a fast-food operation, for a hamburger purchase, the cashier could suggest fries.

Even a "no sale" or a return can become a sales opportunity through suggestion selling. The customer who is looking for a shirt to buy as a gift may not find the right shirt but could be persuaded to buy something else, perhaps a necktie or a sweater. The man who returns a raincoat because it doesn't fit properly still needs a raincoat and could be sold one if the salesperson takes advantage of the opportunity for a suggestion sale.

Equipment Use. Nothing is more frustrating for a customer than to stand at the cash register for what seems an eternity, waiting for the salesperson to figure out how to use the cash register. Before being placed on the sales floor, sales associates should be trained thoroughly in how to operate such equipment as cash registers, credit card machines, and sensor tag removal machines.

The above sections have discussed important elements of a general sales training program, but management must develop a program that specifically meets the needs of the firm and its salespeople. Management must not only be concerned with developing an initial training program for newly hired personnel but also must offer training programs on a continuous basis. As a guide to determining the content of sales training programs, management may study job descriptions and determine the types of skills needed. Obtaining input from sales associates about the areas where they feel they need training is also important. Performance evaluations of sales personnel often reveals areas where improved performance is needed, and training sessions can be developed with these areas in mind.

Compensation Systems

The appropriate method of payment for a salesperson (for example, straight salary, straight commission, salary plus commission, or other options) depends on a number of factors. Because we discussed these factors in Chapter 10, we will not repeat the information here. However, an issue that is quite relevant today is the extent to which increasing numbers of retailers are attempting to link pay to performance.

Many store managers believe that incentive plans are necessary in today's competitive environment and that better customer service depends on relating pay to performance. Stores from Bloomingdale's to Macy's have switched to incentive pay plans in recent years to better compete with firms such as Nordstrom, which built its reputation for service by paying clerks commissions that increase their incomes above the average clerk's wage. In 1987, for example, Dayton Hudson installed a Performance Plus program, whereby salespeople are paid a combination of hourly wages and bonuses for exceeding sales quotas.

However, some companies are discovering that it isn't easy to switch to an incentive pay plan. Not all sales associates are enthusiastic about the change, and some have even attempted to unionize when the firm has moved to an incentive plan. With Nordstrom's sales growth slowing, even some of its salespeople are complaining publicly. Sales associates unhappy with incentive pay plans often say they feel intimidated by unrealistically high sales goals and threats of dismissal. In fact, when Dayton Hudson initially installed its Performance Plus program, many employees were concerned about the method used to determine quotas and the policies that were established; for instance, bonuses could be withheld if employees failed to meet certain customer service standards. As a result of these concerns, Dayton Hudson's management is making many changes in the program. Management is convinced, however, that the program will lead to higher levels of customer service and will also provide sales associates with greater earning capacity.[8]

Retailers must remember that incentive pay plans that work provide benefits for the company, the sales force, and customers. A proper balance must be struck between motivating employees and good customer service. Incentive plans that ignore customer satisfaction can lead to trouble (see Focus 17–1).

Performance Evaluation Systems

A well-designed performance evaluation system can result in improved customer relations and sales force productivity. In developing such a system, management must generate a set of standards against which sales

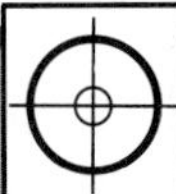

FOCUS 17–1

SEARS ADMITS ERRORS AND ALTERS ITS SALES GOALS

In June 1992 the California Department of Consumer Affairs accused Sears Roebuck and Company of systematically overcharging auto repair customers and proposed revoking the company's license to operate 72 automotive centers in the state. Because of an increasing number of consumer complaints, the department conducted a year-long undercover investigation of billing practices at 33 Sears centers. It found that its agents were overcharged nearly 90 percent of the time, by an average of $223.

Market analysts believe that policies and pressures from corporate headquarters led to the overcharges. The complaints began shortly after Sears established a quota of parts and services and repair sales for every eight-hour shift. Employees were told to sell a certain number of shock absorbers or struts for every hour of work. Sales commissions and incentives, such as free trips for top sellers, also contributed to the high-pressure sales atmosphere.

Sears chairman Edward Brennan admitted that the company's auto service incentive compensation program and goal selling created "an environment where mistakes did occur." As a result, the company has eliminated its incentive program and the 2,700 service advisors now receive a salary that approximates their commissions.

Source: Based on Tung Yin, "Sears Is Accused of Billing Fraud at Auto Centers," *The Wall Street Journal*, June 12, 1992, p. B1; Gregory A. Patterson, "Distressed Shoppers, Disaffected Workers Prompt Stores to Alter Sales Commissions," *The Wall Street Journal*, July 1, 1991, p. B1; Kevin Kelly and Eric Schine, "How Did Sears Blow This Gasket?" *BusinessWeek*, June 29, 1992, p. 38; David Dishneau, "At Sears' Dark Hour, Brennan Invokes Tradition of Trust," *The Birmingham News*, July 19, 1991, p. 1D.

associates' performance is to be measured. Actual performance should be compared to standards to determine areas where a salesperson is performing well versus those areas where improvement is needed. Management should personally meet with salespeople to give feedback. These sessions should be viewed as a mechanism for helping salespeople perform more effectively for their own benefit as well as that of the company. Thus, a well-designed performance evaluation system not only provides an objective way of evaluating and improving performance but also is often useful in helping management discover content areas where training programs need to be conducted.

In the past, most performance standards focused on sales measures. Increasingly, however, retailers are developing standards in a variety of areas, such as those indicated in Table 17–4. Parisian, Inc. is one company that has developed an effective sales associate evaluation system that incorporates performance standards in many different areas. Parisian is a chain of fashion-oriented department stores located primarily in the Southeast. Emil Hess, its chairman of the board, is highlighted in A Profile in Excellence.

TABLE 17–4

EVALUATING SALES ASSOCIATES' PERFORMANCE

Merchandise procedures	Employee's accuracy in counting and inventorying merchandise. Prevents merchandise shrinkage caused by mishandling of merchandise. Keeps merchandise in a neat and orderly manner on sales floor. Knows the design and specifications of warranties and guarantees of the merchandise groups. Gets merchandise on sales floor quickly after merchandise arrival.
Customer service ability	Provides courteous service to customers. Handles customer complaints and service problems as indicated by store procedure. Follows proper procedures concerning merchandise returns and lay-aways when conducted through credit transactions. Suggests add-on or complementary merchandise to customers.
Sales ability	Has strong ability to close the sale. Promotes sale of merchandise items having high profit margins. Acts as a resource to other departments or other salespeople needing assistance. Works well with fellow workers in primary merchandise department.
Product-merchandise knowledge	Knowledgeable of design, style, and construction of merchandise group. Knowledgeable of special promotions and advertised sale items. Knowledge of material (fabrics), color coordination, and complementary accessories related to returned merchandise. Provides accurate and complete paperwork related to returned merchandise.
Store policy	Provides accurate and complete paperwork related to work schedules. Provides accurate and complete paperwork for cash and credit transactions. Shows up on time for work, sales meetings, and training sessions. Accurately follows day-to-day instructions of immediate supervisor. Employee's overall job-related attitude.

Source: Robert P. Bush, Alan J. Bush, David J. Ortineau, and Joseph H. Hair, Jr., "Developing a Behavior-Based Scale to Assess Retail Salesperson Performance," *Journal of Retailing* 66 (Spring 1990), pp. 12–13.

A Profile in Excellence

EMIL HESS

Emil C. Hess and his family moved to Birmingham, Alabama, when he was two years old. He grew up in Birmingham, attending grammar school and high school there. In 1935 Hess started college at Wharton School, majoring in accounting and insurance. He also attended the University of Pennsylvania and graduated in 1939 with a B.S. in economics.

Hess then went back to Birmingham to begin working in his father's business, Parisian. Parisian was originally purchased by Hess' father and William Holiner. When Parisian was first purchased, it was an outlet that specialized in lower-priced women's apparel, millinery, and piece goods. Later, men's and boy's apparel was added to the inventory. In 1945, Hess and Leonard Salit (Holiner's son-in-law) began operating the business.

Emil Hess is a unique retailer. He has several key retailing strategies and philosophies that turned Parisian into the great stores they are today. One of Hess' wisest strategies was to change Parisian's image to a brand-name store offering quality merchandise and service.

Another important strategy is to treat other people importantly and make them feel happy and special. His philosophy is that the customer is by far the most important asset of Parisian. The customer should feel unique and special upon entering a Parisian store. The strategy used in the marketing campaign, "You're Somebody Special," ties it all together. Not only does Parisian advertise this message through a number of communication media, but Hess has also implemented numerous actions to carry out the message. The basic strategy of maintaining quality merchandise is that special people get quality. The store offers free gift wrapping and free mailing to anywhere in the United States. The policy of accepting returns "no matter what" adds to the list of customer service benefits that are consistent with the philosophy of Hess and Parisian.

Finally, store employees share in Hess' philosophy of treating people with kindness and respect. The store's investment-selling program is designed to create a sales force that is customer oriented and that focuses on developing long-term relationships with customers. Salespeople's goals and performance appraisals also focus on developing relationship retailing.

CHAPTER HIGHLIGHTS

- Personal selling is essentially matching customers' needs with the retailer's merchandise and services. Salespeople can play a significant part in generating greater sales and profits for a retailer.
- A number of factors affect the extent to which personal selling is emphasized in a retail firm. One variable is the nature of merchandise sold in the store. The overall strategy of the store also affects the role assigned to salespeople.
- Several types of selling occur in retailing. The easiest type of selling is transaction processing—a situation in which employees serve as checkout clerks or cashiers and do little, if any, selling. Routine selling involves the sale of nontechnical items and requires more product knowledge and a better approach to the sales task than does transaction processing. Creative selling requires the use of creative sales skills, and salespeople need complete information about product lines, product uses, and technical features.
- The job of the salesperson is to lead the customer to buy. A successful salesperson thinks of the selling process as consisting of

the following steps: understanding target customers, approaching the customer, determining the customer's needs and wants, presenting and demonstrating merchandise, answering questions and meeting objections, closing the sale, and following up.

- Because the cost of selling is high, retailers should undertake activities to develop a quality sales force and increase sales force productivity. Retailers should concentrate on better employee selection, providing effective training programs, developing appropriate compensation systems, and installing effective performance evaluation systems.

STUDY QUESTIONS

1. In what ways can salespeople play a role in generating greater sales and profits for a retailer?
2. Under what conditions is the presence of sales personnel most essential in a retail store?
3. What are the various types of retail selling?
4. What is the difference between a service approach and a merchandise approach?
5. How can a salesperson determine a customer's needs and wants?
6. Comment on the validity of the following statement: The best way for a salesperson to deal with a customer objection is simply to ignore it and continue with the sales presentation.
7. Discuss the various ways in which a salesperson can attempt to close a sale.
8. Why is following up an important stage in the selling process?
9. Assume that you have been asked by a retail store manager to describe what an effective sales training program should include. How would you respond?
10. Why should performance standards be established for sales personnel? What are some areas in which performance standards can be established?

A P P L I C A T I O N S

CASE 1: Crate & Barrel: Aiming to Be the Best, Not the Biggest

Would-be imitators of Crate & Barrel stores are not successful because they "miss the point," according to Gordon Segal, founder of the Chicago-based housewares chain. "The point is the quality of the total environment and the objective of serving the customer with a proprietary product at a unique price," Segal explains. "Too many of the people who tried to copy us went for price and did not worry about quality or went for quality and did not worry about price. And usually they did not put the right people together to make it happen. Their goals were not really to serve the customer, but to make money as fast as possible. Our goals are not driven by economics, but by a need to be a superb retailer."

Selling in the store is practiced as an "educational process." Salespeople are expected to know the product and educate the consumer about it, which Segal believes is more effective in creating a relationship than either advertising or displays. "We want our customers for the long term; we don't want them just for the sale of today."

Creating an environment—and an attitude—that keeps customers coming back begins with employees who are enthusiastic about and interested in what they do. Each store functions as its own little company, and each store manager is responsible for hiring and training staff. Crate & Barrel does not hire people who have worked for other retail companies—they may have acquired bad habits. Moreover, every newly hired employee starts the way Gordon and Carole Segal started—doing everything.

"Decentralized management requires, above all, the ability to attract the right people," Segal states. "Most everyone who works in our stores or our corporate headquarters has attended college. Each associate is hired to be a merchant and a future leader, not just a sales clerk. We put our best people on the front line, and that's where we're different. We interview 10 or 12 people for every 1 we hire. We spend a lot of time choosing a certain type of person with a certain talent, taste, and style. The most important ingredient to Crate & Barrel is these associates and the beliefs we engender in them."

Hiring bright young people is one thing. Keeping them motivated day to day and helping them to grow is another. Training, both formal and informal, receives primary emphasis. Responsibility for training is divided between in-store efforts and a companywide continuing education program.

The corporate training program involves three phases. For "Fundamentals of Selling," the first phase, employees travel to company headquarters in groups of about 10 for sessions on corporate structure and philosophy, relating to customers, salesmanship, add-on sales, ways in which buyers find new products, and other topics. Phase two focuses on product information, with sessions broken into different product categories, such as gourmet cookware, dinnerware, and glassware. Phase three covers store design—merchandising philosophy, traffic flow, the effects of high and low crates, window display, and so on.

The constant in all training is the philosophy of customer focus—excellence in product, store, service, and value. As Segal stated, "The great retail companies have a philosophy, a mission, and they take the time to share this with the staff. . . . It amazes me that retailers talk so much about service, but spend so little time bringing up and training their people."

Source: Reprinted with permission from Leonard L. Berry, David R. Bennett, and Carter W. Brown, *Service Quality: A Profit Strategy for Financial Institutions* (Homewood, Ill.: Dow Jones-Irwin, 1989).

Applying Retailing Principles

1. Highlight the unique dimensions of Crate & Barrel that indicate that customer service is first in all dimensions of the organization.
2. What are the dimensions of the Crate & Barrel sales associates program that contribute to an exceptional group of individuals with a continuing focus on customer service?
3. What are the attributes of the successful Crate & Barrel sales associate?

CASE 2: Low Morale among the Sales Staff

After being hired by Whizmart promotional department stores (a chain consisting of 20 units located in the Midwest), Bart Crowder went through 13 weeks of intensive training, along with others hired in the company's junior executive training (JET) program. After training, he was assigned as the manager of the fashion fabrics department in an inner-city store catering to first-generation families of primarily Polish and Italian heritage. Sales associates in that store were expected to speak both Polish and Italian, but in actuality most of them spoke only one of these languages. The sales associates were hired from the neighborhood, and those of Italian or Polish extraction spoke the language of their homeland.

Bart was from a small southern city and had attended college in the East. Finding himself in this environment was different, to say the least. He considered his initial training quite good, though. He had learned systems; he had acquired a good grasp of the company's target market (although he believed that there were some problems with the many varied types of micromarkets in which stores were located); and had trained with good store managers and buyers.

His first assignment as the department manager in fashion fabrics, however, had provided him with some of the best training possible. But the composition of his department and the policies he inherited had caused great problems. He had two full-time salespeople; one person who worked three-fourths time (Crystal); and three part-time women who worked the busy hours during the week. Crystal was the only person in the department who, in addition to English, spoke both Polish and Italian. Her hours had been worked out with the store manager some years previously, and they were the best hours for business. She was the only person in the department on a straight commission. The two full-time women were on a salary plus 1 percent commission on net sales; the part-timers were on straight salary.

Bart hadn't been in the department a month when the two full-time saleswomen asked for a conference. They were vehement, and their complaints were as follows: (1) "Crystal 'hogs' all sales and ties up a dozen customers at a time, and we can't make a penny extra without some commissions." (Bart was not sure whether they knew of the straight commission arrangement, but he certainly was not going to open that up for discussion.) (2) "Crystal speaks all the languages, so she is able to say things we don't understand, and we know she's talking about how good she is and how inefficient we are—she's careful to speak the 'other' language when one of us is around." (3) "The stock work in a fabrics department is tremendous; you always have to be folding bolts, straightening remnants, and so on. Crystal folds *only* her own sales and won't straighten out anything else, so we're always doing stock work while she's grabbing customers." (4) "Crystal sells so much and runs such a good book that we look bad. Even the commissions she 'steals' from us don't bother us as much as how we must look to you and others." (5) "Crystal is so 'sweet' when any of you are around, but when it's just us and customers, she's a real witch." Bart remembers with clammy hands what a difficult position that short conference put him in.

Applying Retailing Principles

1. Is Crystal so valuable that her reactions must be considered?
2. Is it typical to find varying compensation plans within a single department?
3. Are the salespeople's complaints legitimate or emotional?
4. What should Bart do?

Notes

1. This material is reproduced from Bert Rosenbloom, *Improving Personal Selling* (Washington, D.C.: Small Business Administration), pp. 1–3.
2. Terri Kabachnick, "Is Salesmanship the Dinosaur of the 90s?" *Retailing Issues Letter* 3 (May 1991), p. 2.
3. Jacquetta J. McClung, Steven J. Grove, and Marie Adele Hughes, "An Investigation of the Impact and Situational Determinants of Customer Approach Skills in Retailing," in *Enhancing Knowledge Development in Markets,* Paul Bloom et al. (eds.) (Chicago: American Marketing Association, 1989), p. 92.
4. The material on closing the sale is reproduced with modifications from *Marketing Strategy,* self-instructional booklet 1989 (Washington, D.C.: U.S. Small Business Administration).
5. Lawrence B. Chonko, Marjorie J. Caballero, and James R. Lumpkin, "Do Retail Salespeople Use Selling Skills?" *Review of Business and Economic Research* 25 (Spring 1990), p. 41.
6. "Managing Diversity: Retailing's Next Strategic Challenge," *The Retail Report,* newsletter of the Center for Retailing at the University of Florida 5, no. 4, p. 1.
7. The material in this section is based on Terri Kabachnick, "Is Salesmanship the Dinosaur of the 90s?" pp. 3–5.
8. Francine Schwadel, "Chain Finds Incentives a Hard Sell," *The Wall Street Journal,* June 12, 1990, p. B1.

C H A P T E R

18

Advertising, Sales Promotion, and Publicity

THIS CHAPTER:

Highlights the requirements for good promotion plans.

Shows how to establish budgets.

Explains how to allocate a budget.

Introduces the media options available.

Discusses how to determine media effectiveness.

Reviews how to measure the results of advertising.

Explores when to use an ad agency.

Defines the essentials of a good advertisement.

Emphasizes the role of sales promotion and publicity in the retailer's promotion plan.

RETAILING CAPSULE

ESPRIT'S NEW SPIRIT

Susie Tompkins is the co-owner and creative director of Esprit de Corp. She oversees the company's image and product designs. A native San Franciscan, she is often credited with bringing Northern Californian lifestyle to the rest of America through the success of Esprit de Corp.

In 1968 Susie started the Plain Jane Dress Company with her friend Jane Tise. They made deliveries from the back of Susie's station wagon with her two young daughters in tow and opened their first showroom above a massage parlor. Within a year, Susie's husband Doug joined the business and in 1979, the company was reorganized as Esprit de Corp.

The company rose to become one of the world's largest junior sportswear manufacturers. Under Susie's direction, Esprit's clothing and lifestyle designs became industry leaders. Its Real People advertising was reflective of its social conscience—in 1987, Esprit was the first major fashion corporation to address the AIDS crisis, informing its customers of the facts surrounding the disease.

In June 1990 Susie returned to the company after a two-year absence and assumed her current responsibilities. She continues to generate social awareness on local and national levels through personal and corporate commitments to a variety of pursuits as diverse as arts education, AIDS awareness, and environmental responsibility. She is also a strong supporter of San Francisco's Glide Memorial Church, which provides shelter and rehabilitation for the less fortunate of the community.

The Susie Tompkins Collection reflects many facets of her own personal experience. It upholds value, simplicity and elegance in a way that feels appropriate for today.

In a video shown in department stores (and included as part of the video package accompanying this text), images of the Reverend Cecil Williams, minister of San Francisco's Glide Memorial United Methodist Church,

preaching are interspersed with shots of a Susie look-alike modeling the new designs in a meadow. Flash to Tompkins slouched in a chair, talking about her childhood and memories of her mother. "When I was little, I wanted to be a nun, a cow girl, a cheerleader, a professional ski racer," Susie muses. "Mother said to me a dozen times, "You'll never amount to a row of pins.' "

At 49, Tompkins is embracing a panoply of social causes from environmentalism to AIDS to the homeless. And by weaving political correctness into the fabric of Esprit, she hopes to teach the world a thing or two about corporate responsibility."

Esprit in 1992 introduced its Ecollection in four stores in California and 30 Esprit stores in 13 countries. The line is being promoted at the point of purchase with brochures, posters, and counter cards. Management believes the line will be picked up first by "young trendies" and ultimately will have a broader appeal.

Adapted from Esprit de Corp press release, 1992; Laura Zinn and Michael Oneal, "Will Politically Correct Sell Sweaters?" *Business Week,* March 16, 1992, p. 60; Teri Agins, "Calvin Klein's Sexy Ad Insert Failed to Spur Sales of Designer's Jeans," *The Wall Street Journal,* May 5, 1992, p B8.

Susie Tompkins (Exhibit 18–1) is the essence of Esprit. Promotion plans support the positioning strategy of Esprit as an environmentally sensitive and socially active firm. The merchandise is consistent with the core themes of the positioning strategy and is promoted in a sophisticated but low-key approach to the marketplace.

Some people define promotion to include advertising, personal selling, and display, all elements of the Esprit promotion strategy. We discussed personal selling in Chapter 17, and display and layout were explained in Chapter 16. We define promotion in this chapter as including mass media advertising; sales promotions such as coupons, trading stamps, and premium offers; and publicity.

EXHIBIT 18–1

Courtesy Esprit de Corp

By weaving causes from the environment to AIDS into the fabric of Esprit, Susie Tompkins hopes to teach the world a thing or two about corporate social responsibility.

THE NATURE OF COMMUNICATION

One role of retail communication is to **inform,** by providing information on store hours, brands carried, services available, and so forth. Retailers may also seek to **persuade** individuals to do a variety of things such as to make a purchase during a sale. Communication takes place only when the individuals to whom the retailer is sending a message attach a meaning to the message similar to that intended by the retailer.

A familiar model of communication is shown in Figure 18–1. The **source** in the communication process is the originator of the message, normally the retailer. The retailer selects words, pictures, and symbols to present the message to the targeted audience. Composing the message is known as **encoding** and refers to putting together the thoughts, information, or ideas in a symbolic form that is familiar to and understood by the target audience.

FIGURE 18–1 A MODEL OF THE COMMUNICATIONS PROCESS

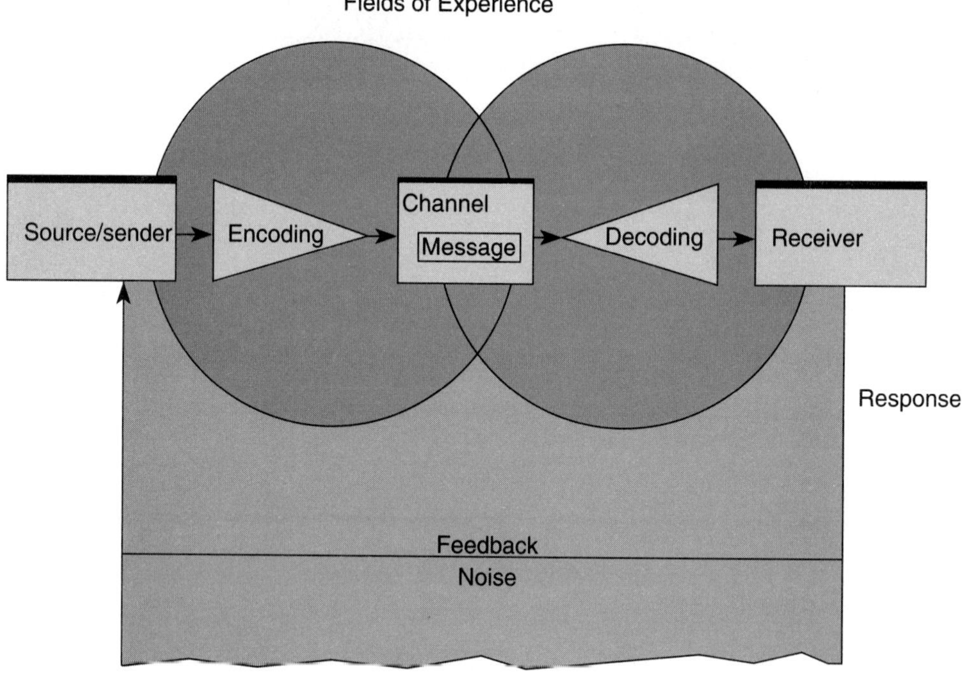

Source: George E. Belch and Michael A. Belch, *Introduction to Advertising and Promotion Management* (Homewood, Illinois: Richard D. Irwin, Inc., 1990), p. 128. Reprinted with permission. World rights reserved.

The **message** is the idea to be transmitted. It may be either oral or written, verbal or nonverbal, or a symbolic form or sign as in the case of McDonald's golden arches. Often, the impression or image created by the advertisement is more important than the actual words.

The next decision after message content selection is the **channel** to be used to communicate the message to the receiver. The nature of communication may be either personal or nonpersonal. Personal channels such as salespeople include face-to-face contact with target individuals or customers.

Word-of-mouth communication by conversations with friends or associates is also a powerful source of information for consumers. Nonpersonal channels of communication include mass media such as radio, television, newspaper, direct mail, or other means of message transmission.

The intended **receiver** is the target audience. Market segmentation plays a particularly important role in this process because segmentation ensures that the message is targeted to a relatively homogeneous audience.

Decoding occurs when the receiver transforms and interprets the sender's message as part of the thought process. The process of decoding is influenced by the individual's experience, attitudes, and values. Active communication is most likely to occur when a common ground exists between the sender and the receiver (represented in Figure 18–1 by the overlapping of fields of experience). Recall again the efforts of Esprit to target individuals with a sense of environmental awareness and concern similar to that of Susie Tompkins.

Unplanned distortion in the communications process is known as **noise.** Noise may occur because of a lack of a common field of experience between the sender and receiver or a failure to properly encode messages, such as the use of signs, symbols, or words that are unfamiliar to the receiver or that have a different meaning than the one intended.

The desired **response** after seeing, hearing, or reading the message depends on the purpose of the promotion program and may include immediate sales, requests for further information, or success in establishing or reinforcing a desired image. Feedback can occur in a variety of ways. The potential customer may ask the salesperson specific questions or in some way reflect nonverbal responses by gestures or facial expressions. Customer inquiries, coupon redemptions, and reply cards are also examples of information feedback.

The communication plan should start with the goals of the firm. Answers to the following questions can help in making such decisions:[1]

- What quality of merchandise do I sell?
- What kind of image do I want to project?
- How do I compare with the competition?
- What customer services do I offer?
- Who are my customers?
- What are their tastes?
- What are their income levels?
- Why do they buy from me?

We will begin our discussion of promotion by starting with advertising, followed by sales promotion and public relations.

ADVERTISING

The American Marketing Association defines advertising as "any paid form of nonpersonal presentation and promotion of goods, ideas, and services by an identified sponsor." The goals of advertising can include the following:

- Communicating the total character of the store.
- Getting consumer acceptance for individual groups of merchandise.
- Generating a strong flow of traffic.
- Selling goods directly.

These goals can be combined with merchandising and store image objectives into the following framework:[2]

How much to spend	Advertising budget
What to advertise	Merchandise
When to advertise	Timing
Where to say it	Media
How to say it	Technique
Whom to reach	Audience
How to provide balance	Planning

Communicating the total character of the store is known as **institutional advertising.** Institutional advertising is designed to enhance the image of the outlet and to communicate targeting and positioning strategies. **Direct-response advertising,** in contrast, induces consumers to take a specific action such as to make a purchase or participate in a contest or giveaway.

Developing the Advertising Budget

Developing promotion strategies to communicate targeting and positioning plans begins with the budget. The budget cannot be developed without knowing the objectives to be achieved and the amount of money available.

Why have a budget? A budget helps retailers plan their promotions. This step alone can go a long way toward better campaigns. Why? (1) A budget forces retailers to set goals so that they can measure the success of the promotions; (2) retailers are required to choose from a variety of options; and (3) budgets are more likely to result in well-planned ads.[3]

Methods of Establishing a Budget[4]

The methods of establishing a budget, including advantages and disadvantages of each, are shown in Table 18–1. No method is perfect for all types of retailing—nor is any combination of methods.

We have combined concepts from several well-known methods of budgeting into three basic methods: percentage of sales or profits, unit of sales, and objective and task. Management needs to use judgment and caution in settling on any method or combination of methods.

Percentage of Sales or Profits. The most widely used method of establishing an advertising budget is to base it on a percentage of actual sales. Advertising is as much a business expense as the cost of labor and should be related to the quantity of goods sold for a specified period.

What Percentage? The choice of a percentage of sales figure can be based on what other retailers in the line of trade are doing. Sample percentages are shown in Table 18–2.

Retailers should not let any method bind them. The percentage of sales method is quick and easy, and it ensures that the advertising budget is not out of proportion for the business. It is a sound method for stable markets.

TABLE 18–1 COMMONLY USED METHODS OF ESTABLISHING A PROMOTION BUDGET

	Advantages	Disadvantages
Percentage of sales	• Keeps spending within reasonable limits. • Simple and easy to implement. • Budget tends to be stable.	• The level of sales determines the amount of advertising. • Does not allow for changes in internal strategy or in strategy of competitors. • Difficult to apply to new merchandise. • Decreases in sales lead to decreases in advertising.
Unit of sales	• Based on experience and trade knowledge. • Permits a good estimate of what should be spent for maximum effect. • Effective when merchandise availability is affected by outside factors.	• Not useful in sporadic or irregular markets or for style merchandise. • Difficult to use when the merchant sells a broad assortment of merchandise.
Objective and task	• Driven by objectives to be obtained.	• Difficult to determine what is required and how much it will cost. • Difficult for introducing new merchandise.

TABLE 18–2 ADVERTISING-TO-SALES RATIOS

Industry	Ad Dollars as Percentage of Sales	Ad Dollars as Percentage of Margin	Annual Growth Rate (Percent)
Apparel and accessory stores	1.9	5.0	8.8
Auto and home supply stores	1.7	5.8	6.7
Building material, hardware, and gardening—retail	3.0	8.4	(11.6)
Catalog, mail-order houses	6.9	17.6	10.6
Computer and office equipment	1.5	3.4	5.9
Department stores	2.8	14.3	4.0
Eating places	3.4	17.4	6.2
Family clothing stores	2.3	6.7	11.5
Furniture stores	7.6	15.8	6.3
Grocery stores	1.3	5.0	4.4
Home furniture and equipment stores	4.9	15.3	11.6
Jewelry stores	3.2	11.3	12.4
Lumber and other building materials—retail	1.6	6.0	4.3
Motion picture theaters	3.2	15.2	(12.4)
Radio, TV, and consumer electronics stores	4.7	18.9	4.5
Shoe stores	4.0	10.8	7.7
Variety stores	1.6	7.1	6.4
Video tape rental stores	4.2	8.3	31.2
Women's clothing stores	3.7	9.7	9.5

Source: Schonfeld and Associates, Lincolnshire, Illinois. Reprinted in *Advertising Age*, July 13, 1992, p. 16.

But if retailers want to expand market share, they will probably need to use a larger percentage of sales than the industry average.

Which Sales? The budget can be determined as a percentage of past sales, estimated future sales, or a combination of the two:

- **Past sales.** The base can be last year's sales or an average of sales in recent years. Consider, though, that changes in economic conditions can make the figure too high or too low.
- **Estimated future sales.** The advertising budget can be calculated as a percentage of anticipated sales for next year. The most common pitfall of this method is an overly optimistic projection of the business's growth. Trends in the industry and in the firm must be hardheadedly assessed.
- **Past sales and estimated future sales.** Future sales may be conservatively estimated based on last year's sales. A more realistic assessment is produced by combining last year's sales with next year's estimated sales.

Unit of Sales. In the unit of sales method retailers set aside a fixed sum for each unit of product to be sold. This figure is based on their experience and trade knowledge of how much advertising it takes to sell each unit.

Some people consider this to be simply a variation of percentage of sales. The unit of sales method, however, does permit a closer estimate of what a retailer should plan to spend for maximum effect. This method is based on a retailer's experience of what it takes to actually sell a unit, rather than an overall percentage of the gross sales estimate.

Objective and Task. The most difficult (and least used) method is the objective and task approach. Yet this method best fulfills what all budgets should accomplish. It relates the appropriation to the marketing task to be achieved.

Allocating the Budget

Once the advertising budget has been determined, management must decide how to allocate it. The most common breakdowns are departmental budgets, calendar periods, media, and trading areas.

Departmental Budgets. The most common method of allocating advertising to departments is on the basis of their sales contribution. Those departments or product categories with the largest sales volume receive the biggest share of the budget.

In a small business, or in situations where the merchandise range is limited, the same percentage can be used throughout. Otherwise, a good rule is to use the average industry figure for each product.

Calendar Periods. Most executives usually plan their advertising on a yearly, monthly, or even a weekly basis. Even a budget for a longer planning period, however, should be calculated for these shorter periods

FIGURE 18–2 A TYPICAL PROMOTION CALENDAR

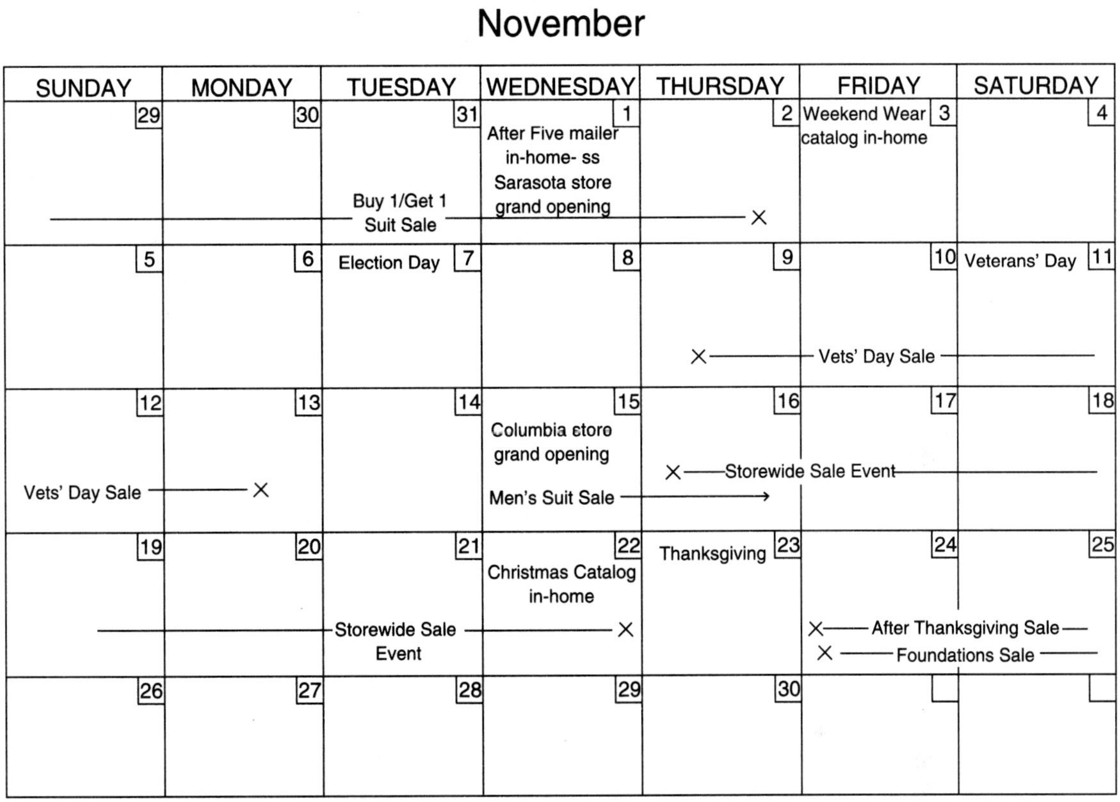

November

SUNDAY	MONDAY	TUESDAY	WEDNESDAY	THURSDAY	FRIDAY	SATURDAY
29	30	31 Buy 1/Get 1 Suit Sale	1 After Five mailer in-home- ss Sarasota store grand opening	2	Weekend Wear 3 catalog in-home	4
5	6	Election Day 7	8	9	10 Vets' Day Sale	Veterans' Day 11
12 Vets' Day Sale	13	14	15 Columbia store grand opening Men's Suit Sale	16 Storewide Sale Event	17	18
19	20	21 Storewide Sale Event	22 Christmas Catalog in-home	Thanksgiving 23	24 After Thanksgiving Sale Foundations Sale	25
26	27	28	29	30		

as well. This permits better control. A typical monthly promotion schedule for a department store is shown in Figure 18–2.

Media. The amount of advertising that is placed in each medium should be determined by past experience, industry practice, and ideas from media specialists. Normally, it is wise to use the same sort of media that competitors use—they are the most likely places where potential customers will look or listen.

Trading Area. Retailers can spend their advertising dollars in established trading areas or use them to try to stimulate new sales outside the primary trading area. It is wise to do the bulk of advertising in familiar areas. Usually, it is more costly to develop new markets than to maintain established ones.

TABLE 18–3

WHERE RETAILERS ADVERTISE

Category	Amount (Thousands)	Percentage
Newspaper	$1,094,000	53
Network TV	366,291	18
Spot TV	240,000	12
Magazine	125,890	6
Network radio	95,000	5
Spot radio	52,477	3
Cable TV	25,206	1
Sunday magazine	25,102	1
Syndicated TV	19,500	1
Outdoor	2,315	
	$2,045,781	100

Source: *Advertising Age,* September 25, 1991. Copyright Crain Communications, Inc., 1991. Reprinted with permission.

Maintaining Budget Flexibility

Any combination of the budgeting methods discussed may be employed in the formation and allocation of the budget. All of them, or only one, may be needed to meet the retailer's advertising objectives. However management decides to plan the budget, they must make it flexible, capable of being adjusted to changes in the marketplace.

To ensure advertising flexibility, management should have a contingency fund to deal with special circumstances—such as the introduction of a new merchandise line or unexpected competitive situations.

Cooperative Advertising

Cooperative advertising occurs when a manufacturer pays part of the retailer's advertising costs under specific conditions. Cooperative advertising can substantially lower the cost for the retailer.

EVALUATING MEDIA OPTIONS[5]

When management decides what they want to advertise and whom they want to reach, they must select the right medium. Most retailers find newspapers, radio, and direct mail (discussed in Chapter 21) the most commonly available choices. However, to reach wider markets, management may consider other media such as magazines, television, and billboards.[6]

As shown in Table 18–3, more than half of all retail advertising is spent on newspaper advertising, followed distantly by network television and spot television.

Spot advertising refers to commercials shown on local stations, whereby the negotiation and purchase of time is made directly with the individual station. Nonnetwork advertising done by national advertisers is known as **national spot advertising,** whereas the time purchased by local retailers is known as **local advertising.**

Media Information Sources

Various sources are available to help retailers develop needed information about media alternatives:

1. **Standard Rate and Data Service.** This service publishes monthly directories of circulation, rates, issues, closing dates, and other information for most major media types.
2. **Audit bureaus.** The Audit Bureaus of Circulation and other bureaus measure, check, and verify the circulation of many business publications, outdoor advertising, magazines, and newspapers.
3. **Advertising Research Foundation.** The foundation publishes a series of continuing studies on newspaper readership, farm publications, business papers, and weekly newspapers.
4. **Media association reports.** The various classes of media all have associations that conduct research and prepare reports on the nature and merits of their media.
5. **Media reports.** Most media provide information on market coverage, rate cards, and studies about their markets. Each medium, of course, tends to present information that is most favorable to itself.

Each advertising medium has its strengths and weaknesses. The characteristics of each one are shown in Table 18–4.

Three general questions can help an advertiser evaluate media:

- Is the audience of the medium appropriate for the advertising campaign?
- Among the available media, which provides the largest audience at the lowest cost?
- Can the medium effectively communicate the sales message?

Advertising can be tricky. However, by establishing specific goals, analyzing various media, and using proven techniques, a retailer can successfully promote merchandise.

Radio

Radio is a relatively inexpensive way of reaching people. It has often been called the "theater of the mind" because voices or sounds can be used to create moods or images that, if created by visual effects, would be impossible to afford.

Buying Radio Time. Management needs to know the type of programming, musical format, geographic outreach, number of listeners, and station ratings.

By getting the station ratings and the number of people it reaches, the retailer can figure out the **cost per thousand** people (CPM) by dividing the cost of a commercial by the number of thousands of people being reached.

TABLE 18–4 ADVANTAGES AND DISADVANTAGES OF VARIOUS ADVERTISING MEDIA

Medium	*Advantages*	*Disadvantages*
Newspapers	Good flexibility Timeliness Good local coverage Broad acceptance High believability	Short life Poor reproduction quality Small pass-along audience
Magazines	Good geographic and demographic selectivity Good credibility and prestige High-quality reproduction Long life Good pass-along readership	Long production lead time Some waste circulation Poor position guarantee
Radio	Mass audience Good geographic and demographic selectivity Low cost	Audio presentation only Lower audience attention than TV Nonstandardized rate structure Fleeting exposure
Television	Appeals to many senses Commands high attention levels High reach	High absolute cost High clutter Fleeting exposure Less audience selectivity Long production lead time
Direct mail	Best audience selectivity Good flexibility No clutter Good personalization	Relatively high cost Sometimes poor image
Outdoor	Good flexibility High repeat exposure Low cost Low competition	Poor audience selectivity Limited creativity

Example. Cost of commercial = $35.00
Audience reached = 45,000 people
Cost of commercial per 1,000 people = $35.00 ÷ 45 = $0.78 per 1,000

Without getting complicated, here are two cardinal rules for radio advertising:

- It's better to advertise when people are listening than when they are not.
- It's better to bunch your commercials together than to spread them apart.

A lot of radio sales reps will try to talk retailers out of advertising during specific times by offering reduced rates for evening hours, for example. This may sound like a good deal, but airing commercials during times when the audience isn't listening is bad advertising.

Because customers can't automatically recall a radio commercial and hear it again, they may have to hear the same commercial two, four, maybe six times before the message sinks in. That's the way radio advertising works. And that's also the way to buy it.

Retailers writing their scripts should remember these basic copywriting rules:

- Get the listener's attention immediately.
- Write in a conversational style.
- Avoid using buzzwords or jargon.
- Repeat the important points.
- Make the ending strong and positive with a call to action.

Television

Television is often called king of the advertising media because a majority of people spend more hours per day watching television than using any other medium. It combines the use of sight, color, sound, and motion. As an item of interest, the most popular television commercials in 1991 included those of McDonald's, Taco Bell, Burger King, and Wendy's.[7] Wendy's has historically featured high-profile commercials, largely because of the creativity of Dave Thomas, the founder (see A Profile in Excellence).

The area that a television station's broadcast signal covers is called the **ADI,** which stands for area of dominant influence. Because television has such a large **ADI,** the stations can charge more for commercials based on the larger number of viewers reached. The cost of television commercial time is based on two variables:

- The number of viewers who watch the program.
- The time during the day the program airs.

One 30-second television commercial during prime-time viewing (8 P.M. to 11 P.M.) can cost 10 to 30 times more than one radio spot during drive time (which is considered prime listening time).

Advertising agencies or television commercial production facilities are the best organizations for creating a commercial that will be effective for the goods or services you are offering. But a well-produced commercial is expensive.

To obtain positive results from television advertising the retailer must have enough money in the budget to pay for the cost of producing a good television commercial (today costs range from $2,500 to $20,000 and above) and to pay for effective commercial time that will reach the viewer at least 5 to 7 times.

Properly done, television advertising is the most effective medium there is. But it is big-league advertising, and a retailer shouldn't attempt it unless he or she has enough money in the budget to do it right.

Television time is normally sold in 10-, 30-, and 60-second time slots, with the 30-second slot being the most popular. The cost of television advertising depends on the size of the audience, which can be described in terms of **rating** and **share.**

A Profile in Excellence

R. DAVID THOMAS

R. David Thomas was born on July 2, 1932, in Atlantic City, New Jersey. He never knew his birth parents, but a couple from Kalamazoo, Michigan, Rex and Auleva Thomas, adopted him when he was six weeks old. Thomas' adoptive mother died when he was five, and his early years included numerous moves from state to state as his adoptive father sought work.

"This wasn't easy," Thomas said. "No roots; no sense of belonging. With all that moving, I didn't get a chance to know kids. I guess that's why work became my constant companion."

In 1956 Thomas opened a barbecue restaurant called the Ranch House with Phil Clauss, his former boss at the Hobby House where Thomas had been a short-order cook. While working there, Thomas met the man who became one of the greatest influences on his life—Kentucky Fried Chicken founder Colonel Harland Sanders. The Colonel was traveling nationwide to promote his new fried chicken franchise. Clauss bought the franchise, and Thomas learned all about the chicken business.

Among the lasting benefits from Thomas's relationship with the Colonel was an introduction to Bob Barney, who ultimately became chairman of the board of Wendy's, as well as a close friend. Barney accepted an offer to work for Thomas and KFC in 1964, and the men's friendship has continued to this day.

After leaving KFC, Thomas helped found Arthur Treacher's Fish & Chips. But as he worked to improve this chain, he remained "drawn to hamburgers." And although critics were quick to point out that the restaurant industry was considered saturated, Thomas opened the first Wendy's Old Fashioned Hamburgers restaurant in downtown Columbus, Ohio. He named the restaurant after his eight-year-old daughter, Melinda Lou, who was nicknamed "Wendy" by her brother and sisters.

In 1981, Thomas first appeared in a Wendy's national advertising campaign. The controversial "Ain't No Reason" campaign featured Thomas relating one of his basic business philosophies in each spot. The controversy stemmed from the use of "ain't no," a colloquial double negative, and generated local and national publicity.

Eight years later, in April 1989, Thomas returned to the airwaves with news about Wendy's latest victory in the hamburger wars. As Wendy's spokesperson, Thomas offered consumers a special moneyback guarantee if they didn't agree that Wendy's has the best tasting hamburgers.

More recent Dave Thomas commercials focus on Thomas's honesty and down-to-earth values. The "Letters to Dave" campaign teamed Dave with soap opera star Susan Lucci. And the "World Tour" spots show Dave traveling the world, sampling exotic cuisine, when all he really wants is a hamburger.

By the end of 1991 Dave Thomas's advertising campaign had provided Wendy's with its highest advertising awareness levels to date, surpassing the phenomenal 1985 "Where's the Beef?" campaign.

A **gross rating point** (GRP) is 1 percent of all homes with television sets in a market area. A program with a GRP of 10 is reaching 10 percent of the television homes. In contrast, a **share** is a percentage of television sets in use that are tuned to a given program. Thus, a program may have a GRP of only 1, for example, at 4:00 on Sunday morning. But it may also have a share of 56.

Cable Advertising

Cable advertising is a lower-cost alternative to advertising on network television. It has many of the same qualities as broadcast television, and, in fact, because it offers more programming, it's even easier to reach a designated audience.

The trouble with cable is that it doesn't reach everyone in the market areas because the signal has to be wired instead of broadcast and because not everyone subscribes to cable. Chances are that cable commercial time will be 10 to 20 percent of the cost of regular broadcast time.

Newspapers

People expect advertising in the newspaper. In fact, many people buy the paper just to read the ads from the supermarket, movies, or department stores.

Advertising is sold by column and inch, instead of just by line. For example, an ad that measures 3 columns across and 7 inches down would be a 21-inch ad. If the inch rate is $45.67, the ad would cost $959.07. In case the newspaper is still on the line rate system, remember that there are 14 lines to an inch. So if the line rate is $3.75, multiply it by 14 to get the cost of an inch rate. (The rate would be $45.50 an inch.)

Here are some other things to remember:

1. Newspaper circulation drops on Saturdays and increases on Sundays, which is also the day it is read most thoroughly.
2. Position is important, so specify in what section you want an ad to appear. Sometimes there's a surcharge for exact position, but don't be afraid to pay for it if you need it.
3. Request an outside position for ads that have coupons. That makes them easier to cut out.
4. Create short, descriptive copy for the ad. Include prices if applicable. Consider using a copywriter or ask the newspaper for copy assistance, which is usually free.
5. Be sure to include the company name and logo, address, and telephone number in the ad.
6. Neat, uncluttered, orderly ads encourage readership. Don't try to crowd everything in the layout space.

Magazines

As with newspapers, a magazine's circulation is usually audited. It is important to analyze circulation by examining the magazine's audit statement.

Some of the larger national magazines sell advertising confined to a particular market or region of the country. The advantage of this type of magazine is that the retailer can advertise in a national magazine, yet pay a lower rate because the ads are limited to particular markets.

Many retailers are now starting to publish magazines known as **place-based magazines** that combine entertainment with a subtle form of marketing. Blockbuster Entertainment's *Blockbuster* is typical of this trend.[8]

Advertising space is typically sold in pages or fractions of pages such as one-half or one-sixth. The rates charged depend upon the circulation of the magazine, quality of the publication, and primary audience.

Telephone Directories

Telephone directories are a source of information for buyers. People who use directories need specific information to complete their buying decision and frequently make decisions based on the information in directories. Therefore, it is good to include as much information as possible in a directory ad.

But costs are reasonable for ads in the yellow pages. A half-column display ad can vary from $50 a month in an area with 15,000 residents to several hundred dollars a month or more in an area of a million people.

Outdoor Advertising

Billboard advertising usually is bought from companies that specialize in leasing sign space to merchants. The typical billboard size is 12 feet by 25 feet. Outdoor advertising signs are bought in terms of showings. A **100 showing** in a market means that advertising space was purchased on enough posters to reach 100 percent of the audience in an area at least once each month.

Nonstandard signs are normally those constructed by the retailer. No standard size exists for such billboards. Retailers arrange with each individual landowner for the space they want to lease.

Specialty Advertising

Specialty advertising incorporates giving gifts to customers. Examples include matchbooks, fountain pens, calendars, and key chains. The gifts typically contain the name of the retailer, company address, and perhaps its logo or slogan. The specialty items chosen should match the type of merchandise sold by the firm.

Evaluating the Effectiveness of Media[9]

Two concepts that are important in evaluating various media opportunities are cost per thousand and frequency and reach. These concepts help establish a price-to-value relationship between media opportunities.

Cost per Thousand

When media opportunities are compared, it is often confusing to determine which one offers the best value. For example, suppose that a retailer is considering two newspapers to carry advertising. Both newspapers cover the market, but they have different costs and circulation, as shown below:

	Cost	*Circulation*
Newspaper A	$100	25,000
Newspaper B	200	60,000

Which paper offers the best deal?

Simply stated, cost per thousand is the unit price of media. It is the cost of advertising per thousand individuals reached by a medium. Cost per thousand is derived by this formula:

$$\text{CPM} = \frac{\text{Cost of Medium}}{\text{Audience or Circulation of Medium}} \times 1000$$

We can now solve the example problem:

$$\text{CPM for A} = \frac{\$100}{25{,}000} \times 1000 = \$4.00$$

$$\text{CPM for B} = \frac{\$200}{60{,}000} \times 1000 = \$3.33$$

Newspaper B delivers its circulation at a lower unit cost than newspaper A. Moreover, newspaper B offers greater circulation than its competitor. From this perspective, newspaper B is the better media buy.

Cost per thousand analysis helps provide a common comparison point for evaluating media vehicles, regardless of the size of the vehicle or its cost. The best use of cost per thousand analysis is to compare similar media vehicles—such as two newspapers—as opposed to completely different media vehicles such as newspaper and radio.

Reach and Frequency

When comparing advertising programs it is important to select the most effective balance of reach and frequency. Reach and frequency are two terms used to describe the overall delivery of an advertising program. **Reach** is the number of different individuals exposed to at least one message over a specified period of time. If a media plan covers four out of five people, it has a reach of 80 percent (4 divided by 5).

Frequency is the average number of times an individual is exposed to a message. If four people see six of an outlet's messages, the frequency is 1.5 (6 divided by 4).

Although separate concepts, reach and frequency are interrelated. Consider the hypothetical following situation as an example. An advertiser who uses magazines for an advertising program has two options:

- Buy one insertion in five different magazines.
- Buy five insertions in one magazine.

Assuming that both options have the same cost, it's easy to see that option 1 emphasizes reach and option 2 emphasizes frequency.

A major cause of failure in advertising programs is insufficient frequency. It is far more effective to reduce the reach of an advertising campaign and add frequency than to reduce frequency and add reach. Unless a product or service is well known and has no competition, increasing the frequency of the advertising message will increase overall effectiveness.

MEASURING THE RESULTS OF ADVERTISING

Management may be interested in the effectiveness of either immediate response ads or image ads. Sales response to ads can be checked daily during the ad period. The effects of image or attitude ads are harder to measure.

Tests for Immediate Response Ads[10]

In weighing the results of the immediate response to advertisements, the following measurements are helpful.

Coupons Redeemed. Usually, coupons represent sales of a product. Where coupons represent requests for additional information or contact with a salesperson, management can decide whether enough leads were developed to pay for the ad.

Phone or Letter Inquiries. A "hidden offer" can cause people to call or write. For example, the retailer may include a statement in the middle of an ad that on request a free product sample or additional information will be sent. Results should be checked over periods of one week through 6 months or 12 months, because this type of ad may have considerable carryover.

Split-Run Ads. Retailers can prepare two ads (different in some way that they would like to test or for different stations or broadcast times) and run them on the same day. Management can identify the ads by the message or with a coded coupon so that they can tell the ads apart. They can ask customers to bring in the coupon or to use a special phrase. Broadcast ads can be run at different times or on different stations on the same day with various discount phrases. Newspapers can provide a split run—that is, to print ad A in part of its press run and ad B in the rest of the run. The responses to each can then be counted.

Sales of a Targeted Item. If the ad is on a bargain or limited-time offer, retailers can consider that sales at the end of one week, two weeks, three weeks, and four weeks came from the ad. They may also need to judge how many sales came from in-store displays and personal selling.

Store Traffic. An important function of advertising is to build store traffic. Store traffic also results in purchases of items that are not advertised. Pilot studies show, for example, that many customers who were brought to a store by an ad for a blouse also bought a handbag. Some bought the bag in addition to the blouse, and others bought it instead of the blouse.

Attitude Advertising

When advertising is spread over a selling season or several seasons, part of the measurement job is keeping records. Retailers' records of ads and sales for an extended time should be compared.

In institutional (image-building) advertising, individual ads are building blocks, so to speak. Together they make up the advertising over a selling season. Measuring the effects of the ads is problematic because they are designed to keep the name of the store in front of the buying public and to position the outlet in a way that harmonizes with overall marketing strategy.

One approach to testing is making the comparisons on a weekly basis. If a retailer runs an ad each week, management can compare the first week's sales with sales for the same week a year ago. At the end of the second week, managers can compare sales with those at the end of the first week, as well as last year's figures, and so forth.

Developing the Copy

Copy can be either rational or emotional. The rational approach focuses on the merchandise characteristics, price, and supporting services. The emotional appeal addresses the psychological benefits that one can obtain by using the merchandise. Normally, a combination of the two possibilities is most effective. For example, product benefits could be both rational (economy) and emotional (appearance). Headlines in the ad can focus on benefits, promises, or even news.

The text of the advertisement can do many things, including (1) stating reasons for doing something (for instance, buying the product or patronizing the store), (2) making promises or giving testimonials, (3) publicizing the results of performance tests, (4) telling a story, (5) reporting a real or imaginary dialogue, (6) solving a problem or (7) amusing the audience.[11]

Elements of Good Copy

The elements of good copy are sometimes summarized in the acronym **AIDCA,** which means attract **attention** develop **interest,** arouse **desire,** **convince** the reader, and get **action.** Effective copywriters make each word count and avoid unnecessary words. Retailers should keep sentences short, use action verbs and terms the reader will understand, and avoid introductions. It is important to get right to the point of the message.

Useful Tips

The following are some tips that can be used when working up advertisements. When properly followed they will help inject selling punch into the advertising.

- *Make your ads easy to recognize.* Give the copy and layout a consistent personality and style.
- *Use a simple layout.* The layout should lead the reader's eye easily through the message from the art and headline to the copy and price to the signature.
- *Use dominant illustrations.* Show the featured merchandise in dominant illustrations. Whenever possible, show the product in use.
- *Show the benefit to the reader.* Prospective customers want to know what's in it for them. Give the customers one primary reason, and then back it up with one or two secondary reasons.
- *Feature the "right" item.* Select an item that is in demand, timely, stocked in depth, and typical of your store.
- *State a price or range of prices.* Don't be afraid to quote high prices. If the price is low, support it with statements that create belief, such as *clearance* or *special purchase.*
- Include store name and address. Double-check every ad to make sure it contains store name, address, telephone number, and store hours.

The Role of the Ad Agency

The function of an agency is to plan, produce, and measure the effectiveness of advertising. Larger retailers with outlets in several communities are more likely to use an ad agency. An agency helps avoid the complication of having to deal with a variety of media in each community.

Advertising agencies typically earn their incomes from commissions. As an agent for the retailer, the agency buys space in a medium. The agency then bills the retailer for 100 percent of the cost and pays the medium, such as a newspaper, 85 percent. The remaining 15 percent is a normal agency commission. Agencies may also take on the accounts of small retailers on a fee basis if the 15 percent commission is too small to make the project worthwhile. In situations such as preparing direct mail advertising, the agency may charge a percentage of the cost involved.

SALES PROMOTION

The American Marketing Association defines sales promotion as marketing activities other than personal selling, advertising, and publicity that stimulate consumer purchasing and dealer effectiveness, such as displays, sales, exhibits, and demonstrations.

Perhaps the best way to introduce the varied nature of sales promotion possibilities is to highlight trends in sales promotion activities by retailers.

Sales Promotion Trends

Promotions may be targeted at either consumers or retailers.[12] Promotions targeted to consumers are known as **pull** promotions, whereas promotions targeted to retailers are known as **push** (or trade-based) promotions.

Consumer-Targeted Promotions

Coupons. Product marketers distribute more than 292 billion cents-off coupons each year. Free-standing inserts account for approximately 80 percent of the total number of coupons distributed.[13]

More in- and on-pack coupon usage is likely, as is continued use of retailer in-ad coupons (retailer coupons paid by manufacturers), and more combination promotions with other devices—premiums, sweepstakes, and refunds.

More Sampling. Use of sampling is increasing, especially to new users or nonusers. Many services now provide selective sampling. Retailers prefer salable samples because they make a profit on such samples. Salable samples are good for manufacturers because they save distribution costs.

Fewer Cents-Off Bonus Packs. Retailers generally resist these promotion devices because they necessitate additional stockkeeping units. They can also be quite costly to marketers because they require special labeling or packaging.

More Premiums. Retailers are lukewarm to premium offers. This is especially true when they are used alone, rather than in combination with other promotion devices such as coupons. Retailers prefer premium offers that do not require their involvement but add excitement and impact to a promotion, create consumer interest, and generate increased product movement.

More Selective Point-of-Purchase Material. Typical point-of-purchase materials include end-of-aisle and other in-store merchandising and display materials. Retailers are highly selective in their use of P-O-P material and prefer displays that merchandise an exciting and interesting promotion theme, support other promotion devices, adapt to storewide promotions on a chainwide and individual store basis, harmonize with the store environment, sell a related product, provide a quality appearance, install easily, are permanent or semipermanent, and guarantee sales success.

More Refunds and Rebates. These devices continue to grow in popularity and use. Refunds and rebates are usually handled as mail-ins with proofs of purchase. They are very effective promotion tools and will be used in more creative ways.

A Question of Ethics

Forward Buying

In a practice known as forward buying, supermarkets take advantage of special deals that offer them 15 percent or more in promotion allowances below the normal wholesale price. The special prices are designed to induce the retailer to promote the product and also to pass the savings to consumers. Retailers, however, normally use some of the funds for advertising and pocket the rest. They do so by stocking up on more merchandise than they plan to sell during the promotion. They then generate a wider margin by selling the remaining goods at the regular price after the end of the sale period. Alternatively, they "divert" some of the low-priced shipment to another vendor who will do the diverting or sell to another supermarket outside its trading area.

Booz Allen & Hamilton, a management consulting firm, estimates that these buying practices account for more than half of supermarket profits. Estimates are that only 30 percent of trade dollars actually reach the consumer in the form of lower prices. One executive complains that it's a marketing expense that is "like pouring sand in the ocean."

Factories have to gear their lines to meet the huge swings in demand caused by the practices of diversion and forward buying. The result is that manufacturers and retailers are always building up toward a surge in demand or drawing down after a surge. Analysts suggest that the inefficiencies caused by forward buying increase costs by up to $3 billion annually, or 2 percent of annual industry sales.

Are retailers acting unethically when they engage in forward buying and diverting?

Source: Based on Howard Schlossberg, "Retailers, Manufacturers Urged to Work Together for Profits," *Marketing News*, November 11, 1991, p. 13; "Not Everyone Loves a Supermarket Special," *BusinessWeek*, February 17, 1992, pp. 64–65.

Fewer Contests and More Sweepstakes. Sweepstakes are generally more popular than contests and are growing in use and importance. Retailers like them, especially when they bring traffic into the store to look at product packages and obtain entry blanks.

Trade-Targeted Promotions

Vendors often advertise directly to retailers to inform them about promotion allowances or other material available. They then seek a commitment from retailers for a specific volume of purchase. Approximately 44 cents of every dollar manufacturers spend on advertising and promotion now goes to discounts and fees offered to retailers.[14]

Forward Buying. Discounts to retailers are often controversial. Retailers, especially supermarkets, are prone to practice forward buying, the practice of stocking up on promoted items at the discounted price at the end of the designated promotion period, and reselling the merchandise at the normal price (see A Question of Ethics).

Slotting Fees. An additional controversial form of trade-based promotion is the use of slotting fees, which are a one-time payment that a retailer charges a manufacturer for access to shelf space to display a new item.[15] Slotting fees are a consequence of the battle for shelf space. Retailers contend that the fees are necessary to offset the expenses associated with bringing new products into the store. However, small manufacturers, contend that fees are anticompetitive because smaller firms cannot afford them. (See A Question of Ethics in Chapter 16.)

PUBLICITY AND PUBLIC RELATIONS

The American Marketing Association defines publicity as any nonpersonal stimulation of demand for a product, service, or business unit created by planting commercially significant news about it in a published medium or obtaining favorable presentation of it on radio, television, or stage that is not paid for by the sponsor. Publicity and public relations are known by various names. Regardless, such activities normally fit into three categories: merchandising events, entertainment, and education or community service.

Merchandising Events

Merchandising events require careful coordination between merchandising, advertising, and publicity. Such events can include fashion shows; bridal fairs; cooking demonstrations; or discussions with celebrity authors, cartoon characters, or sports heroes. They can include exhibits of art, costumes, antiques, or rarities. Merchandising events may also be staged in conjunction with designers such as Gloria Vanderbilt or sports figures such as Michael Jordan.

Entertainment

Retailers seek to build goodwill, store image, and name awareness through entertainment programs. The results from such activities are hard to measure. Macy's Thanksgiving Day Parade is shown on national television.

Education or Community Service

Retailers often sponsor education or community service activities. Examples include fashion advice, career counseling, and even evening college courses, all on the store premises.

McDonald's sponsors an all-American high school basketball team. McDonald's also sponsors the Ronald McDonald houses as homes away from home for families of seriously ill children who are being treated at nearby hospitals (Exhibit 18–2).

EXHIBIT 18–2

Courtesy McDonald's Corporation

The Ronald McDonald House

Globalization and Promotion Options

Global retailers often need to make complex advertising decisions as part of their growth strategies. For example, McDonald's in 1992 launched its first unified global advertising campaign and agreed to be a sponsor of the 1994 World Cup.[16]

The goal of Toys 'R' Us is to have 150 stores operating in Central Europe by the year 2000. The firm recently made the decision to get involved in television, which will include co-op spots with some of the retailer's leading suppliers. Toys 'R' Us targets 110 million inserts annually to German newspapers. Toys 'R' Us Deutschland has responsibility for expansion into central Europe, which includes Germany, Austria, Switzerland, Belgium, the Netherlands, Luxembourg, Hungary, Poland, and the Czech and Slovak Republics.[17]

Chapter Highlights

- Promotion is communication from the retailer to the consumer. Promotion includes mass media advertising, coupons, trading stamps, premium offers, point-of-purchase displays, and publicity.
- All promotion should be in harmony with retailing mix decisions, or a poor image can result.
- Developing promotion plans begins with the goals of the firm. Retailers must decide on who to reach, the message to get across, the number of messages to reach the audience, and the means for reaching the audience.
- Promotion should be viewed as a sales-building investment and not simply as an element of business expense. When promotion is executed correctly, it can be an important factor in the growth of a business.
- Numerous options exist for retail advertising. Media choices include magazines, billboards, newspapers, radio, and television. Over 70 percent of retail ad dollars go to newspapers.
- Media effectiveness is assessed in terms of cost per thousand and reach and frequency. Tests for results of immediate response ads can be in terms of numbers of coupons cashed in, phone or letter requests referring to the ad, sales of a particular item, or analysis of store traffic.
- Advertising copy can be either rational or emotional. The rational approach focuses on the merchandise, whereas an emotional appeal focuses on the psychological benefits obtained from using the product. Headlines in an ad can focus on benefits, promises, or news.
- Many retailers use an advertising agency. The function of an agency is to plan, produce, and measure the effectiveness of advertising. Agencies earn their commissions on advertisements placed for the retailers.
- Retail sales promotions include such activities as couponing, product sampling, cents-off bonus packs, premiums, point-of-purchase materials, refunds or rebates, contests and sweepstakes, and trade-in allowances.
- Publicity includes media exposure that is not paid for by the sponsor. Such activities normally fit into three categories: merchandising, entertainment, and education or community service.

Study Questions

1. Is it possible to increase advertising expenses as a percentage of sales, yet increase the profitability of the firm?
2. Comment on the following statement: The only goal of advertising is to increase sales and profitability.
3. Discuss the following approaches to establishing an advertising budget: the percentage of sales method; the unit of sales method; and the objective task method.
4. Why should a retailer consider using a multimedia mix?
5. Evaluate the following media in terms of their strengths and weaknesses: billboards, radio, television, newspapers, and magazines.
6. What is specialty advertising and how does it benefit the retailer?
7. Why should a retailer consider using co-op advertising funds?
8. What are the various ways retailers can measure advertising results?
9. The text states that the elements of good advertising copy are summarized in the term AIDCA. What does this acronym mean?
10. How does advertising differ from publicity and from sales promotion?

EXHIBIT 18–3

Courtesy United Colors of Benetton. Concept: O. Toscani. Magnum Photos

Benetton's Ad Campaign

APPLICATIONS

CASE 1: Benetton: Socially Aware or Wasted Money?

Benetton's philosophy is not to push a product but to attract attention to its name by addressing social issues, as shown in Exhibit 18–3. A spring 1992 worldwide campaign included images of a dying AIDS patient surrounded by his family; a swarm of refugees clamoring aboard a huge ship; and the shrouded corpse of a Mafia hit victim and a relative's face reflected in a pool of blood.

Critics contend that Benetton is making an effort to present shocking images to attract attention rather than to create genuine product advertising. The Mafia ad, because of its regional significance, ran only in Italy. The others ran worldwide as part of a $60 million "United Colors of Benetton" campaign designed to raise awareness of Benetton's attention to social problems.

French magazines refused to accept the ship ad because of the nation's immigration problems. Magazines in Scandinavia refused to take the ad showing a rear view of a soldier with a gun, holding a human leg bone. The ad showing an AIDS patient on his deathbed surrounded by his family in an Ohio Hospice was banned by the Advertising Standards Authority in the UK.

Benetton's creative director argues that everyone uses emotion to sell a product. He insists that Benetton is simply calling attention to human realities that we are all aware of.

In 1992 Benetton, in another controversial move, launched a plan to distribute free condoms in key stores in Europe and the United States. The condom giveaway was supported by Benetton ads showing different-colored condoms. The ad was rejected by Amica, one of Italy's largest publishing groups, but it appeared in other international markets. Ad industry self-regulatory units in the UK, France, and Spain have also urged magazines to reject many of the Benetton ads as being in poor taste.

Source: Based on Adrienne Ward, " 'Socially Aware' or 'Wasted Money?' " *Advertising Age*, February 14, 1991, p. B4; Michelle McCarter, "Benetton Condom Kindness," *Advertising Age*, February 25, 1991, p. B2; Gary Levin, "Benetton Brouhaha," *Advertising Age*, February 17, 1992, p. 62.

Applying Retailing Principles

1. Is it in bad taste for a retailer to generate the type of controversy associated with Benetton ads?
2. Should Benetton ignore protests of various organizations in its drive to call attention to what management sees as some of the world's pressing social problems?
3. What do you perceive as the relationship, if any, of the ads to the consumer's tendency to purchase Benetton products? What type of image is Benetton seeking to create in the minds of the consumers?

CASE 2: Who You Gonna Call? Bookfinders!

The phone call was from Henry Kissinger's office. He needed help. And then there was the time IBM president Tom Watson, Jr. called for information.

Both were taken care of.

The assistance needed was neither global nor technical. It was literary.

They were among the thousands of customers who contact Bob Ruffalo for help, information, and research to find a book.

Ruffalo's company is Princeton Antique Bookfinders, a throwback to the bookseller out of the pages of Dickens. His rabbit warren of crowded aisles and rooms and buildings lead from one to another in a cramped setting of cobwebs, memories, and the smell of old books. They are filled with beauty, knowledge, and enough inspiration to warm the heart of any bibliophile.

Today, Princeton Antique Bookfinders is the largest out-of-pocket buyer of individual titles in the world. The business began in the early 1970s with Ruffalo's father, who was in the antique business. He sometimes bought complete estates, which usually included a library. He started with an initial inventory of 3,000 books. Now that figure is up to 150,000—and growing.

Need a book on Oriental rugs? Ruffalo has 1,000 for you. Are you a budding apiarist? He has what you want on the care and feeding of bees. And, because he's in Atlantic City, you have your choice of more than 1,500 books on gambling.

Of course, Ruffalo has the most complete collection of literature and memorabilia in Atlantic City. ("See this badge? It was worn by one of the original judges from the Miss America Pageant back in the 1920s.")

How does his business work? Here's a typical story: "A geologist in Houston called for an out-of-print book on Antarctica," said Ruffalo. "Her husband was sent to work in South Korea and she went over there to work with him. She developed an interest in Antarctica. Could we find something for her? We found half a dozen books. Then she asked for more. That was a year and a half ago. We found 650 books on Antarctica. If you want to know something . . . if you want to know anything about Antarctica, we can find it!"

People discover his business through a friend, an advertisement in the *Chicago Tribune, The Wall Street Journal*, or *The New York Times*, or a reference from a publisher. Random House and McGraw-Hill use Ruffalo's service to find books for them (the ultimate compliment).

But what if he doesn't have what you want? He'll find it!

There's a small network of 30 to 40 other out-of-print dealers who call one another to track down what their clients need.

Once a customer finds Ruffalo, all the business is done through the mail. ("Calling on the phone is a waste of time," says Ruffalo. "They're not there. They'll be right back. They're too busy to talk. . . .")

When he finds what you want, he sends you the information on the condition, publisher, publication, number of pages, and other pertinent facts. Cost of the book when he finds it: $35 to a few thousand. You pay only if you want the book. All the customer has to do is okay the purchase order and mail it back in the enclosed reply envelope.

Oh, the books for Kissinger and Watson. What were they about? What did they want?

Ruffalo smiles and answers, "Now I can't tell you that. They're customers. And you don't give away trade secrets. . . ."

Source: Reprinted with permission from Murray Raphel, "Who You Gonna Call? Bookfinders!" *Direct Marketing*, November 1990, pp. 58–59.

Applying Retailing Principles

1. What combination of promotion media is used to build the customer base for Princeton Antique Bookfinders?
2. Do you consider Ruffalo's activities part of data based marketing? Why or why not?
3. What other types of activities can Ruffalo undertake to expand his base of customers?

Notes

1. Ovid Riso, "Advertising Guidelines for Small Retail Firms," Small Marketer's Aid, no. 160 (Washington, D.C.: U.S. Small Business Administration), p. 4.
2. Marvin J. Rothenburg, "Retail Research Strategies for the '70s," in *Combined Proceedings*, Ed Mazze, ed. (Chicago: American Marketing Association, 1975), p. 409.
3. Ovid Riso, "Advertising Guidelines."
4. The material on establishing and allocating the budget is based on Stewart Henderson Britt, "Plan Your Advertising Budget," Management Aid no. 4.018 (Washington, D.C.: U.S. Small Business Administration).
5. Portions of this material are reproduced, with modification, from Edward A. Bruno, *Advertising*, MT-11 (Washington, D.C.: U.S. Small Business Administration); Michael F. Walsh, *Advertising Media Decisions*, MT-6 (Washington, D.C.: U.S. Small Business Administration).
6. Teresa Andreoli, "Media Buys," *Stores*, February 1992, p. 63.
7. Joanne Lipman, "Consumers' Favored Commercials Tend to Feature Lower Prices or Cuddly Kids," *The Wall Street Journal*, March 2, 1992, p. B1.
8. "Retailers as Publishers," *Chain Store Age Executive*, April 1992, p. 16.
9. Walsh, "Advertising Media Decisions."
10. This material is reproduced, with modification, from Elizabeth Sorbet, "Do You Know the Results of Your Advertising?" Management Aid no. 4.020 (Washington, D.C.: U.S. Small Business Administration).

11. William Haight, *Retail Advertising: Management and Techniques* (New Jersey: General Learning Press, 1976), p. 357.
12. For further reading, see "Inside Report: Sales Promotion," *Marketing News*, June 7, 1985, p. 12; Marc Schnapp, "War Games 'In Retailing Promotions,' " *Marketing Communications*, June 1985, pp. 85–88.
13. Scott Hume, "Couponing Reaches Record Clip," *Advertising Age*, February 3, 1992, p. 1; Valerie Reitman, "Turning Coupon Flood into Guided Trickle," *The Wall Street Journal*, June 3, 1992, p. B1.
14. "Not Everyone Loves a Supermarket Special," *BusinessWeek*, February 17, 1992, pp. 64–65.
15. Joseph P. Cannon and Paul N. Bloom, "Are Slotting Allowances Legal under the Antitrust Laws?" *Journal of Public Policy and Marketing*, Spring 1991, p. 168; for further reading, see Kenneth Kelly, "The Antitrust Analysis of Grocery Slotting Allowances: The Pro-Competitive Case," *Journal of Public Policy and Marketing*, Spring 1991, pp. 187–98.
16. "Growth, Expansion McDonald's Only Hope," *Tuscaloosa News*, April 1992, p. E4.
17. Kevin Cote, "Toys 'R' Us Grows in Europe," *Advertising Age International*, April 27, 1992, p. S16.

C H A P T E R

19

Customer Support Services: Strengthening Relationship Retailing

THIS CHAPTER:

Defines the meaning of customer service and reasons for the gap that often exists between customer expectations and perceptions.

Identifies the requirements for excellent customer service.

Reviews the strategic dimensions of customer support services.

Identifies the value of a customer services audit.

Discusses the issues involved in developing retail credit options.

Emphasizes the importance of customer support services in competitive strategy.

RETAILING CAPSULE

CHEAP GASOLINE AND FULL SERVICE? IT MUST BE HEAVEN

Heaven is on a tired, grey stretch of road called the Jericho Turnpike in Commack, New York. It's wedged between a deli called Chef Voila and a swimming pool store.

It's Rudy Massah's service station, called Gasoline Heaven. And it's one of the busiest gasoline stations in the world.

Consider this: Gasoline Heaven pumps 7 to 8 million gallons a year, more than three times the sales of an average neighborhood station. Only a handful of truck stops and megastations do more business.

Gasoline Heaven looks like most of the other gas stations along the strip. But while many of the pumps at the other stations stand idle, there's always a line of cars trying to inch up to one of this station's 34 fuel nozzles.

The secrets of Massah's success will sound familiar to anyone who remembers when service stations sold gas for 20.9 cents a gallon and gave away a free drinking glass with a fill-up: He sells gas cheap, keeps the place clean, gives good service, and gets drivers in and out fast. At a time when Big Oil seems to be taking over and price discounters are disappearing, he flies the colors of a small refinery and routinely undercuts big-name competitors by several cents a gallon.

The only service in many stations these days is self-service, but Massah hires attendants to pump his customers' gas. He also has mechanics, and he'll accept almost any credit card for the same price as cash. He inspects the station's restrooms several times a day and sometimes even cleans them himself.

None of this is done for charitable purposes. Repairs make money. Accepting all credit cards keeps the lines moving: Any credit card will do; just sign and move on, thank you. As for self-serve, slow-moving and inept drivers just take too long.

Massah now can often be seen hanging out the window behind his desk and, like an orchestra conductor, directing attendants to keep the lines outside moving. "This is a hands-on business," he says. And he means it. He won't abide a screen in his beloved office window—it would just get in his way. "I couldn't reach out and touch someone," he says.

A certain military-style neatness prevails at the station, even on the pump islands. Customers don't want to be served by messy-looking attendants, Massah says. Earrings? Not a chance. Studs must be removed (not that Massah is insensitive; he'll allow a newly pierced ear and earring to be covered with a little flesh-colored bandage). And no long hair; "Stuff it under a cap," he tells the pumpers. To his employees, Massah is "Mr. Hyper."

For his customers, Massah uses the homey approach. He and his wife, who keeps the books part-time, plant flowers everywhere they can find an open spot. At Christmas, he gives out calendars, like service stations of yesteryear. And he promises not to raise prices over Memorial Day weekend even though his supplier hiked the wholesale prices. "What he charges is always reasonable," customer Barry Goss, who has been filling up at Gasoline Heaven since 1963, says as an attendant wipes down the windshield. "But you know," he confides, "they don't always wash the windows."

Source: Portions reproduced with permission from Allanna Sullivan, "Cheap Gasoline and Full Service? It Must Be Heaven," *The Wall Street Journal,* May 24, 1991, p. 1.

Rudy Massah is the type of retailer who delights customers by delivering performance beyond expectations. No detail is too small to attract his attention. He competes on the intangibles, which makes it difficult for competitors to copy his success.

The elements of customer care include both objective and psychological dimensions. The objective dimensions include, among others, credit, physical facilities, warranties, repair services, and packaging. The psychological dimensions, which are intangible, include courtesy, attention, knowledge, trust, and a sense of security and confidence.

Customer support services are a primary way in which retailers differentiate their outlets from those of competitors. Many outlets offer the same merchandise at the same price with similar promotion programs. Services provide an opportunity to create a unique image in consumers' minds.[1]

The appropriate level and mix of customer support services varies depending on the retail offering and customer expectations.[2] Consider the following examples:

- **Bergdorf Goodman.** Appeals to the carriage trade by selling $2,000 suits in its Manhattan men's store. Prices are made more palatable by salespeople who will go to a customer's office to measure him for a fit and golf pros in the store to offer clients tips with the help of a putting green.
- **Home Depot.** Guarantees full refunds, no questions asked, to dissatisfied customers. Salespeople are encouraged to spend as much time as necessary, even hours, with customers to address their needs. The salespeople are also required to learn the specifics of every item in their respective aisles and two aisles adjacent as well. Periodic classes are held on new products via an internal television system. Suppliers also give updates and free demonstrations of products in use.
- **IKEA.** Check-out lines are often long and the furniture is of medium quality. Customers come in huge numbers, however, because they perceive that IKEA offers excellent price-to-value relationships. IKEA provides customer services, such as lockers for 25 cents where shoppers can leave their bags and coats.

Understanding Customer Service Expectations

The difference between customer service expectations and experiences, if any, results in a customer expectations gap, as shown in Figure 19–1. The size of the gap depends on the difference between expectations and experiences.[3] Rudy Massah's customers at Gasoline Heaven have high expectations and experience excellent service. Therefore, no service gap exists.

Customer assessments of retailer response depend on their perceptions—which may differ from reality. Customer service expectations are different during the busy Christmas season, for example, than during the slower times of the year. Expectations may also vary by customer.

Management can most effectively address the issue of customer support services by focusing on both customers and processes, which, in turn,

FIGURE 19–1

CUSTOMER SERVICE EVALUATION MODEL

A customer service evaluation model

Consumer expectations	Actual consumer experience: Poor	Actual consumer experience: Excellent
Low	No gap Confirmation of low expectations 1	Large gap Pleasant surprise 2
High	Large gap Unpleasant surprise 3	No gap Confirmation of high expectations 4

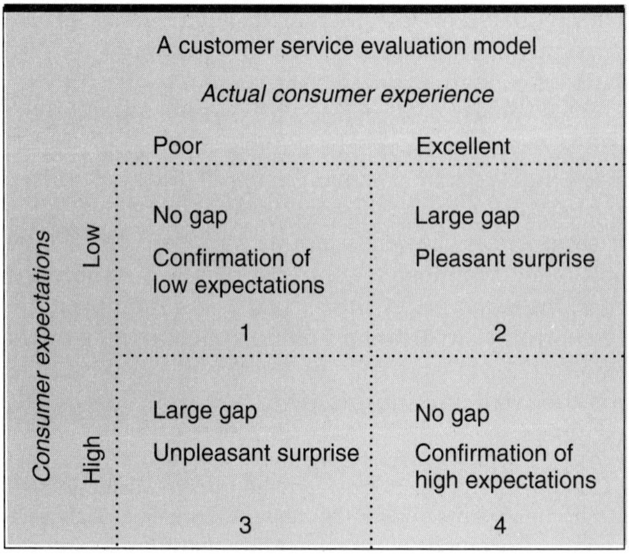

Source: Reproduced with permission from Barry Berman, "Customer Service Strategy," *The Retailing Strategist*, no. 2, 1991, p. 10.

translates into focusing on the outcome. Focusing on the customer means listening to his or her ideas about what constitutes satisfactory service. Focusing on the process means understanding the things necessary to meet customer expectations such as length of time waiting in line, personnel friendliness, and store cleanliness. Focusing on the outcome directs attention to the reliability of the service delivered such as accuracy in repair, delivery when promised, and so forth.

Nurturing the Customer-Focused Culture

Retailers create customer service expectations through advertising, store operations, and everyday marketing activities. The starting point in developing the appropriate customer service mix is a precise definition and understanding of the customer base.[4] One needs to answer the following questions:

- Who are the customers?
- What are their values and attitudes?
- What are their lifestyles?
- What do they need?
- How can they be reached?
- Where do they buy?
- What do they expect?

- What are their perceptions of the store's customer service compared with that of the competition?

To answer the above questions, a retailer must use both primary and secondary research on demographics, psychographics, media preferences, and purchasing habits, as discussed in Chapter 5.

Management also needs a focal point by which to gather, maintain, analyze, measure, and interpret information about customer service expectations.[5] Information may be collected in several ways:

- An analysis of who buys what and where.
- Share of market surveys.
- Consumer shopping panels.
- Analysis of what current customers are buying elsewhere.
- Focus groups (see Focus 19–1).
- Newsletters.
- Employee feedback.
- Sales results analysis, including test mailings and promotions.
- Comment cards.
- Suggestion boxes.

In summary, a customer-focused culture incorporates detailed information about customer lifestyles and buying patterns into competitive strategy.

Closing the expectations gap requires continuous nurturing of the customer-focused culture, as exemplified by Nordstrom (see A Profile in Excellence). Such a culture includes the following elements:

- Commitment of top management.
- Clear organizational goals.
- Specifically assigned responsibilities for each area.
- A focal point for questions and problems.
- Ongoing communication and positive examples.

Strategic Dimensions of Services

Given the above framework, services can now be analyzed on two critical dimensions—value to customers and cost to retailers. Four categories of services emerge from such an analysis, as shown in Figure 19–2: support services, disappointers, basics, and patronage builders.[6]

Support Services. Support services directly support the sale of merchandise. They have high value to consumers, but also a high cost to the retailer. Such services include home delivery, child care, gift wrapping, and personalized shopper services.

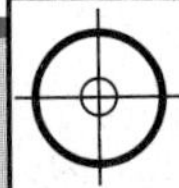

FOCUS 19–1

THE GOLDEN ARCH RULE: KNOW THY CUSTOMER

Manager Gretchen Klobucar of Grand Rapids, Michigan, knows that the best way to discover what customers think about her operation is to ask them. So that's just what she does. And her restaurant's operations, sales, transactions, and customer perceptions are better because of it.

Last spring, she hosted her first customer focus group meeting in the dining room. "I've held crew rap sessions for years," Klobucar says. "A customer focus group is set up very similarly and very simply. I bring a group of customers together and ask them to share their thoughts about my McDonald's and our competition.

"Most of the people were delighted to participate in our hour-long meeting. Many were surprised that McDonald's cared enough to take the time to do this," Klobucar says.

The first focus group was such a success that Klobucar began conducting similar meetings every month. "We schedule them on weekdays in the late afternoon or early evening. To show our appreciation, we serve our guests a complimentary meal immediately following the discussion."

Within a couple of days after the focus group meeting, Klobucar sends handwritten thank-you notes to each participant. When she spots them in her restaurant on subsequent visits, she goes out of her way to stop and chat with them. "I always ask them how they are, and how they think McDonald's is doing. Soliciting their comments gives customers a sense of pride and ownership in the restaurant, and that builds loyalty. They also give us tremendous input," Klobucar notes.

Klobucar also uses the question-and-answer period as a platform to deliver several key McDonald's messages that might not be apparent to customers such as, "Did you know that if we don't serve you in our drive-thru in 90 seconds or less, we feel that we have failed to serve you quickly?"

At the end of the hour, Klobucar and her management team open the floor to any specific questions that the participants may have about McDonald's.

"We've learned a great deal which helps us improve our operation," she says. "Equally important, we've learned a lot about our competition. We have reacted to some of their perceived strengths, such as offering free drink refills, and taken advantage of their weaknesses, such as food quality and service speed."

Says Klobucar, "To satisfy customers, I must know them. To know them, I must talk to them and find out what's on their minds. Then, I take that information and act."

Source: "Face-to-Face—A Look at McDonald's Customer Satisfaction," 1992 mailing to McDonald's shareholders.

Disappointers. Disappointers include layaway and parcel pick-up. These services require high labor effort but return little value to the customer. They are candidates for elimination. An alternative is to restructure them in a way that reduces their cost and increases their value to customers.

Basic Services. Customers take some services for granted. An example is free parking. Retailers often provide such services without giving much thought to their cost, particularly if they are a competitive necessity.

A Profile in Excellence

JAMES F. NORDSTROM

Nordstrom stores are set apart from the pack both in reputation and sales. They pave the way in showing that retailers can flourish by treating their customers well. Nordstrom stores are known for excellent customer service offered in attractive stores with quality merchandise at upscale prices.

Nordstrom's success stems primarily from James Nordstrom's belief that the customer is always right. The chain is legendary for its service. Sales clerks gift-wrap packages at no extra charge and drop off orders at customers' homes. In Alaska, Nordstrom employees have been known to warm up cars while drivers spend a few more minutes shopping. Most important to their success is the store's no-questions-asked return policy.

Second, to maintain the company's reputation, James Nordstrom from the beginning put great effort into recruiting sales associates. Nordstrom rewards them through commissions, profit sharing, and some of the highest salaries in the industry. The pay scale is reportedly 20 percent higher (or more) than the rest of the industry.

Ironically, while other retailers are busy slashing prices, Nordstrom has managed to become a driving force with only minimal promotional events each year. Its pricing policy embodies the belief that a quality item and good service is worth a little more.

A third philosophy of James Nordstrom is his inventory policy. Nordstrom stores carry literally twice the inventory per square foot of most other major retailers. For instance, a new store typically opens with 100,000 pairs of women's shoes and 10,000 men's suits.

Source: Based on Douglas Tigert, et al., "Service, Service, and Service: Why Nordstrom Is So Successful," *Retailing Review* 1, no. 2, 1991, Center for Retailing Education and Research, University of Florida, p. 8; "Why Nordstrom Got There," *Stores*, January 1990, p. 75; "Nordstrom's Gang of Four," *BusinessWeek*, June 5, 1992, pp. 122–23.

Patronage Builders. Patronage builders are the services that receive the most strategic attention from retailers. They include such services as birthday reminders and gift certificates. These services have high consumer value and can be provided at nominal cost. As such, they provide an opportunity to increase the customer base, especially if competitors are unable to provide comparable services at the same price.

Computer technology has allowed retailers to shift more services from the high-value/high-cost category to the high-value/low-cost category. Computerized bridal registries, for example, can be accessed from many store locations, and purchases can be entered on nearly a real-time basis.

Management may want to charge for support services, eliminate disappointers, and use patronage builders as a way to expand the customer base. Regardless, management needs to periodically evaluate services and make sure that patronage builders do not drift into the support services category.

FIGURE 19–2

RETAIL CUSTOMER SERVICES PROFILE

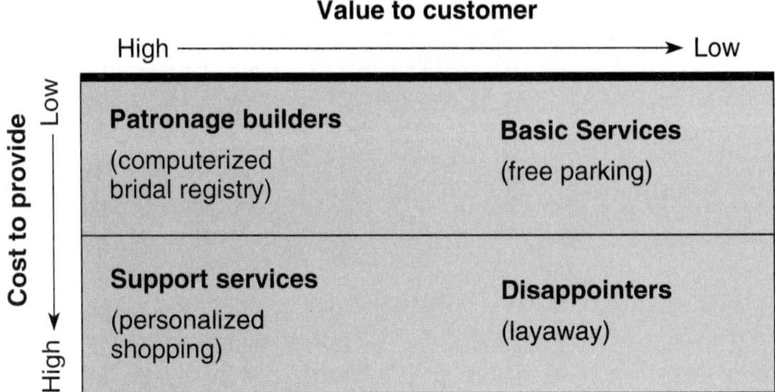

Source: Based on Albert D. Bates and Jamie G. Didion, "Special Services Can Personalize Retail Environment," *Marketing News,* April 12, 1985, p. 13.

SERVICES AUDIT

A services audit can help management respond to customer expectations. Identifying what services consumers really value is no simple task, partly because customers may have difficulty articulating their preferences. In addition, customers often form opinions about the quality and quantity of services by using competitors as a reference point.

Customer services cannot be an afterthought. Asking questions such as the ones listed below can help management integrate services as a strategic element of a customer support plan:[7]

1. What are the company's customer service objectives on each service offered—to make a profit; break even; or, in order to remain competitive, sustain the loss?
2. What services does the company provide (for example, customer education, financing arrangements, pre-delivery preparation, complaints handling, repair service, and so on)?
3. How does the company compare with the competition on the customer services provided?
4. What services do customers want?
5. What are the customer service demand patterns?
6. What trade-offs in terms of cost versus service are customers prepared to make?
7. What level of service do customers want and at what price? For example, is an 800 telephone number adequate or is a salesperson necessary?

Effective implementation of the services support program is critical after the completion of the audit. Services response systems should be standardized whenever possible and a pricing policy should be established in situations where management decides to charge for various services.

Let us now look at the range of services retailers offer to see how they can be developed to meet customer expectations.

RETAIL CREDIT

Credit card billings exceed $366 billion per year.[8] The Sears Discover card in 1990 had more than $19.4 billion in billings, followed by the Sears Roebuck charge card at $16.8 billion, and the J. C. Penney card at $8.7 billion.[9]

Understandably, credit, in one form or another, is one of the most basic customer support services many retailers can offer. The advantages and disadvantages of the various types of retail credit systems are shown in Table 19–1.

Credit is expensive. Still, many retailers believe that granting credit is necessary. The average credit transaction sale is more than double that of cash. Indeed, almost one-half of all sales in department stores are credit card transactions.[10]

Types of Credit

A retailer has two choices in offering credit: in-house credit or third-party credit.

In-House Credit. Management has six choices in offering in-house credit: installment payments, open charge credit, revolving credit, deferred billing payment, layaway, and a store-issued credit card.

Installment credit (a monthly payment account) means that a customer pays for a product in equal monthly installments, including interest. Automobiles and major appliances are often paid for in this way.

Open charge credit means that the customer must pay the bill in full when it is due, usually in 30 days. Credit limits are set that the customer cannot exceed; partial payments on the account are not allowed.

Revolving credit means that the customer is billed at the end of each month on the outstanding credit balance. Such a plan allows the customer to make multiple purchases without establishing a separate contract for each purchase.

A retailer can also offer **deferred billing credit.** Deferred billing occurs when a retailer allows customers to buy goods and defer payment for an extended time with no interest charge. Many stores often advertise this service during the Christmas season, touting "No down payment, and first payment not due for 90 days."

A **layaway plan** is another type of credit. This plan allows a customer to make a small deposit, perhaps five dollars, to hold an item. The retailer retains possession until the customer completes payment. The advantage to the customer is not having to worry about whether the item will be in stock when he or she needs it. And retailers do not have to worry about collection problems.

TABLE 19–1 ADVANTAGES AND DISADVANTAGES OF RETAIL CREDIT

Option	*Advantages*	*Disadvantages*
Maintaining in-house credit	Builds strong identification with customer. Retains customer loyalty. Facilitates customer purchase decision. When outside agency purchases credit contract, bad debt risk is transferred. Special consumers may be targeted with credit plan.	Bad debt may be incurred. Must staff and equip credit department. Clerical work involved with transaction. When credit contract is sold to outside agency, retail firm loses a percentage of credit contract.
Accepting bank cards	Attracts more diverse clientele. Outside agency may accept responsibility for collection of bad debts. Reduces pressure on sales personnel to grant credit. Loss due to bad debts accepted by outside agency. Credit offered to customers who otherwise would not qualify. Steady cash flow can be maintained. Broadens customer base. Supplements firm's credit options.	Fees paid to third party. Clerical work involved with transaction. With large purchases liability for nonpayment may rest with retail outlet if proper authorization, signature, or both are not obtained. Depersonalizes relationship between firm and customer.
Accepting travel and entertainment cards.	Attracts more diverse clientele. Card holders are usually more affluent customers. Broadens customer base. Supplements existing credit options. Responsibility for processing applications, credit authorization, and collection rests with outside agency.	Fee charged to firm for using card. Clerical work involved with transaction. Proper authorization and/or signatures must be secured from cardholder (firm may be liable for debt if not). Depersonalizes customer/firm relationship. Types of purchases may be restricted.
Buying a private-label credit system	Bank handles details of processing, promotion of plan, credit authorization, and collections. Identity of third party is hidden because name of retail firm is on card. Customer loyalty is retained. Strong identity with retail firm is built. No fee assessed firm outside of cost for program.	Up-front fee assessed by firm sponsoring bank.
Payment by check by cash.	Discounts may be given for cash-only purchases. Salesperson-customer relationship enhanced because paperwork held to minimum.	Depending on type of firm, cash-only basis may restrict growth. Bad debt may be incurred with checks. Greater chance of employee fraud. Identification requirements for check writers may diminish store-customer relationship.

Most larger retailers historically have offered a **store-issued credit card.** The reason is clear. Store card holders, compared to bank card customers, spend more per year in using their card, and also are more frequent card users.[11]

In spite of its inherent attractiveness, some retailers are dropping in-house cards. The primary reason is that store-issued cards are expensive. For an in-store card to be successful, it needs to account for 25 to 30

Charge Application

Account Number

Credit Office Use Only

Limit	Auth. By

READ INSTRUCTIONS BEFORE COMPLETING APPLICATION FORM

INSTRUCTIONS TO APPLICANT: (1) If married and you are applying for credit based on individual credit worthiness, do not complete the section for a joint account. (2) If married and you wish to use your spouse's credit worthiness in the evaluation, you must complete the joint account section. (3) Payments from alimony, child support, and maintenance need not be reported as income unless you are relying on such payments in this application. (4) If married and the type of account is marked "JOINT", the credit history of both applicant and spouse will be reported to credit reporting agencies. FRINT CLEARLY. APPLICATION MUST BE SIGNED.

PLEASE OPEN A JOINT ACCOUNT ☐ OR AN INDIVIDUAL ACCOUNT ☐ IN THE FOLLOWING NAME

Name, First | Second | Last | Social Security No.

Home Address, Street | City | State | Zip | How Long Yrs. Mos.

Home Phone No. | Monthly Mtg./Rent | Resident ☐ Own ☐ Rent ☐Other | Date of Birth

Previous Address | Yrs. at Prev. Address | Employer Phone

Employer (Give Full Name) | How Long (3 Yrs. Required) | Position

Employer's Address | Monthly Salary $ | Other Income - Source(s) $

Former Employer | How Long

Name of Relative or Personal Reference | Address | Phone | Relationship

JOINT ACCOUNT

Name of Joint Applicant | Social Security No. | Date of Birth

Employer (Full Name) | How Long (3 Yrs. Required) | Position | Employer Phone No.

Employer's Address | Monthly Salary $ | Other Income - Source(s) $

Former Employer | How Long

CREDIT REFERENCES

Do you presently have or have you ever had an account with ______ ☐ Yes ☐ No

Account No. | Date Opened: | Amount Owing $

Name of Creditors	Important Account Numbers	Exact Name in Which Account is Held	Date Opened	Balance Owed

(SIGNATURE OF AUTHORIZED BUYER OTHER THAN APPLICANT) **X**

The undersigned affirm(s) that the information furnished to ______ by the undersigned in connection with this transaction is true and correct and hereby authorizes ______ to investigate my credit record, and to verify my employment and income references.
The undersigned further agree(s) that if this application is accepted and a Credit Card issued that any use of the card will be governed by the terms and conditions accompanying the card, and the undersigned assume(s), if more than one jointly and severally, liability for all charges incurred in any such use.
Upon approval you will receive a copy of the ______ Charge Agreement to keep.

SIGNATURE IN FULL OF APPLICANTS	**X**	Date	Dr. Lic. No.
	X	Date	Dr. Lic. No.

notice: *The Federal Equal Credit Opportunity Act requires that all creditors make credit equally available to all creditworthy customers without regard to sex or marital status. The federal agency which administers compliance with this law concerning this store is Federal Trade Commission, Washington, D.C. 20580.*

Any holder of this consumer credit contract is subject to all claims and defenses which the debtor could assert against the seller of goods or services obtained pursuant hereto or with the proceeds hereof. Recovery hereunder by the debtor shall not exceed amounts paid by the debtor hereunder.

FIGURE 19–3

SAMPLE CREDIT APPLICATION FORM

percent of all sales in the store. In other words, a $100 million retailer would need at least a $20 million increase in receivables, depending on the speed with which the card holders repay their debt. Operational expenses vary but can total $4 million for a $100 million company.[12]

Managing Internal Credit. Most retailers issuing credit use an application form (see Figure 19–3). The application requests information that helps the firm to decide whether to grant the credit request. The forms may ask for such information as the size of savings and checking account balances, extent of debt, and various other personal information. Often information on the creditworthiness of an applicant is obtained from a credit bureau.

Credit Scoring. Many firms use **credit scoring** in screening credit applicants. This method assigns points to various types of personal information about the applicant. The points are developed from a study of information obtained from good and bad accounts. An example of a credit scoring system is shown in Table 19–2. Depending on the number of points received, a person may be given a certain credit limit or may be rejected. Experience can help decide on the minimum number of points necessary to approve an application.

A credit application is considered by summing the points received based on the application characteristics evaluated. The score may be part of either a single cutoff method or a two-stage process.

In the single cutoff method, credit is granted if the points meet or exceed the cutoff. Otherwise, credit is denied. In a two-stage analysis, credit is automatically awarded if the credit score exceeds the cutoff point and is automatically denied if it is below the cutoff. Additional information is gathered on applicants who meet the cutoff exactly and is added to the initial score based on the application information. A decision on whether to accept or deny credit is then made.

Key Legislation. *The Equal Credit Opportunity Act (1977).* Many retailers shifted to credit scoring because of this act, which states that a person who is denied credit can demand a written statement of reasons for denial. Thus, retailers are under pressure to operate with objective and consistent credit approval policies. Scoring also gives the retailer the following advantages: (1) better control over credit; (2) ease in training new personnel; and (3) a lower cost in processing credit applications.

The Fair Debt Collection Practices Act (1978). Management must be sure its collection practices are legal. This act prohibits abusive, deceptive, and unfair debt collection practices by debt collectors. The law will not permit debt collectors to use unjust means in attempting to collect debt but does not cancel debts that consumers owe.

The Federal Competitive Quality Banking Act (1987). This act allows retailers to charge card holders in any state the maximum interest rate allowed in the state in which the bank is established. Retailers strongly support this act, although some retailer practices have been controversial, as discussed in A Question of Ethics.

Credit Authorization. The retailer also needs to decide how credit will be verified when a credit purchase is made. Some firms still have manual credit verification, whereby a clerk calls the credit department and asks for approval. Some stores set a limit, say $50, above which all credit charges must be approved. All sales less than the amount are approved on the floor.

TABLE 19–2 MAJOR NATIONAL RETAILER'S FINAL SCORING TABLE FOR APPLICATION CHARACTERISTICS

Characteristic	Score
ZIP code	
ZIP codes A	60
ZIP codes B	48
ZIP codes C	41
ZIP codes D	37
Not answered	53
Bank reference	
Checking only	0
Savings only	0
Checking and savings	15
Bank name or loan only	0
No bank reference	7
Not answered	7
Type of housing	
Owns/buying	44
Rents	35
All other	41
Not answered	39
Occupation	
Clergy	46
Creative	41
Driver	33
Executive	62
Guard	46
Homemaker	50
Laborer	33
Manager	46
Military enlisted	46
Military officer	62
Office staff	46
Outside	33
Production	41
Professional	62
Retired	62
Sales	46
Semiprofessional	50
Service	41
Student	46
Teacher	41
Unemployed	33
All other	46
Not answered	47
Time at present address	
Less than 6 months	39
6 months–1 year, 5 months	30
1 year, 6 months—3 years, 5 months	27
3 years, 6 months—7 years, 5 months	30
7 years, 6 months—12 years, 5 months	39
12 years, 6 months or longer	50
Not answered	36
Time with employer	
Less than 6 months	31
6 months—5 years, 5 months	24
5 years, 6 months—8 years, 5 months	26
8 years, 6 months—15 years, 5 months	31
15 years, 6 months or longer	39
Homemakers	39
Retired	31
Unemployed	29
Not answered	29
Finance company reference	
Yes	0
Other references only	25
No	25
Not answered	15
Other department store/oil card/major credit card	
Department store only	12
Oil card only	12
Major credit card only	17
Department store and oil card	17
Department store and credit card	31
Major credit card and oil card	31
All three	31
Other references only	0
No credit	0
Not answered	12

Source: Noel Capon, "Credit Scoring System: A Critical Analysis," *Journal of Marketing* 46 (Spring 1982), p. 85. Reprinted with permission.

A Question of Ethics

CREDIT CARD BANKS

The Federal Competitive Quality Banking Act allows retailers to establish their own credit card banks. Retailers are likely to open credit banks for two reasons: control and profit. The firm can charge card holders in any state the maximum interest rate allowed in the state in which the bank is chartered. (Interest rate ceilings in some states, such as Delaware, Colorado, and South Dakota, are between 21 and 25 percent and as low as 12 percent in others.) The act also allows retailers to operate under one set of rules, rather than 50 sets of rules.

Nordstrom recently opened a credit bank in Colorado. The Colorado interest rate ceiling is 21 percent, allowing Nordstrom to charge that much in all states if it decides to do so. The Limited has also established its own credit bank. May Department stores opened a credit bank in Arizona, where no ceiling exists on consumer credit charges. Circuit City stores also has a credit bank charter, as does Sears.

Retailers contend that they are attracted to credit card banks because they eliminate the hassles of various state regulations, which in turn simplifies their growth strategies. They also help avoid credit card interest rate caps. Retailers argue that a rate reduction caused by a cap would limit the availability of credit cards and could disrupt the economy.

Critics, however, contend that, faced with flat sales, many stores are seeking to generate extra income by raising interest rates on in-house credit. *Money* magazine reported that Nordstrom and Macy's jacked finance charges in some states from 18 percent to 19.8 percent and 21.6 percent, respectively, after establishing credit banks. These increases followed previously announced increases from Dillard's (19.8 percent), Lane Bryant, (22.8 percent), and Lord & Taylor, (21.6 percent).

Are retailers acting unethically in standardizing interest rates across states, or is it simply good business?

Source: Based on Kerry Hannon, "Watch Out for Rising Cost of Store Cards," *Money*, December 1991, p. 33.

Credit authorization is now done electronically by some firms. The clerk enters the account number and the amount of the sale at the cash register. The system then automatically checks the accounts receivable information stored in the computer and indicates whether a credit charge should be approved.

Added-Value Programs. Retailers often entice their core credit customers to remain loyal by creating purchase incentives for them. The key is adding value to the credit card.[13]

Brooks Brothers sends its credit customers a mail-order catalog, invitations to special charge customer shopping evenings before Christmas, special notices of private sales, and postcard mailings with special merchandise offers. Neiman-Marcus implemented a program it calls InCircle. The program allows charge customers to accumulate a point for every dollar in charge purchases. Customers begin receiving benefits and rewards based on their point totals earned.

Third-Party Credit. In a third-party program, firms other than the retailer handle credit applications, credit processing, and authorization; customer inquiries; promotion; and card issuance.

Third-party credit can consist of a **bank card** such as Visa, MasterCard, or Sears Discover Card; a **private-label credit card** for the store, issued by a third party such as a bank; **travel and entertainment cards** such as American Express or Diner's Club; or a **co-branded card.**

The key is that the cards are not controlled by the merchant. Rather, a bank or an entertainment company receives applications and issues cards and is responsible for customer billing and collection. The firms then bill the merchants accepting the card at a percentage of all credit sales.

The General Electric Credit Corporation (GECC) customer credit program is a third-party private label option now used by many retail firms. GECC works with each merchant to tailor a package to the store's needs. Sometimes GECC maintains an office in the store to handle credit processing and collection. Often, customers are not aware that they are dealing with an outside agency.

A co-branded card is a dual-purpose card combining the features of a private-label card and a bank card.[14] The issuer and the retailer each have their logo on the card. An example is the Casual Corner/MasterCard, which can be used at Casual Corner and anywhere else the MasterCard is accepted. Such programs allow consumers to reduce the number of cards they carry and to use the card at outlets that might not accept bank cards. Another advantage is consolidated billing. As with other third-party cards, the retailers focus on their skills—selling merchandise and services—while financial institutions handle the consumer credit issues.

SHOPPING SERVICES

Retailers offer a variety of services for customers who do not have the interest or the time to spend on extended in-store shopping. The most common services are telephone shopping, in-home shopping, and personal shopping.

Telephone Shopping. Telephone shopping is attractive to consumers who have limited time for shopping. Typically, the store will issue a catalog to interested consumers. After looking at the catalog, the customer calls the store, orders the merchandise, and charges the goods to a store account or credit card. The goods are then delivered to the shopper's home by United Parcel Service or a similar shipping service. Some retail outlets also offer toll-free 800 service as a way of increasing sales.

In-Home Shopping. In-home demonstrations remain popular for such services as home decoration. Employees bring samples of draperies, carpeting, and wallpaper to a customer's home. The customer can then see how the materials look under normal lighting conditions.

EXHIBIT 19–1

Courtesy Wal-Mart Stores, Inc.

Hiring older workers: Wal-Mart shows the way by hiring seniors as "people greeters" who meet shoppers at the front door.

Personal Shopping Services. Personal shopping is one of the fastest-growing retailer services. Some firms specialize in assembling wardrobes for professional women and men. The customer goes to the store and provides a list of needed measurements, style and color preferences, and lifestyle information. After that, the person can call the store and indicate which items he or she wants to purchase. The store personnel then assemble several choices and have them ready at the customer's convenience.

OTHER CUSTOMER SUPPORT SERVICES

The customer service possibilities are almost limitless. The type and level of services vary depending on the positioning strategy of the retailer. Some are quite unique, as in the case of the "people greeters" who meet shoppers at the front doors of Wal-Mart (see Exhibit 19–1). The people greeters are one of the most popular customer support services offered by the firm.

Neiman-Marcus is known worldwide for its unique customer services. We have chosen to highlight some of these services in Table 19–3 to illustrate the range of customer support services offered by retailers.

TABLE 19–3

SPECIAL SERVICES AT NEIMAN-MARCUS

Our clientele system requires each salesperson to develop a personal interest in each customer by recording individual taste and merchandise preferences in a clientele book. This record allows the salesperson to use the purchase history to better serve each customer. With this information on file, a customer can keep his or her wardrobe updated without coming into the store. Initiated by Stanley Marcus, the clientele system offers the personalized attention and customer service that make Neiman-Marcus famous.

The "one fitting room" service enables the professional salesperson to fulfill all the customer's shopping needs. Creative selling techniques allow everything—from apparel to the appropriate accessories—to be brought to one fitting room.

The travel service, available in most of our stores, will plan an unforgettable itinerary and take care of the details in order to allow the customer the enjoyment and the adventure of the trip.

The bridal salon makes that special day perfect by aiding in the selection of the wedding and bridesmaids' gowns, answering questions of etiquette, and personally coordinating all wedding activities.

The bridal registry offers assistance in the selection of the china, silver, and items for the home based on a couple's needs and lifestyle. The registry maintains a record of all gifts purchased for each couple. This is a wonderful way to prevent duplication of wedding gifts.

The Neiman-Marcus restaurants offer a fine selection of delectable foods. Customers enjoy the excellent standard of food service and the opportunity to relax during a hectic shopping day.

Personal shopping services, available to all customers, provide expert fashion advice concerning travel, wardrobe coordination, and gift selections. Personal shoppers specialize in being knowledgeable about merchandise from all areas of the store.

The public relations staff informs our customers about upcoming events at Neiman-Marcus. It takes reservations for fashion shows, coordinates special events, and aids salespeople in communicating with customers.

Mail order is the answer for those who wish to shop by mail. Many mail-order customers have never been to a Neiman-Marcus store, but are well aware of our worldwide reputation and our fine quality merchandise. Direct mail order, for our charge customers, offers the latest in direct mail literature including catalogues, charge statement inserts, and special mailers.

The hosiery club offers a wide selection of Neiman-Marcus exclusive hosiery and is a wonderful way to stay well-stocked. A predetermined number of pairs is sent to the customer on a specified schedule.

Gift wraps designed for Neiman-Marcus are world famous. Unique and attractive paper, ribbons, and ornaments convey seasonal themes. Often, recipients are as intrigued with the package as they are with the contents.

The alterations department provides expert alterations on all Neiman-Marcus merchandise.

Fur storage is available at all Neiman-Marcus stores. Upon arrival at fur storage, each fur or fur-trimmed garment is thoroughly sterilized. Alterations such as new linings, repair of worn areas, or a total redesign can be done at this time. There is no charge for estimates, and all work is done in our supervised workrooms.

Local delivery service is provided by UPS at all Neiman-Marcus stores. If specific information is needed, check with the receiving department.

EXHIBIT 19–2

NOTICE

I do not consider a sale complete until goods are worn out and customer still satisfied.

We will thank anyone to return goods that are not perfectly satisfactory.

Should the person reading this notice know of anyone who is not satisfied with our goods, I will consider it a favor to be notified.

Above all things we wish to avoid having a dissatisfied customer.

Courtesy L. L. Bean, Inc.

Notice from a 1912 L. L. Bean circular

Warranties

A strong customer satisfaction warranty forces the retailer to provide high-quality service and merchandise. Anything less than excellence will entice the customer to invoke the guarantee, which can be an expensive process. Thus, guarantees and warranties serve a two-fold purpose: to identify problems with the quality of service delivered, and to force the organization to meet consistently high standards of customer service.[15]

L. L. Bean in 1912 launched its "satisfaction guaranteed, no questions asked" program, which has remained popular with customers even today (see Exhibit 19–2). McDonald's implemented a guarantee at its U.S. restaurants with the promise that "If you are not satisfied, we will make it right—or your next meal is on us." The guarantee applies to complaints ranging from long lines to cold french fries.[16]

Some retailers also offer an **extended warranty.**[17] The store agrees to extend a manufacturer's warranty for a period of time, commonly a year or so. The customer does not have to pay a repair bill during the period, regardless of how much the repair service may cost. Extended warranties are common on major household appliances and consumer electronics.

A service guarantee loses power in direct proportion to the number of conditions it contains. A good service guarantee is unconditional, easy to understand and communicate, meaningful, easy (and painless) to invoke, and easy and quick to collect on.[18]

Extended Shopping Hours

More and more retailers are offering consumers longer shopping hours, either late at night or 24 hours a day. Utility charges are about the same because the equipment runs most of the time anyway. Additional sales generated by longer hours can help spread the fixed costs over a larger sales base.

Retailers should also remember that **blue laws** (laws against opening on Sunday) are enforced in some areas. Such laws are particularly prevalent in the Southeast and Southwest. Enforcement is spotty, but a retailer can wind up in jail if a pressure group pushes the police to enforce the law.

Customers with Special Needs

Opportunities exist to meet the needs of "special" consumers, including those who don't speak English, the aged, and the handicapped (including people who are deaf, blind, or confined to wheelchairs). More than 14 percent of all Americans have physical or sensory disabilities.

McDonald's reintroduced braille and picture menus across the U.S. in 1992, emphasizing its commitment to serving the 37 million Americans with vision, speech, or hearing impairments.[19] Similarly, the Seattle division of Safeway is using closed captions in its television commercials to assist hearing-impaired viewers. (Close captioning is the process by which the audio portion of the television program is converted into written words, which then appear on the television screen.)[20]

Nursery Services

Some retailers are adding nursery services as part of their customer support programs. IKEA, the Swedish-owned home furnishings chain, has been widely noted in the trade press as having an excellent child-care program to encourage parents' shopping (see Exhibit 19–3).[21] Sears has also added a play area in the Kids & More departments in its new power format stores.

Responding to Complaints

Invariably, in spite of a retailer's best efforts, complaints about the merchandise or store policies will arise. The tendency too often is to treat complaints as a nuisance. Such a viewpoint is shortsighted, however. Management should strive, within reasonable limits, to retain customers whenever possible. Customer loyalty and profitability go hand in hand because it costs less to serve repeat customers than to attract new customers.[22]

Customer service breakdowns are especially likely in the following situations: (1) when the service process involves complex scheduling;

EXHIBIT 19–3

Courtesy IKEA US Inc.

IKEA offers a "Ballroom" where kids can play while parents shop.

(2) when a new customer support service is being introduced; (3) when the customer support activity involves high employee turnover; (4) when front-line employees are inadequately trained; and (5) when the retailer is forced to rely on suppliers or other uncontrollable external factors such as the weather.[23]

Retailers can pursue several different courses, as shown in Figure 19–4, in responding to consumer dissatisfaction.[24] Their response can be either passive or active and can reflect either a reactive or a corrective stance from management.

One possibility is simply to deflect complaints by offering an apology, a discount coupon, or perhaps a refund. A second approach is the "lip service" approach. Retailers loudly proclaim their desire for customer feedback. But they have no fundamental system in place to deal with the underlying causes of the dissatisfaction.

Progressive retailers actively seek to understand customers and their dissatisfaction. Such an approach requires a top-down commitment, innovative strategies in responding to dissatisfaction, an investment in customer feedback systems, managerial incentives, and measures that emphasize the importance of customer feedback.

FIGURE 19–4

STRATEGIES FOR DEALING WITH COMPLAINTS

	Company responses: Reactive	Company responses: Corrective
Passive	Deflect complaints	React to needs
Active	Give lip service	Build bridges

Source: Milind Lele, *The Customer Is the Key* (New York: John Wiley & Sons, Inc., 1987), p. 227. Reprinted with permission.

Chapter Highlights

- Customer service expectations vary by type of retailing. The differences between customer expectations and experiences, if any, result in a customer expectations gap.
- Management can most effectively address the issue of customer support services by focusing on both customers and processes which, in turn, translates into focusing on the outcome.
- The starting point in developing the customer services mix is a precise definition and in-depth knowledge of the customer base. The retailer needs both primary and secondary data on demographics, psychographics, media preferences, and purchasing behavior. Management also needs a focal point from which to gather, maintain, analyze, interpret, and measure the use of customer support services.
- Services can be analyzed on two key dimensions: value to customers and cost to retailers. Four categories of services emerge from such an analysis: support services, disappointers, basics, and patronage builders.
- A services audit can help management develop a customer-focused culture. Identifying what services customers really value is no simple task, partly because customers may have difficulty articulating their preferences.
- Many features of a store affect how customers view it and whether they will continue to shop at the outlet. The kind and quality of customer support services are key factors.
- Retailers must consider many factors when they decide whether to offer credit. They can offer in-store credit or have credit handled by an outside agency accepting third-party cards. They may also issue a store card. The pressure to accept bank cards is increasing, and most stores now honor them.
- Most types of credit are offered by the retailer at a loss. However, credit usually is a necessary customer service.

- Retailers can offer a variety of other services as part of the customer support mix. However, it is important to balance revenue against the cost of the services.
- Retailers should closely monitor the legal issues involved in the services they offer.

STUDY QUESTIONS

1. Why should responding to customer complaints be such an important part of the retailer's customer support strategy? What are the possible strategies for dealing with complaints?
2. What are the requirements for excellent customer service?
3. What is the logical starting point in developing a customer service mix? Why?
4. Identify the processes retailers can implement in gathering, maintaining, analyzing, and interpreting customer feedback in planning the customer support service mix.
5. What are the ingredients of a customer-focused culture?
6. Identify the two critical dimensions of customer services and the categories of service that emerge from such analysis.
7. What is a customer services audit, and what is its value?
8. Explain the differences among the following terms: installment credit, open-charge credit, revolving credit, deferred billing credit, and a layaway plan.
9. Explain how retailers use credit scoring to screen credit applicants.
10. What are some things retailers are doing to be more responsive to customers who have special needs?

A P P L I C A T I O N S

CASE 1: Warren's on the Hill

The following situations are problems faced by Warren's on the Hill, a fictitious fine jewelry company.

Mrs. Peck is furious. Tom Davis has been a store manager for 15 years at Warren's. His firm was one of approximately four with similar market positioning strategies in a major metropolitan market. His branch was in a high-income area, and his familiarity with the customers was a matter of pride to him. He worked hard at knowing as many as possible of the "regulars."

Recently, Mrs. G. T. Peck came into the store, visibly furious. Davis approached her and greeted her as usual, attempting not to recognize her displeasure. (She came in frequently and was considered a good customer.) After the greeting, Mrs. Peck lashed out in a virtual monologue—voice shaking, face flushed, words rehearsed!

> Mr. Davis, I can't tell you how mortified I am. My son and his new bride were in the store a while ago. They had been working in their yard and were in their work clothes. I can tell you they didn't look too terrific. But they came in here with the specific purpose of completing their silver. My daughter-in-law has never been into this store of yours; my son never goes into jewelry stores unless someone pulls him in. My husband and I agreed to buy all the pieces they needed for 12 place settings and the serving pieces they needed. Most of their friends don't have sterling, but I think it's important. Well it's important, but I can assure you, neither they nor I will ever set foot in this store again—not any of your snobbish stores! They came in, mind you, with money to buy—a snippy salesperson, without even a courteous greeting, continued working on some forms, and when Cindy said she wanted to discuss an International silver pattern, the salesperson merely handed her a brochure and said, "All of International's patterns, prices, and descriptions are in this catalog. See if you can find what you want." Can you imagine? She hardly looked up—only long enough to see two young people very casually attired. But, Mr. Davis, with a credit card which I am going to make sure is *not* going to be used here. You and everyone else carries International silver. Please close my account at once. I shall pay the balance now. I don't want to deal with people who are so rude and thoughtless.

Michael Overstreet is frustrated. Michael Overstreet's wife, Helen, received a lovely 14-karat gold overlay chain with a lifetime guarantee (so the ads say) in a Superior chain box from her aunt for her birthday. Helen was delighted. She had heard of the name and, more importantly, anything that came from Warren's on the Hill had a mystique for her. She knew it wasn't solid gold, but her aunt always gave nice gifts, and in today's market, even overlay probably was expensive. And Superior was, after all, superior!

One evening at dinner at the club, Helen's chain seemed to "fall apart," as Michael remembered it. Luckily, Helen's dress had a cowl collar that managed to catch the chain intact—it was all there. Helen was also delighted that she had saved the Superior box and Warren's as well. Mike said he'd drop it off at the store on the way to work the next day.

As usual, Michael was running late. He dropped into Warren's in a rush and hurriedly approached the first salesperson he saw. It was early, and the entire staff appeared to be sleepwalking. Mike explained what had happened; the unsmiling salesperson took the chain in hand, examined it, and said, "This isn't a Superior chain. And if it isn't, we have no responsibility for the guarantee. The manager is running late, but when he comes in I'll check with him. Can I have your phone number?"

Michael thanked the rigid salesperson and asked to be called as soon as possible, so that the problem could be solved and Helen satisfied. The salesperson nodded, Mike thought to stay awake. He noticed the salesperson's name as he left. That was fortunate, he thought later, because he received no call from Mr. Davis that day, nor within the next two weeks. Michael called Nancy, the identified salesperson, who said that they were checking and would definitely call.

Three weeks later, Michael Overstreet is frustrated. He has heard that Warren's is top flight. Now he wonders. He calls Tom Davis, the store manager, direct. When Mike begins his story, Tom says he has never heard about the problem. He apologizes. Mike thinks something "smells" and infers as much to Tom. Mike, who never gets angry, says that Mr. Warren and he are members of the same Rotary Club and have been acquaintances for some years. "Shall I call Mr. Warren?" Mike asks Tom.

Mr. Strickland's wife is displeased. Tom Davis wonders how he always gets the hard ones. Recently Warren's on the Hill ran an ad for its inventory sale—everything in the store was marked down appreciably, and all sales were final. Tom worked for some time with Strick Strickland, whose wife was at La Costa in California at a weight-loss clinic, and Strick supposed she was having a miserably wonderful time. He wanted to remember his wife on their anniversary when she was away and wanted it to be something important. He was a man who loved a bargain, and when the word "discount" was promoted, he knew that important jewelry pieces were being offered at great savings; he knew the anniversary gift was in hand!

A particularly dramatic (but as Tom admits privately, rather flashy and tacky) necklace was on sale at $3,500, regularly priced at $7,000. Tom did not hard-sell the necklace, as he was not at all sure that Mrs. Strickland would like it; she had displayed exquisite taste, he thought, and was typically with her husband when anything important was being purchased. Tom also carefully stressed the final nature of this type of sale.

Mr. Strickland loved the piece and the price. The gift was mailed to La Costa, and then the phone started ringing—at both the Strickland's and Warren's. Mrs. Strickland loved her husband and his thoughtfulness, but she hated the necklace. Mr. Strickland called Tom and said, "I know what you said about the sale being final, but since I'm such a good customer, I'm sure you'll make an exception in my case." Davis said he'd check with management. He did. The buyer said that under no circumstances could any exception be made to the established policy.

Tom wondered whether he should call Mr. Warren. What would that do to the decision? Would he tell the buyer to make an exception? Would Mr. Strickland remain a customer under the existing decision? What a problem!

CASE 2: Customer Service: Japan versus the United States

Japan has been able to dominate many U.S. industries by a combination of high quality and low cost made possible by strong vendor partnerships and techniques such as just-in-time inventory management and quality control (QC) circles. Unquestionably, the level of personal service in Japan is higher than in the United States. In Japan, the customer is truly "king." Store clerks and executives, for example, line up to bow to the first customers to enter department stores. Taxi drivers spend time between fares polishing their cabs and often wear white gloves. Efficiency, as well as excellent customer service, permeate the retail service sector, in large part because of pervasive QC programs.

The QC circles at the Mitsukoshi Department store, for example, work to continually modify procedures for gift transaction processing to make them more efficient. Most QC circles meet outside business hours and are largely bottom-up, employee driven groups. In Japan service quality is a primary goal, in contrast to quantity and efficiency in the United States.

Japanese retailers are more prone than their North American counterparts to provide off-site service. Automobile dealers, for example, will pick up and deliver automobiles for repair service customers. They will also make sales calls at customers' homes.

In addition, Japanese retailers spend more time in training customer contact personnel than U.S. retailers do. The instructions go so far as to train customer support personnel how to greet people, what tone of voice to use, and how to handle difficult inquiries. Annual follow-up programs are also held.

Higher service levels in Japan are also obtained by using more people than North American retailers. Japanese hotels, for example, will often have twice the number of service workers per room compared to the United States. Customer satisfaction is also more likely to be quantified and to be a core element of the management process.

Several dimensions of the Japanese culture help make the high service levels possible. Some factors include the loyalty, work habits, and motivation of the Japanese work force. A key underlying element is the tradition of lifelong employment based on the concepts of commitment and hard work that permeate the Japanese society. In contrast, employee turnover is high in the U.S. service industry. Dissatisfied employees will simply go across the street and begin working for a competitor. Furthermore, the Japanese work force is much more homogeneous than the work force in the United States. Finally, the off-site activities of Japanese service personnel would be perceived as intrusive by U.S. customers.

Further factors contributing to the difference in service levels is the inexpensive cost of labor in Japan. Finally, the level of technology in services is also lower in Japan than in the United States. For example, automated check-out and room reservation services are typically not available in Japan.

Source: Based on David Aaker, "How Will the Japanese Compete in Retail Services?" *The California Management Review* 33, no. 1 (1990), pp. 54–67.

Applying Retailing Principles

1. Are the service levels offered in Japanese retailing desirable or necessary in North America?
2. Are U.S. retail customers more likely than their Japanese counterparts to place a premium on convenience and efficiency compared to a higher level of personal service?
3. Why haven't quality circles and similar employee involvement programs become popular in U.S. retailing?

Notes

1. "Their Wish Is Your Command," *BusinessWeek/Quality,* 1991, pp. 126–27.
2. Valarie A. Zeithaml, A. Parasuraman, and Leonard L. Berry, *Delivering Service Quality: Balancing Customer Perceptions and Expectations* (New York: The Free Press, 1990), pp. 24–28.
3. Dean E. Headley and Bob Choi, "Achieving Service Quality through Gap Analysis and a Basic Statistical Approach," *Journal of Services Marketing* 6, no. 1 (Winter 1992), pp. 5–14.
4. This section, with modification, is reproduced with permission from Roy Burns, "Customer Service vs. Customer-Focused," *Retail Control,* March 1989. Copyright © National Retail Merchants Federation. All rights reserved.
5. Bruce R. Matza, "Look at Your Business from the Customers' Point of View," *Retail Control,* April 1991, pp. 11–13.
6. Albert D. Bates and Jamie G. Didion, "Special Services Can Personalize Retail Environment," *Marketing News,* April 12, 1985, p. 13.
7. Hirotaka Takeuchi and John A. Quelch, "Quality Is More Than Making a Good Product," *Harvard Business Review,* July–August 1983, pp. 139–45.
8. Larry Light, Leah N. Spiro, Peter Coy, and Suzanne Woolley, "War of the Plastic," *BusinessWeek,* April 15, 1991, p. 28.
9. Ibid.
10. "Technology: Helping Retailers MAPP out the Future," *Stores,* p. S7.
11. "Store Card Still Strong," *Stores,* January 1991, p. 169.
12. "Retailers Use Bank Cards to Their Credit," *Stores,* February 1992, p. S5; Gary Robbins,

"Scoring: Retailers Finding New Uses for the Technique," *Stores,* March 1992, p. 45.

13. Penny Gill, "Added Value: Relationship Marketing Is One Way for Retailers to Build Loyalty," *Stores,* October 1991, pp. 39–40.
14. "Co-Branding on the Rise," *Stores,* February 1992, p. S7; see also Dan Alaimo, "Wegmans to Use Co-Branded Credit Cards," *Supermarket News,* February 25, 1991, p. 15.
15. Christopher W. L. Hart, James Heskitt, and Earl Sasser, *Service Breakthroughs* (New York: The Free Press, 1990), p. 89.
16. *Birmingham News,* May 24, 1992, p. A11.
17. Laurie Freeman, "Service Contracts and Warranties Impact Bottom Line," *Stores,* January 1992, pp. 122 and 124.
18. Christopher W. L. Hart, "The Power of Unconditional Service Guarantees," *Harvard Business Review,* July–August 1988, p. 55.
19. "Face to Face: A Look at McDonald's Customer Satisfaction," First Quarter 1992 McDonald's Shareholders Newsletter.
20. "Safeway Captions Ads for Deaf," *Supermarket News,* August 19, 1991, p. 58.
21. "Caring: IKEA Sets the Pace," *Stores,* November 1990, pp. 54–55.
22. Hart, Heskitt, and Sasser, *Service Breakthroughs,* p. 31.
23. Hart, Heskitt, and Sasser, *Service Breakthroughs,* p. 31.
24. This discussion is based on Milind Lele, *The Customer Is the Key* (New York: John Wiley & Sons, 1987), pp. 226–33.

Promotions in Retailing– A Variety of Purposes and Approaches

Nike Town, a concept utilizing the store as theatre

(Courtesy Nike, Inc.; photo by Strode Eckert)

(Courtesy Nike, Inc.)

(Courtesy Nike, Inc.; photo by Strode Eckert)

(Courtesy Nike, Inc.)

Promotion to enter a new market

Parisian uses multimedia to enter the Cobb County/Atlanta market.

(Courtesy of Parisian)

(Courtesy of Parisian)

(Courtesy of Parisian)

(Courtesy of Parisian)

EVENT MARKETING—LEXUS "CHAMPIONS FOR CHARITY"

Our Champions For Charity Spokesman's Clothes May Be All Over The Map, But His Heart's In The Right Place.

It's right there. Beating like a big bass drum beneath that loud shirt. There aren't many people with a larger heart than Payne Stewart and that's why we're proud to announce his role as a Lexus Champion For Charity.

Lexus Champions For Charity has helped raise over $12 million for deserving charities.

This year, we're aiming higher. We expect to donate to over 135 charities, including the American Cancer Society, American Heart Association, City of Hope, Leukemia Society, March of Dimes and the Ronald McDonald House.

To help us reach that goal, thousands of golfers will participate in a series of benefit tournaments that culminate in the National Finals held at the La Quinta Resort in Palm Springs. Here, amateur golfers will compete for additional contributions to their local charities.

The Lexus Champions For Charity. It may very well be the only tournament where everybody wins. And one of the few times Payne's heart will get more attention than his wardrobe.

LEXUS
The Relentless Pursuit Of Perfection.

(Courtesy Team One Advertising/Lexus)

Announcement of the event.

(Michael J. Hruby)

Retail-dealer sponsors.

(Courtesy Team One Advertising/Lexus)

The prize.

(Courtesy Team One Advertising/Lexus)

The champions.

Regional shopping center promotion à la Vivaldi "The Four Seasons"

Promotional opportunities for Eastdale Mall in Montgomery, Alabama.

(Courtesy Aronov Realty Co., Inc.)

Winter

(Courtesy Aronov Realty Co., Inc.)

Spring

(Courtesy Aronov Realty Co., Inc.)

Summer

(Courtesy Aronov Realty Co., Inc.)

Fall

P A R T

6

Retailing Issues, Opportunities, and Outlook

The final section of the text introduces you to two significant issues and ends with a focus on the future.

Chapter 20 reviews franchising as a way of owning and operating a retail firm. Chapter 21 reviews services retailing and direct marketing. These are the hottest topics in retailing today.

Chapter 22 assesses the significance of the material covered in the course and provides an opportunity to speculate about trends that can affect retailers in the remainder of the decade.

Retailers, because of their proximity to the customer, have a special opportunity to serve society while earning a profit. Their challenge is to provide good price-to-value relationships while operating in an environmentally sound and socially sensitive way.

C H A P T E R

20

Franchising as a Growth Strategy

THIS CHAPTER:

Explains the importance of franchising in the U.S. economy.

Reviews advantages and disadvantages of becoming a franchisee.

Defines primary types of franchise arrangements.

Identifies the costs involved in becoming a franchisee.

Shows how to evaluate franchise opportunities.

Emphasizes the items contained in a typical franchise contract.

Outlines legal restrictions on franchising.

Highlights the trends and outlook for franchising.

RETAILING CAPSULE

THE FLEXIBILITY OF OPERATING A FRANCHISE FROM HOME

Betty Russotti used to work 12-hour days and travel a lot as a manager for United Parcel Service. Sometimes she went for a week without seeing her one-year-old daughter.

Then, she quit UPS and, along with her husband, started Shipping Connection Inc., a packaging materials retailer in Denver, Colorado. The Russottis have since sold 18 franchises, at least 10 to mothers looking for flexibility. "That's one of the things they like about the job," says Ms. Russotti. "If they want to bring the baby and have him sleep in the back room, that's fine."

As the number of working women with children has risen, the need for flexibility in the workplace has increased, too. But for many women, getting that flexibility has been difficult. As a result, some mothers are starting enterprises of their own, enabling them to be at home more when their children are young. An increasingly popular approach is becoming a franchisee, which lets women start out with a business that is already established.

At Kinderdance International, a firm in Melbourne, Florida, whose franchise owners teach at child-care centers, practically every franchisee is a mother. And Mr. Build Handi-Man Services, a home-repair franchise in Glastonbury, Connecticut, and Decorating Den Systems, a customer home decorating company in Bethesda, Maryland, have also targeted moms as franchise operators.

"You'll find franchise companies beating a path to their door because these women offer past business experience, stability, and motivation," says John Reynolds, a spokesperson for the International Franchise Association, a Washington, D.C., trade group.

Mothers starting businesses face some potential drawbacks. At least initially, many of them will earn less than they did in their corporate jobs.

Building a successful business can also take long hours. And juggling the demands of a crying baby, a ringing phone, and an impatient customer is harder than many people think. The entrepreneurial mother may be tempted to neglect the business while tending to her child—at the risk of lowering her niche, momentum, clientele, and ultimately her investment.

"Some people have the theory that they can work while the child is napping. But that doesn't work because you can't count on the child behaving," says Elaine M. Glasser, a Chicago business consultant who advises on combining work and home life. "It's a creative way to combine more roles and have a bigger slice of the pie. But I don't, in reality, think it works too well."

But for many women, working at home is worth a try. Being the boss also means that a mother can be there for everything from piano lessons to chicken pox but still have a career and an income.

Source: Portions reproduced with permission from Suzanne Alexander, "More Working Mothers Opt for Flexibility of Operating a Franchise from Home," *The Wall Street Journal,* January 31, 1991, p. B1.

Betty Russotti illustrates the reasons why franchising is an attractive business alternative for many individuals. The opportunity to set one's hours, to enjoy a high degree of independence, and to know that one's success is tied closely to one's individual effort is enticing.

In 1991 U.S. franchises sold more than $758.5 billion in goods and services. Additional franchise facts are shown in Focus 20–1. Rapid growth in franchising is expected to continue into the future. A primary attraction is that franchising allows an individual to become an owner or manager with little or no experience and limited capital.

THE HISTORY OF FRANCHISING

A **franchise contract** is a legal document that enables a firm (the franchiser) to expand by allowing an independent businessperson (the franchisee) to use the franchiser's operating methods, financing systems, trademarks,

FOCUS 20–1

Franchise Facts

- Sales of goods and services by the nation's half million franchises reached more than $758.5 billion in 1991, accounting for more than one-third of all retail sales.
- In recent years, franchising has consistently grown at a rate outstripping the American economy, almost 10 times greater than the .9 percent growth in GNP.
- Franchise businesses employ more than 7.2 million people in more than 60 different industries.
- Franchises added 400,000 new jobs to the economy between 1987 and 1989; in comparison, Fortune 500 companies created only 10,000 new jobs during the same period.
- A new franchise opens somewhere in the United States every 16 minutes.
- According to studies by the U.S. Department of Commerce, from 1971 to 1987, less than 5 percent of franchised businesses failed or were discontinued on an annual basis.

Source: Information provided by the International Franchise Association and reported in Mitzi McWhorter, "Franchising Touted as One of the Best Ways to Beat a Recession," *Business First*, April 1992, p. 38.

and products in return for the payment of a fee. Franchisers may sell products or services, sell or lease equipment, or even sell or rent the site and premises.

Franchising is the fastest-growing segment of U.S. retailing and accounts for more than one-third of all retail sales.[1] Annual sales by franchise companies could exceed half of all retail sales by the end of the decade.[2]

Franchising as a business concept expanded rapidly following World War II. Many returning veterans were entrepreneurs who saw franchising as a way to financial success. The problem for many of them was lack of business experience. Established retailers, as a result, began franchising their products and know-how. Franchises exist in virtually every line of trade today. Employment in franchising, including part-time workers and working proprietors, exceeds 7.2 million.[3] The number of companies initiating franchise programs almost doubled during the decade of the 1980s.

Franchising has become a powerful force partly because economic factors have made growth through company-owned units difficult for many businesses. Therefore, by emphasizing independent ownership, franchising provides an effective method of overcoming such problems as shortage of capital and finding and hiring competent employees.

ADVANTAGES AND DISADVANTAGES OF BECOMING A FRANCHISEE[4]

Franchisees enjoy a number of advantages as part of a franchising program. The advantages include training programs that teach the retailer how to operate the business. Such programs allow individuals to enter a business with no previous experience. Less cash is required than in other forms of retailing because the franchiser is often willing to provide credit to a prospective franchisee.

The purchasing power of the franchiser can result in lower costs and higher gross profits for the franchisee. The franchisee also benefits from the national advertising and promotion by the franchiser, which exceeds the advertising of conventional independent retailers. In addition, up-to-date merchandise assistance, displays, and other materials are prepared by the franchiser and distributed to franchisees.

An equally important advantage is the program of research and development that is designed to improve the product or service. Firms such as Wendy's and McDonald's have ongoing programs designed to research and add menu items to help increase the sales base. Franchisees also have access to a variety of fringe benefits such as retirement planning and health insurance at lower rates than are available to independent retailers.

The franchiser can also provide advice for handling special problems. Help is available in site selection, in recordkeeping, taxes, and other issues. As a result, the failure rates for franchisees, around 4 percent, are lower than for nonaffiliated independent businesses. Services that franchisers typically provide to franchisees are listed in Table 20–1.

Not surprisingly, research has shown that franchise sales per store in 1991 either grew faster than their industry sales average or declined at a slower rate than the industry average. As observed, all things being equal, franchisees have more staying power than nonfranchised firms.[5]

There are some disadvantages to franchising. A major problem is the high cost of the franchise. Many franchisees believe that they pay too much for supplies, fees, and other franchise expenses.

The franchisee gives up flexibility in return for the right to a franchise. Operations are handled centrally at the corporate office and cookie-cutter policies apply to all outlets. The rigidity resulting from centralized operations can be detrimental to franchisees who face unusual local market conditions.

Decisions on how profit is to be shared between the franchiser and the franchisee often favor the franchiser because of its financial strength. However, the most frequent complaint is the nature of the contract itself. Often franchisees do not understand the document. They also have problems in terminating a franchise. The conditions of termination frequently favor the franchiser.

The Franchiser's Perspective

From the franchiser's perspective, the primary advantage in franchising is the opportunity to enjoy rapid expansion without decreasing the ownership or working capital of the parent company. However, one of the serious problems facing franchisers is finding management with the ambition and incentive to make a franchise a success. Still, the franchise system is often

TABLE 20–1

TYPICAL SERVICES THAT FRANCHISERS OFFER

General Guidelines

To help franchisees carry out the franchiser's business.

Initial Services

1. Writing business specifications and operations manuals that include the following elements:
   Operational analysis and policy for quality control.
   Control guidelines on standardized operations.
   Accounting overview and expense and income source structures.
   Customer services.
   Personnel management.
   Promotion and public relations techniques.
2. Training for management and key employees.
3. Area selection and unit location analysis.
4. Leasing or purchasing assistance.
5. Providing unit development aid, including design and equipment layout.
6. Advertising support.
7. Trademarks and trade name protection.
8. Mass centralized purchasing savings and other financial assistance.
9. Providing competition analysis.
10. Providing consulting assistance.
11. Ensuring compliance with state and federal registration and regulations.
12. Providing grand opening assistance.

Continuing Services

1. Providing the advice of experience on effective business management and other subsequent management and marketing services.
2. Publishing a company newsletter to keep communication lines open.
3. Conducting in-field reviews and consultations.
4. Providing further education and training.
5. Providing further advertising and promotional support.
6. Providing essential research and development to do the following:
   Develop methods to cut costs and increase sales.
   Expand customer base and discover new markets.
   Provide viable new products and programs.

better than hiring employee managers because the franchisee has a financial investment in the outlet and can benefit directly from its profits.

Legal Restrictions

Some contracts require a buyer to purchase specified products to obtain other desired products. Such contracts are illegal under section 3 of the Clayton Act if a substantial portion of the sales are in interstate commerce and if the effect of the restraint is to lessen competition.

Some contracts tying the franchisee to the franchiser can be legal. For example, a service contract may be required in the sale or lease of a machine if the company's reputation depends on the operation of the equipment. Furthermore, in some situations two products must be used

TABLE 20–2

ELEMENTS OF AN IDEAL FRANCHISE PROGRAM

- **High gross margin.** In order for the franchisee to be able to afford a high franchise fee (which the franchiser requires), it is necessary to operate on a high gross margin percentage. This explains the widespread application of franchising in the food and service industries.
- **In-store value added.** Franchising works best in product categories where the product is at least partially processed in the store. Such environments require constant on-site supervision—a chronic problem for company-owned stores using a hired manager. Owners simply are willing to work harder over longer hours.
- **Secret processes.** Concepts, formulas, or products that the franchisee cannot duplicate without joining the franchise program.
- **Real estate profits.** The franchiser uses income from ownership of property as a significant revenue source.
- **Simplicity.** The most successful franchises have been those that operate on automatic pilot: all the key decisions have been thought through, and the owner merely implements the decisions.

Source: Philip D. White and Albert D. Bates, "Franchising Will Remain Retailing Fixture, but Its Salad Days Have Long Since Gone," *Marketing News*, February 17, 1984, p. 14. Reprinted by permission.

jointly, and one will not function properly without the other. Generally, tying contracts have been found legal only in situations where the franchisers can prove that such contracts are essential to the maintenance of quality.

Elements of an Ideal Franchise Program

Successful franchises have a number of characteristics, as shown in Table 20–2, which can make the concept uniquely appropriate to the services field, the fastest-growing component of business format franchising. The most essential ingredient is a line of merchandise with high gross margins. High margins are necessary to cover the annual franchise fee, operating expenses, and profits. Typically, fast food and personal services have sufficient gross margins to make franchising a uniquely ideal operating vehicle. The overriding advantage of a franchising program is the ability to quickly expand a store network with limited capital.

TYPES OF FRANCHISES

Franchises are of two basic forms. The first form is **product or trade name franchising,** such as that done by automobile dealers and gasoline outlets. The second form is **business format franchising,** in which firms that have developed a unique method of performing a service or of doing business decide to make a profit by selling the rights to use the concept. The business format franchise is the arrangement followed by Holiday Inn, Avis, McDonald's (see A Profile in Excellence), and Kelly Temporaries, among others.

A Profile in Excellence

RAY KROC

At the age of 52, Ray Kroc began revolutionizing the food service industry and changed eating habits and customer expectations throughout the world. In 1954 he bought a typical drive-in restaurant and stripped it to a minimum in service and menu, developing the original eatery of the franchise known today as McDonald's.

Born west of Chicago in 1902, Ray Kroc grew up knowing work as play. He began working at a grocery in grammar school, and in high school opened a music store with two of his friends. In 1922 Kroc abandoned playing the piano and selling ribbon novelties to sell Lily brand paper cups. After years of working his way up the Lily ladder (he became a chief salesperson), he quit his job to become the president and owner of Prince Castle Sales, which sold electric milkshake blenders. It was with this venture that he met Maurice and Richard McDonald in southern California and bought his first restaurant.

Over the years Kroc opened franchise operations across America with the famous golden arches. The keys to McDonald's success stemmed from the corporation's refusal to be a supplier for its operators and to the implementation of the KISS method of operation management (Keep It Simple, Stupid).

Kroc's gospel was "quality, service, cleanliness, and value." If these four words were used and the importance of details were emphasized, Kroc believed the competition would wear itself out trying to keep up with McDonald's. He was committed to making McDonald's one of the biggest and best operations in the country. A total commitment of personal time and energy was (and is) the most important thing required in becoming a McDonald's franchisee. A person need not have more than a high school education, but he or she must be willing to work hard and concentrate exclusively on the challenge of operating the store.

McDonald's today is still being operated under the motto of "quality, service, cleanliness, and value." In 1991 over 12,500 McDonald's restaurants operated in 59 countries.

Product or Trade Name Franchising

Product or trade name franchising began in the United States as an independent sales relationship between a supplier and a dealer in which the dealer acquired some of the identity of the supplier. Franchised dealers concentrate on one company's product line and to some extent identify their business with that company. Typical of this segment of franchising are automobile and truck dealers, gasoline service stations, and soft drink bottlers. Together they dominate the franchise field and account for more than 70 percent of all franchise sales.[6]

Business Format Franchising

Business format franchising is characterized by an ongoing business relationship between the franchiser and franchisee that includes not only the product, service, and trademark, but the entire business format. Such franchises include a marketing strategy and plan, operating manuals and standards, quality control, and continual two-way communications.

Restaurants, personal and business services, real estate services, and a long list of other service businesses fall into the category of business format franchising. Business format franchising has been responsible for much growth of franchising in the United States since 1950 and continues to offer excellent growth opportunities.

According to the U.S. Department of Commerce, large franchisers—those with 1,000 or more units each—dominate business format franchising, with 55 companies accounting for half of all sales and for over 50 percent of all establishments. Thirteen of these large franchisers operate restaurants and 10 are in automotive products and services.

FORMS OF FRANCHISE ARRANGEMENTS

Product or tradename franchises and business format franchises can assume a variety of forms. The franchiser may sell individual franchises to people who will develop each one. Alternatively, franchisers may sell master franchises, or area development franchises.

Master franchisees buy the rights to an extensive geographic area but do not build and operate franchises. Rather, they divide the area into segments and sell the rights within the territory to individual franchisees. Franchisers often are attracted to the master franchise concept because it is easier for corporate management to work with one large franchisee than many small ones. Wendy's and Burger King have expanded rapidly, for example, by selling master franchises. People granted such franchises have substantial financial strength, which increases their likelihood of success.

A second alternative is the **area development** franchise. The franchisees purchase a large territory and in so doing open a large number of shops themselves.

Franchises can assume a variety of formats. In **mobile franchises,** business is done from a mobile vehicle. Snap-On Tools is an example of this type of franchise. **Distributorships** include systems where franchisees maintain warehouse stocks to supply other franchisees. The distributor takes title to the goods and provides services to other customers. An example is Bear Brand automotive equipment.

Co-ownership and co-management franchises are those in which the franchiser has an ownership interest in the operation. Examples include the International House of Pancakes and the Travelodge system. **Service franchises** are those in which franchisers license people to dispense a service under a tradename. Snelling and Snelling, a personnel agency, and H & R Block, a tax service, are examples of this type of franchise.

THE COSTS OF FRANCHISING

Typically, a franchisee agrees to sell a product or service under contract and to follow the franchiser's formula. The franchiser is normally paid an initial

TABLE 20–3

COSTS OF TYPICAL FRANCHISES

Business	Company (Location)	Start-Up Costs
Fast-food restaurant	McDonald's (Oak Brook, IL)	$610,000–700,000
Housecleaning	Merry Maids (Omaha, NE)	$28,500–33,500
Convenience store	7-Eleven (Dallas, TX)	$23,000–155,000
Fitness	Jazzercise (Carlsbad, CA)	$2,000–3,000*
Children's fitness	Discovery Zone	$400,000
Automotive services	Precision Tune (Sterling, VA)	$146,000–163,000
Nanny placement	A Choice Nanny (Columbia, MD)	$40,000
Nurse placement	Nursefinders (Arlington, TX)	$85,000–125,000
Pet stores	Petland (Chillicothe, OH)	$180,000–400,000
Home decorating products and services	Decorating Den Systems (Bethesda, MD)	$15,000–31,000
Chinese food delivery	Ho-Lee-Chow (Ann Arbor, MI)	$160,000–254,000

*Excludes facility leasing; equipment needs are minimal.

fee for the right to operate at a particular location and a franchise fee based on monthly sales. The costs involved in becoming a franchisee can include the initial cost, the franchise fee, opening costs, working capital, premises expenses, site evaluation fees, royalties and service fees, and promotion charges. The costs of typical franchises are shown in Table 20–3. We will briefly describe each charge.

- ***Initial costs.*** Franchisees typically must pay an initial sum for the right to operate under the terms and conditions of the franchise. The amount may be only a down payment with the remainder financed by the franchiser or from other financing sources.
- ***Franchisee fee.*** The right to use the trademark, license, service mark, or other operating procedures of the franchise.
- ***Opening costs.*** Payments for equipment, inventory, and fixtures.
- ***Working capital.*** The operating expenses needed until the business breaks even.
- ***Premises costs.*** The costs of building, remodeling, and decorating.
- ***Site evaluation fee.*** The franchiser's charge to determine the market potential at alternative sites.
- ***Royalties.*** A continuing service charge based on monthly gross sales. In return for the charge, the franchiser provides such services as product research, management advice, accounting services, inventory records, and similar activities.
- ***Promotion costs.*** A percentage of gross sales, normally 1 or 2 percent, to support local advertising and promotion.

Traditionally franchisers have been unwilling to lend money to franchisees for funding new outlets or expanding existing ones. A growing number of franchisers, however, are now offering direct financial assistance to their franchisees. For example, Jiffy Lube International has set up

EXHIBIT 20–1

Courtesy Discovery Zone

Promising franchising concepts for the 1990s

its own small business investment company, licensed and financed by the Small Business Administration.[7]

IDENTIFYING FRANCHISE OPPORTUNITIES

Selected hot new concepts for the 1990s are illustrated in Exhibit 20–1. A Choice Nanny is capitalizing on the millions of working parents with children under age 6 who need help. Discovery Zone is capitalizing on parental concerns about children's fitness. Precision Tune is responding to the tendency for many Americans to keep their cars for a longer period of time.

Franchise opportunities are easy to identify. Choosing the right one is difficult. Franchisers are intensely competitive in attracting interested franchisees. Advertisements for franchise opportunities are common in many newspapers. Franchisers often try to attract franchisees at business fairs. Various publications such as the following are also good sources of information: *Franchising Opportunities Handbook,* published by the U.S. Department of Commerce; *Director of Franchising Organizations,* published

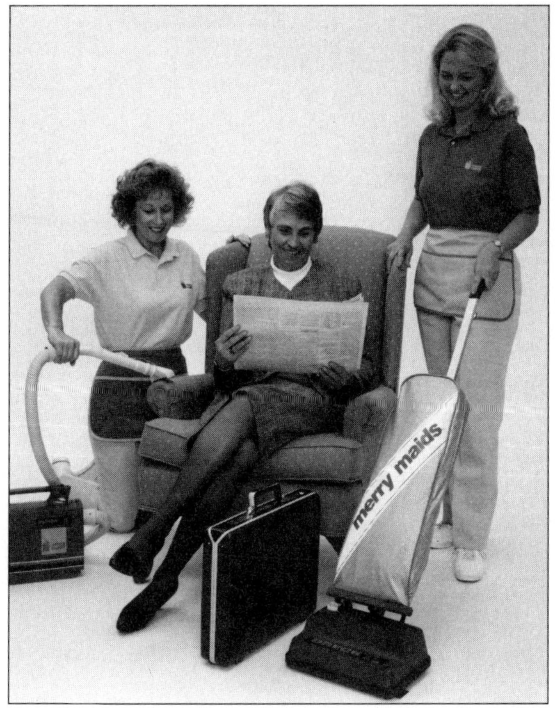

Courtesy Merry Maids

The Merry Maids franchise is cleaning up.

by Pilot Books; and the *Dow Jones-Irwin Guide to Franchises.* Periodicals that contain useful information include the *Continental Franchise Review, Franchising World, Franchising Today,* and *Franchise Newsletter.*

EVALUATING THE FRANCHISE

The number of fraudulent franchisers is growing and continuing vigilance is necessary to help unwary investors avoid the loss of homes and life savings.[8]

Federal Requirements

Federal law requires franchisers to make a disclosure document available to interested buyers before they purchase a franchise. The Federal Trade Commission has issued a trade rule entitled "Disclosure Requirements and Prohibitions Concerning Franchising and Business Opportunity Ventures." The document spells out the information franchisers must provide to interested buyers at least 10 days before the buyer enters into a contract with the franchiser.

The disclosure document must include such information as the following:

Susan McElhinney

Learning how to save a choking baby is part of the training for franchisees at Choice Nanny, a nanny referral service.

- The amount of funds to be paid by the franchisee.
- The level of continuing payments to carry on the business.
- The franchiser's business experience.
- A list of people with whom the franchisee is expected to do business.
- Fees such as royalties and commissions to be paid to the franchiser.
- The litigation history of the franchiser and its executives.
- The restrictions placed on the franchisee's opportunity to conduct business, cancellation and renewal conditions of the lease, the number of franchises in existence, and rate of termination.
- Financial information, including audited financial statements for the last three years.

State Legislation

Some states require a franchiser to register franchise offers with state authorities. They also require the franchiser to furnish the prospective franchisee with a disclosure statement prior to the signing of the contract. The state agency responsible for administering the disclosure laws reviews the financial statements, promotional materials, franchise contracts, and other material submitted as part of the offer. The franchisers may also be required to show that they can provide the financial assistance they promise to a franchisee. The laws also contain provisions on the termination and renewal of franchises.

Courtesy Precision Tune

Precision Tune draws drivers.

Understanding the Franchise Contract

Contract disputes are frequently at the heart of the tension that can exist between a franchiser and franchisees (see A Question of Ethics).[9] The advice of an attorney should be sought before signing any document. Critical areas to be considered include the nature of the company, the product, the territory, and the assistance available.

All franchise contracts contain a variety of provisions to which the franchisee must agree. For example, the franchisee typically must agree to abide by the operating hours established by the franchiser. The franchisee often must also agree to use a standardized accounting system, follow companywide personnel policies, carry a minimum level of insurance, use supplies approved by the franchiser, and follow the pricing policies established by the franchiser.

The franchiser often retains the right to require the franchisee to periodically remodel his or her establishment and to allow the franchiser to conduct unscheduled inspections. Territorial restrictions are typically stated in the contract agreement and provisions for expanding into additional territories are specified.

Some contracts impose sales quotas to ensure that the franchisee vigorously pursues sales opportunities in the territory. Most contracts also prohibit a franchisee from operating competing businesses.

Most franchise contracts cover a minimum period of 15 years. They typically contain provisions for termination and renewal of the contract,

A Question of Ethics

THE WOES OF KFC

The Kentucky Fried Chicken Corporation is battling to make major changes in its contracts with its franchisees. Experts contend that older franchise companies are facing the threat of their lives if they are unable to set and maintain new standards and require franchisees to make necessary investments.

Most contracts with KFC franchisees are for a 20-year period. They grant franchisees exclusive territories and autonomy over investment decisions. Many of the regional stores are now aging and franchisers can't require their franchisees to make the necessary updates in appearance and operations by adding salad bars, for example.

The Association of Kentucky Fried Chicken Franchisees recently filed a lawsuit arguing that KFC had failed to negotiate in good faith. The primary sticking point was the protection of franchisee territory. The franchisee contracts written in 1976 specified that KFC couldn't build a store within one and a half miles (or within a radius containing 30,000 people) of an existing store. The new contracts eliminate that provision to allow KFC corporate management to place outlets in Sears stores on an experimental basis. The franchisees also became concerned when KFC reached an agreement with Marriott to put stores in airports.

The disagreements are not limited to KFC. Holiday Inn Corporation also insisted on new terms and more investment by its franchisees in remodeling and expansion. The franchisees rebelled and Holiday Inn forced some of them to quit. Similarly, Marriott couldn't get many of its franchisees to spend money for improvements at its aging Big Boy Restaurants. Consequently, Marriott sold the Big Boy franchising operation and now operates more than 200 of the chain's outlets as a franchisee.

Are franchisers justified, in the name of keeping a business competitive, in changing the conditions of contracts entered into with franchisees?

Source: Based on Jeffrey A. Tannenbaum and Barbara Marsh, "Firms Try to Tighten Grip on Franchisees," *The Wall Street Journal*, January 15, 1990, p. B1; Scott Hume, "Franchisee to Sue KFC on Territory Rule," *Advertising Age*, May 21, 1990, p. 23; Scott Hume, "Flap Over KFC's Hot Wings," *Advertising Age*, April 9, 1990, p. 4; Glen Ruffenach, "Chicken Chain's Strategy Ruffles Franchisees' Feathers," *The Wall Street Journal*, May 24, 1990, p. B2.

the franchisee's right to sell or transfer the business, and a provision for arbitration of disputes between the franchiser and franchisee.

Termination. Franchise contracts typically contain a provision for cancellation by either party upon 30 to 60 days notice. Normally franchises can only be terminated when the franchisee fails to meet the conditions of the franchise contract, including minimum payments, sales quotas, and upkeep standards.

Renewal. The franchiser can refuse to renew the contract of any franchisee who does not fully comply with the terms of the contract, including maintaining required quality standards. Termination provisions give the franchiser substantial power over franchisees. As a result, many states have passed legislation that limits the right of a franchiser to terminate or refuse to renew a franchise.

Transferring a Franchise. The franchisee normally does not have the right to sell or transfer the franchise to a third party without the authorization of the franchiser. The sale or transfer to a third party typically is not a problem, however.

Buy-Back Provisions. The franchiser often has the option to purchase a franchise unit or the inventory if the franchisee decides to sell. The buy-back provision is an advantage to the franchisee because it can provide a ready sale for the outlet.

Deciding on the sales price is often not easy. Some franchisers will offer a price that covers only the value of the buildings and the equipment and will not pay for goodwill. **Goodwill** is the price set for the intangible assets of a business, including its future earning power and its condition at the time of the sale. Franchisers often maintain that the goodwill of the business is reflected in the trademark or trade name.

Arbitration Provisions. The use of arbitration to settle disputes between franchisers and franchisees is growing slowly. (**Arbitration** is the settlement of a dispute by a person or persons chosen to hear both sides and come to a decision.) Arbitration is faster and less expensive than litigation.

A Few Words of Advice

Talk to current franchisees.[10] A prospective franchisee should talk to other owners and ask them about their experiences regarding earnings claims and information in the disclosure document. They should talk to the franchisees themselves rather than to managers of company-owned outlets.

Seek professional advice. A prospective franchisee needs a lawyer, an accountant, and a business advisor to provide counsel and go over the disclosure document and proposed contract. The money and time spent at this stage may prevent a major loss on a bad investment.

Understand the business. Determine whether the business would be a successful venture apart from the benefits offered by the franchise.

1. Is the product or service offered new or proven? Is the product one for which the prospective franchisee has a solid background? Does the prospect feel strongly motivated to produce the product or provide the service?
2. Does the product meet a local demand? Is there a proven market?
3. What is the competition?
4. If the product requires servicing, who bears the responsibilities covered by warrantees and guarantees? The franchisee? The franchiser? If neither, are service facilities available?

5. What reputation does the product or service enjoy?
6. Are suppliers available? What is their reputation?

Perform a personal assessment. An examination of personal skills, abilities, and experience is perhaps the most important step. Prospective franchisees should determine exactly what they want out of life and what they are willing to sacrifice to achieve their goals. The assessment should be honest, rigorous, and specific. They should ask themselves the following questions:

- Am I qualified for this field?
- Am I physically able to run a business?
- Do I have the necessary experience?
- Do I have the right education?
- Can I learn what I need to know about this business?
- Do I have the financial resources to make this work?

The effects of the decision on one's family should be considered. How will this new lifestyle affect them? Do they understand the risks and sacrifices, and will they support the efforts required to succeed? Beginning a franchise business is a major decision that does not ensure easy success.

Franchisee Associations

Franchisee associations are often formed to represent individual owners in dealing with a franchiser. The purpose of joining together is to allow the franchisees to accomplish common goals and to exert greater power over the franchiser in resolving issues. The franchisees as a group can also support needed legislation, exchange ideas, and generally work to strengthen their position relative to the franchiser.

The Texas franchisee trade group for International Dairy Queen, for example, is in the midst of a battle for control of the more than $7 million a year in advertising funds raised by the Texas franchisees.[11] Similarly, a group of more than 100 Manpower franchisees, shocked at the forced resignation of the chief executive, forced the parent company to rehire the CEO.

The International Franchisee Association has a number of affiliated organizations such as the French Franchise Federation and the Portuguese Franchise Association to assist local franchisees.

TRENDS AND OUTLOOK

Franchising, still in a relative state of infancy compared to the life span of other marketing methods, has played an important role in the evolution of the service sector of the American economy. All trends indicate that franchising will continue to expand rapidly, creating opportunities for existing and new businesses; developing new entrepreneurs, new jobs, new products, new services; and providing new export opportunities for firms engaged in franchising.[12]

Rising personal income, stable prices, high levels of consumer optimism, and increased competition for market share are turning many companies, both small and large, to franchising. Franchising can enable these new franchisers to saturate existing markets or penetrate new markets at minimal cost.

Education will play an important role in the evolution of franchising as programs related to franchising are increasingly being taught in courses in marketing, small business, and entrepreneurship. The study of franchising is becoming recognized as a new and important part of college curricula.

A slowly growing U.S. population, shifting demographic patterns, and the use of new technology has intensified competition among franchising companies. These factors have increased the number of mergers and acquisitions in the franchising system, and it is expected that this will persist during the next few years.

In summary, as we move further into the 1990s, creativity and imagination in the treatment of goods and services will be richly rewarded. Education, computer usage, and the ability to work with and manage people will be requirements for success. All these developments suggest that franchising will be the leading method of doing business in this decade.

International Markets. U.S. franchisers are operating in most major countries or are engaged in negotiations to enter foreign markets. Most nations have welcomed the entry of U.S. franchisers. Franchising already counts for more than 10 percent of retail sales in France and 11 percent in England. Experts suggest that franchising sales may approach 30 percent in such countries. The unification of the Common Market has made franchising regulations even more uniform than in the United States.[13]

Franchising operations in foreign markets involve many of the same problems confronting other business ventures, as discussed in Case 1 at the end of the chapter. Language difficulties, differences in customs, and sometimes unpredictable government decision making are examples of impediments U.S. franchisers encounter when attempting to take advantage of opportunities in other countries. Compared to other service sectors, the problems of franchise companies in accomplishing international transactions are relatively less formidable.

The populations in many foreign countries are young and like to try new products and concepts. In addition, more women everywhere are working outside the home. This trend not only increases the family's disposable income, which is good for franchisers in the service and consumer products business, but it also increases the demand for food purchased away from home.

Many foreign countries are exhibiting the same attributes that fostered the surge of service industries in the United States. These attributes include rising disposable personal income, growing demand for consumer goods and services, expanding urbanization, and high consumer mobility.

Franchisers can enter foreign markets in several ways: by franchising directly to individuals, by opening company-owned operations, by starting joint ventures, or by employing master franchisers. Many franchisers use more than one method in conducting foreign operations, but the most popular, cheapest, and fastest method is the master license technique.[14] The master licensor provides talent that understands the local ways of doing business.

The approach a franchiser uses to enter a foreign market is the first big decision to make. But before any franchiser can consider expansion into international markets, certain basic judgments must be made about the company's operation in the United States. The success or failure of foreign franchising will depend largely on the soundness of the franchiser's domestic market position and on whether the franchiser is capable of providing the necessary expertise to others in another part of the world.

Canada, Japan, Australia, the United Kingdom, and Continental Europe, especially France, West Germany, the Netherlands, and Belgium, are the areas where U.S.-franchised units are most heavily concentrated. U.S. franchisers are attracted to these countries because of the relative sophistication of their economies, fewer governmental controls on investment than those in developing countries, and the generally high level of prosperity of their citizens. Canada is the leading market for U.S. franchisers.

About 75 percent of McDonald's international sales comes from six major markets: Australia, Canada, England, France, Germany, and Japan.[15] McDonald's scored a hit with its nonfranchised Moscow outlet and is seeking to spread the golden arches through joint ventures in Hungary and other Eastern Bloc countries.[16] Baskin Robbins similarly entered Russia through a joint venture.

U.S. companies also have found that franchising is the key to opening Japan's back door. Successful franchisers include Nautilus Clubs, Jazzercize, Domino's Pizza, and others.[17] Southland Corporation's 7-Eleven chain of convenience stores has also experienced major success in Japan.[18]

Foreign-Based Franchising. Foreign franchisers are also entering the U.S. market. Like their American counterparts, they typically are seeking to attract management and capital at a faster rate than they could through company-owned operations. Their franchisees also typically finance their own outlets and fees and royalties to the franchisers.

Examples of foreign-based franchisers in the United States include Food Goemon, a Japanese-style noodle shop in Boston, and Roche-Bobois, USA., Ltd. which has been selling franchises since 1974 that offer leather chairs and other luxurious furniture of French design.

Foreigners most interested in the United States are entrepreneurs from Japan and Canada, where U.S. franchisers have had the most notable success. Canadian examples include Toronto-based Ceiling Doctor International, which has sold ceiling and wall-cleaning franchises in the United States since 1987, and Moneysworth and Best Shoe Repair Inc., also of Toronto, which opened its first U.S. shoe repair franchise outlet in Washington, D.C., in 1989. British franchisees include Fastframe USA., controlled by British shareholders, and Body Shop International PLC, which sells toiletries and cosmetics.[19]

Minority Franchisees. Small investors, especially minority entrepreneurs, often face two major obstacles in their efforts to operate a successful company: inexperience in business and management, and inadequate financing. The franchising system provides a means for lowering such barriers to entry. Under the franchise system, a franchiser usually provides managerial training and assistance on a continuing basis and, in many cases, finances the purchase of necessary equipment. The franchiser may also arrange for property leases, help obtain loans from the Small Business Administration, local banks, or other private investors, and, in some instances, may participate in the venture. In addition, franchisers generally provide such services as location analysis, advertising and merchandising, counseling and assistance, standardized procedures and operations, and, sometimes, centralized purchasing.

Many minority-owned businesses are concentrated in the most popular franchising sectors—restaurants, automotive products and services, food retailing other than convenience stores, convenience stores, and business aids and services.[20]

Chapter Highlights

- Franchising is a way of doing business that allows an independent businessperson (the franchisee) to use another firm's (the franchiser's) operating methods, financing systems, trademarks, and products in return for a fee.
- Franchising is the fastest-growing segment of retailing and accounts for one-third of retail sales. Franchising is forecasted to account for 50 percent of all retail sales by the year 2000.
- Franchises are of two basic types: product and trade name franchises such as automobile dealers and gasoline outlets, and business format franchising, in which firms that have developed a unique method of performing a service or of doing business decide to make a profit by selling the concept to others.
- Sales by product and trade name franchisers have declined since 1972. In contrast, the volume of sales and the number of units owned or franchised by business format franchisers have been steadily increasing.
- The essential ingredient for a franchising program is a line of merchandise with high gross margins. High gross margins are necessary to cover the annual franchise fee, operating expenses, and profit.
- The overriding advantage of a franchising program is the ability to quickly expand with limited capital.
- Franchisers may grant individual franchisees to businesspeople. Alternatively, they may operate as master franchises. Some people purchase area development franchises, which

give them rights to an extensive territory in which they develop a large number of outlets.

- The typical franchise contract gives the franchisee the right to sell a product or service under an arrangement that requires the individual to follow the franchiser's formula. The franchiser is typically paid an initial fee for the right to operate at a particular location and a franchise fee based on monthly sales.
- Federal law requires a franchiser to make a disclosure document available to interested buyers. State laws also require the franchiser to register franchise offers with state authorities.
- Some franchisees have established franchisee associations to represent individual owners in dealing with the franchiser. These associations allow the franchisees to exert greater power in dealing with the franchiser.
- The primary advantage of franchising is the training programs that are available, allowing an individual to enter a business with no experience. The franchisee can also benefit from the purchasing power of the franchiser. Equally important are the programs of research and development that many franchisers have established to improve their product or service.
- The major disadvantage of a franchise is the high initial fee. The franchisee also gives up some flexibility in return for the right to purchase a franchise.
- Some franchise contracts require buyers to purchase specified products to obtain other desired products. Such contracts are illegal under section 3 of the Clayton Act if a substantial portion of the sales are in interstate commerce and if the effect of the restraint is to lessen competition.
- U.S. franchisers are currently operating in most major foreign countries or are engaged in serious negotiations for the purpose of entering foreign markets.

Study Questions

1. What are the differences between product or trade name franchising and business format franchising?
2. Discuss the ingredients of an ideal franchise program. What types of franchises appear to be suited to the elements of such a program?
3. Write a brief essay on the cost elements that are typically included as part of a franchising contract.
4. What are the issues a prospective franchisee should evaluate in deciding whether to purchase a franchise?
5. What are the ingredients of a typical franchise contract?
6. Why would franchisees join a franchise association?
7. Highlight the advantages and disadvantages of becoming a franchisee.
8. What are the legal restrictions on franchising?
9. Discuss the trends and outlook for franchising.
10. Why are franchisers seeking to expand outside the United States?

A P P L I C A T I O N S

CASE 1: The World's Best Yogurt: The International Story

"Every time we go into a new country, it's like September 23, 1981, all over again," says Joe O'Brien, senior vice-president of TCBY International, Inc., the TCBY subsidiary formed in 1986.

The challenges of taking TCBY frozen yogurt to the world have the added dimensions of cultural and language diversity.

The continuing adventure of going international began in August 1987, when TCBY opened its first store outside the United States in Oakville, Ontario, a suburb of Toronto. By 1991 TCBY's global frontier had expanded to 92 stores and points of sale in eight countries outside the United States.

On September 14, 1988, Gordon Rodland opened two stores simultaneously in Nassau, Bahamas. "Our experiences taught us the flexibility required for entering overseas markets with customers even more unfamiliar and challenging."

Signage was a stumbling block in Nassau, a quaint city intent on preserving its old-world ambience. Ordinances prohibited the use of TCBY's signature symbol, the illuminated waffle cone. "We've been able to get traditional signage for the third store," says Rodland. "And eventually, we hope to replace the signs on the original stores."

TCBY's rapidly developing international field staff is learning that flexibility has its place in everything from cosmetic changes—like lowering serving counters for Asians, who are generally smaller in stature than westerners—to allowing for different food choices. Malaysian consumers, for instance, may top their frozen yogurt with litchi, a fruit topping, and Mexico has a milk-based candy topping called *cajeta*.

In October 1988, TCBY opened its first store in the Far East in Taipei, Taiwan. Electing to move into Asia first instead of into Europe was a "pivotal decision," says O'Brien. "We couldn't do both at the same time, and we chose Asia because of the high growth of the countries, the tremendous interest from potential franchisees, and the boom in American products here. Ten years later, the logical choice would have been to enter the European market first."

Forming personal relationships is very important in Japan. Scot Worthington, TCBY International's associate director of operational services, says, "Akio Nakamura, General Manager of Japan's Best Yogurt, decided I looked like Pokochan, a popular Japanese cartoon character. So that's become my nickname, and JBY's daily fax messages are even addressed to 'Pokochan.'"

Becoming acquainted with local customs adds spice to the job of the international team. One of their most intriguing experiences has been with the ancient philosophy of *Feng Shui,* which means "doing things in harmony with nature." A *Feng Shui* (pronounced "fung sooey" and sometimes called a fortune teller) was an unwitting ally of TCBY's on at least one occasion. Wee Pin Lim, associate director of operational services for TCBY International, says, "Before becoming a TCBY franchisee, Jarunan Asdathorn went up into the mountains to visit her Feng Shui—who told her that she would enter into a retail food business with a leading U.S. company."

"We must go to the fortune teller any time we want to lend or buy," says Attakorn Jaruthien. "When we find a store location, we must ask if it is good for selling frozen yogurt. The fortune teller also tells us on which side of the building to place the door and how the furniture is to be arranged."

Not all international challenges are in the Far East. "One of our biggest surprises came in February 1988 when, out of the blue, the Canadian government imposed an import restriction on dairy products coming from the U.S.," O'Brien says. After a lengthy bargaining process, TCBY was given a continued import grace period of 15 months, during which time the company had to build a plant or license a dairy for local production.

"Keeping franchisees adequately supplied with products requires careful planning," says Worthington. "Shipping by ocean freight from America to points east takes a month—and can take as much as two months. Samples are flown to Japan for testing, but sending a full product line by air is too costly."

Source: Based on company promotional literature and conversations with Joe O'Brien, executive vice president for International Operations, TCBY Yogurt, Inc.

Applying Retailing Principles

1. Identify the cultural differences that TCBY encountered in extending its franchising beyond U.S. borders.
2. What legal difficulties has the firm encountered in its global expansion efforts?
3. Why is TCBY expanding so aggressively outside the United States? What countries are likely to be attractive in the future?

CASE 2: Avis Hit by Almost Every Obstacle in the Franchise Book

When Avis entered the quick-lube franchise business, it hoped its parent company's big name in rental cars would help produce big profits in a booming field.

But since then, nearly every problem in the franchise book has dogged the company: its market is creeping toward saturation, competition is fierce, and the Avis unit, which had no experience in the quick-lube field, is having trouble finding sites for its Avis Lube stations. And now, the company that built a name "trying harder" is up against a franchiser's nightmare: a full-fledged revolt of franchisees throughout the Northeast and Florida.

So bitter are franchisees that many are demanding refunds. Some are filing lawsuits, alleging fraud and misrepresentation in the sale of franchises. And one lawsuit, which has hounded Avis Service since its first days in business, charges that the company tricked and destroyed a small competitor to enter the market itself.

Nobody imagined the problems that Avis would encounter. In September 1986, Avis Service and Witco Corp.'s Kendall refining division in Bradford, Pennsylvania, agreed to form K&A Partnership to develop a nationwide chain of Avis Lube centers. (Avis bought out Kendall in 1989 and is its sole owner.)

In many areas, convenience stores and fast-food chains have gobbled up spots with easy access and high-traffic volumes. More often, former gas station sites, common locations for quick-lube stations, have come under stricter regulation because of concerns with toxic contamination.

Many investors complain Avis Service's real estate staff, charged with assisting franchisers in finding and developing sites, didn't do its job.

"There's no doubt I've broken a couple of hearts when I've turned down real estate sites," says Vincent Russo, general manager and a vice-president at Avis Service. But "there are a variety of reasons. . . ." He acknowledges sites have been difficult to find and says some franchisees who counted on a single site were given refunds when none materialized. He says that Avis Service still plans to expand. The company declines to disclose financial results of the operation so far.

Rivals and others say that Avis failed to realize the amount of capital and attention needed to nurture a franchise system. Says John Gallivan, executive vice-president of Grease Monkey International Inc., a Denver chain, "I think they had a rude awakening. It's a long and tedious process to build a successful chain of fast-lubes."

Source: Portions reproduced with permission from Mark Robichaux, "Avis Hit by Almost Every Obstacle in Franchise Book," *The Wall Street Journal,* May 3, 1990, p. B2.

Applying Retailing Principles

1. Identify the conflict issues between the franchiser and franchisees. What likely contributed to the conflict?
2. What are the ingredients of the marketing program developed by Avis?
3. Does the fast-lube concept meet the criteria for an ideal franchising concept as outlined in the chapter?

NOTES

1. "Franchising: Prospects and Problems," *Deloitte and Touche Review,* November 5, 1990, p. 6.
2. C.R. Hartmann, "Franchising Explosion in the 90s," *D & B Reports,* January/February 1990, p. 41.
3. "Franchising: Prospects and Problems."
4. For further reading, see Derrick T. Dingle, "Franchising's Fast Track to Freedom," *Money Extra,* 1990, pp. 35–40; "The Flight to Franchising," *U.S. News and World Report,* June 10, 1991, pp. 68 and 69; Susan Caminiti, "Look Who Likes Franchising Now," *Fortune,* September 23, 1991, pp. 125–28.
5. John R. Emshwiller, "Franchisee Sales Show Benefits of Support," *The Wall Street Journal,* May 19, 1992, p. B1.
6. "Franchising: Prospects and Problems."
7. Buck Brown, "Franchisers Now Offer Direct Financial Aid," *The Wall Street Journal,* February 6, 1989, p. B1.
8. John R. Wilke, "Fraudulent Franchisers Are Growing," *The Wall Street Journal,* September 21, 1990, p. B1; Richard L. Sterne and Reed Ableson, "Franchise Hell," *Forbes,* September 2, 1991, pp. 152–54.
9. Jeanne Saddler, "Franchisees Can End in Suits over Contracts," *The Wall Street Journal,* January 15, 1991, p. B1; "Flaring Tempers at the Frozen Yogurt King," *Business Week,* September 10, 1990, pp. 88 and 90.
10. Portions reproduced, with modification, from *Evaluating Franchising Opportunities,* Business Division Publications, UP26 (Washington, D.C.: U.S. Small Business Administration).
11. Jeffrey Tannenbaum, "Dairy Queen Franchisees in the Lone Star State Revolt," *The Wall Street Journal,* November 1, 1991, B2.
12. Michael J. McCarthy, "When Franchisees Become Rebellious," *The Wall Street Journal,* September 13, 1989, p. B1.
13. Bruce J. Walker, "Retail Franchising in the 1990s," *Retailing Issues Letter* 3, no. 1, 1991, pp. 1–4.
14. "Michael Selz, "Europa Offers Franchising Opportunities to Franchisers," *The Wall Street Journal,* July 20, 1990, p. B2.
15. Ibid.
16. "Establishing Local Relationships, Not Simply Selling Trademarks," 1991 First Quarter McDonald's Stockholder Newsletter.
17. Jeffrey A. Tannenbaum, "Franchisers See a Future in East Bloc," *The Wall Street Journal,* June 5, 1990, p. B1.
18. Ted Holden, Joseph Weber, and Peter Galuszka, "Who Says You Can't Break Into Japan?" *BusinessWeek,* October 16, 1989, p. 49.
19. Jeffrey Tannenbaum, "Foreign Franchisers Entering U.S. in Greater Numbers," *The Wall Street Journal,* June 6, 1990, p. B2; Jeffrey Tannenbaum, "Franchising Opportunities Spread Far Beyond Fast Foods," *The Wall Street Journal,* April 12, 1992, p. B2.
20. Leon W. Wynter, "How Two Black Franchisees Owe Success to McDonald's," *The Wall Street Journal,* July 25, 1989, p. B1.

C H A P T E R

21

Services and Nonstore Retailing

THIS CHAPTER:

Cites differences between service and tangible goods firms.

Describes unique aspects of consumer behavior as related to the purchase of services.

Discusses various decisions involved in developing competitive plans and managing a retail service organization.

Highlights alternative forms of nonstore retailing.

RETAILING CAPSULE

RETAILERS SELLING CONVENIENCE MAKE LIFE EASIER

Demographic shifts, such as the sharp increase in two-income families and households headed by singles, are driving the growth of retail operations designed to meet the needs of consumers for whom time is scarce. A host of new businesses (from those that perform household chores, manicure the lawn, and fine-tune the car, to those that tend to kids and older family members) have sprung up to take care of life's many chores. These businesses have discovered that many people are willing to buy time at a fairly high price.

There seems to be no end to ideas for service businesses to meet the needs of the growing numbers of "time-pressed" consumers. The Busy Body's Helper in New York recruits secretaries, orchestrates household moves, and waters plants. Personalized Services in Chicago will walk the dog, shuttle the kids to Little League, and wait in line for theater tickets. A workout instructor in Hollywood, California, goes to clients' homes for aerobics, stretching, or weight lifting.

This convenience retail industry is experiencing growth in other countries as well as in the United States. A most interesting service is that offered by Japan Efficiency Headquarters. People too busy to visit their aging parents can hire actors to take their place. The retailer charges $385 for a five-hour visit by a "son" or "daughter," $769 for a couple, and $1,155 if a rental baby or child is included. The donors and recipients don't always live that far apart. A Tokyo computer salesperson, for example, sent a family unit of actors to visit his parents, who live only 10 minutes away. The parents enjoyed the visit so much that they decided to forego a vacation in order to treat themselves to a return visit.

Source: Based on Ricardo Sookdeo, "Too Busy with Your Career," *Fortune*, June 29, 1991, p. 13 and "Presto! The Convenience Industry: Making Life a Little Simpler," *BusinessWeek*, April 27, 1989, pp. 86–94.

The Retailing Capsule illustrates that not all retail organizations sell tangible products. Some market services. Because of the growing importance of service retail organizations to the American economy, a separate chapter is devoted to their attention. This chapter also presents information on nonstore retailing—another segment of the American economy experiencing growth. One factor causing this growth has been increasing time constraints among consumers, as described in the Retailing Capsule.

Services Retailing

As mentioned previously, the selling of services is more important to the U.S. economy than ever before. Currently services represent approximately three-quarters of the U.S. gross national product. The Bureau of Labor Statistics estimates that by 1995 74.3 percent of U.S. jobs will be in the service sector and that this percentage will rise to 88 percent by the year 2000.[1] Services are also taking on increasing importance in international marketing. In fact, the United States is the world's largest exporter of services. In many countries, the names of such firms as American Express, McDonald's, and Hilton have become widely familiar.

Fortune magazine defines a **service firm** as one that derives more than 50 percent of its sales from providing services that may involve a combination of both tangible and intangible offerings. Therefore, a service may have both tangible (high goods content) and intangible (low goods content) attributes. Based on the combination of tangible and intangible attributes provided, service firms may be placed along a continuum of no goods content to high goods content. At one end of the continuum would be services that are very low in goods content, such as the services provided by a psychiatrist. On the other hand, services provided by a janitorial service would be high in goods content (physical removal of dirt and trash).

In order to have a better understanding of service organizations, let's look at some of the differences between tangible goods firms and service firms.

Differences between Tangible Goods Firms and Service Firms

Understanding the differences between tangible goods firms and service firms is important in developing successful competitive strategies for service organizations. The following sections highlight important differences between the two types of organizations.[2]

Perishability. Many services are essentially perishable. If a hotel room is empty for an evening, the revenue is lost forever. Dentists, physicians, attorneys, and accountants similarly cannot recover revenue lost because of an unfilled schedule. In contrast, tangible goods not sold on any given day can be held in inventory and sold at a later point to recapture the revenue.

Lack of Transportability. The inability to transport services means that they often must be consumed at the point of production. Medical care essentially is available only at the doctor's office, hospital, or clinic, as are many other professional services.

Small Firm Size. Most service firms are small, single-unit operations. Small firm size limits the service firm's ability to achieve economies of scale. Changes are occurring, however. Sears, for example, offers a variety of services such as insurance and financial services through its department stores. Tremendous growth is also occurring in the franchising of service organizations, such as real estate firms and dental, medical, and legal clinics. Some experts predict that one of the biggest growth areas in the future in franchising will be service organizations in the convenience industry such as child-, car-, and home-care franchises.

Difficulties in Establishing Large Market Share. Service industries typically are characterized by low barriers to entry. Competitors can quickly enter service markets, which keeps any one firm from establishing a dominant market share. The inability to experience economies of scale also negatively affects the service firm's ability to acquire a large market share. Some question whether economies of scale are possible because the cost of some services increases as the firm gets larger. Large, comprehensive-care hospitals, for example, have far greater per-unit overhead costs and labor costs than smaller, more flexible institutions such as emergency clinics and one-day surgery centers.

Labor Intensity. Many service firms are labor intensive—another factor preventing economies of scale. The output of an attorney or a medical doctor, for example, cannot easily be increased. Many services must be personally produced and tailored to the needs of each individual client, which makes application of assembly line techniques and reduction of labor content difficult. Furthermore, the nonrepetitive nature of many services minimizes learning curve effects. Thus, learning and experience do not drive down per-unit costs.

Difficulty in Quality Control. Because service firms are labor intensive and because many services are offered only at the point of sale, standardization in the level of service and quality is difficult to achieve. Fast-food operations, offering a combination of tangible goods and services, are an exception. Such firms have been able to introduce essentially assembly-line techniques to the fast-food business.

Unpredictability of Demand. The demand for services is often more difficult to predict than the demand for tangible goods. Demand for some services can fluctuate widely by the month, the day of the week, or even the hour of the day. Medical offices and ambulance services have problems predicting the number of patients needing their services. The same difficulty exists in forecasting the demand for using telephone services, visiting museum exhibits, and watching ballet performances.

As indicated earlier, competitive strategies of service firms are affected by the fact that they possess some unique characteristics that differentiate them from tangible goods firms. In addition, consumer behavior differences in the purchase of services versus tangible goods affect competitive strategy development in retail service firms.

Consumer Behavior in the Purchase of Services

Many studies on consumers' behavior when buying goods versus services clearly establish that customers view the purchasing of services differently from the purchasing of goods. Some research has found, for example, that consumers seem to feel that purchasing services is frequently a less pleasant experience than buying goods and that consumers perceive higher levels of risk in buying services than tangible goods.[3]

Consumers often face an information gap when purchasing services. A paucity of reliable data on vendors, be they garage mechanics or savings banks, exists. Especially lacking is information to help consumers choose professionals such as doctors and lawyers.

Furthermore, because services are often intangible, consumers find it difficult, if not impossible, to evaluate the service before purchase and also, in many instances, even after purchase and use. Zeithaml has examined this particular issue by reference to three types of product properties: search qualities, experience qualities, and credence qualities.[4] Tangible goods possess **search qualities,** or attributes that a consumer can see, feel, or touch and can thus determine prior to purchasing a product. Services, on the other hand, possess experience and credence qualities. **Experience qualities** are attributes such as taste that can be discerned only after purchasing or during consumption. **Credence qualities** are attributes that consumers may find impossible to evaluate even after purchase and consumption, perhaps because they do not have the knowledge or skill to do so. Services provided by professionals such as doctors and lawyers are examples of services possessing credence qualities.

The fact that services primarily possess experience and credence qualities suggests that the service encounter extends beyond the service-production process. Service retailers should communicate with the consumer beyond the decision by the customer to buy the service and even beyond the completion of the service process. In this communication process, the retailer should establish the evaluative criteria and teach the buyer what to look for before, during, and after the service encounter. In addition, the use of reference groups to present favorable information about the use of a service is an important surrogate for evaluative criteria.

Many other implications exist in developing competitive strategy as a result of the unique characteristics of service retailers and the buying behavior of consumers in purchasing services. These will be addressed in the following section, which focuses on the development of competitive strategy in retail service firms.

Developing Competitive Strategies

In developing a competitive strategy, the service retailer must have a clear definition and understanding of its market and must then develop a positioning strategy to attract this market and to distinguish itself from competitive firms.

Defining and Analyzing Target Customers. Understanding the market is as critical for the service firm as for the tangible goods firm. Management must understand the demographics of the firm's market and the needs, perceptions, and expectations of its client base.

A growing trend is for service firms to segment the market and to target their markets carefully. For example, banks are increasingly trying to build customer loyalty by bundling their services into packages targeted to segments of the population. For some time, banks have been aiming packages at the elderly, the demographic segment with the highest savings. Now, some banks are targeting subsegments within the elderly market because of various age, geographic, and lifestyle differences. NCNB Corp. of Charlotte, North Carolina, aims its financial connections program at young adults just starting careers. Union State Bank's advertisement targeted to young couples is shown in Exhibit 21–1.

Likewise, hospitals are developing offerings targeted to specific market segments. For example, some hospitals are offering luxury suites to affluent patients. A hospital in Los Angeles offers the hospital equivalent of a suite at the Ritz. Wealthy patients pay over $1,000 a night to stay in one of the pavilion suites. The hospital hired an interior design firm to produce suites with "understated luxury." Gourmet food is served on imported china and specially selected silver flatware. In addition, the hospital does not use institutional ads but promotes each area of the hospital (for example, the diabetes unit and the geriatric unit) to the appropriate target audience.

A market segment that some airlines are focusing on more intently is children. Not only are children flying in greater numbers to visit divorced parents or distant grandparents but focusing on children also gives the airlines a chance to win over some steady customers. Northwest Airlines for example, welcomes youngsters by name on the plane's public-address system, and flight attendants give them juice boxes, mini pizzas, crayons, and "Junior Captain" certificates. The company even offered a "Grown-Ups Fly Free" promotion in which adults got a free ride with the purchase of a child's ticket.[5]

EXHIBIT 21–1

Young couples just starting out have plenty of dreams and sometimes a few problems, too. At Union State Bank, we try to help solve the problems and make it a little easier for the dreams to come true. We offer personal one-on-one service from the bank that is involved in the community and wants to see you reach your financial goals. The kind of service newlyweds David and Lisa Reich get from Union State Vice President Wayne Glasscock at our Hoover office. This has been our commitment to the communities we serve since 1903.

We provide a full range of services to meet all your family's growing banking needs. Discover how you too can find a friend at Union State Bank.

Courtesy Union State Bank

Bank advertisement targeted to young couples

The Service Offering. The **core service** of a service firm is the primary benefit customers seek from the firm. **Peripheral services** are secondary benefits sought by customers. The core service for Federal Express, for example, consists of picking up the package, transporting it overnight, and delivering it the next morning. Peripheral services include providing advice and information, providing labels and certain types of packaging, documentation of shipments, and problem solving.

Most service organizations originate with a single core service offered to a single market segment. Initial growth opportunities normally occur through the addition of peripheral services and expansion into new geographic markets. Some service firms have been successful following a strategy of offering new core services for existing market segments, and some have followed a strategy of **concentric diversification,** or moving into different, but closely related, services. Thus, services strategy includes deciding what new services to introduce to which target markets, what existing services to maintain, and what services to eliminate. Decisions on the service offerings then set the stage for decisions on other components of competitive strategy, such as price, promotion, and distribution (delivery) strategies.

In judging a company's service offering, research has shown that consumers are primarily concerned that the service providers give consistently high levels of quality service. However, customers are also concerned with tangibles, such as the appearance of physical facilities, equipment, personnel, and communication materials. The following sections focus on these issues.[6] We also turn your attention to the extent to which service firms can engage in activities designed to achieve greater economies and efficiency without jeopardizing the level of personal attention and quality of service provided customers.

Service Provision. One characteristic of service firms, as discussed earlier, is the principal role people play in the delivery of the service. How can service firms ensure that employees are providing consistently high levels of quality service to their customers? Some companies rely on careful selection and training of employees and the development of programs to build a sense of pride in the service and a sense of identification with the company. Organizations often use both monetary and nonmonetary incentives to encourage employees to provide good service. One incentive is the employee of the month award. The effectiveness of using such an award is enhanced when it is based on customer feedback.

Making the person who delivers the service more visible is another technique. At Benihana, the U.S. chain of Japanese-style steak houses, the chef cooks at a grill in front of the restaurant guests. The chef's visibility and proximity to customers promote a consistently high quality of service.

Often effective in achieving and maintaining quality is peer group control. This is especially relevant where professional standards have been established for a task. In an architectural firm, the existence of a policy requiring partners' review of every piece of work can keep partners and associates on their toes. Surgeons are sometimes assigned in teams to encourage peer group control.

Over the past few years a growing number of service organizations have found that a most effective way to affect customers' perceptions of reliable service is to offer an unconditional guarantee of satisfaction. Such a guarantee promises complete customer satisfaction and, at a minimum, a full refund or complete, no-cost problem resolution to dissatisfied customers. For many firms, such a guarantee has proven to be a powerful tool for building customer loyalty and market share and for improving overall service quality (to see how one firm, Hampton Inn, a low- to mid-priced hotel chain, has implemented such a concept, see Focus 21–1). Management should, however, carefully assess both the benefits and the risks of providing unconditional guarantees. For example, because of the complex nature and unpredictable results of professional services, payouts could be higher than with other services and each payout could be more painful, considering the higher fees and smaller number of clients typical of such firms. Of course, such risks can be managed, but doing so requires great care in the guarantee's design and implementation, as well as in achieving and maintaining exceptionally high service quality.[7]

Importance of the Physical Environment. Because consumers often find the offerings of service organizations difficult to comprehend and evaluate because they are largely intangible, consumers often look for tangible evidence of the intangible to help them determine just what the offering is. Service retailers can provide such tangible surrogate features. For example, a hotel puts drinking glasses in clean paper bags, provides wrapped tablets of soap, and attaches "cleaned" bands across the toilets as tangible evidence that the room has been specially cleaned and prepared for the new occupant. The decor of the salon, the appearance of the staff, and the quality of the appointment cards are all tangible, surrogate product features for the basically intangible product of hairdressing.

Standardization and Specialization in Service Delivery. Increasingly, managers in service firms are engaging in activities to achieve greater economies and higher levels of efficiency. Such activities enable service firms to enjoy not only economies of scale but also more consistent, predictable quality in service delivery. As mentioned earlier, fast-food restaurants have introduced an assembly-line approach to what is a combination of tangible goods and services delivery in an effort to improve efficiency. Other examples of standardized consumer services range from quick auto service providers (such as oil change, muffler, and tune-up shops) to highly specialized medical services, such as centers that treat only one ailment such as hernias or cataracts.

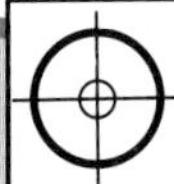

FOCUS 21–1

HAMPTON INN'S UNCONDITIONAL GUARANTEE OF SATISFACTION

In October 1989 Hampton announced its unconditional 100 percent satisfaction guarantee—a first in the hotel industry. The guarantee states that if guests have a problem or complaint at any time during their stay and are not satisfied when they leave, they will be given one night's stay for free.

Management believed that the secret to making the guarantee work was to give employees the authority to implement it. Thus, the program authorizes all employees—not just the manager or front-desk personnel—to take whatever action is necessary to keep the customer satisfied. For example, if a housekeeper notices that a guest is getting frustrated because the door key won't work, the housekeeper won't refer the problem to the front desk or the maintenance department. Instead, the housekeeper will take responsibility for getting a new key, changing the lock, or arranging for a different room. If the guest still isn't happy, the housekeeper may offer, without contacting management, to refund the cost of the room for the night. Before launching the program, training seminars were held for employees. Management also assured employees that they would stand behind their decisions completely.

When customers invoke the guarantee, their complaints are sent to company headquarters in Memphis. The operations staff is thus alerted to quality and service weaknesses and can initiate changes throughout the Hampton Inn chain. In this way, a single customer complaint in one location can contribute to improved service nationwide.

Since implementing the program, management has noticed a definite improvement in employee retention and employee morale. In addition, the program has positively affected the company's bottom line. Research indicates that approximately 2 percent of the system's total room nights are customers who said they stayed specifically because of the guarantee. Research also reveals that the guarantee strengthens customer loyalty—about half of all guests who complain about service problems after they stay indicate they will come back to Hampton Inn. Of the guests who invoke the guarantee before leaving the hotel (the guarantees are in the form of a reimbursement, not a voucher for later use), 86 percent say they will return to Hampton Inn and 45 percent of them already have.

Source: Adapted from "Satisfaction Guaranteed for Customers and Crew," *The Wall Street Journal*, January 28, 1991, pp. A3 and A10.

Standardization of service does not necessarily mean the end of personal attention, which is often a key element the customer seeks from a service firm. For example, trade-offs are successfully being made between standardization and personal service in the chains of legal and dental clinics that offer routine, standardized services to customers in essentially an assembly-line fashion. Emergency medical care centers follow a similar approach. Overhead is low because of the absence of costly equipment, treatment is limited to routine cases, and paraprofessionals are used whenever possible. Other efforts at standardization are evident in banks that offer only routinized services at the branches and handle unusual or complex transactions only at a central office. Banks' use of technology such as automatic teller machines is another way to standardize service delivery and increase efficiency.

Service Delivery. Although service retailers are less concerned with issues such as transportation, inventory, and warehousing than are tangible goods firms, service delivery is an important element of a service retailer's competitive strategy and involves such decisions as channel structure and location.

Channel Structure. Most services are provided directly by the producer to the end user, without an intermediary. Most physicians deal directly with patients, as do attorneys with their clients. Still, some indirect channels are used in service delivery. Tickets to ball games, concerts, and similar events are often sold at locations in addition to the place of performance. Travel agencies serve as intermediaries between the airline and the consumer. Banks extend credit to retail customers who use the bank's credit card, so the bank becomes a third party to any credit transaction a customer has with a retail outlet.

The Importance of Location. Location is an important element of the competitive strategy in a service business. Frequent air travelers are more likely to use auto rental agencies with the largest number of airport locations because such firms are most likely to have an outlet in a major airport. Fitness centers seek locations easily accessible to customers. Dental and legal clinics have found that location is important in attracting customers and are now increasingly moving to shopping mall locations.

Promoting the Service Offering. Effective use of promotion is extremely important for service retailers. Promotion is important in providing tangible "cues" for an intangible offering, in communicating the image of the firm and promoting its individual services, and in communicating with the customer after the service encounter. Let's look at these and other issues in more detail.

Promotion plays an important role in making a service more tangible to consumers. For example, some advertisements associate the service with some tangible object to establish a psychological association between a vaguely perceived intangible and a more easily perceived tangible object. Prudential Insurance's association with the rock of Gibraltar is an example. The rock signifies the solid, unwavering security and peace of mind a consumer desires from insurance. In addition, advertisements may focus on the physical environment in which the service is to be performed in an effort to make services more tangible. For example, a hospital's ad might show pictures of and stress its pleasant birthing rooms. As shown in Exhibit 21–2, the ad for a physical fitness center incorporates a picture of its indoor pool and emphasizes the environment as a factor in workout motivation.

EXHIBIT 21–2

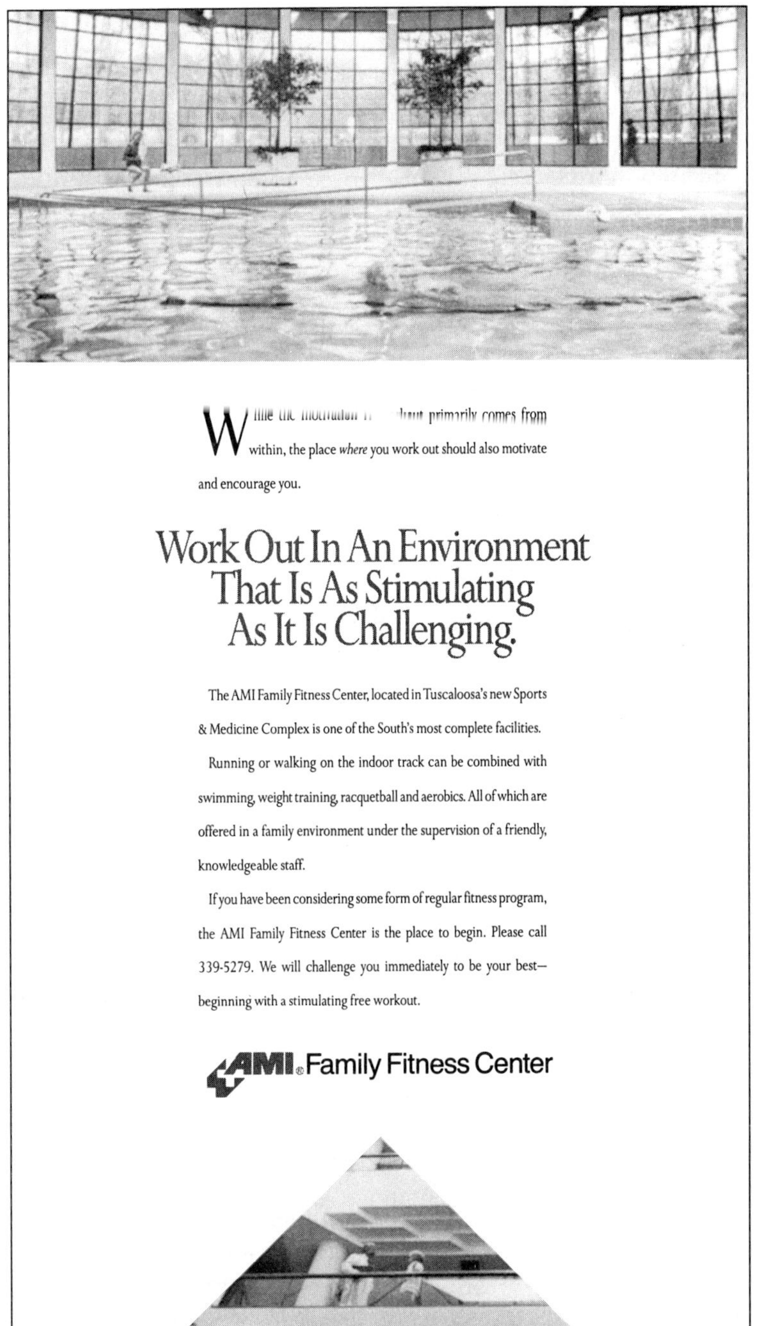

Courtesy AMI Family Fitness Center

A physical fitness center stresses the workout environment.

Service marketers should also try to create a strong organizational image through their promotional efforts. Retailers have long recognized that the quality of a store's services is an important determinant of its image and that store image strongly affects shopping and patronage behavior.

In addition, service retailers should make post-purchase communication a part of promotional strategy. This can be accomplished with postcards, surveys, telephone calls, brochures, or a variety of other devices to show customers that their input is sought and their patronage is appreciated.

Finally, marketing research suggests that consumers of retail services do not rely heavily on traditional, source-controlled information sources.[8] Instead, they prefer more personal sources for obtaining information. Hence, service retailers should try to stimulate positive word-of-mouth communication among present and potential customers.

Pricing. Price is a key element of a service retailer's competitive strategy. Price setting for a service firm, however, may prove to be a challenging task, and in some instances pricing issues have even become the source of controversy and criticism (see A Question of Ethics).

Research has shown that consumers may often perceive a stronger relationship between price and quality for services than for goods. This, together with the difficulties that customers encounter in evaluating services, suggests a greater emphasis and reliance on price as an indicator of quality. It thus becomes crucial that service retailers' prices are set appropriately.[9] However, sometimes there may be no sure way of knowing just what the provision of a service will entail until it is completed; there may be no way of telling the customer what the exact price of the service will be until the service has been provided. In addition, research shows that service retailers use cost-oriented pricing strategies more than competition- and demand-oriented pricing strategies. Costing a service, however, is a difficult and imprecise task because of service intangibility and flexibility. How does one place a value on such things as skill, expertise, and value? Although service costs may be difficult to calculate, service companies are apparently making estimates of costs to be sure that they are covered.[10]

Because of intense competition, slow growth, and other conditions, many service firms are focusing heavily on price as a competitive weapon. Intensive price competition has been evident, for example, in deregulated service industries such as financial services, telecommunications, and transportation. Air travelers today, for example, are faced with a bewildering array of different prices. In fact, the lowest fare may even differ from one ticketing agent to another. Such aggressive pricing is not limited to the service industries just cited. For a more detailed look at issues surrounding price competition in the hotel industry, see Case 1 at the end of the chapter.

A Question of Ethics

PHYSICIANS' BILLING PRACTICES VIEWED AS UNETHICAL

Some medical insurers believe that American consumers are being overcharged for medical services because of the way some physicians are pricing their services. One practice is referred to as "unbundling." Instead of a surgeon's charging for a hysterectomy, he or she bills separately for each procedure that is part of that operation. Billing in this way inflates the fee from $1,200 to $5,000.

To understand the problem better, one must understand the way medical bills are written. The American Medical Association developed a number code for each medical procedure, and the doctor's staff is expected to use the proper code when submitting a bill. Some believe, however, that the rules on how to pick the proper code are vague. The rules require doctors to use the "global" code when appropriate, rather than listing "underlying procedures," but the code does not define which are underlying procedures. An additional problem is the length of the code. The code is contained in a 600-page book that lists more than 7,000 procedures. Although insurers have software designed to detect "unbundling" and other coding problems, billing audits reveal that 40 to 60 percent of the coding submitted by medical providers is inaccurate, resulting in overpayments.

Insurers aren't charging that doctors deliberately inflate their bills because that would be accusing them of fraud. However, some insurers say they know of "income maximization" seminars held for physicians where they are advised to bill at the highest possible rate and, if the bill is not challenged, to keep on billing at the highest rate.

Considering the increasing concerns over rising medical care costs, do medical providers and insurers have a responsibility to monitor the extent to which pricing and billing practices may negatively affect consumers? Do they have a responsibility to develop more effective procedures and controls to ensure that unethical pricing and billing practices do not occur?

Source: Adapted from Rose DeWolf, "Doctors' 'Code Games' Raise Bills by Billions, Medical Insurer Says," *Birmingham News*, July 15, 1990, p. 4D.

NONSTORE RETAILING

Nonstore retailing has experienced phenomenal growth—more than double that of in-store retailing. A number of environmental dynamics explain this growth. Demographic and lifestyle changes, for example, have affected the demand for nonstore retailing. Single-person or single-parent household members lack the time to shop, as do those in two-career families. The "grey market," or the senior segment, is growing and, although such consumers have more disposable income, they are less mobile. Furthermore, some people are afraid to go downtown or to malls and prefer shopping in the safety of their homes. Many consumers also like the idea of shopping 24 hours a day, seven days a week. In addition, advances in the technological environment have spurred the growth of some forms of nonstore retailing. Let's look at the issue more closely by discussing the following forms of nonstore retailing: mail-order buying, direct selling, telephone shopping, electronic shopping, and vending machines.

Mail-Order Buying

Mail order or direct mail is a significant form of nonstore selling. In 1989 consumer mail order sales totaled more than $87 billion; nearly 99 million adults, or over 54 percent of the U.S. population, made a direct mail purchase.[11]

The modern era of mail order dates back to 1872, when Aaron Montgomery Ward published a one-page catalog listing 163 items, most priced at $1. Fourteen years later Richard Warren Sears, a Minnesota railroad station agent, decided to sell watches by mail order. The idea was so successful that he joined forces with a Chicago watchmaker, A. C. Roebuck, to establish a mail-order business. By 1927 Sears Roebuck was mailing 75 million letters and catalogs.[12] Since these beginnings, catalog merchandising has grown significantly, 10 to 15 percent each year for the past five years. Market analysts estimate that between 12 and 15 billion catalogs are mailed each year.[13]

As the number of catalogs has changed, so has their content. Whereas the earlier catalogs contained a wide variety of merchandise, ranging from farm supplies to lingerie, the typical contemporary catalog presents a tightly focused assortment of goods designed to meet the needs of a specific market segment. Lands' End, a company that sells nearly $550 million worth of merchandise through its 90 million catalogs, certainly knows its target market. Nearly 9 out of 10 Lands' End customers have some college education, and the company's customers are five times more likely than the general public to have some postgraduate education. Seven in ten customers are in managerial or professional positions, and 75 percent of their female customers work outside the home. Sixty-five percent of their customers have annual incomes above $35,000. Their customers participate in a wide variety of active sports and travel more than the average American.[14]

Some companies are developing catalogs that focus on consumers' special physical needs. J. C. Penney's "Easy Dressing" catalog contains fashions for arthritic women. The catalog features Velcro fasteners hidden beneath purely decorative buttons. Spiegel has developed a catalog "For You" for those who are overweight. A maker of fashion lines for consumers in wheelchairs sells through its catalog "Avenues."[15]

In addition to focusing the content of their catalogs, companies are using consumer data and technology to develop highly targeted mailing lists. With the use of selective binding, for example, a customer and her next door neighbor might get two different catalogs. Another option is **ink jetting,** which enables the company to print personalized messages within a catalog. Techniques such as these enable a company to treat each customer as an individual. Some industry analysts believe that in a few years, the industry will be at the point where almost every catalog will be for a specific customer.[16]

An exciting development in mail-order retailing is the videolog, a shop-at-home video catalog. Not only do videologs provide a novel method for reaching the consumer, but the approach seems especially appropriate for selling expensive or complicated products. Companies such as Spiegel, Neiman-Marcus, Sears, and Royal Silk have offered video catalogs to consumers. And the results have been favorable. For example, Royal Silk found that video catalog orders averaged $100, compared to $70 for print catalog orders.[17] Even though videologs have attractive benefits, they are not without their drawbacks. An individual tape costs anywhere from $7 to $10. Furthermore, they require more effort to use than a printed catalog.

Even though mail order is experiencing growth, it is not without its critics. Americans receive nearly 63 billion pieces of third-class mail annually, throwing out 10 billion pieces without even opening them. Environmentalists are concerned not only with disposal issues but also with the destruction of trees. Some mail-order companies are attempting to respond to these concerns. For example, Smith & Hawken Ltd., a gardening supply catalog company, promises to plant two trees for each one it uses and offers a $5 gift certificate to customers who send in duplicate mailing labels. Gardner's Supply Company of Burlington, Vermont, set up a program to recycle glossy catalog paper. The company says that it is currently recycling more paper than it uses in its own catalogs.[18]

Another issue of concern stems from those who believe that direct mail organizations should be required to collect use or sales taxes on every order. Even though over 30 states have passed laws over the past five years requiring that out-of-state direct mail companies collect use taxes, the U.S. Supreme Court has restricted the power of individual states to extend their taxing authority beyond their own state borders. The reasoning of the court has been that a company must have some minimum contact (referred to as *nexus*) in the state before taxes can be collected. In a 1967 case, the Supreme Court ruled that the mailing of catalogs and subsequent delivery of goods doesn't constitute sufficient nexus to require the direct mail company to collect the state sales or use tax. Regardless, many states continue to pressure direct mail firms to collect the taxes.

Direct Selling[19]

Direct selling is a method of distribution of consumer goods and services through personal contact (salesperson to buyer) away from a fixed business location. Major modes of direct selling include one-on-one selling and the party plan, in the home or elsewhere. The significance of direct selling is underscored by the following facts. The Direct Selling Association's 1988 industry survey included 175 companies, using 3,996,067 salespeople, or

A Profile in Excellence

JAMES E. PRESTON

James E. Preston joined Avon in 1964 as a management trainee in the company's distribution center in Rye, New York. During the period from 1965 to 1970, Preston served in various management positions in marketing and operations at the world headquarters in New York City. In 1977, he became a corporate executive vice-president and was elected to the board of directors. In November 1981 Preston assumed the additional position of president and chief executive officer, and in 1989 became chairman of the board.

In 1984, after several years of declining profitability, Preston introduced a five-year plan to boost the beauty business. The company changed its marketing strategy, restructured its organization, and began changing the way it viewed customers. A large part of the decline in business came when increasing numbers of women joined the work force. This trend began eroding Avon's core customer base and also diminished the availability of potential sales representatives.

Preston was responsible for a complete change in the business. He realized that the company was serving customers, not distribution systems. Preston believes that the key to Avon's long-term success is the management of the direct selling personnel. He was once quoted as saying, "Direct selling is not a dinosaur doomed to extinction. If anything, it's a phoenix."

an average of nearly 23,000 salespeople per company. Total sales of these firms was $9.7 billion—79 percent occurring through a one-on-one approach and the remaining 21 percent by party plan or group sales.

Four major categories of products and services are sold by direct selling firms. The largest category, accounting for nearly half of all sales, is household products, including cookware, tableware, kitchen and decorative accessories, vacuum cleaners and other appliances, household cleaning products, and foods and beverages. An example of a firm in the beverage line is Pittsburgh Seltzer Works, a company specializing in the sale of seltzer water. Customers leave wooden crates of empty bottles on their porches. The delivery person picks them up and refills customers' orders. The Edelmanns, owners of the business, bought the firm a decade ago when there were only 20 customers. Today the company sells and delivers directly to 700 customers, most of whom are health or recycling enthusiasts (or both).[20]

The second largest product category, comprising about one-third of all sales, involves personal care and beauty items, including cosmetics, fragrances, skin care items, jewelry, and clothing. Well-known firms in the cosmetics and skin care line include, for example, Mary Kay and Avon (see A Profile in Excellence).

Leisure and educational products make up the third product category, which accounts for approximately 8 percent of sales by direct sellers. Products include encyclopedias and other educational publications, toys, craft and hobby items, computers and software, and self-improvement or vocational training programs. The fourth category, accounting for less than 10 percent of direct sales, includes services and product lines that vary widely in character such as cemetery property, foliage plants, and photographic supplies.

Of interest is the fact that many of the environmental dynamics discussed earlier that have led to an increase in demand for nonstore buying have adversely affected direct selling. As the public's fear of crime has increased, fewer people are willing to open the door to strangers. With more single-person and dual-income households, there are fewer people at home. Many direct sellers are therefore attempting to reach consumers during the evening hours and at locations other than consumers' homes, such as work sites. Some are using direct mail pieces and are printing 800 numbers in their literature as well as on product packages to assist customers in reordering products or making contacts. Such companies are quick to point out, however, that customer orders generated by the toll-free numbers or direct mail pieces are turned over to their salespeople to fill. In an attempt to increase sales, some companies are moving into international markets. Amway, for example, has more than 100,000 salespeople in Japan. Avon is sold in more than 100 countries today and earns a substantial portion of its profit from its international operations (see Exhibit 21–3). For a look at what Tupperware is doing in response to these environmental dynamics, see Case 2 at the end of the chapter.

Telephone Shopping

The use of telephones for shopping has become increasingly popular. Telephone selling, or telemarketing, ranges from the acceptance of sales via telephone by store-based or catalog retailers to the advertising of 800 numbers for ordering merchandise to the exclusive use of telephone marketing.

In 1990 American companies spent an estimated $60 billion on telemarketing, up from $1 billion in 1981.[21] According to Congressional testimony, telemarketing sales accounted for $435 billion in purchases in 1990.[22] Consumers are buying virtually every type of product and service via the telephone—from prescriptions to computers to prepared foods. Telemarketing not only gives companies a practical, cost-effective way of interacting personally with customers, but it also gives consumers a chance to ask questions and seek information about a company's offering.

Although some consumers welcome telephone selling, others view it as an interruption and an invasion of privacy. Especially objectionable to many consumers are computerized machines that automatically call and relay messages. They are concerned, for example, that some consumers must pay for calls—people with car phones and pagers are charged for every minute they use a telephone line even if they don't initiate the call. More than a dozen states have passed legislation related to computerized calling. Some versions ban or restrict the hours in which the automatic dialers can be used.

EXHIBIT 21–3

Courtesy Avon Products, Inc.

Women taking classes at an Avon training center in Guangzhou, China, to become Avon representatives

In an attempt to be more sensitive to the needs and concerns of consumers, more and more telemarketers are developing policies and guidelines in order to protect privacy and prevent exploitation. MCI, for example, has developed such guidelines. The company makes all contact through a live operator, they use only equipment that allows immediate disconnection, and they limit hours of calling from 9:00 A.M. to 9:00 P.M. Monday through Saturday, and noon to 5:00 P.M. on Sunday. The company never engages in random dialing, and the company's telemarketers are trained to politely reschedule or terminate a call if the consumer does not wish to take the call. MCI also maintains an up-to-date list of consumers who have asked not to be called and routinely receives the Direct Marketing Association's Telephone Preference Service, a national no-call list to which any consumer may subscribe. Because unsuspecting consumers can be exploited by telephone sales if they misunderstand the conditions of a sale, MCI has developed a verification process to ensure the accuracy of its telemarketing efforts. If a consumer agrees to become an MCI subscriber, an independent company contacts the customer to verify that MCI has accurate information identifying him or her and that he or she understands the terms of MCI's service. If any problems are detected by the independent company, the sale is terminated.[23]

Electronic Shopping

Electronic shopping can assume a variety of forms, including phone shopping from computerized listings, such as Comp-U-Card International Inc.; cable television programs with product and service presentations and demonstrations, such as the Home Shopping Network; and electronic ordering of merchandise from retailers or manufacturers through nationwide computer networks such as Prodigy.

Regardless of the format, electronic shopping has taken on increased significance as a form of nonstore retailing. Over 200 companies are experimenting with ways to use personal computers, videodisc players, and other technologies to improve customer service and provide convenient access to merchandise and product information. More than 5,000 electronic shopping systems now provide information and transaction services to consumers. More than 500,000 consumers shop electronically from their homes through personal computers.

Some market analysts believe that the impending fusion of fiber-optic technology with computer and video technology should make electronic shopping relatively commonplace by 2010. By the year 2000, 70 percent of U.S. households are projected to have computers. Some envision that several basic formats will be widely used then and that electronic shopping will account for 20 to 25 percent of U.S. retail sales.[24] Some believe that such estimates are overly optimistic, but no one can doubt the increasing significance of electronic shopping as a form of nonstore retailing.

Vending Machines

Historians believe that the first vending machine, created by Hero of Alexander in 215 B.C., was a five-drachma machine that dispensed holy water. Since that time, vending machines have been used to sell a wide variety of merchandise, ranging from soft drinks and snack food items to blue jeans to freshly baked pizza. Vending machines have even been used to vend names and telephone numbers of ladies of the evening.

The vending machine industry has experienced tremendous revenue growth. Sales grew from $17.5 billion in 1985 to $24.5 billion in 1989. Because of increasing competition, however, profit margins are usually around 2 to 3 percent. There are over 9,000 vending machine firms in the United States, ranging from mom-and-pop firms to names such as Marriott, ARA, and Greyhound, competing for about 1 million vending locations. Vendors have about 4.5 million machines, which equates to one machine for every 55 people in the country.[25]

CHAPTER HIGHLIGHTS

- The service sector of the American economy is becoming increasingly important. This is evidenced by the fact that 88 percent of U.S. jobs will be in the services area by 2000.

- There are strategic differences between tangible goods firms and service retailers. The competitive strategies of service firms must conform to their unique characteristics. In addition, consumer behavior differences in the purchase of services versus tangible goods affect competitive strategy development in retail service firms.
- Service firms must develop competitive strategies just as firms selling tangible goods do. The service retailer must have a clear definition of its target market and an understanding of that market.
- An element of positioning strategy is the decision regarding the service offering. Here, the retailer must determine not only the core service to be offered but also the peripheral services. Because of the intangible nature of many service offerings, the people involved in service delivery and the physical environment are key ingredients of a service firm's competitive strategy.
- In terms of service delivery, service retailers are involved in channel structure decisions. Although most services are provided directly by the producer to the end user without an intermediary, some indirect channels are used in service delivery. Location is also an important element of service delivery.
- Effective use of promotion is important for service retailers. Promotion is important in providing tangible "cues" for an intangible offering, in communicating the image of the firm and promoting its individual services, and in communicating with the customer after the service encounter.
- Pricing is also a critical element of a service firm's competitive strategy. Because the offering of a service firm may largely be intangible, price is often used by consumers as a surrogate for quality. Price must therefore be set appropriately. However, some unique aspects of service retailing make price setting a challenging task.
- Nonstore retailing has experienced phenomenal growth—more than double that of in-store retailing. Forms of nonstore retailing include mail-order buying, direct selling, telephone shopping, electronic shopping, and vending machines.

Study Question

1. Summarize the differences between tangible goods firms and service retailers.
2. Discuss the unique aspects of consumer behavior in the purchase of services that affect competitive strategy development in service firms. Be sure to include in your discussion the differences between search, experience, and credence qualities of products.
3. What is the difference between core services and peripheral services?
4. What are some service organizations doing to increase service standardization? Are there any disadvantages in following such a strategy? If so, what are they?
5. Comment on the validity of the following statement: Channel structures in service industries are always direct from producer to user.
6. Why is promotion such an important part of a service retailer's competitive strategy?
7. Discuss why pricing is an important element of competitive strategy for service retailers. What difficulties do service firms encounter in price setting?
8. How do present-day catalogs and their use differ from earlier catalogs? What controversial issues surround the use of direct mail as a form of nonstore retailing?
9. What is direct selling as a form of nonstore retailing? What environmental dynamics are affecting direct selling and how are direct selling firms responding?
10. What are the advantages of telephone shopping from the perspectives of companies and consumers? What controversial issues are related to the use of telemarketing?

A P P L I C A T I O N S

CASE 1: Hotels Engage in Price Competition

The hotel industry is in one of its worst slumps ever, partly because of the glut of newly built properties but also because of the nation's recession. In 1990 the industry lost \$5.5 billion; in 1991, \$2.7 billion. Currently, the vacancy rate is 35 to 40 percent. Nearly every part of the business—from bare-bones economy hotels to lush resorts—is experiencing losses.

Out of desperation, many hotels are cutting their rates and actively promoting lower prices. Increasingly, even full-service hotels such as Marriott, Sheraton, Hyatt, and Hilton are running ads touting prices only \$10 or \$20 above that of "roadside dives."

Some people in the industry, however, believe that competing on a price basis creates problems. First, some think that it makes no sense for a hotel that has spent millions on new lobbies, health clubs, and other marketing programs to differentiate itself from competition to focus on price rather than its service. Focusing on price encourages consumers to view hotels as commodities and thus to make their selection only on the basis of price. Another problem is that hotels risk their goodwill by advertising their bargains without highlighting all the restrictions. For example, some prices are valid only for a limited number of rooms and only on certain days, or the advertised rate applies only if two people are staying in the room, each paying the advertised rate.

Source: Based on Pauline Yoshihashi, "Hotel Recovery Will Be a Late Arrival," *The Wall Street Journal,* July 27, 1991, p. B1; Ira Teinowitz, "Sheraton's New Pricing Makes Rivals Cry Foul," *Advertising Age,* May 11, 1992, p. 6; and Jonathan Dahl, "Hotels Take Risks in Touting Lower Rates," *The Wall Street Journal,* September 25, 1991, p. B1.

Applying Retailing Principles

1. What has motivated hotels to engage in price competition?
2. Are there any negative repercussions from competing on the basis of price? If so, what are they?
3. Is there any way a full-service hotel could maintain prices and promote its services when competitors are reducing and advertising price specials? Or is its only effective response to likewise lower prices?

CASE 2: Environmental Dynamics' Impact on Tupperware

Tupperware was a perfect product for the 1950s. Most women were full-time homemakers and they eagerly came in great numbers to Tupperware parties. During the 1960s and 1970s sales nearly doubled every five years, and Tupperware dealers increased steadily in number. Rubbermaid Inc. also sold plastic bowls through home parties but wasn't nearly as successful as Tupperware.

Then in the 1980s things begin to change. Divorces became more common. More customers were single, childless, and working outside the home. Increased use of takeout food and restaurant meals made leftovers a thing of the past. Rubbermaid, seeing these trends, ceased selling through parties and moved its products into stores. Tupperware continued selling through the party format, but sales began to decline. Rubbermaid's current market share of the food storage container market has risen to between 30 and 40 percent from about 5 or 10 percent in 1984. Tupperware's share has dropped from 59 percent to between 40 and 45 percent. Furthermore, since 1986 a quarter of Tupperware's active dealers have left the company.

In an attempt to turns things around, management has engaged in a number of strategies. One is the development of new products such as containers that can be used in a microwave oven. Salespeople are also being encouraged to develop new "twists" on Tupperware parties. They are being held in offices, parks, and even parking lots. They are scheduling "stop and shops" so that people can just drop in, and "custom kitchen" parties that focus on cabinet organizing. To recruit dealers, the company plans to engage in television advertising. The company is also experimenting with a catalog but the mailing list will include only names submitted by Tupperware salespeople. Management has no plans for replacing its current distribution system and sell through stores and insists they will not take any other types of actions that would jeopardize the Tupperware sales force.

Source: Adapted from Laurie M. Grossman, "Families Have Changed but Tupperware Keeps Holding Its Parties," *The Wall Street Journal,* July 21, 1991, pp. A1 and A4.

Applying Retailing Principles

1. Summarize the environmental dynamics that have negatively affected Tupperware.
2. What do you think motivated Tupperware to stay with its distribution system of party selling rather than selling its products through stores, as Rubbermaid did?
3. Do you think that the company's turnaround strategies will be successful? Why or why not?

Notes

1. Peter Nulty, "How Managers Will Manage," *Fortune,* February 2, 1987, p. 47.
2. This material is based on Leonard L. Berry, Valarie A. Zeithaml, and A. Parasuraman, "Responding to Demand Fluctuations: Key Challenge for Service Businesses," in *1984 American Marketing Association Educators Conference Proceedings,* Russell Belk, et al. (eds.) (Chicago: American Marketing Association, 1984), pp. 231–34; Valarie A. Zeithaml, A. Parasuraman, and Leonard L. Berry, "Problems and Strategies in Services Marketing," *Journal of Marketing,* Spring 1985, pp. 33–46.
3. W. R. George, "The Retailing of Services—A Challenging Future," *Journal of Retailing* 53 (1977), p. 86.
4. Valarie A. Zeithaml, "How Consumer Evaluation Processes Differ Between Goods and Services," in *Marketing of Services,* James H. Donnelly and William R. George (eds.) (Chicago, Illinois: American Marketing Association, 1981), pp. 186–90.
5. James Hirsch, "More Airlines Go All Out to Pamper the Junior Jet Set," *The Wall Street Journal,* July 3, 1992, p. B1.
6. Leonard L. Berry, Valarie A. Zeithaml, and A. Parasuraman, "Five Imperatives for Improving Service Quality," *Sloan Management Review,* Summer 1990, pp. 29–38.
7. Christopher W. L. Hart, Leonard A. Schlesinger, and Dan Maker, "Guarantees Come to Professional Service Firms," *Sloan Management Review,* Spring 1992, pp. 19–29.
8. David Mazursky and Jacob Jacoby, "Exploring the Development of Store Images," *Journal of Retailing* 62 (Summer 1986), pp. 145–64.
9. Angela M. Rushton and David J. Carson, "The Marketing of Services: Managing the Intangible," *European Journal of Marketing* 19 (1985), p. 31.
10. Zeithaml, Parasuraman, and Berry, "Problems and Strategies in Services Marketing," p. 38.
11. Stanley H. Slom, "Direct Marketing Faces Hurdles," *Chain Store Age Executive,* September 1991, p. 27.
12. Jill Smoloew, "Read This!!!!!!!!" *Time,* November 26, 1990, p. 65.
13. Marilyn Lavin, "Have Contemporary Consumers Integrated Mail/Phone Order into Their Categorization of Goods and Retailers?" *Journal of Direct Marketing* 6 (Summer 1992), p. 23.

14. Rayna Skolnik, "Selling Via Catalogs," *Stores,* October 1989, p. 47.

15. Kevin Helliker, "Fashion Catalogs Focus on Consumers' Special Physical Needs," *The Wall Street Journal,* November 29, 1990, p. B1.

16. Skolnik, "Selling Via Catalogs," p. 50.

17. JoAnne Lipman, "Need a Commercial Break? Viewers Take Ads Home to Play on VCRs," *The Wall Street Journal,* June 5, 1987, p. 21.

18. Michael W. Miller, " 'Greens' Add to Junk Mail Mountain," *The Wall Street Journal,* May 13, 1991, p. B1.

19. Most of the information in this section is from Thomas R. Wotruba, "Direct Selling in the Year 2000," in *The Future of U.S. Retailing,* Robert Peterson (ed.) (New York: Quorum Books, 1992), p. 188.

20. Gregory Stricharchuk, "Making Money the Old-Fashioned Way: Door to Door," *The Wall Street Journal,* February 19, 1991, p. B2.

21. Michael W. Miller, "When the 'Junker' Calls, This Man Is Ready for Revenge," *The Wall Street Journal,* June 24, 1991, p. A1.

22. *Telemarketing and Privacy: Are Consumers Being Exploited?* (Washington, D.C.: Direct Selling Education Foundation, August 1992), p. 5.

23. *Telemarketing and Privacy,* pp. 5 and 7.

24. "Electronic Information, Transaction Systems Cited," *Marketing News,* March 31, 1989, p. B4.

25. J. Taylor Bucklet, "Machines Start New Fast-Food Era," *USA Today,* 1991.

C H A P T E R

22

Retailing: Trends, Social Dimensions, and Prospects

THIS CHAPTER:

Explores the changes occurring in the external environment.

Reviews growth prospects for the 1990s by retailing sector.

Highlights emerging retailing strategies in response to changes in the external environments.

RETAILING CAPSULE

TERRA VERDE

Katherine Tiddens planned to write a book about the garbage crisis. Instead she opened her 3,500-square-foot Terra Verde store in Manhattan's chic Soho district in November 1990.

All of the 1,000 items sold in Terra Verde—even the shower curtains and paint—are ecologically friendly. Ironically, the store is located in a former leather warehouse, a definite bane to the environmentally correct psyche.

Green retailers such as Terra Verde are emerging as one of the hottest retail formats today, despite a sluggish retail environment. Tiddens attributes the success of her New York City and recently opened Santa Monica, California, stores to a new breed of environmentally aware consumers who not only seek out green products, but also are willing to pay a bit more for them.

"I wouldn't have opened any other type of store in this environment," says Tiddens. Terra Verde, she adds, isn't just appealing to the very socially aware populace surrounding her trendy, downtown Manhattan location. "We not only get the Soho 'green warriors,' but also shoppers from across the area."

Tiddens is more than just a leftover flower child. She has researched and written about the dangers facing the environment since she participated in Earth Day 1970. Although she has no retail background—Tiddens has worked as an editor most of her career—she has a knack for finding products today's consumer wants.

The store stretches beyond the mundane string bags and recyclable paper that have become synonymous with green retailing. The merchandise mix includes books on the environment, light bulbs, furniture, cosmetics, paper, and cleaning products. There are linens and a unique shower curtain from NOPE (non-polluting enterprises) that has become a best-seller.

But mostly, green retailing means green in the cash register. "We've been called the end of retailing as we know it . . . and that makes me happy. We want to show people that green can be beautiful."

Source: Portions reproduced with permission from Faye Brookman, "Terra Verde—NYC Store Features Eco-Friendly Merchandise," *Stores*, January 1992, pp. 126–28. Copyright © 1992. National Retail Federation Enterprises.

Retailing is exciting and dynamic. It changes more rapidly than any other element of the business structure because it is closer to the consumer than any other part of the corporate world. Katherine Tiddens is an example of the type of entrepreneurial response that makes retailing such a dynamic part of American culture.

Retailing during the 1970s and 1980s was dominated by a "field of dreams" philosophy—"Build it and they will come."[1] Consumer demand outstripped supply during this golden era. The number of stores exploded. Growth was fueled by favorable government tax and spending policies. Capital was readily available for expansion, the labor pool was abundant, and women entered the labor force in record numbers. In essence, the excesses of the baby boom generation were in full swing.

But by the mid 1980s the field of dreams philosophy had run its course. Retailers either had to change or file for bankruptcy. Going out of business signs proliferated as record numbers of bankruptcies occurred. Retail strategies had not kept pace with changing business conditions. Past successes bred complacency, which led to failure.

The result is that retailing entered the 1990s with a lot of baggage, as highlighted in Focus 22–1. Specifically, retailing entered the new decade overstored, characterized by a sameness in merchandise and layout, consumers trained to wait for merchandise to go on sale, the absence of a strong customer-focused culture, deficits in equity capital, and uncertainty about the future. The environment today remains intensely competitive and in a state of constant change.

ENVIRONMENTAL FORCES FOR THE 1990s

In this section we will highlight the broad-based environmental forces that will shape retailing in the 1990s. The next section will review changes by industry sector.

Free Market Growth. Eastern Europe and Latin America are now struggling to develop free market economies after decades of central planning. They will provide attractive investment opportunities in the

FOCUS 22–1

THE LEGACY OF THE 1980S

Retailing has entered the final decade of the 20th century faced with enormous challenges from the dynamics of the 1980s:

- **Too many stores.** Throughout the 1970s until very recently, the growth of retail space has consistently outstripped both population growth and consumer spending. We now have significantly more retail square footage than is needed to service the population profitably.
- **Sameness** in merchandise, layout, presentation, and service. Despite a mandate for innovation from retailers seeking above-market growth, many factors have conspired to produce a high degree of retailing sameness. These factors include the temptation to copy the leader—to experience its success by imitating its approach; industry consolidation, which brings more establishments under the same management direction; common vendor merchandising programs; and common technology, especially as related to inventory management, giving all retailers the ability to identify and stock the same best-sellers.
- **Excessive price promotions.** In the mature retail industry, competition for market share has tended to be almost exclusively price competition. Constant price promotions have sapped the meaning of the word "sale." Consumers no longer think of the "regular" price as a "real" price.
- **Poor customer service.** Following a strong focus on productivity in the 1970s and early 1980s, customer service reemerged as a critical issue in the latter half of the 1980s. Despite an industrywide "customer first" philosophy, the level of customer service and satisfaction appears to have improved very little if at all. Very few retailers have been able to successfully execute a competitive strategy utilizing customer service as a differential advantage.
- **A lack of equity capital.** Throughout the 1980s, easy money fueled aggressive and sometimes foolish acquisitions. Many LBOs were not well thought out from a strategic business perspective. They were just financial deals that were highly profitable for the dealmakers. Today, the industry is more highly leveraged than at any other time in its history.
- **A widening gap** exists between the high performers and the rest of the industry; between those retailers who have made long-term strategic investments in the business and those who have made only short-term tactical expenditures. The gap can be defined in terms of technology and good, solid management processes, decision-making structure, and information flow.

Unprecedented uncertainty. Predicting the future is no longer possible. The best senior management can hope to do is to anticipate, prepare, and execute with flexibility. The retail industry is in fragile condition. As a result of the dynamics of the past decade, retailers face enormous challenges as they approach the next century. For many, the 1990s will be a struggle for survival. But a period of high uncertainty also creates opportunity. The major areas of opportunity are not obvious, but the forces of change that will mold those opportunities are very much in evidence.

Source: Reproduced with permission from *Retailing 2000* (Dublin, Ohio: Management Horizons, 1990), p. 3.

future. The return to world peace will positively affect world economic growth over time. The short-term effect will be negative as military bases are closed, armament production lines are shut down, and financial resources are reallocated on an international scale.

Management Decentralization. Technology will allow further decentralization of management decisions. Decisions formerly made by mid-level managers will now be made at the store level because of the availability of detailed, real-time data. Faster and better decisions will result because they are made closer to the consumer.

Geopolitical Trends. American political influence in this decade is likely to decline because of the formation of the European Economic Community, the continuing importance of Japan as an economic power, and the emerging importance of Central and South America as markets. Continuing U.S. need for foreign capital will also make it necessary for the United States to maintain the goodwill of foreigners. Foreign interests, as a result, will continue to make inroads into U.S. markets. During the period from 1984 to 1988, for example, 21 percent of the total dollar value of retail acquisitions in the United States was made by foreign interests.[2] In contrast to political influence, the United States will increasingly assume a dominant cultural role across the world. American-branded goods will continue to enjoy explosive growth on the world market.

Economic Outlook. The economy will experience slow but consistent economic growth in this decade, and will be largely productivity driven. Inflation will remain under control because of the continuing relative softness of the economy. Likewise, merchandise will remain relatively cheap because of the aggressive growth strategies of the newly industrialized nations in the Pacific Basin, Latin and South America, and Eastern Europe. Interest rates are also likely to remain low because of lower inflation and increased savings. The financial system will remain fragile, however, because of the relative instability of key financial sectors such as banking.

Demographic Trends. Population growth will continue at a modest pace, brought about in part by higher birthrates among both legal and illegal immigrants. The heart of the baby boom generation will become the 40-something crowd coping with the demands of family, aging parents, and career development.[3]

Rapid growth in the 45- to 49-year-old age group will result in demands for greater quality and better service. This age group will be a primary growth market for replacement of household goods. Fewer new households will be formed, however. Spending on such items as furniture, home furnishings, and appliances by first-time buyers will thus be sluggish.

The number of 20- to 29-year-olds will decline through at least the mid-1990s. Retailers also will be hard pressed to identify and hire the number of workers they need because of the relative sparsity of this age group.

Contrary to popular opinion, the number of U.S. shoppers aged 60 to 69 will decline through the first half of this decade. This group, however, along with the higher numbers of 45- to 49-year-olds, will reflect a higher savings rate. Both groups will plan with an eye toward retirement. Again, these trends will negatively affect consumer spending.

Value Shifts. Value shifts and environmentalism will continue to be a key concern with most consumers. The so-called green movement is more than a fad and will affect virtually all dimensions of retailing. Some people, however, question the depth of retailers' commitment (see A Question of Ethics). No-smoking campaigns will continue with a vengeance. Likewise, deferred gratification will continue to be the norm as consumers opt for a higher rate of savings.

The conspicuous consumption of the yuppie generation will decline as older, more conservative shoppers express their desire for quality. Convenience will also become an important factor in shopping. Knowledgeable salespeople, effective and quick replacement and repair, and maximum convenience will be consumer priorities, as will truth in advertising, complete information, and product reliability.

In essence, we will see a shift in the 1990s away from the "me generation" narcissism and the dog-eat-dog ambition of the 1980s. Americans are seeking a sense of moral stability as they search for absolute values and a sense of right and wrong.[4] Consumers in this decade will value things that endure, such as a sense of community, the earth, spiritual faith, and the family. Retail winners will be outlets such as The Body Shop, founded by Anita Roddick (see A Profile in Excellence) and discussed in the Retailing Capsule in Chapter 4.

Environmental sensitivity will continue to be strong as reflected in the passage of local antidumping and recycling statutes, retail ads featuring a renewed sense of environmental consciousness, the refusal to use foam trays or cups in restaurants and cafeterias, suburban picketing of incinerator plants, and continuing expressions of anger about the deteriorating quality of life in local communities.[5]

Income Redistribution. More than three-fourths of U.S. wealth is now held by the oldest 20 percent of society. During the 1990s, the distribution of wealth will shift by inheritance to younger people. Experts have labeled the 1990s as the age of inheritance.[6] Income distribution will become even more polarized as wealth is concentrated in the hands of the top 1 or 2 percent of the population. A larger percentage of households will occupy the lower end of the income spectrum, especially because of the continuing influx of immigrants.

A Question of Ethics

STORES HYPE ECOLOGY EFFORTS

Retailers have discovered the endangered Earth—and are turning it into a marketing opportunity.

Wal-Mart Stores Inc. and Kmart Corp. are trumpeting their efforts to get manufacturers to develop products and packaging that don't harm the environment. Lord & Taylor and Macy's are among a coalition of department stores aiding the imperiled African elephant by proclaiming ivory "out of fashion." Patagonia Inc., a mail-order company, began pushing conservation this year in its outdoor-clothing catalogs. And Chief Auto Parts Inc. just started selling "environmentally safe and biodegradable" windshield washer fluid and antifreeze revitalizers, among other products.

For many newly "green" retailers, the Earth consciousness is less altruism than a response to rising concern among consumers. But gimmick or not, environmental marketing works. "It gives consumers a real reason to do business with you," says retail consultant Peter Glen. Adds consultant Sid Doolittle, "It's a motherhood kind of reason."

Low-Cost Kudos

The talk is also cheap. Unlike makers of consumer products, retailers don't have to bankroll product research and development to appear that they're doing the right thing. "That's why it's such a good idea," Glen says.

L.L. Bean Inc., for instance, spent very little to compile a list of conservation organizations needing outdoor volunteers. It sends the information to customers who call a toll-free number listed in its sporting catalogs.

The major department stores aren't risking much either with their anti-ivory campaign. Demand for jewelry made from elephant tusks has declined anyway and ivory sales accounted for a minuscule percentage of total sales at most stores. "Economically, the repercussions won't be especially heartfelt," acknowledges a spokeswoman for Dayton Hudson Corp.'s department store unit, one of the sponsors of a recent advertisement announcing the retailer's stand.

But environmental marketing programs are so easy and inexpensive to develop that some merchants fear they could contain more hype than heft. "As companies compete to look like they're environmentalists, they can cheapen the word," frets Kevin Sweeney, a Patagonia official who oversees the catalog company's environmental programs.

"To stand up and say, 'We're environmentalists, we're good, buy our product,' is wrong," Sweeney asserts. "To teach people about an issue and how they can get active is a better balance."

Environmental activists are also skeptical. "It could all just be a marketing scheme appealing to the genuine desire of people today to do what they can to save the environment," says David Rapaport, an official at Greenpeace, the Washington-based environmental group.

Indeed, few standards exist to judge whether products are environmentally sound. Trash bags made from so-called biodegradable plastic "are really no better for the environment than any other plastic" if dumped in a landfill or incinerator, Rapaport says. But, he adds, "the average consumer isn't necessarily aware of that."

Asked why merchants didn't adopt an environmental slant a decade or so ago, George Hite, an executive at Dayton Hudson's Target discount store unit, says, "The people shopping in our stores in those days weren't as sensitive to these issues as people are today."

A Question of Ethics

continued

Commitment or Hype?

Officials at Wal-Mart and Kmart contend they're deeply committed to selling environmentally safe products and that their ads aren't simply marketing hype. The new environmental program "will do little for us from a marketing standpoint," contends David Glass, Wal-Mart's chief executive officer.

Others disagree. Because Wal-Mart was the first big chain to announce such a program, marketing experts expect it to benefit most from the good vibes the ads give shoppers.

Wal-Mart is attaching tags on shelves to flag products using recycled paperboard or fibers, or products where the manufacturer has eliminated chlorofluorocarbons or reduced solid waste. The company is also considering making its store parking lots into recycling collection points.

But neither Wal-Mart nor Kmart have plans to stop selling any products that are environmental culprits, such as disposable diapers. And a Kmart spokesman acknowledges that questions remain about what types of products are environmentally safe. At this point, he says, "I don't think there are a lot of answers."

Should retailers sell environmentally hostile products, even if consumers demand them?

Source: Portions reproduced with permission from Francine Schwadel, "Retailers Latch on to the Environment," *The Wall Street Journal*, November 13, 1989, p. B1.

Technological Changes. Technology will be even more of a driver of retail success than it was in the 1980s.[7] Technological breakthroughs will be the centerpiece of new marketing strategies and new organizational paradigms. Advances in the application of artificial intelligence to retailing problems are likely to occur; smaller, faster, and cheaper information processing will improve the level of decision making for even the smallest independent retailer.

Continuing technological advances will also make relationship retailing an even stronger core element of competitive strategy. Technology will allow targeting of individual customers at the store level and the development of strategies to maintain strong customer relationships over time.

The Decline of the Shopping Mall. America's love affair with shopping as a form of recreation is collapsing in the 1990s. Fewer free-standing shopping centers will be built. The new facilities are likely to be multiuse complexes that combine living, entertainment, and shopping facilities.[8]

Retail Innovation. Retail innovation will occur at a slower pace during the 1990s than during the 1980s. Less risk capital will be available for implementing new retailing concepts. Rollouts of new concepts will have to occur nationally from the beginning to avoid being copied by competitors.

A Profile in Excellence

ANITA RODDICK

Anita Roddick founded The Body Shop in 1976 at age 33. A former flower child, Roddick always enjoyed being on stage. She was a ham in her mother's pub in England. After college, she pursued several careers, including teaching. She subsequently ran a hotel and then a restaurant. When her husband decided to ride horseback across South America, she was faced with the need to support herself and their children. She thus decided to open a shop to sell her handmade animal-fat–free cosmetics. Her pragmatism drove her to implement the principles that have made The Body Shop such a success today. For example, she only had 600 bottles for her potions and she wanted people to return them. She thus made recycling a cornerstone of the business. Green, a powerful political color, was the only one that would cover the damp patches on the wall in the first store. Anita Roddick had hit a gold mine with her idea that people would buy natural products in small refillable bottles.

By the time her husband returned from South America, she was opening her third store. She had made the decision to open the store before getting word from her husband in South America not to do the deal. Her early partner lent Roddick the funds to open the second store in return for half the company's stock. Today, he owns half of The Body Shop's stock, worth $300 million.

Roddick states that she loathes the cosmetic industries because they are "a pack of lies." She does no advertising, and instead depends on the company's support of social issues to generate publicity. The causes range from saving the whales to the rainforests. The so-called natural cosmetics market she created now controls about 4 percent of the U.S. cosmetics market. The market is growing at a rate about three times as fast as that of the industry as a whole. She says that her business is about two things: "Social change and action, and skin care." She notes that social change and action come first. The Body Shop has become a worldwide phenomenon.

Source: Laura Zinn, "Whales, Human Rights, Rainforest—and the Heady Smell of Profits," *Business Week*, July 15, 1991, pp. 114–16; Jean Sherman Chatzky, "Changing the World," *Forbes*, pp. 83–85; Alan Sloan, "The Selling of the Simple Life," *Worth*, pp. 80, 82, and 84.

Venture capital is more likely to be attracted to Eastern Europe and Latin America because of the stronger growth potential.

The Age of Design. The 1990s have been described as "the decade of design–style, finesse, a refined look."[9] Retailers positioning with superior design as reflected in decor, approach, private labels, and unique products will reap great rewards during the 1990s. Consumers will assume that all retailers offer quality. Style, however, will provide them with an opportunity for lifestyle expressiveness. One special growth area will be in men's apparel.

Home Shopping. Home shopping sales exceeded $90 billion in 1992, an increase of 60 percent from 1980.[10] TV shopping, nonexistent even a decade ago, has passed the $2.5 billion mark.[11] Linking fiber-optic technology with the computer and video technology in this decade will make electronic home shopping relatively commonplace by the 21st century.

Consumer Use of Credit. Less consumer spending and more savings mean that consumers will use credit less often during this decade. This will negatively affect retailing. In addition, modest income growth during the decade will hold down the use of credit and will further serve as a continuing drag on retail spending.

Government Policies. Government policies in recent years have restrained economic growth and will likely continue to do so for the next several years. Prior to the mid 1980s, consumer spending was fueled by a tax structure that made it attractive to hold debt and less attractive to act as a thrifty shopper. Mortgage interest deductibility encouraged people to buy homes, as did the deductibility of consumer interest payments for other big-ticket purchases. Government foreign exchange policies, credit policies, and tax policies since the mid-1980s, designed to lower the trade deficit, have reduced consumer spending in a relative sense. The policies are likely to remain in place until the United States begins to sustain a trade surplus.

The large number of tax increases since the mid-1980s has further hindered consumer spending. Social security payments have increased to the point that, for some households, they exceed personal income taxes. Excise taxes on such items as luxury goods and alcohol have continued to increase, as have taxes at the state and local levels.[12]

Capital Availability. The "go-go" financing years of the 1980s are a thing of the past. Much of the retailing growth in the 1980s was fueled by junk bonds. The junk bond market died, however, when Congress forced the S&Ls in the late 1980s to get rid of their junk bond portfolios. This decision in turn led to the collapse of many thrift institutions and caused the banks to tighten their lending standards. Retailers are now in an era of fiscal conservatism. Mergers and acquisitions are also likely to decline because of the reduced opportunities for creative financing.

Retail Profitability. The retail profit picture, not unexpectedly, will remain dismal, at least through mid-decade. Retail margins have continued to erode since the late 1980s but are now stabilizing. Productivity increases will primarily occur by reducing the total amount of square footage available for retailing. Retailing remains severely overstored. The gross leasable area built by retailers increased by 50 percent during the 1980s. Development often occurred without long-term concerns in mind, and was often driven by limited partnerships as tax shelters rather than by investments that made economic sense.

RETAIL SECTOR GROWTH FOR THE 1990s

The previously discussed scenarios paint a less than optimistic picture for retailing in this decade by industry sector. Exceptions do exist, however. We will briefly review the primary sectors to provide insights into emerging trends.

Supermarkets.[13] Supermarkets will face continuing challenges from formats such as membership warehouse clubs, which offer aggressive price competition. The conventional supermarket industry, however, is responding with savvy by modifying its merchandise mix to improve profit margins and developing portfolios of store types. In essence, conventional supermarkets are positioning themselves as a high-value, one-stop shopping alternative by adding departments and services that encourage cross-category shopping. They are also attracting an additional share of the consumer dollar in higher-margin areas such as cosmetics, flowers, and prepared foods.

The addition of nonfood offerings will come at the expense of the core food offering. Supermarkets will also add such services as grocery delivery (see Case 1 at the end of the chapter), in-store banking, and health screening as a way of increasing their one-stop shopping convenience.

Supermarkets will remain vulnerable to the intrusion of competitors such as discount department stores and deep discount drugstores. Food already accounts for about a third of the sales of membership warehouse clubs.[14] The clubs are also experimenting with perishable food and service departments such as bakeries and delis.

Deep discount drugstores will be primary competition for supermarkets in the sale of over-the-counter drugs and health and beauty aids. These stores have also started to add food products and general merchandise. The combination food and discount store is another threat. Examples include the Wal-Mart Super Center and Kmart Super Center discount and food combination store.

Technological advances will be a primary weapon in the supermarket arsenal. Priority will be placed on establishing automatic product replenishment systems and on automating distribution centers as a way of increasing productivity. These technologies will also allow the decentralization of decision making and better gross margin management. Increased use of informational kiosks, automated checkout systems (Exhibit 22–1), and the expansion of nonstore ways of reaching consumers, such as home shopping via personal computer, are likely. Other technology-driven changes will include greater use of computerized aisle signs, electronic coupon disposal systems, shopping cart–mounted LDC screens, and point-of-sale video checkout systems. Supermarkets will also implement frequent shopper programs as a way of establishing a database that allows management to communicate with individual shoppers and to implement relationship marketing programs.

Discount Department Stores. Wal-Mart, Kmart, and Target have replaced Sears and Montgomery Ward as the mass market leaders. Mass merchandisers experienced major consolidation during the 1980s as a result of mergers and acquisitions, bankruptcies, and unending competition. The top 10 discount department store retailers control more than 85

EXHIBIT 22–1

Courtesy Uniquest

Tests of automated checkout systems are underway in the effort to reduce store-level personnel costs.

percent of industry sales. The "big three" account for nearly three-fourths of the industry volume.[15]

Wal-Mart is the low-cost leader in the industry, but will have to invest heavily to maintain and upgrade store decor and shopping ambience. Target is the leading upscale discounter. The primary question for the 1990s is whether a sufficient market exists for upscale discounters to continue their rapid growth. Kmart is caught in the middle between the low-end Wal-Mart and high-end Target. Kmart management has focused its efforts on diversification into specialty mass market concepts and less on its core full-time discount store business.

A host of new formats is also emerging. Fierce competition is emerging from food and drug combo stores, deep discount drugstores, and membership warehouse clubs. Category killers such as Toys 'R' Us will provide difficult challenges in areas such as sporting goods and toys.

Off-price retailers will also be a source of competition in branded soft goods, and specialty apparel chains offering strong price-to-value relationships will emerge as a competitive challenge. Unknowns in the equation are the extent to which the efforts of Sears and Wards to reposition their firms as promotional mass merchandisers will succeed.

Consolidation and shakeout will continue. Well-known names of the 1980s that disappeared include Gold Circle, Yellow Front Stores, Ames, Hecks, and GeeBee.

Department Stores. Conventional department stores lost market share to discount and off-price stores during the 1980s. Ten department stores control more than 78 percent of industry sales. The leader is J. C. Penney, followed distantly by May Company, R. H. Macy, Dayton Hudson, and Federated.

Dramatic changes in department store ownership occurred during the 1980s, but the scenario has now played out, with few exceptions. May Company merged with Associated Dry Goods, Macy's entered a leveraged buyout, and Dillard's continued the acquisition route and fueled its growth by purchasing, among others, Ivey's. Dayton Hudson similarly acquired Marshall Field's as a growth vehicle. The remaining uncertainties to be resolved include whether Macy's can return to its former financial strength, the success of Carter Hawley Hale in emerging from Chapter 11, and the resolution of the Federated/Allied reorganization.

The strengths of the department stores will continue to be their traditional established presence in major metropolitan areas and a high share of spending in their core merchandise categories. Not to be overlooked is their large credit card base, which provides opportunities for strengthened relationship retailing.[16]

The aging of the population will favor the department stores because of their traditional strengths with middle-aged consumers. However, the tendency of this age group toward increased savings and reduced spending will dampen the advantage somewhat. Customer service, overall, must be strengthened if department stores are to remain a first-choice destination with the middle-aged market.

Technological advances will also be a key to department store productivity increases. Database marketing, communication networks, and quick response systems all need to be enhanced to accelerate merchandise flow, inventory turnover, and strengthened vendor relations. Progress in EDI will help move goods more quickly between the manufacturer and the retailer. Point-of-sale systems will also enable the stores to downsize or eliminate unprofitable departments.

Primary department store competition will come from specialty apparel stores such as The Limited that offer differentiated assortments. Discount department stores will also have access to vendors who previously restricted their merchandise offerings to the department stores. Finally, off-price retailers will continue to upgrade stores and add services, and mass merchandisers such as Wal-Mart and Kmart will make inroads into the home goods market.

Drugstores. Conventional drugstores have the advantage of offering a core destination product—prescription drugs. One might think that the industry would thus continue to grow because of the aging of the population and their need for additional medication. However, traditional drugstores will actually continue to lose market share to grocery stores and discount stores in both prescription and OTC (over-the-counter) drugs. Supermarkets and discount stores offer not only drugs but also other consumables such as photo products, tobacco, greeting cards, and health and beauty aids at better prices than drugstores.

Conventional drugstores are no longer first-choice stores for their core merchandise, except for prescriptions. Even for prescriptions, market share has fallen. In 1990, 57 percent of consumers said they purchased prescription drugs primarily at conventional drugstores, down from 69 percent in 1988. Likewise, in 1990, only 38 percent purchased OTC drugs at conventional drugstores, compared to 51 percent in 1988.[17]

Food and drug combinations, discount stores, superstores, and deep discount drugstores will continue to grow during the 1990s. Such competitors offer one-stop shopping convenience and better pricing. Supermarkets, likewise, will continue to take market share away in such areas as tobacco and alcohol.

Deep discount drugstores have achieved greater consumer cross-shopping for nonprescription merchandise categories than the conventional drugstores. The most successful include Drug Emporium and F & M distributors. The increasing tendency for prescriptions to be covered by third-party payment plans such as Blue Cross/Blue Shield further threatens the margins of the conventional drugstore, although it works to the advantage of the deep discount firms.

In the 1990s keys to success for the conventional drugstores include better use of systems technology, more emphasis on customer service, and targeted merchandise in becoming the outlet of choice for key nonprescription merchandise categories. The firms must also be especially vigilant in developing the technology to profitably process third-party payments.

Specialty Apparel Retailing. Specialty apparel retailing historically has been a highly fragmented industry, although some consolidation did occur during the 1980s. Currently, the top 10 players account for only slightly more than 17 percent of industry sales volume.[18] Leaders for the 1990s include The Limited, Gap stores, and Merry-Go-Round Enterprises. Each firm offers a portfolio of outlets that will remain attractive to consumers.

Specialty apparel retailing growth was fueled during the 1980s by the growth of the women's and children's market segments, the explosion in the number of baby boomers, and increasing numbers of working women. The market fragmented into various consumer groups based on demographics, shopping patterns, and fashion preferences.

The men's apparel market experienced little real growth in the 1980s. The 1990s, however, will see increased emphasis on the male market as reflected in The Limited's Structure (Exhibit 22–2) and Attivo, part of the Merry-Go-Round portfolio. These innovators will lead the way in segmenting

EXHIBIT 22–2

Courtesy The Limited, Inc.

Structure is part of The Limited's diversification strategy through its Express division.

the men's clothing market on the basis of fashion position as opposed to price.

Winners in the 1990s will be the retailers who can quickly test new fashion ideas and adjust production based on demand. Private labels will continue to increase in popularity as a way to protect margins.

Hard Goods Retailers. Hard goods retailers will face difficult times during the 1990s. Furniture and home furnishings are examples of industry segments characterized by maturity and stale marketing concepts. There are some exceptions, as reflected in the success of retailers such as Pier One Imports, the Bombay Company, and Williams-Sonoma (Exhibit 22–3). These retailers have succeeded by developing a focused marketing strategy, superior execution, and a targeted market niche.

Furniture retailers are plagued by their lack of effectiveness in distribution. Consumers don't like the delays between placement of an order and receipt of the merchandise. Many manufacturers and retailers continue to promote furniture as a lifetime investment, which has served to curtail demand, as opposed to enticing consumers with exciting and compelling offerings, thereby encouraging them to change their home environment.

EXHIBIT 22–3

Courtesy Williams-Sonoma, Photo by Richard Gross

Williams-Sonoma has successfully made the transition from a catalog-only company to one with several store concepts.

IKEA and similar stores offering excellent price-to-value relationships in ready-to-assemble furniture are an exception to this trend and have experienced considerable success.

Electronics retailers, in contrast to furniture merchants, experienced explosive growth during the 1980s as a result of the development of category killer outlets such as Circuit City and Best Buy. Growth was further stimulated by the introduction of new products such as VCRs, cellular telephones, telephone answering machines, and CD players. Few such breakthrough products are forecasted for the 1990s. In addition, baby boomers are likely to be more conservative in their spending patterns, and household formation will slow. These factors all contribute to forecasts of modest growth for electronics retailing during this decade. Some shakeout is likely to occur. Currently, the top 10 companies generate only 25 percent of industry volume.[19]

Recreational goods retailers will continue to experience strong growth in this decade, led primarily by the growth of sporting goods superstores such as Sport Mart and Kmart's Sports Authority. A shakeout is likely to occur among the smaller, less well-financed sporting goods chains and the independent mom-and-pop outlets.

Finally, toy retailing merchants will struggle during the 1990s. Toys 'R' Us will continue to dominate and already accounts for one-third of overall toy industry sales volume. Independent operators are having some success by offering merchandise not available in the superstores, a higher level of personalized service, and hometown "boosterism."

Home Improvement Retailing. Home improvement retailing suffered during the 1980s because of the recession, fewer housing starts, and a slowdown in do-it-yourself remodeling work. The outlook is somewhat better for the 1990s. Economic recovery will release considerable pent-up demand. Baby boomers, now settling down, are also likely to increase spending on home decor and fix-up products.

The home improvement industry remains highly fragmented. Independent chains represent almost 94 percent of industry sales.[20]

The primary growth sector is the warehouse home center concept, pioneered by Home Depot. Warehouse home centers take advantage of economies of scale to offer lower prices than traditional stores, and they also provide an exciting shopping experience, excellent service, and wide product selection. The outlets buy directly from the manufacturer and are heavily technology driven through advances in bar coding and scanning.

Smaller chains and independent retailers will continue to find opportunities for growth. Home improvement warehouse centers, for example, sell mass market merchandise. Niche market opportunities exist for retailers offering upscale merchandise. The economies of scale required for home improvement warehouse centers are such that they cannot operate in many small and mid-sized markets. Such markets will continue to provide strong market opportunities for the independents and regional chains.

Convenience Stores. Traditional convenience stores such as 7-Eleven and Circle K will continue to struggle during this decade. They need to establish a clear market strategy, overcome their dated image, and recover from the burdens of debt and bankruptcy filings.[21] The outlets are seeking to recover their market strength by branded partnerships such as 7-Eleven's partnership with Dunkin' Donuts. They are also adding other services such as fax machines, car washes, and automated teller machines to appeal to time-pressed consumers. Experiments are also underway with unattended automated fill-ups.

Gasoline convenience stores (G-stores) are emerging as growth vehicles, as are 24-hour supermarkets. Major oil companies will continue to accel-

EXHIBIT 22–4

THE RISING STARS OF RETAILING

Courtesy Liz Claiborne Inc.

Jay Margolis, vice chairman, Liz Claiborne Inc.

Courtesy The Limited, Inc.

Grace Nichols, president, Victoria's Secret

© Pete Yates/Saba

George Mrkonic, executive vice president, Kmart Specialty Stores

Courtesy Donna Karan Co.

Donna Karan, founder, Donna Karan, Co.

erate nationwide conversions of their gasoline stations to gasoline convenience stores and will take market share away from the traditional convenience store.

Environmental uncertainties make it difficult to establish the overall strength of this industry sector during the 1990s. The likelihood of a federal requirement for underground storage tank population liability insurance could affect their competitive cost structure. Bans on G-stores' selling beer would also have a negative effect, as would legislation designed to protect clerks working in such environments. Recycling and depository laws generally could add a cost burden to these outlets.

THE 1990s EXECUTIVE

Clearly the day of the merchant prince (such as Ira Neimerk, CEO of Bergdorf Goodman, and Marvin S. Traub, retired chairman of Bloomingdale's) is over. As *BusinessWeek* noted, "with their departures, an old way of life is ending—the days when a great merchant saw his store as theater and stocked it with sumptuously presented goods. For these merchant princes, selection of merchandise for their emporiums was paramount. . . . The man with flare for the wares ruled the stores. The old guard were style pickers, not number crunchers."[22]

A new generation of executives is reinventing the industry (see Exhibit 22–4). Some are computer whizzes, others are financial whizzes, and many are women. Above all, the rising group of stars understands the importance of marketing. George MrKonic, Jr., for example, developed membership programs by creating lists of bargain shoppers, sports enthusiasts, and others. He makes use of sophisticated computers and excels in relationship marketing. Donna Karan became successful by designing clothes for comfort. She understands that women today don't buy clothes just because they have a designer's label.

The new executive knows that shoppers won't come to the stores unless they have a reason to do so. Modern merchants extensively test merchandise and retail formats and often use consumer focus groups to identify their strengths and weaknesses as well as those of competitors. A consumer focus and a marketing orientation is occurring even in high fashion, an area that has long ignored the basic premises of marketing.

RETAIL STRATEGIES FOR THE 1990s[23]

We will review strategies for enhancing retail productivity in the 1990s. Companies must focus on six major areas to achieve lasting competitive advantage.

Advanced Merchandising Systems. POS systems have become as basic to successful retailing as cash registers were in the 1920s. Competition has shifted to the development of item-driven information systems in which profitability, inventory status, and rate of sales are known for each stockkeeping unit in the chain.

Competitive Information and Research. Marketing research is not yet a universally accepted tool, even among major retailers. But companies that systematically study the market through consumer research are discovering gems of competitive information (such as unmet needs in terms of style, price point, and size) that can be quickly translated into incremental sales.

Vendor Communication Systems. Leading retailers are electronically transmitting purchase orders, invoices, and advance shipping notices to make buying and allocation decisions much later in the buying cycle and to improve in-stock position as well as inventory turns.

Value-Added Partnerships. Leading retailers are also working closely with key vendors to create a system of virtual integration modeled on the concepts of just-in-time inventory management developed in Japan's manufacturing sector.

Human Resource Programs. Organizational development is perhaps the most elusive of the six goals. A few retailers, such as Wal-Mart and Nordstrom, have achieved levels of employee satisfaction and motivation that are the envy of the retail industry. In a labor market where hourly rates are rising and the traditional retail labor market (18- to 25-year-olds) is shrinking, this is the ultimate competitive weapon.

Customer Service Programs. Retailers that can establish a sense of loyalty in their customers will win big. A lot of customer service is still focused on the basics of merchandising. In contrast, marketing entails positioning the entire retail business, creating a compelling image and rationale, and providing enough uniqueness and value to make the company a top choice, a distinctive retailer.[24]

Although it is vital to survival, improved productivity is not enough. Investors have set some demanding financial targets for retailers to meet. The winners in today's market will be alert to opportunities created by restructuring rather than conducting business as usual.

Perhaps the most powerful change a company can make is to give its employees and key executives meaningful rewards based on performance. The market focuses on cash flow; senior executives should be paid based on their ability to meet or exceed annual cash flow targets. Performance compensation at the supervisory level can also be a potent force for innovation if properly applied.

Obviously, the need for public companies to address these issues is particularly urgent. But for private companies, these initiatives will enhance overall value and increase the chances that a company will be ready when the "big boys" come to town.

CHARACTERISTICS OF HIGH-PERFORMANCE RETAILERS

In summary, successful retailers in the future will share several common characteristics, as discussed in the following sections.

Attention to Detail. Winners not only do the right big things, but also the right little things.

Constant Communication with Customers and Employees. Getting close to the customer is more than just a tired expression. Understanding and responding to customer needs requires close, continuing contact, as exemplified by some of the superior retailers we have discussed.

Market Drive. Retailers such as Wal-Mart will continue to be preoccupied with offering strong price-to-value relationships. Such firms will continue to offer greater value, fashion, and convenience, which will induce customers to spend less time and money at competing outlets.

Strategic Planning. Successful retailers, as we have seen throughout the text, are the ones who are committed to a clearly defined purpose and mission that indicate what they want to be and where they want to go.

Technological Leadership. Retailers will continue to accelerate their moves to an integrated management information system that will link outlying retail outlets and distribution centers with the headquarter's buying and financial functions.

More Micro-Marketing. The post–World War II mass market has shattered into a million pieces. Retailers will increasingly target messages specifically at Hispanics, blacks, and the elderly. They will continue to experiment with new ways to find out just who it is they want to reach, and they will move beyond the use of demographics and psychographics in identifying customers.

Checkout scanner data are feeding the move to micromarketing by providing the types of detailed data requested by retailers. Retailers are no longer passive players, and they are dictating how little or how much space they will give products and will continue to demand a growing list of fees and discounts and more of a partnership role with manufacturers in planning product offerings.

Manufacturing will continue to tailor their market plans to the needs of individual retailers. They will eliminate separate sales efforts at each division in favor of teams who handle broad based top retail accounts.

Listening, planning, and technology will be the key priority words for success in the foreseeable future.

FUTURE CERTAINTIES

Regardless of the changes that are occurring, we can safely make the following assumptions about the future:

- Retailing will continue to grow in importance as a way of facilitating exchange.
- Retailing, to be successful, must continue to anticipate and respond to changes in the environment.
- Retailing will continue to offer exciting, rewarding, and diverse career opportunities. Job opportunities will continue to abound in promotion, personal selling, distribution, research, and various other dimensions of retailing, including competitor analysis, sales management, and corporate training.

Wouldn't you like to be a part of the phenomenal success of firms such as The Limited, Benneton, or The Gap? Or maybe you want to be on the team helping to rewrite competition, as Wal-Mart is doing, or part of a supermarket team working to develop a store of the future, or to help make McDonald's more of a world competitor. Whatever your interests and career aspirations, retailing can play a vital role in your success. We urge you to get on board! You can begin by discussing the specifics of career options with your instructor and by investigating other marketing or retailing courses at your university. Good luck!

CHAPTER HIGHLIGHTS

- Retailing was dominated by a "field of dreams" philosophy during the 1980s. This philosophy has changed during the 1990s as a result of competitive intensity resulting from saturated markets, excessive retail space, and constrained consumer spending.
- World markets are being redefined during the 1990s. Eastern Europe and Latin America are emerging as promising hot spots over the next decade, as is the Far East, especially Japan.
- America's political influence will decline in this decade, although its cultural influence will increase in importance.
- Economic growth will be modest. Inflation will remain under control and interest rates are likely to remain low by historical trends. Income will become more concentrated in the top 1 or 2 percent of the population. The number of low-income consumers will increase.
- The 45- to 49-year-old age group will be the fastest-growing age group. The number of 20- to 29-year-olds will decline in this decade, as will the number of shoppers aged 60 to 69.
- The consumer mood will be more conservative than during the 1980s and will reflect interest in higher moral values, environmental preservation, and truth in advertising.
- Government policies will continue to restrain economic growth as a way of reducing the trade deficit. Retail profitability will be low and capital will be scarce.
- The focus of management will continue to shift from merchandising to marketing as a key to strategy development.
- More and more firms are looking to the long term in developing a strategic view of the business and are focusing on such issues as store positioning, changing consumer lifestyles, and unique competitive strategies.

- Changes in the external environments are also affecting strategy. Key shifts include consumers' greater price awareness and decreasing store or brand loyalty, accelerating technology shifts, growth of the upscale market, time pressures on consumers, slow growth in many market segments, continued overstoring, and growth in small and medium-sized markets.
- Retailers are responding to the changing environments in a variety of ways. The key trends include niching by specialty stores, continued strong success of commodity retailing in selected categories such as food, a strong return to private labels, and continued growth of power retailing.
- A new generation of retail executives is reinventing the industry. These individuals tend to be computer or financial whizzes, and many are women. All of them understand the importance of marketing in retail success.

Study Questions

1. What does it mean to say that retail management is shifting its emphasis from a merchandising to a marketing orientation?
2. Summarize the major changes that the industry projects for the 1990s in retailing competition.
3. Highlight the major competitive strategies emerging among successful retailers in the 1990s.
4. Why do today's winners appear to be such format types as warehouse clubs, deep discount merchants, and category killers?
5. Is it possible for a small, independent merchant to continue to thrive in the environments of the 1990s? If so, what must he or she do to remain viable?
6. Why is the United States forecasted to become less of a formidable political influence in this decade but to have a continuing pervasive cultural influence?
7. What factors are causing service to be a primary ingredient in store choice for more and more consumers?
8. How have government policies influenced retail growth during the past several years?
9. Highlight the role of technology in retailing strategies during this decade.
10. Describe the primary value shifts occurring in this decade and discuss their implications for retailing.

A P P L I C A T I O N S

CASE 1: Groceries by Phone

Delchamps has taken a step back in time in an effort to attract the modern shopper.

The supermarket chain, based in Mobile, Alabama, unveiled plans for a grocery home delivery service. The service is designed to appeal to the elderly, the handicapped, single parents, and two-income families too busy to grocery shop.

In announcing the service, Delchamps president Randy Delchamps noted that his company offered home delivery when it started in the 1920s. Most grocers then provided this service. The practice faded by the 1960s as supermarkets, fed by a more mobile society, replaced the neighborhood grocery store.

"We have always been at the forefront of convenience and we are now adding a service that will offer even more convenience to our customers," said Delchamps, who also is the company's chairperson and chief executive officer.

"With it, we bring service back to another dimension from where we came. Where we once had home delivery, we now have it again," he said.

Shoppers using the new service can either phone or fax their grocery order to a toll-free number in Nashville. Operators there will enter the order on a computer and then fax the order to designated Delchamps stores. Free catalogs listing the products available can be picked up at the stores.

Employees trained as shoppers will then fill the orders, which will be delivered in the afternoon and early evening. Delivery vans will be equipped with special coolers for carrying frozen foods and perishables.

There will be a $9.95 service charge for home delivery and a $5.95 service charge for orders that are picked up at the store.

Aiding Delchamps in the venture is Shoppers Express, a Bethesda, Maryland, company that processes the orders.

Dick Kernan, Shoppers Express CEO, said that his company operates similar firms in 38 markets in 24 states. In addition to offering the grocery delivery service, Shoppers Express also has a similar service for some pharmacies and florists in other states, he said.

Although most might think the service would appeal mostly to the elderly and the handicapped, Kernan said that only about 30 to 35 percent of the shoppers are in those categories. "The preponderance of those using this service are the two-spouse-working family who are too busy for grocery shopping," he said.

Delchamps conceded that the service might end impulse buying. But he said that the service is designed to serve a particular type of shopper, which at least for the time being will be a niche customer for Delchamps.

Source: Portions reproduced with permission from Patrick Rupinski, "Delchamps to Bring It Home," *The Birmingham Post-Herald,* June 16, 1992, p. C5.

Applying Retailing Principles

1. What are the strengths and weaknesses of the grocery delivery concept?
2. What things would you suggest to improve this concept?
3. Are experiments like this one likely to increase in the 1990s? Why or why not? What do you see as the probabilities of success for this initiative?

CASE 2: Consumers Seek Escape from Captive-Ad Gimmicks

Clad in black Spandex, Ina Donath prepares for a Stairmaster workout at one of Manhattan's priciest gyms, the Vertical Club. But something is bothering her.

"It's an invasion of our privacy," the clothing saleswoman fumes. "It's dangerous. It's annoying."

Donath is mad as hell about the banks of television sets, all tuned loudly to Health Club Television Network Inc., flickering from every direction. Similar TV programs, all with a heavy commercial load, have invaded doctors' waiting rooms, supermarkets, airport lounges—anywhere consumers are held captive.

"People are going to become more and more violent in their reactions and in terms of trying to avoid [captive-advertising gimmicks]," predicts Eugene Secunda, an assistant professor of marketing at Baruch College in New York. He expects a trickle-down effect as the complaints of the wealthiest and most educated consumers become more widespread.

Turner Broadcasting System is testing the Airport Channel, with news and commercials, in major airport terminals. Turner also is a partner with Heritage Media Corporation's Act-Media unit in The Checkout Channel, a supermarket checkout TV venture. Lesser known companies are quickly following. Most include a staggering commercial load, often as much as 30 percent of total air time.

"They're coming out of the woodwork. Everyone is jumping onto the bandwagon," says Robert Giacomino, a Grey Advertising senior vice-president. He is bracing for more consumer backlash both because there has been little so far and because so many companies, not all of them reputable, are clawing for their own piece of the captive-advertising pie.

So offensive has health club and waiting room TV become that the ad industry itself has unofficially dubbed it "in-your-face" advertising. Says Giacomino, "One of the big concerns we have is [that] none of these [out-of-home] media vehicles were put up at the request of consumers. Is there a consumer need for it?" That and other questions "haven't been satisfactorily answered," he says.

Joseph Schwartz, Health Club Television's executive vice president, dismisses the group as a bunch of rich malcontents. The club's unusually wealthy profile, he adds, makes it "atypical" of most health-club audiences.

But if Schwartz isn't concerned, some of Health Club Television's advertisers are. "Obviously, we aren't reaching someone if they're annoyed by the message," says a spokeswoman for Dannon of White Plains, New York, which advertises its light yogurt on Health Club Television. She says that the petition will "definitely" be a factor as Dannon decides whether to move beyond the current test run.

At Campbell's Soup Co., Paul Mulcahy, vice-president of marketing services, adds that the brouhaha made the health club test "unreadable" and says that the company must now "regroup."

Source: Portions reproduced with permission from Joanne Lipman, *The Wall Street Journal*, September 3, 1991, p. B1.

Applying Retailing Principles

1. Speculate on whether the Vertical Club controversy is a reflection of wider consumer frustrations over the privacy issue that are likely to be evident during this decade.
2. Should retailers install captive-ad television as a way of enhancing revenue even if the move irritates some consumers?
3. Should consumer views be sought before retailers offer captive-ad programming? What would probably be the retailer's decision process if captive-ad programming was, instead, a proposed new product line?

Notes

1. "From Chaos to Consolidation: Retailing in the 1990s," *Chain Store Age Executive,* August 1991, pp. 11A and 12A; Ina Kalish, "After the Dust Settles: Retailing in the 1990s," *Chain Store Age Executive,* August 1992, pp. 10A–12A.
2. *Retailing 2000* (Dublin, Ohio: Management Horizons, 1990), p. 5.
3. Kathleen M. O'Conner, "Bridging Demographic and Retail Realities," *Shopping Center World,* May 1991, pp. 48 and 50.
4. Jack Eure, "Toward the New Century in Retailing: Survival Strategies for an Industry in Turmoil," *Business Forum,* Fall 1991, pp. 24–28.
5. Eure, "Toward the New Century in Retailing;" "Environmental Audits: The Gold Mind in Green," *Retail Control,* January 1992, pp. 17–20; Randolph B. Smith, "Rush to Endorse 'Environmental' Goods Sparks Worry about Shopper Confusion," *The Wall Street Journal,* April 16, 1990, p. B1; Alison Fahey and Laurie Freeman, "Retailers Adding Touches of Green," *Advertising Age,* December 10, 1990, p. 58; Penny Gill, "Who Supports the Earth. . . ," *Stores,* October 1990, pp. 60–71; Emily Denitto, "Meijer Breaks Storewide 'Earth Friendly' Program," *Supermarket News,* November 6, 1989, p. 1.
6. *Retailing 2000,* p. 8.
7. Robert Zimmerman, "Technology in the Year 2000," *Discount Merchandiser,* May 1991, pp. 76–80.
8. "Retailing: Who Will Survive?" *BusinessWeek,* November 26, 1990, pp. 134–37; "Dark Days in the Shopping Malls," *U.S. News and World Report,* February 10, 1992, p. 14.
9. Fulton MacDonald, "Shake, Rattle, and Roll: The Coming Retail Revolution," *Retail Control,* April/May 1992, p. 21; David P.

Schulz, "Top 100 Retailers," *Stores,* July 1992, pp. 33–38.

10. MacDonald, "Shake, Rattle, and Roll," p. 23.
11. MacDonald, "Shake, Rattle, and Roll," p. 23.
12. Bill Saporito, "Retailing's Winners and Losers," *Fortune,* December 18, 1989, p. 69.
13. Based on Lois A. Huff, "Supermarkets: Prey or Predator?" *Chain Store Age Executive,* August 1991, pp. 16A–18A; Sandra J. Skrovan, "Some Supermarkets Succeed by Wide Margins," *Chain Store Age Executive,* August 1992, pp. 16A–18A.
14. "Supermarkets: Prey or Predator?"
15. Cathy Dybodahl, "The Discount Department Store Industry: The New 'Big Three,'" *Chain Store Age Executive,* August 1991, p. 19A; Margaret Gilliam, "The Future of the Discount Industry," *Chain Store Age Executive,* May 1991, pp. 46–50 and 82; Kimberly D. Hendrix, "Discount Stores Fared Well in the Recession," *Chain Store Age Executive,* August 1992, pp. 19A–22A.
16. Walter K. Levy, "Are Department Stores Doomed?" *Discount Merchandiser,* May 1991, pp. 56–60.
17. Jennifer J. Crites, "The Drugstore Industry: Losing Its Drawing Card," *Chain Store Age Executive,* August 1991, p. 25A; Trevor J. Kershner, "Drugstores Fight Back with Systems and Service," *Chain Store Age Executive,* August 1992, pp. 13A–15A.
18. Amanda Putnam, "Demographic Tailwinds Spur Growth of Specialty Apparel Retailing," *Chain Store Age Executive,* August 1991, p. 29A.
19. Mehul Patel, "Hard Lines Retailers: Wake Me Up When Its Over," *Chain Store Age Executive,* August 1991, p. 32A.
20. Kimberly D. Hendrix, "The 1990s: It's a Tough Time for Home Improvement Retailing," *Chain Store Age Executive,* August 1991, p. 36A.
21. Teresa D. Williams, "Gasoline Fuels Growth of Convenience Store Industry," *Chain Store Age Executive,* August 1991, pp. 37A–38A.
22. Laura Zinn, "The New Stars of Retailing," *BusinessWeek,* December 16, 1991, p. 120.
23. This section on retailing strategies for the 1990s is reproduced with permission from Thomas R. Rauh, "Strategies for the 1990s," *Discount Merchandiser,* July 1989, pp. 52–54. Copyright ©, all rights reserved. See also "Strategies for the New Century," *Chain Store Age Executive,* January 1990, pp. 27–29; John Byington, "Retailing in the 90s," *Discount Merchandiser,* May 1990, pp. 16 and 20; Laurel Cutler, "New Realities, New Challenges, New Millennium—What Lies Ahead?" *Retail Control,* September 1990, pp. 3–9.
24. Eure, "Toward the New Century in Retailing."

APPENDIX

Careers in Retailing

THIS APPENDIX:

Focuses your attention on career development.

Explores the dynamics of the retailing industry and the resulting effects on career choice.

Reviews the characteristics of retailing careers.

Stresses job skills needed to succeed in retailing.

Examines typical training programs and career progression existing in various retail organizations.

Offers tangible tips for career planning and progress.

RETAILING CAPSULE

THE WORLD OF RETAILING

Even though the retailing industry is the nation's second largest employer (manufacturing is first), college students' understanding of retailing is vague and their perception of retailing as a career option is likely to be poor. Students cite long hours and low pay as retailing's main drawbacks. Negatives notwithstanding, retail firms are recruiting more and more college graduates every year. Such companies as Wal-Mart, the May Company, J. C. Penney, Kmart, The Limited, The Gap, Home Depot, and Toys 'R' Us are paying more than ever to get aggressive, retail-minded men and women to sign up. Retailers want careerists who can meet the demands of long hours and demanding customers; people who can get fired up by the challenges of today's market-driven retail business; achievers who see store management or buying as the first step in a lifetime career of accomplishment and reward.

Over the years, the job of the buyer, the retailing function traditionally perceived as the most glamorous, received the major share of interest from college graduates. But, in fact, store management involves the best of two worlds: buying and selling. The person in store management interacts daily with the customer as well as with the merchandising staff.

Students considering retailing as a career possibility may wonder where the jobs are. Department stores, although highly visible, simply offer one source of entry-level opportunities. Retailing takes place in all kinds of operations—specialty stores, discount and off-price firms, food chains, resident buying offices, and national chains. Of course, manufacturers themselves need retail specialists—those who service retailers and those who may function at the retail level in "factory-owned" outlets. Direct selling should not be overlooked either. Opportunities exist in such firms as Mary Kay, Avon, and Amway. The vast and diverse field of service retailing (Pearle Vision, Taco Bell, and the Atlanta Braves) offers another fruitful avenue.

Skills gained in retailing are transferable to almost any field. Retailing can be a wonderful experience for anyone who enjoys buying and selling goods or services. If you get excited about "making your day"—seeing how well you did compared to the same day in the previous year—retailing can be a challenge. If you like to sit at a desk, retailing is not for you. A retail management trainee and potential manager or merchandiser is on the go all the time. Retailers travel, share experiences, meet interesting people, and enjoy immediate feedback on their efforts. If you are prepared to work hard and long, the payoffs can be very gratifying—and after paying your dues, the remuneration is excellent.

We know that not everyone who studies retail management is consciously interested in a career in the field. However, if you are curious about retailing opportunities, this appendix can help you discover what to expect after graduation. In addition, many students will find themselves in careers that interact directly or indirectly with retailing. It is certainly possible, even for those who don't recognize an immediate interest in the field, for this career appendix to spark an unconscious interest.

Students take this course at various stages of career development. The continuum that follows suggests the degrees of career development or orientation that you may be experiencing. You probably have friends in each phase. A "career-disoriented" student, perhaps less disoriented than unconcerned, may not have given any thought to the future. This apparently casual attitude may seem immature, and indeed may be so. Career development is, after all, part of total human development.

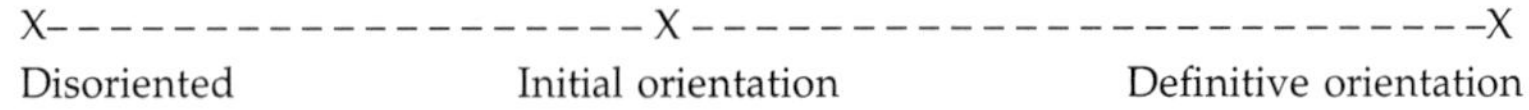

We encourage you to seek career counseling at all phases of your career development, especially when a concern about careers surfaces. If you are uncertain, do not despair. Get to work on helping yourself. Do not confuse "getting a job" with "career development." We suspect that a great deal of early attrition in first jobs results from both a desire to get a job simply to earn money and uncertainty about a career. A job without a career direction tends to prove unsuccessful in the long run. To assist you in finding the right direction for your career, this appendix offers generic career information and focuses on retailing as a career choice.

VIEWING CAREER CHOICES IN A DYNAMIC, EVOLVING INDUSTRY

The dynamic nature of the retail industry is documented throughout this text. However, you may be reading this appendix early in the retailing course, so reviewing certain dynamic changes taking place is appropriate in this discussion of careers. Such turbulence affects career decisions and, ultimately, career paths.

Perhaps the most dramatic phenomenon in retailing has been the merger, acquisition, and leveraged buyout (LBO) activity that has been with us for some time:

- Canadian developer Campeau's takeover of Federated and Allied Department Stores and its subsequent demise.
- Macy's LBO, followed by the sale of its midwest division to Dillard's and its purchase of the Federated divisions of I. Magnin and Bullock's specialty groups in California—leaving Macy's in an uncomfortable financial strain.
- May Company's acquisition of Associated Dry Goods.
- Australian development conglomerate Hooker's acquisition of Bonwit Teller and B. Altman in New York and a partnership in the LBO of Parisian of Alabama (a regional fashion departmentalized specialty store group). Subsequently, Bonwit Teller and B. Altman closed, Parisian management bought back its firm, and Hooker went bankrupt.

The immediate and potential effect that consolidations and divestments have on careers is dramatic. For example, a takeover, friendly or not, brings with it an inevitable displacement of executive-level personnel; corporate consolidations push many unwilling middle- and upper-level executives into the job market. Such disruptions are not unique to retailing. Virtually all industries are affected by the same kind of economic activity. Students need to be alert to such possibilities regardless of career choices. Perhaps the healthiest attitude is to be accepting of such eventualities and prepare for potentially disruptive circumstances, especially when joining a large corporation.

The consolidation phenomenon can have another effect. When two corporate cultures merge, difficulties may result. For basically similar cultures, the natural synergy can be appealing and beneficial to employees at all levels. Two opposing cultures, on the other hand, can be dysfunctional.

On the positive side, certain types of mergers, such as the partnership between a shopping center developer and an anchor tenant, can afford major career opportunities, particularly when the developer is growing. Exciting career opportunities open up, particularly in store line management, as growth takes place. Students would be wise to investigate the structure of organizations in such modes, as it will help predict future advancement opportunities.

Based on another kind of partnership is the cooperative effort of the Kmart-Bruno experiment. This was predicted to offer new career possibilities in the combination general merchandise and food outlets, which are based on the European model of mammoth hypermarkets. This experiment, however, was not successful. Bruno has withdrawn from the partnership and Kmart has dramatically downsized the concept. As a matter of fact, the hypermarket has not been particularly successful in the United States. Critics consider it to be yet another excess of the 1980s. Although some successes will be touted, the basic European model apparently is not acceptable to American lifestyles and shopping behavior. More career dynamics!

Career-oriented students should watch membership wholesale warehouse discounters (for instance, Sam's Wholesale Club, a division of Wal-Mart) whose growth seems ensured; the so-called upscale discounters (Target, a division of Dayton Hudson) that are expanding into new markets; and the diversification into specialty retailing by such corporations as Kmart, J. C. Penney, and Parisian. Each offers career path potential to alert students.

Traditional apparel chains, continuing to grow, offer career opportunities as never before. Many "new" specialists are moving up in size (Benetton and Laura Ashley, for example). Children's specialists have been offering more opportunities as they grow in number (Toys 'R' Us and Kids 'R' Us). Off-pricers, including factory outlets, continue to be a factor (Burlington Coat Factory). Companies addressing customers' desires for home improvement, decorating, and accessorizing (Home Depot and Crate & Barrel) are reported to be on a roll.

CHARACTERISTICS OF THE RETAILING CAREER

One of every eight Americans (approximately 19 million people) works in the nearly 1.3 million U.S. retail establishments with sales revenues of $1.8 trillion. Retail establishments can be found in the smallest rural village and the most sophisticated metropolitan area. The staggering diversity of opportunities can fulfill almost every kind of ability, ambition, and desire.

The dynamics of the retailing industry strongly affect careers. (More on industry dynamics can be found in Chapter 1.) This section reviews the major characteristics of careers that exist within the constantly changing environments and strategies of players in the retailing structure.

Job Security. Traditionally, even during periods of economic stagnation, retailing suffers fewer employment declines than manufacturing or wholesaling. Consumers must continue to buy merchandise regardless of the stage of the business cycle. However, in the wake of the merger and acquisition activity noted above, job security, especially at the middle- and upper-management levels, clearly is less certain than in the past.

Decentralized Job Opportunities. No matter where they live, people require goods and services on a regular basis to maintain their standards of living. This means that you can have a career in retailing even if you do not want to move frequently. On the other hand, people who want to move frequently can find employment opportunities in retailing wherever they go.

Opportunities for Advancement. Because of the large number of retail establishments in the United States, many executive positions exist. As retailing continues to expand, positions in buying and management are created on a basis proportionate to this expansion. But competition for such jobs is intense and performance standards are high.

Because sales and profits can be evaluated daily, retailing offers a daily performance measure. For high performers, such tangible measures are a delight; for the nonperformer, each day is painful. Obviously, not everyone is right for retailing (which, of course, can be said for all career options).

But those who are oriented to retailing can advance rapidly. A college graduate who is a high performer may become a buyer for a high–dollar volume department in a large department store organization within three to five years. As a buyer responsible for producing a profit in the department, such an achiever will really be acting as an entrepreneur within the security of an established firm.

Women in Retailing. Research has shown that the retail industry offers women good opportunities for advancement. Some 20 years ago, they were locked into advertising, publicity, fashion coordinating, or training. Since then, however, women have moved into all middle-management positions and beyond. Today, they hold top management positions in numbers that give evidence that rather dramatic changes have taken place.

Stores magazine conducted an informal survey among the top 25 specialty store chains and the top 25 department store divisions. In all organizations that responded, it was found that women hold the title of at least vice-president—and in most cases, of senior vice-president. In some firms a few have reached the rank of executive vice-president.[1]

Opportunities Opened by Advanced Degrees. Company practices regarding MBAs (or any advanced degree) can vary. Although a few retail companies recruit MBAs for executive training programs, most make no special efforts to recruit advanced degree holders and have no separate training programs for them. Such companies say that they seek top-quality talent, regardless of degrees held. However, the giant conglomerates in the retailing industry see advanced training in business as important for top management positions and especially for fast-track promotions.

The supermarket industry does less college recruiting than most other retailing sectors and has limited interest in MBAs. Instead it places a premium on product knowledge and job experience. Promotions typically are made from within the firm.

Financial Rewards. The opening paragraphs of this appendix indicated that retailers are willing to pay well for career-minded recruits. Those who achieve success in any area of retailing (such as buyers or managers) can expect to be rewarded accordingly. Starting salaries for college graduates entering retail training programs vary widely depending upon the type of retailing; the section of the country, cost of living, and competition for trainees; the experience of the applicant; and the particular company's philosophy. Entry-level salaries range from under $20,000 per year to over $30,000, a situation expected to continue through the early 1990s.

Chief executive officers of corporations such as Kmart, Toys 'R' Us, Woolworth, Sears, and May Department Stores have compensation packages ranging from $1 million to over $3 million (including base salary, bonus, and stock options).

Large retail firms offer the same fringe benefits packages as do other sectors of employment, including vacations, sick leave, college tuition programs, group life insurance, and merchandise discounts. Many retail companies also provide excellent retirement opportunities through stock purchase plans.

Nonmonetary Rewards. Ability and effort—or their absence—are quickly recognized in retailing. The position of store manager appeals to people with the ability to organize and direct the activities of others. As a store manager in most firms, you set your own sales and profit goals, control expenses, compensate employees, and perform other vital management functions. A management career in retailing also offers the opportunity to work with ideas. Managers create ways of increasing sales and profit through imaginative use of the retail mix.

Job Skills in Demand. Mention retailing and many people think of selling or working as a cashier. Yet these positions make up only a small portion of total job opportunities. Consider the need for fashion experts, accountants, advertising and personnel specialists, market researchers, and lawyers. Go even further and think in terms of public relations, engineering, data processing, real estate analysis, and physical distribution. Think beyond the people you typically see when making purchases. Visualize the complex organization behind most retail outlets. Consider the increasing role of technology, which has opened up career opportunities that simply didn't exist a few years ago. Retailing is indeed high tech.

Working Conditions. Working conditions in retailing are comparable to those in many areas of employment. The typical work week is 40 hours

> Parisian will be the leading fashion specialty store for upper-moderate to better-priced merchandise. . . . Our primary efforts will be directed toward the updated and classic customer groups— the fashion leaders. Our secondary efforts will focus on customers with more traditional attitudes toward fashion. Our merchandise mix will include apparel, accessories, cosmetics, shoes, and other merchandise that meets the ego-intensive needs of our customers. In the marketplace, we will create a sense of excitement through visual merchandising, entertainment, theater, and a high level of personal service.

EXHIBIT A–1

Parisian mission statement

with some overtime at peak periods. Hours commonly include work in the evenings and on weekends.

Internships. More and more retail executives prefer management trainees to have prior retail experience. A major way to secure work experience is through experiential education; namely, internships. Students should attempt to obtain such experience. They learn what retailing is really like and will be better prepared to make a good career decision, and retail management observes performance on the job and can make a more intelligent judgment about full-time employment.

TRAINING PROGRAMS AND CAREER PATHS

Parisian. We have selected Parisian as an illustration of a regional chain's training program and career pathing. At a time when many retailers are holding back on expansion, Parisian is taking off in full force. It has doubled its number of stores in the past eight years and plans to add several more each year. By the end of 1993, it was operating three new stores in the metropolitan Atlanta area, plus a number of new stores in major cities throughout the eastern, southeastern, and central United States. In 1992 Parisian employed over 5,500 people. Its mission statement (see Exhibit A–1) clarifies the nature of the company and sets the stage for its educational and training philosophy.

Parisian is committed to providing executives with superior, ongoing educational programs, and career paths that best suit their unique talents. Whenever possible, Parisian promotes from within the company. (See Exhibit A–2 for typical career paths.)

J. C. Penney. To continue our discussion of training programs and career paths, let's look at J. C. Penney, headquartered in Dallas, Texas, employing approximately 196,000 associates, and operating nearly 1,400 department stores stretching across all 50 states and Puerto Rico. Most stores carry

EXHIBIT A–2

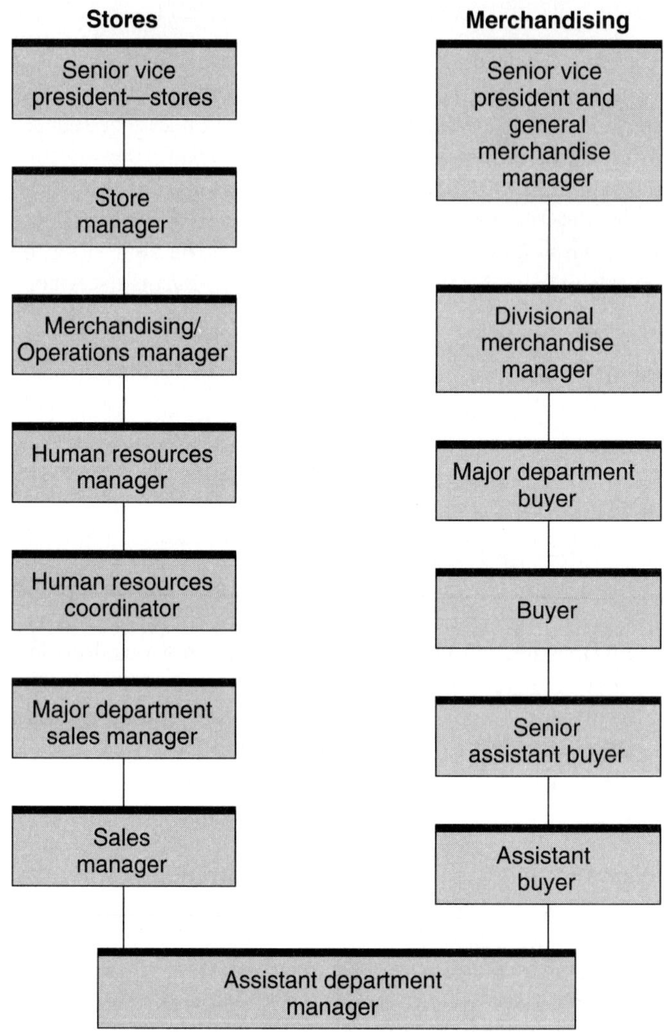

The preferred career path is vertical within the designated division. However, if you have a proven track record in one division, it is possible to transfer to another division.

Other career opportunities

Stores
- Customer service (layaway, credit, giftwrap)
- Loss prevention
- Alterations
- Special events

Corporate headquarters
- Information systems
- Sales promotion/ Marketing
- Distribution
- Finance

Typical career paths

EXHIBIT A–3

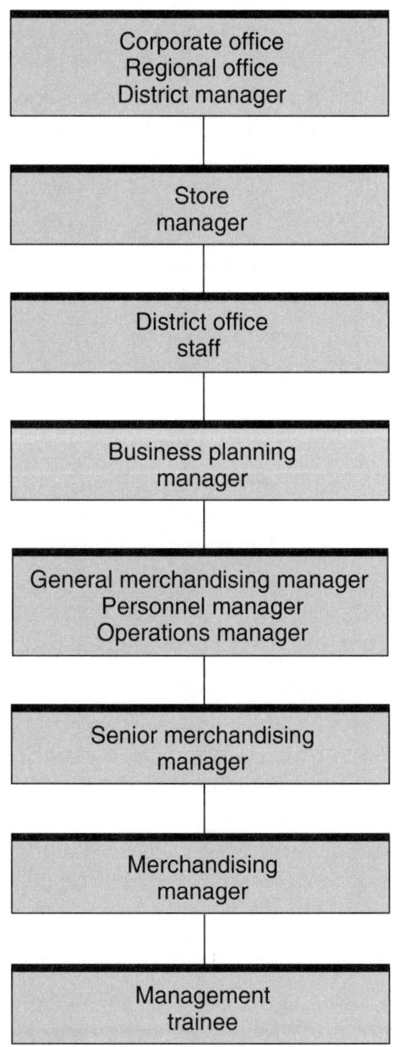

J. C. Penney store management career path

extensive lines of men's, women's, and children's apparel, cosmetics, jewelry, housewares, furniture, and home furnishings. Many also provide custom decorating and styling salon services. In addition to the J. C. Penney catalog division, the company owns the Thrift Drug chain and several specialty retailing operations. J. C. Penney Financial Services markets health and life insurance and various other consumer services. Exhibit A–3 depicts its store management career path.

A comprehensive 12-month program introduces store management trainees to the J. C. Penney culture, including a one-week workshop at one of the development centers. The program concentrates on three primary areas: merchandising, operations, and personnel. The focus of all phases of training is to help each individual develop both manager's sales leadership skills and the skills needed to complete the merchandising process used in J. C. Penney stores.

Career challenges and training also exist in information systems, business services, accounting, auditing, catalog advertising, outlet store management, catalog inventory control, telemarketing center management, and catalog distribution center management.

CHOOSING THE RIGHT COMPANY: TIPS FOR SUCCESS

Neiman-Marcus, a division of General Cinema, has done impressive work to assist students in determining which retail firms can provide the opportunities they seek. Neiman-Marcus believes that the first step toward building a successful career is choosing the right company, one where your abilities will be recognized and your own enterprise will be encouraged, one that is ready for your future, for your need for greater responsibility. Neiman-Marcus suggests that the following questions are useful in evaluating retailers; answering them will provide insights in making choices.[2]

1. Is the retailer investing in the future? Do ambitious plans exist for construction of new stores and expansion or renovation of existing stores? An expanding or modernizing company can capitalize on new markets. A growing organization can give you more opportunity for development and advancement.
2. Is the retailer in a strong market? A retailer's potential depends, to a great extent, on the strength of its market. Retailers situated in areas of the country experiencing growth, particularly those areas attracting people with significant disposable income, are favorably positioned to increase volume and profitability.
3. Is the retailer known for its promotions? Promotional skill reflects a company's merchandising skills and abilities to sell. To be successful, a retailer must capture and hold the attention of its customers. Promotional programs can establish the retailer's leadership in fashion and design.
4. Does the retailer sponsor and support community groups and events? A successful retailer shows commitment to the growth and vitality of the communities in which it operates. Recognizing that an active community has a direct effect on its business, it sponsors or strongly supports activities such as charitable organizations, educational institutions, and cultural groups.
5. How sophisticated is the retailer's technology? An expanding retailer needs to take steps to ensure that productivity and efficiency remain high. Through technology, the extent to which people are involved in processing paperwork and data can be minimized. In addition, rapid change

EXHIBIT A–4

- Develop a profile of the kind of job you want. Where do you want to work? How do you plan to approach the job search?
- Organize your job search. Work as hard at getting a job as you would on the job. Keep detailed records. Maintain deadlines. Follow these key steps:

1. Evaluate yourself: skills and abilities, strengths and weaknesses.
2. Establish career objectives. Next year? Ultimately?
3. Create a company target list. Match company needs to your skills and abilities.
4. Network for success. Utilize anyone who can help you.
5. Prepare your résumé. Learn when and how to use it.
6. Prepare cover letters that will help you get that all-important interview.
7. Make the interview work for you. (See Exhibit A–5 for interviews *dos* and *don'ts*.)

- Utilize all available resources: career centers, employment agencies, and community organizations. The more resources, the better. (See Exhibit A–6 for additional resources.)
- Continually evaluate your game plan and always be flexible enough to modify it if necessary.

Job-finding game plan

Source: *BusinessWeek's Guide to Careers,* Spring/Summer 1984, p. 65; "The Concept of a Job Search Process," *Marketing and Sales Career Directory,* 4th ed., p. 148.

characterizes the retailing field. Technology such as data processing permits a rapid turnaround of information, enabling managers to identify and respond quickly to changing trends.

6. What are the retailer's management needs over the next five years? The retailer's assessment of its staffing needs reflects its perception of its growth potential and indicates the importance it places on human resource planning as a means of achieving objectives. A projected increase in the number of positions at the management level implies a parallel increase in entry-level openings as well as greater opportunities for upward mobility.

The information in Exhibits A–4, A–5, and A–6 is useful regardless of your particular interests. Develop a job-finding game plan for yourself. It can be extraordinarily helpful. The plan in Exhibit A–4 contains four proven strategies to aid you in your quest.

Exhibit A–5 supplies useful tips for interviews, along with typical interview questions to contemplate as you begin the job interviewing process. Exhibit A–6 suggests various sources to get answers to career-oriented questions.

EXHIBIT A–5

Out of 100 bright-as-a-penny candidates who are wearing their best dressed-for-success outfits and have all the credentials necessary to impress St. Peter at the gate of heaven, 99 won't make the effort necessary to answer the following typical interview questions:

- How did you happen to select X as a career choice?
- What are the qualities necessary for success in X?
- What do you consider your chief strengths in this profession?
- What are some of the weaknesses that might hinder your success?
- Why should we hire you rather than one of your equally competent classmates?
- What are your long-term career objectives at this point?
- Why do you think you would like to work for our company?

In no way can you answer these questions without also revealing whether or not you have done your homework about yourself, your career decisions, and the company interviewing you. Here is sound advice from Sydney Reynolds, New York City executive search consultant:

Do

- Anticipate probing questions about any obviously difficult career episode on your résumé, such as a job briefly held, or a summer job that did not result in a permanent offer.
- Control your desire to run the interview. Instead, concentrate on adopting a pleasant and cordial tone throughout.

Don't

- Oversell and make promises you will live to regret once you are actually on the job.
- Project a self-centered perspective, such as, "What's in this for me?"
- Be negative about any employer or company. Don't blame others in the course of explaining situations.

Allan Sarn, a New York-based executive search consultant, sees the mistakes experienced candidates make while interviewing for executive jobs. He emphasizes that candidates must know a number of things about the company before an interview:

Annual dollar sales volume of the company.

Number of employees.

Products and services offered.

Names of top executives.

Scope of the business—domestic or global.

General content of most recent annual report.

Information contained in articles about the company.

Interview *dos* and *don'ts*

Source: Reprinted by special permission from *BusinessWeek's Guide to Careers*, Spring/Summer 1984.

EXHIBIT A–6

- University and college career placement centers.
- College placement manuals—annual listing of companies that recruit.
- Professional placement agencies (''head hunters'').
- Trade associations (e.g., National Retail Federation, Food Marketing Institute).
- Local chambers of commerce.
- Company annual reports and specialized publications detailing training programs and career paths.
- Libraries, especially computer-based search services.
- Guest speakers in classes and student organizations (e.g., Collegiate Chapters of the American Marketing Association).
- Certain interested faculty members.
- State associations of retailers.
- Specialized publications (e.g., *Chain Store Age Executive, Stores, Marketing News, Women's Wear Daily*).
- Publishers specializing in retailing (e.g., Fairchild, Lebhar-Friedman).
- Career fairs sponsored by trade groups.

Sources of career information

Conclusion

We do not believe it is our role to sell you on a retailing career. Instead, we have presented information for you to think about. Retailing has rather definite and understandable career paths. They can well reward high-level performance. Retailing offers many excellent training programs. Evaluate them in terms of your own career aspirations; consider retailing as a career possibility. We ask no more.

Notes

1. "Where Are the Top Women?" *Stores*, September 1990, p. 34.
2. Company brochure, "Neiman-Marcus, An Exceptional Retailer, An Exceptional Career."

Glossary of Key Terms

above-the-market pricing. A pricing strategy in which retailers set prices above competitors' prices.

achievers. Successful career- and work-oriented people who like to, and generally do, feel in control of their lives.

actualizers. Successful, sophisticated, active, take-charge people with high self-esteem and abundant resources.

adaptive behavior. A theory of retail institutional change suggesting that, when an environmental need exists for a certain kind of retail institution, it will evolve; when the need ceases to exist, the institution will disappear.

advertising. Any paid form of nonpersonal presentation and promotion of goods, ideas, and services by an identified sponsor.

aggregation. An approach to target market selection whereby retailers assume that most consumers are alike in their needs and wants.

ambience. The quality of design that expresses the character of a store, resulting in an institutional personality immediately recognized by consumers.

Americans with Disabilities Act (1990). Legislation requiring retailers to make their stores more accessible to disabled shoppers under regulations issued by the U.S. Justice Department.

anchor tenants. The major tenants in a shopping center that serve as the primary consumer-attracting force.

ANSI .X12. The emerging North American industry standard for communicating electronically between retailers and vendors.

arbitration. The settlement of a dispute by a person or persons chosen to hear both sides and come to a decision.

area of dominant influence (ADI). The area that a television station's broadcast signal covers.

area development franchise. A franchise arrangement in which an individual purchases an extensive territory and then opens a large number of franchises within the territory.

assortment. The choices offered within a merchandise line, such as size and color.

at-the-market pricing. A pricing strategy in which retailers set prices roughly the same as those of their competitors.

audit bureaus of circulation. Bureaus that measure, check, and verify the circulation of business publications, outdoor advertising, magazines, and newspapers.

baby boomers. Individuals born between 1946 and 1964, they comprise the largest population segment today.

backward integration. A development that occurs when a retailer or wholesaler performs some manufacturing functions.

balance sheet. A financial statement that shows a firm's financial health on a specific date; it expresses the following equation: assets = liabilities + net worth.

balanced tenancy. A term which means that the types of stores in a planned shopping center are chosen to meet all of the consumers' shopping needs.

basic services. Services that customers expect to have available at all retail outlets. An example is free parking.

basic stock. The amount and assortment of merchandise sufficient to accommodate normal sales levels.

believers. Conservative, conventional people with concrete beliefs and strong attachments to traditional institutions.

below-the-market pricing. A pricing strategy in which retailers offer acceptable quality merchandise at low prices.

benefits. Holidays and paid vacations, insurance, health care, pensions, social security, disability payments, and various other forms of support for employees.

blind check. A checking method in which the checker lists the items and quantities received without the invoice in hand; the list is then later compared to the invoice.

blue laws. State laws designed to regulate or eliminate retail sales on Sunday.

book inventory. A system for controlling the dollar investment in inventory; it enables retailers to know the dollar value of inventory on hand without having to take a physical inventory.

boomers. *See* **baby boomers.**

boutique layout. A store layout in which merchandise classifications are grouped so that each classification has its own "shop" within the store.

bulk marking. A merchandise marking practice (used for items that sell at very low prices and are subject to rapid price changes) whereby items are not marked until placed on the selling floor.

business format franchising. An ongoing relationship between a franchiser and franchisee that includes the entire business format.

cash datings. Payment terms that call for immediate payment for merchandise. Cash datings include COD (cash on delivery) and CWO (cash with order). Cash datings do not involve cash discounts.

cash discount. A premium granted by the supplier for cash payment prior to the time the entire bill must be paid.

cash flow forecast. A method for predicting when retailers will receive cash and when they must make payments.

catalog centers. Centers anchored by one or more catalog showroom stores.

category killers. Merchants offering great depth and breadth in one line of merchandise accompanied by low prices and good quality.

central business district. The area of the central city that is characterized by high land values, high concentration of retail and service business, and high traffic flow.

central buying. A method of buying in which the authority and responsibility for merchandise selection and purchase are vested in the headquarters office rather than in the individual store units that comprise the chain.

central market. The place where a large number of suppliers concentrate.

chain. A retail organization consisting of two or more centrally owned units that handle similar lines of merchandise.

channel of distribution. An interorganizational system through which products or services are marketed.

checking. A phase of the physical handling process that involves matching the store buyer's purchase order with the supplier's invoice, opening the packages, removing and sorting the items, and comparing the quality and quantity of the shipment with what was ordered.

Clayton Act (1914). Declares certain practices illegal even if they do not actually restrain trade or do not constitute a monopoly or an attempt to monopolize.

Clean Air Act (1970). Requires 10-year air quality maintenance plans for various areas of the nation.

co-branded card. A dual-purpose credit card combining the features of a private-label card and a bank card.

co-operative advertising. Promotional programs in which wholesalers or manufacturers pay a portion of the retailer's advertising cost under specified conditions.

co-ownership and co-management franchises. Franchise arrangements in which a franchiser has an ownership interest in the operation.

Coastal Zone Management Act (1972). Designed to preserve, protect, develop, or restore the resources of the nation's coastal areas.

column inch. Newspaper advertising space that is one column wide and one inch deep.

combination check. A checking method that is a combination of the blind and direct checks. If the invoices are available when the goods arrive, the direct check is used; if the invoices have not come in, the blind check is used.

combo card. A combination debit/credit card.

committee buying. A form of central buying in which more than one person shares the buying responsibility.

community center. A shopping center in which

the leading tenant typically is a variety store or junior department store. The typical leasable space is around 150,000 square feet, and the typical site area is 10 or so acres. The minimum trade population is 40,000 to 150,000.

compensation. The amount of salary and fringe benefits to be paid for a particular job.

concentric diversification. A strategy by which a service firm moves into different, but closely related, services.

consignment. A situation in which suppliers guarantee the sale of items and will take merchandise back if it does not sell.

consumer advisory panel. A cross section of opinion leaders in a key market segment chosen to provide a retailer with information on a wide range of issues.

Consumer Credit Protection Act (1969). An act requiring retailers to explain in easily understood language the dollar finance charge and annual percentage rate on the merchandise they finance.

Consumer Leasing Act (1977). An act requiring the leasing company to make an accurate and detailed disclosure of all terms and costs in leasing contracts.

consumer rebate. A sum of money given the consumer by the manufacturer after, and thus separate from, the original purchase.

consumer-dominated information sources. Information sources over which the retailer has no influence. Examples include friends, relatives, acquaintances, and others.

contest. Skill-based competitions for designated prizes.

continuous purchase panel. A group of preselected consumers who agree to record their purchases on a continuing basis.

contribution margin approach. An approach to departmental evaluation in which only direct costs are assigned to departments.

convenience goods. Products for which consumers do not feel it is worth their time to shop around for a better price or quality and thus purchase at the most accessible outlet.

core service. The primary benefit customers seek from a service firm.

corporate culture. The values of greatest importance to the organization.

corporate systems competition. A type of competition that occurs when a single-management ownership links resources, manufacturing capability, and distribution networks.

corporation. A group of people who obtain a charter that grants them collectively the rights, privileges, liabilities, and legal powers of an individual, separate and apart from the individual making up the group. The corporation can sell, buy, and inherit property. The corporation owns assets and is liable for the debts it contracts.

cost per thousand (CPM). A measure of the relative cost of advertising, which is determined by the number of households or persons reached.

creative selling. A type of higher-level selling in which the salespeople need complete information about product lines, product uses, and the technical features of products.

credence qualities. Attributes consumers may find impossible to evaluate even after purchase and consumption, perhaps because they do not have the knowledge or skill to do so.

credit scoring. A method retailers use to screen credit applicants based on personal information supplied by the applicant.

current assets. Assets, such as cash, accounts receivable, and inventory, that are in various states of being converted into cash within the next 12 months.

current liabilities. Debts owed by the business to be paid within the next 12 months.

current ratio. A financial ratio calculated as current assets divided by current liabilities.

debit card. A card that allows funds to be automatically shifted from a customer's account at a bank to a merchant's account at the time of a purchase.

decoding. A phenomenon that occurs when the consumer transforms and interprets a retailer's message as part of the communication process.

deferred billing credit. A payment plan in which a

retailer allows customers to buy goods and to defer payment for a specified time period with no interest charge.

demand merchandise. Merchandise that is purchased as a result of a customer's coming into the store to buy that particular item.

demographics. The ways in which consumers can be described in such terms as age, income, and education.

departmentalization. An organizational principle that determines how jobs are grouped.

dialectic process. A theory of retail institutional change suggesting that retailers mutually adapt in the face of competition from "opposites;" when challenged by a competitor with a differential advantage, an established institutional type will adopt strategies and tactics in the direction of the advantage, thereby negating some of the innovator's attraction.

direct check. A checking method whereby the shipment is checked against the vendor's invoice.

direct costs. Costs directly associated with a department; such costs would cease to exist if the department were deleted.

direct product profitability. Reflects a product's gross margin (selling price minus cost of goods sold), plus discounts and allowances, less direct handling costs.

direct response advertising. Advertising designed to induce consumers to take specific action such as make a purchase or participate in a contest or giveaway.

direct selling. A method of distribution of consumer goods and services through personal contact (salesperson to buyer) away from a fixed business location.

disappointers. Services offered by a retailer that have a high labor content and that return little value to the customer. An example is layaway.

discount center. A shopping center with a strong representation of discount merchants.

distributor allowances. Discounts, extended payment terms, or a combination thereof given to retailers to encourage them to purchase additional merchandise from a wholesaler or manufacturer.

distributorships. Franchise systems whereby franchisees maintain warehouse stocks to supply other franchisees. The distributor takes title to the goods and provides services to other customers.

diverting. The practice of retailers buying merchandise from a vendor at a specially reduced price and then reselling that merchandise at a slightly higher price to another retailer outside its trading area.

dollar control. The way of controlling dollar investment in inventory.

drawing account. A payment arrangement in which a cash advance is made available to retail salespeople at predetermined intervals.

dual distribution. A situation in which wholesalers also operate retail outlets.

EDI/FACT. The international standard for communicating electronically between retailers and vendors.

electronic cash register. A point-of-sale register that uses electronic light beams to enter information at a very high rate of speed.

electronic data interchange (EDI). Computer-to-computer exchange of data.

employee compensation. Wages or salary, commissions, incentives, overtime, and benefits.

encoding. The process of putting together thoughts, information, or ideas in a symbolic form that is familiar to and understood by the target audience.

Equal Credit Opportunity Act (1975). An act prohibiting discrimination on the basis of sex or marital status in any aspect of a credit transaction. The act also was amended to include discrimination based on race, color, religion, national origin, age, and receipt of income from public assistance programs in any aspect of a credit transaction.

Equal Employment Opportunity Commission. An agency of the federal government responsible for eliminating discrimination on the basis of race, sex, color, age, religion, or other variables in job hiring, retention, and promotion.

exclusive dealing. An arrangement in which a

supplier prohibits a retailer from selling the products of a competitor.

exclusive territories. Territories created when suppliers limit the area in which a retailer can sell its products.

experience qualities. Attributes such as taste that can only be discerned after purchase or during consumption.

experiencers. People who are young, vital, enthusiastic, impulsive, and rebellious.

express warranties. Written warranties for products or services.

extended warranty. Warranties purchased by the consumer separate from the product and covering parts, labor, or both for a period of time beyond the duration of an express warranty.

extensive problem solving. A thought process that consumers experience when faced with a first-time purchase in an unfamiliar product category.

extreme segmentation. An approach to target market selection whereby retailers concentrate on a very narrowly defined segment of the market.

factory outlet center. A center consisting of manufacturers' retail outlets that sell goods directly to the public.

Fair Credit Billing Act (1975). An act establishing a billing dispute settlement procedure for open-end credit that also imposes certain other requirements on retailers to ensure fair and accurate handling of credit accounts.

Fair Credit Reporting Act (1971). An act that protects the consumer's right to an accurate, up-to-date, and confidential credit report.

Fair Debt Collection Practices Act (1978). An act designed to eliminate abusive debt collection practices and to protect the consumer from harassment and unfair collection procedures.

fair market value. The price at which property would change hands between a willing buyer and willing seller, both being adequately informed of all material facts and neither being compelled to buy or sell.

fair trade laws. Federal legislation that allows manufacturers to set minimum retail prices for their products.

fashion-oriented centers. Shopping centers composed primarily of apparel shops, boutiques, and handicraft shops carrying selected fashion merchandise of high price and quality.

Federal Competitive Quality Banking Act (1987). Legislation allowing retailers to charge credit card holders in any state the maximum interest rate allowed in the state in which the bank is established.

Federal Trade Commission Act (1914). Legislation passed to create the Federal Trade Commission for enforcing the Clayton Act provisions. The legislation prohibits "unfair methods" of competition as defined by the FTC and gives the FTC the power to prosecute violators.

Federal Trade Commission. An independent agency responsible for enforcing the Clayton Act and other antitrust laws.

Federal Truth in Mileage Act (1986). Legislation requiring both the buyer and seller to certify the mileage reading for a vehicle before a change in title can be obtained.

Federal Water Pollution Control Act (1972). Regulates nonpoint sources of pollution.

festival/entertainment centers. Centers with a strong representation of restaurants, specialty retailers, and entertainment facilities.

financial risk. The monetary loss from a wrong decision.

first-in first-out (FIFO). An inventory costing method that assumes that costs should be charged against revenue in the order in which they were incurred; in other words, the first items purchased are the first ones sold, so ending inventory is assumed to consist of the most recent purchases.

fixed assets. Assets, such as real estate, machinery, equipment, and vehicles, that are used in the operation of a business and are not intended to be resold.

flex-time. A system by which workers arrive at work on a variable schedule.

float. The amount of time that elapses between a consumer's paying by check and receipt of the funds by the retailer.

focus group. An interview technique whereby a small

group of individuals is asked for information about a product or issue in an unstructured format.

forward buying. A retailer's practice, especially supermarkets, of stocking up on promoted items at a discounted price offered by the vendor and then selling the merchandise at the regular price after the termination of the discount period.

forward integration. A situation in which a manufacturer establishes its own wholesale and retail networks.

franchise contract. A legal document that enables an independent businessperson to use a franchiser's operating methods, financing systems, trademarks, and products in return for a fee.

franchisee association. An association of franchisees that represents the owners in dealing with a franchiser.

franchisee. An individual who pays a fee for the right to use a franchiser's product, service, or way of doing business.

franchiser. An organization that has developed a unique product, service, or method of doing business and that allows another firm to use the business concept in return for payment of a fee.

free-flow layout. A layout arrangement in which merchandise and fixtures are grouped into patterns that allow an unstructured flow of customer traffic.

frequency. The average number of times a person will be exposed to a message during an advertising period.

fulfilleds. Mature, satisfied, comfortable, reflective people who value order, knowledge, and responsibility.

full costing approach. A method of departmental evaluation in which both direct and indirect costs are assigned to departments.

functional middlemen. Wholesalers who do not take title to the merchandise they sell.

future datings. A type of dating other than cash datings; includes DOI (date of invoice), ROG (receipt of goods), EOM (end of month), and other datings.

general rate. The advertising rate charged to agencies for national advertising.

general salary increases. Increases granted to employees to maintain real earnings as required by economic factors and in order to keep pay competitive.

generics. Unbranded merchandise that is typically lower in quality and lower priced than brand-name merchandise.

gravity models. Methods of trading area analysis that are based on population size and driving time or distance as key variables.

grey market retailers. Retailers not authorized by the manufacturer or distributor to sell specified merchandise that is offered for sale.

grid layout. A layout arrangement in which merchandise is displayed in straight, parallel lines, with secondary aisles at right angles to these.

gross margin. The difference between net sales and cost of goods sold.

gross rating point. One percent of all homes with television sets in a market area.

group buying. The joint purchasing of goods by a number of noncompeting, nonaligned stores.

guaranteed drawing accounts. A method of compensation in which a company will cancel a salesperson's debt if his or her commissions do not meet it.

hazard communication standard. OSHA regulation requiring manufacturers, distributors, and retailers to train and educate employees about the use of hazardous chemicals.

home improvement centers. Centers featuring a concentration of home improvement or hardware specialty retailers.

horizontal price fixing. An agreement between two or more retailers to charge the same price for identical merchandise.

image. The way consumers "feel" about an outlet or merchandise.

implied warranty. A provision of the Uniform Commercial Code, which requires that all merchandise sold be fit for the purpose for which it is intended.

impulse merchandise. Merchandise that is bought

on the basis of unplanned, spur-of-the-moment decisions.

income statement. A financial statement that shows operating results over a period of time and indicates whether investments in assets and strategy have been successful and profitable.

index of retail saturation. A formula for arithmetically determining whether the trading area of a community is overstored or understored.

indirect costs. Costs that cannot be tied directly to a department, such as the store manager's salary.

initial markup. The difference between the cost of merchandise and the original retail price.

installment credit. A payment plan in which a customer pays for a product in equal monthly installments, including interest.

institutional advertising. Advertising designed to enhance the image of a retail outlet and to communicate targeting and positioning strategies as opposed to inducing specific actions such as making a purchase.

internal data. Data collected by management to determine what is going on within the retail organization.

intertype competition. Competition between different types of retail outlets selling the same merchandise.

intratype competition. Competition among retailers of the same type.

involvement. The way in which individuals identify with a product, service, or outlet and the personal relevance of the purchase to them.

job analysis. A method of obtaining important facts about what a job entails.

job classification. Comparing jobs with the aid of a scale that evaluates job complexity and the length of time the respective responsibilities and qualifications are utilized during an average workday.

job description. The part of a job analysis that describes the content and responsibilities of a job and the job's relation to other jobs in the firm.

job evaluation. A method of ranking jobs to aid in determining proper compensation.

job ranking. Ranking jobs on the basis of their value to the organization and their complexity.

job sharing. A type of employment in which two workers voluntarily hold joint responsibility for what was formerly one position.

job specification. The part of a job analysis that describes the personal qualifications required to do a job.

kleptomaniacs. Persons motivated by an irrational compulsion to steal.

last-in first-out (LIFO). An inventory costing method that assumes that the most recent cost of merchandise should be charged against revenue; thus, ending inventory is assumed to be made up of earliest costs.

layaway plan. A payment plan in which a customer can make a small deposit that ensures that the retailer will hold the item until the customer is able to pay for it.

lead time. The length of time between order placement and receipt of goods.

leader pricing. A pricing policy in which merchandise is sold at less than the normal markup in an effort to increase store traffic.

leased departments. Departments of a retail business which are operated and managed by an outside person or organization rather than by the retail outlet.

leverage. A financial situation in which a business unit acquires assets worth more than the amount of capital invested by the owners; the higher the ratio, the higher the amount of borrowed funds in the business.

lifestyle. A person's pattern of living as reflected in the way he or she purchases and uses merchandise.

lifestyle segmentation. Dividing consumers into homogeneous groups based on similar activities, interests, and opinions.

limited liability company. A form of retail organization that offers the tax advantages of a partnership and the legal safeguards of a corporation.

limited problem solving. Shopping situations in which the consumer is already familiar with the class of product or service and makes a choice between brands or outlets.

local advertising. The purchase of advertising time by local retailers.

long-term liabilities. Debts owed by the business to be paid beyond the next 12 months.

macro environment. The impersonal forces beyond the control of the firm, such as technology or social trends.

Magnuson-Moss Warranty Act (1975). A federal law that regulates express warranties for merchandise.

maintained markup. The difference between the cost of merchandise and the sales retail price.

makers. Practical people who have constructive skills and value self-sufficiency.

manufacturer brand. A brand that is owned by a manufacturer, often referred to as a national brand.

margin. The difference between cost and the retail selling price, or the percentage markup at which merchandise is sold.

markdown. A reduction in the original selling price of an item.

market development. A strategy option that focuses either on attracting new market segments or completely changing the customer base.

market penetration. A strategy option whereby retailers seek a differential advantage over competition by a strong market presence that borders on saturation.

market positioning. Developing a unique position in a market segment relative to other retailers by the use of merchandise, price, hours of operation, services offered, and a clear understanding of consumer demographics.

market saturation. A situation that occurs when such a large number of stores are located in a market that low sales per square foot, compared to the industry average, result.

market segmentation. The process of taking a heterogeneous market and developing homogeneous groups (segments) on the basis of some kind of similarity among consumers.

marketer-dominated information sources. Sources of information under the control of the retailer. Examples are advertising, personal selling, displays, and sales promotion.

marketing. The process of planning and executing the conception, pricing, promotion, and distribution of ideas, goods, and services to create exchanges that satisfy individual and organizational objectives.

marketing concept. A management philosophy stating that all activities of the firm should be organized and executed from the viewpoint of the customer in satisfying the needs identified.

marking. A phase of the physical handling process that involves putting information on merchandise or its containers to assist customers and to aid the store in the control functions.

master franchise. A franchising arrangement in which an individual buys the right to an extensive geographic area and sells the rights within the territory to individual franchisees.

merchandise approach. A retail sales approach that begins with a statement about the merchandise or an open-ended statement related to the merchandise.

merchandise budget. A plan of the dollar amount of merchandise to buy, usually by merchandise classification by month based on sales and profitability goals.

merchandise management. Management of the product component of the retailing mix, comprising planning and control activities.

merchandise planning. Includes all the activities needed to ensure a balance between inventories and sales.

merchandise turns. The number of times the average inventory is sold and replaced in a 12-month period.

merchandising. An operating philosophy in which the firm primarily focuses on having the right merchandise at the right place at the right time in the right quantities at the right price.

merchant wholesalers. Wholesalers who take title to the goods they sell.

merit increases. Pay increases granted to recognize superior performance and contributions.

message. The idea transmitted in the communication process.

mission statement. A statement that indicates what a firm plans to do and how it intends to do it.

mobile franchise. A franchising arrangement in which business is done from a mobile vehicle.

model building. The practice of applying statistical principles and using computer analysis of data to help solve management problems.

model stock plan. The retailer's best prediction about what demand will be at specific times of the year, expressed in unit terms.

motivation. The practice of getting people to want to do what is best for the organization.

national brands. Manufacturer brands such as Procter & Gamble that are sold through a wide variety of retail outlets.

National Environmental Policy Act (1972). An act requiring that proposals for federal action must include an environmental impact statement. Many states have similar regulations.

national spot advertising. Non-network advertising done by national retailers.

natural selection. A theory of retail institutional change suggesting that retail institutions that can most effectively adapt to economic, competitive, social, technological, and legal and political environmental changes are the ones most likely to prosper or survive.

negative cash flow. A financial situation in which cash outlays exceed income.

neighborhood shopping center. A shopping center in which the leading tenant is a supermarket or drugstore. The typical leasable space is 50,000 square feet and the typical site is four acres. The minimum trade population is 7,500 to 40,000.

net worth. The owners' claim on the assets of the business—that is, the owners' investment or equity.

neutral sources of information. Sources of information such as government rating agencies and state and local consumer affairs agencies that consumers perceive as trustworthy and unbiased.

niching. A strategy in which a retailer carves out a narrow position in the marketplace that offers high potential and then specializes in meeting the needs of the consumers in that segment.

Noise Pollution Control Act (1972). Sets standards designed to regulate the quantity of noise emitted by products for sale and by transportation vehicles.

noise. Unplanned distortion in the communication process between the retailer and consumer.

nonguaranteed draw. A cash advance loaned to a retail salesperson to be repaid out of commissions earned in a future period.

nonmarking. The practice of not price-marking individual merchandise items; usually the display fixture will indicate prices.

nonstore shopping. The purchase of merchandise by catalog, telephone, computer, or ways other than physically entering an outlet.

Nutritional Labeling and Education Act (1990). Legislation requiring standardized nutrition and health labels on a wide variety of products sold in supermarkets.

objective and task. A method for establishing an advertising budget by specifically relating the promotion appropriation to the marketing task to be achieved.

objectives. Statements of results to be achieved.

Occupational Safety and Health Administration (OSHA). The federal agency charged with the responsibility of ensuring a safe and healthy workplace for employees and consumers.

off-price center. A center with a high concentration of stores selling brand name goods at 20 to 70 percent off the manufacturer's suggested retail prices.

off-price retailers. Outlets offering well-known brands of merchandise at substantial discounts compared to conventional stores handling the same products.

100 showing. All adults in a trading area see a retailer's outdoor billboard display at least once a month.

open charge account. A charge account in which the customer must pay the bill in full when it is due, usually in 30 days.

open code dating. Dating on containers provided so that the consumer can tell the date after which a product should not be purchased.

open to buy (OTB). A figure used to "control" the merchant's utilization of the planned purchases figure.

operating environment. All organizations or groups that either directly or indirectly are affected by a firm's competitive strategy.

operational evolution. Changing competitive strategy over time by focusing on a new target market and developing a business concept different from the existing one.

order ceiling. A level of stock sufficient to maintain a minimum order point level of stock and to cover sales between ordering intervals.

order point. The level of stock below which merchandise is automatically reordered.

ordering interval. The amount of time between merchandise orders.

original retail price. The first price at which an item (or group of items) is offered for sale.

out-shopping. Traveling out of one's local area to make purchases.

overage. A situation that occurs when the physical inventory is greater than the book inventory.

partial segmentation. An approach to target market selection whereby retailers offer goods and services to most segments of the market, but different versions of the same product or service are offered to each broad segment.

partnership. A voluntary association of two or more people to operate a retail outlet for profit as co-owners. The rights, responsibilities, and duties of the partners are stated in the articles of partnership.

patronage builders. A classification of services that provide high customer value and that the retailer can provide at nominal cost. An example is a computerized bridal registry.

percentage of sales. A method of establishing an advertising budget based upon a percentage of retail sales.

performance risk. The chance that merchandise purchased may not work properly.

peripheral services. Secondary benefits customers seek from a service firm.

personal motives. Reasons for shopping that result from the internal needs of the consumer, distinct from other needs fulfilled in purchasing a good or service.

personal shopping service. A situation in which a retailer will assemble a wardrobe at a customer's request and have the items ready for inspection when the customer comes to the store.

physical handling. Activities involved in receiving, checking, and marking merchandise.

physical risk. The likelihood that a purchase decision will be injurious to one's health or will cause physical injury.

planned shopping center. A shopping center developed with balanced tenancy, parking, and architecture.

POS: A point-of-sale terminal that records a variety of information at the time a transaction occurs.

positioning strategy. An action plan that outlines how the organization will compete in chosen markets and how the firm will differentiate itself from other organizations competing for the same customers.

power marketing programs. Programs in which manufacturers handle everything from price to inventory to display for a particular line of merchandise.

power retailers. Retailers with sufficient financial strength, marketing skill, and reasonably priced, quality merchandise to establish dominance in any market, however saturated, and make a profit.

predatory pricing. Setting prices so low as to deliberately drive competition out of business.

premium. The offer of a free or minimally priced gift to induce sales.

preretailing. The practice of determining merchandise selling prices and writing these prices on the store's copy of the purchase order at the time the order is written.

price discrimination. Varying the prices charged to different retailers for identical merchandise without an economic justification for doing so.

price elasticity of demand. Measurement of the extent to which consumer demand is responsive to price changes; the ratio of the percentage change in the quantity demanded to a percentage change in price.

price lining. Featuring products at a limited number of prices reflecting merchandise quality. Price lining may be instated through either rigid price points or price zones.

price points. Offering merchandise at a small number of different prices; for example, a merchant might price all "good" suits at $175, all "better" suits at $225, and all "best" suits at $350.

price zones. Pricing strategy in which a retailer establishes a range of prices for merchandise of a given quality; for example, prices for "good" suits might be between $175 and $200, and prices for "better" suits might be between $225 and $275.

primary data. Data collected by management because neither internal nor secondary sources can supply the necessary data.

private brand. A brand owned either by a retail or a wholesale firm rather than by a manufacturer.

private-label credit card. A credit card imprinted with the name of the issuing retail outlet whose administrative details are handled by a third party such as a bank.

private labels. Labels that are under the exclusive use and control of a retailer.

product or trade name franchising. A franchising arrangement in which an independent sales relationship exists between a supplier and a dealer but the dealer acquires some of the identity of the supplier. Examples include automotive and truck dealers, gasoline service stations, and soft drink bottlers.

product line. All the products or services offered by a retail firm.

productivity improvement. A strategy that focuses on improved earnings through cost reductions, increased turnover through an improved merchandise mix, and increased prices and margins.

promotion. Any form of paid communication from the retailer to the consumer.

promotional allowance. A discount from list price given by suppliers to retailers to compensate them for money spent on promoting particular items.

promotional increases. Salary increases given to employees assigned a different job and a higher pay level.

psychographics. Ways of defining and measuring the lifestyles of consumers.

psychological risk. The probability that the merchandise purchased or the store shopped will be compatible with the consumer's self-image.

publicity. Any nonpersonal stimulation of demand for a product, service, or business unit by planting commercially significant news about it in a published medium or obtaining a favorable presentation about it on radio, television, or other ways that are not paid for by the sponsor.

pull promotions. Promotions that retailers target to consumers.

push money. Money spent by suppliers to encourage the sale of certain merchandise by paying salespeople a bonus to sell the items.

push promotions. Promotions that vendors target at retailers.

quantity discount. A reduction in unit cost based on the size of an order.

quick response (QR). A distribution method for responding rapidly to customer demands and for improving operations and profitability.

reach. The number of people exposed at least once to a message during an ad campaign.

rebates. The refund of a fixed amount from the purchase price.

receiving. A phase of the physical handling process that involves taking possession of the goods and then moving them to the next phase of the process.

reductions. Anything other than sales that reduces inventory value, including employee discounts, shortages, and markdowns.

regional center. A shopping center in which the leading tenant is one or more full-line department stores. The typical leasable space is a minimum 400,000 square feet, and the typical site is 30 acres. The minimum trade population is 150,000 or more.

regional dominance. A location strategy in which a retailer decides to compete within one geographic region.

remarking. The practice of changing the prices marked on merchandise to reflect price changes.

retail accordion. A theory of retail institutional change suggesting that retail institutions evolve over time from broad-based outlets with a wide variety of merchandise to outlets offering specialized narrow lines and then return to the wide-variety pattern.

retail decision support system. The structure of people, equipment, and procedures that gathers, analyzes, and distributes the data that management needs for decision making.

retail the invoice. The practice of determining merchandise selling prices and writing these prices on the copy of the invoice in the receiving room.

retail markup. The difference between the invoice cost and the retail price.

retail niching. Marketing programs designed to offer customers something unique and thereby carve out a particular slice of the market.

retail structure. The structure comprising all retail outlets through which goods and services move to the ultimate consumer.

retailing mix. Variables including product, price, presentation, promotion, personal selling, and customer services that can be used as part of a positioning strategy for competing in chosen markets.

retailing. Consists of all activities involved in the sale of goods and services to the ultimate consumer.

return on assets (ROA). A financial ratio calculated as net profit after taxes divided by total assets.

revolving credit. A customer is billed at the end of the month on the basis of an outstanding credit balance.

Robinson-Patman Act (1936). The primary law regulating price discrimination. Not all price discrimination is illegal under the Robinson-Patman Act, but management must justify the different prices charged to competing retailers.

routine selling. A type of selling involved in the sale of nontechnical items.

routinized response behavior. Situations in which consumers, because they are familiar with the product class, do not engage in external information search before making a purchase.

safety stock. The level of stock sufficient to maintain adequate inventory for accommodating expected variations in demand and variations in supplier delivery schedules.

sales promotion. Marketing activities other than direct selling, advertising, and publicity that stimulate consumer purchasing. Examples include displays, sales, exhibits, and demonstrations.

sales retail price. The final selling price, or the amount the customer actually pays for merchandise.

sales variance analysis. A technique that enables management to compare actual sales to sales goals.

scanner. A device that emits a laser beam for scanning the bar codes on merchandise and that can provide automatic price readouts, automatic updates of inventory, and similar features.

search qualities. Attributes a consumer can see, feel, or touch and can thus determine prior to purchasing a product.

seasonal discount. A special discount given to retailers who place orders for seasonal merchandise in advance of the normal buying period.

seasonal merchandise. Merchandise in demand only at certain times of the year.

secondary data. Data generated by groups or organizations external to the firm for purposes other than the issue at hand and made available to the firm.

secondary market expansion. Development of retail outlets in communities with populations of 50,000 to 200,000.

self-liquidators. Incentives in which consumers pay part of the cost of a promotion in cash in addition to submitting product labels as proof of purchase to obtain an item.

semiblind check. A checking method whereby the checker is provided a list of the items in a shipment, but the quantity is omitted; the checker's job is to indicate quantities on the prepared list.

service approach. A weak approach in personal selling in which the salesperson simply asks whether he or she can be of assistance to a potential customer by asking a question such as, "Can I help you?"

service firm. An organization that derives more than 50 percent of its sales from providing services that may involve a combination of both tangible and intangible offerings.

service franchises. Franchises in which franchisers license franchisees to dispense a service under a trade name.

service-oriented centers. Centers that depend heavily on service-oriented retailers such as optical, dental, repair, health service, and legal services.

share. The percentage of television sets in use that are tuned to a given program.

Sherman Act (1890). The first law passed to maintain competition; it makes every action to restrain trade illegal.

shopping goods. Items for which consumers carefully compare price and quality differences before making a purchase decision.

shortage. A situation that occurs when the physical inventory is less than the book inventory.

showing. A term used in the purchase of outdoor advertising to depict the percentage of adults in a trading area who see a retailer's outdoor advertising poster at least once each month.

single-price policy. A pricing policy in which all merchandise in a store is sold at the same price.

single-theme centers. Centers offering merchandise in a narrow range such as auto care, home decorating and design, or weddings.

situation analysis. An assessment of internal strengths and weaknesses and external threats and opportunities.

slotting fee. A one-time fee paid by the manufacturer to the retailer for the right to display new products in the retailer's outlet.

social motives. Reasons for shopping that reflect the desire for group interaction of one sort or another.

social responsibility. A belief of retailers that they have an obligation to society beyond making a profit and obeying the laws of the land.

social risk. The likelihood that the merchandise or store will not meet with peer approval.

sole proprietorship. A situation in which the retail outlet is owned and operated by one person who has title to the assets and who is subject to the claim of all creditors.

solo location. A location with no other adjacent retail stores.

source. The originator of the promotion message.

specialization. A principle of organization stating that the content of individual jobs should be narrowly defined.

specialty goods. Products that consumers know they want and are willing to make a special effort to acquire because they will not accept a substitute.

spot advertising. Advertising shown on local stations whereby the negotiation and purchase of time is made directly with the individual station.

Standard Rate and Data Services. A company that publishes monthly directories of circulation, rates, issues, closing dates, and other information for most major media types.

staple merchandise. Merchandise that is generally in demand year around, with little change in model or style.

stock-to-sales ratio. A ratio that reflects the relationship between the dollar amount needed in inventories on the first day of a month to support planned sales for that month.

stockkeeping unit (SKU). A choice within an assortment (for example, a pair of black hose in one size fits all is one SKU).

store design. A term that refers to the style or atmosphere of a store that helps project an image to the market.

store layout. The planned internal arrangement of departments—both selling and sales support—including the amount of space for each department.

strategic planning. The process of defining the overall mission or purpose of the company, deciding on objectives that management wants to achieve, and developing a plan to achieve those objectives.

strivers. People who seek motivation, self-definition, and approval from the world around them.

strugglers. Individuals who are chronically poor, ill educated, low skilled, and lacking strong social bonds.

suggestion selling. The practice of using a customer's original purchase decision as a basis for developing suggestions about related or additional items the customer might like to buy.

supermarket retailing. A type of retailing characterized by self-service and self-selection, large-scale but low-cost physical facilities, strong price emphasis, simplification and centralization of customer services, and a wide variety and broad assortment of merchandise.

supplements. Preprinted pages of ads that are inserted into newspapers.

support. The number of units of merchandise needed to support expected sales of each assortment factor; also known as depth.

support services. Services offered by a retailer that directly support the sale of the retailer's merchandise. Examples include home delivery or gift wrapping.

survey research. Collection of data on opinions or perceptions by the use of a structured questionnaire.

sweepstakes. Games of chance for designated prizes.

syndicated services. Data provided by firms specializing in collecting and selling information to clients.

target markets. The markets that management decides to serve.

tenure increases. Pay increases given to employees for time worked with the company.

theme or specialty centers. Shopping centers characterized by common architectural themes that unite a wide range of retailers who repeat the theme in their spaces.

third-party credit. A financial arrangement in which a customer uses a card such as Visa or MasterCard to charge merchandise purchased at a retail outlet.

time-loss risk. The likelihood that the consumer will not be able to get merchandise adjusted, replaced, or repaired without loss of time and effort.

trade discount. A reduction off the seller's list price granted to a retailer who performs functions that are normally the responsibility of the vendor.

trade regulation rules. Guidelines issued by the Federal Trade Commission that must be followed in selling certain products or services.

trading area. The geographical area from which a store primarily attracts its customers.

trading stamps. Stamps issued with purchases that can be redeemed for merchandise of the consumer's choice.

transaction processing. The easiest selling task, in which the employee serves as a checkout clerk or cashier and does little, if any, selling.

turnover. The number of times the average inventory of an item (or SKU) is sold, usually in annual terms.

uniform communications standard. A computer language used in retailing.

unit control. The way of controlling the width and support aspects of stock balance.

unit of sales. A method of establishing an advertising budget whereby retailers set aside a fixed dollar amount for each unit of the product to be sold.

unit pricing. A pricing policy in which price is stated in such terms as price per pound or ounce.

unity of command. A principle of organization stating that no person should be under the direct control of more than one supervisor in performing job tasks.

universal product code (UPC). A standardized form of product marking for electronic reading of price and other information that is used for food and health and beauty aids.

universal vendor marking. A standard vendor-created identification system for marking merchandise at the vendor level.

unplanned shopping center. Typically a small group of stores and service establishments that have not been developed with a balanced tenancy in mind.

VALS. A trademark program, Values and Lifestyles, developed by Stanford Research International that places emphasis on the psychological underpinnings of consumer behavior.

values. Beliefs or expectations about behavior shared by a number of individuals and learned from society.

variety. The number of different lines of merchandise carried.

vertical price fixing. Often referred to as resale price maintenance, a situation in which manufacturers set minimum retail prices at which their products must be sold.

Video Privacy Protection Act (1988). A law prohibiting retailers from selling or disclosing video rental lists without a customer's permission or a court order.

wand. A portable device used for reading the data contained in electronic bar codes.

wheel of retailing. A theory of retail institutional change suggesting that new types of institutions enter the market as low-margin, low-price merchants that go through a trading up process to emerge as high-cost, high-price, conservative merchants vulnerable to new types of institutions that enter the market as low-cost, low-price competitors.

width. The assortment factors necessary to meet the demands of customers and to meet competition; also known as breadth.

work sharing. An employment arrangement during economic recessions in which employees are required to cut back on their work hours rather than face layoffs.

Index

B

C

E

F

G

H

I

J

K

L

M

N

O

P

Q

R

S

T

U

V

W

Y

Z